CU00734961

THE POTTER GUIDE
TO
HIGHER EDUCATION
1997 ENTRY

by
SHEILA POTTER
and
PHILIPPA CLARE

additional research:
Abigail Chard

DALEBANK BOOKS

FIRST PUBLISHED IN 1988
(annually updated and edited)

© Dalebank Books 1996

All rights reserved. Except for normal review purposes, no part of this book
may be reproduced or utilised in any form or by any means, electronic or
mechanical, including photocopying, recording or by any other information
storage and retrieval system, without the written permission of the publishers.

While the writers have made every effort to ensure that the information in
The Potter Guide was correct at the time of going to press, Dalebank Books
does not accept any liability for errors or omissions.

Dalebank Books
Arden Lodge
Savile Park Road
Halifax HX1 2XR
telephone: 01422 349111

CONTENTS

The unconscious influences of communal life, lived in pleasant surroundings...are as important as the teaching given in the lecture rooms and laboratories, for it is men and women who combine training with vision and human understanding who are most needed...

(Lord Hinton of Bankside)

How to use the Potter Guide

We began the *Potter Guide* in 1987 in the belief that finding the right place to study is as important as thinking about the right course. Over 250 institutions are registered with UCAS. In this edition of the Potter Guide, we cover in detail only the universities and the larger colleges of higher education (those offering a full range of courses); each institution offers a unique living experience. How do you choose between them? Does it matter a lot what kind of institution you choose?

Yes it does: your success academically cannot be separated from the extent to which you are able to settle down and work happily; at the same time, your development in personal/personality terms - equally important to your career - will be conditioned strongly.

The best way to differentiate between the different types of institution is to read a selection of entries from this Guide. For example: The University of Sheffield is a civic university, which received its charter in 1905 - an 'old' university from the period of 'red-brick' expansion; Manchester Metropolitan University received its charter in 1992 - a 'new' university which has a longer history than its university title and which is also a 'civic' institution; The University of Warwick received its charter in 1965 - part of the '60s university expansion programme - and is a greenfield campus; De Montfort University has a number of campuses, each one offering a different experience; Bolton Institute is in the college sector, based in a town; Trinity College Carmarthen offers a more cloistered existence; King's College, London is a University (just to confuse things and slightly more complicated by its being part of the University of London), dating from 1829 and offers a very different environment to the University of Westminster, charter 1992, which is not part of the University of London. Read a selection of universities and colleges at random to see their wide differences.

Universities and Colleges are divided by region in this Guide. The only separate section is given to 'Specialist Colleges' - colleges which offer one area of expertise. These are not given full write-ups here because if, for example, you are determined to study agriculture at a specialist institution, where it is and the student life it offers will be of far less importance than if you were looking at a full range of universities/colleges. You should bear in mind that most courses offered by specialist colleges are also offered through larger institutions, and that some specialist centres have been annexed by universities. Use ECCTIS+ or ECCTIS 2000 to find the full list of specialist institutions available to you.

The Potter Guide should help you to identify a shortlist of institutions which will match your personal needs. You should think carefully, after reading a few entries, about the kind of experience which might suit you and give you the space to progress as a person, as well as to develop through your course.

What each entry includes:

• **PROFILE**: gives you basic information about the university (its address and telephone number, overview number of students).

The Charter Date is included here which tells you when the university was founded: all 'new' universities (those created in 1992 and after) have much longer histories as either polytechnics or colleges of higher education.

• **CAMPUS**: This is a description of the campus: its size, style and layout followed by hard information on academic services, accommodation, life on campus, student welfare, student union, sport, and mature students. Most of these are self-explanatory:

Learning Resources: library, computing, language learning resources;

Culture on campus: drama, film, music, art, entertainment;

Student Union: union welfare provision, trading and business activity, entertainments, clubs and societies;

Sport: information on sports facilities, clubs and training;

Student Welfare: health and welfare, chaplaincies, careers service, special needs provision;

Special Needs Students: outlines information for student with special needs. For further, and more detailed information, contact **Skill: The National Bureau for Students with Disabilities, 336 Brixton Road, London SW9 7AA**. General switchboard number: **0171274 0565**, or there is an Information Service line available from 1pm to 4.30pm daily - telephone **0171 978 9890**.

Accommodation: university owned/run accommodation and private rented accommodation (availability of each and price);

Mature students: the university's approach to mature student access and any facilities for mature students, including nursery provision.

• **THE CITY or town**: describes the city/town to which you will relate as a student. It includes information on amenities, night life, shopping and sports.

• **ESCAPE ROUTES**: surveys the terrain in a 20 mile radius of your campus, and tells you how near you are to climbing, sailing, hiking country and places of interest. This section also gives information on **Communications** - how near you are to motorways, what coach and rail-links are available, whether you will be near an airport.

CAMPUS TYPES

The position of a university or college site in relation to its host town/city will make a very big difference to the lifestyle you will have.

A town/city centre site means that the city/town becomes an extension of your campus amenities: you can escape student life, if you want to, very easily; you can use town/city amenities without having to plan in advance how you are going to get back to campus and will you make your 2pm lecture?

A campus outside the city/town, but within a mile of the centre, allows you the freedom of the city while giving you a more 'ivory tower' existence. The campus is more removed and is likely to generate more of its own entertainment and social life. Student bars and eating places will be more used, because the options are not directly on your doorstep.

A rural campus offers a student life away from the distractions of city living. The sites are often very beautiful, with an environment conducive to study and contemplation, balanced by a strongly site-based social life.

Dual site campuses usually have one site in a town/city centre, and one out-of-town. This can give you the best of both worlds, or can mean you do a lot of travelling. One thing to bear in mind with a dual or multi site campus is where the main part of your course is taught, and where you will be living in your first year. Some sites are split between towns, which are miles apart.

Read the entries, and take distances into consideration.

COURSE CONSIDERATIONS

USING ECCTIS+ or ECCTIS 2000

Your school or college should give you access to ECCTIS. You will probably find the Potter Guide there too, as a fully integrated Associated Service, so that you can cross-reference course and place very easily.

ECCTIS is a database of courses, owned by the Department For Education. You will be able to browse through a range of courses or specifically search out a particular course.

This is not the place to go through the mechanics of ECCTIS. It is the only reliable information source of course information: use it.

Even if you think you know exactly which subject you wish to study, use the 'Overview' browse list, with the 'Expand' key on ECCTIS+ to look at associated alternatives. You might find a subject you knew nothing about which offers exactly the experience you seek. Do not be closed minded in using ECCTIS, or any other information source.

Use the UCAS Handbook (also on ECCTIS) to check on the number of courses being offered in the department/faculty of your chosen course. From the range of courses offered, you should be able to gauge the strength of a particular department and to have an idea about the kind of resources likely to be on offer. If, for example, only one foreign language is offered (French perhaps), you will not be joining a department with resources equivalent to those of a department offering 20+ languages (language laboratories, computer-aided learning, satellite links etc.)

MODULARISATION AND CREDIT ACCUMULATION AND TRANSFER (CATS)

Universities and colleges have 'modularised' some or most of their courses: this means that they are putting value onto separate sections of their courses, making each section a 'module'. The idea is that the 'modules', with their own values, can be built into a degree. There are various ways of 'building': either you can concentrate on a single subject, each module building a greater understanding of your chosen field; or you can, in some universities/colleges, mix your modules to build a wide, broad-based degree - perhaps including a foreign language, or business skills; or you can study two or three subjects in equal depth. The next stage in the idea behind modularisation is Credit Accumulation and Transfer. CATS (the 's' is for schemes) mean that, in some cases, you can take the 'credit' of course modules you have completed successfully to another department/faculty within your university/college and add it into the 'value' of another course - i.e. transfer your credit.

CATS also allow you to move from full-time to part-time study more easily (although you must check on your grant position) because the idea of acquiring 'credits' takes away the rule that you must follow a course from beginning to end without stopping. Some universities and colleges are within consortia which accept module-credits from other courses, provided that the course you have followed elsewhere is deemed 'suitable' for transfer to their courses.

Again, if you decide to change course or institution, you must check on your grant position before you move.

The process of CATS is best used if you have to leave university or college for personal reasons before completing your course. The flexibility of the scheme saves years being lost: in the past, 'dropping out' was often the end of an academic career.

CAREER ORIENTED v 'PURE' DEGREES

Do you want a course which leads to a career? Or are you primarily interested in the pursuit of learning and prefer to think about career options later? NB: it is always possible to 'add-on' a career-oriented course at a later stage.

Career-geared first degree/HND courses fall loosely into two categories: vocational and semi-vocational.

Vocational courses:

These are the first stages of professional qualifications - medicine, law, surveying, town planning, hotel management... The content of the course is overseen by the professional body to which it relates. After completing your first degree, you will have to complete a second stage: either a full-time academic course (law...) or through 'on the job' assessment (architecture...). If a course is vocational, make sure the particular one you choose is recognised/validated by its relevant professional body: some are not.

Semi-vocational courses:

Business Studies, Journalism, Media Studies, Art & Design courses, Computing...all (and more) are semi-vocational courses. A semi-vocational degree will fit you for an area of work, although you will not be professionally qualified, and your first degree will not be a stage of a professional qualification.

Pure degree subjects:

Non-vocational degrees are the pure degree subjects: Chemistry, English, Philosophy, Mathematics...which do not lead obviously to any particular field of work, but which are marketable nonetheless: pure degrees are required for many prestigious careers. It is important to note that over 40% of specifications for jobs available after graduation do not specify any particular discipline.

COURSE INFRASTRUCTURE

● When choosing a course, think about location. This is where the Potter Guide is invaluable. The institution in which you study must also match your personality.

● Make sure that the university/college has the facilities (library, computing, laboratory, workshop etc.) you will need to study your chosen course fully and efficiently.

● Check on the course structure and assessment: if you respond well to exam pressure you should perhaps avoid courses where a large percentage of your final degree result will depend on project work. Equally, if you react badly to exams, do the opposite.

Before you apply for any course, write to the Department/Faculty Secretary and ask about your chosen course's structure and content. There is no overview source at present which gives detailed information.

● Check on teaching 'contact' time. If you need close supervision, apply for courses with almost a classroom-based approach to teaching. If you are interested in pursuing a subject freely, and are self-motivated, look at courses which are supervised on a smaller tutorial basis, and which rely more on your own personal study time in libraries, laboratories or computer centres.

Again, you will have to write directly to the Department or Faculty for this information.

Universities and Colleges must give this information to you if asked: *The Students Charter* states that you should have clear information on which to base your decisions. If you do not want to write to a department which will later assess your application, ask your tutor or parents for help.

GENERAL ADVICE:

● Think more widely about degree course choice than following only the path you feel has been offered by your present exam courses. Look at the Overview browse list on ECCTIS+.

● Look at a number of job areas in which you think you might be interested and find out what qualifications are (a) essential or (b) preferred for entry to their career paths.

● Try to keep your long term options open.

● Remember: genuine enthusiasm for anything is the key to success; don't choose a subject because you think it might be a good idea, have prestige, or might lead to a job, unless you are really happy about studying it.

● If you know yourself to be a high flier, in the long run there is more mileage and more glittering prizes ahead if you pursue a specialised degree structure. If necessary - take a postgraduate vocational certificate/diploma course in a field which attracts you later.

OTHER FACTORS WHICH MIGHT INFLUENCE YOUR CHOICE

● What is the mix of the student population? Is there a full range of courses on offer? What is the largest faculty/ school? Decide your own priorities. What type of people will you want to mix with? Arts types? Boffins? Business students? Medics? Remember, an important part of university and college life is the people you meet. You will find the range of courses offered at each university and college in the UCAS Handbook and on ECCTIS+.

● Do you want to apply for a course with an 'excellent' teaching assessment? You will find a list of 'excellent' institutions in Appendix 3: assessments are given by subject. Do you want to be at a university/college with prestigious research programmes? How can you find out? You can check in the Research Ratings league tables, published every three years. Be careful to check on your own subject, and not on the overall research rating average for the university. Remember that, when published, this table could be up to three years out of date. Treat all other league tables with <u>extreme caution</u>.

● Is there a particular sport or pastime you wish to pursue? Does the university or college have the amenities you need? Does it offer professional coaching? This information is in the Potter Guide entry.

● Will you have somewhere to live? Where will it be? This, too, is in the Potter Guide entry. Look in the Accommodation section for each institution.

● Cost. Can you afford to go to a particular university/ college? Check on the cost of private accommodation. This is your largest fixed cost, and you will have to find somewhere outside the university/college to live for at least one of your years (except in a very few places, or under specific circumstances).

● Send for the Alternative Prospectus from the Students' Union. Not all Unions produce Alternative Prospectuses, but, where available, these will give you a different perspective on the university/college. Do not take all their comments literally: some A.P.s are irreverent to the point of being unhelpful; most are subjective; many are invaluable insights into student life - it all depends on who wrote them.

● Other people's opinions and experiences are, unfortunately, often subjective and outdated. The whole higher education system has changed so dramatically in the past few years that unless your advisor is professionally geared to keeping in touch and up to date, and has kept abreast of all courses and all institution mergers and changes, advice should be handled with care.

Ask as many people as possible, and bear in mind all suggestions. In the end, the only person who will know what is the right course and the right institution for you will be you, provided that you have done your homework.

● **Last year's offers:** these are not a good indicator if you want to guarantee a successful application form. Often, low offers made by a university/college one year attract massive 'safety net' applications the next. The law of supply and demand prevails: offers move upward. Some high demand, prestige courses give low offers to excellent candidates after interview: on paper, if taken as isolated statistics, these 'last year's offers' are most misleading.

ACCOMMODATION

One of the most important single factors of your new life will be accommodation: where you live and how you live will determine your personal comfort, ability to study in your own time, and - above all - how easily you will make friends and join in the social and cultural experiences.

Price differentials are a crucial factor and are very wide indeed. You can still find a room for around £25 per week around some northern institutions; you might have to pay more than £60 per week in parts of the south.

If you are attracted to an institution which will most likely offer you good accommodation, do check what will happen in your second and subsequent years. Accommodation owned by institutions is usually subsidised and can mask an expensive private sector.

You could also run into a problem with accessibility: in some places you might be forced to live a long way from your study centre and have to rely on expensive public transport - or acquire your own wheels.

You should also check on the insurance ratings of university areas. Contact the Union to find out where the most popular 'living out' areas are and check their postcodes against insurance risk. You might find that your belongings cannot be insured in some places, and this might influence your choice of area and, hence, the rent you will have to pay.

THE RANGE OF CHOICE

Halls of Residence

The best choice for most first years. Your room might be small, or shared, the hall noisy, and the food poor. But hall-living is the best way of jumping into student life, learning the ropes and making friends. Fees are usually reasonable and you are usually looked after (rooms cleaned, meals prepared, often some laundry done for you).

It is worth adding that in some institutions halls of residence are positively palatial. They double in vacation time as conference centres, and can provide very comfortable rooms with private bathrooms. Luck of the draw - or sometimes an option to pay extra.

Student flats or houses

You might prefer, or be given, the semi-independence of a shared house or flat. A usual mode is for a number of students (5-8) to have private (or shared) rooms in a flat or house, sharing a bathroom and cooking facilities. You are likely to have to look after yourself (clean, cook and fathom a launderette).

It is a very good idea to learn some simple cooking techniques and do a practice run or two in a launderette before you go.

Head leasing

Some private sector rooms are available on 'head-leasing' (sometimes called 'direct leasing') schemes. Your institution signs an agreement with the owners of houses or flats let to students and collects the rent from you. A good thing for you, since your institution will vet your accommodation and help with any problems.

Lodgings

Here, of course, you will take a room with a family and 'live in' to varying degrees: you might have meals with the family, or make arrangements not to! The advantages are obvious: you might have washing and cleaning done for you and the 'family' will keep an eye on your general welfare. Your parents might like the arrangement, and many of you might also like this halfway independence. Living out, if you are not in student-shared accommodation, can be lonely.

Private sector housing

Similar conditions to institution owned/head leased flats or houses, but the standard and the cost will be variable.

WARNING NOTES:

• You should always check out accommodation before accepting it.
• **NEVER** go alone to view a property; always take a friend, or possibly your parents.
• **NEVER** sign any lease without reading it carefully - and asking advice from your Accommodation Office or Student Union if in any doubt.
• **NEVER** accept accommodation without a written lease and a rent book.
• Make sure, before you take on a property, that the journey 'in' is reasonable; find out how much the bus/train fares will be and add that weekly bill to your rent. Sometimes a cheap place can become expensive if you count in travel, heat and light.
• Make sure you can insure your personal belongings. Some areas in or near big cities are becoming insurance 'no go' zones.

EUROPEAN AND OTHER OVERSEAS LINKS

Where an institution advertises European or other overseas links, find out how many places are available to students from the course for which you intend to apply. The actual number of places can be very limited. Find out also under which scheme the exchange is happening: EC sponsored programmes - ERASMUS/SOCRATES - include support and financial assistance; non-EC exchanges are funded differently. Most universities/colleges have struck individual links with institutions abroad, to exchange students for a term/semester/year. Many courses can include time abroad, some in an educational centre, some in work placements. If this factor will influence your choice, look into the prospects offered:

• the length of the placement
• whether grants are available (non-European links, and indeed some European placements, might depend on your own input of money)
• when the placements are available. If, for example, you will be expected to be away during your final year, how will this affect your applying for jobs?
• the type of institution receiving you. Just because a university/college is Abroad does not automatically mean it is either a 'good' place, in a pleasant city/environment, or that - given an open choice - you would actually opt to go there?

These factors could go into your personal diagnostic menu to help you to choose between institutions. Try not to be drawn into thinking about a course just because it offers foreign travel. As a student, you will have opportunities to travel in the long vacation, cheaply and easily. An overseas placement can simply break up your study routine, take you away from new friends and add little to your understanding of your subject. Think about your own priorities, not just the glamour of going to far-away places.

Further information on EC exchanges and other placements is available from The Central Bureau for Educational Visits and Exchanges, 10 Spring Gardens, London SW1A 2BN.

Before you begin...

Ideally, you should have a copy of *The Working Approach to Higher Education* which gives you a personal programme of study and decision points. Available from Dalebank Books, Arden Lodge, Savile Park Road, Halifax HX1 2XR (NB: the booklet is supplied only in tutor units).

You should look at a copy of the current *Student Grants and Loans: A Brief Guide for Higher Education Students*, available from your school/college or Local Education Authority. Read this booklet thoroughly to assess your financial position.

The UCAS Handbook and other literature will give you clear and full information on the application procedure. At present, you have a maximum choice of six courses. You should aim to submit your application as soon as possible: applications are accepted by UCAS between September 1st and December 15th in the year before you intend to begin your Higher Education career. UCAS literature should be available from your school/college, or from UCAS: PO Box 28, Cheltenham GL50 3SH.

feed the mind

Hungry?

Want to develop your mind?
We can help you.

The University of Sunderland.

One of the most dynamic and
innovative universities in the North
of England.

Excellent choice of over 100 degree
courses and flexible study
programmes in science,
technology, business, education,
the creative arts or humanities.

New riverside campus. New life.

Food for thought?

Phone our special helpline today
for a free copy of our full-time
prospectus, or write to:

**Student Recruitment,
University of Sunderland,
Unit 4B/C, Technology Park,
Chester Road,
Sunderland SR2 7PS.**

☎ **HELPLINE 0191 515 3000**

PROVIDING THE SKILLS FOR LIFELONG LEARNING

NORTH

Bolton Institute of Higher Education
University of Bradford
University of Central Lancashire
Chester College
University of Durham
Edge Hill College of Higher Education
University of Huddersfield
University of Hull
University of Humberside
University of Lancaster
University of Leeds
Leeds Metropolitan University
University of Liverpool
Liverpool John Moores University
University of Manchester
UMIST
Manchester Metropolitan University
University of Newcastle Upon Tyne
University of Northumbria at Newcastle
University of Salford
University of Sheffield
Sheffield Hallam University
University of Sunderland
University of Teesside
University of York

Bolton Institute of Higher Education

Deane Road
Bolton
BL3 5AB
Telephone: 01204 28851

Bolton Institute has about 4,000 full-time undergraduate and HND students. Degrees are modular; students may choose modules to create their own programmes. Subjects are geared, mainly, to the needs of Bolton's local industries - business, engineering and textiles. Assessment is largely by coursework with some examinations. Rhw Institute has three campuses all either in or fairly close to the centre of Bolton. There are 700 places in Institute halls: the private sector has a good supply of rented houses at reasonable rates.

THE CAMPUS

The Institute has three campuses set in and fairly close to the centre of Bolton.

Chadwick campus

Bolton's largest campus, set amid mixed suburban housing about 15-20 minutes' walk and to the east of the town centre. The main building, two-storey glass/coloured-panels/steel, fills a square of respectable period terraced housing: bay windows, gables, trees. The square must have once been pleasant green space. Behind and beyond the square, around a bowling green and into more residential spaces, the campus has developed teaching buildings and a group of halls of residence. All fairly modest in scale and ambience.

Courses here: School of Education and Health Studies, and the Humanities division of the School of Arts and Sciences.

Deane Campus

A similar distance out from the town centre, to the west, is (the main) Deane campus, a compact group of modern buildings bounded by urban streets and car parks and trimmed by green spaces. Bolton's main Queen's Park is close enough for fine day relaxation strolls.

Courses here: Bolton Business School, School of Civil Engineering and Building, School of Engineering, School of Textile Studies, Psychology and Biology Divisions of the School of Arts and Sciences, Mathematics Division of the School of Arts and Sciences.

Great Moor Street

A single building: a rather good example of Victorian red-brick school/institution architecture. The atmosphere is busy and friendly and suits the student mix which ranges from school leavers to adults. Although this is not a main campus it is strongly identified locally with the Institute.

Courses here: Art and Design division of the School of Arts and Sciences.

Car-parking: is not a problem.

Learning Resources

All three campuses have **libraries** which serve their courses: the Deane Campus Library seats 250 readers and the Ryley Library on the Chadwick Campus seats 300. Total bookstock: 100,000 books and 900 journals. Both Deane and Chadwick Campuses have **Information Technology** Centres through which students can access the Institute's mini and micro computers.

The Union

The Union is in the process of moving to a more commodious building. At present, the travel shop and shops on the Deane and Chadwick Campuses are run by the Union. The bar on Deane Campus is the main social centre for Union events: entertainments include discos, live performances and quiz nights. The Union funds over 30 clubs and societies covering political, cultural and sporting activities. The Union newspaper, published monthly, will keep you informed. The Welfare Advice Centre, run by students will give help, support and advice.

Sport

The Institute has a large multi-court sports hall with a fitness room including a multi-gym and a free-standing weights area on the Deane Campus. The hall has a climbing wall. The Institute also has a squash court and playing field and access to all-weather pitches and a swimming pool locally. Coaching and support is available from full-time staff and a small team of specialists whatever your level. Teams compete at regional and local level throughout the year, and there are internal competitions and leagues. Membership of sports clubs or societies carries a small charge; equipment in the on-site sports hall is usually free of charge. The area around Bolton means that you can go fell-walking, sailing, canoeing and rock-climbing - open landscape and waterways are not far away.

Student welfare

The Institute has **counsellors** who can help with a range of issues. Short courses are sometimes arranged. The Anglican **Chaplain**, assisted by a Catholic nun, provides an ecumenical service to people of all faiths and denominations. **Careers** officers are available on all campuses. A Careers Education Programme for each main course includes talks and discussion sessions. The Service has a computerised aptitude test and video playback.

Students with special needs
The Information Officer in for Special Needs will be able to give you individual guidance and will liaise with your intended faculty. The Institute maintains a resource bank of information and works with external agencies.

Accommodation

The Institute has 700 places in two self-catering halls of residence, located on, between or near the campuses. All rooms are single. Costs 1996/97: Hall: £1,580 for 40 weeks; private sector: £34 to £40 per week.

Mature students

The main consideration when Bolton assesses an application from a student over 21 is whether he/she will benefit from and are likely to complete the course. Background and past experience are factors. You should contact the Access Officer in the Marketing and External Relations Unit for further information.

THE TOWN (population: 266,900)

Bolton is one of the satellite towns of Manchester, but with an identity of its own. The town has one of the north's most imposing and splendid town hall complexes, which is quite an accolade since 19th century town halls in the north are the equivalent of medieval cathedrals. The shopping centre is pedestrianised and pleasant, easy and very adequate. This is a typical modest northern town with a good market atmosphere and a friendly disposition, cradled in the west Pennines.

Entertainments: Theatre - The Bolton Octagon is a high quality rep theatre, Albert Halls, in the town hall, houses pantomimes and other live entertainments in a Victorian setting, Bolton Little Theatre houses amateur dramatics; **Museums** - the Bolton Museum and Art Gallery has changing exhibitions; **Cinema** - Cannon Cinema with three screens; **Nightclubs** - eight in all; **Restaurants** - a range.

ESCAPE ROUTES

You are close to the West Pennine Moors and a number of reservoirs with easy access to hill climbing and walking. You are also very close to Manchester and not far from Liverpool. See their escape routes and communications sections.

Communications

There is a frequent service from Bolton to the two mainline stations in Manchester which have regular services to London and all other major UK cities. National Coaches operate services to most major UK cities direct. Bolton is very close to the M61 and M62 which in turn link with six other motorways originating from or passing through Manchester. Manchester Airport is just 30 minutes away by car with flights all over the world.

University of Bradford

Bradford
West Yorkshire
BD7 1DP
Telephone: 01274 733466
World Wide Web: http://www.brad.ac.uk/bradinfo/bradinfo.html

University Charter date: 1966
Bradford is a small/medium-sized university with **just under 6,000 undergraduate** students on full-time degree programmes and **over 800 full-time postgraduate** students. The University is on a single site, just up the hill from the city centre. All degree programmes are divided into 36 modules. Programmes are structured to provide academic coherence within a 'home department'. Assessment is a mix of exam and assessment, with the emphasis being on end of module exams. Your first year assessment will not normally count towards your final degree classification. Many courses have a 'sandwich' element, including one or more placements in external organisations. All single first years who live more than one hour's travelling distance from the University (by public transport) will be offered a place in University-owned accommodation.

THE CAMPUS

Bradford achieved full university status - with the other technologicals - in 1966. In 1957 it became a College of Advanced Technology: an accolade in its time, and recognition of its earlier history of developing technological education to serve a growing industrial community from the early part of the 19th century. The University has built a comprehensive campus on a site contained within a mile of the centre of a city major in its size and amenities.

The site is compact and makes a good job of its limited space by using high-rise functional blocks of concrete, glass and grey brick, separated by stretches of lawn and grouped trees. The campus plan avoids feeling overcrowded, but has a sense of high-density business: the precinct is open to the urban area which contains it, faced by busy shopping parades and the terraced housing of a working northern city. The interest and variety of its layout is helped by the changing levels of its terrain. Campus buildings have all been built since 1965, with the exception of the Phoenix Building, an old mill, now a theatre, which gives the University a nice link with its city's history.

The ambience of the campus is small-scale, informal, good-natured, friendly, with a strong sense of a caring, fairly small undergraduate community. Bradford has high number of mature students (a deliberate policy), who have their own influence on the prevailing sense of purpose, as have the many students of different ethnic origin, who reflect well the style of the city.

The University's strong links with industry are reinforced by its Business Development Service and the developing Science Park adjacent to its campus. Separate from the main campus is the University's Management Centre, set in 13 acres of pleasant parkland.

Cars

There are no problems about bringing your car - other than the inevitable scramble for city parking spaces. There is a termly charge for a campus car-parking permit.

Learning Resources

Bradford has two **libraries**: the recently extended JB Priestley Library (the main University library) and the Yvette Jacobson Library at the Management Centre. Altogether they contain 500,000 volumes, plus 2,500 current periodicals. Open: 8.45am to 9pm weekdays, to 5.30pm on Saturdays and from 1pm to 5.30pm on Sundays. Bradford's goal is for all undergraduates to be computer literate by the time they finish their courses. The **Computer Science Faculty** offers courses in programming and has software self-teach and CAD/CAM facilities. A new cable network covers the University and the Management Centre, providing access to the main computer, available 24 hours a day to all students. You can plug your own computer into the network anywhere on campus, in your hall of residence or at the Management Centre.

The University's **Language Unit** offers teaching in 23 languages. Some courses contain a foreign language module, or you can attend evening classes, supplemented be self-teaching, in addition to your course.

Culture on campus

Bradford has three Fellows to give focus and guidance in Music, Theatre and the Visual Arts.

Drama: The University Theatre Group has its studio base at The Theatre in the Mill, an imaginative conversion of the Phoenix Building (an old mill) on campus. The range of drama is wide and includes work written domestically. The theatre also hosts an exciting programme of visits by professional companies (including London's Royal Court) and amateur groups, and occasionally runs a programme of workshops.

Film: The Film Society screens three/four films per week.

Music: The Music Fellow co-ordinates a wide range of student performance: the main choir is open to all and has an ambitious programme; the smaller chamber choir has entry by audition and frequently performs in public, at home and abroad. The University orchestra has around 50 members and the Wind Orchestra is open to those players who are not in the full orchestra. A varied programme of 'Music for Lunch' and evening concerts featuring artists of international reputation, many of whom give lectures or participate in workshops. Free to students. The Union adds variety with its own programme of weekly concerts and jazz evenings: many top name singers appear. 'In-house' music tuition is also on offer. Studentships and part-studentships are available.

The Union

The Communal Building is the social centre, with three bars (one with a large dance floor), a disco, meeting rooms, snooker room and games room and a travel office. Here too are a print room, common room and the Union's finance, welfare, administration and sabbatical officers. In the Richmond Building, which also houses the University's administrative offices and academic work, the Union runs a bar and a shop. Weekly gigs, concerts, raves and jazz evenings mean that the campus is hopping.

The Union produces a monthly magazine *Scrapie*, a regular news publication *The Bradford Student Hack* and a daily newsheet *Ram*. It also runs *Ramair*, a campus radio broadcasting to halls of residence and beyond. The Union supports a wide range of clubs and activities (over 100) and a well-supported Community Action programme.

Permanent staff: 30; annual trading turnover: £1.5 million; a total of six sabbatical officers.

Sport

The sports centre on campus has facilities for a wide range of physical activity, including archery, climbing, fencing and all the usual pursuits. The small gym is also available for table tennis, fencing and other activities. A new exercise studio facility gives room for dance and the more elegant arts of Tai Chi and Aikido. The weight-training room has a multigym and Olympic facilities. There is a 25 metre swimming pool, sauna suite and solarium, Nautilus Fitness Suite with cardiovascular and resistance exercise machinery, and two squash courts. Facilities can be booked privately during the day; evenings are usually the preserve of student clubs.

Two playing field sites: one close to the campus at Laisteridge Lane; the other four miles away at Woodhall, easily reached by public transport. The Laisteridge Lane site has two netball courts (four tennis courts in summer), two squash courts, two five-a-side football pitches and one full size hockey/football pitch: all are dri-pla or artificial turf surfaces and all are floodlit. The Woodhall site has eight pitches - four football and four rugby - and two cricket squares. There is a pavilion with bar and refectory, as well as changing rooms/showers.

The Athletic Association organises a good range of outdoor pursuits further afield (sailing, pot-holing, golf, hang-gliding...) Coaching classes in various sports and swimming lessons are available. There are about 50 clubs.

Student welfare

The University has a **health centre** near the halls of residence. You should register with a University doctor if you want to use the service to the full. A sick bay with ten beds is available - it doesn't matter who your doctor is - and there is a full-time nursing staff. Student **counselling service** which covers most student problems. The Union welfare office has staff trained to help with accommodation, personal, or any other kind of problem.

Christian **chaplains** are appointed by their churches and work as a team on the University campus. A quiet room is available for Muslim prayer. Bradford offers many facilities for other religious observances.

Careers Service

Bradford courses are all designed to give you a well-balanced base of experience, to increase your practical and transferable skills. The Careers Advisory Service has strong links with the local business community. Careers education happens within departments in addition to one-to-one interviews. The Service has computerised careers guidance systems, runs workshops and 'Insight into Management' courses, and has a well-stocked information area.

Students with special needs

The University has worked on its campus to make it more accessible to students with mobility problems: some residential accommodation has also been converted. Braille facilities provided through the Computer Centre. The University has a Disability Office which will be able to answer your queries. Some courses do present some problems, so you should contact the University outlining your personal needs before you fill in your UCAS form.

Accommodation

Subject to basic provisos (single, home beyond commuting distance, one hour by public transport) - all first years will be offered a place, which must be confirmed by September.

Halls of residence

There are eight halls of residence. Five of the self-catering halls are on the main campus; the other halls are a short walking distance away. Two provide breakfast daily, with evening meals on weekdays and lunch at weekends.

Five of the self-catering 'halls' are in the form of purpose-built terraces of houses. Most rooms are single study-bedrooms. The units have a kitchen/dining room on each floor, or in each house. Amenities vary: you might have a room in a 'flat' where 7 students share communal facilities, or in a block where 24 share 2 kitchen/dining-rooms.

The catered halls are connected by a block which houses dining rooms, common rooms, a small library, a shop, a reading room, two TV rooms, a bar and games room.

Costs (1995/96)

Self-catered halls from £29.35 (shared room) to £48.20 (single, ensuite) per week for 30 weeks

Catered halls: £56.85 per week for 30 weeks

All fees include heating, lighting and the provision and laundering of bedlinen. All halls are warden-controlled.

Private sector

Private rented accommodation is fairly easy to find in Bradford, within close range of the University, and is relatively cheap. The Accommodation Office keeps a list, but does not inspect properties. Usual student housing is a room in a shared house and costs around £24 to £28.

Mature students

A very positive attitude here. You are usually interviewed and, if you lack formal qualifications, you must demonstrate ability and commitment. There are seminars which give information on entry and admissions, child care, fees, grants and loans. You could also contact the Student Recruitment office if you have a specific query.

Nursery

The University runs a day nursery for children between six months and five years old. There are 50 places in all. Open weekdays in term time, and in most of the vacations.

THE CITY (population: 280,000)

Bradford fills a wide, symmetrical hollow in the Pennines. It is a very well-contained city: the crowns of many of its surrounding hills lift empty moorland to the sky. Until the 19th century this was a small rural town, which expanded with explosive energy during the Industrial Revolution. As usual, the Victorians expressed their new wealth, energy and confidence in a collection of buildings which remain a particularly happy result of their competitive civic pride and high-style architecture: the extravagant and famed Gothic City Hall, the flamboyant Italianate Wool Exchange, the solid and functionally excellent St George's concert hall, the cathedral and others. Add to these the pillared and domed Alhambra Theatre, the twin-domed Odeon cinema, the impressive sweep of the National Museum of Photography, the large library and arts cinema (Pictureville): all compensate well for the wide industrial sprawl and labyrinthine streets of the city's approaches.

The shopping centre is good, with new precincts, major chain stores, interesting shops and the specialised markets whose colour and style are so richly influenced by the presence of a large Asian community. The centre is compact, with its facilities well spaced but close, its levels varied: it is not a tiring city to use. If you want larger scale shopping, then Leeds is a mere nine miles away. Prices are very keen, as they are in the good range of restaurants (curries a speciality) and pubs (a happyland for Real Ale).

Theatre: The Alhambra is Bradford's major theatre, recently refurbished. It is the venue for large touring companies, including the RSC, famous variety and comedy acts, opera and ballet. The Alhambra Studio hosts excellent smaller companies and innovative productions. The Bradford Playhouse puts on amateur productions.

Music: St. George's Hall is venue for large concerts, both by well-known groups and singers and by orchestras including the Halle. The Queen's Hall (Bradford and Ilkley Community College's Students' Union) is a more 'alternative' venue. Cartwright Hall is also used for concerts and contemporary dance.

Bradford's musical tradition is varied. As well as indigenous brass bands, the city has a growing jazz community and folk clubs.

Cinema: The National Museum has the IMAX cinema and the Pictureville which is one of the best equipped cinemas in the country. Its collaborative programming in association with Bradford Film Theatre gives Bradford 'a range of film product unmatched outside London'. There is also a range of commercial cinemas.

Nightlife: Good, varied: clubs, discos, pubs with beer from twenty different Real Ale breweries. Bradford is rightly famous for its Indian restaurants.

Sport: Bradford Northern rugby league team, the Yorkshire passion for cricket and Bradford City Football Club provide the city's spectator sports. The Richard Dunn sports centre at Odsal has generous facilities - including speedway; and an ice-rink in the city centre.

Events: The Bradford Festival runs for two weeks in June and takes place, mainly, in Bradford's parks.

ESCAPE ROUTES

The Yorkshire Dales are almost Bradford's doorstep: beautiful scenery, walking country and natural phenomena of tarns, falls and limestone pavements; abbeys, churches and castles. Haworth and Brontë country are also close: the moors here are rugged - very Wuthering Heights. The Worth Valley Railway (steam) is easily accessible.

Close to Bradford is Saltaire, a 'model' village built by Titus Salt for his workers. Salt's Mill, which used to be the work-focus of this development has now been converted. The complex includes the 1853 Gallery, supported by David Hockney and housing a private collection of his work, where you can browse through books and paintings to the strains of opera and the fragrance of fresh lilies.

Communications

Extensive **rail** and **coach services** to all parts of the country, with a fast line to London via Leeds. Bradford has its own **motorway** spur, the M606, joining it to the M62 and thence to the national motorway network. The city is only seven miles from the **Leeds/Bradford Airport**, with its national and growing international links.

University of Central Lancashire

Preston
PR1 2HE
Telephone: 01772 892500

University Charter date: 1992

Central Lancashire is a large/medium-sized university with 12,000 students on full-time or sandwich courses (under and postgraduate) and around 4,000 part-time students. The University has a single, well-developed site close to Preston town centre. A range of degree and HND programmes: the majority of courses are modularised and are part of a cross-curricular CAT Scheme. Assessment methods vary between modules - some are a combination of examination and assigned coursework and some are assessed entirely by coursework. If you live further than 30 miles from the University, there is a good chance that you will be offered University-owned accommodation for your first year. Cost of a room in the private sector: £26 - £40 per week self-catering.

THE CAMPUS

This is a single campus university, occupying a large site very close to the centre of Preston. The campus splits into two major sections, intersected by one of the town's busy circulation roads. The main, original teaching site is set back behind its large car-park, and recessed from the noise by flights of steps. The site is compact and fully built. To the rear is a large car park (used to be a rail yard area), oddly pierced by a finely spired church. This is the face of an old mill town.

The University has inherited or built a collection of 1960s style, flat-roofed, grey-lidded buildings, mostly three storey, in glass and concrete. The original early 20th century building has recently been cleaned and re-faced. Interior spaces are well-lit, surfaced with light warm colour and generating a friendly, well-occupied atmosphere.

Up the flights of steps and across the traffic to the second half of campus and another world. Here, you enter St Peter's Square, faced by terraces of well-kept small houses which is the heart of the University's community life. One side of the square is occupied by a large stone church, now housing the Arts Centre. The church is a listed building (i.e. of special architectural interest) built in 1825. An unusual and stimulating interior.

The centre of the square is paved and stepped down to the polygonal Union Building, large, purpose-built and light-hearted. Set at a rakish angle, its long windows drop two levels to a sunken paved court; its roof rises to a small party-hat pyramid.

The third main building to set the square is the library - new or very recent, large, well-fitted and well-used. Full wall windows give good natural light and deep interior spaces are comfortably lit. Clear plans, well-displayed; photographs of staff help to identify and add to the friendly supportive atmosphere. Working areas are generous. The square also contains a large new teaching block. Beyond, on the fringe of the site, are halls of residence, adding their domestic scope.

The new buildings are smart, substantial and harmonious in line and scale with the original complex. This is a well thought out campus: vibrant and talkative. St Peter's Square has a good balance of green space and trees, and the campus as a whole has a surprising air of space and ease - a real achievement for a relatively packed site in a busy town setting.

Cars
A car would be a good idea: there are very beautiful places nearby, and country worth exploring. Parking is limited, however, and a permit system is in operation on campus and at halls.

Learning Resources

The **library** has over 300,000 bound volumes and 1,100 reading places. It takes 3,000 periodicals. Opening times: 8.45am to 10pm Monday to Thursday; 8.45am to 8pm Friday; Saturday and Sunday mornings.

Computer skills can be a unit in your degree course. The University's 1,000 workstations are dedicated to both academic and administrative use. The University network is accessible through personal pc's in halls of residence.

Through '**Languages for All**', students are able to take up one of 12 foreign languages, or keep up with one they already have. Classes are run on an open access basis and cover skills for beginners up to advanced levels. Ultimately, these courses are intended to be accredited units within main study areas.

Culture on campus

Arts: The Arts Centre, on the main campus, houses a varied programme of theatre, music (including the University Band), art exhibitions, dance and workshops. The Arts Centre serves both the University and the local community. Fringe theatre and music recitals are its main repertory. A purpose-built Music Centre provides rehearsal, practice and performance facilities. Interesting courses are open to all students. The University Singers meet twice weekly, mostly unaccompanied. The University Drama Group (open to all students) has been very successful on the Edinburgh fringe.

You can also eat here. Coffee and lunch are served between 10am and 2pm during term time.

The Union

The Union has its own building. There are five sabbatical officers. The Union runs three bars, three shops, an insurance centre and four catering outlets. Socially it is active, organising live music events, discos, film nights and cabarets. The Union supports 28 sports clubs and 23 cultural and other societies, a student newspaper and a professionally staffed advice service. There is a late-night bus service, with priority for women students.

Sport

The University's main outdoor sports facilities are two miles away from campus. Playing fields and squash courts are nearby and there is a small sports centre on campus. A major outdoor multi-sport complex is due to be developed: £8 million of lottery money has been allocated.

The Union runs sports clubs through its council. There are interdepartmental competitions as well as the national Universities Athletic Union league.

Student welfare

There is a **Health Centre** open full time during term time with four doctors and two nurses who deal with all emergencies. The University has a confidential **counselling service**. Separate debt and legal counselling is also available. The Counselling Service runs sessions and gives advice on study skills and methods, relaxation and meditation techniques, on how to relate to other people more creatively and on exam technique. The University has a **Multi-faith Centre** served by a team representing most major world faiths.

Careers Service

The Careers Centre is open five days a week throughout the year, except during public holidays: literature and material for self-help is on open access. The Service holds workshops on application strategy and interview techniques, and arranges 'mock' interviews.

Prospect-HE is available. The Centre holds information on voluntary work and vacation and part-time jobs.

Students with special needs

The University offers two advisors: one for academic needs, one who deals with problems relating to finance or accommodation or other personal difficulties.

You are advised to visit the University before making your final decision, because some faculties are less accessible than others: the University would like to know of any problems and will try to find solutions.

A Specialised Learning Unit of braille texts and taped material has been included in the main library; hearing loops are installed in most lecture theatres. Some accommodation has been equipped for wheelchair users.

Accommodation

The University allocates hall places to first year students, based on the distance you would have to travel from home. There is University accommodation for 2,000 students. If you live further than 30 miles from the University, there is a good chance you will be accommodated. You should apply in August after Results.

The Accommodation Service provides help in finding private accommodation if necessary and offers comprehensive advice on housing issues. You can stay in University accommodation during your summer search.

Halls of residence

The halls are on the main University site and provide accommodation for 1,500 residents. All places are self-catering. The traditional halls are three storey blocks of single study bedrooms, the cluster flats comprise 4, 5 or 6 single study bedrooms. Both types share communal facilities: all rents include heat and light. The newest halls have ensuite rooms. Prices vary according to amenities.

University residences

Residences house between 12 and 25 students in either single or shared rooms with communal facilities. The University residences are two miles from the main campus.

In both halls and residences, students are expected to clean their own rooms, although communal facilities are cleaned. You can stay in University rooms during the vacations only if you have made arrangements with the Residences Manager first.

University houses

The University owns a number of houses which are each shared by groups of two to six students, the majority of whom will have single bedrooms. Payment is exclusive of electricity and gas.

Costs (1996/97)

Halls of residence:
£1,730 - £1,850 per annum
£2,000 ensuite
Residences : £1,110 - £1,650 per annum
Houses: £1,000 (shared) to £1,650 (single) per annum

Contracts are on a 42 week basis.

Private accommodation

The University has around 1,100 houses on its books. You should contact the Accommodation Service. Lists are not sent out to you, but the Accommodation Service will help you to find approved housing. Lodgings are also available, providing bed, breakfast, evening meal and light and heat.

Costs (1995/96)

The average cost of private accommodation in Preston is around £26 to £40 per week for a room, self-catered. Lodgings are between £45 and £50 (half board).

Mature students

The University works with partner colleges to provide flexible local access to higher education for adults.

Mature students make up a good proportion of the University's students. The University runs a Continuing Education programme for adults who want to return to or continue their studies. Mature students are encouraged to apply for all University courses or you can attend the University as an associate student to develop knowledge and interest in a subject before actually embarking on a degree course.

There is a Foundation Studies programme, lasting 24 weeks, which allows students to experience higher education and the differences between courses. Several Year 0 programmes have been developed for students without degree entry requirements. The Mature Students Society is very active. Lots of advice available.

Part-time courses

The University offers a full range of part-time courses which can be a way through to full-time entry.

Nursery

The Preschool Centre, run by two managers and six nursery nurses (all qualified) takes 68 children between the ages of two and five. There are two sessions a day Monday to Friday. The Centre is purpose built and has a large range of equipment. The facility is open to both staff and students.

THE CITY (population 128,000)

Preston is the administrative centre of Lancashire (Lancaster is the county town - different). Although Preston grew to major size and influence as one of the north-west chain of cotton towns in the Industrial Revolution, it is a town of ancient origins: fiercely loyal Cavalier stronghold during the Civil War and with a history dating back to medieval times. History lingers in its quieter corners in old buildings, squares and terraces, and in the fabric of its life.

'Once a Preston Guild' could baffle you as a benchmark of long time gaps, if you don't know that a Guild is a major celebration, at all levels of activity throughout the town for a whole year - every twenty years! The last one was in 1992. The Guild celebrates the medieval trade guilds and attracts worldwide interest.

The town has a good range of regular markets. One of the best, unfortunately for you, happens only in August: the amazing Preston Pot Fair, a performance fair where crockery is juggled and auctioned.

The centre of the town has been largely modernised: there are two major shopping centres, a covered market, old arcades and many smaller, long-established shops.

Preston was the first town to develop parks for its citizens, and a major one (Avenham) stretches from within minutes' walk of the University down to the banks of the Ribble. The new 'Riversway Marina' re-development of the old docks offers watersports, a floating restaurant a waterside pub, a multiplex cinema with 10 screens and a retail park.

Preston is a well-contained town; you are very quickly out into the fells, valleys and charming villages of Ribblesdale. This is a very lovely area. Go the other way and you can have a brash and noisy outing to Blackpool, with its large funfair, autumn Illuminations and candyfloss atmosphere. You are also within easy reach of the Lake District, Morecambe Bay, The Yorkshire Dales and the city cultures of Liverpool and Manchester.

Museums and galleries: The Harris museum and gallery houses exhibitions of local interest. There is also a military museum.

Music and theatre: The Guildhall (built in 1972) has a theatre and large hall which hosts concerts, snooker tournaments etc. Folk, pop and jazz music is available in the town. The Playhouse accommodates local amateur dramatic clubs.

Cinema: There are two cinemas, one with ten screens, the other, eight.

Nightlife: The town offers a surprisingly good range of restaurants, including a few which are open late at night. The range of pubs, nightclubs and discos is lively for a town of this size.

Sport: Preston North End has its devotees and there are actually plans for a museum of football here. The University has agreements with several local clubs to use their facilities for golfing, swimming and outdoor pursuits. There are two large Leisure Centres.

ESCAPE ROUTES

Preston is the last in the chain of Industrial Revolution developments spreading north from Manchester and east from Burnley and Blackburn. North of Preston, towards the fells and Ribblesdale, is very beautiful, gentle walking country.

You can get up to the Lake District easily either by train or by car. The Lancashire Cycleway - two routes 130 miles long - runs around the northern and southern parts of the County. The routes cross the Pennine moors, travel the tow-paths of the Liverpool-Leeds Canal, wander in the Forest of Bowland and follow the South Pennine packhorse trails. Excellent for mountain bike enthusiasts.

The coast is not far away: Blackpool and Southport are equidistant from Preston. There is sand yachting on the Fylde coast.

Communication

Rail links to Manchester and all points west; effective, and good links up north to the Lake District and beyond. Trains to London, a high-speed link.

M6, access south and north; **M61** direct to Manchester; **M55** direct to Blackpool

University College Chester

Cheyney Road
Chester
CH1 4BJ
Telephone: 01244 375444

> Chester is an accredited college of the University of Liverpool and was a teacher training college whose courses have expanded recently. The College has over 4,000 students and a single 30 acre site half a mile out of the city. Courses are modular and assessed by examination and coursework (often with equal emphasis). The College has halls of residence, housing relatively few of its students and has also arranged a headlease scheme. Most students not housed by the college can find accommodation close to campus.

THE CAMPUS

Chester College was founded in 1839 and officially opened by Gladstone in 1842. It began life as a teacher training college, founded by the Church of England, and was the first purpose-built teacher training college in the country.

The College now, over 150 years later, still occupies the same campus - 30 acres half a mile from the ancient city walls of Chester. Its own walls are high and the approach to the College, some way from the main road, makes it a world apart. The Victorian, redbrick buildings are still used for teaching and administration; many lecture and seminar rooms are housed in the seven storey tower which rises from this original cluster.

As the College has grown in numbers and course scope, new buildings have grown to accommodate the changes. The most recent is a high quality, low-rise Art and Technology building, the science building and refurbished laboratories and new Geography remote sensing suites.

The campus is self-contained, with residential units, sports and leisure facilities alongside academic services and buildings. The College chapel is a focal point, part of the original complex; there are daily services and Holy Communion is celebrated regularly.

Also on-campus are the College's sports pitches, including an all-weather, floodlit pitch; and the Auditorium and Gladstone Hall which host various visiting events.

The English Department occupies a Victorian house just down the road, the only College building off main campus.

The College retains its close contact with the Church of England, although its outlook now is more ecumenical. Chester Cathedral plays a significant role in College life: the annual Valedictory Service is held there, and it hosts the degree ceremony.

One extra feature: the College owns an outdoor pursuits centre at Murton, near Appleby-in-Westmorland (a very beautiful part of the country, with a world and rhythms of its own). The Centre gives you access to the Lake District, Yorkshire Dales, and is close to the highest peaks of the Pennines. The Centre is a base for field work in various subjects, and is available to all students interested in outdoor pursuits.

Learning Resources

The library houses 170,000 items (books, newspapers, journals, videos...) which are listed on a computerised database. Opening hours: late opening on weekdays and afternoon opening at weekends. There is also an on-line link to Liverpool University, and a regular minibus service (Wednesday afternoons and Saturday mornings) if you want to use the University's library.

An Open Access Computing centre was opened in 1995. A range of PCs and Mackintoshes are available, along with course-related software and printers.

All students can study a foreign language module (French, German or Spanish) in their degree programmes. Media Services has video editing and sound-mixing suites, a fully equipped television studio and a photographic workshop.

Culture on campus

The College has a drama studio and strong tradition of student drama. The Molloy Auditorium houses larger touring companies (the RSC occasionally), while the Gladstone Hall is venue for concerts, pantomime, musicals and regular discos. The new Art and Technology building has gallery space both for student work and exhibitions of nationally recognised artists, as well as for some performance art. The College chapel has a strong choir.

The Union

The Union elects two sabbatical officers annually; in all there are 12 executive posts. There is a strong interaction between the Union and the College, including 'question time' in the bar: students can put their queries directly to College staff. Union business is conducted from the De Bunsen Centre, which has a catering outlet and large television room as well as the Union offices. The College Bar and Social Club are not run by the Union, but are used for many social events. You must be a member of the Social Club in order to be able to buy drinks. Entertainments: weekend bands, bops, comedy nights, boat trips; Thursday nights have some planned entertainment. The Union supports 33 clubs and societies, 21 sporting and 12 non-sporting (including Orchestra, Drama and Community Action). Student Union News (SUN) is issued weekly, the College magazine and a fortnightly showing of the Chester College Television videos which chronicle the life of the College.

Sport

On campus facilities include a games hall, gymnasium, squash courts, tennis courts, a weights room, sauna and solarium, a floodlit all weather training area and grass playing fields and a new Fitness and Aerobics Arena. The indoor swimming pool is used by the Department of Physical Education and is used by the Department and by authorised sports clubs. Recreation classes and coaching classes are organised. 21 sports clubs.

Student welfare

Garden Lane **medical centre** is a five minute walk from the College grounds and staffed by the College Sister, available on weekdays. The practice has a physiotherapy service and runs specialist clinics. Five doctors (two female and three male) are available. You can see the **Student Counsellor** at set times. The **Chaplaincy** holds daily Christian service.

The **Careers Service** has a library of information and computerised careers guidance packages. Employer representatives take part in seminars and presentations organised by the service. Careers Education is integrated into the third year of all degree programmes.

Students with special needs
If you want information about facilities available, or wish to visit the College before you apply, you should contact the Registry. Some of the older buildings pose problems for students with mobility problems.

Accommodation

The College has c. 500 places in Halls of Residence. First years who do not get a place are found temporary accommodation and then given a choice of suitable places. Halls are situated on campus and offer full board catering seven days a week. There is also a headlease scheme involving 550 bed-spaces.

Cost (1995/96)
£59.85 pw fully catered for 30 weeks
£40.00 pw self-catering flats and houses

Private Sector
Most students can find housing close to the campus and the Accommodation Office keeps a list of properties available.

Cost (1995/96)
£30-£40 pw for room in house

Mature students

A third of the student population is 'mature'. Access courses are considered along with traditional entry qualifications. If you do not have standard entry qualifications, you should write to the College before applying with details of your qualifications and experience; you will probably have an advisory interview to discuss your course choices.

CITY (population 116,000)

Chester has a very visible history, stretching back to Roman times. Its Roman amphitheatre is the largest yet uncovered in Britain. More famous, however, are the Rows, gantried Tudor buildings which converge in a cross at the centre of the city, now shopping arcades of small boutiques and galleries. The ancient walls contain the city's development, as does the boundary of the river Dee. You can still walk the walls. Also noteworthy are Chester's cathedral, castle and zoo. **Entertainments:** the Gateway Theatre is the main venue and the Little Theatre has its own programme; several museums chronicling the city's long history; cinema - a multi-screen Canon on the city's outskirts and an Odeon cinema in the centre; a selection of clubs, a number of olde worlde pubs (real not refurbished) and a good selection of restaurants; the Warehouse is venue for live bands and there is a lively jazz club. **Sport:** the main sport is the Races (three meets a year) and the Chester Regatta each May. Ten-pin bowling is available just outside the city.

ESCAPE ROUTES

Chester is on the edge of the Welsh hills which rise to become Snowdonia. Excellent walking, climbing and trekking country. You are also close to Liverpool. See the University of Liverpool section.

Communications

Rail-lines to Liverpool, Manchester and Crewe, and from there to the rest of the country. Chester is on the M53 (to Liverpool) and the M56 (to Manchester and the M6 and M62). Air: Speke Airport is the nearest, Manchester Airport is also close and is international.

University of Durham

Old Shire Hall
Durham
DH1 3HP
Telephone: 0191 374 2000

University Charter date: 1832

Durham is a medium-sized university with around 7,000 undergraduates full-time programmes and over 1,000 full-time postgraduates. This is a collegiate university: 12 colleges and two societies in all, scattered throughout the city. All teaching is organised centrally for all students: colleges are, therefore, primarily social units. Degree courses are modular and flexible. Each named degree programme requires you to study specific modules and you are expected to retain compatibility between your modules. There is an additional range of free elective modules. There is guaranteed University accommodation for at least two years of your programme. Students are housed in the colleges.

THE UNIVERSITY

It is impossible here to segregate the University from its city: the colleges and associated buildings, together with the splendid cathedral and the tourism amenities which have gathered round it, are the city.

In this, as in other respects, Durham resembles Oxford and Cambridge (on whom it has always consciously modelled its style). Indeed, Oxbridge students visiting Durham are inclined to remark that the atmosphere here is 'more Oxbridge' than the originals.

The University was founded in 1832. Efforts and plans to create a university here, dating back through many centuries, were blocked by statesmen who wished to preserve the pre-eminence of the two ancient institutions. This legacy of plans (looking to continue old traditions and not forward to the radical shifts in educational priorities, and the explosion into change which came with the surge of the great Civic Universities) has created a university very much in harmony with its surroundings.

In recent years, the University has balanced this traditional image with a number of highly innovative policies - the collaboration with Teesside University, which has led to the founding of University College Stockton, its network of Continuing Education courses, and other changes and expansions - all underpinned by modern financial management systems. The ambience of a collegiate body is preserved, and remains one of Durham's key attractions.

Durham offers a paradoxical university experience: segregation into fairly small college communities which become a strong focus of your life, combined with the concentration of a large student population into a relatively small host city. Every college is unique. Every individual blend of people, architecture and tradition has created an atmosphere of its own.

You must be accepted by a college, as well as an academic department as a condition of entry to the University. Your application will be considered by both your target academic department and a college (if you have not indicated a preferred college, the choice will be made for you). It will be graded according to your merits and, if you make it into the range which relates statistically to the number of offers to be made, you might be interviewed by department and college staff. If your first choice college rejects your application, it will be considered by two other colleges before your fate is sealed.

The University puts a lot of stress on the principle of 'learning how to learn'; whatever the structure of teaching in your faculty, your main aim must be to learn for and by yourself. You will, however, be aided in doing so by you college tutor, who will take a personal interest in your academic progress and general welfare.

The colleges

There are twelve colleges and two societies (one postgraduate, the other offering a less organised lifestyle for the more self-reliant - often mature - students). Two colleges are theological (one is not open to direct application). All but one of the colleges are fully mixed. The significance of the college you choose is entirely social. All teaching in the University is organised centrally for all students. The academic instruction you receive does not in any way depend on the college to which you belong, except for University College, Stockton (UCS) which is a teaching and residential college with its own distinct degree programmes.

Durham colleges are largely residential (the Societies less so), but it would be a mistake to think of them as halls of residence in borrowed robes. The colleges are interspersed through the fabric of Durham as thoroughly as its history and represent the flow of that history in their own styles. Thus **University College** occupies Durham Castle, once a palace of the Prince Bishop and standing twin with the cathedral to symbolise the enormous palatine power vested in Durham for hundreds of years.

The castle, standing on the site of a Saxon church, was founded in 1072. The castle's most beautiful feature is its tiny Norman crypt built in 1080. Because of its history, the castle is open to visitors on three afternoons a week in term-time: a penalty you will have to bear for the privilege of living there. The College provides residential accommodation in the castle, or in new or modernised buildings close by.

St John's College occupies period town houses of architectural distinction, renovated and modernised. **St Chad's College** members live in Georgian buildings close to the cathedral; here there is a strong Anglican tradition together with a welcome for students whatever their religious allegiance. **Hatfield College** buildings range in periods from the 17th century to the 1960s. Most of the other colleges occupy relatively modern premises, some very recent, with all the benefits of purpose-built study-bedrooms (some with en-suite facilities), and design ideas which are known to work well socially (grouping of rooms, provision of common rooms and recreation facilities).

The keynote for Durham's colleges, however, is difference. **St Mary's College** Summer Ball is a major event in the Durham calendar; there is also a carol service, drama productions and special dinners. **St Aidan's** retains a tradition of formal dining once a week: its impressive hall is used for concerts and social events. It has patios, a water garden terrace, tennis courts and a croquet lawn. **Grey** has a theatre, landscaped gardens and a marvellous site with 'arguably one of the finest views in Europe'. **Van Mildert** has a lake - you can skate in hard winter times - and a purpose-built meeting centre. **Trevelyan** has a separate hall for concerts and plays and mounts performance workshops, lectures and discussions.

The list goes on: each college has some special strength or amenity to offer, from gymnasium to organ scholarships, from an exceptionally well-stocked library to excellent dark-room facilities. Many of the colleges have their own chapels and choirs and appoint chaplains whose religious role is extended by pastoral and counselling work. Many offer good recreation facilities and lively clubs and societies (some are particularly good for drama and music). Much of Durham's social life centres on the colleges where there are college bars. High-lights of the social calendar still focus on College Balls.

If you are interested in going to Durham you really should read the college prospectuses (as well as the general University prospectus) and visit the city before applying. One thing to bear in mind while looking at the colleges is that, although no college is more than a mile from the centre of Durham, one or two feel more remote; the walk 'home' on dark evenings along wooded quiet roads and sheltered, tree lined driveways could be lonely.

University College, Stockton

UCS is run by the University of Durham in association with the University of Teesside. It offers a distinct range of courses in European Studies, environmental Sciences, Education and Biomedical Science. The campus in Stockton is purpose-designed and built. Students here have access to their own tailored academic resources, as well as to those of the University. There is a hall of residence on site, although most students here are drawn from the region.Other University buildings

Lecture rooms are on Palace Green, next to the cathedral. The Music School is also on Palace Green, and Law, History, Classics and Theology are housed in the narrow streets and historic buildings nearby. English, Languages, Sociology and Social Policy have modern spaces and facilities in a large modern complex (Elvet Riverside) down by the River Wear. Most social sciences departments live in attractive 18th-century houses in Old Elvet and the Science Departments are grouped on a large site, with new buildings and up-to-date facilities, south of the river. The usual Durham mix of historic and modern accommodation.

Cars

By now you will realise that Durham is not an easy place for domestic parking, or indeed for using your car in the city itself. The University cannot provide for more than a handful of its students and there are virtually no parking places at all for students on the peninsula or in the Elvet area. Regular on-street parking of student cars is not acceptable and most strictly controlled (clamps!), and if you do wish to bring your car, you must make adequate arrangements for parking or garaging before you qualify for a student car badge. Durham is a very small city: you certainly will not need a car to get around it.

Some of the newer colleges away from the city centre have limited parking facilities and this is yet another factor of difference which could influence your choice.

Learning Resources

The main **library** is on the Science Site, close to the six hill colleges and contains collections on all humanities, science and social science subjects (except law, music and education). The library is open until 10pm including the weekends. Law and music sections are housed on Palace Green, close to the relevant departments. Here are special collections of older books and manuscripts. Other archival collections are housed at 5, The College. The University has a total of 900,000 volumes and 2,500 journals.

Each College and many departments have their own libraries, which offer more quiet spaces to work. The library runs instructional seminars and training sessions to improve information-handling skills.

There is a **Computer Literacy Programme**, offering certificated courses: the University intends to ensure that every one of its students is computer literate by graduation. Many of the colleges provide access to the mainframe computer through terminals or micro-computers, and the Computer Centre has an undergraduate 'freelance' terminal room.

There are subsidised courses in French, German, Italian, Spanish and Russian if you already have an 'A' level (or equivalent) and beginner courses in Russian, Spanish and

Italian. There are **language laboratories**, a languages library and class rooms with computer-learning facilities. You may gain a nationally recognised foreign language qualification through the Language Centre: the course take 18 weeks, two hours per week.

Culture on campus

Theatre: In addition to college theatres and drama clubs, the University owns a small theatre in the centre of Durham, well-equipped for dramatic and musical productions, and constantly used by student groups.

Music: Several colleges have halls which are highly suitable for concerts, and regular performances are arranged - open, of course, to all students. Student musical societies are vigorous, with a wide range of interests (Schola Cantorum, light opera, chamber music...). Many professional concerts are organised by the University, the colleges and University societies. The Union has societies which practise ballroom dancing, contemporary dance, folk dance and other musical interests. The Music School and some of the colleges have practice rooms.

The Union Society: The Union Society's primary function is to organise debates. It has strong traditional links with its counterparts in Oxford, Cambridge, Edinburgh and Trinity College, Dublin. Many very famous speakers have debated here. The Society provides club facilities for its members in the North Bailey Club: coffee rooms, licensed restaurant, a reading room with daily newspapers, full bar facilities, snooker and guest rooms. It also provides a good social scene for members: discos, cocktail evenings, videos. The Society also raises lots of money for World Wildlife, Great Ormond Street Children's Hospital and Durham Age Concern. Students and staff may join on a yearly basis, or apply for life membership.

The Union

The Union occupies Dunelm House, one of the most distinguished of the city's modern buildings, gracing a fine riverside site. As in other collegiate universities, the Union operates in tandem with the Junior Common Room committees of the colleges, whose representatives take an active part in Union policy control.

The Union, with four sabbatical officers, provides a confidential welfare and advice (including legal advice by solicitors) service in the Student Support Centre, a large Union shop (selling second-hand books and alcohol, among other things), a travel bureau, a laundry, cheap-rate car and minibus hire service, bars and a cafeteria. Approximately three live 'events' each week - discos, films, live bands and cabarets. The Union also funds over 100 non sporting societies and clubs . Student Community Action arranges for groups of volunteers to help in local projects including a tutoring scheme for GCSE and 'A' level students.

There is a Union Accommodation Office, which brings landlords and students together, and a Welfare Department offering useful information and free literature.

At a more humdrum level, Dunelm House has a photocopier, photo booth and video games. Rooms and halls can be hired and most of the Union services are open to the public.

All this is, of course, in addition to the entertainments, events and support groups available through the colleges.

Sport

Playing fields cover nearly 60 acres: some at the Racecourse, beside the river, and some at the Graham Sports Centre at Maiden Castle; each within two miles of the main University building clusters. A minibus is available. Facilities include a large sports hall, squash and fives courts, an athletics track, an all weather surface, tennis courts, and a number of pitches for rugby, hockey, soccer, cricket, lacrosse and netball. There are small charges for squash and the use of the all-weather surface and floodlights. Facilities are open to the public.

The Athletic Union runs a further 54 clubs. College clubs compete intensely for inter-collegiate trophies.

Many colleges have their own boat houses by the river Wear: rowing is both major sport and pleasure at this university.

There is a sports injury clinic and physiotherapy service at the Health Centre.

University teams have a distinguished record in most sports, particularly in rugby (Will Carling was here), rowing (river facilities are good), hockey, athletics, cricket, fencing, swimming, lacrosse and squash.

Student welfare

The **Student Health Centre** offers a general practice surgery and nursing care. The Centre has surgeries in the morning and afternoon. Also available: a sports injury clinic, advice and vaccinations for overseas travel, Occupational Health services and first-aid training for staff and students.

Advice and **counselling**, including debt counselling, are available from the Student Union's professional welfare officer and the Health Centre. There is a Nightline service. The Health Centre has a psychotherapist and a counsellor.

Most of the colleges appoint **chaplains** drawn from several denominations. The University provides an Islamic Prayer Centre.

Careers Service

The Careers Service runs courses in computing, numeracy, foreign languages, typing and word-processing: these are offered in conjunction with departments and colleges. The Service has five full-time careers advisors, two information officers and good information facilities.

Students with special needs

The Student Health Service has a particular interest in students with special needs; the University Medical Officer is available to discuss any health problems with intending applicants. The Service for Students with Hearing and other Disabilities provides special support. There is, however, a fundamental problem with Durham: the city and University are both very old, many buildings are set on hills and access can be a problem.

Accommodation

The colleges house over 70% of students, but it is usual to 'live out' for one year, normally the second.

Maintenance fee for students in full residence: £1,950 for 28 weeks (1995/96).

Private accommodation is relatively easy to find within a radius of five miles (although accommodation in the city centre is more difficult to track down) and you can expect to pay around £42 pw plus bills for a central site. Costs drop to £25 pw plus bills the further away you look.

Mature students

The University accepts mature students (over the age of 21) if they have the academic qualifications to satisfy the University's general requirements. The University also considers applicants who have no recognised qualifications but who have recently studied on an Access course or who have relevant qualifications or experience.

The University offers an introductory 'conference' before you begin your first year to help with study skills. There is an active Mature Students Association which is also a great support.

Nursery
There is a creche (40 places) for children from six months and school age. Preferential rates for student parents.

THE CITY (population c. 45,000)

Durham stands in the shadow of Newcastle, near enough to shed its wider civic responsibilities onto its larger neighbour; far enough to preserve an island-like sense of wide enclosing space and complete removal from the 'so much to do so little time' pace of our todays.

The ancient part of the town is very nearly an island: the cathedral and castle stand, very impressive statements of medieval power, on the crown of a high bluff, almost completely encircled by the river Wear, and known as 'the peninsula'. Within this charmed ring of water, the river banks wearing a hem of lovely woodland, the ancient city-fortress keeps the dignity and charm of centuries, its narrow cobbled vennels (streets) winding down from Palace Green to riverside and bridge-points. All the clichés of tourism hold good here: there is a sense of time preserved; the city has retained intact the character and fabric of its heritage.

A small city then, permeated by a sense of history, religious life and rural seclusion; a medieval architectural treasure-trove; its cathedral 'one of the great architectural experiences of Europe' splendidly set, with high views over the Wear valley to the hills beyond. Winding narrow ways and wider avenues of period building preserve an ancient calm; shops sell high-class wares to the visitors who fill the summer with pilgrimage. If you feel a positive response to this style and ambience, then no other university in England can match the cloistered calm, the lovely river loop and the magnificent frame of northern hills and dales.

What is there to do in such a city? A wealth of historic buildings to look at: the castle (already mentioned), the cathedral (11th century with many treasures and rare architectural features), three churches dating from the 12th century and one from the 17th, some medieval buildings on Elvet Bridge, the medieval tithe barn which belonged to the abbey, the 14th century Guildhall, the entrance to the former Georgian theatre in Saddler Street.

The riverbanks, Wharton Park and the University's Botanic Gardens provide wooded, green and garden spaces for you to wander.

Durham has an industrial face to its coin. 19th century coal and other heavy industry, now defunct, have been replaced by new high-tec industrial development - television tubes, micro-chips. Old perceived contrasts are no longer brutal.

Music: The Cathedral hosts choral concerts and-jazz!

Nightlife: There is a cinema in the city (two screens), as well as several folk clubs and discotheques. There is a good range of restaurants in the city and its environs: one of the advantages of being a tourist magnet. For more interesting pastimes and 'real city' activities, Newcastle is a mere 16 miles away with a regular 20 minute rail-ride; the last train 'home', however, is at 10.59 pm on weekdays, and 9.30 pm on Saturdays. Shared taxis are an economic option.

Sport: There is an indoor swimming pool, an ice rink, bowling, tennis, putting, cricket and three 18-hole golf clubs. You can hire boats to spend idyllic hours on the river.

Events: Durham has a regatta in June, a Miner's Gala in July, a Folk Festival in August, a Camra Beer Festival in September (in Dunelm House) and the Rolls Royce Rally in September.

ESCAPE ROUTES

Durham stands in some of England's wildest and most beautiful countryside. Encroaching industry from Sunderland and Middlesbrough cuts arcs into the hills: but Durham remains unscathed. To the west are the North Pennines, an area of Outstanding Natural Beauty, still largely unexploited. The coastline east has long sandy beaches and a string of seaside towns. All around is history - churches, castles, abbeys; and industrial archaeology - marking the epochs of the area.

You could also look at the Newcastle upon Tyne University section.

Communications

Durham is on the main **rail** line between York and Edinburgh, has direct services to Manchester, Leeds, Liverpool, Birmingham, Sheffield, Bristol, the South West and Newcastle. Regular trains to London. **Coach services** are extensive and national. The **A1/M** runs close to Durham giving fast access to east Scotland and south to London.

Edge Hill University College

St Helens Road
Ormskirk
Lancashire
L39 4QP
Telephone: 01695 575171

Edge Hill has a total of 6,000 students and is a college of the University of Lancaster. The main campus is just outside Ormskirk; neither of the College's two outposts is used for straightforward undergraduate work. Courses are modularised. An initial broad-based year is followed by specialism in one or more subject areas. Assessment is a mixture of coursework and examination, with greater emphasis on coursework. The College has 800 residential places. Students not placed can find accommodation in Ormskirk, Skelmersdale or Southport.

THE CAMPUS

Edge Hill's main campus is a ten minute walk from the centre of Ormskirk, a Lancashire town inland from Liverpool. The approach to the College on the A570 into Ormskirk takes you through fields and farmland; the College is almost the first building you see before finding the town, on the cusp of urban and rural living. All accommodation, teaching, learning resources and sports and recreation facilities are on this campus.

The central, original College building dates from 1933 and is rather like a stately home-cum-old grammar school. From the entrance and the grassed front areas there is a wide view over Liverpool, the Wirral and out to the Welsh mountains. Inner courtyards are grassed, one with a fountain. Two storeys are raised by the roof, which, with dormer windows, are halls of residence.

Newer buildings on site have grown with the student population, some in keeping with the original building - new halls built as mock stable blocks complete with clock tower, some less so.

A cluster of regimented post-war buildings form almost a 'second campus' behind the 1930s original; this includes the refectory building and the part of the Students Union in a 1960s glass and panel block (another hall of residence).

The two outpost campuses (Chorley Woodlands and Aintree) are not used for undergraduate teaching.

Learning Resources

The new Learning Resources Centre, a modern airy building, houses the library and computing facilities. The **library** has 500 study spaces and 250,000 multimedia items, including books and journals.

There are 150 PCs in the Learning Resources Centre. **Computer Services** have further open access facilities. A full range of induction courses and training, as well as help and advice is available.

The IT Learning Development Service gives assistance with special learning needs with drop-in study skills sessions and specialised help.

A **language laboratory** is available for language student use.

Culture on campus

Drama on campus has a number of homes: the Hale Hall offers a proscenium stage for more conventional productions; the theatre provides an open stage with flexible possibilities; a small drama studio is available for experimental work; and an open air setting in the rock garden is used for Summer productions. Visiting theatre groups perform at the College, as does the Union Drama Group.

Music studios and practice facilities are available. There is the opportunity to learn new instruments and to use recording facilities. Staff in the music department offers assistance.

The Union

The Union elects two sabbatical officers, one a full-time Community Action co-ordinator. Sixteen student representatives in all make up the committee. There are two full-time employees. 'The Venue' is the hub of student life with discos, quizzes, bands, pool and snooker, satellite television, a shop and the Union bar. There are currently 14 non-sporting clubs and 17 sporting clubs, although this changes from year to year.

Sport

From mid-1997, the College will have a new, 25 acre sporting complex with full access for disabled students. The sports hall/gymnasium, weights room, indoor swimming pool, rugby, soccer, hockey and cricket pitches, tennis and netball courts, a floodlit training area and an athletics track are all on campus. All levels of sport are encouraged with the support of specialist PE tutors.

Student welfare

The **Health Care Centre** is open from Monday to Friday 9am to 6pm and is staffed by a Sister. The College doctors hold surgeries three times a week and a family planning clinic is held once a week. The **counselling service** is available by appointment, as well as advice on welfare rights issues (financial, housing etc.) The **Careers Service** offers guidance and advice, videos, visiting lectures and practical exercises.

Students with special needs

College buildings are adapted for wheelchair access; the main building and library have lifts. The Students' Union is very supportive.

Accommodation

The College has 800 places in Halls of Residence. One is new, has 300 places, is self-catering with some ensuite provision; two others are self-catering (one mixed, one female only); and seven halls are catered offering breakfast and evening meal weekdays, brunch on Saturdays and a lunch on Sundays. All halls are on campus.

Cost (1995/96)

Costs range between £31.00 per week (self-catering) to £54.00 per week (fully catered).

Private Sector

Most students find housing in Ormskirk or Skelmersdale, although some plump for the more up-beat character of Southport a little further away. Costs: £30 to £35 per week average.

Mature students

Mature applicants are assessed on ability to benefit from the course, rather than on traditional entry qualifications. You should have recently completed, successfully, a relevant course of study at a Further Education College or through the Open University. Contact the Admissions Office for more information.

THE TOWN (population 17,466) and ESCAPE ROUTES

Ormskirk is a small market town which will provide for your day to day needs. You are quite close to Liverpool which offers the balance of big city life (see the University of Liverpool's entry). Closer to Ormskirk is Southport with its seaside attractions, nightclubs and shopping: this is a popular student 'living out' area. Martin Mere Wildfowl and Wetlands Trust is just three miles away. The Trough of Bowland, Lake District and the Peak District National Park are all fairly near by.

University of Huddersfield

Queensgate
Huddersfield
HD1 3DH
Telephone: 01484 422288

University Charter date: 1992

Huddersfield is a medium-sized university with around 8,500 students on degree and HND programmes. Although, in its self-description, the University claims to have three campuses, in effect it has a single, town-centre site housing the majority of its faculties and recreational facilities. The two outposts are the School of Education, two miles away, and Storthes Hall Park, a residential student village five miles out of Huddersfield. The University offers named degrees which are modular and assessed both through coursework and examination. A number of courses have a 'sandwich' option. First years are given priority for accommodation. Local private rented housing is not hard to find: a single bedsit cost around £30 per week excluding bills.

THE CAMPUS

The Huddersfield Campuses

The campus has grown from the original Ramsden Building dating from 1884 which was Huddersfield Technical College: an impressive Victorian edifice, with small turrets, solid and confident.

The Ramsden Building will not be your primary, or lasting, impression of the University's buildings, which form a campus between the ring-road (a dual carriageway) and the canal. The Central Services building is a piece of monumental late 1970s architecture, well-proportioned with tiered floors. Its walls are light brick and glass, and its lines, stepping down right to the canal edge, are sympathetic to the contours of this hill town. Here are the library, refectory, offices and (some) student accommodation.

This new building is balanced by the University's renovation and conversion of the old Larchfield Mills into teaching facilities, a short walk from the central campus. Canlside West, a former woollen mill, is now the School of Computing and Mathematics and houses the University's general computing facilities. A purpose-built addition is the Business School, across a bridge, across the canal : built in 1984, low-rise and smart. Workshops and the music faculty blocks are behind the Central Services building, rather shadowed and dark.

The campus is well-spaced, with paved areas and walkways. There is not much greenery, however, and nowhere to sit on sunny days, except on the small grass bank outside St Paul's Hall (a converted church dating from 1829), facing the ring-road. From the refectory windows, you will look out over Castle Hill and the hills which hold Huddersfield in their bowl. The canal below is still being restored, and there are narrow boats moored in Aspley marina just across the road.

Huddersfield's other town campus is two miles away at Holly Bank, housing the School of Education and the Centre for International Technical Education. It is a well-shaped site, with large - if not extensive - grounds.

Storthes Hall Park

The University has taken over a Victorian hospital and its grounds in a beautiful valley five miles from the town centre. The site is now occupied by a student 'village' of self-contained, self-catering flats housing 1,500 students. Other facilities include bars, shops, restaurants, a sports hall and an astro-turf hockey/soccer pitch, as well as grass pitches. The University plans a swimming pool here.

Cars

Parking on campus is limited. There is a bus between Storthes hall Park and the Huddersfield campuses.

Learning Resources

The central **library** is on four floors with 750 study places in all. Its book stock is around 300,000 items. There are three other small libraries, one in the faculty of music, one on the Holly Bank campus and a chemistry periodical collection in the Chemistry Building. Open late in the evenings and at weekends.

Computing services offer a comprehensive support service to staff and students. The advisory service can give you advice on specific problems. Computing facilities at Canalside West are open 24 hours a day. Sites are networked and linked to JANET. There are 15 computer labs and over 1,000 IBM PCs.

It is possible to take a language module as part of most courses. The Language Learning Resource Centre has language laboratories and computer assisted language learning facilities.

Culture on campus

Drama: A drama group is run by the Students' Union.
Music: Both classical and rock, is strong here. Regular gigs are organised by the Union. Classical music on campus: Monday lunchtime concerts at St Paul's Hall, evening concerts given by well-known ensembles. The University has a strong music department with a lot of extra-mural musical activity: symphony orchestra, chamber orchestra, wind band, brass band, 20th century ensemble, opera group and coached chamber music. The high point of the year is the annual Huddersfield Contemporary Music Festival, recognised as leading its field.

The Union

The Union is now housed in two buildings and has a pub off-campus. Milton Hall has recently been completed and houses offices, bars, shop, coffee bar, travel bureau, games and television rooms. St Joseph's, a converted chapel, is the present venue for bands and discos - and a curry house! Entertainments are many and varied: quizzes, discos, theme nights, bands and cabaret. Some events happen in the residences, especially at Storthes Hall Park; Hollybank offers a separate entertainments scene. There is a late-night bus with priority for women. Newspaper monthly and an executive bulletin fortnightly keeps students informed. 55 non-sports societies cover most interests.

Five sabbatical officers: Union also employs 23 full-time and 120 casual staff. Advice is available on a range of welfare and legal issues.

Sport

Sports fields are two miles away from the main campus: 3 football and 1 rugby league pitches. The sports hall on campus has a court area the size of five badminton courts. There are two squash courts and several fitness training machines. The gymnasium in St Peter's Hall, very close to campus, is available in the evenings and on Wednesday afternoons. The University also uses local facilities. Other sports grounds at Storthes Hall include two playing fields, an astroturf and second sports hall. 23 sports clubs.

Student welfare

Students can register with the **health centre** on level five of the Central Services Building. Nurses, physiotherapy and a visiting pschiatrist are available and three GPs hold daily surgeries during term time. Two professional **counsellors** are available in the Great Hall. The University **chaplaincy** is staffed by three Christian chaplains.

Careers Service
The Careers Service gives confidential individual advice and guidance, help with self-evaluation and decision making, presentations and workshops, as well as a well-stocked careers library.

Students with special needs
You are advised to contact the University to ensure they have provision for your needs. Wherever possible, arrangements will be made.

Accommodation

The University presently has 2,250 residential places in halls of residence, 1,500 places at Storthes Hall Park. 85% of first years are housed.

Halls of residence
Halls in town are all within a three mile radius of or close to the Queensgate campus. One is part of the Central Services Building and houses 161 students.

Storthes Hall Park houses students in self-contained flats.

There are two main complexes of student houses: one purpose-built (Ashenhurst) and one adopted (Edgerton). The Edgerton houses are all large, Victorian, stone built and substantial.

Costs (1995/96)
40 weeks:
single catered: £60 per week
single self-catered: £32 - £44 per week
double self-catered: £30 - £34.50 per week

Private accommodation
Huddersfield's student housing stock is good. The University Accommodation Office will help you to find the right place for your needs.

Costs (1995/96)
A single bedsit : average £36 per week, excluding bills.

Mature students

The University encourages you to take an Access course in a college in your own area if you have had a long break from regular study. Each student will be assessed on previous academic performance and work experience.

Part-time courses
The University offers day and evening part-time courses of study in a full range of subjects.

Nursery
The day nursery on campus has facilities for 25 children from six weeks to five years.

THE TOWN (population 180,000)

Huddersfield is a wool town, with a fortune built on textiles. The buildings reflect this wealth, solidity and Northern values. The town is set is a bowl of hills, and wherever you are, if you look up, you can see the Pennines. The textile mills are mostly silent now. The town has become, primarily, a shopping centre for a scattered population. The shopping range is good, with several pedestrianised areas and the gamut of high street stores. Byram Street Arcade has a range of smaller boutiques, and is a good antidote to the concept of the mega shopping mall: its interior has been painted, but is otherwise left as it was in the last century.

Huddersfield has two markets: one permanent and covered; the other housed in the old beast market with a shifting population of stall holders.

Greenhead Park is within walking distance of the University and is landscaped and ornamented, with an orangery, a bandstand, bowls and tennis courts. A number of town festivals are held here, including an annual fireworks display.

The town hall and library are the 'town centre'. The town hall is also a concert venue, and home to the Huddersfield Choral Society. The station, in St George's Square, is an example of 19th century flamboyance. Its frontage has now been paved, which gives a clearer view of its structure: more of a stately home than a lesser terminus.

Theatre: The Lawrence Batley Theatre opened in 1994. A Georgian listed building has been transformed into a theatre and a centre for arts and entertainment. The complex is very close to the University.

Music: Huddersfield's musical life is varied. The classical concert programme at the town hall takes in the major northern orchestras and other ensembles.The Huddersfield Contemporary Music Festival happens in November, attracting the leading names in Contemporary Music, and giving space to those lesser known. The last few years have seen Stockhausen, Cage, Boulez, Messiaen, Schnittke and Goreckski. Live music, including jazz, happens in some pubs.

Cinema: one cinema with two screens

Nightlife: Huddersfield has a number of nightclubs, the newest is right next door to the University. Pubs and restaurants: a low-key range.

Sport: The University has its own sports hall and Huddersfield has a large well-equipped sports centre. Swimming pools here and on Cambridge Road. Sports pitches throughout the town: local leagues are very competitive. A new 51 acre stadium is home to local teams and also provides a floodlit golf driving range, bar and restaurants and a rock concert venue. Phase two will include a bowling alley, bingo hall, multi-screen cinema, creche, dry ski slope and gymnastics facilities.

ESCAPE ROUTES

Huddersfield is on the edge of the Pennines, with moorland and hill-walking within minutes of the town centre. 'Last of the Summer Wine' country is just a few miles down the road in and around Holmfirth. The area still bears the traces of its industrial past, from its very impressive stone-built mills to its canals: but the countryside was never fully taken over, and it is very beautiful.

Halifax is about five miles away: its Piece Hall has been converted into galleried shops and a market area; the Hall is an excellent example of re-utilised heritage. Also here, Eureka!, the award-winning museum for children - worth suspending adulthood for; Archimedes drops into his bath, there's a talking tree and a dream cupboard.

As well as its rural setting, its industrial architecture and its own amenities, Huddersfield is about half an hour from Leeds, Manchester and Bradford, so you can take in their culture and nightlife: the trains and buses run until late.

Communications

Direct **trains** to Liverpool, Manchester, Sheffield, Leeds, York and sometimes the North East. Fast links to the inter-city London service via Wakefield Westgate. The Leeds-Manchester link runs every half hour, and late enough for you to have the night out and get home. **Coach links** are extensive and regular. Huddersfield is just off the **M62** and within 20 minutes of the **M1**: fast links to Liverpool, Manchester, Leeds, Bradford and Hull (M62) and straight to London (M1).

University of Hull

Hull
North Humberside
HU6 7RX
Telephone: 01482 346351

University Charter date: 1954

Hull is a medium-sized university with around 9,000 full-time students. The University is on a single, 94 acre site about two miles from Hull. Degrees here are modular with a core syllabus and 'guided paths of optional modules within a named degree programme. Assessment involves examinations and assessed coursework. All single first years are guaranteed a place in University residences.

THE CAMPUS

The University occupies a 94 acre site, fringed with fields and trees: walkways lined with lawns and shrubs; the old buildings decked with vines and creepers. The academic buildings are clustered centrally, and the range of styles is wide: from the ambience of an old, well-off grammar school (administration and Earth Sciences blocks) to the top-heavy white tower of the excellent library and the white 'lego' squares and oblong of the Social Sciences block. Building is mostly in mellow brick, with a variety of height and roof line. The campus is accessibly compact but amply spaced and, as with Hull in general, the feeling is wide and high - the effect of the flatland setting.

Hull seeks to broaden the range and career horizons of its students: every student, irrespective of degree subject, can learn languages (around 50 are taught), acquire computer literacy and enhance life skills. The University generates a sense of sociable, friendly well-being; and inspires in its alumni great affection and loyalty.

The University lies about two miles out of the city centre, to the north. Most of its residential accommodation is not actually on campus: the halls of residence form a student village in Cottingham, two more miles out; most student houses are immediately next to, or within a mile of campus.

Cars

Most of the residential accommodation has parking facilities and, although the roads close to campus get congested, there are no restrictions on bringing your car. However, this is ideal cycling country; storing your bicycle is seldom a problem.

Learning Resources

The main **library** has 850,000 books, takes over 3,000 periodicals and seats 1,300. It is open until 10.00pm on weekdays, 1pm on Saturday. There is a ground-floor cafe. Libraries also in departments and in halls of residence.

The **Computer Department** offers courses for non-computer scientists. Facilities are available around the clock; free access to terminals in all rooms in halls of residence. The Computing Centre is open from 8.45am to 9.30pm Monday to Thursday and until 8.30pm Friday.

The **Language Teaching Centre** is very well-equipped and is open to all students for spare-time study or lunchtime classes, or for courses leading to the University's Certificate in Modern Languages (two languages offered) or for the 'Passport' courses (available in seven languages). You will have access to self-teaching material in over 50 languages. There are three language laboratories and a Computer Assisted Language Learning Unit attached to the Centre.

Culture on campus

Drama: The Gulbenkian at the centre of the campus houses a professional-style theatre. The drama department stages a variety of plays, from the low-budget and avant-garde to presentations of major plays.

Music: The drama and music departments join forces once a year to put on a full-scale opera: soloists from major opera companies sing alongside students. As well as the annual opera, the Music department promotes around 30 concerts each year. The University Choir and Orchestra perform regularly on campus, and sometimes in the city hall. Numerous professional soloists and ensembles visit the University, including the Allegri String Quartet who also give workshops and coaching sessions. There are regular lunchtime concerts (contributions from students and staff).

Regular discos in the Union, as well as films, variety acts and regular concerts by well-known bands.

Art: The University's collection is internationally known and concentrates on British art from 1890 to 1940: the Camden Town Group and Bloomsbury artists are particularly well represented. The gallery is open to the public as well as students. There is also an art and design studio on campus.

The Union

The Union is housed in a large, neatly stacked four-storey building which is presently being extended, at the Union's own expense: two further floors will be in action by 1997. The present building has two bars: one is huge and can accommodate main functions; the other is more relaxed, with various games facilities. A team of six sabbatical officers manage Union affairs.

The University runs two large catering areas in the building, which also houses the University bookshop, dark rooms, a fully equipped (and cheap) laundry, a Union-run shop and travel bureau. Student services are also housed here: careers, accommodation, counselling. A solicitor deals with any student's legal problems.

The Union organises entertainments and runs a range of clubs and societies (54 non-sporting societies) including a strong Community Action Group. Forty social events are organised each term including around 18 live bands. The Union hall will take 1,100 students. There are popular weekly discos - or 'stomps'. The newspaper, *Hullfire*, and student run house-radio system will keep you informed.

Sport

Hull has always had a name for its enthusiasm for the Great Outdoors. 51 clubs are recognised and supported by the Athletics Union, offering a very wide range of activities. On campus: a large, well-equipped sports and leisure centre on three levels houses two large halls with facilities for athletics, badminton, basketball, cricket, five-a-side soccer, hockey, golf, netball, tennis and volleyball. On the second level is the gymnasium, which can be divided to form a studio for ballroom dancing, modern dance, keep fit activities, fencing, table-tennis, trampoline. Also a multigym and facilities for circuit training, martial arts and other pursuits, as well as six squash courts, with a seventh close at hand, and changing rooms. A first floor concourse links gym and sports hall and provides drinks, spectator access and relaxation space. You can buy sports gear at reduced prices here.

Also on campus are playing fields: six soccer, four rugby and two hockey pitches, four cricket circles, three hard and six grass tennis courts plus practice wall. A floodlit all-weather surface, mainly for hockey, caters for other sports and training. Halls of residence have further playing fields and courts.

The University Boat Club has its boathouse on the River Hull - also used by the sub-aqua and canoe clubs.

Professional coaching in a number of sports. Sport is practised competitively within the University as well as in inter-university matches.

The Health and Fitness Centre provides professionally supervised facilities for weight and general fitness training, saunas, solaria, a jacuzzi and relaxation area.

Student welfare

All students are requested to register with a local GP. The Union runs Nightline, welfare advice, minibus service for women and debt counselling. The University runs a professional **counselling service**. Several full-time **chaplains** represent the major Christian denominations and work from chaplaincy centres close to the University. There is a Jewish community house near to the University. The University offers an Islamic prayer room. The city has a small Buddhist community and a mosque.

Careers Service

The University Careers Service is remarkably innovative and student oriented. Quite apart from its very well-stocked library, talks, presentations, management courses, off-campus visits and regular one-to-one interviews, the Service offers a range of careers aids. Vacancy lists and other careers information updated frequently are mounted on the campus-wide interactive computer network. The Service runs 'special skills' courses in numeracy, European languages, typing, computer awareness, and business applications of computers; there is a Numeracy Centre in the School of Mathematics which is financed by a firm of international accountants for students from all disciplines; the Service even has a link with the British School of Motoring to help you pass your driving test. Interview techniques are taught with the aid of video equipment.

The Careers Service also operates a 'Co-operative Education' scheme, which sounds not unlike a sandwich course, but isn't. Students from any discipline can apply for a 'year out' in employment between their second and third years: they are selected for specific 'vacancies' by the normal recruitment processes. If you are successful in your application, the University will keep in contact with you throughout your year; there is no obligation on your employer to offer you full-time work at the end of your contract, nor any obligation on you to accept a post if it is offered: you will, however, have most of the benefits of being employed, including a salary.

Students with special needs

Through its permanent working party on special needs, the University receives regular advice on how to improve its facilities. All departments have a nominated member of staff to oversee the admission and progress of students with special needs. There are specially converted rooms with bathrooms in two halls, and two student-house flatlets converted for wheelchair access. The campus terrain is flat and the grouping of buildings compact, which helps with wheelchair access.

The University will make further adjustments, if given sufficient notice. The University produces a booklet: a *Guide for Students with Disabilities'*.

Accommodation

Hull has accommodation for 4,350 students: 1,585 in halls of residence; 1,635 in self-catering student houses; 288 in on-campus flats and 850 in University-managed (head leased) accommodation. All single first year students are guaranteed places in University residences, except for post-Clearing late entrants who, as in most places, might have to wait in temporary accommodation for a while before finding a University-owned 'home'. There are frequent bus-services to and from campus and fast trains to Hull centre and Beverley.

Halls of residence: Cottingham

There are ten, all of which are mixed. Four traditional halls provide all meals except weekday lunches. Six 'semi-catered' halls are grouped to form 'The Lawns' complex. Each hall has a Warden, Deputy Warden and/or Hall Tutor, and a Senior Resident student. The complex stands in 47 acres of landscaped parkland, containing tennis courts and football pitches. Facilities are open to students of the University who are not Lawns residents. The site is within ten minutes' walk of the centre of Cottingham village, three miles from campus.

The Lawns (semi-catered halls)

The six halls, built in the late sixties, are almost identical. Their design and layout are imaginative and attractive, their facilities good. One hall is entirely self-catering: the other five take evening meals at the Lawns Centre.

The Lawns Centre has a refectory, late night snack bar, colour TV lounges, games and snooker rooms, three bars, a large disco area, a party room, and more. There are regular mid-week discos and an active social life.

Traditional halls

All halls have Junior Common Rooms, television lounges, libraries and self-contained computer studios with PCs and terminals connected to the University's mainframe; indoor and outdoor sports facilities, a wide range of social activities (discos to formal balls), and car-parking.

Each hall is different in character: One (Ferens) is a purpose-built hall; Needler Hall is a converted country house; Cleminson is a mix of modern and Victorian; Thwaite has 24 acres of gardens and a lake, as well as music practice rooms and a traditional dining room with a minstrel's gallery.

On-campus flats: Taylor Court

Twelve 'houses' of three flats each (eight students per flat) grouped around a central courtyard within a minute's walk of most campus facilities. All rooms are single, ensuite, with a private television aerial, telephone point and access to the campus computer network.

Student houses

There are about 210 private residences, specially bought and converted into self-catering accommodation for 1,635 students. Most are in terraced properties immediately adjacent to campus: some a mile or so from campus in 'The Avenues'; a few are large detached houses in their own grounds, mostly in Cottingham.

Costs (1995/96)

The Lawns: nb - 'composite' means with meal tickets
Composite single: £1,610.14 for 31 weeks
Composite shared: £1,534.19 for 31 weeks
Non-composite single: £1,204.35 for 31 weeks
Non-composite shared: £1,128.40 for 31 weeks
Traditional Halls
single: £2,085.37; shared: £1,998.57 for 31 weeks
Taylor Court
single: £2,390.50 for 50 weeks
Houses
single: £1,212.12 ; shared: £1,025.64 for 37 weeks

Head leased accommodation

The University manages 850 places in houses in the private sector, all within a mile or so of campus. c. £30 per week. Private accommodation is plentiful and quite cheap.

Mature students

The University has a well-developed pattern for and commitment to education for mature and part-time students. 'Mature' applicants must offer acceptable qualifications or experience. Students with suitable qualifications might be able to enter the second year of certain courses.

Nursery

The Union administers a purpose-built day nursery for 49 children. The Union subsidises places for students' children. Children are taken from 3 months to school age.

THE CITY (population: 270,000)

Hull has for centuries been off the beaten track except for those connected with its seafaring trades, isolated by its remote setting (the lightly populated agricultural lowlands inland, the wide Humber, only recently bridged, and the legendary wastes of the North Sea). The city has grown where the river Hull joins the Humber, here lined with miles of dockland. Fishing and cargo boats, oil tankers and ferries - the Humber and its docks are still busy.

The old town has a medieval street plan and some interesting buildings: the fine sweep of the Ferens Art Gallery and city hall, facing now a pleasantly geometric panel of gardens, once an inland dock (concerts here in summertime lunchtimes). An ancient fair happens in the city every October.

The chain of docks was built in Georgian times along the line of walls and moat which enclosed the town centuries ago. Some are now closed; one is now a marina; the Princes Quay on Princes Dock and the Fisherman's Wharf are shopping areas: the Princes Quay development is a four storey shopping precinct on stilts and platform over the waters of the dock.

The Humber Bridge, five miles away, has impossibly slender lines traced against the sky: a fine landmark visible for miles. Its centre span (1,410m) is the longest of any suspension bridge in the world.

Theatre: The New Theatre, a converted cinema, presents West End productions, opera, ballet and variety. Spring Street Theatre: repertory and other forms of art in a more intimate space. The home of Hull Truck, the nationally famous theatrical touring company.

Music: The City Hall has a fine concert organ (recitals evening and lunchtimes), an 1,800 seat auditorium and houses concerts by visiting orchestras and internationally famous soloists. Hull has its own Philharmonic and Youth Symphony orchestras and numerous choral groups.

Cinema: The film theatre presents international classics and revivals. Two commercial cinemas, eight screens.

Nightlife: a range of nightclubs, discos and restaurants.

Sport: Spectator sports: Hull City AFC, two rugby league clubs (Hull and Hull Kingston Rovers), rugby union (Hull and East Riding), baseball and cricket (county circuit ground). Beverley racecourse is about ten miles away. Participant sport: there are swimming pools, sports centres, municipal golf courses.

ESCAPE ROUTES

The country of Humberside and the flatlands of Holderness to the north are rich, fertile and open. The coastline shifts, eroding and silting over years rather than centuries. Good cycling; excellent for bird-watching; seaside resorts and puffin haunts close by.

Communications

Two fast trains to London a day: the rest, change at Doncaster (c. three hours). Direct links with Leeds, Manchester and Sheffield. Coach services to most centres. The **M62** gives Hull access to the national motorway network. Evening **sailings** to Rotterdam and Zeebrugge. The **airport** is 19 miles away, across the Humber Bridge. Regular flights to London, Aberdeen and the continent.

University of Lincolnshire & Humberside

Cottingham Road
Hull
HU6 7RT
Telephone: 01482 440550

University Charter date: 1992
Humberside is a medium-sized university with around 10,000 undergraduate and sandwich students. The University is now two: The University of Lincoln is included in the Midlands section of the Guide; The University of Humberside has three sites around Hull. Courses at Grimsby Food, Fisheries and Environmental Studies) will transfer to Lincoln in 1999.University-owned accommodation is limited. Most students are housed in the private sector. Private rented room: £28-£35 per week. Degrees are modularised (unitised) and are offered in single, joint and combined subject programmes. The University also offers a range of HNDs. Units are assessed at the end of each semester. Assessment methods vary: some courses rest entirely on coursework; others have an exam component.

THE CAMPUSES

Humberside University is split over three site clusters in Hull: the Grimsby Campus is being taken over, in the main, by Lincoln University: all students at Grimsby will move to Lincoln in 1999. For Grimsby's description, see Lincoln.

Cottingham Road Campus
Three miles out from the city centre. The buildings are red-brick with a college ambience: grassed quads in front, elegant proportions. It mirrors the original building of Hull University which is just next door, over a high wall. The main administration offices are here, and some accommodation. Hull Business School and the School of Engineering are based here.

Inglemire Campus
This is the home of the School of Social Sciences and Professional Studies. Not far from Cottingham Road and set in playing fields, this site backs onto a convent.

City Centre Campus
Hull City Centre Campus houses two Schools. The School of Architecture is based in the recently refurbished George Street Building. This is an impressive modern building, balanced on pillars, efficient and innovative.

Around the corner is the Queens Gardens site which houses the School of Art & Design. Some courses are based in the Victorian Anlaby Road building.

Learning support (libraries and computing) for the City Centre Campus is housed in the recently restored Hooper Building which used to be a warehouse.

Bishop Burton
A partner college, housing the Equestrian Unit and other agricultural courses.

Cars
Parking provision at the Cottingham Road and Inglemire Avenue, or you must find parking near to where you live.

Learning Resources

Each campus (the City Centre sites have the Hooper Building) has its own **library** relating to its subject areas. Altogether, the libraries hold 190,000 volumes, take 1,000 periodicals and have 500 reading places: because we do not have more site-specific figures, these are not much help to you. Check your own library provision if you are intending to study a book-based subject.

Computing facilities have been developed as a priority. There are microprocessors across the campuses. The city-wide network gives access to your files at all campuses. All students are expected to work with IT.

The Open Access Language Centre has language laboratories, computer assisted language learning and self-teaching tapes in 19 languages.

The Union

There are offices on each campus. Five sabbatical officers and eight other executive officers elected annually.

Some social events happen on the Cottingham Road campus. Here are bars, snack bars and space for regular discos and visiting bands. The Union hires outside venues for large events. Union shops on the Cottingham Road and Inglemire Avenue campuses.

The Strand Close building (previously housing the School of Architecture), near to the city centre, has been converted into a new Union Centre. The building has office space, a completely refurbished bar area and rooms large enough for events and bands. Clubs and societies meet here, and there is an entertainments programme including regular films, discos, bands and comedians. The Student Advice Service is also based here, offering information on welfare issues and a night-line.

Sport

Facilities are related to the individual sites. There are a wide range of sporting activities arranged by the Union, who run a health and fitness club at the Inglemire Avenue site. Here too are pitches, a sports hall, multigym, free weights, fitness machines and a solarium, and daily aerobics sessions.

Student welfare

Nursing officers are on call at the Cottingham Road campus. A **counselling service** is available centrally and the Advice Centre give practical information and help on the range of usual student problems. An ecumenical chaplain is available.

Careers Service
Specialist staff are available throughout the year to give advice and help with applications and interviewing skills. Computerised guidance programmes, Prospect and Adult Guidance are available.

Students with special needs
The University has DART (Division for Assistive Resources and Technology) offering help and advice to students with special needs.

Accommodation

University-owned accommodation is limited: priority is given to non-local first years and overseas students. There are 450 places in catered halls of residence and 200 self-catered places. All halls are warden supervised. The University has an additional 420 (approximately) places in head-leased properties and a further 550-600 places in major developments through approved schemes.

The Residential Accommodation Service has extensive information on the private-rented sector, and - where possible - will give full advice and assistance to students looking for accommodation. Lodgings are approved, but other private sector accommodation is not inspected.

Costs (1995/96)
catered single room: £60.00 per week
self-catered single room: £36.00 to £37.00 per week
Leased (average): £32.00 to £33.00 per week

Private sector
Private sector accommodation is generally available within easy travelling distance. Rooms vary in cost and quality: prices range between £28 and £35 per week.

Mature students

The University has a committed policy of broadening access across all course disciplines. Study programmes can, within reason, be adapted to suit your needs. A high proportion of present students are mature.

THE CITY/ESCAPE ROUTES

See Hull University's entry in this Guide.

Lancaster University

University House
Lancaster
LA1 4YW
Telephone : 01524 65201

University Charter date: 1964
Lancaster is a medium-sized university with around 7,500 undergraduates. A collegiate university on a single, 250 acre site three miles south of the small city of Lancaster. Degrees here are modular with a flexible options system: three subjects in your first year from which you can narrow down to one or two specialisms in your second and third years. Students can study for one or two work-related modules within their overall scheme - the presentation to your 'client' organisation will count towards your final degree. Assessment is by a combination of examination and coursework. The University puts high priority on providing a room on campus, in a college, for all first year students.

THE CAMPUS

Founded in 1964, Lancaster is a capsule of its time, reflecting most purely the educational concepts then dominating university planning: the 'greenfield' setting and the revival of a collegiate system of academic life. The 250-acre campus (Bailrigg) is levelled into the hillside south of the city and close to a small village. The site is landscaped to parkland standard, screened by trees; its buildings are generally low-rise, huddling close to the ground in a well-spaced but carefully interlinked pattern.

Protection from the outside world is in layers: the outer perimeter is ringed by trees and by the sweeping access road which preserves the pedestrian seclusion of the centre by stretching limited-access 'spokes' to the edge of the building complex. The buildings themselves follow a plan of neo-military precision, forming an interrelated series of quadrangles, with sheltered courtyards. There is a central north-south 'spine' (a covered walkway, half a mile long), and, at its core, the University has the amenities of a small town, sustaining its community with banks, a post-office, bookshop, newsagent, chemist, supermarket and a variety of smaller shops and services.

Buildings are modular, symmetrical, light-brick, with white roof-flats; their height is relieved by only one towerblock; their rectangles offset by only the clover-leafed chaplaincy centre, with its upswept roof-lines. The effect could be monotonous, but is in fact light and airy: this is not an over-large campus and its neat layout, in the extravagant spaces of its setting, works well. A new development was completed in 1993, adding more residences and a teaching block

The University is beginning to move into the city: the Department of Continuing Education and the Archaeology Unit occupy a converted Victorian building and some of the new halls of residences are in the city centre.

These developments do not detract from the main citadel of Bailrigg where to the west there are marvellous views across the sea and the Lune estuary; inland rise the fells and foothills of the Pennines; to the north is the spectacular frieze of the Lake District.

The Colleges
Collegesrange in size from 400 to 800 undergraduate and postgraduate students, more than half of whom are in residence. All academic staff and students are members of a college, whether or not they are residents (you will most likely spend your second year living off-campus).

Residential blocks are separate: other buildings include quiet study rooms for living-out members, coffee and snack bars, television and reading lounges, games rooms, utility rooms, licensed bars and common rooms. Most academic departments not needing laboratories are housed in colleges and teach there. You need not belong to the college which houses 'your' department, but the presence of teaching staff, casually and formally, around the colleges, is a strong feature.

Colleges do not control admissions: you apply to the University and will be allocated to a college. They do, however, monitor your general well-being and study-progress through a system of personal advisors. Your advisor will normally be one of the staff teaching in your department. The University houses, in the colleges, pay-as-you-eat restaurants and snackbars. Social life is strongly college-based and is organised by the Junior Common Room committees: films, discos, debates, dinners....

Cars
The shuttle bus between the University and the city is regular. There are also buses between the Campus and Morecambe (one of the main 'living out' areas). Car parking on campus is by permit only. First year students resident on campus are not, in normal circumstances, given permits (unless they are registered disabled).

Learning Resources

The University **library** has 1,000,000 items. The library takes over 3,000 periodicals. There is seating for 820 students. Open 77 hours per week including the weekend. The **Information Systems Services** give general training on use of packages available (word-processing, graphics, data bases and spread sheets) to all students. A large number of networked PCs with Microsoft Windows and Works are available in public areas around the campus 24 hours a day. You can access JANET and the University's central interactive computer through any terminal. The world-wide internet can be accessed from many terminals.

Self-teaching in language is available on the Lancaster Campus in the **Languages Resource Centre** and there is a 'Languages for All' programme which offers regular teaching at low cost.

Culture on campus

Drama: The theatre studio and workshop (the Nuffield) on the Lancaster Campus offers flexible and technically inventive space-uses for a variety of productions by students or by professional or amateur groups: plays, dance, exhibitions, experimental work. The technical standard of the equipment is excellent.
Film: The college JCRs organise film showings; there are cheap film nights on campus on average four times a week.
Music: The University promotes an international concert series, presenting some very famous performers. The Lunchtime concerts given by student soloists and ensembles are arranged by the University Musical Society. Groups include the Choral Society, symphony orchestra and concert band. Music tuition and practice rooms are available.
Art: The newly enlarged and airy Peter Scott Gallery houses temporary exhibitions which focus on contemporary art - photography, sculpture and crafts.

The Union

The Union Offices are in Alexandra Square. Policy is determined at monthly meetings and carried out by six full-time sabbatical officers. To a large extent, the Union operates through the college JCRs: their social (over 60) and sporting (c.36) clubs are financed and co-ordinated by the Union. Commercial activity is limited: two shops and the Sugar House. There are nine bars altogether in the University, but none directly involved with the Union.

The Union does, however, have a centre in Lancaster (the Sugar House) which offers night-club discos on Thursday, Friday and Saturday nights; open until 2am. The facilities are open to the public as well as to students. There is a late night women-only bus which will take students from campus or town to their doors. For live gigs and larger events, the Union hall has a 1,300 capacity, although it does not have its own lighting or sound system.

The Union runs its own radio station, broadcasting to most of the college residential areas, and its own student television service. There is also a Union-produced newspaper (weekly) and occasional creative or special-interest magazines.

The Union offers welfare advice, which includes debt counselling, runs Nightline and produces a very useful, comprehensive Welfare Handbook, covering all likely eventualities.

Sport

Lancaster was one of the first universities to open up its sports facilities to the public, thereby acquiring funds to improve these facilities for students and public alike. There is therefore only a nominal charge for the use of the facilities, but much of the time is already pre-booked by the societies.

Sports facilities are on campus, so you don't have far to go. The sports clubs are subsidised by the University. A multi-purpose indoor sports centre has a 25 metre, ozone-treated swimming pool, a large hall marked for badminton, basketball, 5-a-side soccer, hockey and tennis; a smaller hall (table-tennis, trampolining, judo and karate); eight squash courts, two aeroball courts, weight-training rooms (separate for men and women), a dance studio, sauna and solarium and a rock-climbing wall.

Outdoor fields and pitches for soccer (six), rugby (four) and all-weather hockey (three); a floodlit hard play area, eight tennis courts, a crown bowling green, a cricket square, matting and practice wickets, and areas for golf practice, athletics and archery. Graded jogging routes are marked out on campus and into the surrounding countryside. The boat club has a rowing base on the river Lune; the sailing club uses a large marina in Glasson Dock.

You can book privately or in groups to spend a weekend in the University's remote outdoor centre in the Pennines and you can take up a host of outdoor activities, through various clubs which take advantage of the easy access to the Lakes, fells, pot-holes, sea, river, canal....

The University's Centre for Physical Education offers professional help for beginners and specialist advanced coaching in a range of activities. Competitive sport, serious or light-hearted, has a wide range of permutations in a collegiate system. To add to the drama, there is an annual 'Roses' weekend: Lancaster versus York Universities.

Student welfare

The University has a **Health Centre** on campus, open during the day and staffed round the clock. The University group general practice has both men and women doctors and a sickbay. The University runs a counselling centre

The **chaplaincy centre** at Lancaster is a very distinctive building with three brick drums surmounted by spires and crosses. Inside, the areas achieve a surprising unity from separated chapels. There is also a synagogue, kosher kitchen, rooms for study and prayer for Buddhist and Muslim observances. Access to each part is from a central area which can be opened up for special occasions.

Careers Service
The Careers Service has a wide range of facilities designed to help you to decide on your career path. Computer-aided career matching (your personal characteristics and the requirements of a given career); group exercises to encourage self-assessment and self presentation; 'Insight into Management' courses; assistance in arranging project work in commerce, industry or the public sector as a part of the Enterprise programme.

When you come to applying for jobs, the Careers Service computer can match you against vacancies and give you a personal print-out listing of relevant opportunities. The Service will train you in writing applications and being interviewed. This, as well as a well-stocked information room and computer database, will all help you in your long-term career.

Students with special needs

Lancaster welcomes applications from students with special needs. The University has special experience in working with students whose vision is impaired, as well as links with major disability organisations. Nearly all parts of the teaching and public buildings are accessible to people with mobility difficulties and up to 40 adapted study-bedrooms are available on campus. The University has a Student Advisor for students with special needs.

A Kurzweil text reading machine, a colour CCTV and Braille embosser are in the library and several lecture theatres have induction loop systems. Less formal support is provided by the Union who also employ a Disabilities Officer.

Accommodation

Lancaster puts high priority on providing a room on campus, in a college, for all its incoming students, believing that this sense of security is vital to the settling-in process. In your second year you will almost certainly live out, as secondary priority goes to third-years, overseas students, post-graduates and visiting students. A new self-catering residence has opened by the canal in Lancaster, with 246 rooms, taking 2nd and 3rd years. There is also a head-leasing scheme with 270 places.

The colleges

College accommodation consists mainly of self-catering single study-bedrooms with shared facilities(serving between 6 and 12 students). Facilities do vary and this is reflected in the range of room prices. There are a few double rooms; not all rooms are centrally heated (those without have electricity-metered heating); not all rooms have wash basins.

All social life revolves around the colleges, each of which has its own bar and JCR facilities. You remain a member of your college throughout your three years.

There is no difficulty about living on campus through vacations, although at Christmas and in the summer, you might have to move to another college.

Costs (1995/96)

Single room: £29 - £34 per week

Ensuite: £48 per week

(accommodation allocated for 31 or 38 weeks)

These costs are for self-catering accommodation and include the cleaning of communal areas.

Private accommodation

Off-campus accommodation is likely to be in Lancaster (2 miles) or Morecambe (8 miles away). The Accommodation Officer gives expert advice. Rents are around £30 to £35 a week, excluding heating.

Mature students

The University - with the University of Central Lancashire - administers the Open College Federation of the North-West. If you are over 21, and have recently undertaken an Access course, or followed some other 'alternative route' to higher education, the University welcomes your application.

Preschool Centre

There is a pre-school centre licensed to accommodate 102 children. Students may be eligible for a subsidy on fees.

THE CITY (population c.50,000)

Lancaster city is more like a small county town; even extending the district to include Morecambe and Heysham on the coast, the total population creeps up to merely 100,000. The city is an administrative centre and market town for its region, retaining an unbroken sense of its past; modern change and influence has not been strong enough to counter the feeling of walking historic ways as you pass through old, wandering streets, sometimes cobbled, usually lined with quiet stone houses, most built with a domestic, solid, northern permanence.

The cobbled streets and narrow alleys winding down into the city offer an absorbing browse through antiquarian bookshops, craft and bric-a-brac shops, small coffee houses and restaurants. Most shopping areas are pedestrianised and include an indoor market and fish market.

You can walk by Lancaster's canal (where you can hire a narrowboat or cruiser), or down to the curve of the Lune, the lovely river which gives Lancaster its name. Here St George's Quay, in the 18th century a busy centre for water-commerce, now houses the Maritime Museum in its stone warehouses and Custom House.

A city of changing levels, Lancaster is dominated from opposite hill-sites by its castle and by the Ashton Memorial in Williamson Park. This has been recently renovated and you can now see the surrounding countryside from its viewing gallery. The castle stands symbol to the city's historic dignity, the walls of its impressive shire hall covered by a heraldic display of the shields of every high sheriff and constable since the 12th century. It is still used in part as a prison, but you can visit the hall, the Georgian courtrooms and the medieval dungeons.

Theatre: The Duke's Theatre has flexible staging and mounts imaginative productions.

Cinema: two cinemas; art films shown at the Playhouse.

Nightlife: Good range of restaurants; several nightclubs, one of which is run by the Union; a large number of pubs - a rewarding place for Real Ale seekers.

Sport: The Kingsway Sports Centre offers a full range of facilities. Spectator rugby, football and cricket in the relevant season. Three 18-hole golf-courses and two nine hole. Pine Lake Resort near Carnforth, just north of Lancaster, offers water sports.

ESCAPE ROUTES

Lancaster lies north of the great Lancashire urban landscape, in country which seems far from cotton mills and coal-mines. The valley of the river Lune is green, wooded, idyllic. The Forest of Bowland east and inland is wild. There is still only one road across to North Yorkshire over the moors. The Lake District begins just 20 miles away.

The coast of Blackpool, Morecambe and Heysham attracts tourists with its pleasure parks and fun-fairs: all are within day-tripping distance of the University.

Communications

Rail links to London, to Carlisle, to Leeds and to Manchester: regular, although not frequent and can be slow. **Coaches** run to various centres throughout the country. Lancaster is on the **M6. Ferries** run to the Isle of Man from Heysham (four and a half hours).

University of Leeds

Leeds
LS2 9JT
Telephone: 0113 243 1751

University Charter date: 1904

Leeds is a large university with over 20,000 degree students (under and postgraduate). This is very much a 'civic' university with a single, clearly defined site just outside the city centre. Most degrees here are modular, traditionally academic with a full range of courses on offer, including Medicine. Assessment methods vary, although weight is placed on examinations. All single first year students, from home or overseas, at whatever stage they apply, can expect to be housed in University-controlled accommodation.

THE CAMPUS

The University buildings are packed into a half mile square of land about half a mile from the city centre, and about a mile from the coach/rail stations and the M1.

The facade buildings, in Portland white stone, which flank the main access roads, have a classical dignity which befits the size and importance of a university which has built a solid national and international reputation in many fields since receiving its charter in 1904. Behind the imposing arches of the white Parkinson Building (the Parkinson Tower is the University's landmark) are the original buildings, designed by Alfred and Paul Waterhouse and built between 1877 and 1912. The neo-Gothic Clothworkers Court, Great Hall and Baines Wing are examples of Victorian architecture at its best and have in good measure the dignity which distinguish all the great civic universities.

The University - as all others of its vintage - expanded with explosive energy in the 1960's to accommodate the surging need for scientists and technologists. As a result, the campus is heavily developed.

Most of this building reflects high-density development with solidity and massive use of space. Buildings are high and imposing: the campus is on rising land and its spaces are sculpted by wide flights of stone steps. There is a large square 'lake' (more a patch of water here) to reflect skies and vary the ambience, but generally there are few green areas, except briefly around the more domestic 'absorbed' buildings which line the uphill perimeter. There is rather the feeling of a 'Brave New World' (for those of you who have read the book).

All this is offset by the city centre of Leeds, five minutes away on foot, by Hyde Park which is about a two minute walk away in the other direction, as well as by the large Union - newly refurbished and welcoming - and by the presence on-site of some halls of residence.

Further halls are sited out in pleasant suburbs; at Headingley in particular there is virtually a student-village, with a sense of community, offbeat shopping and the lively pubs students generate.

Leeds offers you a soundly balanced university experience, with healthy lifestyle contrasts.

Cars
No problem at off-campus halls of residence or flats, but city parking is very difficult indeed. Most students walk in or use the bus.

Learning Resources

The University's **library** resources hold over 2,500,000 books and periodicals (9,000 annual subscriptions).

There are two main libraries: the Brotherton Library, extended in 1993 and the Edward Boyle Library, which will extended in 1997 to include a Learning Centre with 100 workstations. The Edward Boyle Library has 90,000 selected course texts, and an audiovisual area with access to material other than the written, as well as the science and engineering research volumes. Altogether, there are study places for around 3,000 readers. The Edward Boyle is open until 10pm weekdays, 10am-5pm Saturdays, 2pm-7pm on Sundays. The Brotherton opens weekdays until 9pm and on Saturdays until lunch time.

There are also faculty libraries, including three main faculty libraries (law, medicine and textiles), and a further 30 departmental libraries on campus.

The University has an extensive computer network on over 50 locations available around the campus, some open in the evenings: space for 1,300 users. The **Computing Service** offers courses for beginners and experienced users, a Help Desk and literature.

The **Language Centre** offers self-teaching audio courses in over 40 languages, available to all students and Computer Assisted Language Learning in all major European languages.

Culture on campus

Drama: The workshop theatre, although primarily a resource for the theatre and drama teaching of the English School, is also open to other faculty staff and students. The Union theatre group organises regular productions and outside theatre groups perform in the Union. Two theatres in the Union, both well-equipped.

Film: The film society shows one or two films per week.

Music: Leeds has an active musical life and the University makes a distinctive contribution. Weekly lunchtime concerts and larger-scale evening concerts present both professional and student performers. The Union organises a very successful series of major gigs, regularly featuring well-known bands. Also an alternative programme of newer, up-and-coming bands: cheaper, good entertainment and a chance to witness the beginnings of fame.

The Union

The Union has been completely refurbished. The outside frontage is as ever. Inside, the reception area is still tiled and functional: down some steps and into the back is a glasshouse extension which lifts the whole atmosphere into a hybrid experience of conservatory/active meeting ground.

There is a good variety of snack bars, coffee lounges and four bars; a bookshop, record library, snooker room and games area; a stationery shop, travel bureau and launderette; a typing pool, print room, supermarket, optician's, Union shop and a daily market selling bric-a-brac, secondhand and clothes, records and trainers.

The Union runs over 150 non-sporting societies and a packed entertainments and events programme attracting famous names, including whole theatre groups. Very active indeed: around 10 special events each week, 4 or 5 discos and a Community Action Group operating 50 projects (and you can help with vacation soup kitchens). The radio station and a weekly newspaper co-ordinate activity.

The Union's Women's Centre provides emergency overnight accommodation and there is a women's minibus which runs into the night. Welfare Services give advice and information on most issues: an excellent service.

The Union has an annual turnover of £6-7 million. A total of ten sabbatical officers.

Sport

All major universities offer a marvellous range of sporting activities: the number of clubs and the range of amenities at Leeds are predictably impressive. There are two large sports halls, one with accommodation for up to 1,500 spectators, a smaller multi-purpose sports hall, a gymnasium and a variety of specialist facilities, including a climbing wall and a rifle range.

At Weetwood, three and a half miles north of the academic precinct, but close to the main halls of residence, there are extensive playing fields: 28 pitches for football, rugby and hockey; cricket squares and a 400 metre track.

Also a full-size floodlit synthetic pitch for soccer and hockey and six floodlit synthetic tennis courts. More tennis courts are at Oxley hall; rowing venues close to campus and at York; sailing on nearby reservoirs and lakes; windsurfing and hang-gliding both have active clubs.

Over 50 sports clubs and societies are sponsored by the University Union.

The University has two outdoor centres, one in the Lake District and on the Three Peaks Walk, both accommodate around 30 people and are available to students.

Student welfare

The **Student Health Service** offers a full range of medical services. The **counselling service** is staffed by professionals and trained student volunteers, backed by support groups and practical help, particularly for women. A thorough welfare survival guide is produced (see also the Welfare provision offered by The Union). You can see **chaplains** from the main Christian churches and the Jewish community.

Careers Service

The University has ten careers advisors in all, and computer resources including Prospect. The service also provides workshops on application and interview techniques and has an Assessment Centre.

Students with special needs

Most University buildings are accessible to people with mobility problems. The University has a brailling and requested-book recording service, and some lecture theatres are fitted with induction loops. The Disability Services Officer liaises with external organisations.

Accommodation

All single first year students, from home or overseas, at whatever stage they apply, can expect to be housed in University-controlled accommodation. The University has around 6,500 places in halls of residence or University flats.

Halls of residence

The 'nearest' three halls are actually on campus (accommodating nearly 500 students); the furthest one is four and a half miles out, and the other three straggle between one and three miles from base.

Halls of residence accommodate about 1,800 students in total and are warden supervised. Each hall provides some meals. More single than shared rooms (shared rooms tend to go to first years) but in a few cases sharing involves three or maybe even four people.

Halls vary in formality, in architectural styles (from a 19th century manor house to purpose-built multistorey) and facilities. All those off-campus stand in landscaped grounds in pleasant suburbs. The larger halls have sports facilities and organise regular social events.

Costs (1996/97)

	On-campus:	Off-campus:
Single:	£2,250 - £2,400	£1,900 - £2,255
Shared:	£1,900 - £2,240	£1,830 - £1,942

Costs include meals, heating, light and cleaning for a session of 30 weeks. On campus halls provide lunch.

University flats

There are around 4,600 places in University flats. Most of the units are within easy walking distance of campus. They range from Victorian town-house conversions to modern four-storey blocks, shared by a small group (from five to twelve). Some rooms have ensuite facilities. Each group of flats has a nonresident 'adviser' (a member of the academic staff) who works with the president of the committee of representatives elected from each flat.

Costs (1996/97)

Single rooms: £1,200 - £2,400
Shared rooms: £786 - £1,215
Married quarters: £1,780 - £2,990 per couple
40 weeks excluding fuel costs.

Private flats and bedsits

Leeds has a good supply of private rented, accessible accommodation. Facilities vary widely, of course; so do prices. Location makes a difference. The Union can give a lot of help, but you should allow good time before the session begins for your search. Rents range from £32 - £46 per week. You will be expected to 'live out' for at least one year of your course. Unipol Student Homes is run by the Universities and Unions of Leeds and Leeds Metropolitan and advertises around 19,000 vacancies a year.

Mature students

You should discuss your intentions with the Admissions Tutor of the course in which you are interested. You can enrol on a recognised Access course on which a conditional offer might be based or aim to meet the requirements of the Mature Entrance Scheme - usually a written examination and an interview.

Nursery

The Fourman Nursery has places for around 50 children, from three months to five years old. A play-scheme during school-holidays takes school-age children (5-12 years).

THE CITY (population: 717,000)

Leeds, a large, prosperous, industrial and commercial city, stands where the bulk of the Pennines subsides into the flatlands of the Ouse valley. The city itself spreads wide boundaries and its western and southern edges are blurred by surrounding conurbations; to the north and east, however, the city quickly gives way to open countryside.

As the city has spread, its outlying villages with their churches and centres have been absorbed, so that the immediate outskirts have their own identities. This is especially true of the area between the University and the halls of residence.

The centre is compact, and divided between the commercial shopping area and the civic buildings, close together, but quite distinct. The Town Hall dominates the civic area, which also houses the City Art Gallery, Civic Theatre and law courts. These are arch-Victorian buildings, with a solidity and confidence. The Victorian ethic continues inside the Town Hall; its main hall is used for the city's regular concerts and above the heads of audiences roll homilies, along the lines of 'Toil is Holy', gilded into pink marble.

The shopping centre is varied: renovated Victorian arcades roofed with modern, startling stained glass; new malls housing an impressive selection of the more select boutiques; pedestrianised areas with all major department stores; the Corn Exchange, complete with life-size World War One plane suspended between the circular galleries of small shops. Add to this the market, selling flowers, fish, buttons and vegetables, and the dark arches beneath the station where you can buy ethnic musical instruments and all kinds of 'objets'.

The development of the city over the past few years has been consistent and high quality. The canal area has a selection of restaurants and bars which give a cosmopolitan atmosphere to its cobbled lanes. New commercial tower blocks have a uniformity of style which is outweighing the excesses of the 1960s and restating the city's involvement in commerce. The new DSS building, love it or loath it, is perched beyond the bus station, presiding over its adopted land and visible from almost wherever you stand.

Theatre: Leeds Grand Theatre is home to Opera North (which has gained an enviable reputation) and accommodates touring national companies. The West Yorkshire Playhouse is the city's main repertory theatre: the Quarry Theatre is here and a smaller studio theatre as well. The Civic Theatre is the city's amateur dramatic centre. The City Varieties Theatre puts on Music Hall variety shows on Saturday nights.

Music: Leeds International Concert season has an interesting programme. Opera North offers varied, sometimes ambitious and innovative seasons. Various large amateur choirs perform. Live music available at many venues, including the Town and Country Club.

Cinema: An out of town Showcase Cinema (12 screens): more centrally - the Odeon (5 screens) and the MGM (3 screens). The Hyde Park, Lounge and Cottage Road cinemas are smaller, and sometimes have art films. The Leeds Film Festival is held in October.

Nightlife: Leeds nightlife is bopping to the early hours, with a full range of nightclubs and restaurants. Leeds is one of only places in the country to have granted all-night licences to three nightclubs. The pubs and bars often have live music, folk or jazz.

Sport: Spectator sports include Leeds United Football Club, Yorkshire County Cricket Club at Headingley, the Wetherby race course just off the A1 and Rugby, also at Headingley. Leeds has eight indoor sports centres with a wide range of facilities. National and international swimming events take place in the international pool. At Beckett Park is an all-weather athletics track. Leeds has 21 golf courses, 180 football pitches, 66 cricket pitches, 33 rugby pitches, 170 lawn tennis courts and 4 hockey pitches.

ESCAPE ROUTES

Leeds is very close to the Yorkshire Dales: beautiful landscapes, walking country, tarns, hills, falls and limestone pavements, small villages, abbeys, churches and castles. The Carlisle-Settle railway line (daily service) is justly famous and the Worth Valley Railway (steam) is great fun. Leeds is at one end of the Leeds/Liverpool Canal. You can hire narrow-boats for trips to Airedale, Skipton and beyond. York is only half an hour away, Bradford about 20 minutes - you could look at their entries.

Communications

National coach networks link Leeds directly with most parts of the country. Excellent motorway access: the **M1** to London ends close to the city centre; the **M62** is five minutes away and links with the **A1**.

The **Leeds/Bradford Airport** is extending its routes constantly and operates a regular service to London as well as other airports in the UK and Western Europe.

Leeds Metropolitan University

Calverley Street
Leeds
LS1 3HE
Telephone: 0113 283 2600

University Charter date: 1992

Leeds Metropolitan is a large/medium-sized university with 20,000 students, around half of whom are half time. It regards itself as a 'people's university' with very flexible degree programmes. Courses can include study support modules; in some cases, students can negotiate individual programmes of study. HNDs are also available. The University has two main campuses - one near the city centre, the other three miles out. Approximately a third of first years are housed in University owned accommodation.

THE CAMPUSES

The University has two campuses: a large 'sixties' block style campus sitting virtually on the inner city ring-road, directly opposite the University of Leeds; and the Beckett Park campus, three miles out, in a 100 acre parkland setting.

City campus

The city centre campus is not quite single-site: the Business School occupies a large and lovely period building with sympathetic modern extensions in Queen Square (this is shared by the Careers and Counselling services, and the Chaplaincy, so you will all come to know it); the School of the Environment has a modern white-with-dark-windows home near the Merrion shopping centre; Accountancy and Finance, Economics and Public Policy live in Woodhouse Lane. This can sound very scattered, but in fact all these buildings are set in the centre most area of the city and are within short, walking distance of the main building.

The main campus building is an enormous, three block structure, multistorey of glass and panels, with interconnecting corridors and staircases. There is a small gallery here, the drama studio and Union facilities, general offices and teaching rooms. This is a functional place with no trimming: the probability of a purely institutional existence is alleviated by a sunken-well meeting-place where you can pause between classes.

The Beckett Park campus

This campus occupies high ground, three miles from the city centre; indeed high enough to lose sight of Leeds, which emerges only as you wander to the edge of the campus. The 100 acre site is well screened by trees and has a woodland/park ambience, although the main cluster of buildings is quite large.

The historic layering is interesting. The earliest building on site dates from the mid-18th century, though much altered a hundred years later; the residential halls were built in 1912, in dignified, old grammar school style; the Carnegie Hall, added in 1933, was designed to harmonise.

The sports facilities here are excellent and are detailed under the sports section, if you are not a sports fanatic, the campus has the merits of its lovely setting, its fine buildings, its large and impressive library and some of the University's halls of residence. The handsome three-storey buildings are set around three sides of a large lawned quadrangle. The mellow old brick, orderly geometry of the layout, and the wide green acres behind, all create a calm, atmosphere of learning balanced by outdoor activity. This campus is an ideal complement to the city campus.

Courses taught at Beckett Park include Teacher Education, Informatics, Leisure and Tourism and Law.

Cars

You do not really need a car in Leeds. Public transport is very good.

Learning Resources

There are three main **Learning Centres**: at Calverley Street and the Brunswick Building on City Campus and at Beckett Park. All are available to all students. Total seating 1,100 places; volumes 500,000; 2,000 periodical subscriptions; open seven days a week.

It is University policy that all students should gain some computer/information technology skills. The **Computing Service** offers detailed manuals, help disks, an advisory service which provides specialist help and advice, and technical maintenance. Facilities are sited at the City campus and Beckett Park, and all suites are networked and have some machines dedicated to open access.

Language laboratory facilities are open to all students. The Language Centre is on the Beckett Park campus and is very well equipped with computer-assisted learning facilities. All full-time students may study a language in addition to their courses at subsidised rates to Language Certificate, Language Diploma and Advanced Language Diploma levels. Many courses do include a foreign language module.

Culture on campus

Drama: The Studio Theatre on the city campus is used by students (who put on two full seasons a year) and takes occasional small touring productions.

The Union

The Union at the Leeds City Campus runs an information service, playscheme, sports office, print room, shop, games room, Student Advice Bureau, Cafe Bar, Entertainments hall and Health and Fitness Suite. New Facilities at the Kirkstall residences include a weight training and fitness studio, cafe and pasta bar..

LMU's Union liaises closely with the Leeds University Union; together they run projects including a summer vacation soup kitchen, the Leeds Student newspaper, Unipol Housing Agency and other welfare services.

Entertainments include discos, gigs, theatre groups, debates and talks by visiting speakers. A women's mini bus offers a door to door service every night and a free mini bus to Headingley (a popular place for digs) is laid on after weekday discos. The Union runs over 60 sports, cultural, political and religious clubs and societies.

At Beckett Park there is an office, a shop and a bar.

Sport

There are 50 sports clubs. The Carnegie complex at Beckett Park has long been nationally famous for the excellence of its sports facilities, and its sporting record. There are acres of fine playing fields, floodlit all-weather areas, an athletics track, a swimming pool, the Carnegie Regional Gymnastics Centre (a large gymnasium and large sports hall, both with state of the art equipment and a climbing wall). The site serves the region as well as the University; schemes are developed jointly with the city council, and supported by Yorkshire and Humberside. Facilities are available for public use in vacations, but in term time all this is your private world. The City campus has some facilities run by the Students' Union which include a Health and Fitness, Weights, two squash courts and Martial Arts/Dance rooms: also a Physiotherapy service. Students can be awarded Sports Coaching and Leadership qualifications alongside their normal courses.

Student welfare

Nurses staff two **health centres** at each major campus. The University has a team of **trained counsellors** available. The **Chaplaincy** offers support to all students: Muslim, Jewish and Christian counsellors are available.

Careers Service
The Careers Service offers help in formulating career plans and has an extensive library. Workshops help to develop your job-searching skills. The Job Shop acts as an agency for students looking for part-time or vacation work.

Students with special needs
A co-ordinator for students with disabilities is available for you to contact before you apply and can all give specific advice on special needs.

Accommodation

The University houses around a third of all first years in University-owned accommodation. Beckett Park residential places are self-catered: up to 70 students share the facilities of each large kitchen. The Sugarwell Court, one and a half miles from the city campus, accommodate 388 students in flats for 4-6 people. These halls are warden controlled and facilities include a laundry, shop, small gym and a non-smoking bar. The new development at Kirkstall Brewery Residences provides study bedrooms and facilities for over 1,000 students.

Unipol Student Homes is an agency giving independent advice to students at both the city's universities. It runs Woodhouse Flats (146 places within walking distance of the city campus) and Eastmoor (187 places, two miles from Beckett Park).

The Mary Morris student residences are reserved for overseas students.

Costs (1995/6)
self-catering single: £32.40 - £51.80 (ensuite) x 41 weeks
self-catering shared: £29.20 - £36.50 x 43 weeks
catered single: £52.90 x 38 weeks

Private accommodation
The Accommodation Office has lists of private housing. Most students live in private sector accommodation; there is no shortage of rented accommodation in Leeds. Single room: £37.50 per week average.

Mature students

The University encourage applications from mature students and accepts non-standard qualifications which prove you have the motivation, potential and knowledge to benefit from a course: 'qualifications' includes work experience and provable interest. The Access and Independent Study Office can design programmes to suit your particular requirements. To help you to demonstrate you 'Prior Experiential Learning', the University runs a 'Making Your Experience Count' course.

Nursery
The Union runs a playscheme at half-terms. There is a Childcare Co-ordinator, who will help you find more regular care.

THE CITY/ESCAPE ROUTES

See the University of Leeds entry

University of Liverpool

Liverpool
L69 3BX
Telephone: 0151 794 2000

University Charter date: 1881

Liverpool is a large university with 10,291 undergraduate students on full-time programmes and 1,791 full-time postgraduates. A city centre single campus covering over 100 acres with a mix of building styles and ages - this is a civic university. Residential accommodation is about three miles out of the city; the University will guarantee accommodation to students who accept an offer of a place by the end of May. Courses are modular; in the main, modules are chosen within a course's options: content and assessment both have the strength of tradition. Assessment varies: all courses include examinations; some course work in some courses is included in the final degree grading.

THE CAMPUS

Founded more than a century ago, the University occupies a 100 acre site near the centre of the city. It has never aimed for an ivory tower image and puts into practice a vigorous policy of integration with the local community. Its unusually active and committed approach to the concept of service marks the University's particular character and shapes many of its courses.

The campus has an interesting locale; it virtually embraces the Roman Catholic Metropolitan Cathedral of Christ the King, a controversial and arresting modern structure; and is close to Liverpool's second (Anglican) cathedral. The precinct has two focal points: the 'original redbrick' Victoria Building, very much a city landmark, which stands at the junction of two main roads; and Abercromby Square, a quiet garden surrounded by elegant Georgian terraces which now house academic departments, and the University's art gallery. These two points symbolise Liverpool's ambience: looking outward to involvement with the city, and inward to fields of study and culture.

The precinct has expanded, mostly into modern buildings, in a reasonably compact area. There are pleasant landscaped walkways, shrubs, cobbles and paving. It is easy to move around the University, and there is an air of a friendly, relaxed, but purposeful community.

Behind and around the Victoria Building, which is a fine example of its period architecture (unusually veering toward understatement and elegance), has grown the cluster of buildings which house the Engineering, Science and Technology Departments, and the Veterinary and Medical Schools. Many of these buildings are new or recent (i.e. post-1960), but are alongside a very large, original complex of Victorian buildings, resplendent with plaques recording early benefactors: statements of civic pride and evidence of turn of the century civic wealth. A stone-fronted-palatial, Georgian style (but actually 1913) building stands entry-guard to an inner courtyard - small lawn and trees - surrounded by more Victorian buildings of extraordinary grandeur.

The University's growth into new buildings and Abercromby Square, from the original grand and imposing complex, gives Liverpool's campus a balance and a rhythm of movement.

Expansion continues. New acquisitions have included: the Liverpool Royal Infirmary Building (Grade 2 listed) which is being converted to house health care facilities, pharmacology and technology transfer; a former chapel, now the Languages Centre; and a new, purpose built Student Services Centre.

The campus as a whole is well-grouped, with lots of space, lots of style, and green areas to grace its vibrant, yet academic, atmosphere. Most academic departments have their own social areas, adding to the social mixing grounds of the Union and the halls of residence.

Cars

The Students' Union issues free permits for precinct parking; you must apply to the warden of your hall of residence for permission to park there. Liverpool is OK for bicycles, but they need watching!

Learning Resources

The **library** has around 1.3 million books and journals, takes over 6,000 periodicals, is administered by a staff of more than 100, and is housed in two complexes: one for arts and one for science. There is seating for 650 readers in the Sydney Jones Library (arts-based), and for 450 in the Harold Cohen Library (science-based). Opening times: Monday to Friday 9am to 9.30pm; Saturday 9am to 1pm. There are also a number of departmental libraries.

Most courses include an element of computing. The **Computer Services Department** provides a central computing service. Personal computer systems located in centres around the University are available for undergraduate use. A new centre has been installed in Derby and Rathbone Hall, available to students outside 'normal' hours. The campus is networked.

The **Language Centre** offers self-access and taught language courses to all members of the University. The language laboratories have audio-interactive video, computer and CD-ROM equipment.

Culture on campus

Drama: There are two theatres on campus: the University Theatre and the Stanley Theatre in the Students' Union. Productions are staged by departments in the Faculty of Arts and by student drama groups. Sometimes the English and Music departments combine forces to stage an opera.

Film: The Union screens films on two nights a week on a very large screen in the Mountford Hall.

Music: There are links with musicians who are members of the Liverpool Philharmonic Orchestra, who give specialist tuition in the Music Department. Music students are encouraged to perform with the University's choirs, orchestra and chamber groups. Big name bands and smaller gigs happen regularly.

The Union

The Union building is in the centre of the precinct and has just undergone major redevelopment creating a covered courtyard, food bar and more shops. A launderette, barbers/hairdressers, stationery shop, photographer, print shop and travel agent are all available, as are five bars, a cafe, television lounge, table tennis, snooker and pool facilities. Also, a large in-Union Monday market.

The Union produces a student newspaper and an arts magazine, and runs 100 non-sports societies; any student may set up his/her own society, provided that s/he can find a group of fellow-thinkers.

The Union arranges concerts and events in the Mountford Hall which has a standing capacity of 1,500. Around 12 bands visit each term, there is a club/disco night at least twice a week and a comedy club every fortnight. Films are shown twice a week.

The Union is enjoying increasing autonomy, employs four sabbatical officers and holds fortnightly meetings of the student body when policy can be discussed.

Other interesting points: a Community Action Group, a free late-night bus with priority for women and a Drop-in Advice Centre.

Sport

The Sports Centre is on precinct, close to the Union building, and admission is free for all students. The Centre claims to have the finest swimming pool in any British university: a six-lane 110-ft pool with a 5m fixed board, and 1m and 3m springboards. The pool is used for many aquatic activities including octopush (underwater hockey).

There is also a large sports hall: 5-a-side football, four squash courts, a climbing wall, dance studio, weight-training and sunbeds.

Additional facilities on precinct are in the Grove Street gymnasium - once a Methodist chapel: a 24 x 12m gym, free weights, four more squash courts. The vaults now contain rifle and pistol shooting ranges.

Sports grounds (extensive) are at Wyncote in Allerton, about three miles from the University, but very close to the halls of residence. There are two floodlit artificial-turf hockey pitches (also used for evening training), and a further 16 grass pitches. Additional playing fields at Maryton Grange (near Allerton) and Greenbank provide seven more soccer and rugby pitches.

The University boathouse is in the grounds of Knowsley Park. There is an outdoor activity centre in Snowdonia, owned by the University, with accommodation for 18 students. There is a programme of recreational classes which make it easy to take up a new sport and there is a Sports Injuries clinic (free treatment). The sailing and windsurfing clubs use the Crosby Sailing Club.

There are professionally-run courses to improve your skills and fitness, and coaching for national student standard competitions. There are more than 45 clubs run by the Athletics Union (47 sports). The University has had major successes over the past years: 1994/95, 25 students represented their country and six became full-time internationals.

Student welfare

The **health service** has moved to new accommodation and now has specialist clinics for family planning and asthma, in addition to general surgeries. There is a 16-bed sick bay at the halls of residence manned by a full-time staff.

The University employs **counsellors** with whom you can discuss personal problems or ask for practical information or advice. There are self help groups. The Union's welfare and NUS officer will advise you on welfare rights as tenants (grants and legal matters). The Union also runs a Nightline service.

The Joint Christian **Chaplaincies** work very closely together on the University precinct, the halls of residence site and in Community Action. There is a Muslim prayer room on campus.

Careers Service

The University has six careers advisors to give you guidance. The Service has a well-stocked careers library, and offers 'Gradscope' and PROSPECT - computer aids.

There is an annual Careers Conference, an 'Insight into Management' course, training seminars, case studies and employer presentations, as well as lots of courses to prepare you for job applications. Each year there are consultations to develop your profile and to help you plan ahead.

Students with special needs

You should write to the Registrar before submitting your formal application, stating your intended course and outlining your special needs. The University will normally invite you to visit your intended department and to meet the Welfare and Accommodation Advisor so that you can discuss provision. Your application will, of course, be considered on academic grounds.

Accommodation

The University will guarantee accommodation to students who accept an offer of a place by the end of May (i.e. before Results) and who return their Accommodation Application Form and Record Card to the Welfare and Accommodation Advisor by 2nd September.

The University offers both catered and self-catered accommodation in eleven halls of residence.

Halls of residence

Most first years are housed in the catered halls which are on two very pleasant parkland sites about three miles out from the University precinct, in an area well blessed with trees and lawns. The halls, in pairs, are warden-controlled. There are special buses morning and evening, and a regular public service.

Two halls have their own cafeteria service for meals - with occasional formal dinners. The main Carnatic site (six halls) has centralised facilities which include four self-service dining-rooms. A large hall is available for formal dinners, formal dances, discos and other activities organised by individual halls.

Six of the halls are mixed, plus two single-sex (one of each). The grouping of the halls, with their good range of facilities (squash and tennis courts, billiard and table-tennis rooms, bars, reading rooms, launderettes, commonrooms, libraries etc.) generates a lively community and varied social life, forming a world complementary to, but separate from, the life of the precinct.

Room amenities vary. Almost all are single study-bedrooms: at best a bathroom separates each pair of rooms; at worst, washing facilities are shared by varying numbers.

Self-catering residences

The self-catered halls (three in all) are actually on campus. Melville Grove, the newest, has satellite television and is networked into the campus computer system.

The flats and houses are mixed, have single study-bedrooms and are shared by groups of between three and ten students. If you apply for an undergraduate course and are allocated self-catering accommodation, the University ensures that you will be in a unit with other first year students.

The three residences have their own management staff; and for first year students there is a Resident Tutor (normally a senior postgraduate).

Costs (1995/6)

Catered single room: £1,911 for 31 weeks

Fees include: breakfast and dinner Monday to Friday. Breakfast and high tea Saturday, brunch and high tea on Sunday.

Self-catering accommodation: £1,482 to £1,560 for 39 weeks

Private sector flats and bedsitters

Most students prefer to live out after their first year. Student houses, taken by groups of friends, are very popular, and in good supply. Equally, there is a good range of bedsitters in very comfortable older houses. The University has joined forces with Liverpool John Moores to set up Liverpool Student Homes which will provide lists of private accommodation. If you want this kind of accommodation in your first year, allow good time for a personal search before term begins.

Rents in Merseyside are comparatively reasonable. Normal rents are around £30 to £32 per week.

Mature students

There are a number of ways to a Liverpool degree if you are a mature student. The traditional entry route of A levels, a successfully completed Access course or Open University module is, of course, open to you. The University has a Mature Students' Adviser whom you can contact; there is also a University leaflet outlining the practicalities of life as a mature student.

Alternatively, you could enter through the University's programme of Continuing Education courses. Courses are available in centres throughout Merseyside, Lancashire and West Cheshire.

The third option is to take the beginning of a degree course through a franchised FE colleges. Four degrees are available at four colleges.

Nursery

A new, purpose-built nursery is planned which will offer a number of subsidised places for students' children and babies. The Student Services Centre can give information on local childcare facilities.

THE CITY (population: 510,000)

Liverpool has a sense of the sea in its air: the wide tidal estuary of the Mersey with its seagulls and ferries; the past glamour from the docks which saw the misery of famine emigration and the wealth (often disreputably acquired via the Slave Triangle) returning from overseas; the imposing white grace of the waterfront buildings - especially the twin towers of the Liver Building, with their famous Liver Birds: a city with spirit and excitement.

In its heyday, Liverpool was a very wealthy city and is endowed with fine, imposing civic and commercial buildings, plus a heritage of rich patronage of the arts.

Close to the University's doorstep is the Roman Catholic cathedral, a controversial and daring design by Sir Frederick Gibberd, with a central altar and circular seating for the congregation. To enter on a sunny day is a stunning visual experience as coloured light spins into wide space through the vibrant stained glass panels designed by John Piper and Patrick Reyntiens. The cathedral was consecrated in 1967, 11 years before the huge Gothic-style Anglican cathedral, designed by Sir Gilbert Scott, built in sandstone, standing quite close to its fellow, and connected by Hope Street (one of the ironies of town planning).

Wandering Liverpool's streets will take you to excellent shopping facilities: modern precincts, large department stores (including a branch of John Lewis), street markets, street vendors, Victorian and Edwardian gin palaces, period pubs and a host of smaller shops and byways.

In the centre are many elegant examples of historic architecture, notably the Bluecoat Chambers. This was once a school and now is a centre for artists and craftsmen; its quadrangle is set back from one of Liverpool's busy shopping precincts and has a curious calm which at once takes you away from bustle. Specialist developments like The Palace and Quiggins cater for more off-beat tastes and bargains are to be had here; both have great bistro-type cafes.

The Beatles, of course, have left their mark and shrines, and their best-known venue, the Cavern, has been rebuilt as part of Cavern Walks, a new building in Matthew Street.

On the edge of Sefton Park, one of the finest urban parks in Britain, quite close to the halls of residence and the most popular area for living-out, is Lark Lane, a lively Victorian shopping street with a range of traditional shops, winebars and eating places. Otterspool Park with its riverside promenade is also nearby.

As modern commerce takes business down river, the old dockland is being redeveloped in imaginative ways as leisure areas: the award-winning Albert Dock redevelopment is Britain's largest group of Grade I listed buildings, with many historic features - its design was revolutionary in 1846. It now houses specialist shops, restaurants and exhibition areas. The Tate Gallery has opened the Tate Gallery Liverpool here, in salute to the port which was source of the Tate family wealth.

Theatre: The Empire - the largest theatre in Liverpool - presents major touring companies for ballet and opera, occasionally performances by the Royal Shakespeare Company, musicals and pop concerts. The Liverpool Playhouse has premiered a number of outstanding plays and presents a good range of drama. The theatre also contains a studio. The Everyman: style of productions is innovative and sometimes controversial. Productions range from classical to modern drama. The Neptune houses both amateur and professional drama. The Unity Theatre takes in small touring companies and is also venue for local amateur dramatics.

Music: There are regular classical concerts by the Liverpool Philharmonic Orchestra at the Philharmonic Hall. Smaller chamber concerts and recitals are held at the Bluecoat Chambers Concert Hall. There are frequent pop/rock concerts at the Royal Court Theatre. Live music issues from many of Liverpool's pubs and clubs. Music on Merseyside is, not surprisingly for a port city, international: Irish ceilidhs to the second biggest Caribbean carnival in the UK.

Cinema: There are two multi-screen cinemas in the city centre and many more around Liverpool. The leading alternative cinema is the Robbins 501; minority interest and art-films are shown in the Film Institute in the Bluecoat Chambers. There is a Showcase multiplex on Edge Lane.

Nightlife: Nightlife is very lively with a good range of nightclubs and pubs. There are some fairly flamboyant pubs: the Philharmonic is a splendidly preserved Victorian/Edwardian bar which has a listed 'Gents', open once a month for inspection to all interested; Ye Cracke, a tiny pub, was a favourite haunt of the Beatles. There are many more. Poetry readings in pubs have a peculiarly Liverpool flavour. The historically-strong presence of the Irish has also made itself felt in the character of many pubs. The city has Europe's oldest Chinatown, containing many fine restaurants. Other restaurants in Liverpool range through all tastes and budgets, perhaps the highest concentration being on Lark Lane.

Sport: Soccer teams Liverpool and Everton are famous, with a large and enthusiastic following. Matches generate a lot of excitement and humour. The Grand National world-famed steeple chase happens here at Aintree in April; Haydock racecourse, too, is only a few miles away. Liverpool Cricket Club has regular matches throughout the season, and is host to several of Lancashire's county games. The area is particularly good for golf, with many Merseyside clubs; there is sailing at Crosby Marina, Salthouse Dock and West Kirby.

ESCAPE ROUTES

At first glance, a map of the Liverpool area seems impossibly built-up, built-on and industrialised. In fact, routes out from the city are straightforward and far-ranging.

The coast (very close) offers Southport, with six miles of sand and two amusement parks, and Formby with its nature reserve where you can see red squirrels.

The Delamere Forest in Cheshire covers 4,000 acres of woodland, with paths and tracks: this is not really hiking country, but not bad for afternoon rambling.

The nearest dramatic countryside, and it is dramatic, is North Wales: you can see Snowdonia from parts of Liverpool. For outdoor pursuits, Wales is the place - climbing, hiking, canoeing... Or north, the Lake District is not too far away.

More locally, Liverpool has a scattering of stately homes, with parks and gardens; or you could go out to the Wirral peninsula - very pretty and with some excellent country pubs.

Communications

Lime Street station has recently been refurbished. Liverpool has fast, direct **trains** to London (two and a half hours) and has direct lines to many other major centres - Manchester, Leeds, Newcastle and Scotland, North Wales, Birmingham, the Lake District. The Merseyrail system extends as far as Southport, Ormskirk, Kirkby and a large part of the Wirral. Most routes are also covered by **national coach services**.

The **M62** links the city with Hull via Manchester and Leeds. The Mersey Tunnel connects with the **M53** and **M56**, opening up the Wirral and North Wales. Along the M62, the **M6** intersects and gives access north to the Lakes and Scotland, and south to Birmingham, London and South Wales. In the summer **ferries** run regularly to the Isle of Man. **Liverpool airport** at Speke has shuttle flights to Heathrow and international airlines.

Liverpool John Moores University

Rodney House
70 Mount Pleasant
Liverpool
L3 5UX
Telephone: 0151 231 2121

University Charter date: 1992
John Moores is a large University with a student population spread over various campuses, most close to Liverpool's city centre. There are two main campus areas and two outposts.Courses are modular and are assessed by examination and coursework - percentage weights of each vary between courses. University accommodation provides 1,650 places in student houses, halls of flats. Priority is given to new first years from more than 25 miles away.

THE CAMPUSES

A glance at the map in its prospectus will show you the scattered nature of Liverpool John Moores 'campus'. It is possible to identify two main clusters of buildings in the city centre, with one or two outriders.

One cluster is set around the academic centre of Liverpool, close to the cathedrals, music, theatre and each other. The second cluster is harshly removed from this world, mainly by the dramatic barricade of ring roads. The two clusters show both faces of Liverpool: one beautiful and cultured; the other grey, neglected and heavily urban.

The analogy with its city's nature is completed by the IM Marsh campus, once a training college, and the halls of residence, which are set in green and affluent suburbs.

Arts and Professional District: the central cluster...

...falls into two halves, but as all the buildings are within minutes' walk of each other, they can be considered together. Five of them, closely grouped, house the disciplines of the School of Design and Visual Arts in fine examples of Victorian school architecture. The University has recently opened its new School of Media, Critical and Creative Arts in the shadow of the Anglican cathedral.

The other 'half' of this cluster is in the same territory as the old University of Liverpool's Mount Pleasant campus. In this area JMU is expanding its newer presence with imaginative design/restoration projects concentrated in the area around Rodney Street which will allow JMU to develop a substantial Arts and Professional campus-complex in the very heart of the city.

The new Learning Resource Centre is a spectacular new-age building in white surfaces, glass and steel. The design of the Centre is appropriate to its purpose- replacing the concept of a traditional library with electronically delivered information. The centre opens onto a small but pleasant tree-shaded square, whose other sides are flanked by university owned Georgian buildings (being recycled for new use) and the Union building.

Here also, in a well-kept Victorian building, lives the School of Law, Social Work, and Social Policy. Close by, in the John Foster Building, built as a convent in 1825, are the Schools of Business and Modern Languages, and Architectural and Planning Studies. The School of the Built Environment is in nearby Clarence Street. The campus is served by Roscoe Court (welfare, counselling, chaplaincy, loans) and the St Nicholas Centre (careers and medical centre), very close to the Roman Catholic cathedral.

Science and Technology: Byrom Street

There is less to say about this not quite city centre University site. Primarily it is functional, and you will come here for the courses. The main 'building' is actually a mammoth complex of three connected buildings. Although within walking distance of the central complex, this is a different world. You will have to make an effort, if you are based here, to use the city and the University's amenities to balance your life away from your immediate course fellows.

The three other buildings in this quarter of the city must have similar problems, but they are smaller in scale and therefore less formidable.

The Byrom Street campus houses Schools of Biological & Earth Sciences, Biomolecular Sciences, Computing & Mathematical Sciences, Electrical Engineering, Electronics & Physics, Engineering and Technology Management and Pharmacy & Chemistry. The three other buildings in this territory house the Schools of Human Sciences, Healthcare and Social Science.

IM Marsh

About three miles from the city centre, in Aigburth, the School of Education and Community Studies occupies a lovely, self-contained site which used to be a teacher (PE) training college. The main building is in Regency style - white and elegant. Facilities here include several gymnasia, dance studios, sports halls, theatres, an indoor swimming pool, and an extensive range of outdoor activities, including an all weather athletics track.

Learning resources

Five site-**libraries**, each serving a particular subject area or areas, all open to all students. The book stock stands at 550,000 items; 3,000 periodical subscriptions; 1,000 study places. Every site has networked PCs. The **Learning Resource Centres** provide user guides, manuals and journals, as well as help and assistance. The university is committed to open learning via electronically - (rather than book) - delivered information. All students can register to use the computing facilities. You can learn a foreign language as part of your degree. **Language laboratories** are open until 7 pm and have an extensive range of tapes.

Culture on campus

Film: Films are shown on Mondays in the Union.

Art: You can learn a range of art skills while at John Moores, including pottery and photography. There are links with professional artists.

The Union

The Students' Union's main building (The Haigh) stands between the two halves of the central cluster, in a three storey, well designed building. The interiors are spacious. A recent development has been to pedestrianise the area around the Haigh and to open Hardy's, a pub/nightclub in a building opposite. Friday night is free entry and cheap drinks. Very popular! The Venue holds an extensive entertainments programme - discos, quizzes, films, live bands, comedians... The Union supports over 80 clubs and societies. *Shout,* the Union's tri-weekly magazine and Shout FM Radio station is open to all student contributions.

There are six sabbatical posts and 13 executive officers are elected through a cross-campus ballot. The Union employs 80 full-time and 150 part-time staff in all. The Union has seven bars (three in The Haigh), six shops, a travel centre, copying and printing services, a pizza bar, banking and a solarium with three sunbeds. Other facilities at the Student Centres at Byrom Street and IM Marsh campuses.

The Union also runs a new Information Resource Unit giving advice on welfare issues. A late night bus service is open to all students, with priority for women, Wednesdays-Saturdays and delivers door to door.

Sport

The University Recreation Service supplements local provision, rather than being the 'prime provider'. The Students' Union funds 25 sporting clubs and societies and has The Base, a Fitness Centre with hi-tech equipment, sauna, MTV and aerobics. The Recreation Service organises other activities for staff and students at all sporting levels in various venues. The Student Pass allows staff and students to have free or concessionary access to some local sports facilities. There are two gyms (at Byrom Street and St Nicholas Centre) and pitches and a swimming pool at IM Marsh available on a voucher system.

Student welfare

The University has two fully-equipped **medical centres** at Byrom Street and the St Nicholas Centre, staffed by nurses and GP surgeries held on all three sites at various times during the week. A **professional counselling service** deals with a wide range of problems. Welfare advice is available on practical issues. The University has four **chaplains**, and also works with local religious groups.

Careers Service

The Job Shop in the Union links students with local employers for part-time and vacation work. The Service gives individual advice and also organises group discussions. In addition, it has information on all major UK employers, and has suggestions for vacation or voluntary work. There are computer-assisted careers guidance programmes. A Keyskill Careers Planning module is available through all degree programmes.

Students with special needs

You should enquire before you apply. There are facilities for students with hearing, sight or mobility difficulties on some courses. Ideally you should visit.

Accommodation

University accommodation provides 1,650 places in self-catering student houses, halls of residence or flats, spread over several sites. All residences have closed circuit television and 24 hour security. Priority is given to first years who come from more than 25 miles away.

Student houses

The University owns 85 newly built houses (each housing five students) directly opposite the Anglican cathedral.

Halls of residence

Two halls: Lime Street, just outside the railway station (indeed part of its facade) which used to be the British Rail hotel – an impressive Victorian building and a Liverpool landmark: houses 242 students. Parkside Hall of Residence in Moseley Hill, three miles out of the city, close to Sefton Park in the desirable part of town: 160 places.

Flats

The University provides accommodation in two high rise blocks of flats, a mile from the city centre. Each block has sixty flats and house, in total, 366 students. Further flats are available in purpose-built complexes on IM Marsh campus (Barkhill Court) and in Laurel Court in Fairfield. The two Courts house 416 students.

Costs (1995/96)

Costs vary between sites. The cheapest rooms are £30, the most expensive are £40 per week for 38 weeks. You might have to pay additional fuel charges.

Private accommodation

All private accommodation is dealt with by Liverpool Student Homes, a service run jointly by both Universities. Rents are around £30 to £32 per week for a room.

Mature students

The University welcomes mature students. Prior learning or work experience will be taken into account. The university is a member of the Merseyside Open College Federation and recognises approved Access courses.

Nursery

There are two nurseries at the University. Mount Pleasant nursery takes up to 32 children aged between three and five years. Tithebarn Street nursery takes 24 children. The University is presently reviewing its childcare policy.

THE CITY/ESCAPE ROUTES

See Liverpool University's entry in this Guide.

University of Manchester

Manchester
M13 9PL
Telephone: 0161 275 2000

University Charter date: 1903: founded 1851

Manchester is a large university with around 13,500 undergraduate students on full-time programmes and c. 3,000 full-time postgraduates. A civic university with a single academic 'precinct' (rather than campus) a mile outside the city centre. Manchester is in the process of modularising its courses to allow greater flexibility of choice. Modules will always be structured into coherent programmes. Some degrees (Medicine, Dentistry etc.) will not be included in the modular structure. Programmes are assessed in various ways: most include a level of project work or continuous assessment; all include an examination. The University offers all first years a place in University accommodation, provided that you confirm your place by 31 August. Private accommodation costs range between £30 and £40 for a room (excluding heat and light).

THE CAMPUS

The University is concentrated in an area intersected by Oxford Road, about one mile from the city centre. It is part of a chain of academic institutions which form the largest education precinct in western Europe: the complex includes the University, teaching hospitals, the Institute of Science and Technology (UMIST), the Royal Northern College of Music, the Metropolitan University, the Manchester Business School, the Manchester Computing Centre and the Manchester Science Park. This quite extraordinary concentration of resources exists within a few minutes' walk of the busy, affluent and stylish centre of what can be claimed, with some justification, to be England's second city. You do not, however, have a dominant impression of being immediately part of Manchester: this is a student state, an academic peninsula.

The main building (dating from 1873) is a large and splendid example of the Victorian, quite literally monumental, pride in civic institutions. In many universities 'the original building' has become a backwater of administration, but at Manchester it remains an organic part of University life, adding its period atmosphere and dignified spaces to the precincts of learning.

Opposite the Victorian splendours of the original building complex, the sophisticated grey brick and stone heights of the tall-towered Mathematics Building and the narrow window lengths of the Computer Building (with its rather sinister enclosed walkways) both make balancing stark 20th century style statements. Both the old building

areas and some of the new are planned to include green inner courtyards - necessary calm and quiet space in a campus which is so large and so heavily built: most vistas between buildings yield views of more buildings.

This is a densely developed sector of central Manchester, and the terrain is flat. The new buildings are slightly off-set so that the originals actually face lawns and trees - as befits their age and grace. It has to be said that some of the newer buildings (no doubt '60's/early'70's) are drab: an old and highly developed university inevitably mixes its styles.

Beyond the glass-and-panels refectory, and the large grey original Union Building, long out-grown, is the Academy, the Union's new extension. This looks rather like a warehouse, with its flat, unrelieved shape and gaudy paint, but it gives much needed extra space for all the things students like to do in Unions (discos, gigs...). Immediately behind is the Contact Company/University Theatre, and not far beyond that, the stately Whitworth Gallery with its superb art areas - so this really is a corner for well-balanced leisure pursuits. Here too are some of the student accommodation units: Toblerone-shapes, green spaces, a more domestic ambience.

The site is well sign-posted, and has clear directions for students with disabilities. In all, a thoughtfully-planned and pleasant campus which includes a useful amenity precinct with restaurants, shops, banks, University offices, linking the main campus with the Business School and the Royal Northern College of Music.

The nationally famous Jodrell Bank radio-telescope is a resource of Manchester's Science Faculty.

Warrington Collegiate Institute's Padgate campus is now a full faculty of the University. Telephone 01925 814343 for details.

Cars

You must have permission to park your car at your residence before bringing it to Manchester.

Learning Resources

Manchester's University **Library**, the John Rylands, is the third largest academic library in Britain. It contains 3,500,000 books, over 1,000,000 manuscript or archival items and 800,000 titles in microform. Most departments also have libraries, of varying sizes. The Library takes over 7,000 periodicals. Opening times: Monday to Friday 9am to 9.30pm; Saturday 9am to 6pm; Sunday 1pm to 6pm. The main library seats 2,445 students.

The Deansgate Building (the original John Rylands Library) is now the Special Collections Division and the John Rylands Research Institute and houses the Library's collections of rare books, manuscripts and archives. The building itself is very beautiful.

You can register at the **Manchester Computing Centre** to use its facilities which are on open access and available all year. All students have their own e-mail address and can use personal computers at the large number of public computer clusters throughout the University. If you need a particular computing skill for your course, this will be taught within your department. The Computing Centre will give you a tailored information pack about University facilities on request.

Students can continue **language learning** through self-teaching. A new Language Centre with self-study facilities opened in 1996.

Culture on campus

Drama: The University Theatre (300 seats) is run by the professional 'Contact' resident company, serving the region with high-quality drama. It is also a social venue for students, with a pleasant bar. The drama department uses it as a teaching aid, and puts on regular productions, as do other departments (notably Languages) on a more occasional basis. The theatre is very well-equipped technically, and extremely flexible in staging capacity: with two automatic lifts and variable sections of seating, productions can be staged in-the-round, in traverse, on a thrust stage, or behind a proscenium arch.

Music: The University presents a wide range of concerts; performers include the internationally famous Lindsay String Quartet, who are part-time lecturers in the music department. There is a University Chorus and Symphony Orchestra who give three or four public performances each session, and a Chamber Choir and Orchestra. There are also excellent concerts in the RN College of Music adjacent to the University, which has acoustically fine auditoria and studios. Lunchtime concerts... performances by the Union's Music Society...never a dull moment. The Union has a number of music venues which host frequent discos and live bands. The large number of students guarantees a lively scene.

Art: The Whitworth Art Gallery belongs to the University and is closely associated with the History of Art department. It is open to the public. Its galleries are harmonious, with beautifully distributed space and light. The gallery puts on about five exhibitions each year, some

from abroad. Its own collection is impressive: outstanding British drawings and watercolours, works by Blake, Turner and the Pre-Raphaelites, prints from the Renaissance, Old Masters and modern Continental drawings, textiles ranging from Coptic cloths to modern fabrics and contemporary British paintings, drawings and sculptures. Recent additions include works by Paul Nash, Matthew Smith, Francis Bacon and Howard Hodgkin. There are strong links with the student community; lectures and events are organised by the Whitworth Arts Society.

The Manchester Museum contains collections of natural history and geology, archaeology and ethnology, coins and archery. There are eight or nine million specimens - excellent resources for research. There is also a special exhibition gallery, open to the public.

The Union

The Union has a total of 14,000 members with a range of services, opportunities and social activities to reflect this magnitude. The Union buildings house: three bars, one open beyond normal time, a large coffee and snack bar, two burger bars, bank, travel agency, hairdressers, optician, two disco nightclubs (The Academy which is an acclaimed live venue with capacity for 1,900 and The Cellar), second hand book and record shop, pool and pin tables, photocopying services, showers, shop, and Advice Centre staffed by two full-time and elected student advisers.

As in other areas, the sheer size of the student community generates a wealth of activity. There are about 150 societies covering cultural, political, religious, academic, dramatic, musical, 'sometimes peculiar' interests. The Union is involved in visiting schools, organising 'Intro Week' and generally providing information about the University through its Alternative Prospectus, its own video and its own award-winning weekly newspaper - the *Mancunion*.

The Union is also closely linked with the local community through MUSCA (a fund-raising group) and Community Action (ten active projects

There are six elected full-time 'sabbatical' officers and an executive of twelve. Decisions are taken by collective executive responsibility and through the General Meeting and by an elected Union council.

Sport

A wide range: 40 different sports clubs operate through the Athletic Union - from archery, fencing, karate, to pistol, speleology and subaqua, via all the usual activities. There are a number of centres off campus:

The Firs Athletic Ground is at Fallowfield, close to the main student residences in south Manchester. Thirty-one acres· of pitches and courts for rugby, soccer, hockey, lacrosse, cricket, netball, four hard tennis courts, two artificial turf areas and a large pavilion;

The Armitage Centre (a sports and conference centre)- a 32 x 36m sports hall, a climbing room, fitness room a sauna/solarium and two activity rooms suited to martial arts, table tennis, a snooker room, keep fit and dance. There are four squash courts close by;

The Wythenshawe Ground - 90 acres with a large pavilion, pitches for rugby, soccer and hockey, six hard tennis courts and three cricket squares;

The Boathouse and Yacht Club - the Boathouse is by Bridgewater Canal in Sale and the Yacht Club is at Pennington Flash, Leigh, 18 miles out of the city. The club sails six Lark dinghies.

On campus is the McDougall Centre, one of Britain's first multi-purpose sports centres. Facilities include a swimming pool, a 90 x 95 ft sports hall, a small gymnasium, a multigym, four squash and two fives courts, an outside court, rifle range, climbing wall and sauna and solarium.

Student welfare

The University does not have its own health centre, so students are advised to register with an NHS doctor close to where you live. Nursing staff and emergency cover for students taken ill on campus are, however, available. Emergency dental care is provided by the University's Dental Hospital. The Student Health Service offers various specialised clinincs.

The University also offers **confidential counselling**, with a team of counsellors, and clinical psychologists.

There are two **chaplaincy** buildings on campus: the RC chaplaincy and the ecumenical chaplaincy, both with large meeting rooms. The latter has chaplains for CofE, Methodist, United Reformed and Baptist students. There is an orthodox Jewish Centre close by the campus and several synagogues in the south Manchester area. There are also mosques in Manchester and a prayer facility on campus for Muslim students on campus. The chaplaincies have good relations with a Western Buddhist Centre.

Careers Service

The University Careers Service has a very large and well-stocked information room, available from the start of your course. You will be asked in to talk to a careers adviser in your second year: The Service arranges a comprehensive range of events and group seminars to help you explore all possibilities.

The Careers Service organises the largest visiting employer programme in the UK. The Service also offers support for those students looking for part-time work during their courses or vacation work.

Students with special needs

There is a lot of help available for students with learning difficulties and for those with sight and hearing impairments. Some student accommodation has been adapted for students with mobility problems.

Accommodation

The University offers all first years a place in University accommodation, provided that you confirm your place by 31 August. Resources are pooled by the University and UMIST so that the range and numbers involved are enormous - far too varied to receive more than a very generalised summary in this space. The unit size ranges from a Victorian house, taking eight senior women students, to the Owens Park complex of flats, on campus, which houses 1,038 men and women and also contains good social amenities.

Many residences are actually on, or within half a mile of campus; most are within one and a half miles. The area a mile or so away is known as the 'student village' - more than 10,000 students live in this area in University-owned and provate accommodation. Only one of the more remote residences (two and a half miles) accommodates first years.

Most residences offer single study-bedrooms, although some do have shared rooms which are usually allocated to first years. Most halls are mixed: two are for women only and three are for men; all single sex halls are catered and relatively small.

Halls of residence

There are 24 halls of residence: 11 are self-catering and 13 are catered. Provision of meals varies, but the norm is breakfast plus dinner, weekdays, and brunch at weekends: sometimes supper or tea is added to this. Some halls have a Christian bias; some are small, with minimal facilities but a quiet, family atmosphere; some are very large with an impressive range of amenities (Owens Park has three restaurants, a library, launderette, bar, hall for discos...).

Within the range, individual halls establish traditions of their own: St Anselm's Hall (men) is 'well-mannered and friendly'; St Gabriel's (women) has a chapel and a Christian spirit, and many social activities; Ashburne Hall has beautiful grounds, garden parties, torchlit bonfire dances and a formal ball.

Students who do not live in Halls may become external members of a Hall.

Self-catering flats

About half the accommodation available to new undergraduates is self-catering. Study-bedrooms are grouped in units varying from 5 to 13 sharing the usual range of amenities: kitchen, lounge, bathroom. Additional facilities can include television rooms, library, dark room, games room, tennis courts. The newer the accommodation the better facilities it will have, including ensuite facilities at the newest.

Costs (1995/96)

Catered hall: £64.00 per week

Self-catering hall: £34.00 per week (shared facilities)

Self-catering hall: £49.00 per week (en-suite)

These prices are guidelines; the range is wide. Lease lengths vary.

Private sector accommodation

The Accommodation Office provides weekly lists of all private sector accommodation and will help you to find a place to live in your second and third years. Private accommodation costs range between £28 and £40 per person per week, excluding heating and light.

Mature students

Applications from mature students (i.e. over 21) are welcomed. You should contact the Admissions Office for advice. A number of courses can be taken part-time.

Nursery

There is a purpose built nursery run jointly by the University and the Metropolitan University, subsidised for students and takes 100 children from six months to five years old. There are playschemes at half term run by the University Union.

THE CITY (population 1,235,000)

Manchester is thriving, growing and enjoying itself. New buildings, worthy of the Milleneum are sprouting: the concert hall complex, new sports facilities, live venues. This, set against its history, rooted in the industrial revolution with its vigorous expression of the engineering, commercial and architectural vision of the Victorian entrepreneurs who laid the foundations of its wealth, makes Manchester a unique experience of a city.

The city has, however, earlier origins. It was a settlement in Roman times and parts of the Roman fort still exist; its cathedral is 15th century; it has a number of 18th century houses. So the thread can be traced. But the vigour, wealth and success of the city, with its reverse side of harsh building and legacies of hardship and poverty are the product of the 19th century.

Canals and viaducts, huge mills, ornate warehouses, theatres, libraries and galleries: extravagant, sometimes eccentric in style - always aiming for excellence. Victorian Manchester is writ large on its townscapes.

But perhaps its strength is its surprise factor: the space-capsule glass and steel theatre built inside the old Royal Exchange building where the high domes and pillared hall (still showing the 'closing prices' on its board) add a dimension to a theatrical experience seldom less than excellent; the unexpected canals; the white ironwork and glass Victorian pavilion revealed behind the shops of St Anne's Square; the imaginative conversion of the old Central Station into the G-Mex Exhibition Centre, retaining much of the remarkable Victorian railway architecture. Perhaps the biggest surprise is the Town Hall, a veritable fairytale palace of civic industry, inside whose walls lurk abbey cloisters, medieval banqueting halls, baroque fireplaces, William Morris drapery and wallpaper, of Gormenghastian proportions: an extraordinary experience and open to Manchester's public.

Shopping facilities are myriad. The question which should be asked of any city is 'does it have a defined centre?' If the answer is 'yes', the city cannot be that large: Manchester has a number of 'centres', each with its own defined character. For student-living Affleck's Palace Arcade will be the place to go: eclectic, idiosyncratic and not a place to take your granny. Back streets of secondhand stores, specialist bookshops, stalls of work by young designers - at affordable prices. There are cafes, bars, restaurants, city pubs, clubs and funny corners. Manchester is a truly cosmopolitan city, a city alive into the early hours where you will find what you want when you want it.

Museums and galleries: An astonishing range of museums and galleries, with a cosmopolitan selection of visiting exhibitions, as well as excellent standing collections. Probably the most student-friendly of art venues is the Cornerhouse on Oxford Road.

Theatres: The Royal Exchange Theatre is a wonderful theatre space with a history of excellence. As we go to press, we hope it has survived the Manchester bomb and will be restored to its former, idiosyncratic glory. The Library Theatre, situated beneath the Central Library, has a repertory company with a high reputation. The University Theatre, with its resident Contact Theatre Company, puts on a range of productions and is attracting excellent touring productions. The Green Room takes in 'minority' touring productions and some very interesting performances - pleasant bar. The Palace Theatre has been expensively refurbished and is venue for large touring theatre, opera and ballet companies, as well as 'star' attractions. The Opera House hosts major productions and national touring companies.

Music: Manchester is the home of the Halle Orchestra and Choir and the BBC Philharmonic Orchestra. By 1997, the new Bridgewater Hall will have opened and, if you are at all interested in classical music, its inaugural programme is historic. With the performances at the Royal Northern College of Music, and visiting orchestras, hardly a day goes by in term-time without a high quality classical concert.

Nationally known venues for rock and pop music are the new Nynex Centre (seating 19,500) Apollo and top clubs like the Hacienda. There are dozens of other venues for live music. The G-Mex Centre is also used for large pop concerts.

Cinema: Central Manchester has a total of 23 screens in various complexes, including the three cinemas in the Cornerhouse complex which specialise in art, foreign and experimental films. The Salford Quays complex, with eight screens, is barely more than a stroll away.

Nightlife: Manchester nightlife is hopping all night: winebars, discos, nightclubs, casinos, cabaret clubs, venues for ballroom dancing, historic pubs with Real Ale... whatever your pleasure. A rich range of restaurants; the widest selection perhaps being in Indian and Chinese food. Manchester has some of the best Chinese restaurants and the largest Chinatown in the country.

Sport: Manchester will host the Commonwealth Games in 2002. Famous football, of course: United and City. Test and county cricket at Old Trafford. Ice hockey and basketball teams have their home at the Nynex Centre. The sports facilities offered by the city include: coarse fishing in Boggart Hole Clough and Alexandra Park; golf at 18 municipal golf courses; cycle speedway at Broadhurst Park. There are football pitches in most of the city's many parks, six cricket grounds, two rugby pitches and four hockey fields. The city also has eight sports centres. Facilities were further boosted as preparation for the Olympic bid. The national cycling stadium opened in 1993 and the Manchester Arena in Summer 1995. The new Millenium Stadium to seat 80,000 is planned.

ESCAPE ROUTES

The city of Manchester stretches far and its internal attractions are many. If you want to get out, the roads and railways are there for you.

South is Manchester's traditional day-trip/weekending territory: the Derbyshire Peak District. Accessible by road and train, this area offers much: outdoor pursuits, history, scenic countryside - some of the most beautiful and dramatic in England. Gorges, crags and moorland make up its terrain, with streams and waterfalls: a centre for walkers. The foot of Mam Tor (the 'Shivering Mountain') is practically the only place in the world where you can 'pan' for Blue John - the semi-precious stone unique to this area - in the cold February streams. North Wales is accessible by direct and fast trainline: day trips to Snowdonia are equally possible.

There are several stately homes with added attractions around Manchester, all within a bus-ride.

Communications

There are two **inter-city rail terminals** (Manchester Piccadilly for London - just over two and a half hours - and the South; Manchester Victoria for Scotland, the North, Wales and Liverpool) connecting Manchester with all parts of the country. Manchester has major city **coach services** to all areas. Within the city runs the new **Supertram** service. The **M62** and **M63** allow fast access to the national motorway network.

Manchester Airport (Ringway) offers regular flights to most parts of the world, and a shuttle service to London.

UMIST

PO Box 88
Manchester
M60 1QD
Telephone: 0161 236 3311

University Charter date: 1905
UMIST is a small/medium-sized university with a total of around 6,000, two thirds of whom are undergraduate. A single campus, very close to the city centre, slightly apart from the main Manchester 'Latin Quarter'. This is a specialist University with courses offered in science and technology, engineering and management. A high number of sandwich courses. Course structures remain traditionally demanding: most are assessed by examination with some coursework/project work included. The University guarantees all single first years a place in university accommodation.

THE CAMPUS

The Institute occupies a 27-acre site in the very centre of the city; it begins the chain of academic institutions which ends with Manchester University itself, but has a clearly marked, separate identity. Life still centres on the original 1902 building, with its Art Nouveau decorative work; housed here are a number of academic departments, the library and administrative offices.

The general ambience, however, is 'new', which is not surprising, since the vast majority of buildings were completed between the early 'sixties and mid-seventies. Shapes are mainly rectangular, surfaces dominantly white; the units rise in clean lines to varied levels, some imposingly high. The set of the blocks, the use of glass, the air of generally well-kept efficiency and the minimal, but effective, landscaping create a sense of dignified space. The Institute succeeds in providing an unexpectedly academic environment within yards of Manchester's main bus and railway stations.

Cars
Parking on UMIST campus is very restricted; permits are issued but demand is very heavy. Public transport is convenient and frequent.

Learning Resources

The Joule **Library** has 252,000 volumes relating to science, technology, management and social sciences and receives 1,100 periodicals. The library is open until 8.45pm on weekdays and from 9am to 11.45am on Saturdays. Closed Sundays. The library has recently been refurbished and computerised, at a cost of £4 million. Remember, you also have access to the John Rylands University Library, Manchester Metropolitan Library, Salford University Library, Manchester Business School Library and to Manchester's public libraries.

Most students have the opportunity to learn programming, numerical analysis and other **computer techniques**. Many facilities are shared with the Manchester University computers for easy mainframe access.

Around 40% of students can learn a foreign language as part of their course. **Language laboratories** are open during the normal working hours of the University.

Culture on campus

Drama: In one of the earliest of the new buildings is the versatile Renold Theatre, used for large-scale demonstration lectures, but also for concerts and drama productions. Manchester University's good theatre is near.
Film: UMIST's Film Society is one of the best in the region.
Music: UMIST organises a programme of lunchtime concerts and organ recitals. The Union mounts frequent discos and live music. There is, of course, ready access to the musical world of the University and of the Royal Northern College of Music.

The Union

Again, the combination of the Institute and its University works to your advantage: there are separate, independent Unions, but students share full use of each other's facilities, and many are used by non students. The UMIST Union runs over 40 societies, and provides a shop, three bars, travel bureau, print shop, television lounge, showers, snooker tables... It also produces a fortnightly newspaper.

The UMIST Union building is well used and has recently been expensively re-furbished. The main bar is open until 11pm Monday to Saturday, 10.30pm Sunday. You can get food from the snack bars in the snooker room (a bar). There is a new cafe and a Union shop.

In total, the Union organises 40 social events per term, including 10 live bands. The hall holds around 550 students.

The Union has its own nightclub venue, the Underground, with a capacity for 900. It is open 9pm to 2am four nights per week, with Thursday being live bands night.

Manchester and Salford students combine to make a lot of money for charities through their joint Rag, which includes a 55-mile sponsored walk: the Bogle Stroll. There is an active Community Action Group.

The Student Advice Centre, offering confidential advice is located in the Union. There is a weekly legal advice session through the legal aid scheme. A women's minibus service is available and women-only taxi services are recommended.

The Union is represented on most University committees, and the Union/University relationship is positive.

Sport

The Sports Office organises the Institute's sports. There are almost 40 sporting clubs and societies. UMIST is involved in intervarsity competitions and the Director of Sport organises recreational sport.

UMIST has its own five-acre sports ground in Fallowfield, two and a half miles from campus, providing pitches for rugby, soccer, hockey and cricket, tennis courts and a modern pavilion with bar facilities. Students can also share the facilities of Manchester University.

Provision for some indoor sports is made in the main building. There are new squash courts, a five-a-side football pitch, tennis courts, aerobics and a multigym at the Sugden Sports Centre opposite the campus.

UMIST enters teams in UAU competitions independently of the University, which means that UMIST students cannot play for the Manchester University teams unless the Institute does not cater for a particular sport. Apart from that restriction, UMIST students can join clubs run by The University of Manchester with equal status.

Student welfare

You will be expected to register with a GP on arrival: information is available in the UMIST *Guide to Student Health*. Counselling is available through the Student Counselling Service on Oxford Road. The Union runs **Nightline** and has a **welfare advice service**.

There is a resident **chaplain** trained in pastoral counselling, and a Roman Catholic chaplaincy on Oxford Road. A room in the main building is provided for use as a mosque.

Careers Service
Students have access both to Manchester University and UMIST's careers information services, both of which are comprehensive and available throughout your course. UMIST arranges the largest visiting employer programme in the UK and has close links with local employers. Students can be helped to find part-time and/or vacation work.

Students with special needs
You should contact the Registrar before you apply. UMIST assesses all applications on academic merit, and - while the Institute undertakes to be as helpful as possible - some of the older buildings do pose access problems. Some residential rooms have been adapted.

Accommodation

UMIST guarantees all single first year students a place in university accommodation providing you confirm your place by August 31st.

UMIST has been building its own residences: students can, however, apply through the University of Manchester as well. A wide range of options on offer. Some residences are on UMIST's campus; some are about three miles away.

Costs (1995/96)
£1,950 catered 31 weeks; £1,175 self-catered

Private accommodation
Costs: £30 to £45 for self-catering accommodation. It is not easy to find accommodation close to campus: give yourself time for your search.

Mature students

Admissions tutors are ready to advise mature students individually about the possibilities open to them. Appropriate Access Courses are considered for entry. There is a four year Integrated Engineering Course for students who are interested in studying engineering but who have inappropriate qualifications.

Nursery
UMIST has a creche on campus which provides 50 places for children (under 5 years old) of staff and students.

THE CITY/ESCAPE ROUTES

See University of Manchester's entry in this Guide.

Manchester Metropolitan University

All Saints
Manchester
M15 6BH
Telephone: 0161 247 2000

University Charter date: 1992

Manchester Metropolitan is a very large university with 30,000 students in total, two thirds of whom are full-time and 60% of whom are undergraduate. This is a multi-site university: seven campuses in all; five in Manchester; one in Crewe; one in Alsager (the old Crewe & Alsager College). Main campus buildings are on Oxford Road, one mile from Manchester centre in the same academic cluster as The University of Manchester, Royal Northern College of Music and the Manchester Business School. MMU offers a wide range of non-modular courses. 'Practically' based subjects (Art & Design etc.) are assessed on course and project work. Other courses are graded both by examination and continuous assessment. University-owned accommodation is very limited in proportion to the number of students (1,433 on the Manchester campuses). Private accommodation: £30 to £40 per week excluding heat and light.

THE CAMPUS

In the centre of Manchester's elongated cluster of academic institutions rises and spreads the impressive main campus of the Manchester Metropolitan University. The University has outposts elsewhere but essentially expresses its style through the buildings which line Oxford Road and face three sides of a re-landscaped Grosvenor Square. You are less than a mile from the centre of Manchester.

The site is dominated by the All Saints Building, rising from a concrete pillared plinth of four-storey horizontals to a central height of five storeys, with service towers to add panache of line. It is a handsome, though plain, structure in warm brick and glass. It houses the main library, drop-in computing centre (from autumn 1996), recreation and sports facilities, and the central administration - so you are bound to spend significant time here.

It is a tribute to its designers and the quality of the All Saints Building's fabric that interiors are spacious, light, impressively well-kept even though they cope with enormous numbers of students. Wide stairways, good modern lines, quarry-tile floors, teak-slatted ceilings, concealed light - all visually stimulating and varied. Wide circulation areas encourage free and comfortable movement, with sociable moments. Not surprising that this building carries a seal of commendation from the RIBA.

The All Saints Building bounds one side of a small square which is open to the constant traffic of Oxford Road. The square is railed and green, with trees and shaded seats - one of the areas of quiet which allow the city student space to breathe.

A new concourse links the All Saints and Loxford Buildings, providing access to a recently extended student refectory, the sports centre and, by the summer of 1996, student services.

Facing All Saints is the Grosvenor Building (Faculty of Art and Design), a grand affair in stone - subdued Gothic-style. The interior is lovely, with pillared high space and roof lights. The Holden Gallery provides fine, extensive exhibition space and has the slightly echoing quality of Victorian halls. The Ormond Building, in dignified Victorian brick; the Bellhouse Building, with its original, beautiful Georgian facade facing the square; the curiously styled large Righton Building (1905) surfaced with green and white tiles and slightly reminiscent of a public baths; the stark, dark brick and severity of the modern Roman Catholic church watching the square: the mix of buildings is eccentric and marks well the history of the University.

Above two of the teaching buildings rise blocks of accommodation - so the touch of domestic life is here.

Across Oxford Road, opposite the All Saints Building and harmonising with it in style is the Martin Luther King (Students' Union) building. Large, purpose-built and very efficient in its ambience.

Courses at All Saints: Art and Design, Science and Engineering, Humanities and Social Sciences

Didsbury

This is one of the largest of the outposts, five miles out from All Saints, in this very pretty urban village, a world away from city sprawl. It will be possible - even too easy - to have a completely independent and pleasant way of life here: there are good sports facilities, including a heated swimming pool, and the site has its own library with a specialised academic collection.

Courses here: Courses in the Faculties of Community Studies and Education

Elizabeth Gaskell

Quite close to the city centre, on a small pleasant campus.

Courses: Department of Psychology and Speech Pathology and courses in law and health care. Well-stocked specialist library.

The Hollings site

Quite close to Elizabeth Gaskell, the building really does look like its 'toast rack' nickname, with its concrete upright supports veering inward and up, then curving free over the top of the building. It is attractively set in a green area of playing fields and leafy avenues. A new library and information centre have, to an extent given the site a new face, without erasing its distinction. Near enough to relate to the main site.

Courses here: Departments of Clothing Design and Technology; Food and Consumer Technology; Hotel, Catering and Tourism Management.

The Aytoun Campus

The Faculty of Management and Business occupies actual city-centre buildings close to Piccadilly Station. Again, within easy range of Grosvenor Square. A new and impressive building opened in 1994 houses libraries, computing centre, purpose-built lecture theatres and seminar rooms.

On the whole, the University is an impressive, well-planned, well provided, well-built institution, with nice historic moments, designed to function well academically and in student interaction.

Crewe + Alsager

Since becoming part of the University the former Crewe + Alsager College of Higher Education is now known as the Crewe + Alsager Faculty. Located on two attractive campuses in south Cheshire, the Faculty gives the opportunity of study in a rural environment, with reasonable range access to Manchester and Chester. The sites include halls of residence, an Arts Centre, excellent sports facilities as well as teaching and learning resources.

Courses here: courses in the Centre for Sports Science, in teacher training and courses in other disciplines.

Cars

Car-parking space is very limited, and street-parking is not easily found. Public transport is excellent. The two campuses of Crewe + Alsager, although six miles apart, are linked by regular and free transport.

Learning Resources

There are seven **libraries**, one on each campus. The main library (recently refurbished) is on the All Saints campus. Overall, there are approximately one million books, 370,000 of which are in the main library. The library subscribes to around 4,700 periodical titles and a range of electronic sources. There is a number of special collections and audio-visual facilities are available at all libraries. Opening times vary from site to site. Some weekend provision is available.

Each site has PCs in both teaching and drop-in **computing areas** (some of which are open until 9pm). Most machines are connected to the University's network, and support staff provide advice and information during the day and on some evenings at most sites. The University offers 'CAL' support for computer literacy courses, and faculty and course inductions.

Support is provided for **language teaching** with drop-in centres and a satellite-viewing centre offering eight foreign languages. A multimedia language laboratory designed for interactive languages learning is also available. The University-wide languages programme offers eight language laboratories and drop-in centres.

Culture on campus

Drama: The University has its own theatre - the Capitol Theatre - at Didsbury, which has productions throughout the year. Crewe + Alsager Faculty has two theatres: the Axis seats 500 and the Studio Theatre 100. There is also a dance studio here, seating 120.

Music: Concerts at Crewe & Alsager. You are, of course, close to the Royal Northern College of Music: excellent.

Art: The Holden Gallery, in the Grosvenor building, and the Rishton Gallery in the Rishton Building have very impressive gallery spaces and a range of changing exhibitions.

Alsager Art Gallery at the Alsager campus holds exhibitions in various media including work by the artists in residence and guest artists of international repute.

The Union

The Union has its own building - the Martin Luther King Building - opposite the All Saints Building site on Oxford Road: this has been refurbished and includes a two tier stage area and a large increase in seating provision. Conference rooms and meeting rooms are available.

Induction loops have been installed so that students with hearing impairment can participate in Union meetings.

There are six full-time sabbatical officers and seven part-time.

The Union runs shops, bars, minibuses, a launderette, travel office, banking and a TV and games room. Offices, shops and bars can be found on most sites.

At All Saints the Union organises events, discos, cabaret, Retro discos, classic film nights and a generally wide range of entertainments, as well as almost 90 clubs and societies, 42 of which are sports clubs.

At Crewe and Alsager, there are discos with karaoke, bar bungees, occasional visiting bands and the Snow and May Balls. Hall capacities are 500 and 600 respectively.

Day-to-day affairs are run by a permanent staff which is answerable to the elected Executive.

Sport

Both the All Saints and Didsbury campuses have their own sports centres. All Saints provides a gym, sports hall, five squash courts, weight-training and a floodlit outdoor area. A multi-purpose sports centre is being developed here. Didsbury has a swimming pool, sports hall, gym, weight/fitness room and tennis courts. The outdoor facilities at the new Carrington Sports Centre (five pitches for football or rugby) to the west of the city and at the Parrs Wood halls of residence. The Rowing Club uses a stretch of the Bridgewater Canal (about 15 minutes from the city centre).

Manchester Metropolitan takes its sport seriously: three lecturers, 34 part-time coaches and nine administrative/supervisory staff are available; together they are responsible for organising and promoting a comprehensive sports/recreational programme. You will be helped whatever stage your proficiency, from beginner to athlete. Inter-site competitions are organised, and league tournaments throughout the year culminate in a prize-giving dinner-dance.

The Students' Union finances over 40 sports clubs which compete at local, regional and national levels.

Facilities are available for casual use when not tied up by classes or tournaments.

The Crewe + Alsager Faculty has excellent facilities available. Outdoor facilities: 32 acres of playing fields (with closed circuit television and pavilion), two cricket squares and nets, 12 tennis courts, a heated swimming pool, a 400m grass track and full jumping, throwing and vaulting areas for track and field events. Indoor facilities: a fully equipped double gymnasium, squash court and weights rooms.

There are sports injuries clinics at All Saints and at C+A.

Student welfare

Students are required to register with a local doctor. There are **branch surgeries** at the All Saints and Didsbury campuses with a clinic open daily. Crewe + Alsager has its own branch surgeries and daily clinics run by nurses.

Student counsellors are available on the Manchester campus and at Crewe + Alsager. At Manchester counselling sessions are held at specific times each week on for outlying campuses. All students will have a personal tutor.

A solicitor's services are available in the Students' Union.

The University has a **Learning Support Adviser** in the Learning Support Unit. You should pick up the *Guidelines on Learning* booklet when you arrive at the University: it has advice on note-taking, revision and exam technique. If you have a problem with learning skills, your tutor will be able to help.

Chaplains, from different denominations, serve all students, of whatever faith, and work with students, either individually or in groups.

Careers Service

You have access to the careers library throughout the year, and to a number of careers computer programmes including GRADSCOPE and SCAN. Individual advisory interviews can be arranged. The Service has a vacancy board for permanent, part-time and vacation work.

A programme of employer presentations, careers fairs and careers workshops is available for final year students. Weekly cv clinics are available for students applying for employment and postgraduate study.

Students with special needs

The University will consider your application on equal footing with those from all other candidates. You should contact the Disability Adviser in the Learning Support Unit to discuss your needs: the University will try to make suitable provision for you if possible.

Accommodation

Altogether, on the Manchester campuses, the University has 21 halls of residence, 14 of which relate to the Crewe and Alsager campuses. The rest are in Manchester: two at the central All Saints site, four at Didsbury and one at Whalley Range. Rooms are mainly single. Most halls are catered and all halls are well served by public transport. This is very limited hall accommodation in view of the number of Manchester Metropolitan's students. You should apply early, although preference is given to first years whose homes are not close to Manchester.

If you do not get a place in a hall of residence, the University has an Accommodation Service and provides a comprehensive list of lodgings, flats and bedsits. There are also sympathetic agencies. In recent years, no student has been without accommodation at the beginning of the year - a good record for such a large University.

Costs (1995/96)
Halls of residence:
Self-catering £1,331.10 for 35 weeks
Catered   £2,031.50 for 35 weeks
             (£5 less for shared room in both cases)

Private accommodation
Over 90% of students live 'out'. Costs vary - Manchester is a big city - from around £28 to £40 per person per week. Allow extra for bills.

Mature students

Entry requirements to the University have, in line with national and local government criteria, widened for mature entrants. The University stresses that this move will not affect the standards of entry but welcomes applications from students with non-standard qualifications and experience.

The Student Services Centre provides study and learning support once you have taken a place on a course and degree routes are accessible through independent study.

Nursery
Some nursery provision (in the Longsight area) is available for children from six months to five years.

THE CITY / ESCAPE ROUTES

See Manchester University's entry in this Guide.

University of Newcastle upon Tyne

Newcastle
NE1 7RU
Telephone: 0191 222 6000

University Charter date: 1963 (the University was a college of The University of Durham from 1852)

Newcastle is a large/medium-sized university with around 9,500 full-time undergraduates and 2,000 full-time postgraduates. It has a single, impressive campus in Newcastle's city centre. A large proportion of student accommodation is five minutes from the main campus; the rest is three miles away. All first year students are offered university-owned accommodation (except, possibly, late Clearing applicants). Degree programmes, although modular, still have a 'traditional' stringency in many areas of study. Flexibility of module choices varies from programme to programme: Medicine, for example, is not modularised. Assessment also varies between courses: examinations - written, oral or practical are now balanced by an increasing weight being given to coursework.

THE CAMPUS

This is among the most impressive of civic campuses: imposing in scale, varied in architectural styles, well planned to combine a sense of space with compact development. The University's 45-acre site forms a handsome part of a generally splendid city centre. Its edges are well defined, preserving a strong sense of privacy and occasionally almost cloistered calm, where Victorian buildings form an inner court of walkways lined by old trees and shrubs. Seclusion is guarded by high, solid new blocks which have their own dignity. This vigorous mix of styles marks the whole campus: the unexpected period grandeur of the Union building is faced by the uncompromising concrete of the Gulbenkian Studio/ Newcastle Playhouse. The campus forms a kind of peninsula, ringed by busy roads, and flanked on opposite sides by the hospital (another fine Victorian structure) and the modern splendour of the Civic Centre - a very impressive building indeed. The city centre complex includes the large University of Northumbria at Newcastle and this whole grouping of civic and academic institutions is a great credit to Newcastle's architectural panache - notable in many fields.

The main campus, and many of the residences, are only a few minutes' walk from the city centre, making it easy to take a quick break from your studies. (The Haymarket Metro and Bus Station are by the main entrance - quick links to the sports fields and some halls of residence).

The University also has two farms and a marine biological station on the North Sea.

Cars
Provision for parking varies. No problems with bicycles!

Learning Resources

The main, recently extended University **library** (the Robinson) has over 1,000,000 books, takes around 5,000 periodicals and seats 1,200 students. The main building houses all faculties except Medicine, Dentistry and Law (which have their own libraries). CD-ROM and subject mainframe databases are accessible. Opening hours: 9am to 9pm Monday to Friday; 9am to 4.30pm Saturdays; closed Sundays. Hours are extended in exam times.

The **Computing Service** runs courses on programming and data processing and there are self-teaching programmes available. Workstations and microcomputers are positioned in clusters all over the campus and in halls of residence. PCs are available on weekdays, some evenings and weekends. All are networked.

The **Language Centre** has open access to all students and offers self-teaching through language laboratories, video aids and computer-assisted language learning software. There are materials in 30 languages. For a small fee, you can enrol in classes in modern languages, including main European languages and some languages of the Far East.

Culture on campus

Drama: the Gulbenkian Studio Theatre, where smaller touring groups perform, is on campus. There is an active Theatre Society, Gilbert and Sullivan Society, Musical Theatre Company and smaller drama groups.

Music: The University Musical Society stages over 100 public concerts a year. There is a large University orchestra and choir, and other smaller groups/ensembles. Regular lunchtime and evening concerts are given by students, professional and visiting artists.

Art: The Hatton Art Gallery, housed in the Department of Fine Arts, has its own permanent collections and hosts touring exhibitions. Student collections are shown and students are able to become involved in the running of the Gallery.

Film: The Union organises regular film nights.

The Union

The Union is ideally located in centre-campus in a large building which has the air of a Tudor palace: rather rambling, with noticeboards round corners and up various flights of stairs. Seven bars, refectory, several food bars - a good range of facilities. There is a bank, travel bureau, secondhand bookshop for buying and selling, a printshop (duplicating, photocopying, printing), an insurance broker, shop, hairdressers, opticians, a debating chamber, one smoke-free bar and a leisure centre with sun beds, sauna, gym, luxury spa-pool, three full-size snooker tables, games and television rooms. The Union even has an international shipping office and a secretarial agency.

The Union owns its own building and running a readers' lounge in the Robinson Library and the postgraduate common room.

The ambitious 'NU Events' programme includes major touring bands, comedians, drama groups, discos and impromptu moments. The Union runs a minibus service from Monday to Saturday which takes students home after events; priority is given to women students. The student newspaper, 'Courier', keeps you informed. Over 150 non-sporting societies include SCAN (Student Community Action Newcastle), which interacts with local organisations to provide voluntary community help.

The Union has six sabbatical officers and nine part-time and is very active politically at all levels, from membership of all major University committees and governing bodies to national campaigns. The Student Advice Centre gives practical guidance on students' usual problems: financial, legal and housing issues. A wide and well structured range of student services in all.

Sport

Over 40 sports clubs and excellent facilities. The Claremont Sports Hall (on the edge of campus) is part of a major sports centre development: a range of indoor facilities here and in the PE centre in the main precinct. Indoor provision for hockey, soccer, netball and tennis, as well as badminton, squash and the usual indoor sports, weights rooms and a dance studio. Classes in 18 activities for beginners and novices in a wide range of activities including jazz dance, trampolining and yoga. Further facilities at the Henderson hall of residence include a floodlit training ground and artificial hockey pitch, netball and tennis courts.

Pitches and courts for outdoor games are on four sites, including the University's country estate ten miles west of the city, which includes an 18-hole golf course and facilities for parties, seminars, conferences (transport laid on, Wednesdays and Saturdays).

Water activities take place in local authority pools: use of these and other LA facilities is included in the Sports Centre membership.

The proximity of the coast and superb countryside inland gives easy access to a wide range of activities. The Boat Club uses the River Tyne, which offers a straight 1,500m regatta course.

Student welfare

Health service: The clinic on Claremont Road provides medical facilities, including a dental practice. A doctor is on duty every morning. The student **counselling service** provides professional help to students and staff in the University. There are **chaplains** from Christian denominations and the Jewish faith, and a mosque on campus. The chaplaincy runs a programme lectures, discussion groups, social events and weekends away.

Careers Service

The Careers Advisory Service runs a range of courses and information services to help you after graduation. The 'Steps to Employment Programme' co-ordinates careers education and helps you to start thinking in good time about what to do next. The Careers Service runs workshops on finding appropriate vacancies, filling in application forms, CVs and interview techniques. You can have personal careers interviews at any stage of your course. The Information Room is well stocked, and includes access to PROSPECT, a computerised careers resource. 'Insight into Management' courses are run in your second year, and the Careers Service runs a 'Volunteering and Work Alternatives Fair', as well as the usual 'Milkround'.

Students with special needs

You should write to the Admissions Office before applying, and indicate which courses interest you, outlining the nature of your special needs. The University all applications on the same academic grounds.

Accommodation

75% of accommodation is reserved for first year under- and postgraduates. Local students may also apply for hall places. You must send in your application by June in your year of entry and your UCAS slip by September 6th if you want to be sure of University-owned accommodation.

Halls of residence

All halls are run by teams of wardens who organise and help. Five halls, all mixed, accommodate undergraduates, postgraduates and members of staff. Three halls (the Castle Leazes complex, all recently refurbished) are very close (five minutes' walk) and two (Ethel Williams and Henderson) are three miles out. Ethel Williams Hall is only a ten minutes' journey by Newcastle's own Metro service. Henderson is near a bus route. The majority of study-bedrooms are single, with washbasins. All halls have recreational facilities and some sports facilities, as well as small kitchens and launderettes.

Costs (1995/96)

Halls of residence: £57.00 per week average including meals, heat and light.

University flats

Five main areas of flats: unsupervised, self-catering, carpeted and furnished. Single study-bedrooms. Number of people sharing central kitchen and common room varies (one to six). Laundry, 'phone box and porter's lodge in each complex. These flats accommodate approximately 2,000 new undergraduates and most are within one mile of the University. The farthest are three miles away.

Costs (1995/96)

(include heat, light and cleaning). 39 week leases: average - £39 per week or £52 per week ensuite.

Student houses
The houses are in a converted Georgian terrace, about 400 yards from the University. Single or shared rooms, although first years likely to share. All houses are self-catering.

Costs (1995/96)
(include heat, light and cleaning): £38 per week average

Private sector
The University leases and sublets some privately owned flats and keeps a record of many more. Rents for this kind of accommodation are relatively cheap (average £32 per week) and easy to find. Costs vary, according to the area.

Mature students

The Admissions Office will send an *Access To Newcastle University* brochure on request which includes details of approved Access programmes, guaranteed place Access schemes and Integrated Degrees in engineering.

Nursery
The University has a Childcare fund to which full-time students can apply. Limited grants are means tested but can cover up to 60% of childcare costs.

THE CITY (population 287,000)

Newcastle is the largest city between Leeds and Edinburgh. Its civic centre is one of the finest examples of modern civic architecture in the country and is justly famous.

The shopping centre is large, and distributed through a variety of areas and well-proportioned streets. Most of the national stores are extremely well accommodated - lots of space for good layout. Many elegant shops, a number of traffic-free precincts, a huge, ten acre covered shopping area (Eldon Square), the largest John Lewis store outside London, the original Fenwick's department store, a fine Victorian arcade, popular markets, including the colourful quayside market (Sunday) under the Tyne bridge. The Metro Centre, the largest shopping complex in Europe, is only a few miles away in Gateshead.

The quayside is one of the city's fascinating places: steep flights of narrow steps, between 17th-century timber warehouses, lead into the castle enclosure, the keep and the Black Gate, built in 1247. The castle itself was built in 1172, and has a massive Norman keep; it can be seen to advantage from Stephenson's two-tier high-level bridge, built in 1849 and part of the river's dramatic skyline. Remains of the medieval walls and towers are worth seeing, as is the Anglican cathedral, with its lantern tower and interesting stained glass, dating from the 14th and 15th centuries. A number of medieval and period buildings are witness to the city's history.

In the 1830s the crowded centre of the city was cleared and replaced by graceful broad thoroughfares: Grey Street and Grainger Street. To walk along these wide streets lined by very beautiful buildings is to step back in time; into the scale and splendour of a more leisured age, spending its new wealth in a display of architectural virtuosity. The same architect, John Dobson, designed the impressive Central railway station, which covers 17 acres and has two miles of platforms!

Town Moor, a large tract of parkland, stretches to the edge of the University precinct. Together with Jesmond Dene (a bird-sanctuary and park) it offers pleasant strolling, a weekly crafts fair and musical events.

Theatres: The Theatre Royal, an outstandingly gracious period building, offers a range of productions including an annual season by Scottish Opera; it is also the northern base for the Royal Shakespeare Company. Newcastle Arts Centre, The Live Theatre and The Gulbenkian Theatre house smaller productions.

Cinema: The Odeon complex has four screens. The Side cinema is independent. The Tyneside cinema, as well as putting on seasons of rare and foreign films, hosts the famous annual Tyneside Film Festival. Two multiplexes: one nine screens, one with ten at the Metro Centre.

Music: The Newcastle Arena seats 10,000 and is venue for visiting big bands and names. The City Hall seats over 2,000 and has concerts given by visiting orchestras and internationally famous soloists, as well as those by its own well-known chamber orchestra, the Northern Sinfonia. The Riverside hosts up-and-coming bands.

Nightlife: Newcastle has long been famous for its nightlife. Local bands, jazz and folk musicians play nightly in pubs and clubs throughout the city. Varied restaurants. Pubs have character: their idiosyncrasies range from the sublime - being housed in a former bishop's residence (the Mitre, Benwell), to the ridiculous - a past landlord being the fattest man in England (the Duke of Wellington in High Bridge).

Sport: Spectator sports: Newcastle United Football Club, Brough Park Speedway and the Gosforth Park racecourse, international athletics at the Gateshead stadium. Leisure centres: five in all. Elswick Park offers canoeing. The Great North Run half-marathon happens annually.

ESCAPE ROUTES

The region around Newcastle is very beautiful and historic: invaded, fought over, guarded by Romans, marauded by Scots and Norsemen, its history is one of conflict, leaving in its wake fortifications and battlements. To the north and west of Newcastle, the wild and sweeping lines of the countryside is still largely empty.

North of Hadrian's Wall and stretching to the Cheviot Hills is the Northumberland National Park: 400 square miles of open space. The Border Forest Park at its edges has been man-made over 50 years from barren moorland and includes Kielder Forest and Kielder Water, both with amenities for visitors: walks, picnic areas, car parks, as well as nature trails (deer, red squirrel and otters).

To the east is the sea. The Tyne estuary and coast includes beautiful beaches. Whitley Bay, two miles north, is a popular seaside resort, with a large amusement park and facilities for golf and sea-fishing.

Communications

The **Metro** is a rapid-transit underground system: the University has its own connection. **Rail:** Newcastle is on the main line from London King's Cross (three hours away) to Edinburgh. **Coach** services extensive. Good **road** links to the A1 and its connections with national motorways. Newcastle **Airport:** flights to Belfast, London Heathrow and Gatwick (all about one hour) and further afield. There are **sea-routes** to Scandinavia.

University of Northumbria at Newcastle

Ellison Place
Newcastle Upon Tyne
NE1 8ST
Telephone: 0191 232 6002

University Charter date: 1992
Northumbria is a medium-sized/large university with 13,000 full-time students and 10,000 part-time, the majority of whom are taught on the two Newcastle campuses - one city centre, the other a few miles out. Two other campuses house some courses: Management and Business in Carlisle and The Business School in Morpeth. Degrees are 'unitised', with four modes available - single, joint or combined honours or an honours programme with 'major' and 'minor' subjects included. Assessment methods vary between units. The University guarantees accommodation to almost all first years whose home address is not in Newcastle.

THE CAMPUSES

City campus

This is a large and handsome campus, relating to the splendid Civic Centre, focal point of the city, in almost symmetrical balance with the University of Newcastle upon Tyne's campus on the opposite side.

The layout is compact and geometric: the central quadrangle, with wide stone steps, is paved and grassed. The campus is bordered by the ring road, but planned to be inward-looking: you are soon unaware of the city around you in this private space. The quadrangle is dominated by the tall, nine-storey library stack, with its narrow windows - 'blind' but book-protecting.

The site is sharply defined. This city campus has a good sense of space, and has set its buildings well. They range through shades of brick or concrete ('stone'), mostly three- or four-storeyed, generally long, but with varied lines. The overall impression is of a well-planned whole, in keeping with the city's reputation for good, workable architectural sense with an undernote of challenge. Quite exceptionally, three sports halls or recreation halls are on campus, a very good art gallery with a lively programme of exchanges and impressive display areas, an extravagantly large and well-fitted Students' Union building in the centre, facing the library, and a medical centre.

The Coach Lane campus

Coach Lane campus is several miles north of Newcastle, towards Wallsend (of Roman glamour-association, completely misplaced). The University's second site creates a quiet, green, wooded village atmosphere around a large teaching block and resources centre. The campus is very well-kept and looks fairly recently built. There are several halls of residence and a health and advice centre, so the ambience is quiet, domestic, welcoming. A regular and free bus service runs to the City site.

Courses at Coach Lane: the Faculties of Educational, Health and Social Work, and (from the Faculty of Engineering, Science and Technology) the Department of Chemical and Life Sciences.

The Carlisle campus

The campus, two teaching buildings and the Students' Union nearby, are housed in renovated 17th century buildings in the old town of Carlisle, part of the Tullie House Museum complex and overshadowed by the cathedral. Facilities include a library, language and computer laboratories, a student common room and seminar rooms. You get a choice between Newcastle and Carlisle...if you are early in applying. Some Business and Management courses are taught here.

The Longhirst campus

This new rural campus, the Business School, is part of the Longhirst Business and Conference Centre, 15 miles north of Newcastle, close to Morpeth. A beautiful area. Longhirst Hall is a listed building and stands in 45 acres of parkland. An initiative with the Wild Life Trust will make this site a centre for environmental excellence. The University's campus is purpose built, next to the old hall. Facilities include lecture and seminar rooms, library, Language and IT laboratories, residential accommodation for 210, sports facilities and a regular bus to and from Newcastle.

Learning Resources

The central **library** has 1,200 study places and 500,000 volumes. There are branch libraries at other campuses and a next-day library loan scheme for their students.

All courses have an IT component and you will be expected to use computers as part of your normal work. The **Computing Unit** has teaching laboratories and networked micros (over 2,500) available at all times.

All students can choose to pursue a language through the **Modern Languages Department**. Tuition is offered at five levels of competence.

Culture on campus

Art: The University Gallery, in the library building, has achieved international recognition through its temporary and touring exhibition programmes and educational and literary events.

The Union

The Union Building on the City campus has a ballroom, a theatre, a bookshop and television rooms. The Union runs three bars, two shops, refectory and cafeteria; there are regular concerts and discos; two nights a weeks, the Reds Bar becomes a nightclub. At least one event a week is organised at the Coach Lane campus, where the Union includes a bar and a shop. A wide range of clubs and societies is sponsored by the Union. One full-time Welfare Officer is available for advice on all aspects of welfare.

A small Union has opened at Carlisle and has a bar, pool room and function room. The 'Guild' here has its own life, events and agenda.

Sport

There are five main sports sites: the sports centre, the Lipman Sports Hall and the Wynne Jones Hall all on the main campus; the Coach Lane campus provision; and the 42-acre Bullockstead sports ground which is five miles from the city centre. Combined, these give you access to squash courts, multi-court halls, tennis courts, soccer, rugby and hockey pitches and cricket wickets. There is a special arrangement with the Tynemouth Sailing Club for use of their facilities. Altogether, there are over 50 sports clubs. The University has a sports injuries clinic subsidised by the Union.

Student welfare

Newcastle and Carlisle have small **health centres** staffed by nurses. **Counsellors** give individual sessions and organise workshops and seminars. The University's Department of Law runs a Law Clinic to advise you on your rights. The **Communication Unit** offers small-group tuition to students, covering study skills. **Chaplains** are appointed by the Christian denominations.

Careers Service
The Careers and Appointments Service has a library of information for self-help, gives workshops on career opportunities and job-seeking skills and arranges individual consultations with careers advisors in your final year. PROSPECT computer guidance system is available.

Students with special needs
The University has a Student Adviser for Students with Disabilities. Some residential accommodation has been adapted. You should contact the Admissions Office and arrange a visit before you apply.

Accommodation

The University guarantees accommodation to nearly all first years whose permanent home address is not in Newcastle. Halls offer 600 catered places and almost 1,400 self-catered. Most hall places in Newcastle are on the main City and Coach Lane campuses. Others are a ten minute walk away at Jesmond or two miles away at Gosforth. 350 places available also in a range of University managed accommodation.

At Carlisle, the Old Brewery Halls of Residence are five minutes' walk from the campus and house 200 students in flats with shared facilities.

Longhirst has accommodation for 210 in six-bedroom, self-catering houses.

Costs (1995/96)
Catered: £42.28 (shared) - £60.76 (single) p.w. - 32 weeks
Self-catering:£37.94 (38 weeks) to £39.48 (46 weeks) p.w.

Private sector
Private sector accommodation is not hard to find in Newcastle. Rents vary according to where you are. Costs: self-catering £25 to £50 per week. All properties advertised by the University are part of the City Council and Universities Accreditation Scheme.

Mature students

The Guidance Centre gives information on Higher Education application, including financial considerations and how to present experience for accreditation of prior learning. There are Foundation courses offered in 28 subjects throughout the North East.

Nursery
The Union runs nurseries at City and Coach Lane for children between two and a half and five years. The University has a childminding scheme for younger babies.

THE CITY / ESCAPE ROUTES

See University of Newcastle's entry in this Guide.

University of Salford

Salford
M5 4WT
Telephone: 0161 745 5000

University Charter date: 1963

Salford is a medium-sized university with around 7,000 students on full-time programmes. The University has recently merged with University College Salford and claims to have three distinct campuses: this is a little misleading since , effectively the campus is on a single site, split by the railway line with two 'satellite' buildings within walking distance. Degrees are modular with core modules building your main degree programme, pre-set by your named course, and optional modules designed to focus your interests on specific areas of your course. Assessment is by a combination of coursework and examination. Salford offers a wide range of sandwich courses. Although there are some arts and social science courses, this is a strongly technological university. University accommodation is guaranteed for first years who have applied before September 8th in the year of entry.

THE CAMPUS

If you are deterred by the urban approach roads to Salford, the University campus comes as a most pleasant surprise. With its stately, turn-of-the-century redbrick original Peel Building still in use, the campus has grown outwards around Peel Park and onto the far bank of the river Irwell: a bridge linking the more recent building with the main blocks is rather a nice feature. Most of the buildings are less than 20 years old; they are mainly rectangular structures with a lot of glass and white surfaces: grouping is well balanced, and the general effect is light.

The site accommodates all the main University buildings, including the Union, sports hall and some student housing.

In the centre of campus, Salford's Peel Park is an enclave of lawns and shrubberies beside a peaceful stretch of the Irwell. The park serves the local community as well as the University, and, with the community playing fields on the other side of the river, provides a good balance to the demands of university life.

This is a neighbourhood in the real sense of the word. It is possible to pass your student years at Salford between a kind of ivory-towered, inward-looking campus life and the attractions of Manchester's city excitement; but you will have a much more enriching experience if you join in the Union's programme of community help, which at Salford is particularly lively and varied.

Salford was one of the technological institutions which became a Royal College of Advanced Technology in the 1950's (a mark of excellence); it has its roots firmly in its community, and maintains strong links with industry in the area.

Cars

Few problems in bringing your car: you must register your vehicle with the University. Parking is limited at some accommodation sites. There is secure space for bicycles.

Learning Resources

Library facilities throughout the campus provide multimedia resources as well as textbooks. Open access computer suites available at scheduled times along with tuition and general support. Language learning is part of the University's crusading approach to Internationalism. Language skills can be acquired through degree module options or via lunchtime/evening courses run by the University's International Institute. There are widespread opportunities to work abroad.

Culture on campus

Drama and Music: Performing Arts courses here generate lively programmes performed within a cluster of venues on campus. Student productions benefit from active links with professional groups and activities range from classical/traditional to modern/pop.

The Union

The Union is large, well organised and operates from four separate buildings three shops, seven bars, a travel bureau, an insurance service, hairdresser's, optician's, printshop and book-bindery, a computer shop and an Interflora flower shop. A music practice room available for use at weekends. The Union runs the Leisure Centre, next-door to the Union building, and produces a newspaper/magazine *Salford Student*, and a twice weekly newsletter..

There is a wide and lively range of entertainments (thrice weekly discos, concerts, cabarets, large balls and a 'Culture Club' which organises other arts events and parties). Discos are held in the SubClub nightclub and the Castle Irwell Pavilion where there is a custom-built video-discotheque. More than 80 clubs and societies encourage a wide range of interests.

The bars are open until 11pm four nights and until 2am three nights a week, and you can get food from the snack bar until 11pm. The Union shop is open until 5pm Monday to Saturday and from 10am to 2pm on Sundays.

The Community Services Group injects student help into local problems with a creative programme which includes organising outings and fun days for local children, working with ex-offenders, or converting pinball machines for use by the disabled. The Union is represented on all University committees except the Senate. The University/Union relationship is generally healthy. There is a professionally staffed Welfare Centre.

The Union's own limited company, SUPER Services, manages an off-campus (but very close) bar.

Sport

There is a leisure centre and squash courts on campus, with facilities for a good range of indoor sports including fencing, weight-lifting, trampolining and a climbing wall. The University's pitches for outdoor sports, with facilities in the pavilion, are at the Castle Irwell student village, about one mile from campus (see Accommodation section). Pitches here include all weather football, hockey and tennis courts and grass pitches for cricket and rugby. There are more than 30 sports clubs: all the 'usual' plus motor-sports, windsurfing and karate. A new swimming pool is scheduled to be in use by the summer of 1997.

There are charges for 'casual-user' use of the sports hall and squash courts. The Union employs an outdoor pursuits officer who organises training in safety.

Traditionally, the University excels in fencing, rugby league, badminton and table tennis. In 1996, the University topped the University League and won the cup in football. There is an annual 'Northern Boat Race' against Manchester University.

Municipal facilities are readily accessible in Peel Park itself (tennis courts and a bowling green) and there is a good swimming pool about a mile away.

Student welfare

The University **Health Centre** provides a full medical practice: you can register here or with a local GP. The Centre is open weekdays; services include professional counselling. Prayer facilities are provided for the University's multi-ethnic student community and nearby Manchester offers more substantial support.

Careers Service
A well-equipped, active service offering advice and professional grooming for job/career searching. Strong links with local employers enhance the usual job vacancy listings and liaison with recruitment organisations.

Students with special needs
All newer buildings have wheelchair access and some residential accommodation has been adapted. Students with learning difficulties/disabilities should contact the Learning Support Co-ordinator.

Accommodation

Accommodation is guaranteed for all first years who have applied before September 8th in the year of entry; and perhaps for one of your later study years. Normally at least 90% of first years are placed. The range and quality of residential provision is unusually good.

Halls of residence
There are three halls - Davy, Faraday and Joule - forming the 'Oaklands Halls' about two miles from the precinct. 540 places. The complex is built on a sloping site of five and a half acres, overlooking the old Manchester golf course, the river Irwell and the Castle Irwell residential development. There is a subsidised bus service to and from campus in the mornings and late afternoons.

The halls accommodate mainly first years, in single study-bedrooms: groups of nine rooms share 'landing' facilities - bathroom and small kitchen. Each hall has its own common room, television room and library; the dining room is in a central block, with a bar, shop and large room for social events. The halls make an effort to cater for the food needs of ethnic groups (though you might need to check). Fees include heat and light and breakfast and dinner on weekdays. You pay-as-you-eat at weekends.

Hopwood Halls of Residence
Catered halls near Middleton in Manchester - nine miles from campus. The Halls are served by trains and a specially provided bus service.

Horlock Court/Constantine Court (also Halls)
Horlock and Constantine Courts are in a central position on campus. 270 places. Easy access to the library, bank, launderette, bookshop and Union shop. All rooms in Constantine Court are ensuite. Both Courts have to be vacated during the Christmas and Easter holidays.

Castle Irwell: Student Houses
Castle Irwell is a residential (self-catered) complex/student village, built on the former Manchester racecourse on a meander of the river Irwell, about one mile from the campus. There are 1,612 places here. The complex takes the form of terraced individual houses, each housing 6, 11 or 12 There is a shop, two TV lounges, a launderette and fast-food available on site. In the central amenities block (the Pavilion) the Union runs a large bar and disco facilities (two discos a week). There are also playing fields.

Student Flats
Trinity Flats: In 15-storey blocks refurbished by the University, less than one mile from campus. Self-catered flats are available for 2, 3 or 4 people (married couples may apply). 600 places in all. Rents include cleaning, heating and lighting. Leases include the Christmas and Easter vacations.

Lester and Colman Courts: Two minutes' walk from campus. These fully refurbished high rise blocks provide places for 750 students in flats for up to four people (single study-bedrooms, bathroom and kitchen.

Direct leasing
Houses: mostly accommodate 3, 4 or 5 students and are situated within three miles of the University. Rent includes a basic charge for heating and lighting; any excess is charged to you. The University also leases two blocks of flats one and a half miles from the campus. The flats take three to five people. The leases for these must be taken by September 6th through to the end of the following June.

Costs (1996/97)
Halls of residence:
self-catering: £39.75 - £47.80 (35 weeks)
catered: £62.85 (31 weeks)
Student houses: £33.80 (39 weeks)
Student flats: £37.40 - £43.00 (39 or 50 weeks)
Direct leasing houses: £32.50 + £5.00 (44 weeks)
Direct leasing flats: £33.50 - £36.00 + £5.00 (44 weeks)

Private sector
The University keeps useful lists and advises you to allow plenty of time. The area most used by students is Higher Broughton. Approved lodgings are visited and checked regularly by the Accommodation Officers. Rents vary according to type of accommodation. A room in a house or flat, self-catering, will cost in the region of £35.00 per week plus bills.

Mature students

Minimum age: 21. Your personal qualities, experience and commitment will be deciding factors, as well as any formal qualifications: so discuss your chances with the departmental Admissions Tutor or the Access Development Unit.

The University runs three Access courses, and offers a number of '2+2' or '1+3' courses in conjunction with linked Colleges of Higher Education. If you pass part I of a course at college, with a high enough standard, you may complete the course at the University. There are many part-time courses: contact Access Development.

Nursery
Nursery provision is offered for children aged between 12 months and five years. The University can supply other information about local child care.

THE CITY (population 247,400)

The University has asked us to stress the proximity of Salford to Manchester - two cities less than a mile apart.

Salford was Lowry's city and its art gallery has the largest collection of his paintings. Its community energy and archetypal Industrial Revolution landscape of canal, warehouses, terraced streets, factories and back-alleys has also inspired the paintings of Harold Riley. From it also has sprung some outstanding drama marked by gritty humour: *Hobson's Choice, A Taste of Honey* and of course *Coronation Street*. This world has almost disappeared (the *Street* is no longer there), although some traces remain, setting their reminders of a grim but thriving past against the new developments which are, in their way, spectacular.

Salford's new style is strong and clean. The shopping precinct offers a very good range of 'town centre' stores and shops, and opens onto the market (partly covered), which is busy with bargains four days a week.

The Liverpool-Manchester Canal which sustained Manchester's prosperity is perhaps a shade misnamed, since Manchester's docks are at Salford. A very large waterside area has been cleared and redeveloped: Salford Quays is stylish and a strong asset; a multi-million pound revitalisation of the docklands area. It includes an eight-screen multiplex cinema, as well as restaurants and bars. The Quays will house the dramatic, Lottery-funded Lowry Centre, together with the University-linked National Industrial Centre for Virtual Reality.

The city has a remarkable sense of its own identity in view of its closeness to Manchester. This stems from its origins: it is far older than Manchester. These origins in a number of villages and communities, although now absorbed into the urban fabric, still mark its style. The edges 'show': parts are very affluent, with pleasant parks; parts are interesting examples of experiments in redevelopment; parts retain the rather odd period dignity of the Industrial North.

The cathedral, art gallery and museums (which include a reconstructed Victorian street) will all well reward time spent there. Other places to visit: Castlefield Urban Heritage Park, Ordsall Hall, Buille Hill Mining Museum and Monks Hall Museum.

A lively nightscene, with many disco - or traditional - pubs and clubs. Worsley Park, within range for a visit to its hall and wooded grounds, offers Jacobean banquets.

Otherwise, if you go to Salford, you will also turn to Manchester for your entertainment, and your excursion territory is mapped out in Manchester University's section of this book. It is worth noting that accommodation here is cheaper and easier to find.

ESCAPE ROUTES

See Manchester University's entry in this Guide.

University of Sheffield

Sheffield
South Yorkshire
S10 2TN
Telephone: 0114 276 8555

University Charter date: 1905

Sheffield is a large university over 16,000 full-time students, almost 3,000 of whom are postgraduates. The University offers an 'academically coherent programme of learning', concentrating on the academic transferable skills of 'learning, analytical, evaluative and presentation skills'. Degree programmes are modular, except Medicine and Dentistry. Within specific courses, students may a few choose unrestricted modules, from any on offer within the University - within certain boundaries. Exams are at the end of each semester. The University has a single campus, one mile from the city centre. All single first year undergraduates will be offered a place in University accommodation, provided that their homes are beyond a reasonable commuting distance.

• *Excellence in Teaching*

In the first rounds of the Funding Council's Teaching Quality Assessment Exercise, 17 out of the 22 subjects so far assessed have been given the rare 'excellent' rating (applied Social Work, Architecture, English Literature, Geography, History, Initial Teacher Training, Law, Mechanical Engineering, Music, Social Policy, Chemical Engineering, English Language and Linguistics, French, Germanic Studies, Hispanic Studies, Russian and Slavonic Studies, Sociology).

• *Modularisation of courses*

All undergraduate courses (except Architecture, Dentistry and Medicine) have been modularised to allow greater flexibility in the choice of programmes studied.

• *Sports Bursaries*

Undergraduate sports bursaries, worth £900 per year, have been introduced to help meet the training and coaching needs of elite sportsmen and women.

• *Student Journalist of the Year Award*

Lucy Cave, a writer on the Union of Students' newspaper, *Darts*, was Runner-up in the coveted Guardian/NUS Student Journalist of the Year award. In the past seven years, *Darts*, journalists have won this award on three occasions, and been Runner-up twice.

• *New Student Facilities*

A new £5 million extension to the Union of Students' building, providing additional social, welfare and retail facilities was opened in September 1996.

THE CAMPUS

The main precinct, on the west (affluent) side of Sheffield, stands on ground rising towards the Peak District hills just two miles away, about fifteen minutes' walk (one mile, slower up than down!) from the city centre. The precinct is split by a busy road, but a wide underpass allows free flow and the sense of intrusion is not strong. The original building, Firth Court, is a fine example of turn-of-the-century architecture and remains the focal point of the University. It is set into Weston Park, with its small lake and its fine art gallery/museum.

The University has spread outward in linear fashion, building new functional academic blocks, of strong individual styles, or occupying large Victorian houses in its path. The mile-long campus avoids the potential oppressiveness of large University blocks and the area into which it spreads is the very civilised end of the city.

With the main halls of residence only a mile away, the student population has helped to create the 'urban village' atmosphere of Broomhill: lively, colourful, with a range of shops, restaurants and pubs. The atmosphere of the University is confident, busy, purposeful; its attitude helpful and efficient with lots of partisan pride.

Central to the campus is the Octagon Centre, impressively equipped, which is also used as a civic venue.

Cars
There are no particular problems about taking cars to Sheffield, although, central parking can be difficult.

Learning Resources

The main **library** (a Grade 11 listed building), together with its three major satellites (the engineering, law and medical libraries), holds about 1,000,000 books, periodicals, microfilms, audio tapes, video cassettes etc. The emphasis is on ready access to information in all library systems. There are seven smaller libraries, all close to the departments they serve. There are few undergraduate courses which do not include some computing. **Academic Computer Services** provides the facilities: 800 networked terminals in open access areas. All students have access to a range of packages including e-mail. The **Modern Languages Teaching Centre** is open to all students. You can learn a language from scratch or pursue the ones you know to a higher level: 30 languages presently available. Modules can be accredited as part of your degree. You have self-access to Computer Assisted Language Learning facilities, course books and a listening/viewing room.

Culture on campus

Drama: The University Drama Studio (in a converted chapel) provides a purpose-designed theatre space and presents a varied programme (about 14 plays per session put on by the Union Theatre Company or Departments).
Film: The Union's Film Unit shows popular and minority films on four nights a week. Cinema capacity- 250.
Music: The Department of Music sponsors 50 concerts a year, including lunchtime recitals and a festival in June. There is a large university orchestra and chorus, a chamber orchestra and choir, early music and contemporary music groups, and numerous student ensembles. An opera is produced every other year. The Octagon Centre is the venue for larger pop and classical concerts (over 70 a year).

The Union

The Union of Students is exceptionally well housed with restaurants, bars and common-rooms which offer light, colour, comfort and high-quality wares, seven days a week. This is a very active, democratically and imaginatively run Union, which administers large sums of money, and organises a host of activities, including 130 non-sports societies. The Union issues a fortnightly student newspaper, a weekly '*What's On*' and an occasional arts magazine using its own a desk-top publishing unit.

A shop, cinema, games rooms, two main bars and many other amenities, even two pubs (run on tenancies) are all run by the Union. Big-name bands perform regularly in the largest of the Union's three venues (1,500 capacity), which offer a lively entertainments programme for six nights a week. An extension to the Union's building (£5 million) has increased even these facilities.

The Union promotes community awareness through systems of 'direct help': hundreds of students work with the mentally ill, the disabled, the elderly, the homeless, and other groups. Affiliated membership is open to Sheffield residents. The Union runs a Student Advice Centre: professional advisers help with problems from financial and academic to housing and other legal issues. The Centre is open daily and is available out of term-time. Nightline is open from 8pm to 8am; self-defence classes; an evening mini-bus door- to-door...

The Union has a massive turnover, a generous grant from the University, a staff of 250 and seven sabbatical officers. Many part-time jobs go to students.

Sport

The University and city's sports facilities are remarkable, partly as a result of the World Student Games in 1991, held in Sheffield. Facilities include an Olympic pool, an all-weather centre, an indoor area for gymnastics, and artificial-surface pitches.

Even before these additions, the existing University facilities were among the finest in the country. The Goodwin Athletics Centre (a few minutes' walk from the main campus) has playing fields, two floodlit synthetic turf pitches with warm-up area, tennis courts, two large sports halls, a heated indoor swimming pool (33.3m), eight squash courts, two weight training rooms (multigym and free-standing weights), an all-weather 500m jogging track and a fitness assessment centre.

In addition, a 45 acre site at Norton, five miles away, provides facilities for soccer, rugby, cricket and lacrosse. You have to go further to sail or row on the Ogston and Dam Flask reservoirs, 20 miles away. The Peak District is an excellent outdoor pursuit resource.

A very wide range of recreational activities flourishes, and the Union of Students' Sports Committee is responsible for organising 57 sports clubs. A weekly programme of over 40 classes from beginner to improver levels cover most sports. If you are in the National Squad at school level or above, you might be eligible for a sports bursary of £900 p.a.

Student welfare

The **University health service** runs a fully comprehensive system of medical care, including dental care and a 16 bed in-patient unit which is attached to one of the halls of residence.

The University's Counselling Service provides confidential support on a wide range of personal and academic issues. Sheffield has a number of **chaplains** from Christian and other faiths. There is an Islamic centre near the campus.

Careers Service

The Careers Advisory Service helps students to decide on their objectives and how best to achieve them; and trains in application and interviewing technique.

The Service has an integrated programme of talks, seminars, courses and confidential discussions. There is a well-stocked careers library, and the Service makes good use of computerised information and careers programs.

The **Enterprise Unit** aims to enhance the personal skills of students as a complement to their academic studies. It concentrates on four areas: teamwork, problem-solving, communication and managing and organising. The Unit works alongside the Student Development Unit, based in the Union.

Students with special needs

The Schools and Colleges Liaison Service will arrange a special visit for you to discuss your individual needs. The University offers adapted accommodation and a range of specialist study equipment. It also has strong links with both the Student Support Service for Hearing Impaired and Sight Impaired Students based in the city. Support requirements are assessed separately from an applicant's academic suitability.

Accommodation

All single first year undergraduates will be offered a place provided that their home is beyond reasonable commuting distance, and they accept an offer by 6th July and confirm their place at the University of Sheffield by 31 August. Post UCAS Clearing: candidates are always housed (if only in lodgings) and are attached to a specific hall of residence.

Halls of residence

The University has six halls of residence. Four halls are about a mile from the main campus; two are a bit further out but easy walking or a short bus ride. Halls are set in pleasant, hilly, wooded grounds in what Sir John Betjeman once described as 'England's prettiest suburbs'. Their sites are en route to the Derbyshire Peaks and moors (part of the National Park lies within the city's boundaries, nearby).

All halls are mixed. They differ in character, but all offer library, colour TVs, bars, sports provision, launderettes, utility rooms and car-parking space. Cooking, heating and cleaning are all provided for you (breakfast and evening meal on weekdays; all meals at weekend). Many facilities are provided, including photographic dark rooms, table tennis, music rooms and pool tables.

Halls have a good range of recreational and sporting activities and inter-hall rivalry is all part of the fun, whether you are competing to raise charity money, or to win something. All halls are warden-controlled.

If you accept a place in hall, you will be expected to live in and pay for it for all three terms, unless there are very exceptional reasons for leaving during session.

Costs (1995/6)

Single room: £61.00 per week
Rents include bed, breakfast and evening meal, seven days a week, with lunches at the weekend.

University self-catering properties

There is a variety of types of self-catering units of accommodation owned and managed by the University, housing a total of 2,086 single students and 145 in family flats. They range from purpose-built flats to specially converted Victorian town houses. The majority of these properties are in a wooded suburb close to the halls of residence and within easy reach of the main campus. Many flats have their own Residents Association which organises social outings, events and sporting activities.

Each unit includes study-bedrooms, kitchen/dining room and bathroom/shower facilities. The majority of study bedrooms are single. Some have wash basins. Common facilities like vacuum cleaners, fridges, irons are provided and there is some weekly cleaning, but to a large extent you look after yourself. The number of students in each unit sharing facilities ranges from three to twelve, though most often six to seven.

Costs (1995/96)

£34.00 to £40.00 per week (excluding fuel); costs vary according amenities.
Family flats: £56.00 - £72.00 per week

You will be responsible for rent for the full term of residence which, for flats, is 39 weeks (from the first Saturday in Intro Week to the Sunday after the academic year finishes). There is some flexibility of contract on double rooms and changes can be made, if the Housing Service agrees.

Alternative accommodation

A wide range of accommodation is available in the private sector, ranging from a single bed-sitting room, or a room-in-a-house occupied by the owner, to a fully independent flat. Facilities, furnishings and rents vary widely, as you would expect. Rents average around £35.00 per week for a single room in a shared house. Around 4,057 properties are inspected and approved by the University Housing Services who check that facilities are adequate and ensure that conditions are suitable for studying - so look at the Service's lists!

You will be more secure in accommodation regularly inspected by the University Housing Services. Sheffield has another large university and other colleges and institutions: the accommodation market is competitive. Allow lots of time for private searching.

Mature students

The University has a Mature Student Liaison Officer with special responsibility for giving advice to mature potential applicants. You apply through UCAS in the normal way. Most mature applicants are interviewed, but the conditions of entry do vary from department to department. You might be asked to undertake work set specifically by the department, supply examples of current academic work, or achieve success in examinations or Access courses being taken. A *Guide for Mature Students* is available from Student Services. There are two autumn Mature Student Visit Days for you to have a look around.

Nursery

The Union runs a nursery with 64 places for children from one-to five-years old and organises playschemes during school half terms for children up to 12 years. Fees are kept low by a joint Union/University subsidy, and childcare grants are available for needs not covered by these services.

THE CITY (population: 540,000)

Sheffield's status as a major city is founded on the wealth and power generated by the Industrial Revolution. Large areas of its outskirts to the south east show the massive scale of the steel industry which thrived here and made the city's name synonymous with high quality. These are the areas seen from the M1 and other access routes from the south, which accounts for the mistaken idea that along with the city's 'brass' goes a large quantity of 'muck'. Enter from other points of the circle and you find a city of parks (there are 52), tree-lined residential areas, and a facility for generating a lively community atmosphere. Two thirds of the City's wider area is in National Parkland.

The separate areas within the city have distinct identities, creating a patchwork of 'village' life which is the key to Sheffield's charm: it is not a homogeneous, bland place. Set in a Pennine amphitheatre of hills, Sheffield is a city of hill-air. Its new housing developments line the hills around the centre with high-rise silhouettes, at night a pattern of lit windows like stained glass.

The city centre has a very efficient layout; one of its main shopping malls, The Moor, is pedestrianised, and a system of flyovers, roundabouts, subterranean ways, piazzas, walkways and passages both separate and interconnect the distinct shopping areas which give the city character and provide a continuing surprise factor. There is a wide range of national chain stores and the host of specialist shops you would expect of Britain's fourth largest city. There are very attractive recent shopping developments in the city. Outside Sheffield, and within easy access because of the special train and bus services, is Meadowhall - an enormous shopping super-centre with all major (and several not so major) stores. Sheffield's 'Supertram' links the University with all major city venues.

Fine civic buildings are not numerous, but the town hall is impressive and the 15th-century church, made into a cathedral in 1913, is interesting. There are a few Georgian houses and 19th century buildings.

The Crucible Theatre occupies a site near to the city library and the civic buildings. The 'square' outside has been cobbled and 'landscaped' to complement the renovated Lyceum Theatre (Sheffield's original theatre) which stands next to The Crucible. A cultured place to pass an evening.

Museums and galleries The City Museum is dedicated mainly to plate, cutlery and metals, although its collection does range beyond with some fascinating artefacts, including a wildlife gallery. Sheffield Manor, used to house Mary Queen of Scots during her 14 years of captivity in Sheffield Castle, is now a small museum. Bishop's House is a museum of local history with changing exhibitions, set in a 15th-century yeoman's house. The Kelham Island Industrial Museum: an insight into Sheffield's industrial past. The Abbeydale Industrial Hamlet: a working museum set and refurbished in a hamlet just outside the city centre - includes a water wheel, forge hammers and an early furnace. The Mappin Art Gallery - largely British art from the 18th to the 20th centuries. The Graves Art Gallery - oriental and European art, and a collection of English watercolours.

Theatres: The Crucible Theatre contains a main auditorium and studio theatre. The Lyceum Theatre was Sheffield's original civic theatre and has recently been renovated beyond its first glory. This theatre takes in touring National Theatre productions as well as ambitious programmes of dance and music, and other touring theatre companies.

Music: The 12,000 Sheffield Arena is one of Britain's premier indoor concert venues, playing host to major names in rock, classical and operatic music. The City Hall has weekly symphony concerts including regular visits by The Halle Orchestra and the City of Birmingham Symphony Orchestra as well as its own Sheffield Philharmonic Orchestra and Choir. Pop and rock concerts are also held here. The city's pubs and clubs have a wide range of live music. The Leadmill is perhaps the best known jazz-spot, venue for regular sessions and concerts by famous musicians.

Cinema: Two Odeons in the city centre and the Crystal Peaks multiplex with 10 screens.

Nightlife: Wide-ranging nightlife, clubs, discotheques, cabaret...good pubs both in the city and in the suburbs. This is Real Ale heartland. For historic banquets, nearby Eckington Hall has it all.

Sport: Two professional football clubs: United and Wednesday. Apart from standard sporting facilities, Sheffield offers trout fishing and coarse fishing; three municipal golf courses; crown bowling in the parks; walking, climbing, caving and hang-gliding in the Derbyshire Peaks. There is a new floodlit 'Ski Village' a mile or so from the city centre, very large and impressive, an imaginative development of industrial waste ground... and of course, the Crucible for world class snooker.

ESCAPE ROUTES

The immediacy of escape from anything resembling a city to the west side of Sheffield is phenomenal. The Peak District opens wide just a few miles from the city centre, and from the University you can walk into the hills in a matter of minutes. The Peaks offer walking, climbing, history, pretty villages, and some very good pubs. Gorges, crags and moorland make up its terrain, with streams and waterfalls.

The Derwent Valley, running close to Sheffield, is a mini, man-made Lake District: its chain of reservoirs, contoured with the valley, are a 'civilised' walking country of circular paths, quite long and invigorating, but not strenuous. The country around is criss-crossed with rights of way, taking you high into the hills.

You are near to the 'Dukeries' (more associated with Nottingham), a string of country estates. Near too is Chatsworth House, Hardwick Hall and Haddon Hall. (One of our joint personal favourites). All well worth visiting at least once while you are here.

Communications

The Supertram is now the communication link in the city. There are, of course, still buses. Sheffield station is on direct lines to most of the major cities in the country. **Trains** run regularly to London St Pancras (2hrs 40mins), Manchester, Nottingham, Bristol, Birmingham and Newcastle. The **bus station** is across the road and the National Coach Service runs buses to most parts of the country.

The **M1** runs along the east edge of the city, giving fast access south. The **M18** branches north east, intersecting the **A1** and connecting with the **M62**. The roads across the Pennines are many, all scenic, and some frequently impassable in the winter.

Sheffield Hallam University

City Campus
Pond Street
Sheffield
S1 1WB
Telephone: 0114 272 0911

University Charter date: 1992

Sheffield Hallam is a large university with around 12,000 undergraduate students on full-time programmes, 2,000 HND students and 500 full-time postgraduates. The University is multi-sited, with main central city campus: outposts are all within Sheffield, the furthest away is Totley, on the way out to Derbyshire. All first years are spent in broad programmes of subjects related to your chosen degree path; second and following years can then be spent either on your named course or pursuing several related courses. Most courses are assessed by a combination of examination, course and project work. Around 30% of first years are housed in university-owned accommodation. For those students not housed, there are House Hunting days organised before the beginning of the academic year.

THE CAMPUSES

Sheffield is one of the largest of the new universities. Its status and strength have always rested on long-standing ambitious support and development input from the City Council. Interaction with the city is still very strong: the University sees itself as a powerful resource for the region and city, offering management and technical training and consultancy services. It also opens its doors to the people of Sheffield for art exhibitions, lectures and concerts.

The University's five sites stretch outward from the large central city campus to the outer limbs where city gives way to open country at Totley. Long-term plans are for a two-site institution; one developed on the existing city campus; the other on a rural site on the outskirts, where residential, sports and social facilities can be more easily established. To this end, the City Campus at Pond Street has developed steadily and impressively over recent years.

Most courses are site-based, so your immediate location and facilities are very important. If your course does operate on two sites, free transport is laid on.

City campus
Sheffield Hallam has spent £40 million on this campus, creating a social and spacious environment. Directly opposite Sheffield's mainline railway station and bus station (both now termed an Interchange), the University's main buildings rise up the hill towards the city centre, which is no more than a five minute walk away. The buildings are high-rise in the style of impressive office blocks, and are well grouped. Changing levels give an interesting shape to access points, wide flights of steps and ramps: an extremely business-like atmosphere, good quality building and a nice sense of space.

The Atrium, the focal meeting point of the campus, has cafes and seating areas and an airy balcony bar. Just off campus is the other main student junction: the Union, in the purpose built Nelson Mandela Building (also recently refurbished).

The most important thing about being based at the City campus is your easy access to the city centre with its social and cultural resources. The Leadmill, for instance, is practically on your doorstep, as are Sheffield's Lyceum and Crucible Theatres..

Schools accommodated here are Construction, Financial Studies and Law, Leisure and Food Management (also at Totley), Science, the Sheffield Business School (also at Totley), Science, the School of Urban and Regional Studies, and Engineering and Information Technology. The School of Computing and Management Sciences occupies a large and very handsome building in Napier Street, quite close (an easy walk) to the main site.

Collegiate Crescent
This campus houses the School of Education and the School of Health and Community Studies. It occupies quite a large site, not far away, in the kind of suburbs where the rich used to live in the late 19th and early 20th centuries. Large houses, gardens creating virtually a parkland setting, the Botanical Gardens nearby. Very pleasant. The site buildings are harmoniously set into this gracious world,

large and imposing in stone, they offer a spacious and quiet study environment. The library looks as if it has served the needs of a college here for a very long time. There is a Students' Union building on site.

Psalter Lane

This is in roughly the same area as Collegiate Crescent, but a little further out and in a later style suburban setting. The building looks like (and probably was) a school or technical/art college built in the 1950s. Its fabric is now the worse for wear, and the interior spaces are also looking worn. The atmosphere is cheerful and relaxed. The various departments of Art and Design operating here are now under the umbrella title of 'School of Cultural Studies'.

Totley

Driving out to Totley is an expedition into another world, and the sense of belonging to a city university is very tenuous. This is a beautiful site, developed around a very old manor house of great charm. On a hill-top, you will be aware daily of the lovely views out to the hills and the superb countryside which will draw you into Derbyshire. The Old Hall houses the Sheffield Business School students (lucky people); other courses here are Leisure and Food Management. The site has some residential halls, a gymnasium and a Union building. Car-parking space is generous, and there are playing fields. A lovely place to study, but very rural and quiet - so if you are looking for the high life, think again.

Cars

Sheffield is a nightmare for cars and car-parking: try not to make it any worse, unless you are based at the Totley campus where a car would be useful.

Learning Resources

Each campus has its own specialist **library** with a combined total of over 500,000 books, the libraries take 2,000 periodicals. The new Learning Resources Centre on City Campus houses the main library complex. All libraries provide facilities for private and group study.

Each campus has its own **computing** facilities with open-access PC rooms and specialist support staff. All students have access to e-mail facilities and to the Internet.

Most students are now given enough flexibility in the curriculum structure to enable them to study one of the main **European languages**.

Culture on campus

Drama: The drama studio mounts small productions. On a grander scale, the University puts on an annual production at the Crucible Theatre.

Art: The University has a small gallery on the Psalter Lane campus, which shows work by students and has visiting exhibitions.

The Union

The central Union building is at the City campus: the Nelson Mandela Centre, purpose-built and well-equipped. The Union runs three bars, shop, launderette, games room, snack bars, bank, travel agency and optician in this building. There is a Union shop on each of the other sites, and a bar run at Totley and Psalter Lane and Collegiate Crescent.

Budget: £1 million. Sabbatical officers: 9. Employs a staff of more than 80. Each site has a permanent rep and some Union facilities. There is a full-time Ents officer, promoting a lively entertainment scene: discos, cabaret, bands... The Union Rights and Advice Unit and the Women's Unit provide trained help daily with welfare issues. The Union magazine keeps you up-to-date.

This is a very active Union, working effectively in an unusual number of fields.

Sport

The Recreation Service Unit promotes and encourages a Sports for All programme. General fitness and recreation classes are provided free of charge. Through the Recreation Service you can hire out facilities including those built for the World Student Games. The University has one of the best indoor climbing walls in the north of England (at Collegiate). Facilities on the City campus include a large sports hall and weight training.

Staff are available for coaching and teaching for most activities. Team competitions are organised at university, school, course and hall levels. Sports on offer range from aikido to weight-training, with the usual and unusual in between.

The Norton playing fields have a good range of sports pitches and a pavilion. Collegiate has a large sports hall, gym, movement studio and weights room, plus courts for squash, tennis and netball (floodlit all-weather). Totley has a gym, squash court and weight training.

Student welfare

There are daily medical surgeries at the two main campuses, and twice weekly surgeries at Totley. The medical centres are staffed by a team of GPs and nurses. There is a doctor available at all times for emergency cover. Students may register with a University GP for their duration of their course.

The University has **counsellors** available for full-time and part-time students. Their office is on the ground floor of the City campus. There are workshops on a number of issues including assertiveness and exam preparation.

The **University Chaplaincy** has two full-time chaplains who will give you access to your own worship needs. The Chaplaincy Centre is at the City campus, and also Collegiate Crescent. There is a Muslim prayer room. Sheffield has a number of Halal meat suppliers.

Careers Service

The Careers Advisors meet students in classes and in groups to discuss career opportunities, and also offer one-to-one careers counselling. Careers counselling covers choice of careers, applications and interviews. You can also take an aptitude test; PROSPECT, Gradscope and Adult Directions are all available, as is a well-stocked careers library. The Careers Service is open all year, closed only at weekends and on public holidays.

The University offers a part-time work bureau (*Pronto*) which identifies opportunities for all students and has links with the local job centre.

Students with special needs

Each School has its own co-ordinator for students with special needs. You should contact the University, outlining your special needs before applying: you will be invited for a preliminary visit to discuss possible provision.

Accommodation

There are no guarantees of accommodation in your first year, although the University helps you to find somewhere to live. Around 30% of first years are placed in hall accommodation: the rest are housed in the private sector.

There are 2,000 places altogether in catered and self-catering managed residences. These figures should be set in context with the very large overall student numbers, of which a significant proportion is 'mature' or drawn from the local community. In both cases, the provision of accommodation is not so great a problem. University accommodation is not available for postgraduate students or for those of you with families, although there is some provision for single parents with children under three years old and for those with hearing difficulties.

All halls are either warden-controlled, or have senior residents on site; all are mixed and offer meals on weekdays only. There are facilities for you to make light meals and drinks.

Halls of residence
Three catered halls with single study/bedrooms. These are at Collegiate Crescent and Totley.

Self-catered complexes
Places are available in purpose built complexes or converted houses at locations easily accessible from the main campus sites. The largest concentration is at Norfolk Park, a few minutes walk from the City campus. There are also converted houses and managed properties on Collegiate Crescent. These residences are all self-catering.

Costs (1995/96)
University catered: £1,566-£1,959 pa
University self-catered: £1,512-£1,748 pa
student house: £1,260-£1820 pa
(lengths of contract vary)

Private sector
The Accommodation Centre maintains extensive lists of private property and organises House Hunting days prior to the start of term. Accommodation, advice and free transport is provided during the search.

Costs (1995/96)
Single room, self-catered, around £30 to £35 per week excluding bills.

Mature students

The University runs its own Access courses in partnership with local FE colleges for those of you wanting to enter specific courses. Other UK Access courses are acceptable, as are non-standard qualifications. The University publishes a handbook for mature students.

Part-time courses
It is possible to study for many of Hallam's degrees through part-time programmes, because of the nature of the University's Credit Accumulation and Transfer Scheme.

Nursery
The nursery is on the Collegiate Crescent site in a large Victorian house with gardens. It takes up to 74 children aged between one and five years. Open: Monday to Friday 8.00am to 5.25pm for 45 weeks a year. 80% of places are reserved for students' children and fees are subsidised. The demand for places, however, is heavy, so apply early. Provision is supplemented by the City Council's various support schemes. Enquire. A half term playscheme is run by the University.

THE CITY/ESCAPE ROUTES

See University of Sheffield's entry in this Guide.

University of Sunderland

Langham Tower
Ryhope Road
Sunderland
SR2 7EE
Telephone: 0191 515 2000

University Charter date: 1992

Sunderland is a large/medium-sized university (15,500 students full and part-time) offering a full range of awards, from postgraduate degrees to further education courses. The University has three campuses, all close to each other: the newest is built on the riverbank.

You are eligible for University accommodation only if you live more than 30 miles from the campus. Private accommodation costs: £38 per week for a room. Degree and HND programmes are modular; assessment happens at the end of each semester and is a mix of examination and coursework.

THE CAMPUS

The University three-campus site, all campuses within walking distance of each other within the town. The university seems to have a clear identity centre at the purpose-built 'Chester Road' campus in the town centre, where academic buildings are balanced by a curving precinct of residential units. This campus occupies a site which is an integral part of the town's central developments, sitting directly opposite the large new complex housing leisure facilities, covered shopping and the bus station. Buildings on site are mainly in the idiom of 1960s/70's blocks - concrete/glass/coloured panels.

The University is a flagship for the area's redevelopment: the large new library, in sophisticated style, and the student housing on the edge of the campus add a good range of higher quality building.

Nearby, Langham complex is set around a very pleasant suburban area: substantial terraces around squares or in tree-set avenues. Gracious though modest in scale. Large houses, hotels and period terraces have been variously converted for University use. Much of the scatter is residential, but some buildings are for teaching, and the University's art gallery is here.

The University's third campus, St Peters, is on the banks of the river Wear. This purpose-built, impressive complex houses the Schools of Business and of Computing and Information Systems together with their libraries and offers a good range of Union facilities. On the opposite bank are new halls of residence, with good river views. The campus is a few minutes' walk from Sunderland's beach.

Cars
Cars are actively discouraged and really are not necessary.

Learning Resources

Four **libraries** on the two main campuses: 300,000 volumes in all and 1,800 periodical subscriptions. 1,200 reading places. Opening hours: 83 hours per week.

Computing: the IT For All Scheme modules are available in all degree programmes. The University has access to the JANET network. One computer suite is open 24 hours a day and others are open until 10pm.

The Open Access Language Centre includes two language laboratories, one with computer assisted learning access. Most courses include an optional language module.

Culture on campus

The University's **Arts** programme includes music, theatre, visual arts, dance and poetry. All events are open to the public as well as to students. The Reg Vardy Arts Foundation at Ashbourne House is one of the University's main venues. All performances are held in the 200-seat Bede Tower Theatre. *The Screen on The River* has opened on St Peter's campus and works in partnership with the Tyneside Cinema.

The National Glass Centre will open on the St Peter's campus in 1997.

The Union

The new developments on St Peter's campus have given the Union space for an adventurous entertainments programme. Manor Quay, the Union's nightclub, holds 1,200; social events five nights a week, regular Club Nights, live bands, jazz, comedians; two bars. Other commercial ventures: a shop, travel office and computer sales desk. The Union brings out a fortnightly newspaper, *Universal Post*. *Wear FM*, a commercial radio station, is based on campus; opportunities for student involvement.

The Union finances five full-time sabbatical posts include welfare and entertainments, and around 100 sporting and non-sporting clubs and societies. The Welfare sabbatical and full-time Welfare Advisors offer advice on any problems students may encounter. Services include Nightline and a free late-night minibus for women. Hardship funds are available, particularly for vacation and accommodation shortfalls.

Sport

University facilities include a 25 yard swimming pool, two gymnasia, a fitness suite and floodlit tennis and netball courts. There are 2 football and 1 rugby pitches on playing fields about half a mile from campus. Teams compete in both the UAU competitions and local leagues. Other activities include swimming, aquafit and a range of fitness programmes.

The University has secured special access for students to use 11 well-equipped local leisure centres at cut-price rates.

Student welfare

The University **health service** also provides general health information and a range of events concerning health issues. Student Services have a counsellor. The University has one full-time **Chaplain** and associations with local ministers who act as part-time chaplains. A mosque is available.

Careers Service

The University has a computer-aided search facility. Group sessions to help develop the skills needed in the competitive search for jobs are arranged

Students with special needs

The Special Needs Unit offers pre-entry advice and each School has a Tutor for Students with Special needs. Many of the University's own residential rooms are equipped for disabled students - alarm cords, points for minicoms, rooms designed for wheelchair use, visual fire alarms... Students with physical disabilities are given priority allocation for University accommodation and, in some cases, can live in hall throughout their courses.

Accommodation

The University has 2,350 bed spaces, and has a supply of shared houses and flats close to the University, plus lists of lodgings. University accommodation is allocated on a first come first served basis. You are eligible to apply only if you live more than 30 miles from campus.

Halls of residence

Ten halls: nine mixed, one women only; five catered, five self-catered. Most halls are on or near one of the campuses.

Costs (1995/96)

Rents in halls vary according to how many students are sharing a room.

Catered:	£42.25 - £53.35 per week
Self-catering:	£24.00 - £35.40 per week

University houses

The University runs a headleasing scheme with 800 places, all within walking distance of campus.

Costs (1995/6)

Guideline prices depending on size of room:
Large: £35; medium: £32; small: £29 per week

Private sector accommodation

A good supply of rented houses and flats in the immediate area, the Accommodation Service liaises closely with the Students Union and gives help and guidance. Rents are reasonable: a room in shared house is around £38.

Mature students

The University has a committed interest in mature students and in students with non-regular qualifications, including Access courses. Attendance modes are very flexible and you can, in some cases, mix day and night attendance. A range of foundation courses are available.

Nursery

Two nurseries which take 85 children from six months to five years.

THE CITY (population c. 300,000)

Sunderland sits at the mouth of the Wear only a few miles from Newcastle's substantial spread: indeed Newcastle is easily accessible for alternative city leisure and cultural time. Sunderland became a city formally in 1992

A large modern covered shopping precinct offers you acres of wares to browse, with greenhouse light and fast food. More traditional shopping facilities stand around this centre and beyond, solid, dignified commercial buildings, some modern stores and occasional exuberant examples of Victorian decorative architecture (the Empire Theatre, several pubs).

The main part of the city is not large; it is bounded to the east by the sea, and to the north by the river Wear. If this sounds idyllic, then beware: the Wear does offer riverside walks, in its deep gulley (not quite a gorge) below the rail and road bridges; but the sea edge is a line of docks, cranes and warehouses. Proper beaches are not far away, and parts of the coast within easy reach are beautiful.

Theatres: The Empire Theatre mounts a varied programme, mostly leaning towards light entertainment, but opera, ballet and concerts take their turn. The Theatre also has a coffee bar and studio cinema. There are two smaller theatres.

Cinema: the Studio has one screen and the Canon two.

Nightlife: The city offers a range of nightclubs, discos, restaurants and pubs.

Sport: Leisure and sports facilities are particularly good. The very large Silksworth open-air recreational complex (used to be a colliery site) has a dry ski-slope, all-weather pitches, boating and fishing lakes. The University's neighbouring leisure complex is one of the largest in the country has a leisure pool, ice rink, sports hall, squash courts, tennis, football and climbing walls.

ESCAPE ROUTES

Sunderland is just south of Newcastle upon Tyne, so read the University of Newcastle entry earlier in this book. The countryside around Teesside is very beautiful, and you have fast access to the seaside.

Communications

Rail services link Sunderland with the major cities of the North and Midlands. Newcastle is 20 minutes away. Extensive **coach** links. Sunderland is served by the **A1(M)**.

University of Teesside

Middlesbrough
Cleveland
TS1 3BA
Telephone: 01642 218121

University Charter date: 1992
Teesside is a medium-sized university with around 12,000 full and part-time students. A wide range of courses offered from diplomas and certificates, NVQ levels 3 and 4 (available through the Centre for Community Education) and HNDs through to degrees and higher degrees. Degrees are modular with the option of an Individual Programme of Study. If you are a mature student with relevant experience, your course may be shortened by accredited prior experiential learning. The University has a single campus close to the centre of Middlesbrough with Flatts Lane, a few miles away, which is for postgraduate and post-experience business and management programmes. Priority for accommodation is given to first years and overseas students. 1,050 places available in University residences. Private accommodation costs: £28 per week for a room excluding heat and light.

THE CAMPUS

The University has two major advantages: it is within five minutes' walk of the centre of Middlesbrough and it is almost entirely contained by a modern campus - much of it newly built, with period trimmings.

The University occupies a 42-acre site and has a consistency of style and harmony of space use which stems from sound planning vision achieved in a relatively short time. The site is compact, which always means that a lot of students are catered for in limited space, so the actual layout and scale of buildings matters a lot.

The campus is dominated by its one multi-storey block (12 storeys), which rises in the centre of the building complex and manages to have a light and airy presence (windows, white surfaces, proportions) in spite of its bulk. The block decants its students into the main quadrangle, reasonably commodious. The building also connects with the block housing the main hall and sports hall. A nicely balanced site.

Indeed, the positioning of the social buildings relates to the teaching blocks in a way which encourages regular movement; the linking access passageways are wide enough to make the movement easy.

The library, a new Open Learning Technology Centre, main hall and sports hall are in the main area; the purpose-built, large and light Union building is on the other side of an intersecting road, together with the academic blocks for Maths and Computer Science and Information Technology. Beyond them is the Health and Fitness Centre.

This pattern will mean a criss-crossing of students en route to class or relaxation which generates a lively campus atmosphere and makes social contact easy. A no-smoking policy operates throughout the campus; smoking is permitted in certain areas of the Students' Union.

Close behind the University is a small park, and a few minutes' walk beyond that is the large Albert Park, with its good-sized lakes, the town's art gallery and museum and the Clairville Athletics Stadium.

A nice frame to your first impression of the University is the residential square opposite the main entrance. Two wings of the square consist of period terraced housing, now student accommodation units.

Cars
Parking permits necessary for parking at the University.

Learning Resources

The main **library** has around 430 study places, over 210,000 volumes and takes 1,804 periodicals. As well as these traditional attributes, the library also provides a world television satellite receiver and an Apple Macintosh laboratory, computerised databases and CD-ROM. The University aims to include a unit of computing in each course, so you should become proficient. The **Computer Centre** backs up computing for teaching, research and administration (special technical manuals, short courses and seminars). You can discuss specific difficulties with staff. The 'drop-in' **language unit** has audio and visual equipment and offers free tuition (beginner to advanced levels) in eleven languages to all students.

The Union

The Union is strong, with a turnover of over £1 million (pa). The Union Building on Southfield Road is two storeys with two bars, one of which doubles as a nightclub. Commercial activity: the Union runs a large bar, a fast food bar, a stationery shop printing service and a recently refurbished nightclub which has a varied entertainments programme. There is a drop-in Advice Centre offering a range of information and advice. A women's centre provides special advice, information and support. The Union funds 65 clubs and societies (both sporting and cultural) and produces a regular colour magazine.

Sport

The main site has a sports hall and fitness centre; 60 acres of playing fields and an all-weather pitch are at Saltersgill, with a sorts pavilion and bar are three miles from the main campus. The Health and Fitness Centre houses a climbing wall, sauna, fitness room, table-tennis, a range of aerobics and martial arts. The University's offers courses in sports training. You can also take an aptitude test programme. Coaching is provided at all levels with particular expertise in squash, tennis and golf, for which there are four high performance centres for students at County Standard. The University hires local facilities for squash, tennis and water sports and has an arrangement for student access with the management of a dry-ski slope near to Flatts Lane.

Student welfare

The **Student Health Service** has a Registered Nurse: drop-in clinics are held daily. The Centre for Student Support provides professional **counsellors** and financial advice: you can contact the centre even before you apply. A full-time Anglican **chaplain** and a number of part-time chaplains from other churches.

Careers Service

The Appointments and Careers Service is well equipped, and offers a range of services, including PROSPECT-HE (a computerised guidance programme). The Service will give you individual consultations, seminars and talks on job-finding, and has closed-circuit television facilities used in interview training. Included in some courses is an Innovative Careers Module with assessment which counts towards your degree or diploma. The module includes constructing a cv, writing letters of application and selling yourself on a competitive job-market. The scheme has been devised by careers staff, employers and consultants.

Students with special needs

The University encourages applications from students with special needs. The Adviser to Students with Special Needs and the Centre for Student Support gives help and advice to students pre-application.

Accommodation

Halls of residence

Priority is given to first years and students from overseas. The University has 1,050 places in official residences. Linthorpe halls and Parkside hall (offering bed and breakfast), with purpose-built flatlets in their grounds, are about half a mile from the main site and border Albert Park. The King Edward's Square halls are furnished flatlets in period houses on the edge of campus.

Costs (1994/95)

Costs vary depending on the type of accommodation. Range: £32.12 per week (sharing a room with two other people) to £43.66 per week (single room in a new hall).

Private accommodation

All accommodation is inspected and all rents are negotiated by the Accommodation Office. Lodgings through to shared houses are offered.

Costs (1995/6)

Self-catering in a shared house: c. £27 per week
Lodgings with full board, seven days a week: £40 to £51

Head-tenancy scheme

The University acts as intermediary between you and the landlord and consequently standards, in general, are higher. This type of accommodation is self-catering. 300 places Prices: around £28 per week.

Mature students

A third of students are 21+ on entry. The University accepts students with relevant experience who do not have conventional qualifications or who have been studying on an approved Access course. Check with your intended course's admissions tutor.

Nursery

The nursery has 66 places for children aged between six weeks and five years, close to campus and open between 8.15am and 6pm Monday to Thursday, and to 5.15pm on Friday. Open all year. You should contact the Student Liaison Officer as soon as possible.

THE TOWN (population: 150,000)

Middlesbrough is quite a large, solid town, typical of the northern industrial towns (if that conjures images for you) which sprang into almost instant and full life in the late 19th and early 20th centuries. Growth here was particularly dramatic: the population in 1820 was lower than 40! Middlesbrough clearly made a lot of money in its heyday and has a good legacy of Victorian buildings, including its fine centrepiece town hall - a veritable extravaganza of style in stone. These buildings bring dignity of scale and size, and, on the whole, much of the town's newer civic buildings have been designed to harmonise. The actual town centre is handsome and has unusually spacious lawned areas.

The 'setting' of the centre is less attractive - residential streets feel cramped and reflect more the poverty underpinning the energies of the Industrial Revolution than its wealth: you have to move out a bit to find affluence and expensive suburban living. As a student you will probably be pleased with the inner town terraces - a happy hunting ground for student housing.

The massive chemical and steel industries which, with shipbuilding and recent North Sea oil have been the base of the town's growth, have also resulted in quite a lot of environmental pollution. This is being combated, but is still a factor to bear in mind.

Middlesbrough has four main shopping centres: one large retail park on the ring-road for mega-stores, and the inevitable covered precinct (the Cleveland Centre) in the centre of town. This has a plethora of chain store outlets, shops and boutiques. In general the town's shopping range is better than adequate, but undistinguished.

The sea border is fully occupied by docks and is definitely not alluring, although the transporter bridge looks quite an experience (a 'tray' suspended from a vast crane carries groups of cars across the Tees).

Theatre: The Little Theatre has changing programmes: a mix of music, drama and dance, classical and popular. Amateur groups also perform. The RSC visits the area once a year.

Music: Concerts - pop and classical - in the town hall (which seats 1,180). The Northern Sinfonia plays regularly. Music Festival in mid-June.

Cinema: There is a four-screen Odeon cinema and a new 14-screen Showcase Cinema.

Nightlife: Good range of restaurants, pubs and clubs - a boppy nightlife.

Sport: A number of leisure centres: Tennis World (one of the biggest in the UK outside Wimbledon); the Cleveland County Stadium, which has squash courts, multigym, track and cycling facilities; the Cleveland Park Stadium (the Middlesbrough Bears Speedway team and regular greyhound-racing events). Plus golf, county cricket, cycleways and footpaths.

ESCAPE ROUTES

Middlesbrough is very close to the northern edge of the North Yorkshire Moors National Park, and to Eskdale - all very wilderness and beautiful. Saltburn, the seaside town, is just down the coast: Saltburn is the mid-point of the Cleveland Way, a long footpath which runs from Scarborough along the coast and then round, inland, to Helmsley. The Yorkshire Dales are also within tripping distance; excellent walking country and very beautiful. The Cleveland International Eisteddfod happens on alternate years, attracting 3,000 competitors...and there is an annual International Folklore Festival. Both take place at Billingham.

Communication

Intercity **trains** run hourly to London from Darlington (about 15 miles from Middlesbrough). Trains also run regularly to Newcastle and further north. Cleveland is linked to the **A1. Teesside** International **Airport** has flights to other British and European airports.

University of York

Heslington
York
YO1 5DD
Telephone: 01904 433535

University Charter date: 1963

York is a small university with around 4,500 undergraduate students on full-time programmes and 1,000 full-time postgraduates. This is a collegiate university; each college has its own range of course specialisms and students are usually allocated to the college with the relevant Director of Studies in residence. The University has a single site and single building style - with a few recent additions. Courses are modular and combine flexibility with academic coherence. Assessment methods vary: some courses have no traditional exams, some mix coursework and examination. All new undergraduates can be guaranteed a place in a University residence for their first year.

THE CAMPUS

The ancient city of York is the religious capital of the North and, like Canterbury and Durham, has always had a strong claim to host its own university, although the University was not actually set up until 1963. The University campus is in Heslington village, two miles south east of the centre of York (there are frequent bus services).

The campus occupies 212 landscaped acres. Its administrative centre is Heslington Hall, a large Elizabethan manor, rebuilt in the 19th century. Although it is good to have this gracious period building on campus, it is set well clear of the main development, and keeps its own space in time, undisturbed, screened by formal gardens.

This is a very beautiful landscaped setting. The artificial lake here is large and shapely, winding through the site, islanded, tranquil, tree-hung; well-used by the architects to create a waterside university. Many buildings have lake-views, and a number have lake-terraces.

The buildings, unfortunately, are not harmonious, although some of you might find the central hall, projecting over the water like a futuristic jetty, interesting. The building mode is rectangular blocks, flat-roofed; materials are concrete, glass, dull brick; pillar-supports are square. Most buildings on site are linked by covered walkways, a good thing since winter weather in York can be very cold.

The University also uses several historic buildings in the city centre.

York is one of the three universities (with Lancaster and Kent) built in the 1960s to echo historic patterns of learning by adopting a collegiate structure. There are seven colleges here (the newest - James College - dating from 1992).

The colleges

Every member of the University, student or staff, is a member of a college: you will join a small, friendly, mixed community within the University's larger framework. Each college has about 600 undergraduates, 150 graduates and 70 academic staff members, and each has equal status in the University. There is a Junior Common Room (JCR) committee to guard and promote student interests; a Senior Common Room represents academic and administrative staff.

With the exception of the sciences, linguistics and music each department has its headquarters in one of the colleges, although the staff resident in each college will be from a number of disciplines. You will almost certainly be allocated to the college where your academic supervisor lives. Thus contact with staff can be maintained easily and informally in social residential time. The colleges have a planned mix of disciplines, years and sexes.

Each college has distinct features.

Alcuin encourages drama and holds regular exhibitions of paintings. Its JCR produces a news sheet and a college magazine. One of the residential blocks is 'quiet'.

Derwent boasts the source of the University lake which flows from a water court in the centre of the College. The central concourse has a snack bar and common-room - open to all students. There are frequent art exhibitions here, and an annual charity barbecue. Four squash courts.

Goodrickes holds a series of general lectures, an annual town/gown evening, and an annual ball. This College is the long vacation home for those students who stay on, and houses the Student Union offices. There are two squash courts and an annual cricket match between College staff and final year students at the end of their time in York.

James, the newest of the colleges houses undergraduate students and has ensuite accommodation throughout.

Langwith has an open-air chessboard and a boule terrain (available for general use and challenge matches). There is a College exhibition, a celebrity lecture, and the JCR organises an annual weekend camp in the Lake District. The College has music practice rooms.

Vanbrugh is centrally placed, and a convenient meeting place for all. There is a snack bar, and the dining hall is used for concerts and drama.

Wentworth has two studios equipped for painting, sculpture and ceramics, and a theatre workshop for music.

Cars
There is no parking on campus for first years, however, there is a frequent bus service and York

Learning Resources

The main **library** houses 480,000 books, government publications, microform and audio-visual materials. It can seat 725 readers and takes 2,600 current periodicals. The six college libraries offer more quiet study areas and are open 24 hours a day. The library in York Minster is also available to students, as are the city's libraries.

The **computing service** runs short courses on programming languages, utilities and packages and more advanced courses as the year progresses. The computing staff also give individual advice. The campus has 500 terminals; some departments also provide facilities.

The University's **'Language for All'** scheme provides classes (free in the first year) in five European languages, Russian, Chinese and Japanese. Classes are offered at various levels and are integrated into the normal timetable. Successful completion is recorded eventually on your degree certificate. Self-access facilities are also available in a smaller range of languages.

Culture on campus

Drama: Student productions in the Wentworth Drama Studio, the Drama Barn, the Central Hall and College Halls.

Music: The music department is separately housed in a building which includes a 450-seat concert hall. There is a specialist area for the study of electro-acoustic/computer music and ethnomusicology. The concert hall is equipped for music-theatre performances and contains a Baroque-style organ by Grant, Degers and Bradbeer and a chamber organ.

There is an extensive collection of orchestral percussion, and an amazing range of specialised and exotic musical instruments. The variety and quality of musical activity is very impressive.

The University enriches the musical life of the city and the region: the various orchestras, ensembles and choirs are open to membership by students, staff and the wider community; students of the department perform regularly with other ensembles. A series of lunchtime concerts and larger concerts in the evening are held on campus.

Art: There are three Art studios in Wentworth College and facilities here can be used by all members of the University. There is an informal teaching programme organised by the Tutor in Art, who also runs recreational classes in pottery, print-making and drawing for members of the Active Arts Society.

The Union

The Students' Union is in the Student Centre and provides a focal point for student activities, clubs and societies. As at other collegiate universities, much of its social function devolves onto the JCR committees. All events are held in the colleges, but are co-ordinated and supported financially by the Union. The Union also provides a legal-aid scheme, welfare advice, hardship loans and minibus hire. One of the Union's most significant functions here is Community Action. A full-time (sabbatical) officer (most unusual) runs a number of student action projects, liaises with various bodies in and around York, and organises the major event - the annual summer camp, when 300 local children are taken on holiday by students.

The Union co-ordinates and promotes sporting events, stages a number of concerts each term and organises other entertainment.

Five discos, two films and a live band are on offer each week. The Union also runs: University Radio York, broadcasting on campus; York Student Television, the University's closed-circuit television system; two student newspapers.

The Union issues a daily information sheet, holds four general meetings each term and is run by six sabbatical officers. There are 60 non-sporting societies, a full-time welfare officer, a nightline service and a free minibus service to and from town each evening.

Alcuin has the largest venue on campus, with space for 420; for bigger live events it has to be York. Large touring bands play at the Barbican Centre and big balls are held at the Racecourse; glamorous!

Union facilities on campus include a shop, a second-hand book mart, a print shop, and a fortnightly market.

The Union is affiliated both to the NUS and to the North Yorkshire area NUS and represents its members with some effect on University committees.

Sport

There are 40 acres of playing fields on campus, with pitches and squares for rugby (2), association football (6), hockey (3 grass), cricket (3). A full-size all-weather pitch provides for match hockey, and is a match tennis court area in the summer, augmenting the six tarmacadam courts (one tarmac court and adjacent grass area are floodlit for winter use). There is provision for golf practice, cross-country running, and orienteering. The sports centre has two halls for archery, badminton (7 courts), squash (4 courts), fencing, judo, climbing, weight-training etc. The range is very wide. There is a sauna and five cricket nets.

Nearby is a 400 metre seven-lane athletics track with full field events provision, including a tartan take-off area for high-jump.

Fulford Golf Club, also nearby, offers restricted membership.

The University lake is a good recreation amenity (fishing, canoeing, sailing, rowing and sub-aqua training). The rowing and sailing clubs have their own purpose-built boathouse on the River Ouse, about a mile away.

The Athletics Union's 40+ clubs take full advantage of the surrounding area: hang-gliding, riding, shooting, gliding. The city's newest three-pool complex is within half a mile of campus.

The collegiate system fosters a friendly competitive spirit; you can join in sports here freely at any level.

Student welfare

The University **health centre** houses both a surgery and a 24-hour emergency service. Nurses will visit you if you are ill on site, and a sick room is available on campus for those students who live out. There are two student **counsellors** and the Union runs a Nightline service. There are three full-time **chaplains** to the University and several part-time chaplains from different denominations can be contacted on campus.

Careers Service

The Careers Service encourages you to start thinking as soon as possible (even from your first year) about your future career. As well as a well-stocked information room, a regular programme of fairs, forums and presentations and an annual 'Insight into Management' course, the Careers Service also offers workshops on how to complete application forms and on how to be interviewed.

Students with special needs

Most of the University's buildings are accessible, with ramps and covered walkways, and there are lifts in the library and in the laboratories. If necessary, students with disabilities can be housed in ground-floor accommodation. Academic departments will usually be happy to record lectures or use other equipment which will aid access to information. The University does its best to resolve logistical problems.

Accommodation

The University has sufficient accommodation to house approximately 65% of all undergraduate students, which means that all new undergraduates can be guaranteed a place in University residence for their first year. In practice most students are able to live in residence for two years.

Colleges

The colleges house almost 2,000 students, mostly in single study-bedrooms, though 10% of first-years will have to share. Meals are paid for separately; there is access to limited cooking facilities, but normally you use the full cafeteria services available in the colleges. Common-rooms, laundries, telephones, television rooms, bars and 24-hour portering are also available in the colleges.

One College, James (the newest) houses entirely first years; its second name is Edens Court.

Costs (1995/96)

Single: £31.00 per week

Non-college accommodation

Six 'outposts' are also offered to first years: Eden's Court - eight houses on the edge of Heslington; Fairfax House set in gardens, five minutes from campus; Garrow House, a converted mansion; Fulford Road and Scarcroft Road Residences, both near York; and Holgate's Hall, 20 minutes' walk from campus.

The York Housing Association provides a limited number of flats and houses for married undergraduates, some large enough for families.

Private accommodation

The Accommodation Office will provide assistance and advice. The University runs a Head-Leasing scheme ensuring a level of safety and quality. Lists of private sector vacancies can be forwarded to you on request.

Most rented accommodation is within one or two miles of campus. Costs an average of £35 per week, exclusive of bills.

Mature students

Minimum age: 21. Various qualifications count, as well as 'A' levels: diplomas from Ruskin Newbattle Abbey and Harlech Colleges, or some of the mature-student oriented Access and foundation courses. Consult the department admissions tutor, and give information about your education/occupational background.

Nursery

The York campus nursery, jointly run by the Union and the University, accepts nine babies between three months and two years and 30 children aged two to five years. The children of students get special consideration and pay a subsidised fee which includes the cost of lunch. The nursery is open weekdays from 8.30am to 5.30pm, 48 weeks a year.

THE CITY (population c. 170,000)

York's history reaches back down millennia: each stage a layer of its foundations, recorded in buildings and stone, remains. The Romans built the fortress of Eboracum here, on the Ouse; the Vikings re-colonised the town; the Normans built a castle, and the wool trade brought medieval prosperity. The city walls run for nearly two and a half miles and date from the 13th century. Walking them is the best introduction to this wonderful city: from their ramparts the inside and outside worlds take on a wholly different perspective.

The Minster is York's finest treasure and England's largest medieval cathedral. But its dominance has far more basis than mere size. Inside, the intricate rose window in the south transept allows a shimmering cascade of light to fall. You must visit the chapter house: its tiny stone carvings are a total capturing of medieval faces, saints with sinners, and there are hundreds of characters all around its walls. The undercroft and treasury under the Minster display the incredible discoveries of earlier cathedrals on this site, found during the reinforcement of the Minster's foundations in the 1970s. (You can also see the modern engineering support structures). The treasury houses some of the Minster's wealth of worldly goods.

York's offerings are many. Its history is in its streets: the medieval Shambles, Georgian Micklegate, small churches, merchants' houses, eccentric squares. All this has been absorbed into a commercial city, with varied shopping facilities. You are not hemmed in by history in York, although you might sometimes feel hemmed in by tourists.

You can take boat-trips from Lendal Bridge and see Bishopthorpe Palace from the river. Rowing boats are for hire during the spring and summer: a fun way to spend the day. Or you could take the Jorvik Tour Bus and have a full guided tour. Jorvik was the Viking name for York: the Jorvik Centre, an 'experience' of the past as much as a museum, is the result of years of excavation, to reveal York's Viking world.

At night, with the Minster, abbey ruins and Clifford's Tower floodlit, and the many church spires illuminated, you will feel you are walking in another world.

Theatre: York's Theatre Royal has a varied programme and high standards, encouraging innovation in direction and production. The recently opened Grand Opera House in an attractively restored Edwardian theatre presents a wide range of performances from ballet to farce. The York Mystery Plays are put on once every four years. Played in the streets, through to sunset, these are a real spectacle.

Music: Concerts concentrate in the Minster, and various concerts are given throughout the city in churches and medieval halls. The York Early Music Festival has international status, attracting the finest soloists, consorts, orchestras and choirs. There is live music in a number of York's pubs, and several folk and jazz clubs.

Cinema: There is a cinema in the city centre with three screens, and the Warner multiplex on the north ring road. The York Film Theatre screens films in the city and at the University.

Nightlife: York has many historic pubs and no small number of newer establishments, you could visit a different pub for every night of the year! There are also winebars and a wide range of restaurants. A few clubs operate, each with its student night.

Sport: Oaklands Sports Centre offers tennis and squash courts and a main hall. Priory Street Sports and Community Centre offers a wide range of sports and social amenities. The well-equipped Barbican Sports Centre is close to the University. There is rowing on the Ouse. Yorkshire cricket and York races are the backbone of the city's spectator sports but you can also support York City football or Ryedale York Rugby League.

Events: There is usually something happening: from the annual Viking boat race to a festival of kites.

ESCAPE ROUTES

The Vale of York covers a vast area of flat, almost unalleviated river plain. Cultural resources of the region drain to the cathedral city. An excellent area for cycling around, a scatter of villages with old churches.

Directly north of York is the abbey-land around Thirsk and Helmsley. This area is very beautiful: far away from anything else; ideal for weekending/getting away from it all. North still are Helmsley Castle and Rievaulx Abbey. This is also good walking country: the Cleveland Way begins in Helmsley. York is only 20-30 minutes from Leeds: look at this section for your nearest 'big city' life.

Communications

York is on the London to Edinburgh line, with a regular, fast service in both directions. There are also direct **trains** to Leeds and Manchester, sometimes Liverpool, Sheffield and the Midlands. Indeed, the rail links from this city are wide-ranging. As are the coach services. The **road** network in York's immediate area is not major. A-roads travel to the A1 and consequently to the motorway network.

Midlands

Aston University
University of Birmingham
University of Central England in Birmingham
Coventry University
De Montfort University
University of Derby
Keele University
University of Leicester
Loughborough University of Technology
Nene College
University of Nottingham
Nottingham Trent University
Staffordshire University
University of Warwick
University of Wolverhampton

Aston University

Aston Triangle
Birmingham
B4 7ET
Telephone: 0121 359 3611

University Charter date: 1966

Aston is a small university with over 4,000 full-time students, undergraduate and postgraduate. Notably, the University does not offer part-time undergraduate programmes: courses are traditional in structure and suitable for full-time study only. Combined honours degrees are available within pre-set limits. Two thirds of students are on sandwich or language courses which involve an industrial, professional or language placement. This is a strongly technological university with strong engineering, business and management links. Degree assessments vary: some involve 'Finals' at he end of the course; others have end of year exams; others are a combination of course/projectwork and examination. The University has a single, compact site close to Birmingham centre. Almost all first years live in University residences: a place is guaranteed provided that your home is beyond reasonable daily travelling distance.

THE CAMPUS

The University has a 40 acre site near a busy flyover, the Aston Expressway to the M6, close to the centre of the city. This is a high-density campus: trees, a small ornamental lake and well-used 'recreation' lawns relieve the severe lines of the geometrically plain buildings, many very high. New concourses channel through original '60s buildings.

The tower blocks accommodate student residential units, stacked to dizzy heights: not a place for the claustrophobic, or those who suffer from vertigo. The University is small and compact enough to generate a friendly, close-knit community. You will not be lonely here.

The campus is, however, strangely isolated by the city around it, and creates its own world. The city centre is only about half a mile away and, probably after you have been here for a while, the busy-ness of the road system will not seem such a barrier.

Cars

There is a bus service, laid on by the University, to and from campus. There is no actual need for a car here.

Academic Services

The library provides on-line access to databases throughout the world as well as books, periodicals and pamphlets. Seats c. 700 students. Opening hours: 13 hours weekdays; substantial parts of weekends.

Computing skills feature in most degree programmes; a local area network links departmental facilities. Each student has an e-mail address and access to the Internet.

Opportunities available to improve your **languages**.

Culture on Campus

Drama: The Guild supports an active Drama society.

Film: The Triangle Arts Cinema is open to the public, with reduced prices for students. As the 'Regional Film Theatre', the cinema hosts the Birmingham Film and Television Festival each autumn.

Music: The Aston University Musical Society runs the University choir and the University orchestra, putting on concerts in a broad range of musical taste.

The Union

Here, the Union opts for the 'Guild of Students' title. There are five sabbatical officers. The Guild produces its own 'Sun' newspaper and a number of broadsheets keep you informed about club and society activities.

There's a purpose-built student shopping mall. In the Guild building is a shop, a post office, secondhand bookshop, computer showroom, insurance service, three bars, games room, refectory, launderette, showers, reprographic service, television, music practice rooms, hairdressers, two banks, a third cashpoint, a bookshop, a hall to seat 400 and a nursery and day-care centre. There are two Union catering outlets.

The Guild organises weekly discos, with regular visits from pop groups. There is a Freshers Ball, a May Ball and a Pyjama Hop, plus one-off events. There are 50 clubs and societies run by the Guild, in addition to the 40 odd run by the Athletics Union. One of the groups engages in Community Action.

Films are shown twice weekly; cabaret and comedy nights and acoustic band nights featuring local and student bands vie for your time.

Sport

Aston has very impressive sports facilities. The main campus has two separate sports centres. Together they provide two indoor sports surfaces for football, hockey, cricket, volleyball, fencing etc., a swimming pool, two squash courts, two multi-gyms, a climbing wall, a sauna and solarium, snooker and table tennis tables and a shop where you can buy sports goods at competitive prices. There are aerobics and keep-fit classes and you can have your fitness activities personally programmed. Clubs use most peak evening time for their activities, but there are ample opportunities for beginners as well as enthusiasts, and for booking facilities for informal games with friends. Swimming instruction is available and you can also practise canoeing and subaqua and life-saving techniques. Outside the two sports halls a three-quarter size synthetic pitch allows soccer, hockey and tennis all year round.

The University's main outdoor sports facilities are a seven mile, twenty minute bus-ride away from the campus. The recreation centre occupies 90 acres of greenbelt in Walsall and is bordered by a working canal: a pleasant retreat from Aston's urban environment. Here there is a cricket square, three tennis courts, fifteen winter games pitches, and two multipurpose hard porous pitches, one of which is floodlit. There are four squash courts. The large pavilion has three bars, a dining room and a social wing, as well as good changing facilities. There is a public squash club and many facilities are open to the general public.

Student welfare

The University has a **health centre** on campus which provides medical care. There is a doctor's surgery and nursing emergency supervision 24 hours a day.

The Guild (Union) has a large **welfare service**, with its own sabbatical officer.

The Guild also appoints **chaplains** of different denominations and supports several religious societies. Religious provision is made for Christians, Jews, Muslims, Hindus, Buddhists and Sikhs.

Careers Service

The Careers Advisory Service provides an accessible enquiry service, gives individual advice and guidance, and runs seminars and skills programmes. The University has computer-aided guidance facilities and a widely stocked information room.

Students with special needs

There are some adapted residential rooms available on the Aston Triangle campus. All buildings have been equipped with lifts and kerbs have been lowered to ease wheelchair access. Contact the Admissions Office as soon as you can to discuss your specific problems.

Accommodation

Virtually all first year students live in University residences; places are guaranteed provided that your home is beyond reasonable daily travelling distance, you have firmly accepted an Aston offer (before Clearing begins) and you have returned your accommodation application form by September 1st. The accommodation ratio is high: the University can house almost two thirds of its students, and you stand a good chance of a further year (usually your final) in a University room.

There are two accommodation sites; the larger on the main campus has 1,470 places; the University Village at Handsworth has 640.

Aston Triangle

Residences consist of three tower blocks and four low-rise buildings. All rooms are single study-bedrooms, grouped in units of three to twelve, sharing a communal amenities. 1,350 of the places are self-catering (you can use the Vauxhall Centre, on campus, for reasonably priced weekday meals). Room cleaning is included in the fees. There are TV/common-rooms and a launderette.

Costs (1995/96)

Self-catered hall: £30.40 pw (38 weeks)

Handsworth Wood University Village

The site, in a pleasant suburb, four miles from the main campus, is set in 18 acres of parkland. The 'Village' centres on the original hall converted now to house 150 first year residents in single study-bedrooms. Breakfast and evening meal are provided on weekdays, and brunch on Saturdays. There are amenity rooms for self-catering.

The Village also offers self-contained flats consisting of six study-bedrooms and shared facilities. These are reserved for returning students.

66 student couples (without children) can be housed in the Village in studio flats. Fees here do not include heating and lighting and you must provide your own bedlinen.

The Village has its own 'inn', several TV rooms, table tennis, badminton and games rooms, a launderette and its own chapel - and a lively Residents' Association.

All residences are supervised by members of staff, and at Handsworth Village a number of staff live in their own houses or flats, on site.

Costs (1995/96)

Catered: £44.46 pw (38 weeks)
Self-catered: £23.40 pw (38 weeks)

Student flats/houses

The Guild of Students has some houses and flats comprising 104 single rooms and 16 shared flats, intended for second and final year students.

Private accommodation

The Accommodation Office keeps a list of accommodation (from whole houses to bedsitters or lodgings). This could be up to eight miles away, but will have regular, fast access into the city, and travelcards make the costs bearable.

Costs (1994/95)

A wide range of prices: average £32 per week plus bills.

Mature Students

You must show evidence of recent relevant structured study. Access courses are considered for entry.

Nursery

There is a day-care nursery run by the Guild. Children are accepted from six weeks to five years old.

THE CITY/ESCAPE ROUTES

See University of Birmingham's entry in this Guide.

University of Birmingham

Edgbaston
Birmingham B15 2TT
Telephone: 0121 414 3344

University Charter date: 1900
Birmingham is a large university with around 15,000 full-time students, of whom c. 3,000 are postgraduate. The University has a single campus (231 acres) about two and a half miles from Birmingham centre. Degrees are traditionally structured and assessment can be by Final examinations, end of year exams building towards your degree or by a mix of coursework and exam. A full range of academic degrees are on offer, including medicine. The University guarantees accommodation to single first years.

THE CAMPUS

Academic origins are in the foundation of a School of Medicine and Surgery in 1828 (later Queen's College), which merged with Mason College (founded in 1875 by a wealthy, self-educated industrialist) in 1892 and became a fully-fledged university, with its own charter in 1900. These origins record the typical birth of a great civic university.

The University today occupies a very large site of 231 acres, about two and a half miles south-west of the city centre. It is well clear of civic bustle, and is surrounded by the green avenues of Edgbaston - wide and tree-lined. At the same time, bus-routes and the University's own rail station balance the suburban quiet with easy access to city amenities.

The central complex of early buildings is extremely handsome: warm brick (its design detail picked out in stone), stone balustrading, 'crowned' domes, the high 'campanile' clock tower, landmarking the site for miles. All is a fine embodiment of principle. The style makes a solid, dignified statement of academic interest, and the scale is impressive, yet stays on the restrained side of architectural extravagance: no trace of exuberance here.

Around it has developed, in varying styles, a modern complex of buildings accommodating a very large number of students and a very wide range of academic and social activities. The site has lost some of its green spaces since we first visited, yet developments retain a sense of order, balance and high quality. The University ambience remains unpressured and very confident.

The size of the site allows an extravagant use of space and a separation of identity for the buildings which mark the University's expansion in the last twenty years. Their functional modern lines serve as strong contrast to the early buildings. Variety of height, line and style avoids the monotony of large campus development.

Cars
Parking on campus is severely restricted.

Learning Resources

The library has more than 2,000,000 printed volumes (including 7,500 current periodicals) and 3,000,000 manuscripts/archives. Most of the books are housed in the main library. There are nine site libraries and access to a wide range of electronic information sources.

The **Computing Service** offers short courses in programming and on the use of the University's computer facilities (which are extensive), as well as providing an advisory service. There are short courses on word processing and spread sheets. Practicals of two hours' backup are timetabled in. The computer facilities are available to non-computer science students from 8am to 10pm if facilities are not otherwise timetabled.

The Modern Languages Unit has courses in nine **languages** at up to six levels of competence. Courses either attract an attendance certificate or can lead to an external qualification certificate.

Culture on campus

Drama: The University runs several courses involving drama, and has two drama studios which are used for courses and productions. The Guild of Students' Theatre Group and the Department of Drama and Theatre Arts put on regular productions in the University's studio theatre. *Music:* The Barber Institute of Fine Arts houses a concert hall. The Music Society gives midday concerts every week during term. The University Choir (220) and Orchestra (100) are the largest student performing groups, but there are many more: smaller instrumental groups and choirs or less regular, ad hoc groups pursuing special interests. The Students' Guild (Union) Opera Group stages at least one work a year. The Barber Institute hall is used for a fully professional opera production every two years, and for a regular series of professional evening concerts and recitals (about ten per year). A very lively and rich musical scene. The University Music Library houses books, scores and audio/visual recordings in the Barber Institute. There is a collection of instruments, some of which you can borrow.

The Union

The Union is known as the Guild of Students. It is exceptionally well housed in a spacious building close to the main campus ring-road. It has its own catering facilities (five outlets) and four bars, bank, insurance, opticians, travel office, shop, printing services, snooker room, committee rooms, television lounges, two nightclubs and two concert venues: very well equipped to fulfil its role as clubhouse and meeting ground. The Guild runs more than 100 societies and a strong athletics union, and provides its own welfare, education and community services. It organises 10 to 12 events per week and has a salaried Entertainments Officer.

On a more enterprising commercial front, there are markets three or four times a week, a weekly greengrocer and an occasional florist.

As well as organising the Freshers' Conference, before the session begins, the Guild will arrange for its members to meet and host prospective students, if asked, and has a reception committee to help new students through any tricky patches as they start university life.

The Guild of Students was set up primarily to advance social interaction between students, and this remains its main function, but student representatives are also full members of all major University committees. The Guild is run through a series of committees, with five principal officers elected annually. Altogether, the Guild employs 100 permanent staff and 400 students. Its income is a combination of University grant and its (large) revenue from trading activities.

The Union has its own TV station and produces a fortnightly magazine.

The University Centre

Another spacious building extends the amenities on campus: main meals and snacks, bars, common rooms and a summer patio. Rooms, and catering, can be hired for private functions. The centre also contains several commercial operations including a travel agent's, hairdressers and banks.

Sport

The University has an extensive range of facilities on offer. Indoors there are two sports halls, a 25 metre deck level swimming pool, a gymnasium, fitness room, weights room, dance studio, squash courts, fives court, martial arts room, indoor climbing wall, saunas and sunbeds, a bar and sports shop. Outdoors there is a floodlit eight lane synthetic athletics track, two floodlit synthetic hockey pitches, a floodlit soccer pitch, a floodlit rugby pitch, tennis courts and cricket nets - all on campus, plus an adjacent canal for canoeing; there are seventy acres of playing fields and a cricket ground less than five miles away. Coaches and minibuses are provided to transport you. 170 miles to the north, at Coniston in the Lake District, the University has an outdoor pursuits centre.

The Active Lifestyles Programme offers 150 instructed courses each term, mainly at beginner and 'slightly better' levels, in a range of sports.

At more advanced levels the Athletic Union teams play in inter-university competitions and local leagues. There is a small charge for some sports facilities and much of the time is pre-booked by societies and the facilities are open to the general public.

Birmingham excels in athletics, hockey, basketball, football, lacrosse and water polo.

Student welfare

The University has a **health centre,** including a GP surgery, with 11 beds. The Student Support and **Counselling Service** offers students emotional, psychological and educational counselling. Professional welfare advice is given here and is also provided by the Guild.

Birmingham provides a large **chaplaincy centre** which is used by a variety of different groups. There is also a daily prayer room in the Union for Muslim students. Hindus and Sikhs go to local temples.

Careers Service

The Careers Centre has six full-time advisors and a well-stocked library. You will have your 'own' careers advisor. The Centre is open to you throughout your course (and afterwards) and arranges seminars and workshops, as well as giving you access to computer guidance programmes.

Students with special needs

You should contact the University before you make your application to discuss your requirements. Some accommodation has been adapted and there is a special print resource centre in the main library. The Sports Centre and swimming pool are both accessible to students with disabilities. The University has a Tutor to Students with Disabilities and is a member of 'Skill', the National Bureau for Students with Disabilities.

Accommodation

The University guarantees accommodation to first years (single or coming up alone), provided that you firmly accept your offer and apply for an accommodation place by May 31st and confirm by September 1st. There are six halls of residence and six self-catering student villages, owned and run by the University.

Halls of residence

Four halls are in 'The Vale', a pretty 40 acre parkland site, complete with lake, immediately north of and a 10 minute walk from campus and about half a mile nearer to the city centre. The four 'Vale' halls have dining rooms and common rooms, kitchens for preparing snacks; shops, launderettes; most have a games room (one has a multigym) and some have library/reading or TV rooms, photographic darkrooms and bars. First years are likely to have to share rooms. Halls are warden/president controlled, arrange social and cultural functions and have a separate community life of their own.

Because of car-parking restrictions on campus you are not allowed to use your car to travel from Vale Halls in the University (which is only a very short walk away).

Two halls remain: one, University House, is a stone's throw from the campus. It is a fine Edwardian building in its own grounds, including its own croquet lawn.

The other, the Manor House (which used to belong to the Cadbury family), is three miles away, adjoining the Griffin Close site. It is based on a period house (built in mock Tudor style), and has large grounds which contain a tennis court and football pitch.

Costs (1995/96)

Costs vary between halls. The maximum charged for a single room ensuite: £2,288; for a single room: £1,928; for a shared room: £1,788. All rents are for 31 weeks and include breakfast daily, with dinner (Monday - Friday) and lunch on Sundays.

Self-catering 'student villages'

Six complexes of student flats. Maple Bank (264 places, all first years) is on the edge of the Vale: students here can take meals as 'guests' in some of the halls. Griffin Close , adjacent to the Manor House three miles from the University, is a much larger complex, housing 1,060 students. A more independent ambience is also fostered by the closeness of the pubs and shops of the outside world.

The 'Tennis Court' site, between The Vale and the main campus, has 622 places. A new development in Edgbaston, The Beeches, has over 200 places and is about two miles away. Hunter Court, next to Edgbaston Cricket Ground, and Queens Hospital Close, two miles from campus and the two newest developments.

All 'villages' have active Residents' Associations which organise social functions and sporting events.

Costs (1995/96)

Costs vary between residences. A standard room is c.£1,259 (excluding heat and light) and an ensuite room is c.£1,954 (including heat and light): all rooms are let for 40 weeks.

Private sector accommodation

A list of lodgings and private flats/bedsitters is kept by the University: all places are visited and approved by senior Accommodation Office staff and are usually within one or two miles of the campus. Average costs: £28.00 to £37.00 plus bills in a shared flat.

Mature students

Minimum age: 21. The University recognises a wide range of non-standard qualifications and runs Access courses in manufacturing, engineering and business studies. It is a member of the Birmingham Access Federation, and also recognises compatible Access courses from other regions.

Nursery

A day nursery is run by the University for pre-school children of students and staff, including fathers. Children are taken from the age of three weeks.

THE CITY (population: 1,006,000)

For some years Birmingham has been in the throes of dramatic and ambitious redevelopment. Old (well not so old) images were of a city beleaguered by ring roads, motorways and fly-overs, occupying an area too vast for its horizons and too much dogged by its heritage of rapid, mass-production-based Industrial Revolution sprawl. Such a heritage cannot easily be dismantled, but the changes already achieved here are dramatic.

Redevelopment of the actual city centre is spectacular. Space-age architecture creates the dramatic new Centenary Square, still presided over by its war memorial and with a number of its more dignified surrounding buildings now stone-cleaned and restored. The extravagant shapes of the International Conference Centre and the new Concert Hall face a square which is mosaic-paved. The Concert Hall offers exceptionally fine musical experience: it houses audiences of 2,200 and has very clever, state of the art acoustics. Here, the City of Birmingham Symphony Orchestra has an internationally celebrated home in which to consolidate its high reputation.

The whole new complex is enormous - in Birmingham, big is beautiful - and includes a tree-lined Mall leading to the canal, and a massive National Indoor Sports Arena.

On a quieter note, the statue of Chamberlain still watches over the sedate and dignified square that bears his name; the Art Gallery, Museum and City Hall still stand in their Victorian stone solidity. Birmingham might be putting on the mantle of a futuristic megalopolis, but its foundations are in its history.

Theatres: The Hippodrome is now a leading opera house, as well as venue for general entertainment and diverse productions. Birmingham Royal Ballet Company has its home here in a specially built extension. The Rep Theatre was recently re-opened and is one of England's famous old provincial theatres, housing productions of musicals, drama, Shakespeare - some en route to London. The Studio is an intimate theatre of innovative drama. The Alexandra has been expensively renovated to welcome the D'Oyly Carte Opera Company.

Music: As well as the Concert Hall and the City of Birmingham Symphony Orchestra, Birmingham offers the gamut of music. The NEC is the venue for top bands and is visited on almost every major tour. The annual Birmingham Jazz Festival attracts top names to the city and Ronnie Scott's (the very famous London jazz club) has opened a Ronnie Scott's in Birmingham.

Cinema: Birmingham has 20 screens in various cinemas. For 'Art' films, go to the Triangle Centre at Aston University and the Midlands Arts Centre.

Nightlife: extensive, with more than a dozen nightclubs offering facilities from winebars to cabarets which attract top names. A very wide range of restaurants is on offer.

Sport: Aston Villa and Birmingham City football clubs, international cricket, athletics, rugby, speedway and greyhound racing are all there for the spectator, and there's the Horse of the Year Show at the NEC. All participant sports are catered for, both inside and out. Thirty indoor sports are on offer at the new National Indoor Arena, and there is figure skating at the NEC.

ESCAPE ROUTES

Birmingham itself covers a vast area, so its surrounding countryside is a wide ring describing counties and miles, from the lowland Wolds to the east, to the rising Marches to the west: with the southern reaches of the Derbyshire Dales to its north and rolling Warwickshire to the south. Stratford is only half an hour or so away (the RSC and Shakespeare); Dovedale and Derbyshire are within easy travelling distance in a different direction; as are the Malvern Beacons (excellent walking country).

Communications

Birmingham's **rail-links** from New Street Station are extensive and serve almost all major centres in Britain. Likewise the coach services are regular and fast to all parts of the country.

Birmingham is, of course, ringed by **motorways** and site of the notorious 'Spaghetti Junction'. The M6, M5 and M40 motorways link the city to the country's motorway system in all directions.

Birmingham International **Airport** is a busy terminal with flights all over the world.

University of Central England in Birmingham

Perry Barr
Birmingham B42 2SU
Telephone: 0121 331 5000

University Charter date: 1992

UCE is a medium/large university with around 11,000 full-time students on HND and degree programmes. Also around 7,000 part-time students and 1,500 further education students. The University has seven teaching campuses: the main site (Perry Barr) is three miles from the centre of Birmingham. Degree courses are modular (with some exceptions and assessment methods vary - from full coursework (most art & design courses) to a mix of coursework and exam. The University has almost 1,000 places in three halls of residence. No guarantee of accommodation to first years.

THE CAMPUSES

This is a difficult one for coherent perspectives: it is either virtually single-sited, or very multi-sited, according to your field of interest.

If you are interested in art and design, there are four distinct and separated sites to consider; if in music, then it's the Conservatoire, in the epicentre of the city. The other outpost is the Faculty of Education at Westbourne Road. Otherwise, all courses are provided at Perry Barr.

The Perry Barr campus

The campus is 3 miles north and a 15 minute bus journey from the city centre.

This main site is quite large, and is purpose built in smart dark brick and dark glass - rectangular blocks of varying height. Paved link areas allow movement to and from the social areas (refectory, bars, a Union shop, bank and small bookshop). The functional, efficient mode is brightened by red railings and lamp-posts. The Coppice, a new student residence complex, is on campus.

The area around the campus is heavily urban, but, as in any city, it is possible to find acceptably pleasant streets to live in; local shops are close and will serve modest day-to-day needs; Perry Barr has a rail station with services to Birmingham New Street.

Birmingham Institute of Art and Design: Gosta Green

BIAD resulted from a union of the Faculty of Art and Design with the Bournville College of Art, and is the largest single unit of art and design in the country.

The main Faculty premises are at Gosta Green on the edge of Aston University's campus. Read its entry in this Guide for an idea of the locale. Courses here: Visual Communication, Three Dimensional Design and Fashion and Textiles.

Margaret Street: the original School of Art

This Victorian Grade 1 listed building is currently being restored to its original splendour. It is very close to the city's Art Gallery and Museum complex. Courses in the department of art are taught here.

The School of Jewellery: Vittoria Street

In the heart of the historic Jewellery Quarter, an area now being developed as a tourist attraction. The School has been rebuilt behind is Grade III listed facade and doubled in size.

The Bournville site

Set in Cadbury's historic complex at Bournville: a pretty, private, cherished 'village' complete with Quaker meeting house and junior school. Created by the Cadbury family for their employees in the better traditions of the paternalistic industrial magnates. Worth a visit if you are not based here. Courses: the Department of Foundation and Community Studies here offers BA courses in Art and Design by negotiated studies and a Design Foundation Diploma.

The Birmingham Conservatoire

This occupies a new, purpose-built suite in an integral part of the central city redevelopment. The Conservatoire moved into the upper levels of its block in 1986. It perches above a covered mall of shops and restaurants, and overlooks a small green and flowered area set with seats, and screened only by railings from a roaring city freeway. The Conservatoire has a close working relationship with the CBSO (about 20 of its principal players teach here). The Sir Adrian Boult Hall offers fine concert accommodation.

Edgbaston site

The Faculty of Education and some Health and Social Science courses live in the green and pleasant suburban landscape of Edgbaston, close to the University of Birmingham and to the self-sufficient High Street amenities of Harborne. Some halls of residence on site.

Learning Resources

Ten **libraries** in total, covering the various sites. The main Kendrick Library is on Perry Barr and houses 300,000 books and 1,200 current periodicals.

Most courses have an element of **computing** work. Each Faculty has its own microcomputer rooms and backup staff from the Information Service who run training workshops.

Culture on campus

Film: The English School runs a film society. Films, mainly 'cinema classics', are shown on one afternoon per week.

Music: The University benefits from its association with Birmingham Conservatoire. The Adrian Boult Hall is a major venue for classical concerts - over 200 events a year. The Opera School presents a production annually. There is a Chorus choir and the pro-am Paradise Sinfonietta to join.

The Union

There are Union Offices on two sites (Perry Barr and Edgbaston); other locations have a site-based Union Officer.

The Students' Union Building is on the Perry Barr campus, has a shop, bar, Student Advice Centre, bank and insurance bureau. Edgbaston has a bar and a shop.

Entertainments: regular events are organised on the Perry Barr and Edgbaston campuses on Friday and Saturday evenings - bands, discos, comedians, quizzes and club nights. A late-night minibus provides a door to door service. The Union runs approximately 35 non-sporting clubs and societies, a fortnightly magazine.

Sport

Sports facilities are out in Edgbaston, on the Westbourne Road campus: two gyms, a multigym, five tennis courts, cricket nets and a grass pitch. The Union hires facilities from the city; if you have a Students' Union Sports Association Card you can use hired facilities free of charge. The Sports Union runs around 37 sports clubs, including aerobics, walking and climbing and women's self-defence, as well as parachute and 'dangerous sports'. There is an interdepartmental football competition.

Student welfare

GPs and a team of nurses run **surgeries** on Perry Barr, Westbourne Road and Cambrian Hall: nursing-only surgeries in Gosta Green and Bournville. Various special clinics including 'Well Woman'. A team of **professional counsellors** offer practical sessions. Both the Union and the counselling service run sessions to improve study skills. Christian **chaplains** represent main denominations. A separate prayer room is available for Muslim students.

Careers Service
The Service runs special sessions on job-hunting and applications, as well as giving individual careers guidance. Careers Information bases are at Perry Barr, Edgbaston and Cambrian Hall.

Students with special needs
Closed loop systems are being designed into new buildings and one hall of residence has a small number of rooms specially converted for students with disabilities. You should write to the Disability Services Adviser before applying, indicating the course you wish to study and the nature of your disability.

Accommodation

Halls of residence
Three halls of residence: one on the Edgbaston site; Cambrian Hall in the city centre close to the Birmingham Conservatoire and to two of BIAD's sites; and a new hall on the Perry Barr campus. Edgbaston has 245 single rooms and 34 shared rooms (two small bedrooms and a joint study); Cambrian Hall has 200 single rooms; Perry Barr offers 432 places.

Costs (1995/96)
£37.00 per week in a hall of residence (self-catering).
£42.00 per week at Perry Barr (self-catering).

Leasing Scheme
The University runs a head-leasing scheme, controlling a number of houses and flats. Around 800 places. Check that you will be near to the site of your course.

Costs (1995/96)
Rents range from £28 to £35 per week, exclusive of bills.

Private accommodation
The majority of students are in private sector accommodation. Either in houses and flats, rented with friends, or in lodgings. The Accomodation and Catering Services has a register. A room costs around £27 to £35 per week plus bills.

Mature students

All applicants without standard entry requirements will be interviewed and you should contact the admissions officer direct before you submit your application. The University runs an Associate Students Programme.

Nursery
There are two nurseries, Perry Barr and Edgbaston: both takes children from two to five years. A half-term playscheme is available for school-age children.

THE CITY/ESCAPE ROUTES

See University of Birmingham's entry in this Guide.

Coventry University

Priory Street
Coventry
CV1 5FB
Telephone: 01203 631313

University Charter date: 1992

Coventry is a large/medium-sized university with 11,000 full-time students on HND and degree programmes. A further 2,500 students study part-time. The University has a single, city centre campus with a temporary outpost for Performing Arts.

Courses are modular: modules are specified within degree programme with some 'free' modules which allow a level of flexibility. A Community Exchange Project allows students to undertake 'live' projects with local community organisations - charitable and other. The projects can be part of your assessed course. Assessment of degree and HND programmes is by combined course work and examination.

Accommodation is guaranteed for all incoming first years, although not necessarily in university-owned or managed properties.

THE CAMPUS

Coventry University is single site, in the centre of Coventry, with the distinction of being directly opposite the city's dramatic cathedral. The campus covers 25 acres; not all major buildings on this site, however, have anything to do with the University. Rather, the University delineates an area of the city's cultural and social life, as well as its own precinct. The city Art Gallery and Museum is between the University's main services buildings and its library; city sports facilities - a large, glass-housed swimming pool and sports centre - are so much in keeping with the University's style that they seem to be part of its buildings. The Odeon cinema is also 'on-site', with student concessions advertised broadly. These, and the cathedral, will give a shifting population access through the University: this is not an isolated or insulated campus.

The main campus, as seen from the cathedral, is a square of block buildings - a site highly developed, without being cramped. The predominant building style of this area is 1960's glass and panel: not a lot more to say about that. There is something about the layering of Coventry's buildings which makes the site seem more enduring than others of similar type. The original Union building is very much centre scene.

The dominating tower block to the north west of the campus is part of Priory Hall - one of the University's main hall of residence.

The University has overspilled the city's ring-road boundary. The Computer Science, Mathematics, and Electrical, Electronic and Systems Engineering areas are housed 'on the other side' in new, purpose-built buildings: all very impressive with clear lines and a sense of meaning business. The divide of the ring-road is not acute: the fast dual-carriageway is overhead, a hum more than a hazard.

Cars

You should not be need a car.

Academic services

The **Lanchester library** is a short walk away from central campus and has over 1,100 study places, houses 300,000 volumes and takes 2,600 periodicals a year. Open until 8.45pm Monday to Thursday, to 5.15pm on Friday and Saturday mornings. Reference access weekend afternoons. The library offers a range of services from the usual to film-processing and tee-shirt printing.

Most courses contain an element of **computing**. There are terminal rooms and computer laboratories available around the campus, some open 24 hours a day, with a total of over 1,500 workstations. The computing advisory service, in the **Computer Centre**, is open every day.

You will use the computers to decide on your course content: the Academic Information System has detailed information on all modules. There are introductory seminars run by computing services at the beginning of your course. The network has an electronic bulletin board updated daily, and twice yearly a newsletter.

You will be able to add on a module of a **modern language** to most courses. Coventry is a leader in using CALL (Computer Assisted Language Learning). All courses are class-taught. Language Laboratories are open on weekdays from 9am to 5pm.

Culture on campus

Drama: The Coventry Centre for the Performing Arts has a studio theatre, a fully equipped technical workshop and a sound and recording studio, as well as two large dance studios and numerous rehearsal and music practice rooms. Students from any discipline can join in; performances are given on and off campus.

Film: The Film Society shows films once a week.

Music: A Concert Band, Chamber Orchestra, Choir and Students' Union Musical Society: a good 'menu'. Four or five informal and two formal concerts (Christmas and Easter) per year as well as lunchtime concerts. Professional performers visit. Instrumental and vocal tuition available. You can use practice rooms in Priory Hall. There is a residential weekend annually for all the music groups, and weekly 'events' - smaller bands or big name bands.

Art: The Lanchester Art Gallery in the School of Art and Design has a funded collection, and houses touring exhibitions.

The Union

Since 1996, the Union has two buildings: the Union building on campus which has three bars, two gig venues, a shop, travel bureau and a take-away snack bar; the new four storey building is an Entertainments Centre with a capacity for 2,000.

Over 80 clubs and societies on offer. The Union is the main venue in Coventry for gigs and cabarets and hosts theatre events and disco, big bands and comedy nights. A full-time entertainments officer (member of permanent staff) maintains the variety and high quality of the programme.

The annual turnover is £1.4 million: five Sabbatical Offices; a good range of welfare and education advice (finance , legal, benefits etc.); twice weekly (at least) social events ('usually something happening every night'). The Union employs 200 students in various capacities.

There is a night-line, run by trained students every night from 8pm to 8am and organises transport every night and after any entertainment, with priority given to women students. There are also classes for women in self-defence.

Sport

Wednesday afternoons are timetabled for sporting activity (if you want to join in). There is help and advice on hand for anyone who needs it, at whatever level your sport.

On the University site are four squash courts, and a hall in the Students' Union suitable for badminton, basketball, volleyball and five-a-side football. The main hall in the original Union building has been converted for fencing and aerobics. The new sports centre, in the Alma Building adjacent to campus, are facilities for weight training, indoor football, table tennis and a range of martial arts.

The playing fields, of which there are 37 acres, are five miles from campus. There is special transport. The playing fields have changing rooms and social facilities. You can play rugby, soccer, netball, hockey, tennis or nine-hole golf.

Altogether, the Union runs around 40 sports clubs and societies.

Watersport facilities are 20 miles away.

Coventry's major Sports Centre is adjacent to the campus. Also close by is the Midlands Sports Centre for the disabled.

Student welfare

The University has male and female GPs with whom you can register as with any other **medical practice** in Coventry. There are two surgeries daily for consultation on any matter concerning life and work at the University: your problems need not be strictly medical. The University has a **counselling service**. There are four **chaplains** with offices in Priory Hall, who can provide links with a number of different religions, with Student Services and other points of Welfare provision.

Careers Service

Careers Advisers are linked to a particular subject area and work closely with your academic staff. The Service runs a comprehensive careers education programme, including guidance on choosing a career, CV and job-hunting skills. There is a well-stocked information room.

Students with special needs

All parts of the campus are accessible to wheelchairs. Computer facilities have been re-designed to help with wheelchair access and problems with other disabilities. Other specialist facilities are available. You should write to the Disabilities Officer to discuss your special needs. A Volunteer Welfare Assistant Scheme is in place to assist with care and study support needs.

Accommodation

Accommodation is managed by Student Services. The University has approximately 2,500 places in halls of residence, University-owned houses and University-managed accommodation. The houses vary in size, and some rooms are shared. All houses and halls are mixed. Accommodation is guaranteed for all first years, although not necessarily in university-owned or managed property.

A majority of students live in private rented accommodation. The housing officers have lists and will try to place you in lodgings or digs if you do not manage to get a place in University accommodation. All recommended lodgings have been inspected by Student Services, and all are near regular bus-routes into the city centre. Some are only walking distance away.

Halls of residence

Priory Hall, on campus, provides catered accommodation and has 547 single study bedrooms, a refectory, television rooms and laundry facilities. There are no facilities for cooking, although every room has a kettle.

Caradoc Hall, renovated in 1994/95, is just over three miles from the main campus and has 64 single flats and 62 two-bedroomed flats. Each single flat has a kitchenette and bathroom, and the two-bedroomed flats have two study bedrooms, a dining room, separate kitchenette and bathroom. There is a hall-superintendent on site.

Singer Hall, opened in 1984, houses 622 students in single self-catering rooms on campus. Bedrooms are in groups of six around shared communal facilities.

University houses

Houses are in residential areas, vary in size and offer single or shared rooms. 320 students in all are housed.

Costs (1995/1996)

Priory Hall: £2,356 (including ten meals per week)
Caradoc Hall: £1,920 (single flat per residential year)
Singer Hall: £1,880 (per residential year)
University houses from £1,040 for a shared room
Contracts for university-owned accommodation are for 40 weeks.

University Property Management

900 self-catered bedspaces are available in small houses managed, on behalf of private house-owners, by the University. You will need to bring your own bed-linen, cutlery and crockery.

Costs (1995/96)

£28 to £31 per week (40 weeks) excluding bills.

Private sector

There is a range of rented accommodation available in Coventry. Begin your search ahead of arriving for your course. The Accommodation Office opens every day from the third week in August to help you in your search.

Costs (1994/95)

The cost of a shared, rented house is around £30 per person per week, excluding bills.

Mature students

The University considers students on past achievement, including non-academic. It recommends that you consider an Access course, and does not specify its own, which run in the Coventry area. The University has links with over 30 partner F.E. Colleges throughout the region. The University also runs an 'Associate Student Scheme' whereby you can attend course elements to find out whether you want to make a full commitment to study. Any course elements passed successfully will count towards your future degree.

Nursery

The nursery offers care for 35 children under five and is open for 48 weeks a year. Places are in high demand.

THE CITY (population 300,000)

Coventry suffered heavy damage in World War II (it was virtually razed in a single night-raid): it has become a folk-image of dark industrial rubble. The city today therefore offers a surprise factor: rebuilding has created a large, traffic-free precinct, over a mile long, terraced and arcaded, with fountains and murals to make a change from the shop windows. Most of the major chain stores are represented here, and there are several department stores.

The imaginative redevelopment is most movingly symbolised by the cathedral. The shell of the destroyed 14th century original leads to the impressive modern cathedral designed by Sir Basil Spence. The interior has a number of rich features: the stained glass of John Piper, throwing slender panels of light towards the altar; the splendid tapestry of 'Christ in Glory', Epstein's 'St Michael and the Devil', among others. A cross made from two charred roof timbers of the destroyed old cathedral has been placed on the original altar, with the inscription 'Father Forgive' carved behind.

There are a few parks around the city: Lady Herbert's Gardens lie between two of the ancient town gates and contain part of the old city wall; Coombe Park, three miles to the east, has 300 acres of formal gardens, woodland nature trails, angling, paddle-boating, birdland: and popular medieval banquets at Coombe Abbey.

A few historic buildings survive. St Mary's Guildhall is one of the finest examples of medieval guildhalls in the country. Its tower once imprisoned Mary, Queen of Scots. The crypt is 600 years old. There are two Tudor almshouses: Bonds Hospital and Ford's Hospital. Spon Street is medieval, lined by 15th and 16th century buildings, now shops and art galleries. Whitefriars: a renovated 14th century Carmelite friary, now a museum.

Theatre: The Belgrade Theatre offers a good range of drama. Every three years the medieval Coventry Mystery Plays are produced in the old cathedral ruins.

Cinema: There are three: one five-screen, one double screen and a multiplex outside the city centre.

Nightlife: There are five nightclubs in central Coventry.

Sport: Fairfax Street sports centre: bowls, badminton, squash etc., plus two swimming complexes with a sauna suite and solarium. Tenpin bowling, golf (three courses) and boating on the canal offer active sport. Those who prefer to watch can visit the rugby union and Coventry City league football grounds, various club cricket grounds, including Courtauld's (county class) and National League Speedway (hot-rod, stock-car).

ESCAPE ROUTES

Your routes south lead to the English countryside of Warwickshire: rich pastureland rilled with streams; historic towns and pretty villages - all very pastoral. Exclusively yours is the tract of castle/literary pilgrimage: Warwick, Kenilworth and Stratford-upon-Avon. Royal Leamington Spa is close to Warwick: you can still take the waters in the Royal Pump Room, under supervision.

Communications

Coventry is on the **main line** from London to Birmingham, with their radial links to elsewhere. The city is also on a direct line to Warwick, Leamington Spa and beyond. **Coach links** are general. Coventry is on the **M6**, reasonably close the M1, M5, M40, M42 and M69. **Birmingham International Airport** has flights all over the world.

Coventry University
Creating **Real World** Success

Everything about Coventry University is geared towards helping you achieve. In life, not just in three or four years. Combining our traditions, reputation, expertise and close links with industry to build you a platform for lasting success in the real world.

Which means offering you practical courses - of real worth to future employers - in subjects directly relevant to the 21st century marketplace. And providing a supportive and stimulating environment that encourages you to generate maximum opportunity from a traditional yet visionary university experience.

- Modular courses to tailor your education to your aspirations

- Guaranteed accommodation for all first year students

- Help and advice in making the most of student life

- First class facilities - educational, sporting and social

- A culture in which the needs of the individual command top priority

We promise you a highly regarded university education that will not only stimulate your mind and personal development, but also create for you a true cutting edge with which to carve out a successful career. To find out exactly what makes Coventry so special, contact us now.

For a prospectus please contact the Corporate Affairs Unit, Priory Street, Coventry CV1 5FB Telephone: 01203 838774 Fax: 01203 838090 WWW http://www.coventry.ac.uk.

Higher Education for all

COVENTRY
UNIVERSITY

De Montfort University

The Gateway
Leicester
LE1 9BH
Telephone: 0116 255 1551

University Charter date: 1992

De Montfort defines itself as a 'distributed' university, with campuses in Leicester, Milton Keynes, Bedford and Lincoln. The University has asked us to give each centre equal weight and status: the write-up here will be under the usual headings and information will relate to each town/city's campuses and amenities. It is not possible to give a single picture of De Montfort's student population: site sizes vary enormously from many thousand students (in Leicester) to a few hundred (Lincoln's four campuses and Milton Keynes).

The campus types also vary enormously. De Montfort, Leicester, has two sites - one city centre and one six miles out; Milton Keynes has a single purpose-built campus with two small outposts; Bedford has three sites in and around the town, and was, until recently, Bedford College of Higher Education; Lincoln is scattered over four sites, one of which is 45 miles from Lincoln, three of which are 'farms' attached to the School of Agriculture and Horticulture, one is the School of Applied Art & Design. When you apply to De Montfort, make sure that you know which of these sites will be your home: you will not mix with the entire De Montfort University population and will have a very different life at any one of the four campus clusters. Accommodation provision varies from site to site.

Degree programmes are modular. Choices increase as you progress through your course; in the beginning you will study core subjects. Modules are assessed by coursework, project work or / and examination.

THE CAMPUSES

Leicester

City campus

The campus is fairly large and compact, occupying a grid of non-busy streets just off the main city access road, and only three quarters of a mile from the city centre.

The style-range of the buildings suggests a time-continuity. Two solid, large Victorian buildings stand watchtower on two of the corners: red brick, stone decoration, roof-top twirls of dome and tower. Between, in bright contrast, rise the high white and elegant lines of the James Went Building. The Kimberlin Library is a smart new building in brick and narrow glass, its interiors well-lit and well-fitted.

The large Fletcher complex, prominent opposite the library, has a medium-rise tower block and a 'skirt' of lower buildings. Its structure is 1960s, but the lines are pleasant enough. Its 'back door' area, close to the river Soar, is occupied by the Union Building.

There is variety in the perimeter settings: one boundary is a busy access road into the city; another is The Newarke - evidence of Leicester's ancient history, with its Newarke Houses Museum. Its old walls and arch lead to a small, pretty close (Castle Yard) which has a few very old houses, a church and the County Court which has been administering justice for the past 500 years.

The rear of the site is bounded by the river Soar and a large industrial area beyond. The river here is more canal than stream, but there is a riverside walk and narrow green margins. A little way along and across the river is the John Sandford Sports Centre. The campus is generally well-supervised, well-kept and welcoming in scale.

Scraptoft campus

The Scraptoft Campus is less than six miles away. You will travel out through the urban sprawl of eastward Leicester until there is a sudden change to an affluent area of wide avenues, gardens and trees: then Scraptoft village.

The rural calm is unexpected. A road off into fields, woodland and birdsong: here is the University's second campus. The buildings are clustered behind Scraptoft Hall, gatehouse and church: there is a preserved air of feudal living about the complex. The campus is quite large, but very well-screened by its wooded setting. Buildings are unobtrusive; there are green quadrangles and the atmosphere is domestic, with more than a hint of a comfortable, reassuring school. You should note how far the campuses are from each other: there are social and welfare facilities on both campuses, and although you will be integrated in the sense that all general facilities are open to all students, it is likely that your life will be campus-based. There is a frequent minibus service between the city centre and Scraptoft campuses, so you can move between the two as you wish.

Courses at Scraptoft: all courses are in the School of Health and Community Studies; Performing Arts; Applied Biology; Teacher Education; Art and Design Foundation; courses in the Department of Public Policy and Managerial Studies.

Charles Frears Campus

A former Nursing and Midwifery College which became part of DMU in 1995 and is now part of the School of Health and Community Studies. The main building is a mock Jacobean mansion with stable block dating from the 19th century. Some additional teaching buildings - 1970's.

Cars

On the City campus map, P stands for paternoster: not a lot of parking here. The Scraptoft campus has three large car-parks and there is a regular bus service.

Milton Keynes

The Milton Keynes' main campus at Kents Hill sits just off one of the dual carriageways, which spin you around Milton Keynes: not far from the M1.

The site is 'greenfield', i.e. open agricultural land. Space, a slight roll to the countryside, space again. The campus buildings add to the general harmony: pale brick, lots of glass, shallow sloping chalet roofs. The atmosphere fairly domestic with carpets, decor and furnishings all new and civilised.

The University also uses two other small teaching sites in Milton Keynes: Chaffron Way is to kilometres and Wolverton is six kilometres away from Kents Hill.

Bedford

This was Bedford College of Higher Education. Two sites here: Lansdowne and Polhill.

Lansdowne is on the west side of Bedford in a quiet, residential area of the town. Campus buildings are modern blocks, with a variety of style and line. Around are landscaped gardens, paved terraces and some avant-garde sculpture. Physical Education, Dance and Sports Studies are located here.

Polhill is on the east side of Bedford in a new housing area. Its buildings are also modern, pleasant blocks set in open grounds with playing fields. Primary Education and Humanities are taught here, and the site is also used for in-service teacher and social worker training.

Lincoln

DMU Lincoln has four campuses - Lincoln City, Riseholme, Caythorpe and Holbeach. The City Campus houses the School of Applied Arts and Design; the others are occupied by the School of Agriculture and Horticulture.

The City Campus is close to the cathedral and castle and to the Usher Art Gallery. Facilities include studios, exhibition and lecture rooms, workshops and a library.

The School of Agriculture's campuses are spread from Riseholme (a mile from Lincoln) to Holbeach, 45 miles away near Spalding. Caythorpe is 25 miles south near Grantham and is the School's administrative centre. Riseholme and Caythorpe offer a total of 490 hectares of estate land: Riseholme's 240 hectares comprise livestock and grassland management; Caythorpe's teaching farm includes a commercial pedigree pig herd and an educational poultry unit.

Learning Resources

Leicester

There are two **libraries**, one at each main campus: their stocks reflect the courses on each site - a total of 260,414 volumes, 2,266 periodicals and seating for 1,111 students. Opening hours: Kimberlin - to 9pm weekdays and Saturday morning; Scraptoft - 8.45am to 9pm Monday to Thursday, 8.45am to 5pm Friday. There is a book shop in each library. All courses have an **Information Technology** component. Access areas are available on each campus, explanatory materials are produced and IT staff will help if you have problems.

Milton Keynes

The 'library' is held in electronic format and is accessible from workstations around campus - not a lot of books here.

Bedford

Each campus has a library offering support for the courses taught on-site. Students have access to both main libraries. Polhill has a Primary Centre.

Lincoln

A library relating to the School of Applied Art and Design at the Lincoln City campus.

Culture on campus

Leicester

Drama: The Phoenix Arts Centre is jointly managed with the city council and shows student productions, as well as hosting visiting companies.

Film: The Department of Performing Arts organises the Leicester Film and Video Festival. The Union has a film club.

Music: A wide variety of events from Early Music to jazz. The University's department of performing arts has pioneered the Leicester International Dance Festival. There are major termly concerts and regular small scale recitals. The University Chorus and Orchestra were founded in 1993 and the University has the Schidlof Quartet in residence.

Bedford

The Bowen-West Community Theatre houses a number of touring productions each year. Larger scale companies mount productions in the Alexander Sports Hall. Polhill has an annual programme of major speakers invited by the Humanities Society which includes talks by experts with national and international reputations.

The Union

Leicester

Union Buildings and Trading Enterprises on both main campuses. The city site Union runs a 'real ale' bar, a long bar (refurbished), coffee bar and snack shop, a shop, two banks, travel shop and print shop and fax bureau.

Scraptoft offers a smaller scale Union building, a coffee bar, pizza bar, travel office, shop, bank, launderette and two bars. Discos and regular band nights and Scraptoft is host to the annual Grand Summer Ball.

The Union has a high turnover of £2,000,000 p.a. and employs 50 full-time staff plus hundreds of students on a part-time basis. Five sabbatical officers, and a ten-strong Executive Committee. More than 100 clubs and societies, sporting and not. This is an interactive, proactive Union, serving its students very well. The usual range of advisory services, and a Community Action Programme.

There are concerts two nights a week (featuring 'the stars of tomorrow'). Discos every Saturday night: 'the best night out in Leicester' according to the Prospectus... and the best student venue in the country, according to John Peel! The Arena has a capacity of over 1,000, and attracts big bands. The Union plans to open a smaller room for comedy and one-man shows. A monthly magazine, *Intasite*, keeps you up-to-date.

Milton Keynes

There is one sabbatical officer who, amongst other things, co-ordinates student representation within the University. The Union has space on the Kents Hill campus and provides a bar, smallish dance area and seating; used for gigs and discos. There is also a small shop.

Bedford

The Union elects three sabbatical officers and seven part-time executives. 15 non-sporting Clubs and Societies supported. The snackbar and shop on each campus provide all basics, food and stationery. The Union runs a bar at Lansdowne and one at Polhill. Entertainments vary, but include a number of live bands each term and weekly discos: Polhill's venue has a capacity of 880. Other attractions have included a hypnotist, theme discos and comedians. Drama and Dance have active societies.

Sport

Leicester

The Centre for Physical Education and Recreation, based at the John Sandford Sports Centre (City campus), has a team of coaches and advisors to enable you to participate in all sports whatever your level of competence. There is a full range of competitive sport . Facilities here: badminton and squash courts, multi-use court, multigym and fitness room, sauna and solarium. There are good municipal facilities closeby: see City section. Scraptoft facilities: gym, fitness studio, solarium, weights area and playing fields.

Milton Keynes

Students here automatically become members of the Open University Club, and have access to various facilities there: bars, restaurants, sports and recreation: the Open University is a very close neighbour.

Bedford

Sporting life at Bedford is active: 40 different sports clubs in all. Facilities are excellent and include a heated swimming pool, three gymnasia, a dance studio, sports grounds and sports centre. Physical education plays a part in many of the degree programmes offered here.

The House of Sport was established here in 1995 with support from the Sports Council. Sports development officers provide coaching and lecturing for students; the College also houses the regional offices of the National Coaching Federation.

Student welfare

Leicester

Leicester Student **Health Service** serves the student populations of both this University and Leicester University. There is a surgery daily at the city campus and three times weekly at Scraptoft. There is also a nursing sister in attendance on both campuses. Sick bay facilities include 12 beds and provide 24 hour care. There is a compulsory charge for this facility paid at the beginning of your course and covering your time here.

If you have legal problems, members of the Law Department staff or senior students can offer advice free of charge. University **counsellors** (3) are based at the city site, and are available on a part-time basis at the Scraptoft campus. The Student Support Unit will give information and advice a range of practical problems.

There are five Christian chaplains available to students of all faiths 24 hours a day. The Chaplaincy Centre has a library and quiet room for services and prayer meetings. The chaplains will put you in touch with your own faith's leader in the community.

Milton Keynes

There is a health centre near to campus where you are encouraged to register. On campus: a full-time counsellor. A University chaplain offers ecumenical support.

Bedford

Campuses have medical centres staffed by nurses. Lansdowne has a resident physiotherapist specialised in sports injuries. A full-time, professional counsellor and a part-time financial adviser are available. A Learning Support Programme helps students with learning concerns. A part-time ecumenical chaplaincy oversees religious welfare.

Lincoln

All centres have close links with local health practitioners.

Careers Service

Lincoln

Seminars and workshops are (often) timetabled into courses: opportunities, choices, interview and cv presentation are some of the topics covered. The main Careers Library is on the City campus; each campus has a careers centre.

Milton Keynes

The careers adviser holds one-to-one interviews and workshops for general advice. Careers library available

Bedford

Both campuses have careers information rooms. Lansdowne specialises in sports-related job opportunities. Polhill has computerised careers guidance programmes.

Students with special needs

Leicester

The Assistant Registrar will give you individual help and consideration. Contact the Course leader or Student Services for more information.

Milton Keynes

The campus offers few obstacles for people with mobility problems. If you have special needs, you should contact the Student Counsellor before applying.

Bedford

The campuses have modified access points for students with mobility problems.

Accommodation

Leicester

Accommodation at DMU Leicester is limited, and rules for allocating its 1,800 hall places are strict. All hall accommodation is given to first years. If you live within a fifty mile radius, it is likely you will be placed in lodgings on a five-day week basis and expected to go home at the weekends. If you live in or near Leicester, you will be expected to make your own arrangements.

Altogether, the University has 20 halls of residence here, 13 city based within three miles of the city campus and seven on the Scraptoft campus seven miles away. The University works a proportional allocation of rooms to different faculties, so you should have a good cross-section of students in hall with you. All halls have a resident tutor who looks after security and discipline and is a steadying influence.

Alternatively, you might be allocated a place in a house with three, four or five students (usually of the same discipline): this type of accommodation is self-catering.

The Accommodation Office regularly publishes a private sector housing list, and you should send for a list if you decide to find your own accommodation. There is also a guide to 'House Hunting in Leicester' for you if you are new to the city: you should send for a guide well in advance. The University runs a 'Find a Home' week over the summer for in-coming first years, to which you will be invited if you are not offered University accommodation.

Traditional halls

11 in all, seven on the Scraptoft campus. These halls provide you with breakfast and evening meals on weekdays. There are limited snack making facilities available for weekend cooking. The city halls vary between functional, purpose-built blocks and rather lovely conversions of old houses.

Costs (1995/96)

Single room:	£49.85 per week
Double room:	£45.80 per week
shared room:	£44.45 per week

Self-catering halls

Nine in all, all on the City campus. These also vary from the purpose built to the converted house. Some units are quite small (20 students); several are single sex.

Costs (1995/96)

Range from £25.60 to £41.20

Head tenancy scheme

The University runs a head tenancy scheme: 100 places.

Costs (1995/96)

£32 - £38 per week excluding fuel.

Approved Lodgings

The University will provide you with a list of approved lodgings.

Costs (1995/96)

bed, breakfast and evening meal
five day week: £38; seven day week: £52 per week

Private accommodation

Private accommodation is not the nightmare it is in many cities. Costs: around £32 per week excluding bills. The University keeps an extensive list of vetted lodgings. You join in the 'Find a Home' week.

Milton Keynes

There is a hall of residence ten minutes from campus and the University leases a range of accommodation from Milton Keynes Housing Association. All accommodation is self-catering. Resident tutors and senior students live at each site throughout the academic year. The Accommodation Office maintains a register of private lodgings and properties to rent. The University advises students to bear in mind the levels of bus service which choosing private accommodation: regularity of public transport varies.

Costs (1995/96)

Hall of residence: £43.00 per week for 39 weeks
Housing Association flats: £35.70 to £43.50 per week
Private sector: £38 to £45 per week

Bedford

440 places in halls of residence. Halls (3) are both catered (2) and self-catering (1). Private accommodation is easy to find. The University leases property and sublets it to students at competitive rents. There is cheap accommodation on offer during August and early September for students looking for a place to live, and the University also runs Find-a Home events here.

Costs (1995/96)

Catered hall (average): £44.50 per week
Self-catering hall (average): £36.20 per week
Private sector: £27.00 to £40.00 per week

Lincoln

Residential centres at Caythorpe and Riseholme campuses can accommodate 800 students. The City campus offers a list of private and approved lodgings, all inspected. Costs: around £30 per week.

Mature students

The University as a whole welcomes applications from mature students. Entry standards required will depend on the judgement of Admissions tutors.

THE CITIES/TOWNS

Leicester
See the University of Leicester's entry.

Milton Keynes (160,000, including surrounding area)

Milton Keynes is considered to be a highly successful version of New Town planning: an architect friend of ours said so, and the range, variety and vigour of the community life recorded in its publicity brochures do seem to validate the notion. If you like New Towns. Many do like the careful planning: non traffic jammed wide access roads which ease you round the city (central shopping pedestrianised, of course); the care with which health and community centres relate to and serve their communities: the well-planned and landscaped, sociologically distributed housing developments. A veritable brave new world, and very attractive in its way; wearing an air of being new.

Range of entertainments from sport to nightclubs, open air concerts in the Bowl arena, leisure centres, cinemas. There will be no shortage of focus for your more frivolous leisure time.

Bedford (population: 138,000)

Bedford is an ancient county town, granted its charter in 1166, built along the banks of the river Great Ouse. The river still plays a major part in the life of the town, and you will be here to witness the annual Regatta each May, and the two day Bedford River Festival which happens every second year over the Spring Bank holiday. The town's buildings are a mix of styles from the medieval through to now. It is very much a county market town with a strong sense of its own heritage. The market is still held on Wednesdays and Saturdays. One of the Bedford's most distinctive features is its Embankment, planted by the Victorians and now a beautiful park.

John Bunyan was born here. The town has a museum and various buildings preserved in his memory. The Cecil Higgins Art Gallery and Museum has a more general collection, including ceramics and glass from the 18th century and a renowned collection of watercolours and prints.

The town centre has the full range of usual high street shops and boutiques set in arcades and boulevards.

Entertainments: theatres - the Bowen-West theatre on Lansdowne campus, the Civic Theatre and Mill Theatre at Sharnbrook (shows some excellent new work); **music** - main venue is the Corn Exchange which houses a full range of entertainment from classical to pop; **cinema** - Aspects Leisure Park has a six screen complex; **restaurants** - a range, American diners, pizzerias, Chinese and Indian; **sport and leisure** - rowing and boating on the river and boating lakes; the Bedford Oasis leisure pool complex; a municipal golf course.

Lincoln (population 90,000)

City in name and status, but medium-sized market town in nature, Lincoln is the commercial and social focus for an enormous region. It rises abrupt - though not very high - from a vast area of low-lying fenland: a wide, empty, rural landscape which surrounds and contains the city and slows its pace.

The ridge, which gives the city its commanding position and lends sky-line drama to its cathedral and castle, originally gave it a safe place above the swampy lowlands. The cathedral is wonderful - one of the country's gems - and the area it dominates, ancient, cobbled, quaint, has great charm. Buildings and remains of buildings, marking the centuries from Roman times to Victorian, cluster around and down the hill.

Beyond the hem of the hill, on land made safe by drainage, the modern quarter, with its industry and commerce has developed. The shopping centre is pedestrianised and offers a good range from quality boutiques to chain-stores. Brayford Pool, in the city centre, is now a marina with facilities for rowing, canoeing and river cruises. It is a reminder of Lincoln's watery past that it was once a Roman port.

Entertainments: the **cinema** has three screens and has recently been refurbished. **The Theatre Royal** offers a varied programme and there is a good range of **restaurants**, particularly in the vicinity of the cathedral, where you can find excellent food in historic hostelries with an atmosphere of olde worlde conviviality. Not a cheap place. There are three **leisure centres** (all affiliated to schools and with only limited open access) and ten-pin bowling.

ESCAPE ROUTES

Leicester

For Escape Routes and Communications, see the University of Leicester's entry.

Milton Keynes

The landscape around struck us as rather flat - or low - rolling - but then, we do live among real hills. Very pleasant in its way, with a number of interesting halls and parks (including one safari) to visit.

Communications: M1 very close (minutes away). Direct rail routes to Birmingham, London and Glasgow. Coach service network. London (Heathrow), Luton and Birmingham airports are within one hour's drive (barring roadworks). If you have a private plane, it can be accommodated at Cranfield airfield, very nearby.

Bedford

The countryside around Bedford is gentle, arable and dotted with limestone villages. The areas history can be chronicled through its churches and old buildings - the medieval Moot Hall at Elstow, Bushmead Priory. Woburn Abbey stately home and safari park is nearby.

Communications: Trains to London take 45 minutes. You can also catch trains directly to the south coast and to most points north. Bedford is between the M1 and A1. Bus services to London and Cambridge are regular. Luton airport is just 20 miles from Bedford.

Lincoln

Lincoln is markedly off the beaten track, and there are not many easy escapes from here. Gentle cycling country with pleasant villages scattered for exploration.

Communications: 15 miles from the A1. A two hour train journey from London.

University of Derby

Kedleston Road
Derby
DE22 1GB
Telephone: 01332 622222

University Charter date: 1992
Derby is a small university with around 4,000 full-time students, a high proportion of whom are mature. The University has four sites: two larger, both outside the town and two Art & Design centres in Derby. Degrees are fully modular with various methods of assessments: there are some examinations for some courses. The University can house 90% of first years.

THE CAMPUS

Derby is one of the newest universities and was unique in being the first CHE which has not migrated up through polytechnic status. The University has four sites, which are linked by several bus routes.

Kedleston Road
Two miles north of the city, by the ring road, the largest of the University's campuses rises above surrounding suburbia. The buildings are set back on grassy banks, landscaped with young trees, beyond grass pitches.

The dominant features of the campus are the 1960's, ten storey, glass and panel teaching blocks. A newer building seems sharply white in contrast, lots of glass and prefabricated panels - a construction widely used in new university development. The new Atrium has made a big difference: with a capacity for 4,000, it is sometimes used for balls - formal and informal.

The central small courtyard has a small fish pond and benches built into brick paving. Main social areas (Student Union, Student Services and Refectory) are grouped together around the courtyard. The refectory is furnished as a 'bistro' and is a pleasant break from an atmosphere which can otherwise seem dominantly functional. The Student Union area (bar and billiards), is small and cramped. Narrow and cramped, too, is the corridor housing some Administration Offices - including Counsellors and the Vice-Chancellor! Some odd contrasts.

Faculties here: Science and Technology, Art and Design and the Business School.

Mickleover
Off the ring road, and down a quiet avenue, is the University's second campus in the modest housing estates of Mickleover, a suburb to the east of the city centre. Mostly single storey, and white surfaced, the buildings are a collection of 1970's-style modular units, good quality and well designed.

The buildings are well spaced and landscaped. The site covers 70 acres and is home to the majority of the University's sports facilities. Playing fields drop away from the buildings on neat terraces which are bordered by agricultural land. Road noise is only a distant hum and does not impinge upon the studious, but relaxed atmosphere.

Faculties here: Education, Humanities and Social Sciences and Community Studies.

City Centre: Green Lane
The Graphic Design and Film and Video departments are housed in an old 19th century building within walking distance of the city centre.

Britannia Building
A converted 19th century mill building which houses a large proportion of the Art and Design School.

Cars
Parking space at Kedleston Road and Mickleover seems ample; at least, we had no problems when we visited.

Learning Resources

A new Learning Centre will open in 1997 on Kedleston Road. Each site has a **library**, and librarians are assigned to the Faculties relating to their own library. Total number of volumes: 250,000; over 1,500 current periodicals. The **Computing Services** are based at Kedleston Road and advice on any aspect of the computing facilities can be obtained from reception here, or from site Help Desks. Most of the equipment is networked and on open access.

Culture on campus

Art: The distinguished Ballantyne Collection of ceramics adds a note of elegance, housed in a spacious gallery and well worth a visit.

Music: The University runs a series of lunchtime concerts given by local musicians, students and University groups.

The Union

The Union's Welfare Officer is available on the various site offices at different times and the Union runs a nightline service, Community Action, Mature Student Groups and Women's Groups. The Union runs two shops and six bars: the latest is the Riverside Bar and the largest, the Richardson, has a capacity of 1,100. Mickleover has a venue capacity of 450 and is used to host visiting bands. Drinks promotions, hypnotists and quizzes are regular features of entertainments. *Eclipse* magazine is produced weekly and distributed to all campuses and halls. The Union sponsors 60 societies.

Sport

The Sports Federation organises the competition of University teams within the UAU and promotes sport at the University. There are 30 sports clubs. A series of fitness classes are run each week. Facilities are split between Kedleston Road (three grass pitches, cinder running track, small gymnasium with 2 badminton courts, 1 basketball court or 4-a-side football. Also a fitness room with multigym and other exercising equipment) and Mickleover (four grass pitches, one Redgra hockey pitch, cinder running track, small gymnasium, basketball badminton and volleyball courts and a 25 metre swimming pool).

Student welfare

A Drop-in Service is offered by nurses at the Kedleston Road and Mickleover campuses; they will visit other campuses on request. Trained **counsellors** and **welfare advisors** provide information and run group workshops on welfare issues. The University **chaplain** runs the Religious Resource Centre. Local provision is good for all major religions.

Careers Service
The main sites have careers information rooms with access to computerised guidance. One to one interviews, talks and workshops are all arranged.

Students with special needs
The University has a Deafness Studies Unit and has special interest in dyslexia.

Accommodation

There are over 2,400 places (accounting for approximately 90% of first years). All places are self-catered and the majority of students are in single study bedrooms. Residences are near both main sites or the city centre and range from new, purpose-built developments with good facilities to converted Victorian houses.

Costs (1995/96)
Single room: £38.92 - £50.96 (ensuite) x 35 weeks
Double room: £33.04 - £36.26 x 35 weeks
Private accommodation: £35.00 - £38.00 per week

Mature students

The University runs a Credit Accumulation Modular Scheme for which you can apply directly. The Foundation stage can be taken instead of Access course. The Pre-Entry Guidance Co-ordinator for Mature Students in the Centre for Access and Continuing Education can advise on suitable entry routes for other courses. The nursery has 40 places for 2-5 year olds.

THE CITY (population 220,000)

Much of Derby today relates to the city's heyday as a centre of the industrial revolution. In fact Derby claims to have been at the very heart of things: the first ever mass production factory (a silk mill) opened here in 1717.

The city centre has remained compact and contains many of Derby's 600 listed buildings. The Cathedral Church of All Saints has a 65 metre tower: a good, quick orientation guide. The Cathedral is at the northern end of the pedestrian precinct, which runs down past the Guildhall (with its ornate clock tower) and the Market Hall. The Victorian market hall has been restored; here and the Eagle Centre market, are good territory for bargain hunting.

You will find splendid clusters of Georgian townhouses as you walk along the streets around the centre. These are intermingled with newer buildings, some not exactly harmonious with their surroundings. Indeed Derby's more modern developments are not very impressive. This is a fairly large industrial town: do not be beguiled by its 'city' status into expecting affluence and high style.

There are three main shopping centres, whose range is repeated on out-of-town retail estates. Derby is a mecca for bargains: factory shops abound and in general the cost of living is low. Older shopping streets such as Sadlergate retain a little of Derby's original character and cater for the more off-beat tastes.

The River Derwent flows close to the city centre. Its banks have been landscaped to form parks and gardens.

Theatre: The Assembly Rooms are the city's main live arts venue. The Derby Playhouse and its studio theatre are in regular use by professional and amateur companies.

Music: The Guildhall has free lunchtime recitals and has Jazz and Folk evenings. The Assembly Rooms' concerts range from classical to rock.

Cinema: The UCI and Showcase cinemas for general releases. The Metro (part of the University's Green Lane site) shows alternative films. Over 20 screens in all.

Nightlife: Derby is a haven for the pub goer: Ye Olde Dolphin is the oldest, dating from 1530. Sadlergate is the centre of the city's nightlife with the most popular pubs, clubs and a wide range of restaurants.

Sport: Two sports centres. Various parks provide two golf courses and tennis facilities. The football team, the Rams, play at the Baseball ground.

ESCAPE ROUTES

The Peak district looms to the north; walks meander through valleys and over hills. To the east, roads become lanes, hedges grow high and villages are charming. Chatsworth is the most famous of the historic houses within range but there are many other halls and gardens. Other attractions include Alton Towers and the Donnington race track for more rowdy outings.

Communications

Derby remains an important rail junction with frequent **intercity** connections to Birmingham, London and Sheffield. The **M1** is 10 minutes away; the **M42** only 20 minutes away. Bus connections are extensive. East Midlands **airport** is about 15 minutes travelling time away.

Keele University

Staffordshire
ST5 5BG
Telephone: 01782 621111

University Charter date: 1962

Keele is a small university with 5,000 full-time students, 4,000 of whom are undergraduates. All teaching and university accommodation is on a single campus (617 acres), two miles from Newcastle-under-Lyme. The principle of Keele's degrees has not changed since the University's inception: students should have a flexible and broad-based learning experience. The majority of students study two subjects and, unusually, can mix science and non-science subjects in joint honours. All courses are modular and are assessed by a combination of coursework and exam.

Most single first years are guaranteed a place in University residences, on campus.

THE CAMPUS

You can see the University from the M6 and the motorway forms the southern boundary of the estate; but access is not as easy as it sounds, since the nearest junctions north and south are some miles away.

The University estate is about two miles west of Newcastle-under-Lyme, on the edge of the sprawling conurbation including Stoke-on-Trent and Hanley. The campus has the good fortune to be over the hill and round the corner from the Newcastle townscape and borders on land which begins to roll.

The estate originally was the parkland setting of Keele Hall, the pleasant sandstone 19th century manor house which now gives the campus its touch of class and architectural interest. The site occupies 617 landscaped acres, including woods and small lakes: this balances out the building pattern which, for such a small university, is intensive.

The campus is well laid out. At its centre is a remarkable, large chapel, built in 1965 in dark brick, a stark rectangle with two end-turrets. This unusual structure gives interest to the focal centre of the campus which it shares with the large Union building, the library, a group of shops (including a bookshop, newsagent and supermarket).

Most of the teaching buildings are grouped west of centre, with the curve of the Chancellor's Building (housing a number of departments) varying the geometric blocks. Some departments are housed in Keele Hall itself, together with one of the refectories and some administrative functions.

The sports centre and playing fields provide a green screen to the north west; the rest of the site blends outward through trees to the staff residences, the halls of residence, the University's observatory on a hilltop, or to open country to the north.

The four student hall complexes are set around the site, to the main compass-points.

A high proportion of the staff live, with their families, on the campus itself, and most of those who do not, live nearby. This means that areas of the site, more peripheral than the student halls, are occupied by small estates of houses and flats for staff.

Cars
Cars must be left in halls of residence car-parks and must display a permit.

Learning Resources

The main **library** houses all books, a total of almost 500,000 and has seating for 650 students. Open late every day, but closed on Sunday mornings.

Keele's **Computer Centre** provides computing services to the whole University. Over 1,000 terminals and PCs are available in departments around the campus and a local network provides access to the Internet and world-wide-web and other facilities. The Computer Centre is open until the late evening.

The University's **modern languages** building has a computer laboratory and two language labs available for private study in French, German, Russian, Latin, Old English, EFL, Spanish, Polish, Japanese and Chinese.

Culture on campus

Drama: The Drama Society organises studio productions and an annual Shakespeare production. A major aim of the society is to encourage original work by Keele students. The Department of Modern Languages puts on performances in French and German.

Music: 'Keele Concerts Society', working with the Music Department, presents an annual subscription series of 14/15 concerts: many feature internationally known artists. The Department also runs an extracurricular lecture programme. Keele Philharmonic Orchestra and Chorus meet weekly and put on two concerts each semester. A variety of other musical activity available.

The Union

The Union organises student social life through societies, events and sports clubs. There are five bar areas (all open relatively late); two venues, one with a capacity of 2,500. A large disco and lighting rig liven up evenings: discos, three films, comedy nights and live gigs each week. Rooms for indoor recreation, television, reading, music practice and meetings. Also a 'daily selection of traders' in the Student Union concourse. Other amenities: a diner, restaurant, two shops, The Golfer's Arms (overlooking the golf course) and a book exchange.

You can join in local community help schemes through the University's Voluntary Service, Community Action and Conservation Volunteers groups. The Union has an Advice Unit which provides information and help on a range of issues. The Job Shop has lists of vacancies on and around campus.

Several Union publications: the usual alternative prospectus and a newsheet (*Junction 15*). The KUBE radio station broadcasts seven days a week.

Sport

The leisure centre on campus has a Fitness Centre which houses sports halls, a synthetic sports pitch, gymnasium, seven squash courts, climbing wall and dance studio. It also has a restaurant, bar and hair shop. There is a charge for the fitness centre and for squash. Playing fields cover 46 acres: an athletics track, lacrosse, soccer and rugby pitches, netball and tennis courts (12 hard-courts), three cricket squares and an all-weather floodlit hockey pitch.

There are over 40 sports clubs and a recreational coaching scheme: archery, badminton, ballroom dancing, fencing, jazz-rock-ballet, roller-skating, and various other sports and activities. Instruction courses carry a small fee.

You can also, of course, use facilities on a private, casual basis.

Student welfare

The University **health centre** offers NHS consultation and a dental service, but not 24-hour cover. A range of specialised clinics is available. The Union runs **counselling services** and Nightline. The University also has counsellors. The chapel is unusually active in Keele. **Christian worship** has been significant in the University since its inception. Three full-time chaplains - Anglican, Free Church and Roman Catholic - in all, with a small but active Jewish Society, an active body of Muslims for whom the University makes prayer rooms available.

Careers Service

The Service offers individual interviews, group sessions on study skills and runs workshops on interview technique and filling in application forms, as well as Insight into Management courses; has computer-assisted systems and a well-stocked information room.

Students with special needs

Access to some buildings might pose difficulties. You should contact the Admissions and Recruitment Office before you apply. There are some specially adapted ground floor rooms and kitchens and the University will try and assist you if you require a Community Service Volunteer. Accommodation on campus is guaranteed for the duration of your course.

Accommodation

Most single first year students are guaranteed a place in University residences. If you hold Keele as either your firm or insurance offer, the University will place you in University accommodation if you return your form by the end of August for the first and at least one other year of your course. Clearing candidates are not guaranteed accommodation, but the University makes every effort to find accommodation for you.

Halls of residence

The four halls (between 600 and 1,100 places each) consist of groups of residential blocks: three are on campus, one is in Keele village. Accommodation is in study-bedrooms. Each hall elects a council which organises regular social events, including sports and discos, balls and films. Facilities include music rooms, bars, games rooms, television rooms, computer suites, launderettes, bicycle sheds and car-parking places. Some rooms in Lindsay Hall and Horwood Hall have ensuite facilities. All rooms are self-catering, or you can eat in the restaurants on campus. Security is looked after by Assistant Wardens.

Costs (1995/96)

Halls of residence: £27 (basic) to £43 (en suite) per week for a 38 week session including heat and light.

Private accommodation

Private accommodation is available, but the best is snapped up quickly. The main student area is Silverdale, two miles from the University. Costs range from £30 to £40 per week in a bedsit.

Mature students

You need not have passed the normal examination hurdles; you must be able to demonstrate academic commitment by having recently taken a systematic course of study. A majority of Keele's mature students opt to take a four year course, including the Foundation Year. The University runs an Open Lecture course, a programme of Adult Continuing Education, and supports recognised Access courses.

Nursery

Close to the centre of campus. Run for children of staff and students. Places for 50 children of students from three months to five years. Early application is necessary.

THE TOWNS

NEWCASTLE-UNDER-LYME

(population: 119,000)

Newcastle-under-Lyme is your nearest population centre. Its main street is pedestrianised with a market place in the centre, making the street's width of boulevard proportions. This is the traditional market centre for the region. The buildings flanking the market place have a Victorian solidity, with varying roof-heights. Recent development has increased the town's shopping facilities by a third. The shop range here is reasonably wide, with national names vying with local traders. The town has the aura of a place unruffled by outside influence, and, considering its population, its sense of permanence is not surprising.

STOKE-ON-TRENT

(population: 244,000)

Your nearest large centre is Stoke-on-Trent, an amalgamation of the six towns (don't let Arnold Bennett confuse you). Stoke's population is 245,000 and its people are still employed in the old pottery industries for which the area is famous. The city has reclaimed much of its old industrial 'eyesores', which are now grassed and planted. The canals, once industrial waterways, are now open for leisure cruises, although you can still see working barges. Here, there are theatres, concerts and lively nightlife. The six towns retain their identities and facilities; the area's main shopping district is Hanley, where you will find most major chain stores. Each of the six towns has its own market.

Theatre: The area depends largely on amateur dramatics. There is the Theatre Royal in Hanley and Queen's Theatre in Burslem. The Victoria Theatre at Hartshill was the first professional theatre company to play in the round and has been internationally acclaimed.

Music: Concerts are held at the Victoria Hall in Hanley. There are various folk and jazz clubs in the area, including a Morris and clog-dancing workshop.

Cinemas: The Regional Film Theatre is in Stoke, and there is a new eight-screen cinema in the Festival Park Leisure Centre. Otherwise you should go to Hanley which has a commercial cinema.

Nightlife: There are 12 nightclubs in the area, and beyond the towns are country pubs down country lanes.

Sport: The area has a number of sports clubs, including a ski-club and speedway stadium. Newcastle has a golf club. The Festival Park Leisure Centre has a 'Waterworld', dry-ski slope, snooker club, 30-lane tenpin bowling, bars and a restaurant.

ESCAPE ROUTES

Staffordshire is synonymous with the Potteries, with the Industrial Revolution, but that was all a long time ago, and Keele is right on the edge of very beautiful countryside. The north east of Staffordshire is open moorland and the bottom edge of the Peak District. The valleys of the rivers Manifold and Churnet are exceptionally beautiful. Along the Manifold gorge, bones and teeth of ancient beasts have been found. The area has some pretty villages.

Stoke-on-Trent is your nearest city, although there are several conurbations to go at in the area. This is home to some of the most famous potteries in England, including Wedgwood, Royal Doulton and Spode. Nearby, at Smallthorne, is an Elizabethan mansion - Ford Green Hall - which is now a museum.

West of Stoke is Cheadle, which has - two miles northeast - the Hawksmoor Nature Reserve. This covers 250 acres of moorland and marshes, with nature trails and a large population of bird life. East again is Alton Towers, one of the country's great pleasure parks set in the parkland of a 'ruined' Gothic 19th century mansion. The gardens offer much: exotic plants, fountains, conservatories, as well as miniature railways and boating lakes. And now there is the fun park; a good break from study.

Communications

You will have to go to Stoke for your **rail connections**. From here, access is fairly comprehensive.

Coach links, likewise, become more far-reaching the further you travel to a large centre. The **M6** is your fastest route to everywhere else.

University of Leicester

University Road
Leicester
LE1 7RH
Telephone: 0116 252 2522

University Charter date: 1957

Leicester is a medium-sized university with c.7,000 undergraduate students on full-time programmes and c.2,000 full-time postgraduates taught on a single campus one mile from the city centre. The University offers a full range of academic degrees, including medicine. Most programmes are modularised. Assessment is by various examination types; some practical exercises might be included. Accommodation is guaranteed for first years who live beyond a reasonable commuting distance from Leicester and who confirm their places by August 31st.

THE CAMPUS

Leicester remained a small provincial university college from 1921 to 1945, when it began to expand, receiving its charter in 1957. The rate and nature of its growth have allowed it to retain, as a matter of committed philosophy, good features of its collegiate atmosphere.

The University stands only about one mile from the city centre, but wide surrounding fields and a large cemetery opposite the main building cast a deceptive aura of country calm. Standing on slightly raised ground (local hills are not high), the shape of the campus controls the distribution of buildings so that no complex can become oppressive.

'Arrival' impressions are of elegance - the original 1837 building is a very fine example of Georgian architecture in vine-covered, light-grey brick with white edges. The rest of the site is modern, often dramatically so; dark glass and steel, prism roofs, a light brick and glass high-rising (architecturally distinguished) engineering block, a 'suitable' white tower block for the arts. A well-set campus.

Cars

You may bring your car to a hall of residence if the warden agrees (check first). The University site is open to cars after 5.15pm on weekdays and all weekends. No problems with bicycles - this is good cycling country.

Academic services

Leicester's main **library** is a modern five-storey building with a good atmosphere. Over a million books, as well as other forms of information; 4,500 current periodicals; seating for over 1,100. Three main branch libraries: Clinical Sciences, Education and Chemistry Library. The main library is open until 10pm during the week, until 6pm on Saturdays and from 3pm to 9pm on Sundays.

Computers: The Computer Centre offers certificated courses in Information Technology to non-computer science students. Open access computer laboratories are available in the main teaching buildings, in some cases, for 24 hours a day. The campus network has access to the world wide web.

Languages: The University has a Language Centre aimed at increasing language proficiency amongst staff and students, and used by the local business community. The Centre has three laboratories and an 80 place self-access area which you can use for a small subscriptions.

Culture on campus

Drama: the University has working links with the Haymarket and Phoenix theatres in Leicester as well as its own theatre. Student productions are often staged.

Music: Campus concerts are frequent: lunchtime recitals by student ensembles or visiting artists. Two student orchestras, choirs and a wind band. The University has practice rooms and can arrange tuition for instrumental and vocal training. There are a number of music scholarships for first year students of any discipline in the form of free tuition: you must have reached Grade VIII or equivalent before you are eligible for a scholarship.

Art: The University Studio has facilities for painting and sculpture open to students: tuition in sculpture, drawing and painting techniques can be arranged.

Film: The Union runs a film club, with weekly showings.

The Union

The Union is housed in the Percy Gee building (centre-campus). It contains the Pitt Stop Food Court, a bar, two nightclubs - the Asylum and the Venue, a hall (for general meetings, bands, film shows..), common rooms, TV rooms, music practice rooms, launderette, shop, travel agency, bank and legal advice centre.

The Union sponsors around 100 non-sporting and 40 sports clubs and societies, and runs a community action group - 'Contact'.

Also, three welfare officers who are particularly helpful on practical issues, such as housing. The Union takes its welfare role seriously and regards it as one of its main functions. It runs a range of welfare services, has a hardship fund for students in dire straits, a Nightline service and support groups in a number of stress-related areas. Self-defence classes and a night minibus are available for women. The Education Unit gives help with course decisions. As a final flourish to taking its role admirably seriously, the Union runs a property management scheme which inspects private rented accommodation.

A very lively entertainments programme: over 100 bands a year, up to 20 big-name bands in one term, 8 discos a week, Mega Discos, termly balls, cheap beer evenings...The Students' Union newspaper *Ripple* publicises all events. The Union runs various commercial services, hires out its building for social functions, and employs over 50 full-time members of staff.

Sport

Two large sports halls (one adjacent to the Oadby halls of residence; one on the main campus) and a sports studio offer indoor facilities for table tennis, squash, snooker, an activities studio, two weights rooms etc., and a full range of outdoor activities is promoted by the Union's Sports Association (40 affliliated sports clubs).

Two sports grounds (25 acres in all): one at Wigston and, near the halls of residence complex at Oadby, a second, which includes one of the finest athletics tracks in the Midlands, an all-weather area, a good physiotherapy service, modern dressing rooms, a large number of tennis courts and five-a-side football pitches.

You will have to purchase a Sportscard annually, for a modest fee, which entitles you to use all the facilities, hire equipment and to attend coaching and fitness courses (a Fitness Programme runs alongside the Coaching Programme: eight weeks' coaching in your chosen activity). A full programme of aerobics and circuit training is run at Oadby and the main campus, early morning, lunchtime and evening.

Student welfare

The **Student Health Service is** run along the lines of an NHS group practice, and caters for the needs of De Montfort as well as Leicester University. The surgery is just off-campus and is open twice a day. The Sick Bay is in the same building and provides in-patient care, with nursing staff available throughout the day and night. The University has a professional, confidential **counselling service**, covering health problems and special needs including dyslexia. **Chaplaincies:** Each of the principal Christian denominations appoints a chaplain There are representatives of the Jewish and Hindu communities and an advisor for Muslims. They share The Gatehouse on campus. A room is set aside for prayer and meetings.

Careers Service
Each department has a careers tutor who keeps a monitoring eye on the vocational implications of your course. Departments organise careers talks and seminars on job applications.

The Careers Service has computer-aided careers advice and information on vacation work, courses and experience. The Service offers mock interviews and workshops which include 'Being interviewed' and 'Making successful applications'. Resources are shared with De Montfort University so you can attend their events too.

Students with special needs
The University is home to the Richard Attenborough Centre for Disability and the Arts. Some accommodation has been adapted for students with special needs. The Study Support Centre gives help, assistance and advice.

Accommodation

You are guaranteed a place in University accommodation if you live outside reasonable commuting distance, have firmly accepted your place by May 31st and confirmed this by August 31st. Altogether the University has 1,841 places in halls of residence and 1,980 places in University houses (3,821 places in all). In addition, the University has recently begun to lease flats from Leicester City Council, in Goscote House, a tower block near the campus.

Halls of residence
There are six in all: five in a complex at Oadby (four kilometres from campus), which includes a new annexe of 150 ensuite rooms and one at Knighton, halfway between Oadby and campus. There is a special bus service morning and evening, a frequent normal service, and a women's minibus at night.

All halls are warden-controlled. They vary in size (276-418 places) and in facilities offered: mostly single study-bedrooms (some first years can expect to share); full board (except weekday lunches); some kitchen facilities, sporting and social activities (from discos to formal balls; from soccer to chess), common rooms, TV rooms, bars.

Hall buildings are a mix of large Edwardian houses and purpose-built blocks, adding their own beautiful grounds and sports fields to their suburban environment.

Costs (1995/96)
For three ten-week terms excluding vacations:
Single room: £1,849 - £2,125
Double room: £1,579 (at most)
Costs include heating and cleaning.

Student houses
Self-catering (or cafeteria facilities on campus or at the Knighton complex). The largest of the self-catering complexes is at Knighton (one and a half kilometres from campus), others nearer. The vast majority are purpose-built, but some are older houses, converted to provide similar facilities.

Each house contains ten single study-bedrooms and a shared kitchen, bathroom and utility room. Each site has a launderette.

The Ratcliffe complex at Knighton has a takeaway food service, as well as a self-service restaurant, a bar, a common room and a shop. Sporting and social activities are organised.

Costs (1995/96)
Single room: £1,284.78 for 38 weeks, including Christmas and Easter vacations.
Putney Road houses: £39.90 per week for either 38 or 51 weeks.
Costs include heat and light.

Student flats
The flats in Goscote House are self-contained with private kitchen and bathroom. There are bedsits, and one-bedroomed flats which are suitable for two people. The flats are let for 52 weeks.

Costs (1995/96)
£48 to £63 per week, inclusive of heat and utilities

Private accommodation
Average rent around £32 per week. There is an information service. The University and Students' Union are both very helpful.

Mature students

Pre-entry advice is available (Introduction to the University of Leicester, budget planning etc.) The Admissions Office will send you a Mature Students Booklet. An active Mature Students' Association. The University may subsidise childcare: this is means tested.

THE CITY (population: 286,000)

The western suburban approaches to Leicester stretch green, tree-spread avenues close into the city: by the time you reach the urban core of backstreet housing, you are very close to the city centre. Eastern approaches are less pleasant, but again, quickly give way to leafy suburbs and patches of open country. There is no sense of entering an overwhelmingly dense city landscape: indeed someone who lives here said recently that Leicester is more village than city, and that people at bus-stops are very nosy. Comfortable in scale, varied and idiosyncratic in its development - a city to receive you with ease. Its railway station is charming: old mellow brick and graceful lines.

Leicester is an ancient city; traces of its history turn up in odd corners and balance its modern developments. Near de Montfort University there are almshouses founded in the 14th century, the Newarke Chantry House (built in 1512), an old stone arch leading to the small but very pretty Castle Yard Close which contains a few lovely old houses. The excellent market has occupied the same site for more than 700 years; the medieval Guildhall is one of the most remarkable in England.

New Walk offers a vista of beautiful Regency and later buildings and was laid out in 1785 to link the fine De Montfort Hall with the city centre. The Hall stands on top of a hill (by Leicester standards) and faces the wide green field-spaces of Victoria Park - a medium sized affair with tree-ways planted in straight lines. The road down to it has buildings which remain gracious and domestic above their office or shop function. From the hill you can see straight across the city and the rolling countryside beyond looks very near.

New buildings and precincts in and around the city centre have livened the rather bland face of its shopping facilities - which are very good. The central area is largely pedestrianised and mixes new arcades with by-ways of secondhand shops. It manages to retain the air of a large regional market town (which it is) more than of a large modern city.

Leicester is Environment City on a World League scale and is certainly the most environmentally/eco-friendly city in the UK, with a number of 'green' experiments and initiatives to its credit.

Theatres: The Haymarket Theatre and Studio is Leicester's main entertainment centre and venue for touring companies. A varied programme, with a positive policy to encourage new drama. The Phoenix Arts Centre has a lively, interesting range of 'in house' productions, touring groups, film and music.

Music: The De Montfort Hall holds concerts of classical music. This is also the main venue for rock and pop concerts. Leicester has several jazz and folk clubs, with events most nights of the week.

Cinema: The Phoenix cinema (in the Arts Centre) shows an excellent programme of 'art' films, foreign, avant-garde, new and classic, and is Leicester's Regional Film Theatre. Two Cannon cinemas and one Odeon: 9 screens in all.

Nightlife: Leicester's nightlife is varied, with discos and dinner dances, casinos and winebars.

Sport: For spectators, Leicester offers Leicester City Football Club and Leicester Rugby Club, county cricket and a racecourse, American football and basketball. For those more active, the city has eight swimming baths, rollerskating, cycling, athletics, two 18 hole municipal golf-courses, tennis, bowls, squash and badminton. Close to the city campus are the City's swimming pool, athletics track, cycling track and all-weather pitches.

ESCAPE ROUTES

The countryside around Leicester is rolling, green and pleasant with a maze of country lanes flanked by hedgerows. Charnwood Forest, covering thirty square miles, lies north and west of the city. The area is ideal for easy walking and cycling. Less than 20 miles away is Rutland Water, one of Europe's largest man-made lakes, where you can sail or water-ski or picnic.

Leicester has fast access to Birmingham and Nottingham with their nightlife and activity, as well as to Warwickshire and Stratford.

Communications

Leicester is on the main line from Sheffield to London St Pancras, with **trains** running hourly. Direct lines to Birmingham and the Midlands, as well as Nottingham and Derby. **Coach services** are extensive. The **M1** runs close to Leicester and the **M69** links with the **M6** just south of the city. Fast access both to the East Midlands **Airport** to the north and Birmingham **Airport**: the first has flights to places in both Britain and the rest of Europe; the second has major international services.

Lincoln and Humberside University (Lincoln)

Lincoln University campus
PO Box 182
Lincoln LN2 4YF
telephone: 01522 882000

This is a new University campus which will open for the 1997 intake of students. It is the twin of the Humberside campus of the University of Lincoln and Humberside and will adopt Humberside's courses from Grimsby by 1999/2000. The site is presently being developed in Lincoln's city centre. The campus will take 1,100 full-time students in 1997; the population will rise to 2,400 by 1999/2000. Degrees will be modular within a subject framework and be assessed by a combination of coursework and examination. All first years will be guaranteed accommodation, either in halls of residence or in approved rooms.

THE CAMPUS

This completely new University results from a new kind of partnership between local government, local businesses, community groups and European funding bodies. The campus, on riverside land around Brayford Pool in the city centre is still in its early stages of development. We have not yet visited, but shall do so before the next edition. The siting of the University means that the city will be on your doorstep. Courses at Lincoln: Communications, Criminology, Economics, Health Studies, Humanities.

Grimsby

The School of Applied Technology, presently sites at Grimsby will transfer to Lincoln in 1999. Students entering in 1997 will spend two years on the Nun's Corner site, just outside Grimsby, reached through leafy suburbs. This site is very much a 1960s college, with playing fields but no architectural distinction. Grimsby itself is small, with little active nightlife; you will rely on the activities of the Student Union.

Student Life at Lincoln

Student life, at present, is all to come. Sports facilities might be provided by the University of by the kind of association with other local organisations which is the founding spirit of place here. Advice and counselling services are taking root and an ecumenical chaplaincy is in place. No medical services as yet: you will have to go local.

A careers service is stocked with appropriate literature and computer assisted guidance; advisers will visit the campus on a part-time basis. Special needs applicants should contact the Division of Assistive Resources and Technology who will assess and advise and can provide support equipment for a number of disabilities.

Accommodation

The University guarantees accommodation to all first years, either in halls of residence or in approved student rooms. Halls of residence on campus provide 322 self-catered single study-bedrooms (280 ensuite) in groups of five or six sharing.

Costs (1996/97)

ensuite: £44.00 per week x 42 weeks
partial ensuite: £40.00 per week x 42 weeks
Fuel costs included.

Private accommodation

Houses or flats, checked and approved by the University in consultation with landlords. £30 - £35 per week excluding light, heat and water rates.

Lincoln (population 90,000)

City in name and status, but medium-sized market town in nature, Lincoln is the commercial and social focus for an enormous region. It rises abrupt - though not very high - from a vast area of low-lying fenland. The cathedral is wonderful - one of the country's finest - and the area it dominates, ancient, cobbled, quaint, has great charm.

Beyond the hem of the hill, on land made safe by drainage, the modern quarter, with its industry and commerce has developed. The shopping centre is pedestrianised and offers a good range from quality boutiques to chain-stores. Brayford Pool, in the city centre, is now a marina with facilities for rowing, canoeing and river cruises. The campus is on its banks.

Entertainments: the **cinema** has three screens; **The Theatre Royal** offers a varied programme; a good range of **restaurants**; three **leisure centres** (all affiliated to schools and with only limited open access) and ten-pin bowling.

Loughborough University of Technology

Loughborough
Leicestershire
LE11 3TU
Telephone: 01509 263171

University Charter date: 1966

Loughborough is a medium-sized university with around 8,500 full-time students, around 1,000 of whom are postgraduates. This is a strongly sporting and technological university. A single campus of 216 acres a mile from Loughborough. Degrees are modular with a level of flexibility in module choice; assessment is by coursework and examination. Almost all students can spend two years in University residences (unless they come from nearby).

THE CAMPUS

The University is set one mile west of Loughborough - a small, comfortable town whose clear shape allows the campus a sense of open space and harmonious development unrestricted by invading suburbs.

There has been a major college at Loughborough since 1909: the maturity and space of its grounds (216 acres) and the style of its original building provide a base-sense of security and order which mark that period at its best. A second factor is the long established fame of that college for excellence in national and international sport. This has given the University its quite extraordinary range of cherished, numerous and beautifully set playing fields, pitches and sports buildings. And all on campus! As well as their functional excellence, the playing fields give the campus its calm green ambience: Loughborough is unique among our universities in this sense.

The set and distribution of buildings on the campus is thoughtfully planned. Angles vary, heights are generally low-rise (no more than six storeys), often domestic and with only an occasional group of towers for dramatic relief. The large library, in centre campus, has an interesting cantilevered shape, with white surfaces. One, however, has to admit that the Union building is stark, and some of the accommodation blocks tend towards the claustrophobic; not, however, true of the newer buildings.

The University houses a high percentage of all its undergraduates on or very close to the campus: accommodation units are an integrated part of the scene, set in groups around and close to academic and amenity units. The result is a very close-knit, though large, community, living what is virtually a special kind of village life. It is true that you can turn easily and quickly to the cultural and social life of Leicester and Nottingham, but for the casual hour, or local evening, the town offers little, the University much. If you come to Loughborough it is important that you should know yourself able to enjoy and benefit from the intense and centripetal student life.

Because the site is large and generally flat (though it does ruefully boast the steepest gradient in the area), and parking space is limited on campus, a bicycle here is a worthwhile investment. As well as campus-hopping, it will help you to explore the area.

Learning Resources

The Pilkington **Library** houses over 600,000 volumes, seats 700 students and takes 3,850 journals. Opening hours: until 10pm Monday to Friday, 12.30pm Saturday and 10am to 9pm Sunday (reference only). The **Computer Centre** provides access to, and advice on, a wide range of personal computers and software. There are extra courses in computer literacy and a network of over 2,000 terminals. Most facilities are open for 24 hours a day. The University is fully networked with access to the Internet and world wide web. **Language laboratories** are available for self-teaching in the European studies department, at no extra cost to students. Many degree courses have an optional module of either French, German or Spanish.

Culture on campus

The University Arts Centre, on campus, houses a photographic darkroom and studio equipment, a record and cassette library, amplifiers and other facilities for music, microcomputers for music synthesis, colour graphics and 'computer-discovered' poetry. There are evening classes in pottery and painting, and a series of poetry readings.

Drama: the drama studio (seating 150) is also used as a television studio; the larger Sir Robert Martin Theatre (seating 300) has flexible staging facilities: both are used occasionally by visiting professional companies.

Music: A choir meets weekly; an orchestra thrives. A wide range of musical tuition is available, instrumental and vocal, to students who have already achieved a reasonable standard. An annual award of £500 is given for outstanding performance. There is an opera workshop and practice facilities as well as formal and informal concerts. The University has its own record label - Quarantine - which produces CDs of student bands.

The Film Society shows four recent release feature films a week. Small annual membership fee with admittance free.

The Union

The Union Building has recently been extended and now includes a Student Advice Centre adding to the wide range of services and activities on offer. Shops sell sports goods, stationery, groceries and second-hand books, a travel agency, academic bookshop, insurance brokers and banks.

The Union, after its extension, is the largest music and dance venue in Leicestershire. The auditorium can seat 450 and has a concert capacity of 2,000. There is also a 400 capacity nightclub. Entertainment almost every night during term time with five licensed bars operating nightclub hours during the latter part of the week. Weekly pop concerts, discos (three) and comedy shows. Many 'big name' stars have appeared here.

Students have every opportunity to 'get involved'; you can organise one of the 152 clubs and societies, write a column in the Union newspaper, do a piece for campus radio or organise the Real Ale Festival.

Most students get involved with Rag, a very lively and inventive affair, which raised £204,800 (1994/95) for charity. Others take part in Community Action, whose activities include visiting the elderly, people with disabilities and children.

Sport

The specialised Department of Physical Education, Sports Science and Recreation Management ensures that high-level tuition and coaching is always available. The University's sporting prestige also enables clubs to attract other high-calibre coaches.

Loughborough's achievements in competitive sport at all levels within the University, nationally and internationally, means that other universities compete for second place in many areas! The list of successes is too long to repeat here but includes winning the men's overall BUSA Championship for 15 and the women's BUSA Championship for 17 consecutive years (say no more).

Sporting facilities include three sports halls, two gymnasia, a dance studio, fitness centre, two swimming pools, seven squash courts, two floodlit all-weather areas, an all-weather athletics stadium and numerous major games-playing pitches, all-weather tennis courts and a four court indoor tennis centre.

All sports facilities except squash and swimming, for which there is a small charge, are free to those in the SU, although a high proportion of time in the indoor facilities is pre-booked by clubs.

Annual £1,000 sports scholarships are available to outstanding students.

Not all sport is serious: intramural leagues exist in 37 sports (with rules excluding top sports students from competing in their own sports) and a range of recreational courses are offered.

Student welfare

The University **medical centre** is staffed by three doctors and a nurse, and has four sickbeds. Open 24 hours a day in term time. The service is free. A physiotherapy service is available. **Counselling:** the Student Advice Centre offers financial, personal and legal advice, and the University has a professional counselling service. The University offers individual and group sessions to help with study problems. There are also workshops covering how to listen, stress management and assertiveness training. Relaxation training is available. The **Chaplaincy Centre** is used for group meetings as well as worship. Chaplains are available to all members of the University. There is a room for private prayer and a suite of purpose built rooms for Muslim students, including a prayer room for 100.

Careers Service

The Service offers one-to-one careers interviews and careers workshops, presentations and talks to help with job-hunting, applications and interviews. There is an 'Insight into Management' courses run in your second year. There is a well-stocked information room and the Service has PROSPECT, computer-aided guidance, which will help you with self-assessment.

Students with special needs

The University has a Special Needs Sub-committee which initiates action to improve residential and academic facilities, and is affiliated to Skill and to the Midlands Forum for students with special needs.

Accommodation

The remarkably high number of accommodation places (70% of undergraduates can be housed in halls of residence) has already been mentioned. This does not mean that everyone automatically has a place - those of you who live nearby, for instance, might have to live at home, or think about lodgings. Mostly, however, the position here is much better than elsewhere; nearly everyone can stay in rooms for two years if they so wish, and some can stay for three. It is likely, however, that you will actually want a change of environment at some stage: the Student Housing Office will help you to search. Accommodation is not hard to find and is usually only half a mile from campus. Rooms are allocated automatically in August/September and there is no special application procedure; so if you do want to state a preference, write to the Halls Accommodation Office in good time.

Halls of residence

All halls are mixed and all are warden controlled. Various meal deals are available including full board and you pay in advance. All halls have some catering facilities.

Costs (1995/96) £50.80 to £69.16 per week (30 weeks, full board)

Self-catering accommodation

Self-catering 'courts' are organised into units containing five, six or eight students in (mostly) single or (a few) shared study-bedrooms.

Costs (1995/96) £32.55 to £43.40 for 39 weeks

Private sector

A shared house costs around £28 to £35 per week per person. It is not too difficult to find accommodation within two miles of the University.

Mature students

Minimum age for mature students is 21. You must show your ability to take a degree course and sustain its pressures successfully. Access courses are acceptable. A Guide for Mature Students is available from the Admissions Office.

Nursery

The nursery has been purpose-designed to high standards for children from 3 months to 5 years old. 64 places allocated for the use of students, staff and local people.

THE TOWN (population: 46,000)

Loughborough is a small, compact, well-kept and very pleasant market town, set in an open, lightly wooded, mild and rolling rural landscape. Very English. Very Midlands at their best. The area provides the best hunting terrain in England and is home territory to the famous Quorn Hunt. The setting is actually known as 'Charnwood Forest' although, like most of our ancient woodlands, mere traces remain. Enough, however, to provide variety and line to horizons which could become monotonous. And good walking, cycling and wandering country, with a number of country pubs.

The town has a traditional market with ancient origins, a quietly dignified Town Hall and square, more than its share of pretty parks and green spaces, modest but agreeable new shopping areas and the 47-bell carillon in Queen's Park, built as Loughborough's war memorial. There are regular 'bell recitals'. The carillon is particularly aptly placed since Loughborough's John Taylor Foundry has been casting bells for more than a century and is world famous. In the Town Hall, the Charnwood Theatre offers drama, dance or musical entertainment; nearby is the town's five-screen cinema . There is a large November Fair, again of ancient origins. The parish church, All Saints, virtually restyled in 1862, has much earlier origins (14th century) and evidence remains. There are a number of old churches, schools and other buildings of interest in their own right, adding their reward to a wander around the town.

More energetically, there is a leisure centre which has good facilities, and 'The Mill' health club has a gym, exercise classes, sauna and jacuzzi.

ESCAPE ROUTES

Whether or not you regard local countryside as hilly depends very much on your concept of a hill; but the pleasant lines of the Wolds, with the Soar and Grand Union Canal winding close to the town adding the fascination of waterways and locks, provide peaceful settings for a scattering of very pretty villages. At the weekends you can experience the style of yesteryear on the Grand Central Railway, an enterprise run by volunteers, which puts great old steam locomotives back on the rails for trips of five and a half miles.

Loughborough's expedition territory, however, generally overlaps with that of Leicester and Nottingham, which also provide their own city-scale amenities and entertainment.

Communications

Loughborough is on the main London (one and a half hours away) to Sheffield line, with hourly services and occasional express **trains.** Northbound there are trains to Nottingham and Derby, then a network of link services. South and only a short trip is Leicester. The **M1** passes close by, and the **A6** and **A60** give Loughborough access to Leicester and Nottingham. The East Midlands **Airport** is only seven miles from Loughborough. British and European services, holiday charters and air taxis operate all the year.

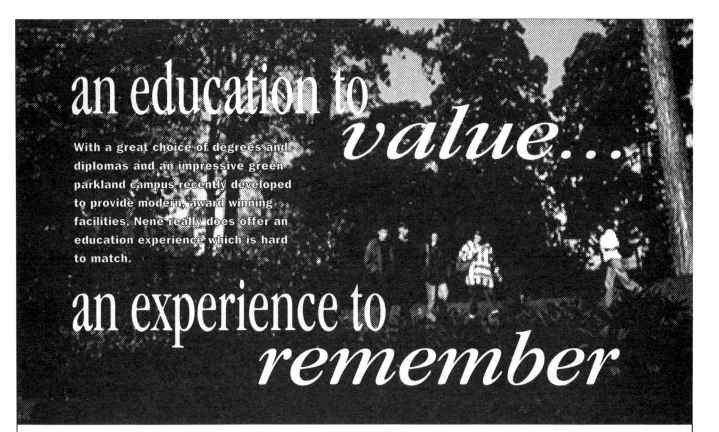

an education to *value...*

With a great choice of degrees and diplomas and an impressive green parkland campus recently developed to provide modern, award winning facilities, Nene really does offer an education experience which is hard to match.

an experience to *remember*

Come and experience Nene for yourself at one of our Open Days

An opportunity to come and see the campus and talk to tutors and current students about your chosen course and what life's like at Nene generally. You'll be introduced to all the main teaching and learning resources, accommodation and the Students' Union.

Wednesday 11 September '96 • Saturday 26 April '97 • Wednesday 10 September '97

BA/BSc Combined Honours Degree Programme with a choice of over 300 subject combinations

Single Honours Degrees and Higher National Diplomas in over 100 subjects including:

Accountancy & Finance	Education (Teaching)	History	Nursing & Midwifery
American Studies	Energy & Wastes Management	Industry & Enterprise	Occupational Therapy
Art & Design	Engineering	Information Systems	Podiatry (Chiropody)
Biology	English	Languages	Psychology
Business & Management	Environmental Sciences	Law	Sociology
Construction & Surveying	European Business	Leather Technology	Sport & Recreation
Computing	Fashion	Management Science	
Drama	Geography	Media & Popular Culture	
Economics		Music	

Halls of Residence places on campus for most 1st year students. Friendly, lively and easy to get to.

For further information on Open Days or for a copy of our prospectus, 'phone Wendy in Marketing on the number below.

0 1 6 0 4 7 2 2 1 8 0

NENE ◆ NORTHAMPTON
College of Higher Education

Nene College of Higher Education, Park Campus, Boughton Green Road, Northampton NN2 7AL.

Nene College of Higher Education is an exempt charity offering Undergraduate and Postgraduate Degrees and Diplomas.

Nene College

Moulton Park
Northampton
NN2 7AL
Telephone: 01604 735500

Nene has around 8,000 undergraduate/HND students and 300 postgraduates. Two campuses: the main campus is three miles from Northampton town centre; Art, Design and Technology are housed two miles away (a mile from the town). Degree programmes are traditionally organised: Combined Honours allows cross-faculty subjects. Assessment is by coursework and examination. 1,400 first years can be accommodated in halls of residence.

THE CAMPUS

Nene College was formed from a merger of the Northampton Colleges of Art, Technology and Education in 1975 and has grown to include the St Andrew's School of Occupational Therapy and the Sir Gordon Roberts College of Nursing and Midwifery. It now operates on two purpose-built campuses, and two town buildings which house single subjects (Podiatry and Occupational Therapy). There are plans for a 180 acre park to connect (or nearly) the two main sites.

Park Campus
The campus sits on the edge of Northampton's modest urban and light-industrial sprawl. The affluent host suburban village, Kingsthorpe, provides a comfortable sense of order and, beyond, open countryside stretches to shallow horizons. You are three miles out from Northampton's centre.

The College has recently spent £35 million on developing this 70 acre site - and it certainly shows. This is now a 'designer' campus where good quality new buildings occupy well-planned, landscaped space in remarkably harmonious balance. There is a sense of commodious provision: car-parks for students are large; there is a generous belt of new or recently built halls of residence; borders are green, cultivated and nicely ornamented by touches of sculpture; trees are mature.

The refectory is spectacular: dark glass walls, white supports, a soaring roof; computer building and sports hall more severely handsome.

Not all is photogenic, inevitably: Nene has been offering Higher Education provision since 1972. Out of central focus is a work-a-day area of elderly greenhouses, 'temporary' buildings and '70s low blocks.

The campus is large enough to accommodate a good range of academic and social facilities and provide the frame for a lively student ethos, yet small enough for you quickly to feel easy and at home.

Courses here: all except Art, Design and Technology, Podiatry and Occupational Therapy.

Avenue Campus
Here are the origins of Nene College. About one mile from the centre of Northampton and two miles from Park Campus, the two original 1930s buildings which were Northampton's Colleges of Art and of Technology are bridged by a large 1960s block - glass, concrete, flat roof.

The campus faces a large open grassed 'park', known as the Racecourse, and occupies 24 acres - a compact and fully-built site. The buildings behind facades are industrial in style. Definitely a workshop bias experience here, matching the courses on offer. Major up-grading proceeds.

Courses here: Art, Design and Technology.

Car-parking
1,000 car-parking spaces. First years in halls of residence may not bring a car onto campus.

Learning Resources

Each campus has its own library. The bookstock totals over 185,000 volumes and the libraries subscribe to over 1,000 journals. There is a special collection of School Experience material, and materials on Leather Technology. The College is the Northamptonshire region's European Reference Centre. There is a programme underway to link all faculty buildings and accommodation units into a multi-site computer network. The Information Technology Centres offer a 24 hour drop-in service and over 1,000 workstations. You can take an introductory training course in the College's computer systems, and there are facilities for independent learning. A new drop-in Language Laboratory with tutorial support is open to all students.

Culture on campus

The Dramatic Arts Centre on campus is venue both for student drama, and for professional touring companies who visit the College. Nene has a brass band, choir, symphony orchestra, chamber orchestra, and a changing number of student rock and jazz groups. Regular evening and lunchtime concerts. The Film Society shows films on most nights. The College organises guest lecturers and speakers.

The Union

A Union building on each of the two sites. Park Campus Students' Union was opened in 1993 and houses two bars and a snack bar, eating and lounge areas, pool tables and games machines, a shop and a small bank. The Students' Union on Avenue Campus provides bar areas, snack bars and a disco area. The Union entertainment programme means that there is something happening almost every night of the week - discos, band nights and alternative events. A student newspaper keeps you informed. Around 40 clubs and societies in all covering a wide range of interests. You can get advice on a number of subjects (personal, legal and accommodation).

Sport

The College has two sports halls, one on each campus, a dance studio and on-campus playing fields. You can work for certificates in coaching or refereeing in a number of sports. If you are interested in canoeing, mountaineering, parachuting, flying...there are Union-run clubs for you to join. The College has teams in football, rugby, basketball, hockey and cricket.

Student welfare

The College has a **Health Service** run by two nurses: one is the practice nurse, the other is the Occupational Health nurse who is available on both campuses at different times. Three trained **counsellors** are available on Park Campus. First years can join organised self-help groups, steered by second years on the same course. Second and third years are also trained to help more formally in the Learning Support Centre. The **chaplaincy** is an ecumenical team who arrange services, talks and missions. The main restriction to students with **special needs** is the campus buildings, some of which are not accessible to wheelchair users. You should discuss your particular requirements with the Tutor Responsible for Students with Special Needs.

Careers Service

The Careers Service is based at Park Campus; the Avenue Campus has a part time office. The Service offers personal guidance, visiting speakers, information booklets and a range of other facilities.

Accommodation

1,400 first year students can be housed, mainly in single study bedrooms (two thirds with ensuite facilities) in six halls on the Park Campus. If you are not allocated a room, you will be offered a place in the private sector. The College aims to visit all properties offered to first years. Second years onwards find housing in the town or surrounding area; the Accommodation Office will help in your search.

Costs (1995/96)

£25 per week (shared) ranging to £39 - £49 per week (single for 39 or 52 weeks.

Private sector: £25 - £45 per week excluding bills.

Mature students

Nene positively welcomes applications from mature students. Past experience, interest and commitment are all important. Many courses are flexible in their entry requirements. Access courses validated through a recognised consortium (from anywhere in the country) are normally acceptable entrance qualifications.

Nursery

The College has childcare provision for 16 children aged between two and a half and five years, available for two sessions a day (9am to lunch, lunch to 5pm).

THE TOWN (population 185,000)

Northampton is an old market town, serving a quietly tilting and folding county without drama, but with its fair share of charm in small villages, interesting old churches and historic buildings. In spite of a later disaster (fire in 1675) Northampton retains one of the largest of the country's old traditional market squares.

Entertainments: the Royal Theatre presents repertory theatre, studio productions and touring companies; Derngate - a 1,400 capacity purpose-built entertainment centre - houses ballet, opera, concerts, sports events, theatre; Cinemas: MGM (nine screens), Cannon (three screens) and The Forum (art and foreign films). There is a jazz club (membership only).

Two leisure centres, including a water flume, another swimming pool, a Golf Complex and a 24-lane ten-pin bowling centre, as well as a stock car/hot rod racing stadium, Northampton football, rugby and cricket clubs, Towcester race course and Silverstone Racing Circuit.

ESCAPE ROUTES

The countryside around Northampton is undulating and gentle. Althrop House is here. You are near to Warwickshire with its castles and the tourist attraction of tourist attractions, Stratford upon Avon.

Communications

Northampton is on Network South East and has a regular service to London Euston. Services too to Birmingham and Rugby. Very close is the M1 (three junctions in all). Near too are Luton and Birmingham Airports.

University of Nottingham

University Park
Nottingham
NG7 2RD
Telephone: 0115 951 5151

University Charter date: 1948
Nottingham is a large/medium-sized university with over 13,000 full-time students taught mainly on a 330 acre campus three miles from the city. The University offers a full range of academic, modularised degrees; Medicine is not modularised. The percentage of coursework included in overall assessment varies: all degrees have a strong element of examination. Accommodation is guaranteed to first years who confirm their offers by August 1st.

THE CAMPUS

This is a very handsome campus, set on rising ground, well landscaped with lawns and trees; its graceful white central buildings, built in the 1920s, look out over a strip of parkland (complete with large lake) and a wide boulevard, across the broad expanse of the Trent valley. The view is heavily urban and industrialised, but a sense of space prevails. The 330-acre site grew from a gift of land, three miles west of the city, by Sir Jesse Boot (founder of the Boots Company). The University can trace its origins back to 1798: its royal charter was granted in 1948.

The University responded to the demands of the 'sixties by building 'Science City' - a large complex of scientific and technological buildings, later extended by the new Medical School and associated teaching hospital. The concentration of these high-density functional block developments on the extreme eastern edge of the campus has had the virtue of letting the rest of the site retain its civilised parkland ambience.

Grouping of the other buildings on campus is singularly attractive. Centrally set is the large library, an elegant white structure with long slender window panels. Nearby is the Hugh Stewart Hall of Residence, a particularly lovely period hall, domestic and imposing, surrounded by lawns and covered with creepers. In the main, the halls of residence form a comfortable screen around the campus, only a few minutes' walk from the working buildings. Because 'home' can beckon so easily, and most halls provide full board daily, there is a strong tendency for life to centre on the halls - producing a generally quiet campus.

The University's Faculty of Agricultural and Food Sciences has its own 400-acre 'campus', ten miles south of Nottingham at Sutton Bonington. The School has its own accommodation hall and social life, turning to the Nottingham campus, or Loughborough, for a wider student community.

A minibus service connects with the main campus.

Cars

You must not bring a car to Nottingham unless you have a concessionary parking permit (only given to students with special needs or if you live more than 3 miles away). Parking at Sutton Bonington is not a problem.

Learning Resources

The library has a total stock of over 1,000,000 volumes and pamphlets and takes over 5,000 periodicals. The library is 'federal': different departments are housed in different buildings; in all, the library can seat 2,360 students. Opening hours: Monday to Friday to 9.45pm; Saturday to 5pm; open Sunday during pre-exam months.

The Cripps **Computing Centre** runs several courses and lectures through the year for non-computer scientists, covering a variety of languages and other facilities. Public access areas are on a number of locations, most give 24 hour access.

The Language Centre has three teaching laboratories, four satellite dishes and TV and audio studio facilities. You can learn a language through the 20-place self-access tape library with a tape archive of 3,000 tapes in 30 languages, including EFL. Or you can enrol in a night class: the Centre runs classes for the local community.

Culture on campus

Drama: The English Department teaches drama as a performance art, and sponsors a drama production each year. Productions can be set in the main hall, or, less formally, in a smaller workshop/studio.

Music: A full programme of recitals by visiting professional artists is organised by the Music Department; there are also special guest lectures. The University's Recital Hall seats 190. The Department of Music owns many period instruments for performing Renaissance and Baroque music in its original mode. There is a choir (120 strong), orchestras and a chamber orchestra.

Art Centre: The Arts Centre contains the Department of Art History and Music, art galleries (with year-round exhibitions), the Recital Hall and a visitors' centre.

The Union

Union offices, and some comfortable social areas, are in the Portland Building, whose amenities - the refectories, the University bookshop, and a ballroom available for social functions - are run by the University. The two main bars have been taken over and refurbished by the Union (large enough for gigs and discos). The Union also provides a shop (stationery and groceries), a travel shop and a printing and desk-top publishing service, newspaper (*Impact*), a campus radio and a fleet of minibuses. The Union organises large concerts, cabarets and discos. Its Student Community Action group works in problem areas; 2,000 students join in this work.

The Union funds over 200 clubs and societies ranging through sport, religion, politics and hobbies. Its annual turnover is £2.5 million. There are five Union sabbatical officers.

Sport

There is a large indoor sports centre, ten squash courts and some outdoor pitches on campus, and more outdoor facilities at Grove Farm, one mile away, and at the Sutton Bonington campus (where there is a second sports hall).

The sports centre is built around the frame of an old aircraft hangar: there is one very large hall, where two full-size tennis courts are laid out, with equivalent space allowing badminton, basketball and volleyball courts; a smaller hall can take four badminton courts (or equivalent games space) and has a climbing wall. The centre 'spine' of the building houses two practice rooms (judo, table tennis, weight and circuit training). A large lounge-balcony adds a bar and snack bar. Opposite the Sports Centre is the new 25 x 18 metre swimming pool.

Outdoor sports include access to the 2,000 metre international rowing course at Holme Pierrepont, near to campus, and sailing on the river Trent, where the University has a well-equipped boathouse, or on the University lake (also used by members of the public). There is a new floodlit artificial turf hockey pitch and additional pitches for hockey, rugby, football and lacrosse.

You will have to pay to use the sports facilities; you can buy a reasonably priced season ticket. The Union organises a wide range of sporting activities including an inter-hall sports league.

The University has solid sporting achievements in many UAU championships. If you are County Standard or above, you may be eligible for a sports bursary (maximum £750 per year).

Student welfare

Health service: There is a University health service which provides medical care and a dental service. You have to pay a small Health Centre fee to be eligible for in-patient care in the Centre's accommodation. The Student Advice Centre offers advice on all usual problems. There is a **counselling** service for students with more personal concerns. **Chaplaincy:** The University has a number of Christian chaplains. There is a chapel in the Portland Building and a prayer room for Muslim students. The University also has a rabbi and a Muslim consultant.

Careers Service
The Service has a variety of computerised advice packages. There are sessions on handling application forms, one-to-one interviews and group selection interviews, as well as two residential 'Insight' courses during the vacations. The Careers Service has a well-stocked Careers Information Room.

Students with special needs
The University has a co-ordinator for disabled students The University has a braillink to the computer, a braille embosser and a Xerox Kurzweil Personal Reader. On campus, there is an Institute of Hearing Research and a Blind Mobility Research Unit. There are some problems with access to a few buildings. The University is a member of Skill.

Accommodation

The University guarantees first years a place in University halls or flats (unless they live locally) providing they have accepted an offer firmly by May 15th and applied for a place by August 1st. The University is aware of the special problems facing later applicants on the scene, and tries to make sure that these difficulties are kept to a minimum. If students do not have hall accommodation when they arrive, they are likely to be placed within four weeks.

Halls of residence
There are 12 halls of residence (3,000 places) on main campus, varying in style and amenities, but generally carrying a sense of affluence and comfort. As terms include full board, you will find much of your day's pattern is influenced by returning to your hall for meals and spending social time in the rooms there, or the common rooms/bar. This pattern is beginning to relax as more halls (five at present) introduce 'pay as you eat' schemes. Halls cannot cater for special diets. **NB: Halls have no self-catering facilities.**

All halls provide and launder bedlinen and arrange room cleaning; most have laundry facilities, a small shop, library, TV and quiet rooms, and all have bars. There is usually a small pantry on each floor.

Three halls are for women, three for men, so only six are mixed: you must expect the possibility of being allocated to a single-sex residence. The majority of rooms are single study-bedrooms, but there are a number of rooms shared by two students and these, inevitably, will generally go to first years.

Costs (1995/96)
single room: £1,920 (full board)
shared room: £1,728 (full board)
30-week session
Pay-as-you-eat accommodation is initially cheaper (until you buy food!).

Broadgate Park flats
The flats, a short walk away from University Park, offer self-catering accommodation in units of five or six single study-bedrooms with shared kitchen/dining room and bathroom. All rooms are suitable for single students only. The complex has its own shop, launderette and social centre. Presently there are places for 1,400 students

Costs (1994/95)
Single room £1,350 self-catering, 44-week session (includes heating and hot water).

Sutton Bonington
One hall of residence, with 260 places. £47.17 per week.

Private accommodation
The Accommodation Office acts as an information bureau, putting you in touch with housing associations, owners, landladies and estate agents who are prepared to let rooms to students. The Office does not inspect or approve this accommodation.

Students live in various areas of Nottingham, within two miles of the University. Accommodation is not hard to find.

Costs (1994/95)
Average rents: shared house: £37 per week excluding bills.

Mature students

Students without traditional qualifications should write to the Admissions Tutor for the course in which they are interested. Departments may arrange interviews, set essays or tests, or ask for coursework examples. A special prospectus, Entry at 21+, is available. The Mature Students' Guild is part of the Students' Union.

Nursery
A purpose-built, 50 place nursery on the main campus takes children aged between six months and five years. Students have priority for two thirds of places. A playgroup is available for children aged two and a half to five years. The Union runs a playscheme during half term holidays for children aged between five and eleven.

THE CITY (population 280,000)

Nottingham is the largest city in the East Midlands, with a history rich in legend, as well as trade and industry. The Domesday Book recorded the settlement as a flourishing trading community with its own mint. The Industrial Revolution brought the explosion of population and wealth common to the northern cities: lace-making, hosiery, tobacco and bicycles were some of its foundations.

Nottingham has a rich legacy of very beautiful period buildings: street after crescent after alleyway of the kind of finely designed and meticulously worked factories and warehouses, mostly dating from the city's prime time in the wealth-generating craft of lace-making.

The legacy of wealth is also woven into the city's domestic architecture - many areas, particularly the rich inner suburbs, have wonderful, ornate villas and whole private squares of Victorian terraces and gardens. A city of lovely parks too - 2,600 acres of them.

The Theatre Royal, resplendent white, pillared, Victorian (classic mode) has had the lines of its structure skilfully extended to incorporate a new and acclaimed Concert Hall. The Theatre peers down a narrow road to Slab Square - a wide, paved central area dominated by the domed City Hall, the square is a focal centre around which the city weaves its roads.

Nottingham's castle, set on a hill and a landmark, originated in 1068, and after many ruinings and rebuildings was finally restored in 1875: this is the building standing today, more of a manor house than a castle.

More modern is the covered market, part of the Victoria Centre in the city centre, which houses, on its ground floor, the ingenious Waterclock, designed by Rowland Emmet.

Hockley, on the fringe of the city centre, is the brasserie and small boutique neck of your woods: student land.

In October the city swings into action with the three day Goose Fair, which was originally a hiring fair and autumn market in medieval times. Today, the skyline is alight with 18 acres of fair-ground rides - some Edwardian, some space-age: a spectacle to behold in your first weeks.

Theatres: The Theatre Royal is a venue for large touring companies, from opera and ballet to pantomime. The theatre has been refurbished and is part of the impressive Royal Centre, along with the Royal Concert Hall. The Nottingham Playhouse is a high-quality repertory theatre which has productions ranging from Shakespeare to farce. The Lace Market Theatre and the Co-operative Arts Theatre are both amateur venues where local talent thrives.

Music: The Royal Concert Hall, in the Royal Centre, has a large auditorium for classical concerts from major symphony orchestras, including the London Philharmonic Orchestra, and large rock concerts from big name bands. Rock City is also venue for gigs, large and smaller.

Cinemas: The city centre Odeon cinema has 7 screens, the MGM 4 and the Broadway Media Centre shows art and minority films. The Showcase Cinema, just out of the city, has 10 screens.

Nightlife: The city has a wide range of restaurants, nightclubs and discos, as well as pubs. A lively nightlife.

Sport: The city is home to Nottingham Forest FC, and the Nottinghamshire County Cricket Club, which plays at Trent Bridge. Also motor-racing at Donington Park and the Ice Stadium, where Nottingham Panthers ice-hockey team plays. There is a dry ski slope and ten-pin bowling. We have already mentioned Holme Pierrepont, the National Water Sports Centre where University teams row. On this stretch of the Trent there are year-round training courses and facilities include Olympic rowing, water-skiing, windsurfing and fishing.

The city has a full and wide range of leisure facilities.

ESCAPE ROUTES

Set in the Trent valley, Nottingham lies in country once thickly wooded and is close to the Dukeries, a series of stately homes. Robin Hood still haunts the region's tourism; Byron and D.H. Lawrence, in their ways, put their marks on the landscape. From the city you can easily get to the southern reaches of the Derbyshire Dales, to the cycling country of Leicestershire, to parkland and estates.

Close to Nottingham are Eastwood (birthplace of DH Lawrence, complete with museum) and Newstead Abbey (ancestral home of Lord Byron) with its 25 acres of gardens and lakes. Byron is buried in Hucknall, three miles south.

The Trent river and associated canals offer boating trips and narrowboat excursions, as well as a wealth of industrial archaeology built into their banks.

Communications

Nottingham has good **rail links** with the whole country, and fast regular trains to London, Birmingham and Sheffield. The coach network is extensive. **Road:** The M1 runs close to Nottingham, and the Midlands junction of the M1/M6/M5 in Birmingham is 40 miles south west via the M69 or M42. *Air:* The East Midlands Airport 11 miles away has both inland flights and flights to Europe.

The Nottingham Trent University

Burton Street
Nottingham
NG1 4BU
Telephone: 0115 941 8418

University Charter date: 1992

Nottingham Trent is a large/medium-sized university with over 15,000 full-time students (HND, undergraduate and postgraduate) and around 4,000 part-time students. The University is effectively dual campus - one in the city centre and one four miles out at Clifton. Clifton Hall (close to the Clifton campus) houses the Faculty of Education. Courses are modular. Assessment methods are generally a mix of coursework and exam; some 'practical' courses (art & design for example) are assessed by coursework only. Priority for the 2,800 residential places goes to first years.

THE CAMPUSES

City campus

The University occupies an extraordinarily large and consolidated area which is virtually part of the city centre. The site is unrivalled in the new universities' world in terms of its buildings' quality and historic range and the city on its doorstep.

The main Newton Building directly faces - admittedly the rear of, but nevertheless - the Concert Hall and Theatre Royal. The building is 'senate' in style. Imposing in its white stone bulk, its central tower rises high, a dramatic skyline feature. Immediately behind stands Nottingham Trent's answer to a number of older universities' Victorian architectural jewels: the Gothic Arkwright Building.

Across the street (the campus is intersected by a number of city streets) is the library, impressive, large and modern. Across another street the Bonington Building, home of many courses in art and design, with its galleries, exhibition spaces and sculpture court.

The whole campus has an air of confidence and panache; its buildings are impressive in scale and quality and in the positive flair of their design. The historic mix continues through large, recent or newly built complexes in centre campus (which include a medical centre) to the domestic Victorian terraces on the edge which are drawn into the functional net.

The balance of the world you learn in will depend on whether you choose to walk out into the city to the University's fore, or into the lovely Arboretum Park (with lake) behind. There are residential units on the edge of campus (a hall and flats).

Courses here: Art and Design, Business, Environmental Studies, Law, Economics and Social Sciences and Engineering and Computing.

Clifton campus

The University's second campus is about four miles away, set on high ground with free views over the sweep of the Trent valley. The site is quite heavily built, but retains a sense of space. Large teaching blocks are offset by groups of domestically scaled student houses, set in terraces and squares around wide lawned areas. The site is edged by playing fields. The large Science and Mathematics Faculty complex (the Erasmus Darwin Building) is sited here, as is the second medical centre, large library, theatre, Students' Union and the new Science block (opened 1994). The atmosphere is lively yet relaxed; there is a good balance between work/leisure/sport/private living, which makes the campus its own world. This was a College of Education and retains an air of conviviality.

Courses here: Humanities and Science and Mathematics

Clifton Hall

Close to Clifton campus, this large Georgian manor house, with new extensions, is home to the Faculty of Education. High views over the river Trent, with a green and wooded setting, make this an idyllic place to learn. The Hall is part of Clifton village conservation area. The village has a green and old rectory - all very picture postcard.

Cars

Car-parking is limited. You can apply to the Union for a car-parking permit.

Learning Resources

Two large **libraries**: one on the city campus, and one on the Clifton campus housing a total of 400,000 volumes, 2,500 journals and seating for 1,000. A new library on the City campus plus an extension to the library on Clifton campus will be completed by 1997 with learning resources structured to accommodate new information media.

The University-wide Academic Computing Network has around 5,000 workstations with 7,000 access points in total. Each workstation is connected to the global internet. 30 Student Resource rooms, some available 24 hours a day.

Language tuition is available in nine languages and at six levels, in a variety of courses. The open access laboratory at the City site offers audio-visual material in the afternoons and evenings. A University Award involves three hours study per week and termly assessments.

Culture on campus

Art: The University in partnership with the Henry Moore Foundation has established the Bonington Gallery. Used to show art and design exhibitions, the gallery also plays host to contemporary music and performance artists.

The Union

Two Union Buildings: Byron House on City Campus and the new Benenson Building at Clifton. Byron House offers the state of the art 'SUB' nightclub (which includes a diner and bar) and Le Metro, a quieter venue with regular live jazz. The Benenson Building, part of Clifton's new student village, has a newsagents, tobacconist, stationers and shop, as well as Student Union Administration, the Student Advice Centre, Ticket Express, TUBES (the Student Employment Bureau) and the Student Information Desk. Also a diner, takeaway service and Brubeck's Bar; a TV viewing area and meeting rooms.

The Union has five sabbatical officers and a high annual turnover. The weekly newspaper, *Platform*, is produced in collaboration with The Evening Post.

A good range of welfare services available from the two advice centres: debt, legal and housing, self-defence classes, hardship fund management, and a women's minibus which gives a city-site-to-home-door service after library and pub closing times for a nominal charge. TUBES has already been mentioned: this offers courses to help with the experience of work as well as being a 'job shop'.

Altogether, there are 90 clubs and societies, including sports clubs. Entertainments: frequent - SUB has live bands on Fridays and PURE dance nights Saturdays. There is a regular bus service from Clifton to the City campus, but Clifton campus generates much of its own activity: weekend events, film nights, keep fit classes.

The commercial wing of the Union is becoming increasingly successful and the Union has recently spent over £2 million on refurbishing social areas and offices.

Sport

In addition to sports facilities on both main campuses, Wilford Lane Sports Complex, two miles from the city campus offers pitches which students can use, free of charge, during the day. One of the Union's most successful ventures are the health and fitness studios now on both main campuses offering excellent facilities at concessionary student rates. The Union offers 28 Sports and 13 Outdoor Pursuits societies.

City campus facilities
A large sports hall with indoor cricket nets, a climbing wall and court provision for badminton, volleyball and/ or tennis. There are also two squash courts with changing facilities. The Victoria Hall has a small gym equipped for martial arts and weight training.

Clifton campus
Two gyms - one for indoor games, the other with gymnastics and trampolining equipment; a 12-station multigym; two squash courts and changing facilities; pitches for rugby, football, hockey; tennis and netball courts; an all-weather sports area; athletics track.

Student welfare

The University has two **health centres**, staffed by five doctors and nursing staff. A physiotherapist is available for consultation at Clifton twice weekly and once a week at the city site. There is a team of professional counsellors on both sites. **Chaplaincies**: Christian chaplains + Muslim, Sikh and Hindu religious advisers are available.

Careers Service
The Careers Advisory Service works with groups of students within departments, giving advice on careers decision-making, job hunting, writing application forms and preparing for interviews. You will have access to computerised careers databases.

Students with special needs
The newer University buildings have been designed to cater for students who have limited mobility. Other buildings, however, present problems. You should visit. Some accommodation has been adapted for students with special needs. Some lecture theatres have loop systems; also, facilities for visually impaired students.

Accommodation

By 1997, there will be over 4,000 bedspaces available in halls of residence and through a headleasing scheme.

Catered halls
Only one hall, on the Clifton campus is catered: this houses 331 students. Breakfast and evening meals on weekdays. Costs (1995/96): 32-week contract: £64 per week

Self-catering halls
Nine self-catering halls, five offering ensuite rooms. All have been recently refurbished or are purpose-built. Costs (1994/95): 40-week contract £48 - £51 per week.

Private sector
The Accommodation Office keeps a list of private rented flats or bedsits and lodgings. If you do not get a place in hall, come up early to find a 'home'. Costs average £30 - £40 per week (plus bills).

Mature students

A booklet - Access Steps to Higher Education - is available from the Centre for Access and Continuing Education. The Centre also give advice on Accreditation of Prior Learning. Support services include: a Mature Students' Handbook, pre-enrolment meetings, a Mature Students Welcome and monthly informal support groups.

Nursery
Two playgroups - one on each campus - 50 places in all for children from 18 months to 5 years old.

CITY/ESCAPE ROUTES

See the entry for The University of Nottingham

Staffordshire University

College Road
Stoke-on-Trent
ST4 2DE
Telephone: 01782 294000

University Charter date: 1992
Staffordshire is a large/medium-sized university with 11,600 full-time undergraduates and HND students, 1,200 postgraduates and 3,700 part-time students. The University has two sites: one campus in Stoke, the other in Stafford. Degrees are modular with flexible programmes allowing open options throughout your course. Assessment is a mix of examination and coursework. 75% of the University's 2,500 residential places are reserved for first years.

THE CAMPUSES

The University has two sites. One is the Stoke campus, which is actually as close to Hanley (the city centre of Stoke-on-Trent) as it is to Stoke (which confusingly isn't). The other is a short distance out of Stafford, the county town. There is a free regular minibus service between Stoke and Stafford.

The Stoke campus

The setting of the University's larger campus is modest, flanking the Stoke-on-Trent railway station and backed by an area of early century working-class terraces.

The main (original) building dates from 1910, a period when most towns of any size had public spirited men of industrial wealth, who gave some of it to their communities for the education of their people. This is where this University - and many others - has its roots. The interior of the 1910 building is quite stately: pillars, scrolls, marble surfaces. But access to the main library, at the rear of the building, is very 'tradesman'. The 'open' until you know your way around: apparent ways through are dead-ended. The library has a good working atmosphere and a lot of private study areas, although the passing road is quite noisy.

Across the road is the six-storey concrete and glass 1963 Mellor Building (the Physical Sciences are stacked here); behind that, the recently built smart and large Union of Students' Building and refectory. The Flaxman and Henrion Buildings house the Schools of Arts, Social Sciences and Design & Ceramics. There is a small gallery and the Regional Film Theatre perches in front.

The Bookshop and HE Shop are alongside the railway station - a very fine example of turn of the century railway architecture.

The campus has a second site, Leek Road, a short walk away, where it has already built new academic and sports facilities. Further developments have just been completed. The Students' Union has extended social facilities, including a new venue (capacity 2,000), where it will be able to book bigger bands, and generally make merry on a larger scale. There are also four 200-seat lecture theatres, and a range of general teaching rooms.

The Leek Road site is being developed in collaboration with the National Rivers Authority, to create a pleasant riverside complex. New accommodation blocks will be linked to the existing halls by a small bridge across the river Trent. Amenity value will be enhanced by playing fields.

Both sites are within reasonable walking - or better, cycling - distance of both Stoke and Hanley. Hanley Park is nearby.

Schools here (both sites): Arts, Design and Ceramics, Sciences, Social Sciences, Business and Law.

The Stafford site

The campus is set back from the road, on rising land on the final edge of suburban spread, and about a mile and a half out from the (County) town centre. Its outlook in the main is over beautiful wooded hills and open country. This is a very quiet site; the whole area has a deep rural peace. The campus is spacious, with wide lawns and a scatter of trees mature enough to give summer shade.

This was originally a purpose-built 1960s college. The site has been developed recently: the new Octagon Computing Centre adds a state of the art touch to this well-ordered campus.

The Students' Union offices are cluttered and friendly; the inner courtyard relaxed and pretty: a community which respects its habitat. The campus has its own library and refectory.

The Engineering laboratories behind the main blocks are single-deck and have unsightly roofing which works extremely well to let in lots of sky-light. Behind this there is a mini-village of wooden 'terrapin' huts, operating as teaching rooms.

Departments based here: School of Computing, School of Engineering, some Business School courses, School of Health.

Cars

A car would be an advantage at the Stafford site. Car parking facilities are available at both sites, but on-street local parking is very limited. Public transport is reliable and not expensive.

Learning Resources

The three site **libraries** have a total of 310,000 books and electronic media and take almost 2,100 periodicals, and a growing number of video materials. There are 1,300 study places altogether, including seminar rooms.

Computing Services staff give advice and assistance. Training courses on computing and software packages are run. Access to the University's networked computer system is during working hours, into the evenings and on Saturday mornings during term time. In all there are over 2,000 pc's, many on open access, 800 of which are in the Octagon, and 120 in the main library.

For advanced work high performance workstations are available. Study of a **foreign language** is an option in any modular degree structure. You may also take short certificated courses in addition to your main degree programme. Language Laboratories are open from 9am to 9pm weekdays. There is a wide range of tapes.

Culture on campus

Drama: There are four student productions per term.
Film: The Regional Film Theatre is on the College Road site. It shows films of special interest. The student Film Society shows four films a week.
Music: There are several student bands, and the University Sinfonia. Regular classical concerts - with some famous performers- at the Octagon in Stafford. The Pavilion at Stoke holds Jazz nights bi-monthly (broadcast on Jazz FM).
Art: The University has two galleries: the Shelton Studio is run by students and shows their work. The Flaxman Gallery has a lively programme of exhibitions, both specially commissioned and touring. The University offers art tuition via 'Community Classes', open to students.

The Union

Union facilities on all three campuses are open to all students. Leek Road facilities include a concert hall and the College Road bar has recently been refurbished.

The building in Stafford town centre provides a sports hall, squash courts, social facilities and bar.

The Union runs two shops, two travel bureaux, two snack bars and four bars which serve subsidised beer. The entertainments programme includes discos and gigs, balls and famous-name bands.

A full range of clubs and societies.

The Union employs a full-time Welfare officer, and represents your interests on campus and nationally. *Get Knotted*, the Union magazine, is produced regularly.

Sport

There are sports facilities on both sites, open to all students. Both campuses have fitness suites.

Stoke

College Road has a sports hall complex and playing fields at Leek Road, including a full-size all-weather pitch.

Stafford

An all-weather floodlit synthetic pitch on site. The sports hall and squash courts are in the Union building in the town centre.

The Recreation Service promotes involvement in sport and helps to develop skills, as well as arranging competitions both in leagues and informally. There are 25 sports clubs.

Certificated courses run in a number of sports for those wishing to become coaches. Students from the University won gold medals (Athletics) in the last two World Student Games.

Student welfare

There is a **surgery** on each site staffed by nurses. Each site has a physiotherapist, specialised in sports injuries.

The **counselling service** offers support and advice, including on debt and legal matters. self-help groups are also available. There is a Nightline listening service.

Chaplaincy rooms are open to students of all faiths or none. The University has one full-time chaplain and four part-time. Islamic and Jewish societies invite their religious leaders on site: special provision is made for Muslim students on the Stafford site, and on request at Stoke.

Careers Service

The Careers and Appointments Service has libraries of careers information on both campuses. Advisers are available for discussion, CV preparation, mock interviews and group sessions.

Students with special needs

You should send for a booklet provided by the University which covers the provision made for students with special needs. There are 20 rooms in halls of residence suitable for students with mobility problems and a good range of equipment for sensory impaired students. The university runs a Volunteer Scheme, which recruits, trains and manages full and part-time volunteers to pair up with students who request support.

Accommodation

The University has over 2,000 accommodation places, most of which are in single, self-catering rooms in halls of residence, custom-built houses or adapted houses or tower-blocks. 75% of this accommodation is reserved for first years. If you do not get a place in hall, or want to live out, the Accommodation Offices hold a large register of private accommodation. Rents in this area are very reasonable. Each Accommodation Office has local lists.

Costs (1995/6)

Rents range from £25 (shared) to £40 per week in University accommodation. Costs include heat and light.

Private sector accommodation

This is not hard to find around either of the University's sites. Stoke's average £32 per week; Stafford £33 per week.

Mature students

For many courses, you can enter without standard qualifications if you are aged over 21 by December 31st in your year of entry: consideration of your application will take account of maturity and experience, motivation and commitment as well as any previous study experience or qualifications (including UCAN certified Access courses). The Mature Students' Association brings students together from all courses. The Higher Education Shop on the Stoke campus will give help and advice.

Nursery

The University has two nurseries, one on each campus. Stoke takes children from six months to five years; Stafford from two to five years.

THE CITY (population: c 250,000)

Stoke-on-Trent is an amalgamation of six towns. Its people are still employed in the old pottery industries for which the area is famous. The city has reclaimed much of its old industrial 'eyesores', which are now grassed and planted. The canals, once industrial waterways, are now open for leisure cruises, although you can still see working barges. Here, there are theatres, concerts and lively nightlife. The six towns retain their identities, and facilities; the main shopping district is Hanley, where you will find most major chain stores. Each of the six towns has its own market.

Stafford is a market town, very pretty and rural with a range of shops and pubs.

Stoke

Theatre: The area depends largely on amateur dramatics. The Victoria Theatre at Hartshill was the first professional theatre company to play in the round and has been internationally acclaimed. The Stoke and Newcastle Arts Project Ltd promotes professional music and drama events.

Music: Concerts are held at the Victoria Hall in Hanley. There are various folk and jazz clubs in the area, including a morris and clog-dancing workshop.

Cinema: The Regional Film Theatre is in Stoke, and a new eight screen cinema in the Festival Park Leisure Centre. Hanley has a commercial cinema.

Nightlife: There are 12 nightclubs in the area, and beyond the town are country pubs down country lanes.

Sport: The area has a number of sports clubs, including a ski-club and speedway stadium. Newcastle has a golf club. The Festival Park Leisure Centre has a 'Waterworld', dry-ski slope, snooker club, 30-lane tenpin bowling and bars.

ESCAPE ROUTES

Staffordshire is synonymous with the Potteries, with the Industrial Revolution, but that was all a long time ago, and Keele is right on the edge of very beautiful countryside. The north east of Staffordshire is open moorland and the bottom edge of the Peak District. The valleys of the Rivers Manifold and Churnet are exceptionally beautiful. Ancient teeth and bones have been found along the Manifold Gorge. The area has some pretty villages.

There are several conurbations to go at in the area. This is home to some of the most famous potteries in England, including Wedgwood, Royal Doulton and Spode. Nearby, at Smallthorne, is an Elizabethan mansion, now a museum.

West of Stoke is Cheadle, which has - two miles north-east - the Hawksmoor Nature Reserve. This covers 250 acres of moorland and marshes, with nature trails and a large population of bird life. East again is Alton Towers, one of the country's great pleasure parks set in the parkland of a 'ruined' Gothic 19th century mansion. The gardens offer much: exotic plants, fountains, conservatories, as well as miniature railways and boating lakes. And there is the fun park; a good break from study.

Communications

You will have to go to Stoke for your **rail** connections. From here, access is fairly comprehensive. **Coach** links, likewise, will probably require a change. The **M6** is your fastest route to everywhere else.

University of Warwick

Coventry
CV4 7AL
Telephone: 01203 523523

University Charter date: 1965

Warwick is a medium-sized university with 8,100 undergraduate students on full and part-time programmes and 5,300 postgraduates: there are relatively few part-time undergraduates. The University has a single greenfield campus (550 acres) with two off-shoots - Westwood (Education) and Gibbet Hill (Biological Sciences and Maths) ten minutes walk away. The campus is just outside Coventry at the beginning of the Warwickshire countryside. Courses are traditionally structured, each including a wide variety of options. Assessment mainly by examination, some including an element of coursework/project/dissertation.

All first years who accept a place by the end of August are guaranteed a place in University-owned accommodation

---

THE CAMPUS

Warwick has a most impressive campus occupying 200 hectares at the point where Coventry's city boundaries merge with the open countryside of Warwick. Although so close, the grey conurbation, of which Coventry is the southern boundary, does not cast its shadow. Most of the campus is centrally grouped and quite compact, except for the Education Faculty, with the Westwood halls of residence, which is a short distance away from centre (15 minutes on foot, less on a bike), and the Maths and Biological Sciences units are at Gibbet Hill, 10 minutes' walk away (footpath and cycle track).

Dominant buildings are white, rectangular, flat-roofed. The general effect of the main building-area is harmonious and open, although a factual description might not convey this.

However, the off-setting shapes of the Arts Centre, with its eccentrically (and no doubt scientifically) piled series of dark roof-platforms (brightly edged), and the twisted stack-tower of the Union building, with its dramatic glass face, are strong features.

Further variation comes with the curved shapes of lawns, the warm-brick, traditional pitched roofs, and the white verandahs of the social studies building. The close setting of the buildings is thus not allowed to feel overpowering; the campus is not too large (having skilfully distanced two of its units); green spaces surround. The atmosphere is informal and friendly.

Links with the community are impressive - in research work, practical liaison in areas where talking to people working 'outside' is mutually beneficial (management studies, social studies etc.), and in the sharing of cultural and sporting facilities.

Cars

Car-parks on campus are pay and display, and rates are not outrageous. You can apply for a permit on medical, academic or compassionate grounds. For those who live off-campus, the University has arranged special rates from bus companies with passes which allow unlimited local travel.

Learning Resources

The library has over 800,000 volumes and seats 1,227 students. Open seven days. Total of 5,000 periodicals taken. Westwood has its own library.

The Computer Centre is a resource for the whole University and beyond, with a large variety of languages, libraries and applications. The Centre maintains work areas in all faculty buildings. The campus network is linked into the global internet.

The Language Centre offers daytime and evening courses in major European and Oriental languages. Facilities: four teaching laboratories, a multi-media private study section and a recording studio. The facilities may be used by any student with an interest in languages; you may even borrow a portable mini-laboratory to use in your own room. The tape library is stocked with audio-visual study courses in 22 languages, both general and specialised. You may build a foreign language into your degree programme or, for a small fee, enrol on a 'leisure course'.

Culture on campus

Warwick's Arts Centre is justly well known, and regularly is the setting for concerts, dance and shows. It serves both the University and public in a large complex which also houses the University bookshop, conference room and sculpture court.

Drama: There is a main theatre (570) seats, visited by major touring companies. The range of productions is unusually wide, from very powerful drama to comedy. A smaller studio theatre (150 seats) provides for smaller scale and more experimental productions by visiting companies and student societies. Student drama thrives, with a good range, from Brecht and Strindberg to the annual children's Christmas Show.

Art: The Mead Gallery is an important regional venue for national and touring exhibitions. An attractive use of space here.

Music: The Centre's hall seats 1,500 and offers an acoustically fine auditorium. Concerts here attract top orchestras and performers. Student music groups offer the symphony and chamber orchestras, led by the resident Coull Quartet, and the University Chorus, all of which tour abroad, and give concerts in the Arts Centre and elsewhere in Britain. Other music groups: Brass Ensemble, University Consort, Early Music Group, a concert band, an informal chamber music group and choir and a Gilbert and Sullivan Group. Practice rooms and facilities are very good: two concert grands, a two-manual Gable harpsichord, virginals and early music instruments and an electronic studio. Subsidised tuition is available. An occasional keyboard- and a number of choral- and instrumental- scholarships are awarded by the University and there is a scholarship in electro-acoustic composition.

Film: There is a purpose-built Film Theatre with a varied and adventurous programme. The Union Film Society shows up to 50 films a term for about £1 per showing.

The Union

The Union here is lively and active in all areas. Dynamic and democratic.

Its building is one of the most striking features on campus and, mounted above its flight of steps, keeps tower-vigil over the main access road and main entrance. Residences cluster to the rear and sides: the main University buildings stretch ahead and out, with the arts complex and Senate House as no-man's land in between.

The Union runs over 200 clubs and societies: sports, recreation and arts, academic and political, and ethnic and religious. An unusually large number and wide range: home-brew, science-fiction and fantasy, alternative music, alternative technology.

The Warwick Student Union Services Ltd. provides 8 bars, a Union shop, two launderettes, a coffee bar, a snack bar, a vegetarian outlet, a pasta restaurant, a pizza delivery service and a travel bureau. There is also an optician, insurance office and building society branch on campus. The company has a turnover of £5 million per annum and a permanent staff of 100. We can report that the standard of service and food is exceptionally high.

One unique trading activity is 'Warwick Study', a pioneer in the field of student academic services. It provides personal computer technology either at discount prices or on loan, a fully computerised second-hand book service, a professional CV service and a past-exam papers service for student revision. Innovation indeed.

The Union arranges entertainments, including discos and concerts most evenings. The Union also supports an independent newspaper *The Warwick Boar* and the Union building accommodates the campus radio, which broadcasts across campus for 18 hours a day. Unitel is the Union's own television broadcasting service.

Students also operate their own law centre, housing advice service, counselling and Nightline. The Rights and Advice Service incorporates an Employment Service. You can help with community problems through the Community Services Group, which works with the Cyrenians and the CAB, helps in schools and in an adult literacy scheme.

The Union is represented on most important University committees and its campaigns on student issues, both local and national, are high-profile. It has a thoroughly democratic constitution: meetings are once a week, which is about twice as regularly as in most active Unions.

Sport

Sport and recreation activities happen in two areas, separated by a 15 minute walk.

The sports centre has a 25-metre, six-lane swimming pool, seven squash courts, a fitness room, a weight-training room, an activities room for fencing, judo etc., a climbing wall, a sauna and a large multi-purpose sports hall (badminton, volleyball, netball, 5-a-side football etc.). There are pitches, courts and squares for soccer (7), rugby (3), hockey (2), tennis (12), cricket (3); plus one all-weather pitch and a croquet lawn. Outdoor facilities at Draycote Water allow you to sail, row and canoe. Staff of the P.E.Department give tuition at beginner and improver levels in a wide range of activities. 69 sports clubs in all.

A Trim-Track, with exercise stations, takes in hills, fields and woodlands along a five-kilometre route.

An eight-lane Olymprene all-weather running track, shared with Coventry Godiva Harriers, attracts famous sportsmen and women to its events.

At Westwood (the secondary site) close to the halls of residence, there is a games hall, a second swimming pool, a facility for Olympic gymnastics and a dance studio.

Student services

There are two general practices which operate from the **health centre** on central campus which has a full-time nurse, seven doctors and a dentist. Open from 9am to 5pm on weekdays. A psychotherapist attends the centre occasionally, and a physiotherapist is there twice a week. Three trained **counsellors** are available for your problems, and the Students' Union has a welfare advisor backed up by student volunteers. There is a **chaplaincy centre** on campus, used for meetings, relaxation and worship. Anglican, Roman Catholic, Free Church and Jewish chaplains provide pastoral ministry and services.

Careers Service
There is a booklet available at the beginning of term about part-time work on campus. Careers staff are available to discuss implications of course changes, vacation work or even your project topics. You are encouraged to start thinking about your career in the second year: PROSPECT (pioneered in part by Warwick) is available for computer-assisted careers guidance. The Service runs an sessions on application forms and interview techniques. The Careers Room is well-stocked.

Students with special needs
The campus is generally accessible to students with mobility problems. You should contact the Senior Tutor before you apply so that your individual needs can be assessed. A visit is always recommended.

Accommodation

Accommodation is offered to all students who have accepted a place here by the end of August, provided that they have applied by then. More than half the student population is housed in University-owned accommodation - six halls of residence and four groups of flats all on campus. Nearly all first years will have a University room, if they wish, and many students are able to return to University residence (usually the final year). Most first years will share double rooms, and a few post-Clearing candidates might have to face a possibly difficult two or three weeks in lodgings until the term settles down. They can expect campus rooms by the end of four weeks at most.

If you are allocated a room on campus, you are not allowed to bring your car.

All accommodation is self-catering.

Halls of residence
Six halls, including International House, for which all students can apply: resident tutors and warden keep a protective, caring eye on things. Bedlinen, basic cleaning and laundry are provided. Each study-bedroom has a washbasin and halls have common-room areas.

Costs (1995/96)
single £30.85-£45.00 ensuite per week (30 weeks)
shared £25.40-£28.80 per week (30 weeks)

Campus flats
Groups of 5, 6 or 12 students. Rooms are grouped around kitchen and bathroom.

Costs (1995/96)
single : £30.70 - £33.85 per week (39 weeks)

Private sector
The Accommodation Office operates a property-leasing scheme and keeps a list of addresses (mainly in Leamington Spa, Kenilworth and Coventry) of flats, bedsits and lodgings.

Costs (1995/96)
shared house: £30 to £35 per week excluding bills, but including Council Tax.

Mature students

The University encourages applications from mature students. Minimum age: 21. There are no set entry requirements. You should apply through UCAS, and your application will be considered on its merit.

Access courses are available in association with local colleges in law, social sciences, science and business studies.

There is a Mature Students' Society .

Nursery
There is a creche at Westwood for 25 children aged one to five years. Children of students are given priority. Professionally run, with part-time help. Efforts are made to keep the price down, and students can qualify for help from a discretionary hardship fund.

There is a half-term playscheme - free - run by students.

Coventry and Escape Routes

The University is closer to Kenilworth, and relates socially more to Leamington Spa than to Coventry; this is, however, your nearest large centre.

See The University of Coventry entry.

University of Wolverhampton

Wolverhampton Main Campus
Wulfruna Street
Wolverhampton
WV1 1SB
Telephone: 01902 321000

University Charter date: 1992

Wolverhampton is a large university with 23,000 students, around 13,000 of whom are on undergraduate programmes. Students are taught on five sites, however, making their totals less formidable. Two campuses in Wolverhampton (most courses), others in Walsall, Dudley and Priorslee (Shropshire). All, with the exception of the two in Wolverhampton, are quite a distance from the others. Degrees are modular, offered in single and combined programmes.

Accommodation preference is given to first years who live more than 75 miles from Wolverhampton.

THE CAMPUSES

Note: these campuses are scattered and each is a self-contained unit in many ways. You should think about your course and campus in combination: your life will be very campus-centric. The majority of courses are taught at Wolverhampton, and this is, in effect, the University.

Wolverhampton campus

The main campus occupies a large site on both sides of the town ring road which splits it into north and south sites. The split, however, is not very deep: the ring road is quite narrow and the University's buildings large enough to overleap the gap - metaphorically speaking. There is an underpass wide enough to serve the needs of Saturday football fans as well as students: the Wolverhampton Wanderers Football Stadium is virtually on campus.

The south half of campus consists mainly of the original building and its more recent extensions. From the ring road, you will pass between the high, grey block of the north campus and the modern, austere brick walls of the library and Students Union Building on the south side. The old face of the complex, between the ring road and the city centre, turns inward towards the ancient church and other important town buildings.

The original building is solid and handsome, built in 1931 and typical of large, mainstream educational institutions of its period. Three storeys high, it has a marble-lined entrance hall, complete with sweeping staircase and potted palm. The building has a studio theatre in its lower depths.

The campus complex was built up around the original building. Its central open space is paved and utilitarian. Very back-doorish. The Union is large, new and efficient-looking. The site's atmosphere is welcoming; the scale undaunting.

On the northern half of the campus, the tall dour building (housing art and design) is backed by descending modern blocks. The most recent, in dark brick and glass, is very distinguished. The chaplaincy, the Randall Lines Hostel and a cluster of smart new residential halls complete the downhill development.

There are three pubs actually on campus: this might suggest the advent of football crowds more than student habits, but this area is strong on its Real Ale.

The one 'outpost' in the town is just around the corner from the south campus; a highly decorated and charming old original 'polytechnic' building dated (we think - the numbers were very enscrolled) 1895.

The Compton Park campus..

..houses the Wolverhampton Business School, about three miles from the centre of Wolverhampton and occupying space in an affluent suburb, with gracious period houses, parks and pubs. It is linked to the main campus by your own energy, or by a good bus service or by the University shuttle. Close by is the Compton Activities Centre which has extensive sports facilities.

The Dudley campus

Six miles from Wolverhampton and a ten-minute walk from Dudley town centre. If students have split-site lectures there is a free inter-site bus.

The campus has expanded on a very pleasant suburban campus around a handsome 1930s building similar in style to Wolverhampton's main 'original'. Developments are low-rise blocks, nicely lawned around the edges. Money has been spent on high-quality new building for the Students' Union. Sports fields give a touch of green space; the campus has the University's biggest sports halls (over 600 square metres), and tennis courts, and the complex is comfortably scaled. It has a rather remote feel, although the town is not far distant (a reasonable walk or ride), partly because of its quiet, leafy suburban setting. The atmosphere is collegiate/large established senior school.

Courses here: Humanities and Social Sciences

Walsall site
Seven miles from Wolverhampton and eight miles from Birmingham.

The campus very much retains the scale and atmosphere of its college origins. The buildings are concrete, flat-topped with black steel/white framed window walling. The grouping is skilfully planned so that, in spite of the modular uniformity, there is a good sense of space created by the long shallow horizontal lines. The ambience is domestic - there are a lot of accommodation units here. The campus has its own swimming pool, large playing fields, gymnasium, tennis courts and running track; a theatre, library, dance studio, tv studio and bookshop. A well-equipped college environment. The campus immediately neighbours the town's Rugby Club grounds, in a particularly pleasant, long-established residential area. Some houses nearby are Victorian or early 20th century; many are large with big gardens: it all helps to create a good general ambience.

Walsall itself is just over a mile away.

Courses here: Education, Sports Studies, Music, Religious Studies and Dance.

Shropshire campus (Priorslee, Telford)
This new campus is built around a small stately home in a greenfield site close to the centre of Telford and includes purpose-built accommodation blocks, library provision and a refectory. We have not yet visited Priorslee, but it sounds a spectacular change from the original site occupied here, which we did visit.

Courses offered here include those from the Wolverhampton Business School, the School of Computing and Information Technology, the School of Education and the School of Humanities and Social Studies.

Cars
If you are based on the Wolverhampton campus, parking is a problem. Dudley and Walsall have limited parking on campus. All University hostels have parking space for a limited number of cars. You should apply for a permit as soon as you arrive from your own site.

Learning Resources

Every campus has its own **learning centre**. The main library is on Wolverhampton's main campus, and here too there are specialist libraries for law and art/design.

The Wolverhampton philosophy is one of active learning, and improvement of learning materials and experiences. To this end, **Learning Centres** are being established on each campus: these will combine library facilities with 'a growing range of learning technologies' (this usually means computer-delivered information). Around 400,000 volumes, 3,500 periodicals taken and 1,405 seating places over all sites.

The **Computer Centre** is a central resource for the student community. There is a multi-site network with 1,500 workstations. The Computer Centre has a library of manuals and 750 of the workstations available for student use. You are encouraged to call on the expertise of staff if you have difficulties. IT skills can be acquired during any course.

Courses in **European languages** are available to all students, whatever your discipline.

Culture on campus

Again, we must insert the caveat that life will very much depend on which campus is your base.
Film: The Wolverhampton campus has both a film society and a 35mm cinema. There are film societies at all campuses.
Art: The Arena Theatre and Lighthouse Media Centre in Wolverhampton are the main arts venues. There are eight or nine student productions per term, along with professional productions.

The Union

The Union operates on all sites and runs ix bars in all and five shops, one general and one travel. The Union buildings on the main sites are new, and built to last. There are around 30 clubs and societies and a lively entertainments programme - something happening every night of the week, including a regular club night. Free inter-site transport means that entertainments are accessible to students from any campus. The Advice Unit, staffed by professional welfare advisors, provides advice and assistance on welfare issues. The Union also provides paid work for students, as well as training and support. The Union produces *Cry Wolf*, a monthly magazine.

Sport

Each site has its own facilities:
Wolverhampton - a large sports hall and squash courts and a new fitness suite with weight machines and aerobic classes.
Compton Park - tennis courts and sports fields.
Dudley - a (very) large sports hall, well-kept sports pitch on campus and tennis courts.
Walsall - a swimming pool, dance studio, tennis courts, running track and sports fields.
Shropshire - all indoor and outdoor sports take place at the local sports centre.

A fee of £5 buys you an annual sports card which gives you admission to all facilities, otherwise you pay a small charge for occasional use. Coaching and training are available for competitive athletes.

Student welfare

Health care: You should register with a doctor close to where you live. Consultations are available with a doctor who visits the Wolverhampton site weekly. There is a personal **counselling service** run by the University, and a specialist financial counsellor is available. Workshops are organised to help with personal problems like eating disorders, exam anxiety, assertiveness etc. **Chaplaincy Centre** is based on the Wolverhampton site with offices at Dudley and Walsall. There is a Church Studies option in the modular degree scheme. The Centre has meeting rooms, and coffee bar and lounge. You can find out here where you can worship if you are a non-Christian.

Careers Service

Careers advisors give practical help in application procedures, going for interview and presenting CVs. Workshops on presentation skills and how to be interviewed are run throughout the year. There is a well-stocked information room and access to GRADSCOPE and PROSPECT. The service also runs the University's Student Employment Bureau which advertises part-time and vacation work.

Students with special needs

Wolverhampton has an on-going programme of adaptation of the campuses for students with special needs - induction loops in major lecture theatres and minicom phones being two additions. There is a visual language centre for the deaf / hard of hearing and special support for the dyslexic. There is a Disabilities Advisor who is there to improve access and admissions for students with disabilities.

Accommodation

The University has a total of 2,300 accommodation places on its five campuses and preference is given to first-year students who live more than 75 miles from Wolverhampton. All hostels are centrally heated and fully furnished. There are Resident Assistants in each hall, second-and third-year students, who sort out minor problems and liaise with the site managers. All halls have launderettes or are close to laundry facilities.

The University also carries a large list of lodgings - over 4,000 bed spaces and is increasing the number of addresses carried for self-catering accommodation.

Halls of residence

All halls are on or close to campuses, most are self-catering and most have single study-bedrooms. Half of each hall is set aside for non smokers. Students are expected to clean their own rooms and to take on responsibility for the communal kitchen areas. If your room is ensuite, you will be expected to clean your own bathroom. A charge is made if your standard of cleaning is not acceptable.

There are two complexes on the Wolverhampton campus. Both have kitchen facilities shared by between either nine or 12 students. Both are mixed. The two are close to each other and within a ten-minute walk of the town centre. Randall Lines and Lomas Street Hostels house 300 students each. New ensuite blocks will house a further 400 students.

Compton Park Site accommodates 130 students about one and a half miles from the town centre.

Dudley hostels house 380 students all in single study-bedrooms. Four halls are catered: prices include a meal voucher which can be exchanged in any University refectory. Two of the catered halls are Edwardian buildings (with mainly double bedrooms), another is late Victorian. The refectory on site is open until 6.30pm Monday to Friday and offers a range of food, including vegetarian.

Walsall campus accommodates 360 students in 15 mixed blocks, all single study-bedrooms and all self-catering.

Shropshire campus accommodates 477 students in nine blocks. All rooms are single with en-suite facilities. Kitchen facilities are shared between six students.

Costs (1996/97)

Self-catered, single: £1,459.40 per year
En-suite: £1,677.90 per year
Catered (Dudley only): £1,714.20
(based on 39-week contracts)

Private accommodation

Each campus has its own 'living out' areas: you are likely to live within three miles of your campus base, in many cases nearer. The housing stock in this area is varied. The Accommodation Office maintains lists of vacancies for both single students and groups.

If you need to spend time here to find suitable accommodation, the University keeps a hall of residence open during the summer so that you can have a base from which to search. Suggested hunting grounds: shop windows (particularly newsagents'), the local paper (*The Express & Star*), estate agents and the student grapevine (if you have friends here already). You are advised to steer clear of accommodation agencies.

The Union has a contract for private sector accommodation: very useful. The University operates a 'team up' system which makes sure that you do not have to view properties alone. All good policies.

Costs (1995/96)

Shared house/flat: around £27.00 per person per week.

Mature students

The University has a Higher Education Shop in the centre of Wolverhampton which is, in effect, an advice centre for mature students. You can come here for information, or counselling on higher education and your own route through. The University is also a member of the West Midlands Access Federation.

Nursery

There are two playgroups for children aged between two and five years. One is on the Wolverhampton campus, the other is at Dudley.

THE CITY/TOWNS

Wolverhampton (population 240,000)

Wolverhampton is the largest town in England not designated a city. Which does not mean it is huge. It stands, apparently untouched by the proximity of Birmingham, on the brow of a hill on the edge of some extremely beautiful countryside. Its immediate environment is one of ranging suburbs and redbrick.

The town buildings are comfortable, solid and some unconsciously elegant: the white courthouse, corner pubs, red banks. The streets are not wide, but even on a busy day - and we were here for a teeming conference once - there is room to move.

The University's 'old face' is part of a complex which holds the atmosphere of Wolverhampton. The civic buildings downhill are good examples of modern civic architecture - approachable, with clear lines and well-spaced. There are green bits between the concrete, and the green bits are tended. The church, directly opposite the University's main building, is a remarkable building, black stone without being forbidding; inside, light pours through its magnificent stained glass. The gallery next to the church has the eccentricity of up-dated Victorian buildings which have not been refurbished, only re-adopted.

The shopping centre is well served with a range of national chains and smaller, very Wolverhampton shops. The hillside setting gives shape to developments, and there are still squares, alleys and ginnels.

The Grand Theatre is right next door to the (1895) University Health Sciences building. It is a fine example of Victoriana, with a flamboyant exterior which really should have a civic square in front, but unfortunately looks out only to the access to the new bus-station.

If you take a bus out of town, you will find (if you go in the right direction) the canal which has pretty walks along its banks.

Theatre: The Grand Theatre has a changing programme of visiting productions, many on major national tours. The theatre is impressive, and refurbished. The Arena Theatre on campus has studio productions of new drama.

Music: The Civic Hall stages large concerts. A smaller hall, the Wulfrun, offers more intimate evenings.

Cinema: The Lighthouse Arts and Media Centre has moved to a new town centre site and now has two screens showing mainstream as well as minority interest films.

Nightlife: Wolverhampton has several new nightclubs and live music venues. A good range of pubs: an excellent area for Real Ale. Restaurants cater for most styles and budgets.

Sport: Wolverhampton has a new swimming pool which also offers 'keep fit' classes. There is also a new football stadium at Waterloo Road. The Dunstable race track is floodlit and has a turf and an all-weather track.

Dudley and Walsall

Dudley and Walsall are both a lot smaller than Wolverhampton and offer a much more 'town' life. Dudley is an old market town, overlooked by the its castle. Its amenities are cosy, if not extensive - although it has a 10 screen cinema. You can visit the Black Country Museum (an interesting experience) and the zoo. Walsall is more a Birmingham suburb than either Dudley or (certainly) Wolverhampton.

Telford

Telford is a new town with an ice-rink, bowling-alley, 10-screen cinema and indoor rackets centre. It is close to the Ironbridge Gorge with its 10 museums and World Heritage site.

ESCAPE ROUTES

Wolverhampton is just twenty minutes out of Birmingham (Dudley and Walsall are closer; Telford a little further away). The area immediately around the University's scattered campuses is suburban, with tracts of rolling farmland.

Further afield, you can visit Ludlow Castle, out west towards Bridgnorth - an impressive fortress; or travel into Shropshire, a very lovely county.

Simply visiting the University's various sites will give you some idea of the area's topography, history and variety.

Communications

Wolverhampton

Rail-links are wide, and easily link into the going-everywhere Midlands network. **Coaches** also travel all over the country. Wolverhampton is close to both the **M6** and the **M54**, with easy access to the whole country. **Birmingham International Airport** is near enough to be useful.

Dudley and Walsall

Walsall has a **railway station**, Dudley does not. Walsall acts as a branch station. Walsall is just off the **M6**, and Dudley not far off the **M5**.

SOUTH

Anglia Polytechnic University
University of Bath
Bath College of Higher Education
Bournemouth University
University of Brighton
University of Bristol
Bristol, University of the West of England
University of Buckingham
Buckinghamshire College
Canterbury Christchurch College of Higher Education
Cheltenham and Gloucester College of Higher Education
Chichester Institute of Higher Education
University of East Anglia
University of Essex
University of Exeter
University of Hertfordshire
University of Kent at Canterbury
Kingston University
The LSU College of Higher Education
University of Luton
Oxford Brookes University
University of Plymouth
University of Portsmouth
University of Reading
University of Southampton
Southampton Institute of Higher Education
University of Surrey
University of Sussex

Anglia Polytechnic University

Chelmsford Campus
Victoria Road
Chelmsford
Essex
CM1 1LL
Telephone: 01245 493131

University Charter date: 1992

Anglia is a medium-sized university with around 7,000 full-time undergraduates taught on two main campuses: one in Cambridge and one in Chelmsford. The University's third campus is in Brentwood. Courses are modularised in 'families'. Assessment is largely by coursework, although there are some examinations. Accommodation: the University runs a reservation service which includes halls of residence, University-controlled rooms and rooms in the private sector.

THE CAMPUSES

Anglia, as it is now, was formed in 1991 by combining two major colleges, plus two smaller centres. The Cambridge College of Arts and Technology (CCAT) has long had a high reputation in its field; the Essex Institute of Higher Education (in Chelmsford) has long served its community comprehensively and well. In 1992, Anglia became a university, along with the other polytechnics.

Courses are generally based on a single campus and the two main campuses are very dissimilar, so the location of teaching for your subject will be very important here. The distance between the two is long and the roads tedious.

Two smaller campuses complete the institution: Brentwood (which houses the Department of Education and the Department of Health, Nursing and Social Work) and Danbury (Conference Centre).

Smoking is not permitted in university buildings, except in specially designated areas.

The Cambridge campus

A wide, shallow flight of steps takes you into the main, original building: a square-set block built in warm russet brick. The interior has a quick sense of affluence and quiet learning. Buildings to the rear create the ambience of a mini-scale campus, built mostly in the idiom of local domestic architecture - pale brick with darker trim-lines. The Computer Building strikes a contrasting modernistic note through its glass-capsule mode, enclosing a vivid spiral staircase. Some of the site's buildings are less than pleasing, but on the whole this is a well-spaced, visually harmonious campus with a consistently gracious atmosphere. The enclosed quadrangles, though small, create an overall impression of civilised learning.

The Mumford Building houses a well-used bar and canteen and the University's impressive theatre, is one of the best in Cambridge. The library areas are equally successful: carpets, wood-panelling, interesting artwork on the walls, good lighting. The ground floor allows 'quiet discussion' of work. In other areas, a working quiet prevails. There is a separate students' social club in a 19th century building, reminiscent of a small chapel, tucked into nearby Grafton Street.

Courses here: Broadly speaking: the majority of Language-based courses, Pure Sciences, Music, Business & Economics and Humanities.

The Chelmsford campus

The integration of the college here with the community it serves is immediately apparent from the location of its site: it sits directly opposite the Council Offices, bus station and railway station, depending on which of its perimeter roads is your point of reference. You can feel the ease with which the people from the town or surrounding area, in search of learning, could converge on this institution. Buildings are closely set around a small grassed square and along adjacent roads, moving from 1930s civic-institution-brick, through 1950s four-deck rectangles, to domestic housing.

In October 1994 a secondary social 'campus' (Rivermead) opened on a riverside site in Chelmsford, a 10 to 15 minutes' walk from base. It has its own Learning Resource Centre, accommodating the library and computer terminals, as well as 500 residential places in purpose-built halls of residence.

A small park beyond the dual carriageway (the campus boundary) and some green space behind the University-owned houses help relieve the modest town setting.

Courses here: Built Environment, Business, Computing and Planning, Health, Housing, Law and Technology.

Brentwood campus
The Brentwood campus, also in Essex, (closer in to London) is housed in an Edwardian country house with some new, purpose-built accommodation. This site has its own theatre, a developed arts programme, some accommodation and a nursery for 40 children.
  Courses here: Teacher Education

Cars
On all sites, a bicycle would be more of an asset.

Learning Resources

There are two main **libraries** (Cambridge and Chelmsford) and other site libraries. All libraries are linked by computer. Overall the libraries stock 300,000 items which include audio-visual materials. The University offers courses in computing to all students and the **Computer Service** has support staff available to all users. Facilities on open access are available on all three campuses. The new Learning Resources Centre at Chelmsford brings together the library, computer and media resources. **Language centres** at Cambridge and Chelmsford are designed to enable you to learn languages in your own time and at your own pace with the aid of audio-visual material and *ad hoc* tuition given by qualified staff. All courses give the opportunity of taking a Language module.

Culture on campus

Drama: The scope for dramatic involvement on any campus is very wide. The Mumford Theatre on the Cambridge campus is well equipped, with an apron stage which becomes an orchestra pit at the flick of a button. The number of productions on this campus is dazing. Brentwood also has a small theatre, not as ambitious but no less used. Chelmsford as yet does not have a theatre (but what institution of this size has three in all??), and uses the local Cramphorn Theatre for its productions.

Music: Chelmsford campus offers music lessons and has a collection of instruments you can either have on loan, or rent for longer periods. The Cambridge campus has lunchtime concerts. You can join the University orchestra, college choir, chamber choir, chamber orchestra, wind band, jazz orchestra... Wide opportunity for involvement.

The Union

Anglia Students' Union operates on each main campus (including Brentwood). The Union runs about 70 clubs and societies, including sports clubs, on all campuses; runs a bar and recreation areas at Cambridge and a bar at Chelmsford; organises a varied entertainments programme (no grand venue, so mainly up-and-coming acts or 'the best of the has-beens') and produces a student newspaper. There is a Student Advisory Centre at Cambridge and at Chelmsford.

Sport

Chelmsford campus: the campus has a sports hall/ gymnasium: local facilities used for pitch games.

Cambridge campus: Sports facilities include a multi-gym and two hard tennis courts. As in all Cambridge educational establishments, rowing is a strong sport. Off-campus there are playing fields (four pitches) and a cricket square.
  There are limited facilities at Brentwood.

Student welfare

There are fully equipped health and **medical centres** on both main campuses offering GP, nursing and consultant psychiatric advice services. The University has a **counselling service** whose orientation is preventative and developmental as well as supportive.

  Both main campuses have links with local **chaplains**, including ordained members of the academic staff at Chelmsford, who will oversee your spiritual welfare. Cambridge University's Fisher Society opens its doors to all Catholic students who are Cambridge-based.

Careers Service

The Careers Service offers personal interviews, has a well-stocked library and advice videos. You can also use CASCAID-HE, a computer-assisted guidance programme. A Student Employment Office at Chelmsford will help you to find part-time and vacation work.

Students with special needs

The University asks you to contact the Admissions Office before you apply to Anglia, and offers as much assistance as possible to your application - although some buildings are not suitable for students with mobility problems. In collaboration with the RNIB, library work-stations are being installed at both main campuses for students with vision impairment. Cambridge already has a Kurzweil scanner, a braille embosser and other brailling facilities. A warden-controlled hostel in central Cambridge has specially designed accommodation and a trained carer is on hand if needed. This amenity is shared with Cambridge University. Further adapted accommodation is available at other hostels in Cambridge and Chelmsford.

Accommodation

The University runs a reservation service which includes University halls of residence, managed rooms and rooms in the private sector. If you are not offered university accommodation, the Accommodation Office (open at Chelmsford throughout the summer, full-time) will provide lists of suitable rooms and advice.

Cambridge campus

The University has an Accommodation Service which keeps a register of available accommodation and will give you as much assistance as possible. Unfortunately, if your offer depends on your 'A'-level results, you will not have the lists until your offer is confirmed, which does not give you very much time.

  There are 225 places in halls of residence on the Cambridge campus. Cambridge-based students generally rely on alternative accommodation stocks.

  The University manages around 620 places in student shared houses.

  Generally, Cambridge is not an easy place to find accommodation. If you are thinking of coming here, make sure you will have time before you arrive to come and look for somewhere to live. The Accommodation Office lists about 1,000 places in bed and breakfast or full-board accommodation. Costs are high.

Costs (1995/96)
Single room: £39-£55.25 per week

Private sector housing: self-catering is around £45 - £57 per week in Cambridge, excluding bills

Chelmsford campus

The Rivermead campus accommodates 503 students; an older hall houses 105, mainly first years.

The University also owns some shared houses in Chelmsford and Brentwood.

Costs (1995/96)

Halls of residence and University controlled houses:
Single room: £34-£51 per week (Chelmsford)
Single room: £39-£55.25 per week (Cambridge)

Private sector housing: self-catering is around £38 - £42 per week in Chelmsford, excluding bills, and £45 - £57 per week in Cambridge.

Mature students

Anglia has a strong commitment to mature students, and a high proportion of students are over 21 on entry. All levels of University advice services are used to handling the specific needs of mature students. Entry requirements can be fulfilled by vocational courses, non-examined courses or relevant skills, or an Access Certificate. The University offers a wide range of part-time courses.

Nursery

Three on-campus nurseries: one at Cambridge, one at Chelmsford, the other at Brentwood, take children aged between two and five years of both staff and students.

THE CITIES

Cambridge (population: 102,500)

See The University of Cambridge's entry.

Chelmsford (population: 152,000)

Chelmsford is the county town of Essex, medium sized and undistinguished. It serves a large and heavily populated area and consequently has its fair share of standard chain stores, plus quite a lot of cheap eating places/pub food. There is a quite pleasant cathedral close, a quiet enclave very close to the town centre, where shops are a little more old-fashioned; the cathedral itself is squat and unprepossessing from the outside; we did not go inside. There is, inevitably, a large covered shopping area.

Theatres: Chelmsford has two theatres, one with a professional company and one (smaller) for community use.

Music: The Chancellor Hall is venue for a range of concerts - rock and jazz. There are two jazz clubs.

Sport: Chelmsford has a leisure centre with an ice-rink, swimming pool and extensive sports facilities. The town is the home of Essex County Cricket Club.

ESCAPE ROUTES

Cambridge

See the University of Cambridge's entry

Chelmsford

This part of Essex is not particularly wonderful: the stretch between Chelmsford and Cambridge is flat and built on, with commuting road networks. There is the distinct feeling around here that most of the population leaves in the morning and comes home to sleep - dormitory living. We know it quite well, and at risk of causing offence, cannot think of anything to say.

At the eastern edge of the county you are near the villages of Suffolk and Suffolk's winding lanes: contrary to the Essex Man/Woman myth, this end of the county opens easily into the counties where the pace of life slows markedly. You can also travel north to the town of Saffron Walden, rich from the wool trade over centuries, and the scattering of pretty villages nearby.

The Essex coast runs down to Southend (and beyond) with its pub and club life. You are not far out of London.

Harwich (ferries to Holland and Belgium) is not far away by train: fares to Amsterdam are still very reasonable.

Communications

Cambridge

See the University of Cambridge's entry.

Chelmsford

Chelmsford is on the **commuter line** to London, as is Brentwood, which means the Big City is only 35 and 25 minutes away respectively. **Coach** links are wide-ranging. Fast (when not jammed) **roads** into London, and out into the rest of Essex.

UNIVERSITY OF
BATH

Claverton Down
Bath BA2 7AY
Telephone: 01225 826826

University Charter date: 1966

Bath is a small university with around 5,000 undergraduate son full-time programmes and 1,000 full-time postgraduates. All part-time students are on postgraduate programmes. The University has a single, greenfield campus (200 acres) two miles outside Bath. Most courses here include a 'practical element' and most are also available as sandwich options. This is a technological university where the majority of subjects taught are scientific or engineering based; languages and social sciences balance the scales but no traditional 'arts courses' are actually offered as degrees. Assessment is usually a combination of examination, coursework and research projects.

All first years are offered a place in University accommodation on campus.

THE CAMPUS

After the granting of university status to major technological institutions around the country, a suitable home was found for the institution which became Bath University on a hilltop, 200 acre greenfield site where building began in 1966.

The University is set rather less than two miles (and a steep hill) out of Bath, but feels more remote than its distance. First impressions on arrival are of a campus exposed to the elements, although it is rimmed with trees. There is a lot of green space around. The buildings are uncompromisingly rectangular and set in neat, regular patterns; the symmetry and varying profiles (none too high) create, on the whole, an efficiency of ambience which suits well the role of the University: halfway between the academic and commercial/industrial worlds. There is an aesthetically light feel to the use of pillared spaces, areas of glass and the pleasing shades of surface materials - although it is an unfortunate truth that the 'sixties concrete can rapidly appear rather shabby, if one insists on looking closely. The main buildings run continuously along, or are closely connected with, a central 'pedestrian deck' which forms a social spindle for the campus, where students and staff can meet informally and around which are shops, bars and teaching facilities. On campus there are: several shops, four banks, a post office/newsagent, three launderettes and a general store.

Two well-spaced 'high-rise' (but not very high) blocks of residential accommodation are stacked above the central deck. Two more housing units, in neatly set, three-storey blocks, separated by a small copse, mark the northern edge of the campus. South of the main complex there is a landscaped hollow containing a small lake (always a

decorative environmental plus). This is overlooked by a small amphitheatre, an unusual feature which adds interesting scope for open-air student drama. Playing fields and tennis courts complete the sense of space and green calm. The University is small and its atmosphere combines an air of quiet, steady work with well-organised leisure, all on a fairly domestic scale.

Cars

You are unlikely to be given a permit in your first year. There is ample parking on campus for disabled drivers.

Learning Resources

The University now has a Learning Resources Centre open 24 hours a day. The main **library** has over 300,000 volumes, subscribes to nearly 2,200 periodicals and seats around 1,200 study spaces.   **Computing:** The newly opened 24-hour Learning Centre houses over 300 open access PCs, networked with access to the world wide web. Also here, a Help Desk and Computer Shop. You can take a language option in most degree schemes, and there is a **language laboratory** available for self-teaching.

Culture on campus

Extracurricular activities which are organised by specialist staff who run workshops and give expert tuition. The development of a new **Arts Centre** is underway: its Arts Theatre is now complete.

Drama: enthusiasts can work on productions on an experimental scale in the Barnor, before a larger audience, in the Arts Theatre. There are workshops, an Arts Weekend in the spring, regular theatre trips and visits to campus by professional companies each year. Opportunities also for dance under the tuition of a professional choreographer.

Music: The University actively encourages musical skills, A professional leader directs the student orchestra, which performs a wide and ambitious range of work, often with the Choral Society. There is also a concert band, a barbershop group and a musical and operatic society. The University sponsors a professional chamber group (the Herschel Ensemble) and arranges regular lunchtime and evening professional concerts, held in the University or in Bath. The Union Music Society currently has 15 bands using its facilities. The University subsidises lesson charges, and you can borrow from a good range of musical instruments.

Art: Again, amateur activity flourishes: there are weekly classes, workshop weekends and private working facilities; studios and workshops; personal or group tuition by practising artists. Exhibition space in the library displays domestic work and work by professional artists, and houses travelling exhibitions.

The Holbourne Museum in Bath is administered by the University. Group visits are arranged by the Union to the museum and the Crafts Study Centre housed there, where you can study and handle fine 20th century craft-work. The museum contains a wide and interesting collection of paintings, Italian maiolica, Renaissance bronzes, porcelain, silver, miniatures, furniture and glass. This was originally a private collection and has its own marks of idiosyncrasy. The building itself is a lovely example of 18th century elegance.

The Union

The Union operates during the week from an area at the base of Norwood House accommodation block. Services include Student Support Centre, Travel Shop, coffee bar, Discount Shop, 24 hour games area, bar and Ents venue. The Union employs 35 members of staff .There is currently a total of over 100 societies.

The University ENTS committee organises a range of events, including major gigs and cabaret, and works with four of Bath's nightclubs which offer student discounts.

The Welfare department has full time members of staff and a visiting solicitor gives free legal advice once a week. There is a nightbus, which runs between 11pm and 1am. and has a women priority policy.

The Community Action Group works with the elderly, underprivileged children and the mentally handicapped. A Learning Together scheme encourages students to spend two hours a week for ten weeks in a local school, taking a tutor group, consequently earning a certificate and a letter of recommendation.

Publications: The Union produces a newspaper and a weekly, well produced magazine, *Spike*. The Campus radio station broadcasts in the mornings and in the evenings during the week and all day at the weekend. CTV, the Campus television network, broadcasts every evening and gives a lot of time to student productions.

Sport

The University held the 1995 European Youth Olympics: an eight lane athletics track, an Astroturf pitch, eight new tennis courts and an indoor tennis hall were some of the facilities built for the occasion.

The University takes its sports very seriously, having a formally constituted Sports Development and Recreation Department. There are excellent facilities and tuition available on campus, free to students and open to the general public, for around 50 sporting activities: a sports hall, a 25m swimming pool, four squash courts, archery and rifle ranges, grass ski-slope, an equestrian cross-country course and dressage area and 85 acres of playing fields allow ample scope for recreation. At a second level, students who are working academically on physical education, recreation and sports technology are given every support. The staff of the department are active in various research fields and their expertise and skill reinforce all the work they do; they are backed by a team of 50 specialist coaches.

Bath has been designated one of the country's seven national centres for coach education. There are various coaching qualifications you can take, and a scheme which offers periods of instruction in a wide range of physical recreation pursuits, open to all staff and students. You will be encouraged to join in.

The University offers sports scholarships (allowing a year of high-pressure training for exceptionally gifted athletes) and bursaries (to help with high level training and coaching).

Student welfare

The University **health centre** is just off-campus on Quarry Road. The centre is staffed by three medical officers, three qualified sisters and a psychiatrist. It is staffed 24 hours a day and has a (term-time) sick bay. There is a **counselling service** available on campus from 9am to 5pm. The Union runs a Nightline and has access to legal advice. The **chaplaincy centre** team includes Anglican, Roman Catholic, Baptist, Methodist and Society of Friends members. There is a prayer room in the University for Muslim students and a mosque in Bath. The nearest synagogue is in Bristol, but there is an active Jewish Society.

Careers Service

You can discuss your plans with a careers advisor, or use computer programmes which guide 'occupational interest' or test aptitude.

Students with special needs

Contact the Director of Admissions outlining your disability. All Union facilities have lift or ramp access: access is not, however, easy for students on Biology or Biochemistry courses. Some residential accommodation has been built specifically for students who are wheelchair-bound: disabled and able-bodied students share communal facilities. There are 'talking book' facilities in the library.

Accommodation

There are over 1,874 places in accommodation blocks on campus. All first years are offered places in University accommodation, on campus; if you are a very late entrant, however, you may be housed in University accommodation in the city rather than on campus.

The siting of the University creates a wide divergence of life patterns between the students who live on campus and those who have accommodation on the outskirts of the city or in small villages scattered around Bath.

Halls of residence

Between 8 and 13 study-bedrooms are grouped around a communal kitchen. You can self-cater if you wish, or use the main refectories. A senior resident and resident tutor live in each complex.

Costs (1995/96)

self-catering: single: £1,477 (39 weeks) or £1,212 (32 weeks)

Private accommodation

Private accommodation is hard to find. Costs range above £40 per week. Where rooms are three or four miles away, the University tries to ensure that only a single bus journey is involved. The University will help and advise in your search and offers a free agency service.

Mature students

Minimum age for mature students is 21. The University does not run an Access course, but there is an arrangement with Bath College of Further Education, which offers Access courses leading to University admission for degree courses in Sociology. You do not have to comply with standard entry requirements, but should be able to demonstrate necessary ability, study skills and appropriate level of knowledge of any subject listed as a course requirement.

Nursery

There is a day nursery on campus open from 8.45am to 12.15pm and from 1.45pm to 5.15pm. The nursery has a limited number of places for children aged between two and five year. There is invariably a waiting list.

THE CITY (population: 79,965)

Bath is the most beautiful and complete Georgian city in England. It had the rare good fortune of having its streets planned and its buildings designed by an architect of genius, John Wood (and his talented son). The wealth necessary to create and sustain the high style of the city runs with its history. Its early origins as a Roman settlement, already famed for its warm mineral springs, are marked by the best preserved Roman baths in England. These are now the centrepiece of a museum, where exhibits give a vivid impression of life 2,000 years ago. Medieval Bath has left the borough walls defence ramparts. But the city's real fame began in the 18th century through three happy coincidences: Dr Oliver (of Bath Oliver fame) built a bath for the treatment of gout; John Wood found moneyed backers for his visionary schemes; and Beau Nash, a talented dandy of the time, brought London's elite to a world of 'the waters', balls, assemblies and promenading which grew increasingly rich, making Bath a byword for elegance and fashion. The aura and charm which still mark Bath today were distilled through the novels of Smollett and Fielding, Jane Austen and Dickens: few cities can have benefited from such a hype in days when the word had not been invented. No wonder tourists flock here!

Add to this a unique Robert Adams bridge over the Avon - a stone road of shops; a very beautiful abbey, founded in 1499 (rebuilt in the 17th century and restored in the 19th); the nearby 18th century Pump Room; the imposing Upper Assembly Rooms; a wealth of fine Georgian buildings and streets; and the sublime splendour of the Circus and Royal Crescent, where the fine proportions of Georgian architecture are revealed in the honey-gold local stone.

There are disadvantages: Bath's fame rests on its air of genteel calm, period retirement and quiet streets. There are thousands of tourists every year, crowding the peace that attracts them, competing for amenities and sending up prices. The Bath Festival is a marvellous bonus with its 'feast of culture', but again the city overflows at a time when end-of-year exams turn you inwards: the University's eyrie setting will be welcome. Glastonbury festival is also accessible.

The city offers excellent shopping facilities, including expensive boutiques and unusual high-quality craft work. Winebars, pubs, restaurants and tea-rooms are absorbed into Bath's cobbled ways. A city to yield lovely images which will haunt a lifetime, offset by a lively night-scene.

There are three markets open daily, and a flea market on Saturdays. Also an area of shopping well geared to student life: vegetarian food, ethnic goods. All worth a browse and a balance to the general affluence.

Theatre: The Theatre Royal is one of our oldest and most beautiful theatres; it presents pre-West End productions, opera, ballet, musicals and shows. Two smaller theatres: the Ustinov Studio and the Rhondo offer amateur and alternative shows.

Cinemas: Bath has three cinemas with six screens in all. Two cinemas are in converted theatres.

Music: Bath has a Choral Society, Symphony Orchestra, Cantata Group and City Orchestra, plus visiting performers. There is an active Gilbert and Sullivan group, a Bach Choir, jazz, Indian and Irish music. Each November a Mozartfest attracts leading international musicians.

Nightlife: Half a dozen nightclubs, good pubs with live music, and good restaurants.

Sport: Good spectator Rugby, three golf courses (2x18 and 1x9 hole). There is a sport and leisure centre.

ESCAPE ROUTES

The country around Bath is very beautiful, undulating and green. You will have no trouble in finding things to do should you wish to explore: the Cotswolds with their honey-coloured villages; the Mendips, with Cheddar Gorge, Ebbor Gorge and Wookey Hole; Wells Cathedral (the other half of the bishopric of Bath and Wells); Glastonbury Tor topped by the abbey...The Boathouse at Bath: the only punting reach left in the West Country. You can hire traditional wooden Thames skiffs, punts and canoes.

Have a look at the University of Bristol entry in this Guide: Bristol is not far away at all, and you will have easy access to the city.

Communications

Bath is on the main line **rail-link** between Bristol and London (Paddington). There is also a direct line to Exeter and the West Country. Coach services are very good. The city has reasonably fast access north to the **M4** and thence to London, Bristol, South Wales and, via the **M5** link, to Exeter or to Birmingham and the North.

Bath College of Higher Education

Newton Park
Bath
BA2 9BN
Telephone: 01225 873701

> Bath College offers modular degrees, either as combined honours, sometimes across disciplines; single honours are available provided that there are sufficient modules available to make up a degree. Assessment is by a combination of exam and coursework.

THE CAMPUS

Bath CHE has two campuses: Sion Hill in the centre of Bath and Newton Park four miles away.

Sion Hill
Sion Hill is housed in a beautiful Georgian Crescent, of the Nash variety, and a large modern building. The campus is in Lansdown on the north side of Bath quite a way from the city centre. Its grounds are landscaped - a pleasant feature in this residential area. The Faculty of Art and Design is here. The campus includes studios, workshops, a lecture theatre and student facilities. Residential accommodation is a short distance away in Somerset Place.

Newton Park
All other courses are located at Newton Park, the larger of the two sites. This estate is leased from the Duchy of Cornwall and is most gracious: the countryside around is open; the campus, a stately Georgian manor house. The older buildings have been adapted to house teaching space. Newer buildings have grown around the original and include the Michael Tippett Centre, with an auditorium and large rehearsal space, beautifully designed. Student residences, social and sports facilities are all on site: Newton Park offers a very contained student life. The grounds include a nature reserve, woods and farmland, as well as formal gardens. Four miles is not a great distance from Bath; you have the best of both worlds.

Transport
There is a Sion Hill-Newton Park shuttle which runs for students with lectures on both sites. It is used solely for this purpose and cannot be 'jumped' for a free ride into town. Students must be listed as 'inter-site' and their transport needs registered by their tutor. The Nightbus is run by the University of Bath, but is open to BCHE students. Priority is given to unaccompanied women. For general journeys, the Union recommends local taxi services (the 'shuttle service' from Newton Park to Bath is 70p one way), which actually work out to be cheaper than the bus.

Learning Resources
There are **libraries** on each campus: the Sion Hill library houses a bookstock and slide collection specialising in Art and Design; Newton Park's library supports subjects taught there and includes a listening library for Music and Schools' Resources. The Open Access **computing** room is at Newton Park and is available for individual work. Sion Hill has a Macintosh workshop for Art and Design. Somerset Place also has its own library and computing services for use by its residents.

Culture on campus
A series of concerts (Rainbow over Bath) are arranged jointly with the University of Bath. Twenty-five professional concerts are mounted during the academic year and range from early music to jazz to world music and contemporary music.

The Union
The Bath CHE Students' Union elects two sabbatical officers annually, a President and Vice-President, and has an Executive of fourteen. It employs six full-time members of staff, to administer the Union finances, run the bars (one on each site) and the Union shop at Newton Park.

There are a number of part-time employees. Although most social events happen at Newton Park, Sion Hill is also a venue for some BCHE SU happenings. There are at least two events a week: a live band, at least once a fortnight and regular disco nights on both sites. A fortnightly bulletin - Ents Info Sheets - is available around the College. Big events include the Christmas Party, Summer Ball at Newton Park and the Graduation Ball at Sion Hill. The Union runs a range of clubs and societies: all have a nominal joining fee. You can form your own society with just 13 like minded people, provided that you are all willing to donate your joining fee.

BCHE SU regards welfare as one of its primary functions. Training is provided for volunteers and one of the sabbatical posts is devoted to welfare provision. The half-

Bath) and Student Community Action are all run by the Union. You also have recourse to Nightline, presently run by the University.

The Student News Magazine (AP'A-THY) is independent of the Student Union and run as a Society.

Sport

The Sports Hall is on the Newton Park campus, as are other sports facilities. Sports offered vary each year: football, rugby, netball, cricket, aerobics, jiu jitsu and horse-riding are listed by the 1993/94 Athletics Union. To join the Athletics Union costs £5 for a year, or £2 per society if you are interested in only a couple of particular sports.

Student welfare

The Union offers welfare advice and counselling, and the College has a Welfare Officer. The careers reference room is at Newton Park. The Careers Service has strong links with the University of Bath.

Accommodation

The College has 600 places in Halls of Residence of which 50 rooms are doubles. Halls are situated on both campuses and all are self-catering. Cost £33.20 - £37.70 pw for 40 weeks (1995/96).

In the private sector most students can find rooms in shared student housing. £38-£43 pw for room in house

Mature students

Mature students with recognised, kitemarked Access courses are welcomed. If you are over 21 and do not have standard entrance qualifications, the College will consider your application on an individual basis.

CITY/ESCAPE ROUTES

See the University of Bath in this section.

Bournemouth University

Talbot Campus
Fern Barrow
Poole
Dorset
BH12 5BB
Telephone: 01202 524111

University Charter date: 1992

Bournemouth is a small/medium-sized university with around 7,000 full-time students (undergraduates - c. 6,000, postgraduates and HNDs). The main campus is two miles out of Bournemouth; the Bournemouth 'campus' is a cluster of buildings in the Lansdowne area of the town. A flexible course structure allows units to be built through full or part-time study. Learning support is available if you have problems. The University will house you in your first year in the student village, in hotels, guest houses or lodgings. You are assured of a place before you arrive.

THE CAMPUS

The Talbot Campus

Two miles out of Bournemouth, towards Poole (during your time here you will probably relate to both towns). Much of the building is new, high quality and with a 'college' atmosphere. The original buildings are functional '60's blocks. Spaces are well-kept and clean and the large windows allow in plenty of natural light. New building on campus has added smart five-storey teaching and library blocks.

As well as administration offices, and departmental teaching rooms, the Students' Union, refectory and sports hall are housed here.

The 'other half' of the campus is very new. A polygonal courtyard has flower beds and benches and is a pretty space enclosed by low rise staff offices and teaching rooms. The other pod-type construction houses the library, conference centre and lecture theatre. The interior is airy and light. Proportions here are domestic and friendly. Paths between are paved and bordered. We were impressed.

The new buildings help to cope with expanded student numbers, but the scale of the site is small in relation to the number of full-time students it serves.

Another impressive aspect of the university's development is its student village, on campus. This is much more a 'village' than many other euphemistically named student habitats, which are, in fact, self catering halls of residence.

This village is a mini housing estate, with starter-home ambience. The squares around which the houses are built have the brick-sets and grass verges of high-quality developments. The students around seemed very much at home. The new Student Centre houses, amongst other things, the medical centre and chaplaincy.

The immediate area is a surround of new housing estates. The University is 12 minutes walk from Winton which will cover most of your shopping needs.

Courses here: all those not recorded for the Bournemouth campus.

Bournemouth Campus

The University has acquired a number of buildings around the Lansdowne area of Bournemouth's town centre. Central administrative offices are here.

Courses here: courses in the Schools of Business Studies, Design, Engineering & Computing and Conservation Science.

Cars

Only those with special needs may park on or within one mile of campus. A park and ride scheme operates and cycle tracks have been laid.

Learning Resources

The **libraries** on the Talbot campus are purpose-built and well-planned. Bournemouth campus also has a library which serves the needs of its departments. Altogether, the libraries hold approximately 140,000 volumes and 1,500 current periodicals. The Campus Wide Information Service gives access to internal and external electronic information sources. The University aims to integrate **computing** into all aspects of life. The site has over 2000 personal computers. Open access is available in three large laboratories. There are 200 workstations on 24 hour access.

All students can develop **languages** through open learning methods using books and tapes, supported by group tutorials weekly. If you do well, you can qualify for an extra-curricular certification of language competence. French, German, Spanish, Portuguese, Dutch, Italian and Russian are all available.

Culture on campus

Drama and music: The Community Arts programme invites touring companies to perform on campus. Performance (theatre, musical, dance) are open to students, staff and local people.

The Union

Talbot Campus

'The Herb Garden' bar serves snacks during the day and 'Dylan's Joint' has a more substantial range of food. There are a couple of pool tables and games machines, and a small travel centre operates near the foyer.

The Union's main venue, the Sugar Mine, has a capacity of 800. Entertainments each weekend include live bands and discos. Wednesday events, of either live music or comedy, are held at 'Dylan's Joint', whose smaller bar is a good place for a quiet drink. The University bars are open every night and offer the cheapest prices around. Larger events are held at venues in either Poole or Bournemouth.

Bournemouth Campus

The Union and University recently acquired Bournemouth's Old Fire Station in the centre of town - an excellent and unusual social venue which now houses a nightclub and bar, a bistro and the longest fireman's pole in Britain! Most entertainment happens here.

There are approximately 20 societies funded by the Union. *'Nerve'* is the Union's regular magazine.

Students are represented on many of the University's committees, including the Board of Governors. The Union and University jointly employ a professional Welfare Administrator, one sabbatical officer is in charge of welfare and the Union runs a nightline.

Advice on any financial, personal and academic difficulties you may have is available on weekdays.

Sport

On the Talbot campus, the sports hall has two squash courts and a multigym next door to the student Union. There are several floodlit all weather courts with multipurpose pitch markings. You can indulge in most sporting activities in the surrounding area, if not on University owned facilities. Full-time instructors organise fixtures, give coaching in all activities and arrange fun sports for those of you who are serious, but not that serious. There are eight sports which have UAU fixtures.

Wall-climbing facilities are available.

Clubs take part in Bournemouth and Dorset County Associations matches.

Student welfare

In the new purpose-built Medical Centre on campus, local GP's hold surgeries for students who register with them. **Medical assistance** is available for accidents or emergencies. There is also a qualified nurse on site and dental treatment available.

The University provides a **counselling service**, and workshops covering some aspects of welfare are run through the Health Service. Anglican, Roman Catholic, Free Church and Jewish **chaplains** are responsible for your religious welfare and for ecumenical services. A common room in the new Student Centre is used, and is open to all.

Employment and Occupational Guidance Centre

The Centre provides help in deciding career plans and finding employment. Advice can be sought at any time.

Students with special needs

Applications from students with STFT are welcome. You should contact the University at the time of your application to discuss your particular special needs.

Accommodation

The University guarantees a place to live for all incoming first years in either the student village, hotels, guest houses or lodgings.

Student village

The student village, directly opposite the campus, can house 250 students; places are allocated on a first come first served basis, and chances for first years are slim.. Leases run for 40 weeks and all houses are NON-SMOKING. A launderette is available on campus.

Costs (1995/96)

Self-catering: £45 per week

Other Halls, Hotels and Guest Houses

Hurn House, in the Lansdowne area of the town, offers 144 self-catered places all reserved for first years. The majority of first years are housed in small hotels in various areas of Bournemouth and along the coastal developments. Most clusters of accommodation are within four miles of the University. Most also are well served by shops and pubs - so you can soon join a student mini-community.

The Accommodation Service has negotiated prices and checked facilities, and will book a place for you. Termly contracts give you more flexibility of movement: a good thing as you make new friends.

Costs (1995/96)

Hurn House: £48 per week
Hotels and Guest Houses: £45-£66 per week

Private accommodation

Easier to find than in many student areas. You have both Poole and Bournemouth to explore. Boscombe is a popular student area. Rents are medium range to high, but properties will be of higher quality in the main. The Accommodation Service maintains a register

Costs (1995)

Self-catering: £35 to £50 per week

Mature students

Normal entry requirements do not apply if you are over 21. You should contact the Admissions Unit early, so that your application can be assessed before you apply through UCAS. A flexible range of qualifications will be considered. The policy for accrediting prior learning and experience is generous.

There are extended courses in Engineering and Science if you are qualified to pursue a degree course, but less than confident about your scientific or numeracy competence.

Nursery

There are 30 nursery places on campus for babies from six months old to children of five years. If lectures are timetabled late, the creche stays open until 6.30pm. The Union runs a half term playscheme.

THE CITY (population: 159,000)

Bournemouth, with its wide sands and mild climate, is a haven for holiday-makers: entertainments, pleasure beaches, outdoor sport of every kind and fashion are here. The town retains its open spaces: 2,000 acres of parks and gardens, which give the air of a relaxed, spacious resort, rather than a kiss-me-quick rollercoaster ride.

The town is built in a bowl, roads climbing out of the basin bottom. Small alleys and narrow lanes are lined with small shops and restaurants. If you come here, there is a danger that you will feel too much on holiday, especially on bright winter days when you will have the whole place to yourself.

There are a lot of hotels of the 'English Riviera' variety, and the town's clientele is sedate.

Shopping is generally small scale and quite elegant: its suitability will depend on how you regard student living.

A two mile walk east, via Hengistbury Head, brings you to Christchurch, set on two estuaries and an excellent place for bird-watching. Christchurch priory church dates from Saxon times and architecturally spans through to the Renaissance. The town also has a ruined castle, a Norman house, and a monument to Shelley.

Museums and galleries: The Russell-Cotes Arts Gallery and Museum covers the general history of Bournemouth and has changing art exhibitions; the Bournemouth Exhibition Centre has changing exhibitions.

Theatre: Bournemouth International Centre has two halls for theatrical performance, hosting touring shows, ballet and drama; the Pavilion Theatre presents summer spectaculars; so does the Pier Theatre.

Music: The Bournemouth Symphony Orchestra plays regularly in the Winter Gardens. There seem to be rather a lot of **festivals**: a music festival in May which has classical and jazz events, a 'Music Makers' Festival' from 25th June to 9th July (out of term, but you might still be around), and the annual International Festival in June. There are also Summer Illuminations, which include a candle lighting ceremony. The International Centre is a major stop on the big name band circuit.

Cinema: two cinemas: an Odeon (five screens) and a MGM cinema (three screens).

Nightlife: the town has a large and popular nightclub called the Cage/Zoo club (student night - Monday). Other clubs are less flashy, but give you variety. Pub life flourishes in central and suburban Bournemouth, and there is a good range of eating out places.

Poole...

....has a more ubiquitous pub life, plus a mega-club with three levels and many bars. Popular for balls. The UCI has 10 screens and is part of the **Tower Park complex,** which has a skating rink, bowling, Lazer Quest, swimming pool and other amusements ...plus fast food burgers, bars and a night club.

The **Arts Centre** has a cinema showing less mainstream films, cafe, exhibitions, theatre and live bands.

Sports: Bournemouth has facilities for golf, bowling, ten-pin bowling and all major sports. **The Dolphin Leisure Centre** has a near-Olympic size swimming pool with high diving boards, a solarium and gym. Student discounts on offer. The **Bournemouth International Centre** has a leisure pool and limited sports facilities; more extensive are those at the **Littledown Centre** two miles out of town.

Poole Harbour is a major centre for watersports and sailing.

ESCAPE ROUTES

Bournemouth, itself a major resort, has access to much of southern England's holiday-making area. Apart from the coastal attractions, which are many, Bournemouth is close to the **New Forest**, famous for its ponies. The forest was named 'New' by William the Conqueror (some short time after 1066 and all that), so it should not be regarded as a recent greening. The New Forest has excellent facilities for walking and riding.

You can take a boat to the **Isle of Wight** from Southampton, or to the Channel Islands and **Brownsea Island** from **Poole.** Brownsea Island is now a nature reserve, but used to be a reserve for boy scouts: there is an open amphitheatre on the island which stages annual productions in the summer. Poole, your other 'centre' is Britain's largest natural harbour, and is one of the largest in the world. As well as these outdoor wonders there is a huge sports centre with facilities comparable to what is on offer in Bournemouth. Beyond is the **Isle of Purbeck**, designated an area of outstanding natural beauty. You should visit **Stonehenge**, about an hour's drive away- as is **Salisbury**, with its wonderful cathedral and ancient graces.

And more... In **Southampton,** not a long drive away, is the **Hall of Aviation** (the official memorial to R.J.Mitchell, designer of the **Spitfire**).

On your doorstep are miles of sandy beaches and a wealth of watersports: you will have to remind yourself daily that you are here to study.

Communications

Rail-links are extensive, although not particularly speedy. Talbot Campus is a seven minute drive from the station; Bournemouth campus is a five minute walk. **Coach** services likewise. Bournemouth is not easily linked into the country's main **motorways**, but by-passes and newly improved A-roads make journeys easier. Hurn **airport** has a range of inter-European flights.

University of Brighton

Mithras House
Lewes Road
Brighton
BN2 4AT
Telephone: 01273 600900

University Charter date: 1992

Brighton is a medium-sized university with around 7,000 undergraduate students on full-time programmes, 750 HND students and 400 full-time postgraduates. The University has four sites, each very different from the others - three in and around Brighton, one in Eastbourne. It is very important that you find out at which campus the course you wish to study is based: we have not found it easy to sort what is where...there are indicators in the text below. Courses are modular and offered in single and joint honours programmes.

Limited University accommodation is mainly occupied by first years.

THE CAMPUSES

This University exists on four quite separate campuses, entirely distinct in character and setting. Three are within reasonable striking distance of each other; the fourth is twenty miles away, in Eastbourne. It is quite difficult to identify a 'main campus', since each of the three Brighton sites can lay some claim: the Falmer site is purpose-built and has the mix of academic, residential and amenity buildings, grouped on a defined 'greenfield' plot which fits the image evoked by the word 'campus'; the Moulsecoomb site fits another stereotype image: twin multistorey, functional blocks faced by a rather forbidding building which houses most administrative and management services; the Grand Parade group of buildings occupies the very centre of Brighton and is a significant presence in the life of the town.

Eastbourne, of course, was once an independent college; student life here is strong, although you will be a full member of the University community and have access to all facilities - just as Brighton students have access to Eastbourne.

Let us start in Brighton, and move outward.

Grand Parade

This is a handy umbrella title for the group of buildings strung along the A27 main access road. The largest building almost directly faces the famous Pavilion. It is quite a large modern block, accommodating the University's own theatre (a professional-looking affair), the spacious art gallery, and the academic pursuits of 1,000 students. It has a small lawned inner courtyard, with a few seats. Clustered more or less nearby are several buildings, some nicely period and domestic in style, which make up the rest of this 'precinct'. Most courses here are in the fields of visual and performing arts.

Courses here: mainly Art, Design, Humanities, Performing Arts, Sculpture. Also Catering, Urban Studies, Computer Centre, Photography and Fashion Textiles.

The Moulsecoomb site

Leave the grand bits of Brighton behind, take the road to Lewes into an area faced by housing estates and a large complex of retail stores, and the University lifts its solid bulk in two tall buildings: dark brick, white concrete and glass. This is the largest of the sites, and the circulation areas within are very busy. The recessing of the site from the road is too shallow to achieve any calm, but some effort has been made to plant trees and create green margins, and the atmosphere is energetic and talkative. The Students' Union offices are here, and across the road Mithras House contains most of the University's administrative offices. The road into Brighton can be very congested, but you can use rapid rail instead: the rail line runs alongside the site and Moulsecoomb Station is immediately behind.

Courses here: Engineering (range), Pharmacy, Computing, Finance and Accounting, Mathematical Sciences, Architecture and Interior Design, Construction, Geography and Surveying.

The Falmer site

This greenfield campus is large, but dwarfed by the scale of the campus of the University of Sussex, on the other side of the shallow valley. You reach the site via a long country lane (Village Way) lined with parked cars in term time. Buildings here are dark brick, topped by concrete-faced or white-painted 'flats'. The style is low-key, and the scale and ambience friendly, its domestic note enhanced by the complex of residential units on or close to the site, and by the easy presence of sports facilities.

Housing two University campuses, the Falmer site composes a curious island of student-living in an empty landscape. The frontier between the two campuses is marked by the rail line, and Falmer Station links you with Brighton (four miles) and Lewes (about three miles away).

Courses here: Community Studies, Languages, Education, Library and Information Studies, Maths and Science Centre, Literacy Centre and Teacher Training.

Eastbourne site

The Eastbourne 'campus' occupies a collection of large villas with beautiful gardens, the buildings faced with red tiles and mock-Tudor gables. The area is thick with private schools and carries the mantle of long-established order and trained courtesy (the first 'Please wipe you feet' mat we have used on our travels). The large gardens, tall trees and well-kept lawns provide a gracious setting for your studies, and the most westerly group of villas is within minutes' walk of the seashore, the promenade, and the footpath along the shoreline to Beachy Head.

The Chelsea School of PE, Sports Science, Dance and Leisure here is a designated centre for the National Coaching Foundation.

Courses here: Podiatry (at the Leaf Hospital), Physiotherapy, Physical Education, Dance, Sports Science, Business, Hospitality and Tourism, Food Retailing and Food Studies.

N.B. The identification of courses with campus sites is not entirely accurate, since course components are sometimes dispersed. You should check if you are concerned about your base: they are all very different!

Cars

Not really recommended, but very useful.

Learning Resources

Each site has its own **library** with stock suited to its subjects. The total number of items in all libraries exceeds 500,000 - including 3,000 current periodicals. Eight libraries in all. Opening hours at the Moulsecoomb site library are Monday to Thursday 8.30am to 9pm, to 5pm on Friday and on Saturdays 9am to 1pm. Other site libraries do not have such generous opening times. The library on the Moulsecoomb site is new.

The **Computer Centre** serves all sites and there are special documents to help new users come to grips with the system. Facilities are available in some halls of residence. Members of the User Services Section provide advice and consultancy services: a member of the Service is at each site (two at the Moulsecoomb campus).

The modular course structures allow you to slot in a language option if you wish- check on modules available.

Culture on campus

The prospectus is not clear about what exactly happens at which campus, so we have had to be general here. If it matters to you greatly, check activities on the site at which you will be based before you apply.

Much of the information we do have has come from site plans, and looking at notice boards.

Drama: The University theatre is on the Grand Parade campus. There is a Drama Society, and contemporary dance lessons are given weekly

Art: The University's gallery at the Grand Parade campus holds exhibitions throughout the year. Themes often relate to the subjects of the popular Open Lectures, delivered by guest speakers. Student works are regularly shown.

Music: A University Orchestra and Choir work towards performances each term.

The Union

The University of Brighton Students' Union (UBSU) operates on each campus with a total of six sabbatical officers and 14 assistants.

UBSU is limited in the range of events it can hold: the Union has no main hall and so must use venues in Brighton to hold larger events. There is a shuttle service between Eastbourne and Brighton. The Union runs bars at Falmer and Eastbourne, both offering food, discos and club nights. The Basement nightclub in Brighton is also run by the Union.

38 societies are funded by the Union, mainly religious, political and cultural interests. The Union produces an annual handbook, and a handbook covering sports. *Grapevine*, weekly, carries an entertainments listing, club and society news and classifieds. *Spoof*, a monthly magazine, includes many general interest features.

The Welfare and Advice Unit is staffed by full-time advisors: available at Moulsecoomb every weekday and for one day per week at the other campuses. A women's bus runs to town.

Sport

Sport activities offer one of the few ways in which students from Eastbourne and Brighton can easily mix. Few teams are now campus-specific. There are around 40 clubs covering the normal, rugby and football, to the not so, kite flying and kayaking. An interdepartmental competition has an emphasis on the social side of sport and the University Recreation Service runs Health and Fitness, Sports and Outdoor Pursuit courses. Introductory courses are run for beginners. Sports facilities include hockey pitches, lacrosse, football and rugby pitches, athletics facilities, tennis and netball courts, indoor swimming pool, gymnasia, saunas and sunbeds, dance studios, a climbing wall, floodlit training areas and extensive playing fields. Facilities are mostly at the Falmer and Eastbourne sites. Recently women's teams in hockey, football, rugby and basketball have been very successful.

Student welfare

Each campus has a **surgery** run by a local GP and a University nurse. You must register with one of these, or with another local practice. Professional **counsellors**, **psychologists** and **psychotherapists** can be seen by appointment on each campus. The Welfare Service offers wide-ranging practical advice at each campus.

The University has **chaplains** who provide friendship and support, regardless of your faith. Services arranged include daily worship for Muslim students at Moulsecoomb.

Careers Service

Available on all four sites, the Service runs workshops on application and interview techniques and arranges interviews. Resources include a well-stocked careers library and PROSPECT-HE. A fortnightly newsletter of employment news is produced.

Students with special needs

Access and resources vary from site to site: you are advised to visit before applying. A separate assessment interview can be arranged to determine the feasibility of following a chosen course on a particular campus.

Accommodation

University-owned accommodation

First years occupy the majority of University accommodation, although you might opt to live in town in one of the many lodgings or self-catered properties available. Offers are made according to how quickly you respond to your academic offer from the University. Each site has accommodation nearby, mostly self-catering

Costs (1995/6)

Halls of residence:

Self-catering single:	£42 to £53 per week
Catered single:	£63 per week

Private sector accommodation

The University keeps a list of about 3,500 landlords/ladies who offer lodgings or self-catered accommodation (flats or houses). Costs (1994/95): shared self-catering: £43 per person per week (excluding bills) maximum.

Mature students

The University welcomes applications from all students, regardless of age and formal qualifications, provided that you have evidence of relevant work experience and can convince Admissions you are able to follow a course. The university is a member of the Southern Access Federation (SAFE). The University's Access Co-ordinator will advise you on SAFE courses. You will be in a stronger position if you have followed, or are taking, some course of study before applying.

Nursery

There are 35 places available at Moulsecoomb and 40 at Falmer for the children of both staff and students. Children between the ages of two and five are accepted. A new nursery at the Eastbourne campus has ten places.

TOWNS/ESCAPE ROUTES

See the University of Sussex' entry.

University of Bristol

Senate House
Tyndall Avenue
Bristol
BS8 1TH
Telephone: 0117 928 9000

University Charter date: 1909

Bristol is a medium-sized university with 8,500 undergraduate students on full-time programmes and around 2,000 full-time postgraduates. This is a civic university with a campus just outside Bristol's centre, heading towards Bristol's bohemia. Courses give traditional academic options with unit values. Assessment is mainly by exam, but might include coursework or a project/dissertation.

The University guarantees accommodation to all first years who normally liver outside the Bristol area and who apply to the Accommodation Office by July 31st.

THE CAMPUS

University College Bristol was founded in 1876. The College merged with the Merchant Venturers' Technical College in 1909 to become a University.

The University, in the main, occupies a hill half a mile from the city's waterfront, and is an integrated part of the city scene. The majority of the buildings are grouped around the lovely centrepiece of Royal Fort Gardens, the setting for a graceful 18th century merchant's house, currently the University's Department of Music.

The precinct does not have clear edges; its buildings spill out into nearby squares and streets and its spaces are intersected by two highly exclusive shopping ways, Queen's Road and Park Street, although the 'precinct' itself feels very removed from the hurly-burly of city life, a remove enhanced by the number of trees.

The University adds its touch of drama to the city skyline with the Gothic-style Wills Memorial Building (completed in 1925), which has the lines and space normally appropriate to a cathedral. This is one of the most 'landmark' of University facades, and a good place to meet.

The precinct harbours a rich range of architectural styles: the Arts Faculty occupies a number of Victorian villas, linked together but preserving their gardens and period dignity; the Science buildings have modern, regular, geometric lines, although some are in early century, purpose-built faculty buildings of redbrick; there is the inevitable presence of harsh functional blocks, one of which is the library, but interiors are gracious. The Social Sciences block, built in the 1990's neo-domestic style, picks up and echoes the lines of the large house around which it extends. We were impressed by the quality of this building, and indeed by the quality of all Bristol's buildings.

As a student, you will probably relate more to the 'village' of Clifton and the area up to Redland than to the city centre: both are doorstep distance. Clifton gives you an ambience of minor bohemian living which balances well the go-getting hustle of the city.

One point: the Union Building is a ten minute walk from the main University buildings. It felt further, perhaps because we had not quite cracked the labyrinth of roads between the two sites. The building itself is a 1960's block, and its swimming pool makes the inside very warm.

Cars

A general rule: first years - no cars.

Learning Resources

Bristol has 14 separate **libraries**, all with different library regulations. The University's total number of books and periodicals (6,000 are subscribed to) exceeds 1 million volumes; 25,000 are added each year. The 14 libraries seat over 2,000 readers in total.

The **Computing Service** provides lectures and general help, as well as a variety of support services, including a Help Desk with a special device to communicate with those who are deaf or hearing-impaired (TDD) and Help Desk for Undergraduates. Facilities available include microcomputer laboratories located around the campus and in halls of residence - eight or more offering 24 hour access.

The **language laboratories** give you access to a library of over 3,000 tapes in a range of languages at a variety of levels. Languages include Arabic, Catalan, Hebrew, Finnish, Serbo-Croat (decide which...), Welsh, Chinese and Swahili, among many others, and the standard European fare. The Language Centre provides teaching and resources for language units in degree programmes.

Culture on campus

Drama: Drama is particularly strong in Bristol. There are three theatres: the Wickham Theatre is used for the Drama Department's own productions and by small-scale visiting professional groups. The larger Winston Theatre in the Students' Union accommodates various student drama groups, and the Victoria Rooms (built in 1842) offer a larger (700) auditorium for large-scale productions (e.g. by the University Operatic Society). Student productions have a presence at the Edinburgh Festival. There is a theatre-in-education programme run by students.

Film: A wide variety of films is shown at different venues within the University, about four a week.

Music: The University has four orchestras and choirs, and a number of smaller scale ensembles. Fifty concerts a year include lunchtime concerts and a range of other recitals and performances. Currently major concerts are set in the University Great Hall or various city venues but from January 1996 musical activities will be centred at the Victoria Rooms following the Department of Music's relocation there. Recitals will take place in the Regency Room, which will be re-equipped with a range of excellent instruments including a Chamber Organ. Larger concerts will be performed in the main 700-seat theatre where versatile staging will accommodate a large symphony orchestra or opera productions.

Groups associated with the Music Department include various Music Ensembles and the Corradini (Baroque string) Ensemble. At the end of the year, orchestras and choirs combine in a gala concert and there is a soiree in the gardens of Royal Fort House.

The Union

The Union building is a plain, but well-proportioned six storey block . There are three bars, one preserved for discos and functions, a restaurant and snack bar, a shop, a travel bureau, a launderette, a video and record library, a hair salon, a theatre, art/pottery rooms and a swimming pool. The games room has video games and snooker and pool tables. The Union runs a book exchange/selling scheme.

150 clubs and societies and the second largest Ents venue in Bristol. A free late night bus service will take women students from the Union to their homes. There is also a bus shuttle service, running throughout the evening between the Union and the halls of residence.

There are six sabbatical officers and 30 part time posts. Union welfare provision includes a well-stocked welfare and advice centre.

The Union produces a fortnightly newspaper, *Epigram*, which was shortlisted in the Guardian/NUS Media Awards.

Sport

The Indoor Centre at Woodland House, close to the precinct, houses a sports hall and trim-gym fitness room. Many indoor activities are on offer: squash, five-a-side soccer, basketball, volleyball, badminton, tennis, cricket and climbing practice (there is a climbing wall).

Playing fields at Coombe Dingle accommodate seven soccer, five hockey, four rugby, six cricket pitches and a floodlit artificial grass pitch. Twelve of the University's 16 tennis courts are here. Buses to and from the sports grounds run hourly (including weekends); otherwise you could jog the two/three miles.

The sailing club is on the river Avon at Axbridge and the boat club is at Saltford.

The University has a 33m swimming pool, under the Student Union building. The pool is open to the public, on a restricted basis.

Facilities are hired for dance activities and exercise classes.

There are, in all, 46 sports clubs. Over half the clubs have coaches. The Department of Sport Exercise and Health Sciences organises activities. The Advanced Sport Squad caters for talented sports people. The University offers sports bursaries.

Student welfare

The **Students' Health Service** has six doctors and four nursing sisters. It provides a full general practice service which includes advice and help with foreign travel immunisations, sports injuries, contraception, exam stress and pre-employment medicals. The **Student Counselling Service** is a confidential service for all students, offering help with work related or personal issues. The Union runs Niteline and also offers welfare advice. There are **chaplains** from all the main Christian denominations. Students from other faiths can be put in touch with their religious leaders in the city. An Orthodox Jewish rabbi is responsible for the University's Jewish students and the Ecumenical Chaplaincy Centre is staffed during weekdays in term time.

Careers Service

The Careers Service runs an extensive programme of events and activities, Insight courses into management and the media. Help too with application forms, workshops with video cameras on interview techniques. Skills training workshops run in conjunction with employers on subjects including leadership and presentation skills. All this on top of individual counselling, computer-aided guidance programmes and placement systems.

Students with special needs

You should outline any special needs requirements on your application form. Some University accommodation has been adapted for wheelchair users. Three residences have been identified as most suitable for visually impaired students. Practical support and information is available to all students with disabilities. Deaf students may choose between a range of provision: sign language, interpretation, computer-aided note-taking and radio aids. Contact the Disabilities Unit in the Department for Continuing Education for more information.

Accommodation

Bristol has 3,932 University-owned accommodation places and guarantees accommodation for all new undergraduates who have applied to the Accommodation Office by July 31st and who live outside the Bristol area. All accommodation is within two and a half miles of the main campus.

Halls of residence

Nine halls of residence, six in the Stoke Bishop complex and three in Clifton: five catered and four self-catering: three of the self-catering halls are arranged in flats of five to seven students. Some rooms have ensuite facilities.

All halls have social and sporting facilities: TV rooms, bars, launderettes.

Costs (1995/96)

Catered halls:

single:	£1,976 - £2,202 (30 weeks)
shared:	£1,574 - £1,765 (30 weeks)

Self-catering halls:

single:	£1,232 - £1,711 (30 or 38 weeks)
shared:	£828 (30 weeks)

Student houses

Student houses are owned or leased by the University and house between ten and 125 students per 'house' and are self-catering. The houses are usually within the immediate University area. Rooms are either single or shared. Kitchens and communal facilities are shared.

Costs (1995/96)

single:£1,330 - £2,489 (38-50 weeks)
shared: £893 - £1,140 (38 weeks)

Private accommodation

The majority of Bristol's students (around 7,000) live in private sector flats or bedsitters, with some in lodgings with families.

The areas most used by students living out of hall are Clifton, Cotham and Redland: all are within walking distance of the University. Students usually have to pay full rent over the summer. Rents are high.

If you do not want a place in University-owned accommodation, or are not placed, you will be asked to go down to Bristol to look at the noticeboard where vacancies are displayed. You will have to arrange for your own accommodation during the time you are searching.

Costs (1995/96)

£42 to £47 a week for reasonable accommodation.

Mature students

Mature students (over 21) should show evidence of recent academic work to complement any relevant work/life experience. The University accepts validated Access qualifications.

Nursery

The University Nursery Parents' Association runs a nursery for children from 18 months old.

THE CITY (population 384,422)

Bristol is a mix of the old and the new. The city grew up around its harbour on the river Avon and has been a flourishing commercial port since the 10th century.

The Avon is an attractive river and its deep gorge (good for rock climbs) just below Bristol at Clifton is spanned by the fine sweep of Brunel's famous suspension bridge. A very affluent city where Georgian terraces, medieval churches and many other listed buildings mark out the city's past and balance its modern, pedestrianised shopping centre. There is an imposing cathedral which was founded in 1148 as an Augustinian monastery.

As with many of Britain's port cities, Bristol's waterfront areas are being redeveloped for their amenity value. St Augustine's Reach, just off the 'Floating Harbour', is one of the centres of activity - exhibitions, fireworks displays, races - and home to the Watershed and Arnolfini Centre, both of which are innovative experiences of the worlds of media and modern art.

Between Bristol University and its Stoke Bishop halls of residence lie the 442 acres of rolling Clifton downland, protected by ancient law, and stretching into the city itself.
Theatres: The Theatre Royal, dating back to 1766, is the oldest working theatre in the country. Restored to its former glory in the early seventies, the building now also houses a small studio theatre, the New Vic. The Theatre Royal is home to the Old Vic Company. The Bristol Hippodrome seats 2,000 and hosts opera, ballet and touring productions.
Music: The Colston Hall is the city's main music venue and houses concerts ranging from rock to Mozart, including the Bristol Proms.
Cinema: Bristol has 12 in all, including two at the Watershed and one at the Arnolfini Arts Centre, both of which show art and minority films.
Nightlife: Nightclubs and discotheques, wine bars, restaurants and picturesque old pubs: Bristol is a lively city after dark. Student residential areas in particular generate a good community spirit. Perhaps the best known pub is the Llandoger Trow on King's Street, a timbered 17th century house.
Sport: Spectator sports: Gloucestershire Cricket Club; two football teams (City and Rovers); and the Bristol and Clifton Rugby Union Clubs. Excellent tennis facilities: Redland Green is famous for the international tennis championships held annually during the week before Wimbledon; there are numerous private tennis clubs and most parks have good public courts. There are ten public swimming pools (the pool at Clifton is open-air). There are four Sports Centres, an ice rink, two dry-ski slopes and several golf courses in the area around the city.

ESCAPE ROUTES

The area surrounding Bristol is rich with history and varied natural beauty: the Cotswolds with their villages, small churches, steep-sided beech-wooded valleys; the Mendip Hills - Cheddar and Ebbor Gorges, Wookey Hole; Wells Cathedral; the city of Bath; Glastonbury Tor... A good area for walking and exploring.

Across the river Severn you will find the Forest of Dean and the Wye Valley complete with Tintern Abbey (don't forget your Wordsworth). You also have easy access to South Wales - see the Cardiff and Swansea entries.

Communications

Bristol is just south of the **M4/M5** intersection, giving fast access to London, South Wales, the Midlands and the West Country. The National Express **coach network** links Bristol with most major cities. **Rail services** to London (1 hour and 40 minutes) and easy connecting routes to most major cities. Bristol **Lulsgate Airport** has scheduled connections

University of the West of England

BRISTOL

Frenchay Campus
Coldharbour Lane
Bristol BS16 1QY
Telephone: 0117 965 6261

University Charter date: 1992

UWE is a large university with around 11,000 undergraduate students on full-time programmes and 1,000 full-time postgraduates. A further 2,000 students are studying on undergraduate programmes part-time. The University has five campuses satellited around Bristol: none is far from the city centre. Degrees are modularised within faculties. Coursework is the main component of assessment, with some exams, projects or dissertations also included.

There is no guarantee given by the University of a place in halls of residence or houses: the Accommodation Office provides addresses of lodgings and shared houses/flats.

THE CAMPUS

There are five campuses in and around Bristol.

The Frenchay Campus

Frenchay Campus is the largest site, purpose-built in 1975, to the north of Bristol, not far from Bristol Parkway station.

A busy carriageway borders its northern edge; the predominance of tarmac rather distracts attention from the urban-country landscape immediately around. Frenchay Campus' buildings are all modern, in varying degrees of blocks: the campus has evolved a series of interconnected inner walkways and gantries, some concrete, some brick, some glass; parts look like enormous greenhouses.

The effect is of cluttered space: the atmosphere is positive, busy and friendly. This is a large institution, but personal. Rather daunting, large refectory-type services are off-set by small departmental recreation rooms; the mini-mall of shops and bank, centre campus, is both useful and a meeting ground.

There has been considerable expansion here: a new building for the Faculty of the Built Environment, lecture theatres, a computer centre and extended library facilities.

It is perhaps interesting to note that the Higher Education Funding Council building is on this site, and is the first building you will see: an impressive facade.

Students services include the Chaplaincy Centre (a pleasant, low octagonal building), main library and computer centre, and a full range of welfare and advisory services. This is something to bear in mind if your course is based at another of the sites. Facilities also include a computer shop, a sub-Post Office, a Travel Office, an insurance bureau, a launderette, and a Union shop. Two student villages on campus and a regular bus service into the city centre.

There is a regular bus service into the city centre.

Courses here: the Bristol Business School and the faculties of Applied Sciences, Built Environment, Computer Studies & Mathematics, Economics & Social Science, Engineering, Law and Languages and European Studies. The central administration, Students' Union and the Centre for Student Affairs also live here.

Bower Ashton Campus

South of Bristol, across the river. The Faculty of Art, Media & Design is here. The site borders Ashton Court Estate, so you have open country on your doorstep. The building is multi-storey glass and panels: a modern art school.

Redland Campus

The Faculty of Education lives out at Redland Hill. This building, a modern high-rise block, is set in its own (small) grounds. The area around is one of period houses and on the very edge of Durdham Downs - gracious and beautiful.

St Matthias Campus

St Matthias - the nearest site to Frenchay Campus, we have taken you full circle - houses the Faculties of Humanities and Health and Social Care. A listed building: grey, stone, gabled, set in suburbia. A small campus with green, well-kept lawns, tennis courts and two halls of residence.

Glenside Campus

Set in pleasant grounds in Stapleton, the campus houses the Faculty of Health and Social Care, with its own substantial library. Plus self-catering Units for 310 students.

If your course is not based at Frenchay, make sure that you visit the campus relevant to you on an open day.

Cars

Parking on all campuses is very limited and the University operates a permit scheme.

Learning Resources

The main **library** is on the Frenchay campus. Each campus has its own library relating to its subjects. You can also access computer based information. A total of 357,000 volumes, 2646 periodicals and 1,167 seating places. The library at Bower Ashton has special collections of exhibition catalogues, fashion patterns, slides and illustrations. Redlands library has a large collection of children's books.

You can take an extra curricular course in computer appreciation or programming. Programming support is available on all sites. **Computer Services** holds regular seminars on specialised computing areas, which can be arranged at any site. Two terminal rooms on the Frenchay campus are available continuously: these are open to all students, wherever you are sited.

The **Language Centre**, on the Frenchay campus, is open to all students for private study. It has a large selection of foreign language tapes. Self-study materials are available in 20 languages. As well as specialist language degrees, the University offers foreign language modules on many degree and diploma courses.

Culture on campus

Drama: You can join the Centre for Performing Arts which promotes all forms of artistic expression. The Centre is at Frenchay, and part of the activities of the Octagon Centre.
Music: Musical groups on offer to students are an orchestra, a chamber orchestra, a choir, instrumental trios and quartets. The University Singers and the University Symphony Orchestra are supported by the Centre for Performing Arts. Concerts are given three times a year. There are also weekly programmes by visiting performers during term time at Frenchay and fortnightly programmes at Redland. Every Spring a musical is presented and a number of minor operas are produced annually. Friday lunchtime entertainments (free for students) at the Octagon, include jazz, classical and contemporary music, drama and poetry. Music tuition is available to students at concessionary rates and there are practice rooms at Frenchay, Redland and St Matthias. Choral scholarships are available at Bristol Cathedral and the Centre for Performing Arts plans to offer music bursaries.

The Union

The Students' Union has its own building on the Frenchay Campus and offices on other sites. The building at Frenchay is very lively, with a positive, friendly atmosphere. There is a bar at each site and some entertainment events are organised at sites other than Frenchay. However, most students converge on the main site for the Friday night entertainment programme.

There are entertainments on all campuses, including comedy, film nights and bands. The Union runs its own nightclub in Bristol - the Tube Club - which is open five days a week. Two bars on the Frenchay campus. *BACUS*, the Union magazine, has details of entertainments, as well as articles of interest and concern to students at UWE and in Bristol. The usual full and varied spectrum of non-sports clubs and societies is available.

The Union Education, Welfare and Information Department provides support for students at an academic and welfare level, as an alternative to the University's Centre for Student Affairs (CSA).

Sport

The University uses pitches for soccer, lacrosse, cricket, American football and rugby at Beggan Bush Lane and St Mary's Rugby Club.

The Redland and St Matthias campuses each have a gymnasium. St Matthias also has two soccer pitches and a cricket square. On the main Frenchay campus the Recreation Centre is accessible through membership or a 'pay-as-you' play scheme, and is open for public use. Other facilities here include a floodlit artificial pitch, four squash courts, a weight/fitness room and a sunbed.

There are around 40 Union sports clubs.

The Centre for Physical Recreation organises courses and activities throughout the year for both staff and students of the University, including, during the summer term, sailing in the City Docks.

Student welfare

The University has three **health centres**, staffed by one full-time and two part-time doctors, supported by three nursing staff. You are advised to register with the University's GP if you live on campus, or with a local doctor. **Counsellors** are based in the Centre for Student Services at Frenchay and serve students from all campuses. The **Chaplaincy** base is the Octagon Centre, which is also used for other activities: drama, music and worship. It does have a special atmosphere, and offers a place of quiet for relaxation. The Chaplaincy reflects the ecumenical nature of the University's population.

The Centre for Student Affairs provides special support for any student wishing to improve **study skills**. A fortnightly programme of meetings during your first two terms include organising time, writing essays and preparing for examinations. Special assistance is given to full and part-time students on an appointments basis.

Careers Service

The main Careers Centre is on the Frenchay campus; other campuses have Careers Rooms relating to the subjects taught at that location. The Frenchay careers library has a number of computer programmes (including 'Jobs', PROSPECT HE and ROGET Scan) to help with planning and identifying vacancies. There are a number of careers events put on throughout the year, some in conjunction with the University of Bristol.

Students with special needs

There is a resource centre for disabled students with staff available for advice and guidance. The University produces an information pack for disabled students. Some facilities have been modified to suit the needs of particular students - the libraries at Frenchay and St Matthias have p.c.s with scanner, voice synthesiser and braille embosser. Four study bedrooms at Frenchay have been adapted for students with wheelchairs and space may be provided for personal care assistants.

Accommodation

Accommodation can be a problem in Bristol, although because of the location of Frenchay campus, you are not competing directly with the University of Bristol, and have easier hunting grounds. The University's own accommodation provision is limited. Responsibility for finding somewhere to live lies with you, so start early. Over 90% of University halls and houses are reserved for first years. There is no guarantee given by the University of a place in halls or houses. The Accommodation Office provides addresses of lodgings and shared houses/flats.

University listed accommodation has not been inspected. You should contact the Accommodation and Welfare Office for information and advice.

Halls of residence
The University offers 1,116 places in halls of residence. There are two self-catering halls : one (154 places) on the Redland campus, one (86 places) on the St Matthias campus. Two student villages on the Frenchay campus: Ashley village (238 places) and Carroll Court (294 places). Rooms are let for a full 40 week period. Halls are warden controlled.

Costs (1995/96)
Halls: £34.80 to £37.60 per week, single room, self-catering

Student houses
The University offers over 1,200 bedspaces in university managed houses in popular student areas of Bristol. These are let for a fixed period, usually 45 weeks. £35 to £44.75 per week (1995/96).

Private accommodation
The University Accommodation Guide gives you clear and comprehensive guidelines on how and what to negotiate before you agree to rent a room and information on various residential areas of Bristol. Self-catering: £35 to £40 per week exclusive of heating, electricity and gas (1995/96).

Mature students
The University welcomes enquiries from 'mature' students (those over 21 in the year of entry), and will consider your overall experience as well as academic achievement. Access courses run locally through Colleges of Further Education either guarantee a place at the University on successful completion or - at least - favourable consideration. There are study days where you can assess your own ability to pursue a degree course.

The Centre for Student Affairs runs specific events for mature students who have been accepted: workshops, study assistance and Open Days.

Nursery
The Union runs a nursery for up to 28 children from six months to five years old. This is based at St Matthias campus. The University's Staff Association runs a nursery for children aged between two and five years on the Frenchay campus. Both are open to students and staff. Fees are means tested.

Play-schemes for school-age children are run by the Union in half-term holidays at Frenchay, Redland and St. Matthias campuses.

THE CITY / ESCAPE ROUTES

See Bristol University entry in this Guide.

The University of Buckingham

Buckingham
MK18 1EG
Telephone:01280 814080

University Charter date: 1983
Buckingham is a small university with around 900 undergraduate students on full-time programmes and 100 full-time postgraduates.
NB: Buckingham is independent of direct government funding. Course fees for the 1996 session are £9,460, of which students eligible for a mandatory award will pay £7,284. Fees must be paid for each of the two years of your course. The University has a single campus on the edge of Buckingham. Courses run for two years, with four terms per year (including over the Summer). Humanities, Business and Law degrees are offered in flexible patterns.
Accommodation is guaranteed for first years.

THE CAMPUS

The University is situated on the edge of the quiet market town of Buckingham and is housed in an attractive mixture of sympathetically renovated old buildings and purpose-built new blocks, located on three precincts, one still in the finishing stages. One set is landscaped around the river Ouse, where an old mill is now used as the Students' Union; a former Franciscan monastery is the focus of the second. The third, the Chandos Road Complex, occupies renovated red-brick Victorian factory premises. The central library, a large lecture hall and computer rooms will be housed here. Because the University is so small, it has been possible to retain the character and human scale of the original buildings, and limits to expansion have been set that will preserve the atmosphere of the campus and the relation of the University with the town.

Buckingham is a small and friendly community with a strong international flavour. Although some of the mature students especially have sacrificed a great deal to go to university, there is - as you would expect - a general sense of affluence among students here.

Learning Resources

The **library**, containing 65,000 volumes, is divided between the two sites, according to the subjects taught in each of them. Open until 10pm. 202 study places in all.

While students studying **computing** have first call on the laboratory's facilities, the 47 terminals are open to all students and all courses provide opportunities for work on microcomputers. The facilities are available between 7am and 11pm. Tutorials are available in computer use.

Learning a language is an option for all students, whatever course you are taking (English if it is not your native language). The **Language Centre** has a self-access resources centre for audio and video recorded language material; there are two new audio-active comparative language laboratories, a video library covering all major languages, and computer-assisted learning.

Culture on campus

Drama: The Drama Society puts on productions of Shakespeare, Eliot, Brecht etc. in the Radcliffe Centre and sometimes in the open air.

Music: Lunchtime and evening concerts are sometimes given by visiting musicians, often students from the London music colleges. There are practice rooms and the Union has its own instruments for jazz.

The Union

Because the University is a private institution, wholly subject to market forces, the voice of the students is accorded a weight it does not always have in state universities. The students are represented on the Council and Senate.

The Union has a permanent manager and two staff, and sponsors a variety of clubs and societies, many of them catering for the needs of overseas students.

The Union organises regular social functions and special events such as the Graduation Ball and RAG Week. There are about 40 societies.

There is a shop, where you can buy secondhand books and the JCR with pool and video games. A late-night minibus service operates between library and 'home' villages/town at exam times and on social events nights.

Sport

The University Sports Association promotes various activities including rugby, hockey, cricket, tennis and soccer. There are all-weather tennis courts and an all-weather five-a-side pitch. Indoor activities include martial arts, aerobics, fencing, table tennis and snooker. There are 12 sports clubs on campus and other clubs and centres in the neighbourhood which students may use on payment of membership or booking fees.

The University's new sports field, a mile from the town offers rugby, hockey and a floodlit training area.

Student welfare

Students must register with a general practitioner, either locally or with the University medical officer. A **medical officer** and a colleague each hold a **weekly surgery**. There is a student **counselling service** whereby students can discuss personal problems with the student counsellor.

A **prayer room** is provided for Muslims and Halal meals are available in the refectory. The town offers Christian churches of many denominations, where students are welcome, but for mosques, a Sikh temple or synagogue you must go further afield to Milton Keynes or Oxford.

Careers Service

The Careers Service recommends an exploratory interview before beginning in-depth careers thought, 'to get to know yourself': or you can read the section of a recommended workbook which helps you to do the same thing. You can also use 'CASCAID - Higher Education'. Careers advisors will then help you to structure your CV, employers' application forms and covering letters. There is a well-stocked information room.

Students with special needs

There is a special tutor for students with specific learning difficulties.

Accommodation

The University has approximately 450 single rooms on or around campus; others are in the town. All accommodation is self-catering.

Accommodation is guaranteed for first year students; second years should expect to find their own. No problem about remaining in residences over the holidays, for an additional fee.

Student residences

The majority of rooms are in purpose-built halls of residence: others are in shared flats, refurbished cottages and off-campus houses. All kitchens are equipped for limited self-catering.

Costs (1995/96)

An average of £58 per week during term time and £30 per week during vacations. The rent varies according to size, facilities and location.

Private accommodation

Lodgings and rented accommodation are available in nearby villages. The Accommodation Office provides information. Costs: £45 to £80 per week (1995/96)

Costs (1995/96)

Private accommodation: £45 to £80 per week

Mature students

Mature students will probably be better able to meet Buckingham's fees. For admission, the University assesses educational background and personal experience.

Nursery

There is a full-time day nursery close to campus.

THE TOWN (population: 8,000)

A thriving town in Saxon times, Buckingham was made a county town in 888 when England was divided into shires. Its decline began in Tudor times when the wool trade was in recession and the assizes were moved to Aylesbury. Despite the recovery of the assizes after Viscount Cobham had built a gaol for the town and succeeded in getting through an Act of Parliament, the assizes later reverted to Aylesbury and Buckingham became a backwater.

The town is an architectural delight: several old buildings survived the disastrous fire of 1725, and the elegant Georgian houses and public buildings that were erected after the fire have not been swept away to make way for concrete shopping precincts.

What nightlife the town might once have had has been siphoned off by Milton Keynes, some 14 miles away, where there are cinemas, pubs, restaurants, discos. In Buckingham itself, a local Association, the Friends of the University, promotes social and cultural events, but to a large extent you will rely on local pubs and a scatter of restaurants. The indoor and open-air swimming pools are open for student use.

ESCAPE ROUTES

This is a quiet area, with stately homes and gardens and a gentle landscape. Your nearest larger centres are Aylesbury and Bicester, which are not very large. A place of retreat and bicycle rides.

Communications

The nearest **railway station** is in Bletchley, 12 miles away. Buckingham is about 15 miles from the **M1**, from which there is fast access to London and the North. Local **bus services** link Buckingham with Oxford, Bedford, Aylesbury and Milton Keynes. London is 60 miles away.

Buckinghamshire College of Higher Education

Queen Alexandra Road
High Wycombe
HP11 2JZ
Telephone: 01494 522141

Buckingham has around 4,000 undergraduate students on full-time programmes, 1,300 HND students. The College is a College of Brunel, The University of West London - all degree courses are validated by the University. Courses offered are in Social Sciences and Humanities, Business, Leisure and Tourism, Health Studies, Art &Design and Technology.

THE CAMPUS

The Buckinghamshire College can trace its origins back to 1893 to a School of Science and Art established in High Wycombe. The ideas adopted by this first College are still followed by Buckinghamshire today: aiming to link courses with the industries they serve.

The College now has three sites in all: the Main College and the Management Centre's Wellesbourne Campus, both in High Wycombe (which also is home to the John North Centre); and Newland Park near Chalfont St Giles.

The Main College is a purpose-built campus of modern buildings, serving the courses taught there (Art and Design; Arts and Social Sciences; Built Environment; some business/management courses; Computing, Engineering and Technology; Furniture).

Newland Park is a country campus twelve miles away. Here, new buildings cluster around the original 18th century mansion set in 200 acres of parkland. Half the park is farmland, which means that the remaining 100 acres is a marvellous amenity for Newland Park students. The grounds are landscaped and have extensive sports grounds. (Courses offered here: The Business School; Health Studies)

Courses are structured so that you will spend all your time on one or other of the campuses, and will not have to travel between them. The life style you will have on each of the two sites is so very different from the other your course campus will be your College experience.

No undergraduate courses are taught at the Management Centre. Buckinghamshire College is now a College of Brunel, The University of West London. This means that degree courses offered by the College are validated by the University, and that when you graduate, you will receive a Brunel, The University of West London degree.

Learning Resources

Each site has its own library with resources (135,000 volumes and 1,600 current periodicals in total) tailored to the course needs of the campus. All libraries are open each weekday and on Saturdays. The Information Technology Service provides a suite of personal computers with various software packages.

Culture on campus

There are recreational facilities on both main campuses, and services are organised by specialist staff. Newland Park has a purpose built theatre on site, and the Union runs a Drama Club. Films are shown by the Union, and there is a Musician's Society. The Student Centre on the Main College campus is the focal point of student life in High Wycombe: it houses a bar and various amusement machines.

The Union

Entertainments: The Union organises a programme of regular entertainments, including bands, discos and films, and holds two Balls a year, one at Christmas and one in the Summer (the Newland Park campus is an ideal venue). A wide range of sporting and non-sporting societies are available on each campus.

There are three elected full-time officers (President, Entertainments Officer and Education and Welfare Officer) and a large team of part-time officers. Elections happen every six months, giving you more opportunity to join in. There are close links with other College/University Unions, and with the NUS. The Union works with the College directorate and departmental staff 'whilst retaining complete autonomy' (Prospectus).

The Union can give advice on finance, welfare, housing, medical concerns, legal problems and the Council Tax. It runs several minibuses and a satellite television station on the Newland Park campus.

Sport

The College is a member of the Southern England Students Sports Association, and are authorised as a Fit for Life centre. You can be assessed for fitness and training programmes, and have the opportunity to pursue a range of sports. Programmes are arranged for all levels of ability and interest.

There are sports facilities on both main campuses. The College has agreed special rates with local providers for facilities it cannot offer (e.g. squash courts). At weekends, trips are organised for outdoor pursuits: these are very popular.

Student welfare

There is a nurse available on the High Wycombe site every weekday. You are advised to register with a local GP for more general health care. Newland Park has a fully-equipped medical centre and a local GP acts as College Medical Officer. The Students' Advisory Service offers counselling, including group personal development sessions to help deal with problems, as well as individual, confidential discussions. The College aims to provide specific services for students with special needs; you should contact the College before you apply should you have any specific requirements and discuss what is available.

Careers guidance is given both through individual interviews and small seminars. The Service has computer-aided guidance programmes and video facilities.

Accommodation

The College does provide some accommodation for its students. There are 100 study bedrooms a mile from the Main College in High Wycombe in a purpose-built self-catering hall. Places are allocated to full-time students who are following 'advanced level courses' (degrees and diplomas). 90 of the rooms are available to first years.

A further 455 places are available on the Newland Park campus, the majority of which are allocated to first years studying courses based there. A third of these rooms are catered (three meals weekdays and two at weekends), and two thirds are self-catering. Rooms range in age and quality. There is a well-equipped social centre for all students on campus.

A new, purpose-built hall of residence in High Wycombe town centre provides 400 contained self-catered rooms. More student accommodation is planned in High Wycombe for 1997.

Cost (1995/96)
Self-catering £43.75 - £46.50 pw
Catered single £59.50pw; double £53.50 pw

Private sector
Pressures on private sector housing in South Buckinghamshire are heavy. This is not a cheap area to find housing. Both the Main College in High Wycombe and Newlands Park have Accommodation Services where you can pick up information on available lodgings, houses, flats, rooms and bedsits.

Cost (1995/96)
£40-£45 pw for room in house

Mature students

The College acknowledges Accreditation of Prior Learning for mature students. You should send for the College brochure which will tell you about arrangements for 'accreditation'. The College assesses your previous learning and experience if you are thinking about becoming a part-time or Associate student, or if you have gained a place on a full-time course.

THE TOWN/SURROUNDINGS:

See The University of Reading's Escape Routes

Canterbury Christ Church College of Higher Education

Canterbury
Kent
CT1 1QU
Telephone: 01227 767700

> Canterbury Christ Church has around 5,000 full and part-time students. A purpose-built campus minutes from the city centre. Degrees are not modularised: Students take two subjects in the first year and have the opportunity for greater specialism in the second and third years.

THE CAMPUS

Canterbury Christ Church College has a purpose-built, low rise campus, brick and glass, minutes from the city centre. Centre campus is the College chapel and the central quadrangle with an open air stage and square pond. The music department is housed in an old building which was once part of St Augustine's College. (St Augustine's was the Abbey on whose foundations Canterbury Christ Church is built). The College has also taken over St Gregory's church nearby, and converted it into a performance space.

Learning Resources

The College library houses 180,000 books. You can also use the Cathedral and the University of Kent's libraries. College departments have micro-computers which are available to all students, as well as the computers in the Information Technology Building. Most are linked into the College's computer network. The Language Centre is available for learning or improving a foreign language.

Life on campus

The Drama Society mounts full scale productions, as well as holding weekly workshops and play readings. There is a range of musical societies, including the College orchestra which plays both in Canterbury and elsewhere (sometimes abroad). The College Choir sings in the cathedral. The C4 Video Club shows a selection of films each term.

The Union

The Union organises a range of activities, sporting, social and cultural. The hub of College 'life' is the Student Building which has two bars, a dance floor, a disco, music room, a video games room, a games room with pool tables and table football, two TV rooms and a Quiet Lounge.

Sport

The college has a gym, squash courts, tennis courts and 16 acres of playing fields (the playing fields and not on campus, but are not far away).

There is a range of sports clubs and societies, including fencing, karate and horseriding, as well as the usual range of football, hockey, netball, basketball etc. Annually, the College holds a staff v student tennis match.

Student welfare

The College medical centre has a surgery and bed spaces. Male and female doctors work with the College's Medical Officer. The College's runs a course in study skills throughout your first term and offers a counselling service. The College is an Anglican foundation: services held in the chapel daily.

Accommodation

The College offers room in halls of residence to as many incoming first years as possible: it also leases houses in the city for student-share renting. You can eat in College whether you live on site or in the city.

Cost (1995/96)
£66.00 pw catered; £45-£51 pw self-catered

Private sector
Canterbury is a small city; you might have to think in terms of travelling in from surrounding towns and villages. Prices range up from around £45.00 per week for a room.

Mature students

If you are a mature student, you must provide evidence of successful study, an approved Access course for example.

City and Escape Routes:

See the University of Kent at Canterbury's entry.

Cheltenham & Gloucester College of Higher Education

PO Box 220
The Park Campus
The Park
Cheltenham
GL50 2QF
Telephone: 01242 532700

> Cheltenham & Gloucester CHE has around 4,500 full-time undergraduates, 800 HND students and 350 full-time postgraduates. Degrees are modular and include both vocational and non-vocational subjects in two main fields of study. Each module is assessed by 'continuous or progressive assessment'. Priority for the college's 500+ bedspaces is given to first years, overseas students and students with special needs.

THE CAMPUSES

Cheltenham and Gloucester College of Higher Education, as it is now, was formed in 1990 as a result of a merger between the College of St Paul & St Mary and the higher education sections of the Gloucestershire College of Arts and Technology (GlosCAT).

The College has three main campuses in Cheltenham, and one or two smaller sites also in Cheltenham.

The three main sites are diverse in architectural style. Because of the modularisation of Cheltenham & Gloucester's courses, you might spend time on all three. All are close to the town centre and within easy cycling distance of each other. The College provides a free inter-site bus service at 15 minute intervals throughout the College day which connects all College campuses and has a town centre stop.

Park campus

This main campus is the most spacious and gracious of the College's sites. It is set in 30 acres of grounds, planned originally as the Gloucestershire Zoological Gardens and Botanical Gardens to the south of the town centre. The campus is surrounded by affluent houses with fine gardens. The dignity and elegance of their style touches the College through the large period villas in academic use on campus. The College's newer developments range through '50s and '60s blocks to the sweeping lines of the new lecture block, multi-purpose hall and Student Union building, all opened in 1994. On campus are also residential halls and houses.

All teaching facilities and social/residential amenities are clustered together and balanced by playing fields, two hard tennis courts, a pretty lake with its quota of swans and ducks, and beautiful, well-tended grounds. A calm, orderly environment for study.

Courses here: Faculty of Business and Social Studies and the Humanities & Religious Studies and Professional Education programmes of the Faculty of Arts & Education.

All main sites have a student bar, restaurant facilities, library and information technology facilities.

Francis Close Hall

This is the closest site to the centre of Cheltenham and houses the Faculty of Environment & Leisure. The original buildings form a beautiful cloistered complex, in Victorian 'Gothic Revival' style. A handsome library, wood-panelled corridors, lawned courts and a fine chapel all weave a mantle of calm contemplation - the more arresting since the immediate surroundings consist of Victorian terraces on a modest scale. The old buildings have recently been refurbished and house the Department of Geology & Geography. New buildings, harmonious with the old in design, house Hotel & Catering Management, Management Studies and the Department of Countryside and Landscape.

The Hardwick Campus

A smaller site, just around the corner from Francis Close Hall, has residential blocks and a splendid sports hall, with new (1994) Sports Science laboratories. A short distance away lie the College's main sports grounds. Sport and Leisure Management are taught here.

Pittville Campus

This complex of modern buildings is set in respectable suburbs a little to the north of Cheltenham's centre. The fairly routine concrete blocks of '60s style (or lack of it) are dramatically relieved by the startling lines of the new (1993) Media Centre: open metal stairways; wide and high spaces. The interiors of the buildings are functional and efficient, offering impressive space for art and photography exhibitions. The art, media and fashion programmes of the Faculty of Arts and Education are housed here.

All main site have a student bar, restaurant facilities, library and information technology.

Learning Resources

The College has integrated its **library**, information technology and media service into three Learning Centres - one on each main campus. Each holds books, journals, computers and media equipment specific to the courses taught on site. A total of 350,000 books and other publications and almost 1,900 periodicals. Each main site also has its own Information Technology facilities: microcomputers and networks for both teaching and individual student use. Media Services offer video editing suites, available to students, and there are four language laboratories.

Culture on campus

Drama: the new multipurpose hall on the Park campus operates as a flexible, large-scale theatre, hosting performances by touring companies, student groups and societies. The studio theatre on the Pittville campus houses smaller touring groups and performance productions.

Art: Pittville Gallery on the Pittville campus presents work from range of artists, emerging and established, College and outside. The atrium space at Pittville provides a less formal exhibition area. Sculpture exhibitions, live art performances, photography and graphics presentations - all are held regularly here. Electronic arts are promoted by Video Active, an outreach facility which offers community and education workshops. It also operates as an in-house unit for the development of multi-media installations, live art and performance productions.

Music: a varied programme is organised by the Musical Society and the Director of Music. The College Choir performs regularly, as do various ensembles and the College orchestra. There are also concerts given by visiting musicians and groups.

The Union

A total of four sabbatical officers are elected annually. The Union has a full-time, sabbatical Social and Communications Officer who is responsible for organising entertainments and events. Also responsible is the ENTS committee, open to all students. There are weekly discos across all sites, as well as quizzes, comedy, live music, karaoke and balls. The College Rag Week coincides with the Cheltenham Gold Cup; Rag events always include a sponsored hitchhike - previous destinations have been Paris, Amsterdam and Dublin. The College Summer Ball is held at Cheltenham Racecourse. There is a range of clubs and societies, and funds available should you wish to start your own. The present list includes Student Community Action, Green Awareness, Drama and others.

The full-time Welfare and Research Officer holds surgeries on every site, and helps to deal with your problems either with direct advice or referral. Professional advice on grants, debt, benefits and legal problems is available. The Union also produces a number of advice packs (Housing, Students and Benefits etc.).

The Union runs a number of commercial activities. It manages all on-site bars, site shops, laundry facilities, vending and games machines.

Sport

College facilities include a sports hall, gymnasium, tennis courts, hockey, lacrosse, rugby and football pitches and an indoor swimming pool. Where there are no College owned facilities, you can use newly extended sports provision in Cheltenham. You have fast access to the Cotswolds for orienteering, camping and climbing.

The College offers a number of coaching awards in a range of sports. The Union is affiliated to the University Athletic Union. You can represent the College at local, regional and national level. The College has a very active sporting history. Sports clubs are co-ordinated by the Union's Leisure Services sabbatical officer.

Student welfare

The College has a medical centre staffed by a team of doctors, two nurses and a Student Health Adviser. There is a confidential counselling service in addition to your timetabled academic counselling. Two full-time chaplains provide formal and informal worship and organise a wide range of events from prison visiting to retreats. Students with special needs are supported by Student Services who provide pastoral care, practical help and advice.

Careers Service

Guidance Services are based at Francis Close Hall campus and provide reference material on employers, computerised careers guidance programmes (including Job-File Explorer and Adult Directions). The Service also organises group talks on information sources, CV writing, job application and interview technique.

Accommodation

Priority for on-campus accommodation is given to first years, students with special needs and those from overseas. All halls are mixed: some self-catering, some catered. There are 500+ bed spaces: 230 places are at the Park Campus residences. Francis Close Hall has a small number of rooms in one of the original buildings. New residences have recently opened at Hardwick and Pittville; there are 254 ensuite rooms on the Pittville campus. Catered leases run for 34 weeks and self-catered for 40 weeks.

Costs (1995/96)

Range from £53.00 per week self-catered to £67.00 per week (half board).

Private accommodation

Student Services have lists of flats, houses and bedsits available in the area and the College runs a 'property leasing scheme'.

Costs (1995/96)

£40 - £45 per week self-catering accommodation
£60 - £65 per week for lodgings

Mature students

The College accepts Access courses and other non-traditional entry qualifications. You should contact Student Services to find out the range of facilities available to mature students before you apply.

Nursery

There are two pre-school centres for children of staff and students, and provision at half-term for children aged over four years.

TOWN

Cheltenham is a Regency spa town, made 'Royal' in 1788 with a visit from King George III and prosperous as a result. The Promenade is probably the most impressive of the town's many Regency terraces: elegant, white and imposing. There is a good range of shops, erring to the expensive, including a non-chain department store which still has quirky interest. The general atmosphere is affluent and leisurely, with a gentleness of light.

Entertainment: restaurants, nightclubs, wine bars and olde worlde pubs. Festivals: Literature in October and the Cheltenham International Festival of Music in July. The town is home to Gloucestershire's professional repertory theatre, the Everyman, and has a cinema.

Sports: a newly extended leisure centre, and, of course, Cheltenham Racecourse, home of the Gold Cup. Cheltenham on Gold Cup Day is jammed.

Cheltenham is just off the M5. Its other main road is the A40. There is a direct train line to London and to Birmingham, and others.

ESCAPE ROUTES

See the University of Bristol's entry.

Chichester Institute of Higher Education

The Dome
Upper Bognor Road
Bognor Regis
West Sussex
PO21 1HR
Telephone: 01243 865581

Chichester has a total; of 3,600 students of whom 1,000 are part-time. The two campuses are sited in Chichester and Bognor Regis, not too far from each other. Chichester's degree programmes are modular and assessed by both examination and coursework. First year students can expect to be housed in Institute residences if they wish to be.

THE CAMPUSES

The Institute is based on two main sites: Chichester and Bognor Regis. Degree programmes are taught at one or both of the campuses; free inter-site transport is provided. The two sites are not very far from each other; amenities on one campus can be used easily by students based at the other.

Chichester (Bishop Otter College)
This campus was one of the constituent colleges of the Institute. Bishop Otter College was founded in 1839 as a Church of England teacher training college and retains its Anglican links; the most startling building on campus being the modern chapel. The 38 acre site is occupied by some of the original 19th century buildings, and a neat array of modern additions. On campus are playing fields, two gymnasia, a dance studio, a music block, craft centre, residences, as well as other teaching and social resources. The Chichester Festival Theatre is just across the road, and the campus is close to the city centre.

Bognor Regis
The Bognor Regis College, another college of the Institute, was established in 1947. Its campus is a beautiful terrace and crescent of Georgian mansions, built in the 1790s as a home for the Prince Regent. These original buildings are the core of the campus behind and beyond which have developed a range of more modern teaching and residential blocks. The 33 acres campus has landscaped grounds and playing fields. It is a ten minute walk from the sea.
The College of Nursing and Midwifery is sited both at Bishop Otter College and at Southlands Hospital (Shoreham on Sea).

Learning Resources

Each of the main site has its own library, with a total of over 170,000 books. The Institute subscribes to 750 periodicals. The libraries are open during weekdays until 9pm (5.30pm on Fridays) and on Saturday mornings. There are open access information technology areas on each campus.

Bishop Otter College will open a £4 million Learning Resources Centre on campus, housing its library, media resources and computer centre. The Art Gallery will be relocated here.

Culture on campus

Drama: The Institute has a close association with the Chichester Festival Theatre. In addition, there are a number of dramatic entertainments organised by students. The two main campuses each have a hall equipped with a stage, sound system and lighting.

Music: There are purpose-built music studios and suites of music practice rooms. The Orchestra and Choir rehearse in Chichester. Institute staff direct jazz, improvisation and non-European music groups. The Institute's collections of musical instruments are available to students, as is an electronic studio with recording facilities and highly qualified technicians. The Institute's chapel houses concerts, as does Chichester Cathedral: student and professional concerts combine to offer a year-round programme.

Art: The Institute has a collection of art and artefacts, some of which (pieces by Henry Moore, John Skelton and Geoffrey Clarke) are distributed around the Chichester campus, both inside and out. The Mitre Gallery on the Chichester campus houses changing exhibitions.

The Union

The Union is represented on many of the Institute's committees, including the Board of Governors. The bars on campus, regular dance and discos and various social events are all organised by the Union. Welfare information is available. The Union supports a range of clubs and societies.

Sport

Each campus has sports fields on site. Chichester accommodates a dance studio and two gymnasia; Bognor Regis has tennis courts and a sports pavilion. Team sport is encouraged and many sports clubs run both male and female teams.

Student welfare

Each campus has a health centre with fully qualified nursing sisters in residence during term time. There are also professional counsellors available. The Chaplaincy is based at the Chichester campus: the chaplain sets out to offer positive Christian guidelines to students. The Institute careers adviser offers advice and guidance; both campuses have careers information rooms.

Accommodation

Chichester: 240 places in halls of residence on campus, all catered.
Bognor: 230 places in halls of residence on campus, all catered.

Costs (1994/95)
£54.40 pw on both campuses.

Private sector
Chichester: most students find lodgings. Costs £45 pw self catered; up to £70 pw fully catered.
Bognor: most rooms are within two miles of the campus. Costs: £40pw self-catered.

Mature students

In some cases, standard application qualifications are waived for mature students who can offer relevant alternative qualifications or experience. The Institute was a founder member of the Southern Access Federation and in involved in launching the Wessex Access Federation.

Nursery
The Pavilion Nursery is based on the Bognor Regis campus and offers 22 places for children aged between 0-5 years. You will have to book a place in advance.

THE REGION

Chichester is a beautiful Georgian city within ancient city walls. Its cultural and leisure amenities include The Chichester Festival Theatre, internationally famous, and the Minerva Studio Theatre which shows alternative productions and films. The city centre offers a range of shops, restaurants and pubs.

Bognor Regis is a seaside resort, a small town which overspills into surrounding villages. An ideal place if you enjoy windsurfing or sailing.

See also the entries for the University of Southampton and the University of Sussex.

University of East Anglia

Norwich
NR4 7TJ
Telephone: 01603 56161

University Charter date: 1963

UEA is a medium-sized university with over 5,000 full-time undergraduates and 1,200 full-time postgraduates. The campus is a single site of 320 acres two miles from Norwich. Degree programmes are modular and very flexible - and always have been (this was one of UEA's founding principles); many courses are interdisciplinary. Assessment is both by coursework and examination at the end of each semester - i.e. no 'finals'.

All first years and overseas students are guaranteed a place on campus.

THE CAMPUS

UEA, University Plain, set two miles out of Norwich, is compact and well designed, in 320 acres of parkland overlooking the river Yare. The buildings are grouped together along a multi-level paved precinct of irregular shape, and look - from the outside - a space-station citadel. The University Plain acts as a small town, with shops and banks, as well as eating places and coffee bars. In keeping with the style of its foundation time (1961), its concrete and glass surfaces enclose its community in functional, well-kept units.

The precinct really has two sections: the amenity buildings (library, restaurant, music centre, University House, sports centre, shops) which are separate blocks around, or just aside from, a sunken area - the 'Square'; and the 'Teaching Wall', an aptly named continuous structure of several storeys housing the majority of UEA's Schools. The sunken area is a general meeting place and in the summer is a mini-suntrap. The facades of the surrounding buildings are uncompromising, but pleasing in their lines. UEA, built on a flat site, is visually arresting in its use of changing heights and levels.

The 'Teaching Wall' is initially daunting, with high-level walkways giving you only one way in and out. However, the structure is convenient: nowhere is very far away and the funnelling effect of the gantries is efficient at rush-hours as long as you are going in the right direction! Opposite the 'Teaching Wall' is Norfolk Terrace: residences which actually overlook the University parkland, and are usefully close to your morning's travails. Running parallel with the 'Teaching Wall' is a development of academic buildings. The Sainsbury Arts Centre, set at the far end of the 'Teaching Wall', has been accoladed (and not) by commentators on architecture. It does look like an aircraft hangar from the outside: a rectangular block of aluminium and glass with interior walls of louvre blinds. All very airy.

Set in the grounds of the University, a short walk from the main campus, is Earlham Hall, dating from the 16th century. This houses the School of Law and its ivy-clad walls contrast with the University's designed planes.

The parkland around is landscaped and open, with its very own Broad - a Norfolk word meaning, in this case, 'a large lake' - for amenity value and nature conservation.

The campus atmosphere is open and friendly with strong, positive interaction between students and staff.

The University prides itself on being a regional centre, as well as a national institution with international links. This local interest includes research projects which help local industries, and substantial interaction with the cultural and social life of the region.

Cars

Students resident on campus are not normally allowed to park cars on site unless they have special dispensation (e.g. disabled drivers). All other students must register their vehicles. A bus-service to Norwich takes 15 minutes.

Learning Resources

The **library** houses over 700,000 volumes and has a large audio-visual section. It will seat almost 1,000 students and is open during the evenings and at weekends. Students have access to a full-time advisory service which also offers data-preparation services.

The Computing Centre offers 'casual access' to 250 PCs. Its Help Desk augments teaching through the Schools and provides self-teaching packages.

The James Platt Centre for Language Learning provides **language learning** facilities to all members of the University on a self-teaching basis. There are tapes of language courses, drama, poetry and current affairs in 40 languages. There is a small fee. Classes are available for all levels of language ability.

Culture on campus

Drama: The Drama and Theatre Society puts on several productions a year, offering production as well as acting possibilities. The Studio (200 seat with sprung floor) houses student drama and a wide range of public events.

Film: The Film Society screens over 60 films a year, covering most tastes.

Music: The University Music Centre, opened in 1973, is well equipped with practice and rehearsal rooms, a listening room and a recording and electro-acoustic music studio of professional standard, as well as a small concert hall seating 150. The small concert hall is used for chamber concerts and recitals. Larger concerts organised by the University are held in the 500 seat lecture theatre on the University Plain, in Norwich Cathedral, or in St Andrew's Hall in the city. The Student Music Society promotes a series of lunchtime concerts and evening events. The University Choir performs regularly, often supported by a professional orchestra. The University Orchestra gives two main concerts a year, with a wide programme. The Music Society organises a chamber choir and chamber orchestra; and there is the Student Opera Society. The University has a chest of viols (for which tuition is available) and Renaissance and Baroque instruments, plus a full range of modern percussion instruments. There are strong links with Norwich Cathedral and the annual Aldeburgh Festival. The University also has an extensive programme of nationally known bands and rising stars playing to packed houses.

Art: The Sainsbury Centre for Visual Arts, opened in 1978, was built to house the Sainsbury Collection. This collection, acquired since the 1930s, is particularly known for its tribal artefacts, but is diverse, including major modern Western works: Henry Moore and Francis Bacon are among those well represented. Some vivid pieces are rather subdued by the decor of the Centre's exhibition areas. The Centre also houses the UEA Collection of non-figurative art, and the Anderson Collection of Art Nouveau. There is a programme of special exhibitions. The Art History Library and a section of the School of Art History and Music adds a working atmosphere to the gallery. The coffee bar is very pleasant and an alternative to the central restaurant/buffet facilities. The Sainsbury Research Unit for the arts of Africa, Oceania and the Americas promotes teaching and research.

The Union

The Union has its offices in Union House, the University's social centre. The executive has annual elections for nine part-time and four full-time posts. Union House has common rooms, quiet rooms, TV rooms and writing rooms. The print room produces the official SU paper fortnightly, and the weekly independent *Concrete*. The student-run TV station, Nexus, broadcasts news and documentaries on student affairs and there is a radio station, Livewire.

The Union administers the 100 clubs which cater for all interests - cultural, political or sporting. Between five and ten events are promoted each week, from films to discos and gigs. UEA is 'on the circuit' for nationally-known bands and runs a lively scene. The 'Waterfront' in the city is run by The Union and attracts very big names.

SUS (Student Union Services) Ltd runs the campus supermarket, post office, travel shop, secondhand bookshop and games room.

Sport

The sports centre on University Plain houses a sports hall with facilities for golf-driving and cricket practice as well as volleyball, basketball, tennis and badminton. The practice hall caters for judo, trampolining, fencing and aerobics. There are six squash courts, a gym including weight training, multigym and isokinetic equipment. The facilities are open to the general public. The only charge to students is a small one for the squash courts. Outside and adjacent to the centre is a synthetic grass area for hockey, soccer and general games, as well as 12 tennis courts. Coaching is provided in most activities by the Physical Recreation staff and local coaches.

Less than a mile away are the University playing fields, 30 acres of grounds. Rugby, football, hockey and lacrosse are available here. There are three cricket pitches and a new pavilion. The county athletics track is on campus.

Water sports are available on the Norfolk Broads: canoeing, sailing, rowing and windsurfing. There are around 40 sports clubs which offer parachuting, taekwando and gliding, plus a range of usual sports.

Student welfare

The University **health service** is on the main campus. Normal NHS-type problems can be dealt with here, although there is a small charge for any services not included under the NHS umbrella. There is a part-time dental service, a sick-bay, and a 24 hour nursing service. The Dean of Students Office and the Student **Counselling Service** helps students with problems ranging through the social, educational, personal and emotional. The Union runs Nightline and a personal counselling service. There is a meeting room in the **chaplaincy** building for worship of all faiths. Chaplains represent the main Christian branches of the Church, and other religious bodies.

Careers Service

The Careers Service holds workshops on application procedures and interviewing techniques, including the use of closed circuit television. You can take part in careers discussions, and will have access to a well-stocked library and to computer-assisted guidance material. The Service also organises talks and visits.

Students with special needs

Some accommodation is adapted for wheelchair access. The University will do its best to accommodate you, if your application is otherwise suitable.

Accommodation

Almost half of the 3,000 residential places on campus have been built in the last four years. Many are ensuite. Accommodation priority is given to first year and final year students. As a first year you are guaranteed accommodation as long as your home is more than 12 miles from the University and you have committed yourself to a place by the around 12th September in your year of entry.

Halls of residence

The accommodation on the University Plain is almost all in single study-bedrooms. The number of students sharing kitchen and bathroom facilities in some residences ranges from five to 15. Some of the newer units provide ensuite rooms.

Costs (1995/6)
Single room: £34.90 per week
Single ensuite: £50.30 per week
University Village: £46.45 per week

Private accommodation
Most second and third years live in the Golden Triangle between UEA and the city. You should allow enough time before you come to UEA if you wish to find suitable accommodation in the private sector. If you would normally be guaranteed accommodation as a first year, but wish to live 'out', you must let the Accommodation Centre know that a room in residence is not required.

Details of lodgings are on display in the University's Accommodation Centre. Most lodgings are within walking distance or a short bus ride of campus. The average weekly rent for a private room ranges from £30 to £45 per week.

Mature students

Mature student minimum age: 21. If you lack adequate qualifications you must show intellectual interests You might be interviewed, and perhaps asked to take a written test. The University accepts validated Access courses. Apply early.

Part-time courses
A very wide range of courses is available for part-time study, to degree level. To qualify for part-time courses, you must be at least 23 years old, live within travelling distance of UEA, and persuade selectors that you have the intellectual capacity to pursue the course successfully.

Nursery
The University runs a nursery providing care for children from the age of six weeks to five years. Charges are made, but there is a hardship fund for those who need it.

THE CITY (population: 124,300)

Norwich is a very beautiful cathedral city, the commercial capital of East Anglia and has just celebrated 800 years of city status. Set in the flat-lands of Norfolk, the city is unexpectedly hilly, with streets travelling up towards the cathedral and castle.

The city has strong medieval roots, apparent in its castle and cathedral, both Norman. The castle was the county gaol from 1165/6 to 1887, and is now a museum and art gallery. Its moat is a garden, with walkways and lawns. The cathedral, dating from 1096, is magnificent and quiet, with an air of harmony and peace.

Norwich integrates its past with its present, living with rather than exploiting heritage and carrying traditions, buildings and lifestyles through the centuries. Walking the winding streets you will pass shops and houses from different periods, including timbered cottages and Regency terraces. There is a large open air market outside the City Hall with bright canopies and a jostling mix of stalls.

The shopping is as mixed, with chain stores and a wealth of specialist boutiques. The city's pace is leisurely, easy; there is time to explore, and space. Although Norwich is one of England's more interesting, historic and intact cities, it is off the beaten tourist track, so you will have it largely to yourself even in the summer. After dark, whole streets are floodlit, making daytime landmarks magical by night.

The river Wensum meanders around the city and has a walkway taking you past some historic landmarks. For centuries Norwich has been known as a 'city in an orchard' with over 800 acres of parkland and gardens within its boundaries and the wide farmlands without.

Theatre: The Playhouse, which opened in 1995, offers rep. The Theatre Royal seats 2,000 and houses visiting companies and artists. The small Maddermarket Theatre is modelled on an Elizabethan theatre. The Sewell Barn Theatre (110 seats) is a converted traditional Norfolk barn.

Music: The Arts Centre has a programme of rock, jazz and chamber music. Regular musical events in the cathedral. St Andrews and Blackfriars Halls, both medieval, are venues for choral, philharmonic, band and pop concerts - as are the Assembly Rooms.

Cinema: Seven screens altogether plus the regional film theatre - Cinema City - housed in the ancient Stuart and Suckling Halls with bar and cafe.

Nightlife: Norwich offers a full range of nightlife, from romantic evening strolls down illuminated streets to rocking discos. More than 200 pubs include picturesque, ancient, historic hostelries, many offering live music. Wide range of restaurants. Most nightclubs offer Student Nights.

Sport: Norwich Sports Village houses a competition-size swimming pool and an Aquapark. There are close links between Norwich City Football Club and UEA students.

ESCAPE ROUTES

Norwich on a map is the centre of a wheel with road spokes reaching outward through the counties of East Anglia.

The Broads offer boating and watersports, cruising and weekending on 200 kilometres of navigable water, moving from rivers to shallow lakes. Some Broads are nature reserves with observation hides. Also good fishing-grounds. The Norfolk coast between Cromer and Great Yarmouth is empty and fairly unexploited. Excellent cycling country - but not for mountain bikes.

Norwich is a secure island amid very flat Norfolk: other places (King's Lynn, Cambridge, Colchester, Ipswich) are a fair distance away.

Communications

A regular **train** service runs to London. The line to Peterborough connects with northbound services. **Coach** services are extensive, although not comprehensive. Norwich is not near the national **motorway** network.

University of Essex

Wivenhoe Park
Colchester
Essex
CO4 3SQ
Telephone: 01206 873333

University Charter date: 1965

Essex is a small university with 4,100 full-time students - a fairly high proportion of postgraduate students on campus. Essex has a single campus, set in the 200 acre Wivenhoe Park three miles from Colchester. Degrees have flexibility within the first year of degree programmes followed by specialisation. Assessment can be by a combination of coursework, project/dissertaion and examination.

First years are guaranteed a single study/bedroom.

THE CAMPUS

Essex University is one of the smallest universities in England and Wales. It was planned to be one of the largest in Europe when its charter was given in the mid '60s, but stopped expansion fairly quickly. The result is a University site with parkland large enough to accommodate far more building, and a rather curtailed precinct: the flip side is that the amenities you have were designed for more students than are here - a good thing - and have been opened to the public which will give you a more mixed environment. The University, although in a populated area, feels a long way away from anywhere else.

Essex campus is set in Wivenhoe Park (200 acres), which occupies a valley down to the river Colne. and a great asset. The University's buildings are compact, leaving green space and pleasant wooded parkland for your leisure time. Buildings are functional, set on a 'high street' of square terraces, each stepped up from the last. There are five in all, slab-paved and generally unrelieved from straight lines. Around each of the squares is a range of 'businesses': shops, a central launderette, the Union, restaurants, post office, teaching and administration offices, research accommodation, all housed together to encourage the general mix of University life.

Above these buildings, still on the same continuous concourse, are the library, theatre and small art gallery. The library is a block construction, with large windows which overlook one of the park's three lakes. The general lines of the University campus are lowered and softened for the gallery and theatre; raised again by the tower-block residences which stand against the skyline.

Colchester is three miles away, within cycling distance. There are buses between the town and campus.

Cars

The University requires you to register your vehicle. All cars on campus - whether belonging to staff or students - are treated equally.

Learning Resources

The Albert Sloman **Library** has over 540,000 books and pamphlets, and takes over 3,000 periodicals. Study space for 700 students. Opening hours: 9am to 10pm Monday to Friday; 9am to 6pm Saturday; 2pm to 7pm Sunday.

All students have access to central **computing facilities**. There are three UNIX and three PC laboratories, and all terminals may be used to communicate with the campus-wide mail system, or JANET (links with other universities). The laboratories are open seven days a week from 6am to 2am, and are available to you, except when in use for teaching. The **Computing Service** gives advice and provides training in the use of the facilities.

You can opt to take a module of **language study** in most degree programmes. Courses are offered in French, German, Spanish, Russian, Portugese and Japanese. The University has three language laboratories, including computer-assisted learning programmes.

Culture on campus

Drama: The Lakeside Theatre is well equipped, for its size. There is a Theatre Writer in residence and the termly programme has a core of student productions (The Theatre Society rpoduces 10 shows a year). Visiting companies are encouraged to provide open rehearsals and workshops during their time at the University.

Film: The Film Society shows two films a week at subsidised rates.

Music: The University offers fortnightly subscription concerts which attract international artists: these are supported by the local community. There are also weekly lunchtime concerts given by young professional musicians. The University Choir is open to students, staff and local residents and mounts two concerts a year with professional choirs and soloists. A small orchestra is active on campus, again open to both students and non-students. You may take subsidised music lessons and the Music Society has practice rooms.

Art: the small gallery on campus has changing exhibitions. The Art Society has its own pottery room.

The Union

The Students' Union runs and organises over 100 clubs and societies and has 80 permanent members of staff including five sabbatical officers. Turnover is around £2.5 million. Facilities on offer to societies include secretarial help and a print shop, as well as meeting rooms and transport. A Union newspaper comes out fortnightly and the fully-equipped radio station broadcasts round the clock. The Entertainments Officer organises a varied programme of events: Union venues include The Level Two nightclub and caberet and three bars. Also: a travel office, shop, stationery shop and secon-hand bookshop.

The Student Advice Centre is run by two permanent members of staff as well as trained volunteers and offers help on a variety of problems. A nightbus is organised for, mainly, women and black students and generally serves off-campus accommodation.

Sport

Forty acres of Wivenhoe Park are used as sports facilities, including five football, three hockey and two rugby pitches, and two cricket squares. There is an athletics track, three all-weather tennis courts, archery facilities, a Trim Track fitness circuit and an 18 hole frisbee golf course. The lakes provide a venue for beginners' instruction in windsurfing and canoeing. For the winter, Essex has a synthetic all-weather floodlit area, used mainly for football and hockey: in the summer this is converted into eight additional tennis courts.

The Sports Centre has six badminton courts, a tennis court, trampolining and judo. There are five squash courts here, with an additional four squash courts on campus. The gymnasium has a climbing wall and is equipped with a fitness/training room, aerobics studio and fitness testing laboratory.

The University has 12 dinghies at Brightlingsea for your continued sailing. Also at Brightlingsea are the wind surfing and canoeing clubs. The University Sailing Association has been recognised as a sailing school and can therefore give RYA certificates of proficiency.

Swimming, riding, gliding and sub-aqua are off-campus.

Essex has a director of physical education who organises and co-ordinates the student sports clubs of which there are around 40. Although the University is small, its sporting achievements are highly respectable.

Student welfare

The University **health centre** is on campus, with daily GP surgeries. The student **counselling service** organises group sessions as well as individual advice.

The **Chaplaincy Centre** offers support to a range of religious faiths, including Jewish, Muslim, Sikh and Buddhist groups. There is a large Multi-faith Centre and a Religious Studies library. Seven Christian ministers.

Careers Service

The Careers Advisory Service has a microcomputer room and video room, as well as the Careers Information Library. The Service runs workshops on applications and interviews, and gives talks on careers.

Students with special needs

The University is very suitable for students with mobility problems: the campus is accessible and a number of ground floor rooms have been adapted for students in wheelchairs. Eight rooms, specially designed for wheelchair users, are available in The Houses. You should state your personal needs on your UCAS form, and you can write to the Admissions Officer if you want more, or more specific information.

Accommodation

The University can house around 50% of its students, and as first years you are guaranteed a single study-bedroom. You have your room for the full 39 weeks of three terms and the Christmas and Easter vacations.

All accommodation is self-catering. Study-bedroom complexes have a mix of students from the first and third years, overseas students and postgraduates. Married students may have difficulty in finding suitable accommodation although provision by the University is more generous than most. You should contact the Accommodation Office as soon as possible to find out about accommodation provision.

Halls of residence

University halls of residence all have study-bedrooms grouped together in flats, with shared kitchen and bathroom facilities, and a sitting area in most cases. Costs include heating, hot water, light and electricity.

On campus are the Towers and Wolfson Court. The number of rooms in each flat ranges from 13 to 16. Wolfson Court has two two-storey blocks with flats each containing seven students. Together, the Towers and Wolfson Court provide accommodation for 1,150 students.

The newer halls on campus, known as The Houses, are built in flats for four to six students. All rooms are single and en-suite. South Courts development opened in 1993.

The other halls - Avon Way (one mile north), Forest Road (one and a half miles north) and Greenstead (one mile west) - are run along similar lines. Greenstead has corridor amenities instead of grouped flats, with 9-15 on each corridor. Avon Way and Forest Road have flats for between 4 and 6. All rooms are rented for 39 weeks, which include the Christmas and Easter vacations.

A further 458 rooms will be available for the 1996/97 session.

Costs (1995/96)

Prices range between £33 and £52 per week according to the room and its amenities.

Contract houses and flats

Not generally given to first years. The University sub-lets furnished flats and houses from private landlords. Most bedrooms are single. Students share bills other than rent.

Costs (1995/96)
£30 to £40 per week per student (excluding bills)

Lodgings
The University has a list of approved lodgings, providing bed and breakfast. You are strongly advised to inspect the room and meet the householder before accepting a University lodging. Most are at least two miles from campus.

Costs (1995/96)
Average of £40 per week bed and breakfast

Private accommodation
You may arrange your own accommodation, providing it is within 25 miles of the University. The Accommodation Office has lists of houses/flats/bedsitters in the area. Average rent is £30 to £40 per week.

Mature students

Minimum age: 21. It is recommended that you do an Access course, or some return-to-study programme should you intend to go to University after a long study gap. If you are interested in more information, you should contact the Admissions Officer. The University organises an Advisory Day in November.

Nursery
There are places for 96 children aged under five years on campus. Fees are means tested, so you could get reduced rates on a hardship allowance. You have to book in advance of your course. The nursery is new and purpose built. There is a play-scheme for primary school children at half-terms.

THE CITY (population: 150,000)

Colchester has a thoroughly mixed commercial life and layered history. It presently houses a permanent garrison, has a strong base of industry - heavy and light - and retains its traditions as the heart of the British oyster trade. The Oyster Feast, which takes place in October, is unique: a quirky start to your University career.

The town was built on the river Colne. Its oldest part, still fully circled by its Roman wall, stands above the river. The Norman castle, built by William I in stone from the Roman fort, has the largest keep of its kind anywhere. This was the county jail for two centuries (17th-19th) before becoming home to the Colchester Library and Museum. Beneath the keep are Roman vaults.

The streets of old Colchester still follow the Roman plan, and there are houses dating from the 17th century and Regency and Georgian periods. The influx of Flemish refugees in the 17th century is architecturally recorded in the 'Dutch Quarter' of the town, with gabled roofs and colour-washed frontages. However, Colchester's atmosphere is predominantly modern, with shop fronts rather obscuring the town's old elegance, and the new rampart of ring-road walling in the shopping centre. Shopping here is good, much of it pedestrianised, with plans in operation for new arcades. The town is a regional centre with most chain stores represented.

Altogether, Colchester has 180 acres of public parks and gardens including Castle Park.

Theatres: The home of the Colchester repertory company is the Mercury Theatre, built in 1972. It has a fairly wide-ranging programme.

Music: Small concerts are put on at the Colchester Arts Centre. Most regional musical events are organised by the University.

Cinema: The Commercial cinema (five screens) and St Mary's Arts Centre both show films, commercial and minority interest.

Nightlife: Colchester has a varied nightlife with some historic and interesting pubs, and nightclubs (historic only in the fabulous sense).

Sport: The town has a professional football team and a county cricket ground. The sports centre offers facilities for squash, badminton, 5-a-side football, trampolining and weight-training, with a sauna, solarium and massage. There is a swimming pool. A new leisure and sports complex opened recently.

ESCAPE ROUTES

Colchester stands inland from the salt-marshes of the Essex coastline and on the underbelly of Constable country. Around are small market towns and seaside places.

You are near the villages of Suffolk, and Suffolk's winding lanes: contrary to the Essex Man myth, this end of the county opens easily into the counties where the pace of life slows markedly.

If you do want the publife and clublife, Southend is not far away, nor are the other notorious haunts of this maligned county.

Communications

There is a half-hourly, fast **train** to London Liverpool Street (takes one hour). Also easily accessible are Ipswich, Norwich and Cambridge. **Coach services** are extensive, although some require changes. Colchester is not near any motorways: its A-road links are fast. Felixstowe and Harwich have regular **ferries** to northern Europe: fares to Amsterdam are cheap, and there is a through train service.

University of Exeter

Exeter
EX4 4QJ
Telephone: 01392 263263

University Charter date: 1955

Exeter is a medium-sized university with 8,000 full-time and 2,500 part-time students. Officially, the University has three campuses: in effect, there is a single main campus of 245 acres just a mile from Exeter with two outposts - the School of Education half a mile away and The Cambourne School of Mines in Cornwall. Degrees are modular, allowing a level of flexibility within a coherent framework. Assessment is a mix of coursework and examination.

The University will find accommodation for all first years and can house 3,400 students in University-owned accommodation.

THE CAMPUS

Streatham Campus

The University's main Streatham campus lies within one mile of the city centre. In most cities this would lead to close integration, but Exeter's size (not much bigger than an average town) and location allow the University a sense of remove and rural calm. The very beautiful hillside site had its origins in the house and gardens of Streatham Hall (now named Reed Hall), given to the University in 1922. The gift formed the nucleus of the large, 245 acre estate owned by the University. The original hall gardens were laid out in the late 1860s and reflected the keen interest of that period in exotic plants from all over the world; much of the character has been retained and has marked the style of later developments, so that the University estate has become a major extended botanical garden, with trees and shrubs brought here from many faraway lands.

The parkland ambience is helped by the very mild maritime climate: the region has its own 'mini-climate', cast by the rain-shadow effect of Dartmoor and the prevailing south-west winds. The University site adds to this its south-facing slopes and generates a sense of relaxed well-being; it will be an effort not to feel on perpetual holiday and to get the necessary work done! It is good to have access, out of season, to an area so beautiful.

The site is well landscaped, accepting the clean lines of its modern buildings into its gentle slopes, and grouping them to give variety of angle and to release significant blocks of space for gardens and arboretum. The original hall is 19th century (Italianate) and there was some early development in the 1930s. But the vast majority of the buildings date from the decade 1958 to 1968, so their style is homogeneous (light brick) and typical of the better-quality buildings of the time (Exeter has a general sense of affluence). Two streams flow through the site, dammed to form a series of ponds, stocked with fish and providing a habitat for waterfowl. The streams, with their water-meadow, form part of the green circle of playing fields, botanic garden and University-owned farmland which promotes so strongly the air of civilised and civilising calm which hallmarks the campus.

The halls of residence and complex of University flats lie on opposite sides of the campus perimeter, tactfully separated from the academic and amenity buildings. In the centre of campus, in the main grouping of amenity buildings, there is a shopping centre with supermarket, bank, bookshop etc.

St. Luke's

The University School of Education, the second largest in the country, is housed at the St Luke's site, once a separate college of education, half a mile from the city centre. There are good facilities including two new buildings and an independent community life. A frequent minibus service runs between the St Luke's and Streatham campuses.

The Camborne School of Mines

The Camborne School of Mines is now a department of the Faculty of Engineering at Exeter University: if you apply to Exeter for Camborne's specialist range of engineering, science and technology, you will find yourself on their modern campus in Pool, Redruth, Cornwall. The School has two underground test mines, worldwide close links with the minerals industry, is internationally famous and offers 'very applied' courses.

Two miles from the mainline rail station in Redruth, and two miles from the nearest beach.

Cars

Parking space on University property is limited and the issue of permits is strictly controlled. Permits will not be issued to students in hall, in self-catering accommodation or in private accommodation within 1.5 miles of the campus (unless disabled or with other special needs). If you want to take a moped or motorcycle onto the main estate, you must register ownership. There is no parking available at the St Luke's site. For parking at halls off-campus, apply to the warden.

Learning Resources

The University has over 800,000 volumes and subscribes to 2,820 current periodicals. In addition to the main **library**, there are faculty and department libraries, including those at St Luke's and Camborne. The main library seats over 550 students, and the faculty libraries a further 698. Opening hours: weekdays to 10pm; Saturday to 5pm: Sunday closed. The University is responsible for running the Cathedral Library and the library of the Devon and Exeter Institution.

The **Computer Unit** operates a policy of open access to computing facilities; five rooms are available 24 hours per day. The Unit runs courses covering all aspects of the service which are open to all students, and also runs specialist courses for computing in the arts. There is a campus-wide network of over 800 microcomputers which are linked to distributed and central computing facilities, and to national and international networks.

The **language centre** is open to specialist and non-specialist students alike. The self-instructional laboratory offers more than 9,000 tapes in over 40 languages, including the exotic: you can begin a new language or increase your competence in a more familiar one. There are courses for those who prefer to be taught by humans rather than machines.

Extracurricular qualifications can be gained in both languages and computing.

Culture on campus

Drama: The Northcott Theatre seats 433. The theatre is a regional centre for the arts in the south west and has its own professional company, offering a range of drama to suit most tastes. Also performances by major national touring opera and dance companies, film weeks and late-night films. The theatre provides for amateur dramatic productions by local groups and student societies.

Music: An annual series of University subscription concerts featuring distinguished chamber groups and soloists; also regular concerts by the Bournemouth Symphony Orchestra and the Bournemouth Sinfonietta, as well as fortnightly lunchtime recitals, and performances by student societies. For performers: large choral, chamber, madrigal and Gilbert and Sullivan; a symphony orchestra, a chamber orchestra and numerous smaller ensembles. The Symphony Orchestra holds an annual course in the week before the beginning of the autumn term.

The Cathedral Library

The University administers the Cathedral Library, founded in the 11th century by the first Bishop of Exeter, Leofric, and now housed (printed books) in the Bishop's Palace. The library contains the 'Exeter Book', the largest single collection of Anglo-Saxon poems, the Exeter Domesday Book and other rare manuscripts and books.

The Union

The Guild of Students (Students' Union) is housed in two large buildings, Devonshire House and Cornwall House. Both houses have a range of facilities: Devonshire House - a refectory, bar and coffee bar; Cornwall House (near to the University flats) - a bar, bistro and coffee bar and a restaurant (wholefood/vegetarian). The Guild runs a print shop, travel shop, secondhand bookshop and a shop selling stationery and sports equipment.

The School of Education has its own common room bar, launderette, shop and cafeteria.

The Guild organises discos on Friday and Saturday nights, books an impressive range of bands and organises an annual Summer Ball.

100 societies are funded by the Guild. The Community Action Group works with Age Concern and organises a half term playscheme and a baby-sitting service.

A joint counselling service is organised with the University, including a Family Centre and a Welfare Advice Centre. At Camborne, the Guild provides Welfare Advice and Counselling (with the University).

The newspaper, *'Exepose'*, is published weekly.

Sport

On the main campus there is a large sports hall, providing for tennis, basketball, netball, volleyball badminton and small court games, indoor cricket nets and a practice climbing wall. A secondary area gives space to fencing, table-tennis and a fitness room: there are eight squash and two fives courts, and a six-station multigym. There is an outdoor swimming pool.

A mile away, at the School of Education, there are two gymnasia (one fully equipped for gymnastics; the other marked for volleyball, basketball or badminton), weight-training facilities and an indoor heated swimming pool.

There are 64 acres of playing-fields: three all-weather pitches (two on the main site - one floodlit - and one at the School of Education) and more than 20 tennis courts. The Athletic Union runs 49 clubs - sailing, rowing, gliding, parachuting, golf, rifle-shooting, cross country; and because of the University's site and setting, between sea, river and moorland hills, these can all be enjoyed fairly close to base. The sailing club keeps six lark dinghies on the Exe estuary and the Boat Club has a well equipped boat house on the Exeter Canal.

Membership of a club costs around £15.00 - this makes you, automatically, a member of the Athletics Union.

Camborne also has many sports facilities and is in the middle of excellent outdoor pursuit country.

Student welfare

There is a **student health centre** on campus, with a group of part-time medical officers and two full-time nurses (similar facilities at the St Luke's site).

The Guild provides a range of **welfare services**, mainly operating through advisors - legal, financial, emotional. The student counselling centre gives confidential support to those with personal or emotional problems. Counselling in study methods is also available.

There is a University chapel, a Roman Catholic chaplaincy and an interdenominational chaplaincy room. Muslim, Buddhist and Jewish students have their own societies and there are worship centres in the town.

Careers Service

The Careers Advisory Centre offers advice on employment and careers, and arranges talks and visits. Individual interviews are offered and the service also provides short training courses, psychometric testing and arranges guest speakers.

Students with special needs

The University has an Advisor to Disabled Students. Before you submit an application to UCAS, you should write to the Admissions Officer outlining your requirements. The Exeter site is hilly, and the University does not have extensive facilities for students with special needs. There are special facilities in three halls of residence, and rooms can be adapted for the deaf and the blind.

Accommodation

The University can house around 4,200 students in University-owned accommodation: about half of these are self-catering flats and are reserved for older students, including 'mature' first years. The rest are in traditional halls. Priority for hall places is given to students who accept a firm offer of a place by May. The University, however, 'will find accommodation' for all first years.

Halls of residence

The 13 halls are on, or immediately adjacent to, the main site, except St Luke's Hall, which is at the School of Education site. They vary in style quite a lot; the estate retains a number of period houses and some of these form the nuclei of clusters of annexes and extensions which become halls. The original houses provide a pleasantly domestic ambience.

Halls are fully catered, which means that a return to base at mealtimes is a regular part of your day. A lunch ticket system allows some flexibility as to where you actually eat. All halls have libraries and common reading rooms; most have bars, some have their own tennis courts.

St Luke's Hall is worth a special note: because it was an independent college until 1978, it is unusually well-endowed with various facilities (see Sport section): the Hall accommodates 130 students in a self-contained, friendly environment. Some rooms here are ensuite. It is far enough from the main site to be its own world (two miles), and close to the city centre (half a mile).

Accommodation at Camborne is in two modern self-catering hostels with 53 single study/bedrooms and communal facilities. Half are allocated to first years. Some (not very much) 'hall' accommodation is in attached lodgings in nearby houses, which provide sleeping accommodation: in all other respects, residents are full members of their halls.

A majority of hall rooms are single study/bedrooms, but quite a number are shared by two students: you should expect to be asked to share.

Halls are warden controlled.

There is provision for vegetarians in the full board accommodation.

Costs (1996/7)

£77.35 per week, single (30 week session)
£71.68 per week, shared (30 week session)
£85.26 per week ensuite (30 week session: St Luke's only)

Costs include full board, cleaning, heating and laundry of bedlinen. St Luke's students can use meal vouchers in the University refectories.

University flats

First years aged 19 and over may apply for a place in University flats. Over 2,000 students can be accommodated in self-catering flats, on the main site and at the School of Education. Single study/bedrooms, in groups of up to 12, share a communal kitchen/dining room and other facilities. Four newer buildings offer ensuite accommodation, with groups of six sharing kitchen/dining facilities. Cornwall House is very close, providing common rooms, bar, launderette and food in term-time, if you don't want to cook. There is also the swimming pool mentioned earlier. At the School of Education, students are arranged in groups of five and nine. Although there is some cleaning (fortnightly for rooms, daily for communal areas) you are not so cosseted as in halls. You also have to take your flat-space for 39 weeks (including Christmas and Easter vacations) and it is possible to stay for the whole year (at extra cost) if you so wish. The flats are controlled by the Director of Domestic Services and staff tutors are in residence.

Costs cover heating, lighting, some cleaning, hot water and the use of basic kitchen equipment.

Costs (1996/97)

£40.95 per week (39 week session)
£49.21 to £54.25 per week (new flats: 39 weeks)
£50.57 per week ensuite (34 week session)

Off-campus accommodation

Many students choose to live off campus; the Accommodation Office keeps lists of lodgings and self-catering accommodation in Exeter or the surrounding villages. The main areas occupied by students are St James'/St David's, just off campus; and Newtown close to the School of Education campus. Students in lodgings are associate members of a hall. Shared house or bedsit: £40 to £45 per week

Mature students

Various qualifications are accepted for mature students, including Access courses which are run by the University, or are otherwise accredited. The University will also take experience since leaving school into account. There is an Associate Student Scheme, whereby students can 'sit in' on lectures, without commitment.

Nursery

The Guild runs a family centre for children between six weeks and five years old. Places are limited and you should apply as soon as possible. Also a half-term playscheme for older children and a baby-sitting service.

THE CITY (population: 100,000)

Exeter is an ancient city, sheltered by surrounding hills, set inland, but close enough to the mouth of the Exe estuary to be invigorated by maritime air. Built on the river Exe, its history is one of merchants and seafarers.

Its cathedral, founded in 1050, miraculously survived the Second World War bombing raid which, in a single night, virtually wiped out the centre of Exeter. Its two towers are Norman and its building is on the Grand Scale of Britain's Great Cathedrals. Inside is a treasure trove of detail, in both stone and woodwork. Outside, in the Cathedral Close - an interesting run of houses from different periods set around a green - is 'Mol's Coffee House'. Now a jeweller's, this building is reputed to have been the meeting place of Sir Francis Drake and his fellow seadogs. The Elizabethan Ship Inn on Martin's Lane was another of his haunts.

Exeter's city walls are a fusion of history: the original Roman buttressed by the medieval. The walls are a sporadic reminder of Exeter's past. Two medieval aqueducts can now be explored as part of a system of underground tunnels.

The Guildhall, one of the oldest still in use in England, is now rather surrounded by shopping developments. Exeter has a good range of shops. Precincts and malls have gathered the larger stores into a compact area. The city is pleasant to use; it is hilly, but not exhaustingly so; you can feel very quickly that you have moved district rather than just turned a corner.

The quays down on the Exe date from the 17th century when Exeter again became a port after much medieval wrangling. Walks down by the water are easy and very pretty, or you can hire rowing boats from the Exeter Maritime Museum. Despite the bombing raid, Exeter still has a number of old buildings - Georgian terraces, 15th century almshouses. Most are still used: Wynards Almshouses built around a beautiful courtyard is the co-ordinating centre for voluntary organisations.

Theatres: The Northcott Theatre on the University campus serves the region. The Exeter and Devon arts centre has a small theatre, the Cafe Theatre, which can be hired for shows. The Barnfield Theatre takes in small theatre and one-man shows. The city is host to the Other Theatre Season, a season of plays put on by professional touring companies.

Music: Apart from the regular concerts at the University, the cathedral has a concert programme which includes symphony concerts by the Bournemouth Sinfonia and the Royal Philharmonic Orchestra. The Plaza is venue to rock and pop concerts. Exeter has a number of folk clubs and jazz venues, and many pubs have live music.

Cinema: Exeter has one major cinema with a total of four screens. The Northcott shows minority films and 'art' hits, and has a late night programme.

Nightlife: Apart from live music issuing from the many clubs and pubs, Exeter offers nightclubs and discos. Four are on the quay, adding the atmosphere of waterside living.

Sport: Greyhound and speedway racing, and horse racing at Newton Abbot and Haldon racecourses are the main spectator sports on offer. And, of course, football. Exeter has four sports halls and the city swimming baths and Fitness Centre. Outdoor tennis is available in Heavitree Park. The Plaza Leisure Centre offers a 'wave' pool, squash and a large indoor sports area.

ESCAPE ROUTES

Around and beyond Exeter is the West Country, some of the most beautiful and unspoilt land in England. Dartmoor Forest, the Exe estuary, the rolling hills of central Devon surround the city.

To the west of Exeter, some miles away, is the open wild land of Dartmoor. The coastline in this area is known as the Devon Riviera. Torquay is the largest resort in Devon; its setting is marvellous - wooded hills behind and the sweep of sea before - and the weather here is very mild.

Exeter's environs have many pretty villages of 'cob' cottages, built from a mixture of clay and straw, which give a sense of timelessness. The whole area is one where you can escape easily from the pressures of University life.

Communications

Exeter's **rail links** are extensive, linking to London, the West Country and the north. **Coach services** likewise. Exeter is the southernmost end of the **M5**, which gives fast access to Bristol and the **M4** and links with the **M6** in Birmingham.

University of Hertfordshire

Hatfield Campus
College Lane
Hatfield
Herts AL10 9AB
Telephone: 01707 284000

University Charter date: 1992

Hertfordshire is a medium to large-sized university with 10,500 undergraduate students on full-time and sandwich programmes. There are four campuses: main campus in Hatfield; Business School in Hertford; Humanities and Education in Watford; Law in St. Albans. Degrees here are not modular. A high proportion of courses are offered with a 'sandwich' element. Assessment methods vary but are usually a combination of examination and coursework.

Accommodation priority is given to first years, overseas students and students returning from overseas placements in halls, flats, houses and approved lodgings.

THE CAMPUSES

The University is very largely centred on its main site at Hatfield. Courses are site based and students do not move between campuses. Your experience, therefore, will depend very much on where the course you choose will be taught.

The Hatfield campus

The campus occupies 93 acres in a low-key suburban setting on the edge of south Hatfield, about two miles from the railway station (trains to London take 25 minutes), and within yards of the A1, which is mercifully recessed into a cutting. This is a very large complex of modern buildings, dating from 1952 (when the University opened as a college), and stretching in changing building styles across the years between.

The most recent additions are three large new buildings in today's modes of pitched-roof-and-brick or window-walling with gaudy paint; they face and dominate the facade of the main entrance block. Most of the campus buildings are low-rise; the few higher blocks do not add much visual weight. There is a spaciousness about the site - good expanses of lawns, lots of trees - which cancels the near-presence of the A1, and survives the presence of quite a lot of temporary classrooms which occupy courtyard spaces. Turning a blind eye to these, one sees a very pleasant site, with pathways climbing wooded slopes across to the on-campus residences (a substantial group), set at a comfortable remove from your centres of work.

The library occupies one of the large new buildings in front of the site. The Students' Union building, known as The Elephant House (we come across some odd names; apparently this sobriquet comes from the building's likeness to the Elephant House at London Zoo), has been refurbished and is the venue for gigs and concerts. The Faculties of Engineering, Health and Human Sciences, Information Sciences and Natural Sciences (more than 3,500 students) are based here.

Meridian House

A new off-campus centre for Nurse education has been established at Meridian House in Hatfield itself.

School of Art and Design

This School has moved from St Albans to a new site in Hatfield, across town from the University's Hatfield Campus. The buildings it now occupies were the design offices of British Aerospace, and give the School the scope to co-ordinate facilities and to integrate its activities. Also on this site (Hatfield Business Park in fact) is the University's Conference Centre - the Fielder Building. Across the road is a large new shopping centre, the Galleria, and the UCI multiplex cinema centre.

The Hertford campus

The Hatfield Business School lives at Balls Park on one of the most beautiful sites we have seen. Recent buildings extend from a lovely old mansion (dated 1640), large, gracious, calm; its old brick suitably crumbling; its restoration unobtrusive. Beguiling to know that tutorials and some teaching happen in such a setting and some residential units are in its outbuilt quarters. The newer buildings make no concessions to line or ambience, but they are all in one heap, and leave most of the campus free.

St. Alban's Campus

The Department of Law is housed here is a modern block in the centre of St. Alban's. The building has a Learning Resources Centre with computing facilities and a specialist law library.

Surrounding the complex lies a parkland of 100 acres - vistas of landscaped lawns and trees, shady walks, pond, quirky topiary. You are free to wander through this idyll. Yet you are only a short walk from the centre of Hertford, and a mile and a half from Hertford North station (regular service to London). You are, however, ten miles from Hatfield and although there is a bus service, students told us they seldom visit the main campus except for major social events.

Facilities on site are excellent, partly because the immediate neighbour is a large and well-equipped comprehensive school. Balls Park students 'police' the school's swimming pool, and have use of it in non-school time.

Other facilities include a refectory, students' common-room and bar, an auditorium, a bookshop and general shop, a weights room, and (shared) use of tennis courts and playing fields.

Courses here: The Business School.

Watford campus

Another very beautiful academic oasis. Out from Radlett, through a pretty village (Aldenham), along a tree-clad country lane, and you are on this most rural campus. You are in fact a mere two miles from Watford and very near to the outer edges of London's sprawl, but the atmosphere here is, again, remote.

The splendour of the grounds reflects the pretensions of the original mansion - built in castle-style in 1799. It is now backed by a range of purpose-built teaching blocks, library and residential units.

There is a day nursery here, and a Hertford County Council nursery school uses the site. Numbers of small children were playing on the lawns in front of the 'castle' mansion when we visited. The gardens here have been developed as a sculpture park, under Hertfordshire's Art in Public Places initiative. Facilities here: library, computer centre, student residences, refectory, bar, tennis courts, playing fields and an outdoor swimming pool.

Courses here: the School of Humanities and Education.

Field centre

The University has yet another rural retreat to offer: this time it is their observatory and field station in the grounds of Bayfordbury House (between Hatfield and Hertford). Glasshouses, lake, woodlands and farmlands are all used for field research; the observatory for teaching and research.

Cars

There is limited car-parking provision at Hatfield campus, none at all at Watford, none at Hertford. Students are not encouraged to bring cars when living in Residence.

Learning Resources

All **libraries** are open for 12 hours a day during term time and each site library caters for the subjects taught on campus.

Almost all courses contain an element of **computing,** and introductory courses are regarded as necessary in schemes of study. Every campus has a computer service, open seven days a week, late into the evening. Every centre has an open access area for all students. Assistance is usually on hand. The campuses are all networked.

French, German and **Spanish** are available to all students. The Business School offers Japanese.

Culture on campus

UH *Arts* promotes a programme of music, drama and dance on all main campuses. Lunchtime concerts, famous speakers, public lectures on the visual arts all contribute to variety. There are opportunities for student drama; many student productions even tour overseas. The John Lill Centre for Music on the Hatfield Campus is the focus for music making. The University Choral Society (on the Hatfield and Watford campuses) presents concerts twice a year; the University Orchestra also performs; there is a Big Band with a big touring schedule.

The Union

The Union represents students on University committees and has a Students' Union Council which meets regularly and is made up of elected members from each division. There are over 80 clubs and societies and an active social programme: there is a social happening every night except Sunday. There is a regular student newspaper, a campus radio station and satellite television. Each site has a bar, and the Union runs a snack bar, shop, insurance and travel offices and a games room. Also a Welfare Service: its Resource and Advice Centre is on the Hatfield campus. The central hall at Wall End has a sound and lighting system. A fortnightly newsheet, *Vibes*, lets you know what is happening.

Sport

The University has almost 60 sports clubs which welcome beginners as well as catering for those of you already expert. There are trips and tours for outdoor pursuit-type sports - canoeing, climbing and ski-ing. Local facilities are hired to supplement the University's own provision.

The Hatfield campus

This campus has a large sports hall with sprung wooden floors, electronic scoring and information devices. The main hall has equipment for basketball, volleyball and badminton. The upstairs balcony is used for judo, fencing, karate, Wu shu Kwan and keep-fit.

There is a climbing wall constructed from natural rock. Adjacent to the sports hall are two squash courts and there is a mini-gym next to the halls of residence. Here too are floodlit tennis/netball courts and playing fields. Changing rooms and a weight training area in the multigym. Sand-filled artificial hockey pitch, rugby football and cricket pitches also here.

The main sports ground is at Angerland Common, a 15 minute walk from the campus. The Hertfordshire Indoor Cricket School is in the middle of the campus, and its facilities are open to the University.

Hertford campus

This campus has an indoor heated swimming pool, gymnasium and outdoor sports grounds for pitch games, tennis and netball. Also, a Fitness Centre, small weight-training area, a trim trail around the parkland, floodlit all-weather courts for training and recreation and a golf practice area.

Watford campus

A hockey pitch and football pitches, an open-air swimming pool, one floodlit tennis and netball court outside: a gymnasium and a Fitness Centre offering a range of activities.

Student welfare

There are **medical centres** on each main campus, with nursing staff and doctors' surgeries up to three times a week, and daily at the Hatfield campus. The University runs a confidential **counselling service**. A full-time **chaplain** at Hatfield.

Careers Service

You will have access to PROSPECT, the most recent computer-assisted programme. The Careers Service runs various workshops and educational sessions including an 'Insight into Management' course.

Students with special needs

The University has considerable experience of students with special needs. Some accommodation on campus is specially adapted, and special examination provision is made for students with physical difficulties in writing. There is a braille output computer terminal, a Kurzweil reading machine for the visually handicapped and teletext for the deaf. There is a Disabled Students Officer and each faculty has a Disabled Students Co-ordinator.

Accommodation

The University has a total of around 4,000 accommodation places. Priority is given to first years, overseas students and students returning from overseas placements in halls, flats, houses and approved lodgings. Locations vary from campus-based, to town centre, to village residences (sometimes period picturesque), to short-distance-out. The university's campuses are fairly scattered, and their accommodation trawling is correspondingly wide and diverse.

Halls of residence

A total of 1,106 places in halls of residence, about 900 of which are reserved for first years. Most rooms are single with communal kitchens. Facilities include games rooms, TV rooms and laundries. Each hall has a resident tutor.

Costs (1995/96)

Single room self-catering: £44 per week
Double room self-catering: £38-40 per person per week

University houses and flats

The University has a further 1,220 self-catering places in houses and flats at Hatfield. Watford has 200 places.

Costs (1994/95)

£46 and £50 per week for 40 weeks excluding bills.

Rented houses

The University runs a head tenancy scheme through local landlords in towns and villages nearby. Rents: £40 - £45 per week.

Mature students

The University runs preparatory courses and pre-entry workshops for mature students. University Access are offered courses through associated colleges as well as on campus.

Nursery

The nursery is fully equipped for children from small babies to five year olds. There are 47 places at Hatfield and 26 at Watford (for two- to five-year olds).

THE TOWNS

Hatfield (population: 25,000)

There is not a lot to say about Hatfield. It serves its community through a complex of orthodox town centre High Street precincts: nothing special, but adequate facilities. There is better style, quality and scale in Welwyn Garden City, close enough to use easily.

Hatfield Old Town, on the other hand, offers the historic fascination of Hatfield House - magnificent late Tudor/Jacobean: still in the grounds are the early Tudor remains of the original House where Elizabeth I spent her early years. The Old Town is a delight: beautiful old houses and olde worlde village charm. If you come to the University, visiting here is a must.

The UCI multi-screen cinema at the Galleria is a night-club (with 16 screen video wall) in Welwyn Garden City; various 'shows' at the Forum in Hatfield; amateur dramatics and films (often art films) at Welwyn Garden's arts complex.

Hertford (population: 22,000)

Hertford is an old market/county town. It retains its old period quarter with atmosphere fairly intact, and has developed good modern shopping facilities alongside. One is very quickly out into rolling landscapes with streams, woods and a sense of deep rural seclusion: it is difficult to believe that London is a mere 30 minute rail trip away. There is an open market on the streets on Saturdays, but generally the town is fairly quiet. There is a museum, a gallery and an indoor swimming pool.

Radlett & Watford (population: 74,566)

You can reach both Radlett and Watford by bus from Aldenham. Each is about two miles away. Radlett is pretty but little more than a good, old-style High Street. Watford is a large, busy town with the range of shopping and amenities you would expect from a mixed urban community.

ESCAPE ROUTES

Hertfordshire is one of the Home Counties, a place of pleasant countryside and rolling hills, very green between the urban moments. The county's history is layered; there is a wealth of Elizabethan and Jacobean houses, many still unspoilt villages, very beautiful churches. You will be circled by New Towns and Garden Cities, which, in themselves, are not of any great interest. If you are sited anywhere which is not St Albans, you should visit that campus if only to look at the Abbey; likewise Hatfield, to see the House. North London is only 30 minutes away.

Communications

This depends on which campus you are based. You will have access to either the **M1** or **A1**, both of which will take you into north London. You are close to the **M25**.

Rail-links: trains on the Network South East will take you around the region, although in and out of London are the most regular services.

The University of Kent at Canterbury

Kent
CT2 7NZ
Telephone: 01227 764000

University Charter date:1965
Kent is a medium-sized university with around 7,000 full-time undergraduates. This is a collegiate university on a greenfield site
Campus type: collegiate university with a 300 acre greenfield campus overlooking Canterbury. Degrees are divided into two parts: Part I - first year and flexible - and a specialised Part II. Most courses have end of year exams: assessment methods otherwise vary.

Most first years live in university-owned accommodation. All students are guaranteed one year of accommodation on campus.

THE CAMPUS

The approach roads to Canterbury pass through the low-lying quiet landscapes of rural Kent, gently rolling and scattered with small villages.

The University has occupied its site and deployed its buildings in a manner worthy of our most ancient traditions. On a low hill, overlooking the city, its colleges are ranged in a protective screen, shielding the University's academic, amenity and services buildings from the outside world. In terms of daily living, the peripheral, south-facing set of each college allows its residents to enjoy open views and a feeling of space.

The 300 acre site has ample room for the main buildings to be grouped around well-kept lawns and well-proportioned paved areas; the general air is quiet and dignified: a civilised community in a well-groomed, sophisticated setting. More than in comparable modern universities the atmosphere is donnish. The student atmosphere created within this framework is outgoing, confident and sociable.

Building styles vary: two of the four colleges (Eliot and Rutherford) are each constructed in four units around a central courtyard; Keynes College is more open in design, with inter-space lawns and gardens which don't quite become courtyards, and the visual plus of a pretty pond; Darwin College, rather austere, has a more compact plan and its rectangles form a functional Y shape. Accepting the architectural differences, the campus is a homogeneous whole, its styles thematically linked by recurring elongated panels of grey brick and slender longitudinal panels of glass.

The rest of the site, where buildings are more functionally designed, is well-screened by mature woodland. There is a two and a half mile nature trail through these woods and around the grassy slopes and ponds which give the University its secluded calm.

The Colleges
The collegiate principle aims to bring together under one roof, 'teaching and research, residence and catering', in order to create an ambience where students can 'integrate intensive study with the social and recreational aspects of university life'. Allocation to a college is in the hands of the admissions/accommodation staff; you may indicate a preference (if you have one) although there is no guarantee that this would be a successful move.

You will remain a member of your college, and able to use its amenities and join in its social, cultural and sporting life even in the year or years that you will have to spend in off-campus accommodation. You will not be taught exclusively in your college: classes will take you to other colleges, or specialist buildings.

Although the college units create a club-like, centripetal social life, there is a certain amount of intermingling as friendships form across college boundaries. Each college has developed special features.

Darwin College has interlinked student kitchens and lounges where residents can cook for themselves. There is also a large party room, with its own cooking facilities.

Eliot College is the base for a number of student societies and activities; there is a dark-room for the Photographic Society, the student newspaper offices and the University's radio station transmitter. The Great Hall is used for concerts and one of the lecture theatres can become a small playhouse. Drama and Music Society offices are here, and Eliot has its own chapel (a conversion of the northern cloister). It is fitting that this first of the colleges, bearing the name of so great a poet and seeker after spiritual truth should be the religious and cultural focus of the University.

Keynes College has a smaller-scale dining hall and common room, and its social life is diffused through the system of kitchen/common-rooms serving blocks of 12 study-bedrooms. A more domestic scene. There is a house in Canterbury, regarded as part of the college, which takes 18 students.

Rutherford College has a very grand College Hall, offering space for orchestral and pop concerts, and its Junior Common Room accommodates discos and dramatic productions. College premises include the School of Continuing Education, responsible for adult education in Kent.

Cars

If you are living in College, cars are not permitted. Off-campus students can bring cars, but make sure you can acquire the necessary parking permit.

Learning Resources

The main **library** has around 900,000 items and takes around 3,000 current periodicals. Seating for over 1,000 students. The library is open until 10pm from Monday to Friday; until 7pm on Saturday; and from 2pm to 9pm on Sundays. The Cathedral Library and its collections of early books is administered by the University. The colleges also have libraries. The **Computing Laboratory** runs courses for students interested in computing, and computing can be an option in a joint degree. The campus computer network has over 1,400 connections and permits access at any time. The facilities of the **language laboratory** are freely available to all students, and many subjects can be studied in conjunction with a language. The Languages Building contains laboratories with computer-assisted learning facilities and TV reception from Europe.

Culture on campus

Drama: The **Gulbenkian Theatre** (seat 342) is a resource for the community as well as the University. Its presentations are wide-ranging and performances divide fairly evenly between those by the University and student groups, and visiting professional companies. Major national touring companies appear here, as have leading smaller experimental groups. Regular comedy nights. Less formal student productions happen in the colleges.

Music: There is no music department at Kent, but a Director of Music, working closely with the Students' Union Music Society, promotes a flourishing programme of musical activities, including lunchtime concerts, featuring professional performers and members of the University. There is a University Symphony Orchestra and University Chorus (each presenting a public concert each term). Once a year there is usually a major musical event in the Gulbenkian Theatre and a summer Opera Project each June. All students can book piano/practice rooms for private use. There is a chamber choir, chamber orchestra, a Jazz and Blues society with a big band and other groups.

Film: Kent's **film theatre** (Cinema 3) is the region's only film theatre and presents programmes of independent/restricted release films. The Union shows recent commercial films on three evenings a week during term.

The Union

The Union building is small and unobtrusive. The Union functions, which are powerfully centralised in non-collegiate universities, are here dispersed around the college Junior Common Rooms. The Union building accommodates the administration offices, from which the Union officials conduct business affairs (organising and financing the hundred-plus student societies; providing legal and other advice; running a shop and a travel service).

Junior College Committees (JCCs) deal with domestic college matters and meet fortnightly with the Union executive to keep the student body on a common course. College social life is organised by the JCCs and runs parallel with the entertainment programme (theatre, dance, exhibitions) organised by the Union. The Union runs video games and pool tables in each college JCR, a second-hand bookshop, a free research and rights service, and a secretarial service to societies.

Its entertainments programme is extensive, with a social event almost every night of the week, and live bands booked for 50 nights every term. The hall used on campus has space for 1,500 students. Several bars are not run by the Union; one (Woody's), however, is.

Sport

The sports centre, conveniently set midway between the colleges and the Park Wood courts (residential complex), operates a Sports for All policy. There is a large sports hall (badminton, ball-games, cricket nets and a climbing wall). An additional gymnasium provides two multigym-gyms and free weights. There are some (limited) facilities for the disabled, and there is a boxing ring. Country dancing, keep fit, a sauna and a solarium cater for the less dedicated.

There are six squash courts on campus and tennis courts near the sports centre. Playing fields and graded jogging routes mark the beginning of open country and offer a range of pitches, with a floodlit all-weather playing area which converts into an athletics track.

Off-campus, University clubs offer rambling, camping, gliding, mountaineering (Kent is a long way from anything resembling a mountain), riding, rowing, shooting and swimming.

You can be as competitive as you like at university or college team level. Coaching is available to a high level in boxing, cricket, soccer and squash, and all martial arts; or you can seek more modest advice on general physical fitness. There is a sports injuries clinic in the centre.

Sports bursaries of £500 are awarded to applicants who show outstanding sporting ability - provided they accept Kent as their firm offer by May 15th!

Student welfare

The University has an NHS **medical centre** on campus with full GP and emergency services. Five beds available in the 24-hour sick bay. There is a confidential counselling service, independent of the University, a visiting psychologist and psychiatrist and a daily walk-in service for crisis counselling.

Resident fulltime, part-time and visiting **chaplains** cover most denominations. The Jewish Society is active: there is a visiting rabbi and another who is a member of staff.

Careers Service

The Careers Advisory Service gives you a Personal Development Workbook in your first year. In the second and third years, talks and seminars cover cv writing, application forms and interviews. You will have access to two computer-assisted guidance programmes.

Students with special needs

You should write to the Advisor to Disabled Students before submitting a formal application. You will be encouraged to visit the University.

Accommodation

All first years are guaranteed University accommodation, provided that places have been firmly accepted by September 10th. The University has 3,400 places: 1,500 catered and 1,900 self-catering. First years usually live on campus in either in or near a College or in Park Wood, a 'village' of self-catering houses.

The Colleges

Each college has a large number of study-bedrooms, grouped in corridors or staircases; a large dining hall, common-rooms, coffee bars, shops, bars, television and games rooms, spaces for quiet study, and a small library, as well as the facilities for academic life already mentioned. Rooms can be single, or twin-bedded, or bunk-bedded.

Costs (1995/96)

Single room: £46.48 per week
Ensuite (Becket Court): £60.76 per week
(30 weeks)
Includes breakfast and an entitlement to reduced price meals in college during term time.

Park Wood Courts

A village of five and six bedroomed terraced houses built in 'courts' of about 20 houses. If you are in Park Courts, you may use the facilities of your college (of course).

Costs (1995/96)

£38.15 per week inclusive of bills: you have to pay for your accommodation over the Christmas and Easter vacations.

Private accommodation

Second and third years often live in the coastal towns of Whitstable and Herne, five or six miles away. The journey can take between 20 and 40 minutes. Season tickets help a lot. The University keeps lists of properties and landlords.

Costs (1995/96)

Average rent is £40 per week in lodgings.

Mature students

The Mature Student Entry Scheme is based on interview and completion of a written assignment. The University also considered Access qualifications.

Nursery

The University runs a day nursery for children aged between six weeks and five years. A Union subsidy allows a concessionary fee for students.

THE CITY (population: 36,000)

Canterbury: ancient city (the site was already an old settlement when the Romans came), cradle of Christianity in Saxon England (its first cathedral, nothing of which survives, was built in AD 597 by St Augustine) and home now of the splendid cathedral which is Mother Church of Anglicans throughout the world. Today Canterbury retains much of the grace and character of its history, particularly around the cathedral, where a maze of narrow lanes, overhung by old houses, retains the sense of cluttered medieval living. The city hasn't grown with the times: its population is still that of a small town.

Long stretches of medieval (13th and 14th centuries) city walls, partly built on Roman foundations, survive in an arc to the south and east of the city centre, double-traced now by the ring-road; the 14th century west gate, the only survivor of seven former gates to the city, now contains a museum of arms and armour.

While the city has many interesting and lovely buildings from many periods, all is shadowed by the magnificent cathedral: to enter is to be filled with wonder (if you are susceptible to the marvels of stone, wood and glass which are its glory).

The old part of the city is beautiful, wearing its history with calm dignity, its main ways lined with small, decorous, expensive shops in suitably period style, and comfortable inns (with the occasional incongruous fast-food take-away). There are intersecting water-lanes edged by gardens, alleys and by-ways - attractive wandering terrain. Modern developments on the outer edge of the city have brought big stores and modern chains.

Theatre: The Marlowe Theatre presents a mixed programme of drama (mostly light), musicals, comedy, ballet and regular classical concerts. The city's other theatre is the Gulbenkian on campus, already mentioned.

Music: In addition to the musicals and concerts at the Marlowe, music is sung and performed in the cathedral. Concerts and other events in the annual Canterbury Festival are held on the University campus.

Cinemas: There is one (Cannon) with two screens in the city, and of course Cinema 3 on campus.

Nightlife: There is a good range of restaurants, pubs (many with live music) and winebars in the city. No suitable venue for big bands.

Sport: Spectator sports: City Football Club, Kent Count Cricket Club and greyhound racing. The range of activity-involvement is good: two swimming pools, golf, river trips/rowing and facilities for ball games and gymnastics at the Canterbury Sports Centre.

ESCAPE ROUTES

Kent is the Garden of England. Think of the Darling Buds of May and you're there; there are still villages with oast houses and still fields of hops and orchards. The north Kent coastline has sandy beaches, good bathing and a low rainfall record. Cliff walks and paths follow the coast from Folkestone to Dover from The Warren, a basin of rare plants and trees between the water and the rising cliffs: you will find fossils here. The coastline stretching across to the Isle of Sheppey includes Whitstable, one of the areas used by the University students for accommodation. This is a small oystering port with old streets and inns; an excellent place for sailing, wind surfing, fishing and golf. The rest of the coast is pretty and increasingly caters for tourists. You will have it to yourselves out of season.

Communications

Canterbury has two stations, both with regular **trains** to London. Dover is reached from the East Station and Ramsgate and Ashford from the West, and there is the Channel Tunnel link. **Coach** services are extensive: Canterbury is on the **A2/M2** which links London and Dover. There are continental **ferries** and **hovercraft** services from Dover, Folkestone, Ramsgate and Sheerness.

Kingston University

Penrhyn Road
Kingston Upon Thames
Surrey
KT1 2EE
Telephone: 0181 547 2000

University Charter date: 1992

Kingston is a medium/large university with 13,000 full-time students (including HNDs) and 4,000 part-time. The University is distributed around four main sites all a short distance from each other in Kingston. Degrees are modularised and assessed by a mixture of methods.

All first year students are guaranteed hall accommodation, provided that they apply before the first week in September.

THE CAMPUS

The University is distributed around four main sites and uses its split site so creatively that the units can operate as a part of a whole. They are strongly subject oriented, which could tend to be divisive, but distances between sites are short enough to allow a University minibus to shuttle round every hour.

The prospectus gives equal weight to the four sites, but since Penrhyn Road accommodates the largest number of students, and administrative offices, we shall start there. Each site has its own library, refectory and Students' Union bar. The newly-occupied Roehampton Vale site is slightly less accessible (distance and traffic!).

Penrhyn Road

The main complex towers beside Penryhn Road, a major thoroughfare. The cluster of buildings here fills a very large area, creating institution scale vistas of offices, teaching rooms, corridors...a veritable labyrinth. To the rear, the new Sopwith Building has added a touch of dash and colour with its white walls, dark glass and bright green metal framing, but the bulk of the complex is constructed in 50s and 60s modular, repetitive style, mainly four storey with a tower block; spaces which in a less expensive urban site would be green are here in use for car parking. The Students' Union building is a recent, smart block.

The complex sits almost opposite the splendidly imposing County Hall buildings. Behind the campus are avenues of very pleasant, roomy Victorian semis, with roads of more modern, mixed housing. The site is only a few minutes' walk from the centre of Kingston.

Courses here: the whole Faculty of Science, the Faculty of Human Sciences; all Schools of the Faculty of Technology except for the School of Mechanical, Aeronautical and Production Engineering.

Knight's Park

A short walk from the Penrhyn site, along and over a blue bridge crossing the Hogsmill river (more a stream), you are in the Knights Park campus. Although so close, the ambiences of the two sites are very different. Knights Park was originally an art school and its setting, lines of building and interior spaces create harmony: its early function does mark its style. The stream, with its green and flowered margins, is a great help: the Students' Union refectory and bars run in gallery fashion along its bank.

The basic building is in 'functional block' mode, but its contrasts of shade and texture and its tower, rising in dark brick and white trim achieve visual stimulus. Inside, a spacious art display in the reception area, an inner court of lawn, flowers and bushes, seats and display cabinets in corridors create a relaxed and communicative atmosphere.

Courses here: Faculty of Design (including Sculpture).

Kingston Hill

The prettiest of the University's sites, three miles from and above Kingston, on the A3 towards London. This used to be a college and occupies 50 parkland acres, landscaped, with old trees, green space and steep terracing. The site has grown around a lovely old large white manor house. More modern developments are distinctly utilitarian - the most recent, good quality, prefabricated units are sharp in outline. The steep rake of the site (lots of steps to consider) and the tree-screening soften the lines. The Students' Union building looks very war-time, with its entrance of painted brick and its main area in Nissen hut curved corrugated aluminium. Very dark interior. Was it an air-raid shelter?

The campus' Rehearsal Studio is orchestral size and fully equipped as a professional recording hall.

The setting of this campus is very affluent; a 'parkland' created by large suburban gardens and many trees.

Here: the Faculties of Business and Healthcare Sciences and the School of Music.

Roehampton Vale

Set back (but not very far) from a fearsomely busy dual carriageway, and practically nextdoor to a large ASDA store, this building was previously a manufacturing base for high-tech mechanical systems. Its ambience therefore will not be too dislocated by its new role, housing Schools in the Faculty of Technology. A functional, compact, smart building, with its own Union facilities. Not a lot more to say...

The site is over a mile from Kingston Hill, which makes it four or five miles from Kingston town centre: rather in the no-man's land of outer London's fast link roads.

The building is connected into the University circuit by the shuttle bus and public transport. This really is a busy road, particularly at come and go times. Don't bother to bring a car.

Courses here: School of Mechanical Aeronautical and Production Engineering

Cars

You would be better without a car. Transport is good: the University shuttle 'Hoppa' connects all the main sites with a free hourly service.

Learning Resources

Each site has its own **library**, geared to its own courses. You can use all libraries which have a total stock of over 350,000 books and 2,300 current periodicals.

There are introductory courses run by **Computing Services** at the beginning of each academic year open to all students. Each site has its own Advisory Service. The Computer Education Centre gives general and specialist short courses.

The **Interactive Learning Centre** at the Penrhyn Road Centre has two language laboratories and facilities for computer-aided language learning: you will be able to learn at least one foreign language and gain a certificate as well as an employment-related report.

The various services are integrated as a central services cluster, which is open from 9am to 9pm weekdays, 10.15am to 3.45pm weekends (term-time).

Culture on campus

Music: The University's range of musical experience is open to all students, staff and often the local community. You can learn to sing or play instruments with professional staff (subsidised, but there is a fee). You can join big band jazz, early and new music ensembles, brass group, orchestras and choirs. There is a full programme of lunchtime and evening concerts.
Film: The Student's Guild shows films weekly.

The Union

(Kingston University Guild of Students - KUGOS)

The Guild has four full-time sabbatical officers, 27 employees and employs over 250 casual student helpers. Annual turnover: £2.5 million. Around 80 clubs (sport and social) are supported at present.

Each site has its own Guild office, bar and weekly disco; Penrhyn Road has an all-day snack bar and Knight's Park has a travel office. There are three shops, two on the residential sites. All facilities are open all year round. The Guild (Union) has negotiated general advice from local solicitors either free or at cheap rates.

Entertainments feature both established and up-and-coming bands; also comedy shows, cabarets and club nights. 19 events, including quizzes, films etc. , happen every week. For larger events (over 500 audience) the Union hires a hall in Kingston. A late night bus service runs, with women priority.

Publications: weekly newsheet (*Rumours*) and free press magazine (*Tzar*).

Sport

Coaching is available at all levels in eleven sports: all the major ones plus sub-aqua and martial arts. The University Sports and Recreation staff run courses in many sports and fitness activities. There are 33 sports clubs.
Facilities: fitness centre, aerobics studio and gymnasium at Kingston Hill, playing fields at Tolworth Court Sports Ground, tennis courts at Tolworth and Kingston Hill. Penrhyn Road has a fitness centre and two solaria.

Student welfare

The **Health and Counselling Centre** on each site provides medical care. Specialised clinics are held in the **Health Centre** at Penrhyn Road. Health Centre services include osteopathy, aromatherapy and chiropody at reduced prices. The University has a professional **counselling service** and there is a student-run Advice Centre. One full-time ecumenical chaplain and two part-time **chaplains** (including a Jewish rabbi) see to religious needs.

Careers Service

The Careers Service helps with applications, interview techniques and psychometric tests. There is a well-stocked Information resource base, including computer-assisted guidance programmes. There are close links with local employers, which helps when you are looking for part-time evening or vacation work.

Students with special needs

The University has a Special Needs Co-ordinator for disabled students who is part of the consultative admissions procedure. You are encouraged to contact her to arrange an information interview to discuss your needs.

Accommodation

The University guarantees accommodation in hall to all first years who request it before the first week in September. There are now 2,266 places in halls of residence. Halls all have pleasant locations within a few minutes' walk of either the town centre or a campus. Some rooms are ensuite. Each hall has a manager and resident second and third year students.

The University has a vacancy list of private rented accommodation and shared houses, and a head tenancy scheme for 650 second and subsequent year students.

Costs (1996/97)

Halls of residence: single, self-catering: £2,200 - £2,400 for the full session.

Private sector and lodgings: £45-£50 per week self-catering.

Mature students

The University is the administrative centre for the Surrey and South West London Access Agency. It organises Access courses and 'return to study' programmes. Prior learning can be accredited under the CAT scheme. Support services in the University are geared into the needs of mature students.

Nursery
Children aged between two and five years are eligible for the University nursery, which serves staff, students and the public.

THE TOWN (population 132,547)

Kingston is one of the only four towns in the country to have Royal Borough status. It has a lovely setting: bounded to the west by the Thames, with its rivercraft and riverside walks, and surrounded by major beautiful parks and commonlands. Hampton Court's Home Park is just beyond Kingston Bridge, and both Richmond Park and Wimbledon Common are close to the town's edges.

The shopping centre came as a surprise: we have not visited the town since it launched a major programme of demolition and rebuilding. The centre is now dominated by two giant stores: an enormous John Lewis complex, impressively New Age in style (like or hate it); and a balancing enormous re-born Bentalls, designed with some echoing elegance of the old stores. The old familiar (if you knew Kingston) original face of Bentalls is being preserved as facade to a large new indoor shopping centre. There is still a quiet area around the church, and the Market Square retains some of the town's old charm. There is one three-screen cinema, and two night-clubs, and a very good range of (mainly expensive) restaurants. Kingston caters for a very well-off community.

ESCAPE ROUTES

You are in the middle of the Royal tract of Surrey, close to Hampton Court and its famous maze, and to the Royal deerparks of Richmond Park and Bushy Park. There are famous houses, beautiful galleries, landscaped gardens, river walks and boating. You are near also to Twickenham, which is, of course, synonymous with Rugby Union. Bring your warm waterproofs for the season.

Communications

Kingston is very much on the inner edge of London's outer rim and communications are mainly to and from London. Once you are in the metropolis, you can get anywhere. Kingston is near Heathrow Airport, erring towards Gatwick and close to the M4 and M25.

LSU College of Higher Education

The Avenue
Southampton
SO17 1BG
Telephone: 01703 228761

LSU has around 1,900 full-time undergraduates. The College has a small single site just outside Southampton centre. Most courses are modularised and are offered either as 'minor/major' options, equally balanced subject options or combined honours. Assessment is a mixture of coursework and examination in varying proportions: in some cases assessment is 100% by coursework.

The College aims to provide all first years with accommodation.

THE CAMPUS

LSU was founded almost a century ago by the Sisters of La Sainte Union. This is a single site college. The campus is compact, ten acres in all, and set just outside Southampton's city centre: Central Station, the coach station and civic centre are just a five minute walk away. Student residences, those owned by the College, are on or near campus. This means that although the College is very near the city centre, it retains its own strong social life and identity. Campus buildings have generally been modified to blend with the original building - roof gables and college squares. The spacing of the buildings creates a pleasant living and working environment.

The site is shared by St Anne's School.

Cars: parking on campus is very limited.

Learning Resources

The library, housed in the Resources Complex, contains over 115,000 items and takes 500 current periodicals. Opening hours: 8.45am to 9.30pm Mondays to Thursdays, 8.45am to 6.30pm Friday, 9.00am to 4pm Saturday. The Computing Centre is open to all students and runs introductory courses in information technology and computer use. The Media Resources Centre has a closed-circuit television studio and audiovisual workrooms.

The Union

LSU's Union has two sabbatical officers and eight executive officers who are elected annually. The Union Building is a large house on campus; its offices and the Board Room are both used for meetings and Union business. The Coffee Bar, also in the Union Building, serves food from 10am to 4pm Monday to Friday.

There are 30 clubs and societies (sporting and non-sporting), including a Theatre Workshop who mount termly productions, and Channel 5, the television production society.

Sport

The Union co-ordinates a number of sporting clubs and societies. If you have an interest which is not represented, the Union will probably fund a new departure - provided that you can drum up enough support. On campus: two gymnasia and an indoor swimming pool.

Student welfare

The First Aid Centre is staffed by a full-time nurse from 9am to 5pm every day. The counselling service offers individual help and acts as an information and resource agency. The chaplaincy centre is open daily and is open to all. The Careers Service offers workshops on cv writing, job hunting and interview techniques.

Accommodation

The college owns 750 accommodation places (494 catered and 256 self-catered), all within five minutes of the campus. Two new halls of residence (one self-catering and one full-board) opened in 1995. All rooms in the new halls have ensuite facilities. The college is able to house all first years.

Costs (1995/96)
New hall: £64 pw catered; £49 pw self-catered (ensuite)
Old hall: £58.50 pw (catered)

Private sector
The Accommodation Office compiles lists of available properties. Rents: around £35 to £42 per week plus bills

Mature students

Non-standard entry students are expected to show evidence of recent academic study, including Access courses or Foundation Years. Places are available in the nursery on campus for children aged between six months and five years of staff and students.

City/Escape Routes

See the University of Southampton's entry.

University of Luton

Park Square
Luton
Bedfordshire
LU1 3JU
Telephone: 01582 34111

University Charter date: 1994

Luton is a medium-sized university with a total of 14,000 full and part-time students following a courses leading to a range of awards, including degrees and HNDs. The University has fourcampuses, three in Luton and one four miles out. Degrees are modular and flexible; all programmes include six free modules. Units are assessed by project and coursework and written tests.

Most first years will be offered a place in University residences.

THE CAMPUS

Park Square

This is the main campus, and the most central, next to the Arndale Centre, the hub of Luton's shopping area. The campus area is bordered by busy roads and its boundaries are the town's pavements. As a result, security is quite thorough, with Student Cards doubling as ID.

The main buildings are five- and six-storey 1960s blocks and the adjoining scientific laboratories are mainly single-storey. Interior spaces are well kept and clean; rows of lockers down the corridors give a school type atmosphere. Newer extensions have been designed to blend in with the overall pattern of the site; the glass atrium at the main entrance feels quite futuristic: bright colours, steel seats and a TV monitor flicking from scene to scene around the campus.

The main entrance, the concourse (again under glass and by the main lecture halls) and the main refectory are all close together and are the main social mixing areas. The predominance of glass creates an airy feeling, helped by the strictly enforced no smoking policy. The newly refurbished Learning Resource Centre incorporates the library which is very spacious; arrays of plants and a big glass roof create an atmosphere you would not usually associate with a library. Noise levels in this very open plan area were surprisingly low; students must take note of the many 'silence' signs.

Faculties here: Science and Computing, Business, Design and Technology and Health Care and Social Studies.

Castle Street

This single large building is a ten-minute walk from Park Square. This too dates from the '60s. The main entrance has glass panels and dark colours; elsewhere in the building interiors have been softened with the use of carpeting and light ceiling covers. You are a little further from the town centre here; the bus depot is next door and industrial units rather than shops surround the building.

Faculty here: Humanities.

Putteridge Bury

Four miles from Luton and connected by a University bus service. This campus is dominated by a large Victorian manor (designed in the style of Chequers). Its landscaped gardens give beautiful views of the surrounding countryside.

Putteridge Bury is a conference centre; however, the Faculty of Management is also based here.

Dallow Road

We did not visit this site in the town centre. The prospectus describes this building as having Victorian origins. Courses here are affiliated to the Faculty of Art and Design.

Cars

There is little provision for car parking.

Academic services

Housed in the Learning Resource Centre on Park Square, the **library** (and the four on other sites) hold a total 135,000 volumes, takes 1,400 periodicals and has over 450 study spaces. Opening times: 8am to midnight (issue desk to 10pm) Monday to Thursday, 8am to 6pm on Friday, 9.30am to 12.30pm on Saturday and 10am to 5.30pm on Sundays. **Computing:** Over 700 computer workstations and terminals are available, and specialist staff give help and advice. The computer centre is open 24 hours a day Monday to Thursday, and closes at 7pm on Fridays and weekends. The University is networked and on the world-wide web. **Languages:** A language can be studied as part of a modular degree at one of six levels. Two language laboratories available. A **Maths Learning Centre** offers help in maths and statistics and runs on a drop-in basis. A study skills team offers help and advice.

Life on campus

The University Orchestra is made up of students and staff. An annual concert is performed at Putteridge Bury and the orchestra performs at other University events. The Gilbert and Sullivan Society presents two or more productions a year.

The Union

The Union building is on the Park Square campus. Four to five entertainments are put on each week; the Underground is the nightclub in the Union and aptly named. There are two other bars, one no-smoking. The Union sponsors around 20 societies. There is a Nightline service, a minibus available for use by clubs and societies and a late-night minibus service runs from the Union until late at night. A free monthly magazine, *Juice*, includes job vacancies as well as the usual editorial-interest content.

Sport

The University has two gymnasia, a weight-training room and changing rooms at Park Square. One gym is used for table-tennis, aerobics ('sweat sessions') and martial arts, the other for small court games. At Stopsley the University has playing fields, club room and a squash club. Use of these facilities is restricted to members of the Sports Association. Many sports are played in University and local leagues. A sport injury clinic is available - £5 per half hour. The University has a Fitness Suite open to all students, for a small fee.

Student welfare

The NHS Medical Centre in Castle street is open to students. Qualified **counsellors** are available on a personal or group session basis. The Advisory Service will give advice on grants and legal issues.

Careers Service
There is a careers library which gives access to a number of computer programmes. Personal interviews are available, as is a 'drop in' service at lunchtimes. The University is developing a career development module, dealing with application strategies and other aspects of Careers work, which might eventually be integrated with the Modular degree scheme. There are also courses in **Study skills**: essay writing, computing, problem-solving. The Service has an a Job Agency run in collaboration with the Brook Street Bureau: their agency can help you to find vacation work in your home town.

Accommodation

University owned or managed
Most first years will be offered a place in a hall of residence. All halls are self-catering and are very near to, or no more than a mile and a half from, campus. Halls range in size from a large Victorian house offering places for 14 men, to a purpose-built hall for 440 students. Older house-halls have resident wardens and groups of new halls have a site warden. Hall bills include heating and electricity costs. The University also handles a head-lease scheme with 800 places in 200 houses, all within a two mile radius of campus.

Costs (1995/96)
Self-catering halls: c. £45.20 per week (40 weeks)
Head-lease: £32 to £40 per week (bills not included), depending on distance 'out'

Private accommodation
The University Accommodation Office can supply lists of bedsits, lodgings or shared houses. A room in a shared house averages £37.50 per week.

Mature students

The Luton Access programme has evolved into a foundation year for the Modular Degree Scheme. You can therefore register immediately on a degree scheme or, if you prefer, do the foundation year but keep your options open. Your programme of study can be built to accommodate nursery hours and school holidays.

Nursery
There is a nursery for 36 children aged from two to five years. Demand for places is high and an early application is advised. Opening hours: 8.30am to 5pm.

THE TOWN (population: 174,000)

Luton had a very quiet pre-20th-century history. The market town was noted for its straw hats and is still a major national supplier. The decision by the Vauxhall Motor Company to set up its headquarters and factory here dramatically changed the shape and style of the town. Other industrial developments, the building of the airport and close proximity to London have brought a number of large housing estates.

The town centre has been radically rebuilt to serve the needs of this quickly expanding population, so much so that very few original buildings remain. The centre of town is compact. The shopping area, University, railway and bus station are all a couple of minutes walk of each other.

'Shopping' here means the Arndale Centre! This huge complex seems to have entrances on every street, and the indoor market has over 80 different traders. Next to (and dwarfed by) the Arndale is the pedestrian precinct with wrought-iron benches and flower boxes.

Within half a mile of the centre is Wardown Park and within the town's boundary is Stockwood Country Park.
Theatre: The St George's Theatre hosts a range of drama; the 33 Arts Centre has occasional theatre nights.
Music: The St George's Theatre has a programme of Music on Mondays. Regular jazz at The 33 Arts Centre .
Cinema: A three-screen Cannon. Both the St George's Theatre and the 33 Arts Centre have film evenings.
Nightlife: The usual range of pubs, clubs and restaurants.
Sports: There are a number of sports centres, some with swimming pools. Stockwood Country Park has an 18-hole golf course, athletics track and grass pitches; Wardown Park has tennis courts and boating. Luton Town Football Club is in the First Division.

ESCAPE ROUTES

There are several country manors and parks close to Luton. Luton Hoo is the nearest; its extensive gardens were landscaped by 'Capability' Brown. Within ten miles there are three animal parks: at Woburn, Woodside and Whipsnade. Knebworth House, the venue for occasional mega-gigs, is within the vicinity too.

Communications

Trains run regularly to London (Kings Cross is 30 minutes away) and there are also direct connections to Derby and Sheffield. **Road:** Direct links with the M1 at junctions 10 and 11. Junction 8 cn the A1 is not far either. **Air:** The airport is 10 minutes by taxi: daily international flights.

Oxford Brookes University

Gipsy Lane Campus
Headington
Oxford
OX3 0BP
Telephone: 01865 483030

University Charter date: 1992

Oxford Brookes is a medium-sized university with around 7,500 full-time undergraduates. The University has three campuses, two close together, a mile from Oxford; the third, five miles away in Wheatley. Degrees are modular: indeed, Oxford Brookes was one of the pioneers of flexible, modular degree programmes. Assessment is a balance of coursework and examination.

First years are given priority for hall places: there are c, 2,200 places available.

THE CAMPUSES

Oxford Brookes has three campuses: Wheatley is five miles from the city centre; the other two are very close to each other and only one mile out.

Gipsy Lane

This is the main campus, housing the majority of Schools on a compact site just a mile out of Oxford centre. Blocks are medium rise, well proportioned and stratify the University's development. Not much space to mingle.

Academic services are part of the main building (early 1960s glass and panel; was the Oxford College of Technology), as is the refectory, bookshop, main lecture halls and the library.

Behind the departmental blocks are playing fields swathed between the University and Cheney Hall and the new sports centre.

The Headington area is very much suburbia. The University is surrounded by houses; one edge borders a town park ; around the corner is a road of small shops. A world apart from dreaming spires.

Headington Hill Hall

Headington Hill is about a three-minute walk from Gipsy Lane, across an iron bridge over the Old London Road. The Students' Union facilities are based at this campus.

Courses here: parts of the School of Business, and the School of Art, Music and Publishing.

Wheatley

Oxford's third campus is five miles from Gipsy Lane and feels further. The Schools of Education and Business are here. This was the Lady Spencer Churchill College of Education taken over by the University in 1976. The campus has a rural setting; its 65 acres stretch into surrounding fields. Buildings are quite severe blocks, apart from the original redbrick college, now a hall of residence. Teaching areas are low-rise and less daunting. Most administrative offices and sports facilities are here.

Oxford Brookes' modular structure means that, should you opt for a component of either business or education, you are likely to use both the Oxford and Wheatley sites. The University provides free transport between the two. The journey takes less than twenty minutes.

Cars

Student parking at Wheatley. Most halls of residence have a 'no cars' rule and no parking the other campuses.

Learning resources

The main **library** (Gipsy Lane campus) has 620 reading places; Wheatley's library is dedicated to its own site's courses, and has places for 170 readers; Dorset House library serves the School of Occupational Therapy. The combined library stock is around 250,000 volumes. Opening times at Gipsy Lane, weekdays to 10pm, weekends to 4pm.

The **Computer Centre** facilities are open to all students and most courses include some use of computers. 23 open-access PC rooms are spread across the campuses. The Computer Services and Help Desk Services are available in term time, providing documentation and advice. Courses on specific skills are run by Schools.

Languages: you can opt for a foreign language unit or learn a language as well as your other specialisms. The Languages Centre offers facilities for all students, which include audio and visual aids as well as computer-assisted language learning. The School of Languages has strong links with both the Goethe Institute and the Maison Francaise d'Oxford (sponsored by the French government).

Culture on campus

Drama: The Students' Union Drama Society and the Fortune Players put on around six plays a year. The Drama Society has 'The Drama Hut', a small theatre at Gipsy Lane.

Music: Music can either be integrated into your modular programme, or is open to all students. Leading musicians spend time here as lecturers or part-time teachers. Performance activities include an Orchestra, Choir, several Chamber Groups, Jazz and Rock bands.

Art: The Department offers evening classes in drawing, painting, pottery and calligraphy, and has its own electronic studio.

The Union

The two main sites, Wheatley and Oxford (Gipsy Lane and Headington Hill) have their own Union facilities. The Oxford campuses' Union building is on the Headington Hill Hall estate; Wheatley's Union Building is purpose built. As well as the total of four bars (two of which serve snacks and meals) there are three shops (Gipsy Lane, Wheatley and Cheney Halls).

An event happens every night (darts competitions and quizzes fill in the non-disco nights). At Wheatley there are regular weekend discos, live bands and comedy evenings. Venue capacity, 1,200. 65 clubs and societies are active.

The fortnightly magazine - *The Last Edition* - covers a wide variety of issues in its 50 (approx) page format, giving scope for contributions from a good cross section of the student body.

Sport

There is a new Centre for Sports on the Gypsy Lane campus: new five-badminton-court-size sports hall houses a heavy weights room, dance studio, health suite and a dedicated climbing wall and tower.

Most of the University's outdoor facilities are on the Wheatley campus. The intersite bus service comes into its own! Facilities include a cricket pavilion, sports changing block, pitches for football, hockey and cricket, squash and tennis courts, pitch and putt golf and a fitness trail. Six of the tennis courts are floodlit. A boathouse on the Isis provides rowing and canoeing

The University offers a full slate of sporting activities (c.35 clubs in all) and competes at all levels with first, second and third teams. Opportunities for involvement here are excellent.

Student welfare

The **Medical Centre** on the Gipsy Lane campus offers nursing care, and there are two doctor's surgeries daily for which there is an appointment system. The Wheatley campus has a doctor and nurse available at certain times.

Two **counsellors** are available to discuss all problems, academic and personal. In your first term, you can join in a short series of workshops aimed at improving study skills: organising yourself, note taking, advanced reading, easy writing and preparing for exams; all very useful.

The University's **chaplaincy** team includes an Anglican and a Catholic priest, and URC and Methodist ministers as well as its chaplain. The Chaplaincy Room is available for prayer meetings and study groups. Provision for most major faiths is good in the city.

Careers Service

The Careers Centre offers an extensive education programme for students, with discussions and workshops. You can build careers education into your modular programme, taught through workshops, seminars and projects. For all students there is a timetable of conventions, practice interviews and computer-aided careers guidance. The Careers Centre runs 'Insight into Media' and 'Insight into Management' courses.

Students with special needs

The advisory service for students with a disability takes you through from pre-application to graduation. The service organises induction programmes, provides advice on special equipment, makes special exam arrangements if necessary and acts as a point of reference for external agencies. The University has adapted residences with accommodation for carers.

Accommodation

First-years are given hall priority; however, it is essential that you apply for a hall place as soon as you have firmly accepted an unconditional place.

Halls of residence

The University has six halls of residence of various sizes, with approximately 2,200 places in all, 455 places are in catered halls. All halls, with the exception of the Lady Spencer-Churchill Hall at Wheatley, relate to the Gipsy Lane campus. The majority of places are in single study bedrooms. Leases run for 42 weeks.

Small/Medium Halls

The University has six smaller Halls, five of which are in a two mile radius of Gipsy Lane. All are self-catering; all have single study bedrooms, shared communal facilities. Leases are for either 42 or 50 weeks.

Costs (1996/97)
self-catering: £1,750 p.a. average
catered: £2,650 p.a. average

Housing Association and Private Accommodation

The University has around 350 places in shared houses: these are also open to first years, especially to mature students: but you must apply early. Leases run for 46 weeks. Rents: £41 to £48 per week. Private rented flats and houses are hard to find at the beginning of the academic year. First years tend to stay in lodgings. Cheaper rooms in town are £40 per week; an average is £48 per week. The area around Oxford Brookes is a little cheaper.

Mature students

The University runs study skills programmes and an Engineering Foundation Programme from which you would automatically proceed to your degree or diploma course. You can enrol as an Associate student. Access courses are accepted as entry qualifications.

Nursery

There is a purpose-built nursery on the Gipsy Lane campus for 48 children aged between two and five years. Fees for students are means tested.

THE CITY/ESCAPE ROUTES

See Oxford University's entry in this Guide.

University of Plymouth

Drake Circus
Plymouth
Devon
PL4 8AA
Telephone: 01752 600600

University Charter date: 1992

Plymouth is a large university with around 10,000 full-time undergraduates, 1,000 HND students and 650 full-time postgraduates. The University has four campuses: the main campus in Plymouth houses most courses: Seale-Hayne near Newton Abbott houses Agriculture, Food and Land use; Exeter campus houses the Faculty of Art and Design; Exmouth campus houses education, the School of Humanities and Performance Art. Degrees are modular within set patterns, with some free options where you can, for example, include a foreign language. Assessment is a mix of coursework and examination.

Accommodation varies between campuses.

• *New courses for 1997*

BA (Hons) International Relations, DipHE Nursing, BA (Hons) fine Art Contextual Practice, BA (Hons) Language and Fine Art.

• *Teaching excellence*

Sociology has been given the accolade of 'Excellent' for its teaching by the Higher Education Funding Council. This follows the 'Excellent rating given to Environmental Science, Geography, Geology and Ocean Studies last year.

• *Nursing Contract*

The contract for nurse education across the South West was awarded to the University. Bases for teaching are located in Cornwall, Somerset and Devon.

• *Funding Allocation*

The highest allocation for 'Quality Research' from the Higher Education Funding Council of any of the new universities was received.

• *CD Prospectus*

The Faculty of Science has produced its own interactive CD prospectus. This is the second in a series being produced and follows the success of the CD prospectus from The Faculty of Agriculture, Food and Land Use at Seale-Hayne, Newton Abbott .

• *Open Day*

The annual open day will be held in June 1997.

THE CAMPUSES

The University of Plymouth was born from a merger between Plymouth Polytechnic, Rolle College in Exmouth, Seale-Hayne Agricultural College and Exeter College of Art and Design. The four sites remain federal, and act federally. This is, in the true sense, a regional university.

Plymouth

This remains the University's main campus. Five of the seven faculties operate from here: Technology, Science, Human Science, the Plymouth Business School, Postgraduate Medical School.

Plymouth's buildings have very much the campus atmosphere of an active university. The campus itself is compact. You can see it easily from the ring-road. Its blocks are functional and have developed with the University's own expansion. Faculty offices have overspilled into surrounding 'villa' type housing, which balances function with domesticity. The original building is in the glass/panel idiom of technical institutes and forms one side of the quadrangle which is your between-lectures meeting ground: you will have to walk across here to get to the Student Union building and the library. In fact, the Student Union is underneath this precinct; its coffee lounge roof is a pyramid of glass which from 'ground' level seems a piece of modern sculpture.

Another balance to prevalent concrete is the old school building, now absorbed, rebuilt Georgian in white stone. This is the building which faces onto the ring-road, the blocks behind forming a backdrop to its 1812 charm. The Sherwell Church has recently been redeveloped and now provides two lecture theatres and an exhibition hall.

The workshops on campus are built as a mini-factory, complete with triangulated glass roofs. These are opposite the new faculty building for Technology, yellow brick, with softer lines than its 1960s counterparts.

Perhaps something to note: security here is good; there are closed-circuit television cameras installed on most buildings and the security staff are friendly but firm.

Seale-Hayne

This site is a remarkable contrast to the Plymouth campus. It is set outside Newton Abbott, west of the town. Before you go and look at it, contact the University for directions: it took us a long time to get there. The original building is in the style of an Oxbridge college (one of the redbrick, neo-Elizabethan sort built in 1914), very beautiful and set in 240 hectares of Faculty-managed farm and woodland. New extensions do not impinge on the air of affluence and old English stateliness. Down tracks are working farm buildings where you will learn your craft. Our only problem was that we kept meeting tractors. There are regular bus services to Newton Abbott, Exeter, Torbay and Plymouth... although, with the exception of Newton Abbott (not a large town), none of these centres is very near.

Faculty: Agriculture, Food and Land Use

Exeter

This campus was Exeter Art College, and still very much is Exeter Art College. It is well equipped, purpose-built, with a small Union/recreation area. The campus is about two miles out of Exeter's city centre.

Faculty: Arts and Design.

Exmouth

This campus used to be Rolle College, and still specialises in teacher training. The campus is set on a hill above Exmouth town. It is a series of low rise buildings, with an atmosphere of a small, friendly student community. From the drive you can see the sea. Surrounding houses are Victorian, large, affluent.

Faculty of Education, School of Humanities and the Performance department of the Faculty of Arts and Design.

The campuses are federal: there is transport between them, but the journeys are not easy. You must remember where you will be sited when you decide to come here: the lifestyles offered are very different.

Cars

If you want to belong to the University fully, a car is essential. Parking provision does vary from site to site: the largest car-park is on the Exeter campus. But cars are not prohibited on any campus.

Learning Resources

The University has four **libraries**. Materials information for all can be accessed through the library computer system. Altogether, the University has 400,000 books and subscribes to over 3,000 journals. Each individual library reflects the atmosphere of the site: Plymouth's obviously is the largest, with a busy, almost bustling (strange word for a library) ambience. Other libraries are smaller and more focused.

There are **computing facilities** throughout the University, and computers play a large part in most courses. The **Computing Service** provides information and help at all stages of your initiation into new systems, including short courses, seminars and workshops. Facilities are accessible until 10pm weekdays and 5pm weekends.

Foreign languages can be studied as part of some courses.

The University runs a **satellite television** service which makes and beams educational programmes across Europe from the University's television studio.

Culture on campus

Drama: The Drama Society aims at putting on at least two productions a year and runs workshops on acting skills and backstage craft (lighting, sound, set building...). There are plans afoot for street theatre too.

Music: Plymouth campus offers a range of music: the University Choral Society is based here; there is a string orchestra and various small ensembles which will depend on your fellow students. At least once a year, the students put on a musical. A part-time music tutor organises tuition for those of you interested. There is also a wide variety of musical activities at the Exmouth campus, including collaboration with the community to mount events for the Exeter Festival, or concerts in Exeter cathedral.

Art: There is a small gallery at the Exmouth campus which exhibits the work of local or home-grown artists.

The Union

The slant of the University of Plymouth Union is very site focused, which is not surprising: the sites are a long way away from each other. Each of the four campuses has its own site students' union, complete with a president and executive. Here we concentrate on the Plymouth Union.

This is a tardis of a building; much of it is underground with skylights. The Union Office itself is buzzing, and officers are very helpful. An insurance bureau, a games room (with pool, video and pinball), a launderette, a print/ reprographic unit and a shop are here, as well as a travel office, with good local travel information. There are two bars, one of which has become a fully fledged nightclub. The Union also runs a bar in the Main Hall, a no-smoking coffee bar and a lounge. There is a lively social scene with parties, discos and bands. The Union has recently appointed an Entertainments manager.

The Union funds over 100 clubs and societies. Plymouth campus weekly magazine is *Fly*, with contribution boxes all over campus. The magazine is also available on the internet (fly @ plym.ac.uk)

The Union has a small-holding on Dartmoor; small plots are available for lease.

The welfare team is available for private, confidential advice, and have a stock of backup leaflets and books. The Union runs Nightline on two campuses, available as a drop-in or telephone service, and a women's minibus.

The overall decision-making body of the Union is an amalgamation of these site unions, brought together as Union Council. Union facilities at other sites, though smaller, offer a range of services.

Sport

Sporting activities are co-ordinated through the Union. The Plymouth campus offers two gymnasia and three squash courts. Larger scale facilities are on the outskirts of the town: a fully equipped sports hall (badminton, basketball, tennis, table-tennis, five-a-side soccer, fencing and cricket practice); a floodlit, all-weather area; a pavilion with changing rooms, showers and a refreshment room. Here too are pitches for soccer/rugby/cricket/hockey, a five-hole golf course and an athletics practice area. There is a programme of fitness and coaching classes.

The University also has a watersports base just a few minutes from Plymouth campus. The Diving and Sailing Centre has 150 boats (dinghies through to a yacht). You can learn sub-aqua to advanced diver standard here (not something offered at many institutions: the University claims it to be unique among universities. You can also learn to sail, canoe, water-ski and board-sail.

Exmouth has a 13 acre playing field with soccer, rugby and an all-weather pitch. Here too: two netball courts, six tennis courts and a games area. The campus has a gymnasium and multigym used both for teaching and recreation.

Seale-Hayne has facilities for rugby, football, hockey, cricket and athletics; an indoor sports hall with squash courts and a multigym.

Exeter campus has a recreation programme based on local facilities.

Student welfare

Services vary from campus to campus. Medical provision, generally, is made locally. The three main campuses have **medical centres** with nursing advice and provision; Exeter relies entirely on local services. There is a team of **professional counsellors** at Student Services to help with your problems. The University has a team of men and women chaplains. The Plymouth **chaplaincy** is next-door to Student Services. Chaplains are co-ordinated, ecumenically, by a full-time minister.

Careers Service
The Careers Service helps with application procedures and gives individual counselling. You will have access to computerised careers information. The Service runs an Insight into Management course.

Students with special needs
There are some purpose-built residences for students with disabilities on both the Plymouth and the Exmouth campuses. Access to older buildings can be a problem. Contact the University Registry for fuller information.

Accommodation

Plymouth
The recent completion of the Robbins Conference Centre has given the Plymouth campus 430 new places in halls of residence - all of high standard (160 ensuite). There are also 1,180 self-catering places for first years, all within three miles of the campus. Some are shared rooms, but the majority are single. Buildings range from 11-storey blocks on campus to Victorian/Edwardian houses. A Georgian terrace next to campus houses women only.

Seale-Hayne
There are over 200 places for first years, some self-catering, some catered and some optional. There are 18 places in a Head-Lease-type scheme.

Exmouth
Over 220 places in halls and houses, most of which have wonderful views over the sea. A third of the residences are self-catering. Most rooms are shared. First years have priority.

Exeter
There is a head-lease scheme exclusively for first years.

Costs (1995/96)
Costs vary from campus to campus:
Hall fees for a single self-catered room range from £1,528.80 to £1,960 (ensuite). Fees relate to a residential year of 35 weeks.

Private sector
The Student Accommodation Service provides information to students who do not wish to/cannot have a place in hall. Accommodation varies from lodgings including meals to self-catered accommodation in a landlord's home or student shared house. High standards are set by the University and students based at any of the four campuses can usually find suitable accommodation very quickly. For students unable to get to Devon to arrange their own private accommodation there is the 'approved and arranged' service whereby high quality accommodation is allocated to a student according to the information he/ she provides.

Costs (1995/96)
These will, again, vary. A room in a shared house in Plymouth or Exeter could be £38 plus bills. This figure could drop by £8 to £10 at Seale-Hayne and Exmouth.

Mature students

A 'return to study' course is recommended. If you are interested in applying to the University of Plymouth and would like to check on the validity of an Access course in your area you should contact the University's Continuing Education Department. Many mature students begin studies near to home at one of the University's Partner Colleges and then progress to one of the main University campuses for later stages of study.

Nursery

There is a nursery on the Plymouth campus for 26 children from three to five years old. Places are limited.

THE CITY (population: 250,000)

The Exeter and Exmouth campuses both relate to Exeter which is covered by the Exeter University section. Seale-Hayne relates to Newton Abbot which is very small indeed: if you opt for this campus you definitely do not want a city life. So, here we shall concentrate on Plymouth.

Plymouth is an old port, famous for the Spanish Armada and its Hoe (Drake and the bowls if you remember). The Hoe is still there, as is an enclave of Elizabethan houses. The rest is, unfortunately, history. Plymouth suffered bombing in the last big war and much redevelopment since: this redevelopment continues. New buildings are in the idiom of neo-warehouses constructed in glass and green piping. The shopping areas are a mix of the last decades' blocks and paved precincts. The range of shopping is good: Plymouth is the commercial centre of the West Country and the only city of any size west of Exeter.

The Hoe is a space of green beyond city ramparts overlooking the English Channel. It is quite a pleasant walk, and only a short distance from the University. The Barbican is a small area of quaint shops and restaurants, also not far from the University.

Plymouth's surroundings are its saving. The river Tamar runs wide into the city. To the west are Cornwall and Dartmoor National Park and, in all directions, the clear beauty of the West Country.

Theatre: The Theatre Royal houses touring productions of drama, ballet and opera, many on their way directly to or from the West End. The Plymouth Arts Centre, the Barbican Theatre, the Drum Theatre (part of the Theatre Royal) and the Athenaeum Theatre (local amateur productions) are all small venues for alternative drama.

Music: There is a regular programme of classical music at the Theatre Royal, and the Bournemouth Symphony Orchestra has concerts at the Plymouth Guildhall.

Cinema: Plymouth has two cinemas with a total of five screens. The Plymouth Arts Centre shows of art films.

Nightlife: A range of nightclubs in Union Street and pubs in the Barbican. There is a full range of restaurants to suit all tastes and finances.

Sport: Watersports abound, as you would expect. There is a main swimming pool (33m) used for national competitions, and the Plymouth Pavilions have a landscaped pool and ice-rink.

ESCAPE ROUTES

Plymouth is in one of England's deservedly most popular holiday areas. The Devon coast is very beautiful, as is the country inland. This will be one of the shortest 'escape routes' sections in this book, not because there is nothing to do, but because there is so much: if you enjoy being outside or exploring small villages; if you enjoy walking or sailing or riding or gliding, then this is the place to be.

Communications

Plymouth is on the **main line** through to Cornwall and has **trains** through to all major centres: the journey can sometimes take a long time (but it does rather depend where you come from). **Coach links** are extensive. The new coast road will make a difference to Plymouth's access routes. The nearest motorway is the **M5** at Exeter, about 45 minutes away. **Ferries** travel to Santander and Roscoff.

University of Portsmouth

University House
Winston Churchill Avenue
Portsmouth PO1 2UP
Telephone: 01705 876543

University Charter date: 1992
Portsmouth is a medium/large university with around 9,000 full-time undergraduates, 744 HND students and 300 full-time postgraduates. The University has three campuses, although most courses are located on the main campus in Portsmouth. Degree programmes are modular, single subject or multi-disciplinary. There is a variety of assessment methods for each course.

The Accommdation Office reserves a high propotion of its rooms for first years.

THE CAMPUS

The main Guildhall campus is set in a large and reasonably compact, quiet area in the bottom left hand corner of Portsea Island, which is separated from the mainland only by the A27 (becoming the M27) running as a causeway through narrow, shallow waters. The academic buildings are serried behind the original Park Building (still in use), early-century classical-style, which landmarks the University's position in this flat peninsula. The campus is split into two halves by road and railway in an area pleasantly green, its buildings flanked by the spaces of Victoria Park, naval sports grounds and the University's own private green and shaded Ravelin Park. Buildings are generally modern-functional; not in themselves particularly appealing, but well-grouped. Their setting is shared by a number of the city's buildings, including Portsmouth's Victorian castle of a city museum and art gallery. These merely add variety and touches of period charm to what is - in effect - an academic precinct: the University dominates its environment in much the same style as a city-integrated university.

The Union building is very large and very busy, and manages to look well-used without looking well-worn.

Well worthy of comment is the Frewen Library, actually built on and into Ravelin Park; if you look up from your books, you will have views of lawns and trees. The building style is dramatic if you respond well to its geometrics: a cropped pyramid of tiered galleries - particularly impressive when lit. Its outside is white with dark blue edge; its interior has exposed pipe-work, painted in vivid primary contrast colours.

You can walk right round the main campus in about half an hour. Some Schools are outposted: the School of Education and English on the Langstone campus (3 miles); and the Business School on the Milton Campus (2 miles).

The Langstone Campus has halls of residence and its own student support services; it is also the location of the University's main sports fields. The Milton Campus has its own library, refectory and Students' Union facilities. Halls of residence are scattered around the southern bulge of Portsea Island: no distances are great.

Cars
A free minibus service runs between the three campuses and direct public buses travel between the University and the town.

Learning Resources

The **libraries** house around 600,000 volumes in total and take 3,300 current journals. There are two main libraries, the Frewen Library on the main campus and the Goldsmith Library on the Milton campus. The Frewen Library is open for 76.5 hours a weeks, and the Goldsmith Library for 56 hours. The Frewen Library has places for 840 readers.

The Portsmouth campus is networked. **Computer Services** offer computer literacy courses to all students, as well as advisory services and seminars on software, system utilities and user interfaces. Courses on specific computing applications are run within departments.

Supplementary **language courses** are available through the Language Centre as part of most courses and an Institution-wide Language Programme. All language courses are taught; language laboratories are available only if supervised.

Culture on campus

Film: The Rendezvous Cinema has its 'house' in the University's School of Art, Design and Media and shows films on six evenings a week. Films shown are a mix of art/minority productions and those which have already been on general release.

Music: The Nuffield Centre on the Guildhall Campus houses most of the musical activity at the University. There is a Musical Director who supervises tutorial and practice facilities; you can hire instruments. The Dramatic and Musical Society produces an annual Gilbert and Sullivan opera and the Choral Society and Orchestra perform regularly.

The Union

The Union has six full-time, sabbatical officers elected annually and employs 60 members of staff.

Alexandra House (the Union building) has three bars - one of which doubles as a nightclub, a refectory, shop, insurance and travel bureau, and general offices. The Milton site Union also has offices, a coffee shop, cinema and a bar. The Union runs a bar/common room at the QEQM Hall of residence. As well as over 100 clubs and societies, the Union ensures a wide variety of entertainment on campus, with 40 social events organised per term.

Services include a Rights and Advice Centre, a typing and publication service, newspaper with fully-equipped newsroom, student radio station (PURE FM), lift-sharing scheme and a Jobshop. The Student Development and Support Unit offers training courses and experiential learning opportunities, including Community Action.

Sport

Portsmouth University has very good sports facilities and 60 sports clubs. There is a Sports Manager who works closely with the Students' Union Sports Officer.

The University sports hall has three cricket bays, basketball and volleyball courts, badminton, football, hockey, netball and tennis. The University also has squash courts and outdoor tennis courts. A two room multi-gym offers 28 exercise stations in addition to the weights room. For ladies there is training assistance, on ladies-only evenings. There is black belt coaching in both judo and karate, and a resident instructor for the martial art of WUSHU (the instructor is described as 'strict' in the prospectus!). And a coach for the fencing club.

Outdoor pitches are near the residential area by the shores of Langstone Harbour: provision for cricket, hockey, rugby and soccer. Watersports are very strong here. The University has a fleet of Larks and Lasers on the Solent, and in both classes Portsmouth students are British student champions. There is windsurfing instruction for beginners and sea canoeing. The Canoeing Club organises regular weekend trips to rivers for more straightforward paddling.

Worthy of note: the University is a badminton Centre of Excellence. The resident coach is a former England international and team manager.

Student welfare

The University has a fully-staffed, residential **sick bay** at the Langstone campus for students both in halls or living in the private sector. Two General Practice surgeries have associations with the University and are situated close to campus. There are four **counsellors**: two men and two women. The University also has a legal service and a Financial Aid and Advice Centre.

The **University Chaplaincy** has both full and part-time chaplains and serves all students, whatever your religion - or no religion at all.

Careers Service
The Careers Centre works closely with departments to provide careers information relevant to you. Careers advice is available to you (on request) from the beginning of your course. The Careers Service has close links with local employers; there is a Job Shop advertising part-time vacancies in the Union. You will have access to PROSPECT-HE, a careers computer programme.

Students with special needs
You are requested to contact the Assistant Registrar (Admissions) before you apply. Some residential accommodation has been adapted.

Accommodation

The University offers a high proportion of its hall places to first years. If you do not find a place in hall accommodation, the Accommodation Office will allocate a place in approved lodgings to you before you arrive. 'Approved lodgings' means the lodging has been visited by the University Accommodation staff and passed as suitable.

Halls of residence
The 11 halls of residence can accommodate 1,782 students. Two halls are 'traditional', offering meals. Each hall has a committee of students who organise social events. The newest hall opens in October 1996: the rebuilt Victorian Royal Pier Hotel on the seafront with 270 ensuite rooms.

Costs (1995/96)

Single room catered	£60.00 per week
Double room catered	£58.00 per week
Single room self-catering	£40.67 per week
Single room (en suite)	£44.59 per week
Double room self-catering	£37.00 per week
Leases: 39 weeks	

Headleasing
The University offers 700 places in 200 houses. Costs: around £40 per week.

Private sector accommodation
Flats and bedsits are in high demand in Portsmouth and the supply is limited. Details of accommodation are available in a daily bulletin from the Accommodation Office. Costs: £36 to £40 per week.

Mature students

The University encourages applications from mature students. If you do not satisfy normal entry requirements, you should contact the admissions tutor in the department in which you are interested. A Mature Student's Guide to Higher Education is available from the Academic Registrar.

Nursery
The nursery takes children aged between six months and five years open between 8.30am and 5.30pm. There is a half-term playgroup run by the Union.

THE CITY (population 179,000)

Portsmouth has been designated a Millennium City: £112 million will be used to convert Portsmouth Harbour into an International Maritime Heritage Arena.

The city in the main is surprisingly modern in ambience, and must have undergone massive redevelopment after the 1939-45 war. It has a number of large shopping centres and precincts, a traditional fruit and vegetable market, and good browsing territory for antiques and bric-a-brac. Balancing areas of lovely old Georgian and Victorian buildings remain to anchor the city into its history. The splendidly ornate white pillared and domed Victorian Guildhall, faced by an impressive modern civic complex with a wide, piazza style pedestrianised area between, gives the centre great dignity and a fine symbolic linking of old with new.

You never forget that Portsmouth is a naval garrison city, which means that its lifestyle can be very vivid indeed. Here, the presence of such an army of seafarers will mean that you must find your own land-legs pretty quickly, and be careful about your social wanderings until you have acquired some local lore. No shortage of clubs, pubs, discos, casinos here - "the fleet's in" has always been a classic call to high and wide living. Clarence Pier has a fun-fair open from May to September.

The harbour has historic ships permanently moored: the Mary Rose (the Tudor ship salvaged with its artefacts intact), the HMS Victory (Nelson's flagship and the ship on which he died), the HMS Warrior (the first iron-clad ship).

Theatres: The King's Theatre has touring productions and is architecturally interesting. The Theatre Royal is a small theatre housing children's shows and others of more general interest. Portsmouth Arts Centre and the Hornpipe Arts Centre are venue for touring companies of more 'alternative' theatre. The Wedgewood Rooms have a programme of 'alternative' comedy and bands.

Music: There is a full programme of music on offer at the Guildhall, from classical to pop. Touring folk, jazz and blues bands often use the pubs.

Cinema: Portsmouth has three cinemas, two Cannon and an Odeon, all with three screens. A multiplex cinema with 10 screens is planned in Port Solent.

Nightlife: A lot of nightlife here. Nightclubs are mainly around the South Parade Pier (discounts for students). Restaurants are mainly in Southsea. Pubs, everywhere.

Sport: The main sports centre is the Mountbatten Centre which provides facilities for most sports, except swimming. The Victoria swimming pool is the deepest civic pool. The Pyramids Resort Centre is an indoor swimming complex with wave-machines and flumes, a pool-side cafe and restaurant; not perhaps for the serious swimmer. The sea and coast provide enormous scope for watersports and the facilities on offer are excellent.

ESCAPE ROUTES

The south coast to the east and west of Portsmouth is varied and changing: its naval history is dramatic; its beaches are famous; and its waters offer some of the best sailing in England.

You are close to the New Forest which covers 145 square miles inland : facilities for walking and riding.

Salisbury is within easy distance: a very beautiful city in its older parts. West and north are Salisbury Plain and Stonehenge: a bit of a trek, but certainly worth the effort, especially if you manage to make it before sunrise... Close too is Winchester, with another fine cathedral city.

Across the Solent, with a good ferry service, is the Isle of Wight, now owned largely by the National Trust.

Communications

Rail links travel along the south coast and north to London and beyond. London is 80 minutes away. **Coach links** are extensive. The **M275** links with the **M27** which is the fastest route from London to Southampton. The north/south throughways are not straightforward to this part of the country. There are **ferries** to the Isle of Wight which take only 15 minutes. Ferries too to Cherbourg, Le Havre, St Malo, Caen, Bilbao and Santander.

University of Reading

PO Box 217
Reading
RG6 2AH
Telephone: 01734 875123

University Charter date: 1926

Reading is a medium-sized university with around 7,500 full-time undergraduates and 2,000 full-time postgraduates. The University has a single 300 acre campus just outside the town centre. There are two outposts: the Faculty of Education and Community Studies is a mile away; the University's farm (2,200 acres) are near Reading on the Downs. Degrees are offered in a flexible unit structure within widely based faculties. End of year exams plus Finals (end of course examinations) can sometimes be augmented by some coursework.

Applicants who have firmly accepted a place by the end of June will be offered a place in hall. Later applicants may be placed in hall or will be helped to find accommodation.

THE CAMPUS

Reading's original site was at London Road, half a mile from the present campus, and still in use. The move to Whiteknights Park gave the University a most beautiful site. About one and a half miles south of the centre of Reading, Whiteknights was once part of a medieval manorial estate, landscaped in the 18th century, with further ornamental development in the early 19th century.

Today, the site offers 300 acres which the University has been developing with great care since 1954, occupying older houses (often fine examples of grand Victorian villas), adding new buildings with an eye to harmony; even the presence, inevitable in a long-growing University, of worn 'sixties blocks is not obtrusive... And always as much as possible of the beautiful parkland setting has been preserved, with its lake and trees and conservation area, rich in fauna and flora. The site generally is flat, but the campus has good visual variety with wild meadowland beyond the wide gracious lawns, set with magnificent mature trees: images of summer shade and idylls.

Not 100% idyll of course; on the western edge, screened from Wilderness Road (evocative names here) is a group of dismal single-storey blocks which carry the (lack of) style of 1940s make-do. They are about to be re-developed.

Most new development has been kept to the perimeter. In these hard times, expanded student numbers have led to the packing of space on many campuses: this one remains implausibly spacious.

The academic buildings, with the Students' Union and the Senior Common Room, cluster around the library in centre campus; the halls of residence stretch along the northern perimeter and into nearby streets. Separating the two are the sports grounds and open green spaces.

The general atmosphere is confident, unstressed, well ordered: no doubt a result of so harmonious a setting.

Outposts
The University's Faculty of Education and Community Studies is at Bulmershe Court, a mile from the main Whiteknights campus. This campus is pleasantly set where suburban villas give way to housing estates. Courses: Education and Community Studies; Film and Drama.

Farms for agricultural teaching and research (2,200 acres in all) are near Reading, on the Downs.

Cars
Parking space is limited; this is good cycling country however, and the campus has many cycle-parks.

Learning Resources

Reading has a main **library** and three branch libraries (covering Music, Agriculture and Education) with a total of almost a million books and pamphlets. It takes 4,000 current periodicals. Seating for nearly 1,000 students in all. Opening hours: Monday to Thursday to 10pm ; Friday to 7pm; Saturday to 12.30pm ; Sunday 2pm to 6pm .

The **Computer Science Department** teaches a first year course on programming and systems to non-computer scientists. Computer facilities are available all day every day, and time allocation is operated on demand. There are extra courses for all students on aspects of computer literacy. Access to the campus network is possible from PCs in departments and the halls of residence.

The University has four **language laboratories**. Tapes, textbooks and satellite television are available. You can study a language from scratch; some extracurricular courses are certificated by the London Chamber of Commerce (Languages for Industry and Commerce).

Culture on campus

Drama: Several productions are staged each term by the drama society; and by the French, German and History departments, one a year each. There is a theatre on the Bulmershe Court site.

Film: Showings in the Palmer Building twice a week represent the 'best of cinema', organised by the Reading Film Theatre.

Music: The music department organises regular concerts and recitals for students and the public. There are performances by the large University Choral Society and Orchestra, a chamber orchestra and a chamber choir. There is also a music club, the University Singers, an opera society, which gives a stage performance each year, a series of lunchtime concerts and a chamber opera performed every other year. Two further groups have been set up recently - the Navara String Quartet, which is the University's quartet-in-residence, and the Thames Chamber Players, who are department-based, but tour in the region. A wide range. Music tuition is available. Regular discos are run by the Students' Union.

The Union

The prospectus describes the Union building as 'substantial' - the entrance is unprepossessing with harsh lights and a sense of cramped space. Outside there is a large paved area with wooden seats and tables, commanding pretty, peaceful views over lake and woodland. The Union building contains shops, travel and insurance services, and some indoor sports facilities. The committee runs more than 30 clubs and societies, sports, entertainment, discos, welfare (advice, debt counselling and Nightline) and all necessary administration.

There are two bars, and a third at Bulmershe, recently refurbished, which hold 400 and 200 students. The hall used for gigs holds up to 1,300. There are between 10 and 12 bands booked per term, mostly from outside the University.

The Union employs 37 full-time and 14 part-time staff, and six sabbatical officers.

Sport

Both the main sports centre and the University's playing fields are on the Whiteknights campus. The Wolfenden Sports Centre has facilities for a wide range of indoor sports - badminton, volleyball and five-a-side football. There are aerobics and fitness classes, and the University offers coaching in a range of sports.

An extension to the sports centre has recently been completed. Provision now includes a fitness room, a martial arts/dance studio, full changing rooms and a walkway to the adjacent Squash Centre (eight courts).

The main playing fields have a full range of pitches, a floodlit hard porous surface and floodlit hard courts for netball and tennis.

There are sports facilities at the Bulmershe Court campus which are available in the evening and at weekends: a sports hall, gymnasium, climbing wall, mini ski-slope and playing fields.

The University has facilities for rowing, sailing, canoeing and wind surfing at bases on the Thames and the Kennet.

Reading is represented in all UAU competitions and many clubs participate in local leagues.

Student welfare

The University has a **medical centre** just off campus. GPs, physiotherapy, a Sports injury clinics, immunisation and dental care are available. There is a sick bay with beds, if you need 'residential' care. All for a small fee. **Counsellors**, psychologists and psychotherapists are provided by the University. At the **Chaplaincy Centre** a team of Christian chaplains work together and have links with the Jewish chaplain. There is a mosque on campus. A room is set aside for quiet space and thought. There is also a meeting room, a small library and a small kitchen.

Careers Service

Many of the Careers events are part of an optional module run between the Careers Advisory Service and the School of Applied Management Studies: these are mainly 'Insight' courses designed to give you an introduction to management and to management skills. The Careers Service works with departments and will come and see you during your second year.

Students with special needs

Some residential accommodation has been adapted. There is a booklet available with information about facilities provided by the University: you should write to the Co-ordinator for Students with Special needs. The University produces a large print abstract of the prospectus.

Accommodation

There are 4,577 places in University residences, mainly in traditional halls, although a very small number of self-catering places is available to first years. With the exception of Bulmershe Hall and Mansfield Hall, all are within 20 minutes' walk of Whiteknights. Applicants who have firmly accepted a place (and returned the accommodation form) by the end of June will be offered places in halls.

If you apply later and are not offered hall accommodation, the University will offer you University lodgings, or help you find a place in the private sector. A house-hunting weekend is organised in September.

Halls of residence

The halls of residence vary in size and style since their architecture spans quite a long period from 1900 to 1994. Other variations which might influence your choice are the setting (two overlook the lake; three are close to the sports ground, etc.) and amenities (some have music rooms, games rooms and tennis courts).

Each hall has a library, a central dining room (except self-catering halls) serving three meals a day on weekdays and two at weekends, common rooms, a TV room, a bar and a laundry. Most rooms are single study-bedrooms, with shared bathrooms and pantries but - as in most universities - where there are double rooms, it's the first years who share. An increasing number of rooms have ensuite facilities. All halls are warden controlled.

Much social life centres on the halls: formal balls, special dinners, an international evening, a summer concert.

Costs (1995/96)

catered single room: £74.00 inclusive of 19 meals per week
self-catered single room: £39.00

These are typical. Prices vary according to facilities - obviously, shared rooms are cheaper and ensuite rooms more expensive.

Private Sector

You should be able to find accommodation within a mile of the campus. Private accommodation, self catering, is around £40 per week, excluding bills.

Mature students

The minimum 'mature' age is 21. Generally the University looks for traditional (O level, A or A/S level) qualifications, but if you write to the sub-dean of your target faculty, special pleading and/or an interview might yield a more flexible approach. Access courses are acceptable but you might also have to take a written test.

Nursery

The Union runs a nursery for 22 three to five year olds open 8.30am to 5.30pm Reading University Playgroup (run by parents) takes three to five year olds on weekday mornings during term time.

THE CITY (population: 250,000)

Reading is a large county town (700,000 people in its catchment area), 40 miles west of London, on the Thames where it joins the river Kennet. It is chiefly distinguished by being an old crossing. There is little of note in the town: there is a pleasant park, Forbury Gardens, near to the ruins of the abbey, founded in 1221. This was once one of England's larger and richer abbey complexes: Henry I was buried here.

There are one or two interesting old and reconstructed churches and period civic buildings. There is Caversham Court, just north of Reading, which has terraced lawns sloping down to the river, where plays, dancing and garden fetes happen in the summer.

Reading claims to be one of the best shopping centres in the south of England. It does have a good range of shops, but like all towns so close to London, much of the panache and style seems to drain to centre. There is quite a good market and a large covered shopping precinct.

Reading is regarded as a 'typical' British town. For the purpose of marketing surveys its residents are thought to represent the nation's shoppers. We are not sure if this is a plus or a minus. You might find some unusual 'experimental' clothes in the chain stores.

Theatres: The Hexagon entertainment centre (1977) has a large (1,700 capacity) auditorium and immensely flexible staging. It puts on a range of spectator events: drama (mostly light), opera, discos, concerts, exhibitions, craft fairs, films, dinner dances and world class snooker. Performances can be either amateur or professional. There is also a bar, wine bar, food and foyer exhibitions. The Hexagon is part of the civic centre complex - rather awkward and forbidding outside but successful interiors.

Music: There is the Reading Symphony Orchestra, Operatic Society, Amateur Theatrical Society, a number of choirs and harmony groups, plus lighter concerts.

Cinema: The Reading film theatre is in the Palmer Building, on campus. There are two cinemas, six screens in all.

Nightlife: Reading nightlife is not extensive. The better restaurants are out of town, as are the more interesting pubs and inns. There are five nightclubs and a casino.

Sport: There is an excellent range of sporting activities and facilities, including Palmer Park with its banked cycle track, a six-lane athletics synthetic track, a floodlit area with football and tennis... This is also excellent golfing country, with a number of clubs around Reading welcoming new members. For spectator sports you have a wide choice. The river offers regattas, including Reading's own. The city has three rugby clubs: Abbey, Old Readingensians and Reading. Berkshire County Cricket Club plays the minor counties championship and Reading Football Club is 'spirited'. There is speedway and greyhound racing at the speedway stadium.

ESCAPE ROUTES

The area around Reading, cut through by the river Thames, is pretty, rolling, historic, rich and very well-kept. Although this is now Commuter Land, many settlements are well-preserved, retaining their quiet rural charm. The landscape undulates, controlled and wooded, with a sense of being an extended park.

Reading is on the river, or rather, two rivers, so the opportunities for messing about in boats are abundant. Down-Thames, the waters widen to one of the most gracious stretches of this royal river. Henley, famous for its July Regatta, lies a few miles north east.

Further downstream, is Windsor. The largest castle in England, official residence of the Queen, dominates, indeed is, the town. Windsor Great Park covers 4,800 acres and is pleasant walking country. Windsor Safari Park, just south west of Windsor, is open daily.

Further afield are the Vale of the White Horse, historic and picturesque; the university city of Oxford; the upper reaches of the Thames. And with London less than half an hour away by train, your leisure hours should be quite happily filled. This is also a marvellous area for riverside inns and country pubs.

Communications

Reading is on the Western Region's **intercity** routes between Paddington, the West of England, South Wales, Bristol, the Midlands and the North. There are regular, frequent trains to both Paddington and Waterloo. At best the service takes only 22 minutes.

National bus routes to all parts of the country come through Reading. 'Express' buses to London pass the University; the service runs hourly with extra buses at peak times. Reading is on the **M4** London-Bristol and South Wales. There is a direct bus service to **Heathrow**, which takes 50 minutes, and a direct rail link to Gatwick.

University of Southampton

Southampton
SO17 1XB
Telephone
01703 595000

University Charter date: 1952

Southampton is a medium-sized/large university with almost 9,000 full-time undergraduates and 1,750 full-time postgraduates. The University has a main single campus: 'offshoots' on Southampton Water Front - the Docklands campus - and the new Avenue Campus which houses the Arts Faculty close to the main campus. All courses are assessed by examination: some include an element of practical or written work from your course. Southampton offers a full range of academic subjects, including Medicine.

Most first years are guaranteed a place in University hall.

THE CAMPUS

The University stands on a mark-out line where large suburban houses with good gardens and lots of trees meet the area of more urban housing, reaching out from the city centre two miles away.

The University is a mix of graceful older and more modern buildings grouped in a landscaped valley. Most buildings are three or four storeys, light in appearance, with regular geometric proportions. New buildings include the School of Physiotherapy and Occupational Therapy and the Baroque-revival style Arts faculty.

The more 'sociable' areas are grouped around less geometrically: the University's theatre, concert hall and art gallery (all serve the region's community as well as the University), and the health centre, refectory and Students' Union. There are lawns and shrubs; the Botanical Gardens on campus are a protected oasis.

Academic dignity is preserved in a large complex of older, redbrick buildings built in 1927, well-kept, lawn-edged, wearing an atmosphere of studious calm.

The University precinct is surrounded by streets whose reasonably commodious houses absorb some of the overspill teaching and accommodation needs. Very close to the precinct is Southampton Common, a large, open, wooded area which balances the compact campus.

Outposts

The new Avenue Campus, neo Georgian and housing the Arts Faculty is close to the main campus.

Docklands Campus is on Southampton Water Front and houses the departments of Geology and Oceanography and the Underwater Acoustics groups of the Institute of Sound and Vibration.

Cars

Parking space at the University is limited, so first years are not allowed to bring cars. Bicycles and motorcycles are permitted.

Learning Resources

Main **library** services are provided in the Hartley Library in the centre of campus. It has 900,000 books, seats 1,300 and has over 100 staff. The library is open seven days a week for most of the year. Five branch libraries serve Biomedical Sciences and the outpost campuses.

Computer facilities are available from 8am to 10pm Monday to Saturday. Courses are offered to non-computer scientists. PCs and some high performance workstations are available on a casual use basis on all campuses.

Most courses can include a unit of a modern language. The **language centre** has recently upgraded its facilities. 30 languages are now available for self-study and there are voluntary courses also available. Computer-assisted teaching can be accessed anywhere on the computer network.

Culture on campus

Drama: The Nuffield Theatre has its own repertory company, and hosts visiting companies (drama and dance) including the University Players.

Music: The Turner-Sims concert hall, purpose-built, is venue for international artists, as well as for the University. There are many recitals and concerts, including two lunchtime recitals each week in term time. Student musicians play a major part here; there is a pre-session music course for those interested in becoming involved. The Union runs the orchestra and Chamber Choir.

Film: Union Films - with its on-campus cinema - has won the British Federation of Film Societies award three times. There are two sessions of 36 films annually: cost, £9 per session (25p per film!).

The Union

The large, four storey Union building is the campus' social focal point, near the refectory and across the road from the library. The ballroom has a capacity of 800 (venue for live bands and departmental balls). Also housed: an impressive Debating Chamber; two licensed bars; a coffee shop; a bistro; a well-stocked shop; travel centre; launderette; a bank; two television rooms; pool and snooker tables; and a music practice room. The Union runs a mini-market weekly where you can buy music, crafts, clothes and posters.

There is a total of six full-time and eight part-time sabbatical officers, including an Entertainments Officer. Several big name acts are booked each term; smaller events happen in the bars, an event a night - quizzes, comedy, bingo, discos and smaller bands. The Film Society gives a 'professional' service (a front of house and refreshments) and shows films on four nights a week.

Larger events are organised by the 200 societies (80 of these are sporting). The Union hires out to societies facilities and rooms, and the Entertainments team will give all assistance to make an event 'happen'.

The Community Care Scheme is active, offering students the chance to become involved with the city. Whereas most universities organise a Rag Week of frenetic fund-raising for charity, Southampton's Rag fund-raising runs all year - which seems much more sensible.

The Debating Society, as well as having enviable facilities, publishes its own newspaper. The Union's own newspaper comes out every fortnight; also the fortnightly bulletin of committee news and the yearly handbook.

The Welfare Sabbatical Officer is supported by two advisors (one full time, one part-time) employed by the Union. Leaflets on welfare issues, as well as a small legal fund, a half-term play scheme, study skills and typing courses are all under Welfare's umbrella. A nightly safety bus for both men and women runs from campus to town and to halls.

Sport

There is an indoor sports centre which includes a 60' x 100' sports hall, squash courts and rooms for table-tennis, martial arts, outside climbing wall and a range of fitness training. Outdoor facilities (boatyard, rifle range and excellent sports grounds) are all within easy reach of the campus - one of the bonuses of the University site's being on the edge of the city.

The sports grounds have a pavilion which serves drink and food, and there are 16 changing rooms.

If you want to swim, you can use the several pools in the city. The sea nearby offers a full range of watersports.

The Department of Physical Education works closely with the students. The professional staff and many specialist part-time instructors offer instructional courses and organise intramural competitions in many disciplines. Courses for all ability levels are free of charge.

There are around 80 sports clubs organised through the Athletic Union. The University excels in sailing, table-tennis, American football and skiing.

Student welfare

There is a **Health Centre** provides a full GP service on campus open between 9.30am and 5.00pm. You may register here if you live within two miles of campus. Outside these hours there is a GP on call.

There are four fully trained **counsellors** on the campus who can be contacted through the Students' Union, or by making an appointment at their offices. The confidential sessions run into the early evening.

The University **Chaplaincy Centre** maintained by three full-time chaplains. There is a common room with a library and coffee bar where all are welcome for a chat.

Careers Service

The Service has five full-time careers advisors. There are computers with self-assessment careers programmes, including PROSPECT-HE and the Service also offers practical help in writing CVs and management competencies. The Service publishes a weekly 'Careers News' during term time.

Students with special needs

You can make arrangements to visit the campus through the Admissions Office; you will be met by an advisory team, including the University's Adviser to Disabled Students. There are some specially adapted rooms on campus and a 24 hour care service is provided.

Accommodation

First years who accept Southampton as their firm offer and meet the terms of their offers are guaranteed a place in University residences.

There are 3,825 places in University residences. Halls of Residence are mixed with single study bedrooms; flats or corridors are usually single sex. All have a balance of students from all faculties, planned to broaden your social contacts. The halls are generally set in very pleasant surroundings and are within walking distance of campus (except the family hall which is two miles out).

Traditional halls

Warden-controlled. Five halls. Breakfast every day, with lunch on Sundays, evening meal on weekdays. Between 10 and 20 minutes' walk from campus. Mostly single rooms. Halls are grouped on two main sites, Glen Eyre and Wessex Lane, each of which have Junior Common Rooms (to which you must pay a subscription for the upkeep of social facilities), bars, TV rooms, games rooms, libraries, squash courts and outdoor sports facilities. Other facilities include shops, music rooms and launderettes.

Self-catering halls

These have a Warden or Senior Resident on site. Groups of students share the facilities, and group sizes vary, as do facilities. All rooms are single. There are 96 places for families or couples.

Costs (1995/96)

Traditional halls, catered:
Single £64.35 to £68.55 per week (30 weeks)
en suite £78.70 per week (30 weeks)

Self-catering halls:
Single £33.80 to £38.00 per week
en suite £47.50 to £49.00 per week
Studio flats £57.30 per week (usually for postgraduates)

Private accommodation

Private rented accommodation (flats and houses) is available, but is hard to arrange unless you are in Southampton to negotiate well ahead of term time. This is not really feasible for most first-years. For second and subsequent years, the Accommodation Office attempts to match students to suitable accommodation and provide booklets, leaflets and maps. There is an Accommodation-dedicated telephone service during the summer vacation.

Costs (1995/96)

Average £38 plus bills per person per week for rooms/bedsits.

Mature students

Minimum age, 21 (23 for law). Each case is considered on merit: evidence of recent study is important: passes at 'A' level, an Access course, or an OU foundation course, for instance, would be acceptable. The University runs some 'Return to Study' courses.

A range of degree courses is available through part-time study.

Nursery

The University runs a nursery for children aged four months and five years. Student places are subsidised by the Union. The nursery is open between 8.30am and 5.30pm, term and vacations.

There is a half-term play-group and a babysitting circle.

THE CITY (population: c 197,000)

Much of Southampton was destroyed during the Second World War. The 12th- century city walls with their old merchants' house-fronts and early gunports are well preserved, along with a wealth of other relics of the city's long and interesting history. The waterfront has a busy charm, with pier head, the regular ferries to the Isle of Wight, and the new 'Ocean Village', which offers a marina, shops, restaurants, a multiplex cinema and disco. Shamrock Quay is worth finding: busy, with shops and restaurants among the restored dockland warehouses.

The city centre, however, was rebuilt in post-war utilitarian style and has the atmosphere and appearance of the southern New Towns. The shopping parades and pedestrian precincts accommodate a reasonably good range of shops and chainstores. The city is a good mixture of the new and the old, with more than a thousand acres of open spaces, large parks in the city centre, rock gardens and riverside walks. The common, north of the city, has nature trails and the Common Studies Centre, with a display of local wildlife.

Theatre: The Nuffield Theatre on the University campus serves as Southampton's repertory theatre and hosts professional companies. The Mayflower Theatre is the largest provincial theatre south of Manchester, acting as home to various events from the visiting Bolshoi Ballet to an evening with Des O'Connor, taking in serious theatre in between. The Gantry Theatre behind the Mayflower is the venue for more alternative theatre. The Solent People's Theatre is a professional street theatre company which tours the pubs and schools of Southampton.

Music: The Guildhall is a large general venue for orchestral concerts. An elegant, period building with a large seating capacity. The Civic Art Gallery hosts concerts by the Bournemouth Symphony Orchestra. The Mayflower Theatre stages rock concerts as well as touring opera companies, West End musicals, variety shows and general theatre. The Turner Sims Concert Hall, on the University campus, has good acoustics and is the city's main centre for classical music events. The city has live music sounding from its pubs, including folk clubs and jazz.

Cinema: A Cannon 5 screen multiplex has opened at the Ocean Village development. Alternative film showings go to the Gantry Theatre.

Nightlife: Southampton's nightlife is lively, the focus is not the city centre but around the areas where historic pubs have survived, some traditional, some with live music (The Frog and Frigate brews its very own ale); student-oriented nightclubs and discos have sprung up in the areas with popular pubs. There is a wide range of restaurants and fast food outlets.

Sport: For spectator sports, Southampton offers its football club, the 'Saints'. Hampshire County Cricket Club plays regular fixtures. The city has two local teams for American football. There are three sports centres, the largest covering 300 acres of ground with facilities for most sports including petanque. The Bitterne Leisure Centre houses indoor sport. Southampton also has a dry ski-slope centre and ten-pin bowling. This is an excellent sailing area, on Southampton Water and the Solent. Facilities cater for all-comers. The nation's largest annual boat show is held in Southampton; and there's Cowes Week, in August.

ESCAPE ROUTES

Southampton exists because of the sea. The south coast to the east and west is varied and changing: its naval history is dramatic and rich; its beaches are famous; and its waters offer some of the best sailing in England.

You are close to the New Forest which covers 145 square miles inland: facilities for walking and riding. Salisbury is within easy distance: it is a very beautiful city in its older parts, and the cathedral is practically the only one in England to be conceived and built in a single style - it is singularly magnificent. West and north are Salisbury Plain and Stonehenge: a bit of a trek from Southampton, but certainly worth the effort, especially if you manage to make it before sunrise... Closer to the University is Winchester, another fine cathedral and historic city.

Communications

Southampton is 70 minutes away from London: hourly non-stop and hourly semi-fast services run to Waterloo. **Direct rail links** with many other cities; a local service takes you along the coast. **Coach services** are regular to London, Heathrow, Gatwick and Paris. Southampton has close access to the **M3** and **M27**, which links with the **M25** and the national motorway network. Regular flights from **Southampton Airport** to Amsterdam, Guernsey, Paris, Jersey, Brussels, as well as other parts of Britain. A local **ferry service** runs between Town Quay and Hythe Pier. A regular service to Cowes on the Isle of Wight.

Southampton Institute of Higher Education

East Park Terrace
Southampton
SO9 4WW
Telephone: 01703 319000

Southampton Institute has 5,000 full-time undergraduates, 2,000 HND students and 100 full-time postgraduates. The Institute has, effectively, a single city centre campus; the second campus is devoted to non-HE students. Degrees are modular; assessment is by continuous assessment and end of semester exams. The Institute awards Nottingham Trent University degrees.

The Institute's halls of residence are reserved for first years and students with special needs: 2,350 places by 1997.

THE CAMPUS

East Park Terrace Campus

The Institute occupies a city centre site, developed densely with modern blocks. Halls of residence are only a few minutes' walk away from the main buildings - lecture halls, the library, Union and bars. East Park faces the west boundary of the campus, so part of your city outlook is green. A policy of 'no smoking except in designated areas' operates on campus.

All undergraduate courses are taught here.

Warsash Campus

The Institute's second campus at Warsash (ten miles from Southampton) is now dedicated to non-degree level studies, short courses and business linked events. Some specialist resources and facilities remain here to support the Maritime Faculty based on the main campus.

Learning Resources

The library offers 1,000 study places and a well-developed system of information retrieval via computers. There are three IT Resource Centres, with advice desks, open to 9pm. More than 500 networked PCs and 100 Applemacs, as well as 150 portable computers available for student loan.

The Union

The Students' Union Building on campus has a TV and coffee lounge and three bars open all day, plus entertainments: DJs, bands, cabarets, hypnotists etc. in the evenings; big name bands for the various balls. Southampton Guildhall is used for large-scale events. The Union also runs an Advice Centre in collaboration with Institute counsellors and includes debt, legal and stress counselling.

A good range of clubs and societies supported; the Union magazine, *Exposed*, will keep you informed.

Sport

The recreation centre has a sports hall, fitness suite and sauna/solarium. Playing fields used are four miles out of the city; additional fields at Warsash, ten miles away. Sailing, canoeing and windsurfing facilities are also at Warsash where the Waterborne Activities Centre, offers dinghy, keelboat and powerboat courses. The Institute is a centre for National Coaching Foundation courses, offering instruction classes which lead to national awards.

Student Welfare

One of the halls of residence has an NHS surgery. The Institute's counselling service offers workshops on a variety of problem areas. There is an ecumenical chaplaincy team. The Careers Service offers talks and training (CV writing, interview technique etc.). The Institute runs a Job Shop which advertises jobs on campus and liaises with local employers. Special needs: many areas of the campus have been adapted for use by students with disabilities, including some residential rooms.

Accommodation

By October 1997, the Institute will have 2,350 places in halls of residence; most are reserved for first years and students with special needs. The Accommodation Office keeps a list of private rented accommodation. Costs: range from £45 pw (shared) to £56 pw (single, ensuite); private sector: £35 to £45 pw plus bills (all 1995/96 costs).

Mature students

The Institute has links with various local colleges and looks favourably on Access courses. A free Study Assistance service supports students with learning problems - from basic study techniques to dyslexia.

City and Escape Routes

See The University of Southampton's entry.

University of Surrey

Guildford
Surrey
GU2 5XH
Telephone: 01483 300800

University Charter date: 1966

Surrey is a small university with 7,500 undergraduates and postgraduates on full and part-time degree programmes (no part-time undergraduates). The University has a single campus in Guildford. A number of degree programmes have been modularised within named course patterns; others follow 'traditional' lines. Some programmes can be taken with sandwich options. Assessment methods vary. This is a technological university offering mainly science, engineering and business oriented degrees.

The University guarantees a place in residence for all first year undergraduates and can accommodate many final year students.

THE CAMPUS

The University was founded in 1966, and most of its buildings were purpose-built in the late years of the decade. The site is now well developed and has acquired, with surprising rapidity, an air of maturity: trees look thoroughly at home, and lawns are really green. Restricted space here is used to maximum effect. The campus climbs a shallow hill, which mildly dominates Guildford. No attempt is made to space out developments: buildings are grouped, stacked, balanced... connected by stairs, ramps, gantries, walkways at various levels, flyover corridors - all quite dynamic and active. Buildings are plain and functional, well-proportioned, flat-roofed rectangles, mainly four storeys or less. The general impression is helped by light brick, concrete and glass surfaces and by the changing levels of the site.

Little space separates the academic and amenity blocks from the residences, serried above them. The effect could be claustrophobic, but the University is relatively small; it's all a matter of scale - and on this scale it works. The halls of residence add pitched roofs, climbing tiers of light on winter evenings, and the domestic dimension which gives a smallish campus good balance.

Space in front of the campus is effectively graced by pretty ponds, contoured lawns, weeping willows, a small waterfall... again, very small scale, but a good antidote to suburban Guildford (the town centre is a mere ten-minute walk away).

The campus was quiet by the time the early winter evening settled: there was very much a sense of home-going, no doubt fostered by the campus residences.

The University is dominated by the large modern Guildford Cathedral, which becomes its landmark, and where degree ceremonies are held.

Cars

Cars may not be parked in the vicinity of the residences except at Hazel Farm. This means that for first years it's no cars - unless you choose to live off campus or at Hazel Farm, in which case you can apply for a permit to park on the main site. Using local car parks off campus is not recommended. There is a park for motorcycles and bicycle racks around campus are often immediately outside, and in full view of, classrooms. This looks a good safety factor.

Learning Resources

The main **library** houses 325,000 books and can seat 550 students. Opening hours: 10am to 10pm Monday; 9am - 10pm Tuesday to Friday; 1pm to 6pm Saturday; 2pm to 6pm Sunday. The University takes 2,600 periodicals.

Most undergraduates use **computers** as part of their formal training, and all students have the opportunity to attend optional computing courses. You have access to well over 1,000 terminals throughout the campus 24 hours a day. The campus is networked with access to the world wide web.

In addition to the combined language degrees, students in all departments are encouraged to study a foreign language. The European **Language Teaching** Centre's activities include language proficiency testing, available to all Surrey students. The course of study can lead to a Certificate of Proficiency. Language tuition is available at four levels. Self study courses are available too.

Culture on campus

Drama: Student groups put on productions ranging from the classics to musicals and farce. Workshops and evening classes further develop the skills of any students interested in drama.

Film: The Oscar Film Unit and Arts Cinema provide a full programme ranging from Hollywood blockbusters to film festival entries.

Music: A series of public concerts organised by the Music Department brings well-known musicians to the campus, often to perform alongside the University's own choir and orchestra, or the professional musician-academics who teach here. Less formal music of all kinds, played by music students, can be heard on campus, especially in the series of lunchtime concerts. The Union books major bands to play in the Great Hall; smaller bands play in the Union.

Dance: Professional dance groups visit the campus frequently, at the invitation of the Dance Studies Department, who also display their own skills in lunchtime workshops and evening shows. A range of dance and physical theatre classes are on offer: the Department aims to make dance accessible to all.

Art: The Performing Arts Technology Studios, built and equipped to high professional standards, are used by students in the Music and Dance Studies Departments, and by other students interested in the performing arts. There is an annual Poetry Lecture, given by a distinguished poet, and various other eminent poets and playwrights visit the University to give readings of their work, or pre-performance lectures. There is also a series of literature lectures. Exhibitions of paintings, photographs and sculpture are mounted in the University's gallery and in other suitable spaces around the campus. Evening classes allow you to try your hand at painting, drawing, jewellery making, sculpture or pottery.

The Union

The Union building offers a social haven from the academic day in its lounge areas and three bars, and in the cultural and social activities it generates through its Entertainments Officer. As well as representing students' interests, taking an active concern in welfare, the Union runs a wide range of clubs and societies. A weekly newspaper and campus radio station keep you informed. The University and Union both use the Internet as a communication tool.

The Welfare Officer gives a range of advice on personal, academic and finance/legal problems: Niteline helps with more personal problems. Students can help in local community work by joining voluntary groups organised by the Union.

Sport

High standards prevail in a number of sports where the University is successful in competitions. About 40 classes and short courses are available: the sports programme caters well for beginners.

Sports clubs (over 50 in all) also offer tuition; activities include gliding, martial arts, water polo, fencing, archery, aikido - the range is wide. Some clubs arrange trips - rugby tours, sub aqua 'dive' holidays and outdoor pursuits in the Lake District. There are non-serious (or perhaps very serious) competitions between students and staff at lunchtimes. The main focus is on fitness and health.

Campusport offers a wide range of aerobic classes and Campusdance offers classes for all from ballet to Lambada and street jazz to Israeli folk dancing.

General facilities include a large sports hall, dance studio, table tennis room, three squash courts, aeroball court, sunbeds and a 180ft climbing wall with over 50 different 'climbs'. Off-campus (about half a mile away), the Varsity Centre is home to all student pitches, and has competition squash courts, nine all-weather tennis courts, a licensed bar and a floodlit artificial turf pitch.

Student welfare

The University **health centre** has medical and nursing staff, and a trained nurse is on duty 24 hours a day in the sick bay. Two professional **counsellors**. The Union and University Welfare Offices run a joint service. The University **chaplains** have a significant pastoral role on the campus.

Careers Service

The Careers Service offers seminars, presentations, group work and information. In the final year, you can attend careers talks and take aptitude tests. PROSPECT - a computerised careers programme - is available.

Students with special needs

You should write to the Student Advice Welfare Office in Union House before you apply and explain your needs. There is a leaflet outlining the University's facilities and further details of admissions procedures.

Accommodation

The University guarantees a place in residence for all first year undergraduates and many final year students.

The courts

There are seven courts of residence on the slopes of Stag Hill on campus and further places at Hazel Farm approximately three miles away. They provide accommodation for over 2,600 students, mainly in single study-bedrooms. All the courts have self-catering facilities; meals can also be purchased in the restaurants on campus. Each court has an amenity building with reception lounge and television. 500 rooms in the newest Courts are ensuite.

For each group of rooms there is a kitchen/breakfast room (KUB) which provides modest cooking facilities and a meeting place. Each court is warden-controlled and, generally, each KUB group contains a final year student.

Hazel Farm

The University has a purpose-built estate of 50 student houses about three miles from campus. Each house offers between six and eight study-bedrooms and a kitchen. A regular, free bus service operates to and from campus. Hazel Farm residents are responsible for their own cleaning; rents are lower to allow for this.

Costs (1995/96)

Costs average £42 per week (single room). Semester only (28 weeks) or sessional (38 weeks) residence is available.

Private accommodation and headleasing

The University manages flats and houses off-campus for students. The Accommodation Office also keeps lists of private rented property and inspects as many of the properties as possible. Many students live in Woking or Godalming - cheaper than Guildford. Rents average £45 per week, excluding bills.

Mature students

If you do not have 'normal' entry qualifications, you can offer OU credentials or other courses designed for 're-start' academic study. Access courses in Science, Engineering and Sociology are run in conjunction with the local FE college. Other courses or experience, including NVQs, might be acceptable: write to the Undergraduate Admissions Officer if you are unsure.

Bridging courses

Bridging courses and an integrated foundation year in Engineering and Science are available for those students who do not have the required subject combination or level of qualifications for entry onto other Engineering and Science courses at the University.

THE TOWN (population 63,000)

Guildford, the county town of Surrey, is centrally set in the county, where the river Wey flows through a break in the chalk of the North Downs. It is surrounded by lovely landscapes, richly wooded, and bears the marks and character of its history, which stretches far back in time. There was a royal mint in the town in Saxon times; silver pennies were struck here in the 10th century.

The town remained small until expansion came with the railway in 1845: this destroyed much of the charm and created the commuter element in Guildford today.

Guildford's history patterns the fabric of its town. The tower of its oldest building, St Mary's church, is a rare relic of Saxon architecture; the surviving keep of the castle was built in the early days of Norman rule; undercrofts below High Street buildings indicate an affluent medieval town; the 1620 Abbots Hospital remains one of the finest buildings in Surrey; 17th-century locks and river improvements make the Wey today an attractive and well-used amenity; the Guildhall, built in Elizabethan times, was refaced in 1683 (and embellished by its landmark projecting clock). The town has much period charm, although its historic centre is now surrounded by substantial modern developments, far less attractive but bringing very good shopping and commerce. This is a wealthy area. Guildford has its share of affluent commuters and offers beautiful surrounding countryside with small hidden villages and hamlets which feel a world away from the metropolis: such is the power of Green Belt preservation and town planning.

Theatre: The Yvonne Arnaud Theatre has a pretty, willow-screened setting by the river. A range of professional drama here: many productions connect with the West End. The Mill Studio in the adjoining Town Mill offers lunchtime and fringe theatre. The Bellerby Theatre also presents professional and amateur drama.

Music: The Guildford Philharmonic Orchestra (the 'top professional orchestra of the south-east': Official Guide) gives a full programme of concerts from September to May, in the civic hall. Here also are rock concerts, musicals, operatic performances, dances, antique fairs, film shows - even wrestling. A good range of civic interests. There are regular concerts and recitals in the cathedral.

Cinema: one, with four screens.

Nightlife: three nightclubs, an excellent range of restaurant styles (and prices) in and around the town, and 'popular' student pubs.

Sport: River activities: narrowboats, rowing, canoes and punts. In addition to the usual sports centre facilities, the Guildford Spectrum Leisure Complex offers a range of sporting activities, including ice-skating, ten-pin bowling, an athletics track and swimming and diving pools. Guildford Lido: lawns, trees, flowerbeds surround the main pool-diving and water-chute - and two paddling pools. Heated. Crazy golf and refreshments. Open from April to September.

ESCAPE ROUTES

Surrey, so close to London, has retained much of its natural beauty, despite population by London commuters who perch here between evening and morning rush-hours. The countryside around is open heathland, with the Hog's Back to the west and the Pilgrim's Way winding across the hills.

You are close to Windsor Great Park, to the lure of the Thames, and to the magnet of London.

Communication

Guildford has a fast line to London and very regular **trains** (to Waterloo - 34 minutes, last train back leaves just before midnight). It is also on lines to the West Country and east to Kent, the coast and the ferries. **Coach** services are wide-ranging. Guildford is close both to the **M25** and to the **M3** to Winchester. The M25 circulates to the rest of the country's motorways. You are within easy reach of both Gatwick and Heathrow **airports**.

University of Sussex

Sussex House
Falmer
Brighton
BN1 9RH
Telephone: 01273 606755

University Charter date: 1961

Sussex is a medium-sized university with around 6,500 undergraduate students on full-time programmes and 1,500 full-time postgraduates. The University has a single campus, four miles from Brighton. Degrees are modular, within course patterns, and assessed by end of year exams, with an element of dissertation or coursework.

Nearly all first year undergraduates do live in University-managed accommodation, but students are free to make their own arrangements if they prefer.

THE CAMPUS

The campus is four miles out of Brighton (and four miles to the other host town, Lewes) set in empty, open, rolling Sussex downland: a designated area of 'Outstanding Natural Beauty'.

The University occupies a 200 acre site in a lovely, remote rural setting where the downlands begin to roll and rise out of the flat coastal plain. Its buildings are densely clustered along a central spine. The layout was originally planned for ease and convenience of communication and access - close grouping, a grid of link-walkways, and the use of small courtyards.

Buildings are plain, in local russet brick, flat-topped and generally rectangular. The original complex includes heavily arched concrete horizontals: this is perhaps the most familiar face of the University and is rather daunting in its scale. There is, however, a lot of space available here, so buildings need not (and do not) rise to any great height. Beyond its building clusters the campus has wide green spaces and is well wooded, especially on its margins.

The campus is a self sufficient community with a general store, travel agent, newsagent, student co-op, greengrocer, large bookshop, post office, four banks, insurance broker, launderette and a pharmacy. More than a dozen eating places and the many residences on campus (including family units) make this more of a way of life than solely a learning environment. Falmer station is almost on campus with trains to Brighton and to Lewes.

Conference centre
The University is fortunate in having the White House Centre, on the Isle of Thorns estate in the Ashdown Forest, 20 miles from campus. Facilities include golf, tennis, an open-air swimming pool and an indoor recreational area.

Cars
There is provision for parking on campus and there are no problems about bringing your car, although space is rare at busy times. You need to register your car.

Learning Resources

The **library** has over 700,000 books, 850 seats and takes over 3,500 periodicals. Opening hours: Monday to Thursday to 9.30pm; Friday to 7.30pm Friday; Saturday afternoon; 11am to 6.30pm Sunday.

The University **computing service** offers introductory courses on applications packages and programming languages. There are many open-access suites on the campus (open until 11pm six nights a week) and in the Computer Centre.

The **Language Centre**'s facilities are open for students to teach themselves; courses are run over lunchtimes and evenings. Facilities include 5,000 tapes in 60 languages, three audio-active comparative language laboratories, satellite TV booths and computer-assisted language learning.

Culture on campus

Drama, music and art: The Gardner Arts Centre houses a 500 seat theatre for plays and concerts, studios and two galleries. Activities here include plays, dance, classical music, jazz, exhibitions and workshops, with artists and performances both national and from many other countries. Student art activities too are encouraged by the staff of the Centre: the Drama Society stages several plays a year; the University Orchestra holds its concerts. Music flourishes through the good range of musical societies - from jazz and folk clubs to choir and orchestra. There is a February 'Music Breaks Free' Festival which attracts major

performers. The University offers 'in house' music tuition. The Arts Federation organises a range of activities, workshops and one day courses in the practical art studio: pottery, wood-engraving, life drawing...
Film: A double bill of alternative films every Wednesday.

The Union

The Union is run from Falmer House and has six sabbatical offers, two of whom are concerned with welfare.

A varied entertainments programme. The Mandela Hall has hosted some big-name acts (Courtney Pine and Pop Will Eat Itself), but is more a place for a rave. The Crypt nightclub (on campus) has discos catering for different styles each night. Two other bars close to the residences offer a wide variety of promotions, free bands and quizzes. Every summer, a marquee is erected for a four day carnival and the Summer Ball is a highlight of the year. Big events are held at venues in Brighton.

The Union runs two shops, a cafe, pool tables and games machines around the campus, a print shop and secondhand bookshop.

The Welfare Centre provides support and information on a full range of issues - including legal and financial; a Nightline service and various childminding schemes.

Radio Falmer, the commercial campus radio broadcasts for 18 hours a day, seven days a week. A weekly newspaper, *The Badger*, keeps you up to date with Union news and local events, and the magazine *The Pulse* covers local, national and international issues.

Sport

The Student Union Sports Federation combines with the University's Sports Service to offer a full range of organised sport (40+ clubs in all), team games, intramural competitions and more casual recreational activities. Instruction available in a range of physical activities from aerobics to yoga, as well as good coaching and general advice on fitness training. Use of sports facilities carries a minimal charge.

The sport centre contains two multipurpose sports halls, a gallery, a sauna and solarium with built-in cassette-player, a gymnasium/weight-training room, four glass-backed squash courts and cafe/bars.

The sportsground, on the north edge of the campus, provides 14 acres of playing fields, a floodlit all-weather playing surface, six tennis courts, cricket nets, a grass running track and long and triple-jump pits with a special foam landing area for highjump and pole-vault. The pavilion here has five more squash courts and catering and bar facilities.

The Sports Service provides a sports injury clinic for Brighton and the surrounding area.

Student welfare

The University **health service** has doctors, dentist and nurse, a sickbay for emergencies and childcare facilities. An academic and personal **counselling service** works either with individuals or in groups.

The University Meeting House has a chapel which is used by a wide variety of religious groups. An ecumenical team of chaplains appointed by various churches and by the Jewish community work together. There is also a Muslim student centre on campus.

Careers Service

Each School has an academic tutor who acts as careers tutor. The Careers Advisory Service has a large Information Centre where you can access a number of computer-assisted guidance programmes, including PROSPECT. The Service offers workshops on job-search, self presentation and communication skills and a range of specific focus workshops. There is a Workshadowing programme.

Students with special needs

The University has some modified and specially designed housing on campus for physically disabled students. Students with disabilities who need assistance in day-to-day living may apply to live in Kulukundis House, which has been specially designed to meet their needs.

There is a tactile guide to the campus for blind/partially blind students and tactile paving and handrails; a CCTV enlarger and a Kurzweil reading machine available in the library; apply to Admissions. Guide dogs for the blind are permitted on most areas of the campus. Support for deaf students is available locally.

Jubilee scholarships are available to physically disabled students who are Sussex County residents. There are also awards to assist blind students.

Accommodation

The University undertakes to provide a place in University-managed accommodation for all first years who firmly accept an offer of a place by the end of June. Most first years are in fact housed, even if they apply later.

All University accommodation is self-catering. On-campus housing ranges in size and amenities between the five Park Houses, each with 100 single rooms, and houses and flats which take between six and twelve students each.

Off campus, the University owns a number of properties in Brighton and Hove - each four miles away. These also range widely: Holland House, a former hotel, has 100 rooms; most properties are more domestic in scale - houses rather than hostels.

There are about 100 family flats in University-owned properties, the majority of which are on campus. All are in heavy demand and are let only to families with children.

Costs (1995/96)
single: £42.25 to £45.00 per week
shared: £30.25 to £38.00 per week
Costs normally include electricity.

Private accommodation

If you do decide to live out, you are likely to be about four miles away from the campus. Costs for non-University accommodation in Brighton and Hove average £43.00 per week plus bills and travelling expenses.

Mature students

You must be able to demonstrate that you are capable of University study. There is a special selection procedure for candidates with no recent qualifications; this includes a preliminary piece of work set by the University and an interview.

Nursery

There is a creche, a playgroup and a nursery school for the under-fives, and a playground near the residential area. There are plans for a new centre.

THE CITY (population: 200,000)

Ones immediate image of Brighton is the Royal Pavilion, flight of architectural fancy of the Prince Regent, given glorious shape, in the style of an Indian prince's palace, by John Nash (who laid out Regent's Park and its beautiful terraces in much more restrained style) in 1812.

The Regent's fond interest set the style of Brighton today: it became one of the country's leading and most fashionable resorts, creating a legacy of fine buildings and high class shopping.

Older times left the famous Lanes, originally 17th century fishermen's cottages and now a treasure-trove of boutiques, antique and book shops. There are guided walks. Modern times have added their less attractive candyfloss layer of seaside tripper paraphernalia.

The town has a solid core of business men and women who commute to London daily, and a crowd of tourists and trippers bringing exuberant life in the summer months; equivalent hordes of conference-goers through the winter keep the pace fast and varied: the social scene never flags, and the sociological profile is unusually varied and interesting. Typical of the pattern is that the large student lodging quarter doubles as a holiday flat area during the long vacation.

With Hove, the town offers seven miles of shingle beach. It has a long promenade, two piers and a Sea Life Centre. Georgian and late Victorian houses grace its streets, and it has two churches containing rare examples of Pre-Raphaelite art: Rossetti and William Morris designed the windows in St Michael's, and Burne-Jones the altarpiece in St Paul's.

Shopping facilities are excellent, the Lanes have pretty but quite expensive shops; behind them the North Laines offer a rich collection of ethnic, secondhand and oddball shops: great for browsing and bargains.

Theatre: The Theatre Royal offers productions of London standard, often indeed transferring to the West End. A wide variety of drama: serious plays, comedy, the odd musical. The theatre dates from 1774 and has a Victorian red plush interior.

Music: The Dome, a large concert hall seating 2,000, presents entertainment from classical concerts to circus via popular shows, and is also a conference centre. The Brighton Centre seats up to 5,000 and presents concerts, sporting championships and exhibitions.

Cinema: The Cannon film centre has three screens, the Odeon six, the MGM Multiplex eight. The Duke of York's has a film club at the Duke of York's.

Nightlife: Pubs, a great many from the glitzy to the spit-and-sawdust type. Clubs likewise: Brighton is quite a magnet for revellers, which unfortunately makes it expensive unless you wisely use the many student promotions that are on offer. Restaurants...whatever style you like and can afford, you will find here.

Sport: Active sport: a large indoor swimming pool complex, with all the trappings of holidays and seaside, is close to the Pavilion. Hove, too, has an enormous leisure centre: leisure pools, water flumes, sauna and solarium, ten-pin bowling, indoor bowls, two sports halls... Brighton's yacht marina is the largest in Europe. Horse-riding, watersports, ice-skating: the list is long. Spectator sports: Brighton and Hove Albion football team; Sussex County cricket; Brighton racecourse; Hove's Coral Greyhound Stadium. There is of course all the fun of the seaside you would expect from a resort as catholic in its pleasures as Brighton.

Festival: Brighton has its own arts festival in May. There is also an Autumn women's arts festival: cabaret, music, poetry-reading and exhibitions.

Lewes (population: 14,971)

The alternative centre for students on campus. Lewes is a historic county town, complete with the ruins of a Norman/medieval castle, Anne of Cleves' House, a medieval priory demolished by Oliver Cromwell, a number of beautiful old buildings of note, and the passing through of the Greenwich Meridian.

The High Street is photogenic and marks the passage of its history in plaques to commemorate famous people, or notable martyrdoms or other ancient sufferings. Shopping facilities are wide-ranging and very good. There is a livestock market and auction on Mondays.

Theatre: There is a small theatre club (Lewes Little Theatre) which runs a 158-seat auditorium and occasionally offers after-show suppers. Membership is about £3 for students.

Music: Concerts in churches.

Cinema: There is a cinema club, showing minority interest art films.

Nightlife: A good range of restaurants, hotels and pubs. This town is small but affluent.

Sport: The Lewes Leisure Centre has swimming pools, flume, four badminton courts, projectile hall for archery, shooting, golf etc., gymnasium and health suite.

ESCAPE ROUTES

Sussex is an easy county of wealthy seaside towns, small villages, timbered houses, rolling downland, a scattering of Iron Age Forts and old routes and ways. Should you wish to wander from Brighton, the options are pleasant: the coastal resort names have the memory of bathing machines, Royalty and gracious living. You should explore the banks of the River Arun, and Arundel Castle.

Communications

Brighton has an extremely efficient **rail service** to London: this is commuter land. There is also a direct line running east and west, not always hugging the coast, but never far from it. **Coach services**, as you would expect, are far-ranging. The **A23** links with the **M25** eventually. Otherwise the road-system is fairly parochial. Newhaven has **ferries** to Dieppe.

Oxbridge

If your school already has a tradition of sending students to Oxford and Cambridge, there will probably be enough information and lore to hand to give you all the guidance you need. If, moreover, you have acquired a dedicated determination to go to one or the other, you will probably be unswervable, and the only decision to be made is - which college. (Even that might be part of your ambition-target.)

No other university can match the layers of myth, image, prejudice and reputation built up by Oxbridge: they have had many more centuries to acquire patinas and for much of their time have had a national monopoly of academic excellence. If you are moved by a sense of history and would feel privileged to tread where so many of our great and famous men have walked the corridors of time, power and learning, then no other university can compete.

Do not, however, be put off by the legends; nor too influenced by those who would diminish the glamour or belittle the prestige. (Why anyone today should wish to reduce the power of international renown is a mystery to us.) It is true that a large proportion of the undergraduate population still comes from the public schools, which have a long history of special coaching for entry, and strong links with individual colleges. But the Universities are actively looking for high-quality students from all kinds of backgrounds, and certainly cannot afford to discriminate against the new educational centres: the promising scholars who came naturally through the old grammar school system are still making their way through the comprehensive schools. Some of you might find your school has little experience in putting forward candidates; some of you will find actual opposition to the 'elitism'. The two Universities have been mending the ways of their entry methods, to remove some of the mystique. Academic standards are certainly very high: but so they are in other high-demand courses and institutions.

If you really want to go to Oxbridge and feel you can achieve very good grades - then have a go. The significant phrase here is 'really want to go'. This is a very special academic and social world. You must be sure that you can cope with its intensity and pressures, as well as enjoy its delights. The next sections should help you decide.

Applying

Both Oxford and Cambridge operate their admissions procedure through their colleges. You must apply to be interviewed and accepted (or not) by a college, not by the University. If you do not wish to specify a particular college (or colleges) on your application form, you can pass your application through the central office which will allocate you to a college which is 'light' on candidates for your chosen subject. You will probably see at once (being a promising sort of person) that this process can work to your advantage, since colleges do not know that you are an 'allocated' rather than a 'preferred choice' candidate. (The forms are completed for you). On the other hand, an informed and determined choice of college could give you a flying start on interview.

Interviews are a vitally important feature of the selection process and colleges of each University might use written tests additional to 'A' levels to help them identify more finely the intellectual qualities they seek. The selection procedures at both Universities are more flexible than the 'straight' UCAS 'conditional offers' system, in that, here, the candidate with exceptional flair, or potential, who might not be a broad spectrum achiever at 'A' level, can be recognised.

In their detail, however, the application procedures are far from identical, and will be dealt with in the separate sections.

You may not apply to both Oxford and Cambridge unless you are aiming at a choral award.

It is important to remember, if you do go to either Oxford or Cambridge, that - while they do not by any means monopolise the brightest school-leavers - there is a higher concentration of brilliance here, than in other universities. You must be prepared for the competitive edge. If, however, you do not aspire to be a highest flier, you will easily find other levels at which to cruise happily. The Universities have a wealth of special experience beyond the purely academic.

University of Oxford

The Oxford Colleges Admissions Office
University Offices
Wellington Square
Oxford OX1 2JD
Telephone: 01865 270000

A total of 10,500 undergraduate and 4,200 graduate full-time students. 30 of the 39 colleges admit undergraduates, as do the five permanent private halls established originally by religious sects (although now admitting some lay students). Most colleges accept students in most disciplines, and offer a good social and academic mix. Undergraduates take two sets of examinations during their courses - the first and Second Public Examinations. The First exam (Prelims or 'Mods') is usually taken during the first year: the Second exams are, effectively, Finals. Degrees are awarded and classed on the results of the Second Public examination.

THE UNIVERSITY

This is the oldest University in the English-speaking world, with its beginnings in the misty times of the 12th century. The slow growth through many centuries has graced the city with examples of architecture from many periods: each college founded and built with a splendour of fabric and scale. The colleges are set around a fairly small area of the city, presenting imposing facades, frames of lovely inner quadrangles and gardens, intersected by narrow medieval ways. To walk the byways is to pass through a literary and cinematic series of images which should adorn your memory for a lifetime, particularly since, as a student, you will catch the glories of changing light as the seasons turn or as you wander the shifting times of day.

Not, of course, entirely a city of dreams. The city goes about its business with a notable disregard for its University, and many of the colleges surprise you by resting among shops and premises whose function is far from academic. Indeed, relations between town and gown here have traditionally been less than easy: reading the history of the place, studded with bizarre anecdote, is an entertaining way of preparing yourself for the idiosyncrasies of its way of life.

The colleges are autonomous, and it is they (or one of them) who will select you, stand dragon over your academic progress and keep a watchful eye on your welfare and well-being. The University itself is 'a matter of function rather than of buildings' (postgraduate prospectus). It provides general administration, laboratories, central lecture halls, the great libraries and museums; it specifies minimum entrance requirements (each college/course will have its own, beyond base); prescribes courses and syllabuses; sets, controls and marks University examinations; and awards degrees. It works through a structure of 16 faculties, and through these you will have the chance to meet fellow-subject-students from other colleges.

A good thing, since in most ways your life will be strongly college oriented: you will be accepted by and identified with your college; you will live in its halls or houses and eat mainly in its dining halls; your learning patterns will be monitored through tutorials where one or two of you will meet weekly a tutor who will normally be a member of your college. It is natural, in such circumstances, that friendships will be formed and fastened largely within college walls.

Choosing your college

There are 39 colleges, 30 of which take undergraduates, and five Permanent Private Halls.

Colleges vary in size: you might like to think about the numbers of fellow students you are likely to have in your college and year group, and within subject intake within that. College numbers of students range from 211 to 420.

There are location differences: here the city and its University are intermingled. This means that from some colleges you can walk out into the busy world of high-street shopping. Other colleges occupy remote and beautiful settings by river, in meadow, or are part of a conglomerate of colleges which form their own historic area and ambience. The original women's colleges (only one, St Hilda's, remains for women only) are (surprise) on the very edge of the college clusters and enjoy what can be a welcome sense of remove and calm.

If you like the idea of Oxford but do not want to live in crumbling ancient splendour, Keble and the original women's colleges are late 19th century, and two colleges are new - St Catherine's (1963) or 'new'- St Peter's (1929). They could offer the best of both worlds: as could the many old colleges which have modern, well-equipped accommodation halls.

You can take into account these various factors but, for many of you, the choice will remain difficult. So, in the end, you really will have to read as much as you can and then go and look around.

Application procedure

Oxford offers a conditional offer route, not entirely unlike the normal UCAS process. You must complete a UCAS application form and an Oxford Application Card and send them 'home' to UCAS or Oxford between September 1st and October 15th. You can state one college or make an open application.

This is close in style to normal UCAS offers, but an interview is also part of the selection process. In addition, some colleges, or certain courses, may set pre-interview written tests or might send for one or two examples of your work in advance of the interview.

If you are successful, you will receive an offer; the most common is AAB, but many are ABB, a few are AAA and some are lower (if your performance has been exceptionally good).

You should apply through the Head of your school or the Principal of your college. If you have left school, write to the College Admissions Office explaining your circumstances.

University academic services

The library

The principal University library, the Bodleian, is world-famous. Opened in 1602, its old, original building is one of the most beautiful in Oxford, with an immensely strong sense of time-past: the Latin names of the old schools are still written in gold above the doors of its central quadrangle. This is a copyright library, and contains many millions of volumes; it occupies several buildings and offers a number of reading rooms, including one for blind students. The Bodleian is not a lending library: you borrow books from the libraries of faculties, departments and colleges.

There are four libraries dependent on the Bodleian, with specialist collections. The Radcliffe Science Library has 22 miles of bookshelves (!) and can seat 600 readers. It is the largest general scientific library in Great Britain, apart from the British Library. The Bodleian Law Library seats 340 readers and houses 250,000 books; it also houses the Law Faculty (academic rooms and facilities). The Indian Institute Library has 90,000 volumes concerning India and parts of SE Asia. The Rhodes House Library houses collections on the history and social sciences of the Commonwealth, the USA and sub-Saharan Africa.

As well as the Bodleian group of libraries, the Hooke is a lending library for science undergraduates; the Ashmolean Library has a collection specialised in Oriental and Western art and Egytian, Near Eastern and classical archaeology. The Taylor Institute (the Centre for modern European languages and literature) has a research library, as well as being the undergraduate lending library for the Modern Languages Faculty. It is the largest library of its field and type in Britain.

In addition to their wealth of reference books, faculties have their own distinguished and substantial lending collections, as does each college, which often holds rare and valuable books (not available for loan) in tandem with a lending/working library.

Museums

Again, the University predictably offers an exceptional range. **The Ashmolean Museum of Art and Archaeology** was the first museum in Britain to open to the public (1683). The collections are nationally and internationally famous: they range from an ancient skull (6000 BC), to examples of contemporary art displayed in the museum's McAlpine Gallery. Great benefactions and centuries of learned acquisitions have created a place of pilgrimage here for museum lovers.

The museum is also a research centre, and has four specialist Departments (Antiquities, Western Art, Eastern Art, Coin) and the University's centre for Egyptology: each has its own rich reserve and study collections.

The Museum of the History of Science (housed in the old Ashmolean Building): scientific instruments of historical interest - mathematical, time-telling and surveying; clocks, watches, astronomical and optical instruments, chemical apparatus and cameras. There is an associated research library.

The University Museum: extensive scientific collections of zoology, entomology, geology and mineralogy, second in importance in the UK only to the Natural History Museum in London. Parts of all collections are in the Museums Court exhibition to illustrate undergraduate teaching: most specimens, however, are in storage, reserved for reference and research. The museum houses the Hope library.

The Pitt Rivers Museum: (part of the Department of Ethnology and Prehistory). Very important collections illustrate the history, typology, distribution and technology of the world's principal arts and industries (excluding the age of mass-production). Amulets, charms, arms and armour, lighting and fire-making appliances, textiles and musical instruments - a specialised and fascinating journey into the makings of civilisation, worldwide. The Museum is served by the Balfour library.

Computing

The central facilities of the computing service include the computing teaching centre, which provides a wide range of introductory and advanced courses on most aspects of computing for all members of the University. You can also arrange to learn in your own time, through videotape or computer-based course-forms, backed by an advisory service.

Language facilities

Students can continue to teach themselves languages in the language laboratory. There are audio, visual and textual materials covering 86 languages and computer assisted language learning facilities.

Life in the University

Social life

Generally your microcosmic college world will be the focus of your social activities. You can also share the activities of other colleges: join their choirs, play in their bands and orchestras, star in their productions...

Debates

On a University scale, perhaps the most famous body is the Oxford Union Society - not to be confused with the actual Student Union. The Society is primarily a debating society and has provided a forum for some of the most illustrious thinkers and eminent politicians to indulge in pyrotechnics of wit, learning and intellect since it was founded in 1823. And it continues... The Society has its own premises and operates also as a club, offering a large lending library, restaurant, bar, jazz cellar, billiards, newspapers, television, regular videos and social events.

Drama

The University has two dramatic societies: the Oxford University Dramatic Society (OUDS) and the Experimental Theatre Club (ETC). They are extremely competitive, since many of Oxford's students are drama-ambitious, and star quality here can give you straight access to national recognition. Each puts on two or three major productions each year, plus several occasional productions - revues and experimental plays. OUDS, based in the Burton Taylor theatre, mounts in all 16 plays per term and hosts an annual Drama Festival and a New Writing Festival. Student drama is also presented at the Old Fire Station (now a new studio theatre). The Playhouse seats 650 and presents six student productions a year.

There is also a University Opera Club, staging productions, and some modern-language departments stage plays in foreign languages. Standards are high, and if you add in the host of college-based productions, there is a range of drama here equalled probably only by Cambridge. Particularly pleasant are the open-air productions in the summer.

Music

Orchestral players can join the University Orchestra (almost entirely University members) or Philharmonia, or the Oxford Symphony Orchestra (mainly city musicians). Both give instrumental concerts and accompany choral concerts. Again there is a wealth of musical opportunity through various student orchestras, bands and chamber-music groups. The University Music Society and college music societies promote solo and group performances, amateur and professional. The scene at college level shifts with each year's talent pool: many students initiate, organise and direct their own musical performances and standards can be very high. Singing? Well, there is the Oxford Bach Choir (200-300 members), the Oxford Harmonic Choir (about 100 members), the Schola Cantorum (a select University choir) and several college choral societies. College chapels offer the peace of sung services.

Professional concerts (a large number): orchestral, choral, chamber concerts are organised. And there are regular visits by the Glyndebourne Touring Company and Welsh National Opera.

Sport

Again, sport is predominantly a college activity and intercollegiate rivalry adds competitive drive and lively spirit. Most colleges have their own sports grounds, boat houses and squash courts, and because the University owns so much of the suitable (and otherwise) land in Oxford, and the river is never far away, you don't have to go very far to pursue your chosen sport.

However, central facilities cater where colleges do not, and offer common ground. The large University parks, bordered by the colleges and by the river Cherwell, offer space for the University Cricket Club, University croquet, petanque and men's/women's hockey and lacrosse clubs.

The Iffley Road sports complex caters for athletics, association football, rugby and lawn tennis. The sports centre has a large multi purpose sports hall and many specialist rooms. Also a synthetic all weather track, squash and Eton fives complex, an indoor cricket school convertible to a small-bore rifle and revolver range, and a lawn tennis pavilion. Two rugby fives courts and a rowing tank, with ergometer testing room and gymnasium have recently opened...and there is a traverse climbing wall.

Roger Bannister became the first athlete to break the 'four-minute mile' barrier here, on the old cinder track - but you can't expect many historic highs like that. The regular peaks of the sporting year are, inevitably, the traditional Boat Race and the Varsity rugby match at Twickenham, both against Cambridge. These time-honoured rituals have recently been extended by the Varsity Games (a dozen minor sports in Oxbridge competition) and - more innovative - a Town and Gown annual competition.

JCRs

Junior Common Rooms are the college equivalent of undergraduate Students' Unions. The University Students' Union here is separate again: so you have two routes through to political experiment. Each represents your interests at its own level.

The Union itself has four sabbatical officers and is represented on many University committees. There are four student publications, including a literary magazine and a weekly newspaper. The annual turnover is £350,000. The University Rag raised £50,000 last year.

There is a nightline.

Accommodation

This is a key aspect of college life which could help you in the dilemma of choosing a college for your application. An increasing number of colleges can accommodate all (or nearly all) undergraduates for all three years; more can offer two years in residence, plus a fair chance of a third; a third group are non-committal about how many of you will have to 'live out'. All first years are accommodated in college.

Private accommodation in Oxford is expensive - and you can't roam far afield in search of cheaper accommodation. It actually costs more to live out of town, and, in any case, college regulations optimistically demand that you live no further than six miles from the city centre, in accommodation which has been approved by the college. Help is available from the colleges and the University Accommodation Office. Prices vary enormously, but the cheapest is around £50 per week.

College accommodation itself is kaleidoscopic in type and quality. New blocks give you warm, civilised space, sometimes with private bathrooms, often with low-ratio sharing (two or three); old college-fabric rooms are usually large, generally comfortable and make up in their historic continuity and atmosphere what they might lack in amenity. The term 'college-owned accommodation' can mean annexes and houses around the city where room and amenity quality is variable. Those of you who have a strong ambition to come to Oxford will be largely attracted by its historic style and atmosphere, and will want to live in the old rooms, in spite of any possible discomforts.

Costs

Living costs here are conditioned by a range of variables almost as wide as the number of colleges. As with other aspects of life here, you will have to check in detail for yourself those aspects which particularly concern you. An 'average' here would be only the roughest of guides. Maintenance charges vary from college to college, quite widely. You should send for a copy of the Alternative Prospectus from the OUSU, which will give you information on the full range of accommodation charges.

Private lodgings could cost much more.

College fees

In addition to your accommodation costs, colleges charge for tuition and academic facilities. If your tuition fees are paid by your LEA, college fees are also covered. If you are self-financed, remember to take them into account.

Student welfare

Welfare

Understandably, the small college worlds put 'welfare' into different perspective. The domestic pattern, plus the virtually private tutorial system, should make it very difficult to build up problems unremarked. So the college is your first framework of care; but the Students' Union and the University itself do provide welfare and advisory services if you need an 'outside' ear.

Available are two full-and three part-time counsellors and a medical consultant on two mornings a week. There is a code of practice on harassment.

Religious welfare

The University itself and most of the colleges were religious foundations and have separate places of worship where Church of England services are regularly held. The Roman Catholic chaplaincy provides a focal point for Roman Catholic members of the University and the Orthodox Church maintains a centre serving Greek and Russian Orthodox students. The Oxford Jewish Centre provides for the religious and spiritual needs of Jewish students and also offers advice and counselling. It contains a synagogue where both orthodox and reform services are held. There is a mosque in the city which is used by students and a prayer-room is available at the Islamic Studies Centre attached to St Cross College. There is also an active Buddhist Society run by the University.

Careers Service

The Careers Service has extensive programmes of careers education, including training in application and interview techniques.

Students with special needs

There are access problems with the ancient college buildings: newer colleges are easier. Get in touch with your chosen college or department as early as you can. A hostel, Taylor House, provides proper care including transport. A special guide, Oxford for the Disabled, is available from the Oxford Council of Voluntary Services, St Aldates Oxford OX1 1DY.

Mature students

Only around 2% of the undergraduate population is 'mature'. You follow the same application procedure as anyone else: A levels or Access course qualifications are a very good idea, although calibre of employment and professional qualifications will be heeded. If you are self-financed, do bear in mind the extra cost of college fees. All colleges are willing to consider applications from mature students.

Nursery

There are two nurseries which together take 72 children aged three to school age. Fees are high (£76.90 per week) but subsidies might be possible. Six colleges have access to nurseries run by their own members, and the SU has established a childminding network.

THE CITY (population 130,400)

One of the significant differences between Oxford and Cambridge is the nature of their host cities. There is a curious balance here between a city which has an independent sense of its own importance, with a large working community to cater for, and an ancient University whose beautiful, golden stone buildings manage to retain their veils of time and dignity even when they stand interlaced with the shops, banks and offices of busy workaday Oxford. It is easy to forget the balance, if you side-step from the main streets and enter precincts of ancient calm, or find the green acres and river ways where generations of students have wandered, dreamed, brawled, punted and suffered crises; because the University does dominate (and own) the spaces of central Oxford. There are 653 listed buildings within a single square mile. The history of the place is not exclusively academic; this was a Royalist stronghold in the Civil War and both city and University have set their style through the ages in support of the Establishment and Roman Catholicism/High Church influences. One cannot, in this inner sanctum, raise one's eyes, cross a road or turn a corner without encountering majestic and compellingly beautiful images of the past.

At the same time, the city expands through major industrial development: once the huge car works at Cowley; today more likely the new hi-tech industries which crowd to the University's magnetic fields of research excellence. These bring a different style of living, different types of people, and an eclectic range of shops to cater for their needs. So beside and among the famous bookshops and the long established providers of college scarves, are scattered the predictable shops, varied eating places, chemists, boutiques, chain stores and the inevitable shopping precincts. Good city life prevails.

Theatre: Oxford Playhouse houses a range of touring productions. The Apollo offers opera, ballet, pantomime, musicals and big concerts. Seats more than 1,800.

Music: a wealth of music here, including many visiting renowned orchestras and smaller groups.

Cinema: two MGMs (four screens) show national releases; one independent shows more variable fare, and there are two 'membership only's which are cheap to join.

Eating out, pubs and nightclubs: very wide range of restaurants; actual nightclubs are thin on the ground.

Sport: Spectator sports: Oxford United and Oxford City Football clubs, or you can watch Oxford's Rugby Club. Greyhound and speedway racing at Cowley Stadium.

ESCAPE ROUTES

The country around Oxford is soft, cultivated: the towns and villages have a secure air of being The Country and quite safe from marauding hordes. The north Cotswolds to the west, the Vale of the White Horse to the south, the leafy Thames Valley to the east: idylls surround you.

Communications

Rail links are national, and London is only an hour away. Coach links likewise. **Road:** Close to the M40, which links to the M25 and M42.

Cambridge University

Intercollegiate Applications Office
Kellet Lodge
Tennis Court Road
Cambridge
CB2 1QJ
Telephone: 01223 337733

A total of 10,000 undergraduates and almost 4,000 postgraduate degree students. Mature students: 8%. Of the 31 colleges, two admit graduates only, two admit (a few) 'mature' undergraduates, and one (Homerton) offers only teacher education. All colleges accepting undergraduates offer all subjects (or very nearly); and again you must check for yourself on the size of your own subject intake, if this concerns you. Courses are structured in a unique system: all have two parts; each part is examined separately and the two parts do not necessarily have to be in the same subjects or even associated subjects. Major examinations (Tripos) are held at the end of each Part , sometimes at the end of each year: some courses include a dissertation towards your final result.

THE UNIVERSITY

Cambridge is slightly younger than Oxford, but in time perspectives, a hundred years or so hardly matters, and most of the actual college buildings are similar in age and style, although there are more here which are new, or date from the 19th century.

What are the differences which could help you polarise if your ambition is 'Oxbridge' undefined? Well, the first and main one is the town of their setting. Cambridge colleges do not, in the main, weave in and out of the city's ways. They form a University world more separate, more beautifully defined by its river and water-meadows, yet (scale is small here), easily reaching into the facilities of the town.

This is both an attraction and a deterrent. Both Universities have short, intense, 8 week terms, where academic and social pressures are high and concentrated. If you add to that an environment which is heavily student-filled, and where it is difficult to pop out without encountering a dozen friends/acquaintances, then a greenhouse can become a hothouse. In this climate you will either blossom and flourish, or the reverse. Certainly the sharp, close focus will create three completely unforgettable years.

Traditionally here, more than at Oxford, town has served gown. For centuries the University was the major employer here, and its presence/stature has remained unmodified by a large urban population with its own things to do. The town also serves an age-old shopping and market function for a vast, sparsely populated area surrounding it. Its character is hence more quiet, lower-key, more 'county' and more rural than Oxford's. The isolation of fen and lowland is in the air, which in winter is frequently spiked by icy winds from Siberia (the Cambridge student believes there to be no barrier between). This can be a viciously cold place, but fenland mists or frosty brilliant skies can make the beauty surreal.

Things are changing. Oxford might have attracted new hi-tech industry to its research-lights; Cambridge, always ahead on scientific reputation, has done so to a degree where the magnetic pull on new industry is known as the 'Cambridge Miracle'. This is changing the old balance between town and gown and should improve/extend the range of things to do. The University here, more than Oxford, has hitherto turned into itself for cultural and social life; rich and varied though that be, it is good to have alternatives.

A corollary which hardly needs to be pointed out is that it is not so easy to vary life here by excursions into the region around.

The river, and its dalliance, is more linked with the college landscape here than at Oxford. The Backs (now officially preserved as an Area of Outstanding Natural Beauty) put a hem of lovely meadowland, full of daffodils in spring and ducks all the time, between the main road world and a range of colleges of surpassing beauty, including the matchless (hard to avoid superlatives here) King's College Chapel (foundation stone: 1446). Do not miss Evensong here, even if you come merely to look round.

Through the Backs wanders the Cam, sluggish and sludge-filled as only torpid fen waterways can be, but nevertheless passing fair beneath its willows and its graceful bridges. Some bridges are closed at night by high iron gates of portcullis-style impregnability, to remind the world that the colleges are private domains.

Like Oxford, Cambridge attracts its full share of look-there's-a-real-student tourists; so you will have to be good at dodging, or ready to look thoughtfully into cameras. This can actually be a real nuisance in the peak times.

Some things are similar to the Oxford pattern. The University provides lectures, practical classes and demonstrations; central facilities like libraries, science and language laboratories and the computing service; a counselling service, a dental service and an excellent careers service which you can continue to use long after you have left the University. The University works through its faculties, each containing a number of departments, sets and marks examinations and awards degrees: like Oxford. It also presides over the Fitzwilliam Museum, the Cambridge University Press, the Botanical Gardens, Addenbrooke's Hospital, various Medical Research Council units, and the Local Examination Syndicate.

Choosing your college

The range of styles is more eclectic here than at Oxford, since more colleges (though still not many) have 19th-century, or 'new' buildings. New accommodation can be very smart indeed. Send for individual college prospectuses. Security of accommodation provision is a major factor and can be checked. Distance out is not relevant, since you have to 'keep term' within three miles of the centre of Cambridge (actually Great St Mary's church). You could check on the number of graduate students in your subject (which equals availability of 'home' supervisors); on whether a college has a Director of Studies in your subject; on how many women students/academics there are; how long the college has been mixed (ambience is slow to change); sports facilities and strengths; accessibility of the college library; renown of the college choir. Decide what is important to you. The size of the college matters (they range here from 200 to 600 undergraduates).

Much of what we write about Oxford is relevant here.....and if you still find it hard to choose, you can leave your application form college section blank and be computer-allocated (see Oxford).

Cambridge is a hard-working university, traditionally more so than Oxford: courses here are intensive, as well as 'uniquely flexible' (Prospectus). Examinations (called Tripos examinations here - after the three-legged stool on which students sat for oral examinations) are taken in two parts. The pattern has a number of variables. Part I might be set at the end of year 1 or year 2; in some subjects Part I is subdivided into IA and IB, which ensures a major exam in each year; if Part I is at the end of your second year, you should expect to take a preliminary examination at the end of year 1, to monitor your progress.

'Uniquely flexible' means that when you come to take Part II, you may choose either to specialise in your original chosen subject (often through a project or dissertation combined with some exam papers); or you can switch course to explore another intellectual avenue, not necessarily related to that of Part I. You will need the approval of your college and grant-awarding body, and there are two inaccessible subjects (medicine and veterinary science): the chance of such a pattern cannot be found elsewhere. It is based on the premise that study here is so intensive and fast-moving that you have covered 'all aspects of the subject' (Prospectus) in two years, at least to the point where you have been trained enough for the quality of your learning thereafter to be a matter of extension and depth which does not have to be subject-oriented. Some subjects can only be taken as a Part II course.

Your degree document will not record subject or class, although you (and everybody else - results are on public display here) and your Director of Studies will know how you fared in each major exam; and for career purposes you will be able to claim the class achieved in Part II. All undergraduate degrees, regardless of discipline, are BA (except for the BEd at Homerton), almost invariably with Honours: a 'Special' means that you have virtually failed, but the University seldom puts a 'fail' label on any student who has made it through selection procedure and full term of a course. Additional flexibility features here at square one when your college might agree (if you are persuasive) to a switch of subject from the one in your original application.

We turn here to the primary issue of admission standards, mainly because the trend toward iconoclasm which could distort your view. 'I got here so anyone can' does not survive the statistical evidence of grades achieved by entrants here. The most frequent grade-run requested (and got) is 'AAA', with perhaps the odd 'B'.

One thing is apparent: the interview at both is of great importance and can be the deciding factor; and each University has a keen eye for the candidate interesting in ways other than academic. Rumours about the value of one's capacity to boost a college's sporting reputation have always been rife, but equally, you might win a music scholarship, or have some other skill that singles you out.

At the end of the day, the colleges guard the mystiques of their selection processes and it is quite likely that none can actually be identified. Many universities accept that there is a 'right type' for them; at Oxbridge colleges there are more facets to be considered and matched up.

The teaching pattern

The University will provide lectures and (sometimes) seminars (small teaching groups), which will be intellectual meeting grounds in your subject (the year number admitted to your college might be very small). It also provides for laboratory work. Less formally, your college will arrange for your 'supervisions' ('tutorials' at Oxford). They are more frequent here (up to three a week, and lasting for about an hour). You could be in private session with your supervisor; more commonly there will be two of you, and occasionally as many as four.

Where possible, your supervisor will be a Fellow of your college, but your Director of Studies will ensure that you are placed with someone who is expert in your particular chosen topic, so you might well be visiting another college for supervisions. Your supervisors will change, of course, from term to term, but your Director of Studies will remain your academic mentor throughout your undergraduate years. It is a good idea to check that a college does have a Director of Studies in your subject, before you choose your application list; it can make a difference...

Application procedure

You must send your application to your chosen college, not to the University; or you can send a non-college-specific application to the Cambridge Intercollegiate Applications Office. Your applications (to UCAS and to Cambridge on the PAF - Preliminary Application Form) must be received by the 15th October. PAFs available via your school, or from the Admissions Secretary at any college, or from the CIAO. Interviews are held in Cambridge between September and December and contribute enormously to the success (or otherwise) of your application. You should know your 'result' by January.

If you have made a non-college specific application or are rejected by your chosen college but are a strong candidate, you will be 'pooled' - computer allocated. Two 'pools': the Winter pool, post application and interview decisions, and the Summer pool, post-Results.

Interview

You will **not** normally receive an offer without interview (exceptions might be made for overseas applicants, and at the post-A level results pool procedure). Colleges have their own ways: you might be interviewed by two or three people together, or by different people at separate times. Background, motivation, enthusiasms, general interests, academic potential and knowledge: all will count. Be prepared. If the subject you are applying for is not a linear progression from your schooling, you might be set a short written test.

Unconditional offers

If you already have 'A' level results you must apply for an unconditional offer: i.e. dependent on interview and other assessable factors. You will not normally be expected to take 'S' or STEP papers at this stage, which in some ways makes life easier for you than for earlier-stage candidates.

If your 'A' level results turn out to be good enough to make you think 'Why not Oxbridge?', you must apply by the following October 15th for entry in the next academic year.

Conditional offers

Conditions will relate to grades to be achieved in examinations. The normal level of a conditional offer will be in the range of 26 to 30 points on three 'A' level, or equivalent, examinations together (Prospectus) - i.e. ABB - AAA. In a number of colleges, you will also be asked to take one or two 'S' or STEP papers. Offers are assessed in tandem with interviews.

STEP (Sixth Term Entrance Paper) is conducted by the Oxford and Cambridge Schools Examination Board. No knowledge beyond 'A' level work is needed (regardless of syllabus); the papers are 'free standing' and can be used alongside other admissions criteria. Each subject is tested by a single paper. Papers are taken in your usual exam centre (your school/college) shortly after the last A level exam at the end of June. You must enter for STEPs by February 21st in your year of entry.

You may not have to take a STEP paper, but you should know about the possibility. Any enquiries about the exam should go directly to the Examining Board (STEP Office). Questions are designed to complement mainstream exams. An advantage to colleges over 'A' level and 'S' papers is that scripts are available to them, so that candidates who quite achieve grades set, but whose performance-patches indicate high potential, can still be properly evaluated. Although Cambridge insists this is not an entrance exam, STEP does fill the gap left by the CEE.

Academic services

The enormous **University Library** is a copyright library and contains many millions of national and foreign publications. It receives a copy of every book and periodical published in the UK. Your faculty will also have a large specialist, accessible library, and your college will complete the range with its own domestic library/ies - often impressive and with priceless collections. There are about 100 libraries in total. All very much as at Oxford.

The University **computing service** gives a good range of short courses to foster every level of proficiency (or just learning). There are specialist courses for arts students, as well as for scientists (one assumes a difference of level). Many undergraduates now use the mainframe computer, and colleges are increasingly meeting the demand for provision of equipment.

If you wish to develop skills in a **language**, you can take, in parallel with your course, the 'Certificate in Competent Knowledge', in any of the languages offered in the modern and medieval languages Tripos. A 'demanding and respected qualification' (Prospectus). Multimedia courses are offered in over 100 languages and learning facilities are computer assisted.

Museums and art: The University-linked Fitzwilliam Museum is a gracious, neo-classical building with a really good cafe (a mark of class in museums these days). One of the most important museums in England, it contains a marvellous range of exhibits (antiquities, medieval work, coins, ceramics, glass, armour, sculpture and paintings of all schools and periods). It also has visiting exhibitions. A place of calm for the spirit if life gets too hectic.

The Sedgwick Museum (on Downing site) is the University geological museum with specimens, fossils and dinosaurs. The Museum of Classical Archaeology on the Sidgwick site (Arts) has displays of Greek and Roman casts, vases and other artefacts.

Museum of Archaeology and Anthropology (Downing site) has shrunken heads, totem poles, native dress, and archaeological finds both international and local.

Whipple Museum of Science in Free School Lane illustrates the history of science, and has a large collection of scientific instruments.

Museum of Zoology (New Museum site) has stuffed animals and birds, and wonderful skeletons of whales swimming through space.

Life in the University

A similar scene here to Oxford. Your college and its bar(s), friends' rooms, various societies and clubs: these will be the frame for your social hours. Bops, parties, May (and other) Balls, general celebrations of life. Things can be as much of a social whirl as you wish; it is probably more difficult to avoid being sociable!

Debates: The Cambridge Union Society has no connection with the Students' Union. It is the parallel, august debating body, nationally famed for the quality of its debates and the illustriousness of its speakers. It is an accolade to be invited to debate here. The Society's facilities include squash courts, a bar, library and 'free' films.

Drama: Cambridge drama wins national and international acclaim, and the list of its ex-members who have won lasting fame on stage and screen is long and starry. Notably, groups from Footlights have been the main source and setters of the high style of satire. However, talent ebbs and flows and it does depend on the flair apparent of your particular time. The ADC (Amateur Dramatic Club, which has its own theatre) is the leading University-based group, but many colleges and other groups offer experimental, ambitious, or just lively participation: quite a few colleges have their own theatres. Standards can be very high: drama here is competitive and talent widespread. Lots of scope for the technicalities too - and the prospect of idyllic outdoor performances if the summer weather is kind.

Music: A whole section of the Official Prospectus is devoted to the provenance and quality of college organs. Such specialist devotion and wealth of fine instruments is a good indicator of the quality of musical activity here. You will be able to join, or listen to performances by, orchestral, operatic and choral groups, college choirs, jazz players...all sounds of music from an Elizabethan gavotte, performed by costumed dancers, or madrigals sung from river craft as the light dies - to the most exhilarating displays of new music pyrotechnics. Music is part of Cambridge excellence. The Music Society has two orchestras and a choir. There is also a splendid chamber choir.

The Union

JCRs here are Junior Combination Rooms. These are the bodies nearest to a Students' Union (the actual SU has limited functions); they represent your interests and help your social life in college.

The Students' Union has five sabbatical and eighteen other members of its Executive. The Union has very little influence in University management committees. A network of women's groups is growing (sometimes men can be members!) in colleges and in the Union. Women have their own Newsletter and Council which meets twice a term.

Clubs and societies

Many are college based but there is also a very wide range (250) of University clubs, including 58 for sports.

The Cambridge Student Rag raised more than £70,000 in 1993, and there is a big Student Action Group.

The famous Student newspaper, *Varsity*, is independent (not controlled by the Union).

Sport

Most colleges provide sports grounds and facilities varying from superb to adequate - you must check on your own particular interest. Most facilities, including boat clubs, are close at hand. Most are excellent. The range and level at which you compete/learn/try are as wide as you could wish. Intercollegiate competition is fierce and there are the high spots of the big matches and races against Oxford. The University is not a member of the UAU but teams are beginning to compete in their matches.

Student welfare

You should register with a doctor in Cambridge. Colleges have their own in-house **health care**, which varies. The University has a dental service. You will be allocated to a **tutor** in your college who should keep a parental eye on your welfare and well-being, and be a tower of strength should you have problems. There is also the University **counselling service**, and 'Linkline', a student-run listening/information service.

Most colleges have their own chapel and **chaplain** sustaining an ancient tradition of Anglican worship. There are **religious societies** which cross college frontiers and operate University-wide, such as the Christian Union, the RC Fisher Society and groups associated with the Methodist, Quaker, Baptist and United Reform denominations. There is an active Jewish Society, running a local student centre and synagogue, and a Progressive Jewish Society with a reformed style of worship. The Buddhist Society is in evidence. There is an Islam Society and a mosque.

Careers Service

The Service arranges talks and courses as well as providing advice for individuals. There are computer-assisted guidance programmes and a range of aptitude tests.

Students with special needs

A hostel has recently been opened for students with physical disabilities. There is a Disability Advisory Committee.

Accommodation

A good proportion of the colleges (14 in all) provide accommodation for all three undergraduate years; some even house you entirely within the college itself, although it is more common to provide extension hostels and college-owned houses. Many of the rest provide at least two years 'in' (with a good chance of a third) and provide suitable lodging arrangements for exiles. Very few leave you to find your own accommodation - which is not easily available and can be expensive. If you are prepared to be cramped and squalid, you could find a room at £35 pw but the range you can expect is £40 to £50 pw in the town.

An average is £45 including bills.

College accommodation costs vary and need to be inspected individually to be properly assessed. Apparently cheaper meals, for instance, can become less of a bargain when you add in the fixed kitchen charges (an amount you pay each term towards the running costs of the kitchens). Some colleges absorb these charges into the costs of meals, some add meal tickets in with room rent - so you have to do the sums.

The standard of accommodation varies enormously: there are pleasant 'sets' (a single study and a bedroom) with minimally shared (with two or three) bathrooms; in the newer colleges you could have a good-sized, expensively equipped study-bedroom with a private shower (these are fitted out with an eye to attracting conferences); in the ancient Courts (Quadrangles in Oxford) you could have a large, atmospherically worn, too-large-to-heat, but enchanting room, reached by foot-hollowed stone steps. On the other hand, you could have a modular cell in a modern block, or a nondescript (even drab) room in a college-owned house (with multi-shared facilities). In a few cases you have to search for your own lodgings.

Costs vary enormously as you would expect, even within colleges. It will, in part, depend on how many meals you are obliged to take in College. You should check. Remember the terms here are short and remember those kitchen charges. The Alternative Prospectus is helpful about accommodation.

College fees

Payable to your college for its academic services and paid by your LEA if you are on a grant. These too vary slightly between colleges.

Mature students

2% of the Cambridge intake is 'mature' (over 21). Most colleges admit a few, but Lucy Cavendish was founded entirely to take mature women; Wolfson and St Edmunds accept only graduate and mature undergraduates. You might be asked to take 'A' levels or STEP exams (see 'Application procedure'), or be set a written test. There is a separate application procedure (a form to be returned by the end of October) and - as normal - a UCAS form must be sent by October 15th. You will be considered on a personal basis.

THE CITY (population: 110,000)

Origins go back to AD 70 and a Roman (later Saxon) settlement: the Cam is still locally known as the Granta - its British name. The twin functions of the old town grew side by side: scholars and students clustered into groups to settle and build until the first college we would recognise (Peterhouse) was founded in 1284; the town developed its own affairs, becoming a commercial and cultural centre for the wide regions of rural lowland which enclose it.

The University's power, wealth and fame brought disproportionate notice to this quiet backwater, as it grew to accommodate its own intellectual energies, and attracted increasingly tourists and visitors. Only in the last decade has its influence become more indirect, as new industries (although - true - still in measure dependent on the University) offer employment, money and social layers which are an alternative to the old town/gown division.

The central distribution of the beautiful old colleges, surrounded and shaped by river and meadows - the Backs, Pieces and Commons - remains the main attraction of Cambridge.

The city generally blends in with the quality of honey-coloured light caught by the colleges' stone; one 'finds' shops, often set in a run of mixed properties, sometimes in elegant terraces, crescents or 'passages'. A very lovely city. Shopping can yield delight; wandering certainly will. The market adds its colour, life and an extraordinary range of goods on six days of the week. The inevitable new shopping mall is well removed from the historic areas and does not impose a conflicting atmosphere.

Colleges and churches fill the city's main spaces with their academic calm, their marvellous architecture, their entrance arches and their secret worlds of inner courts and fine gardens.

Museums and galleries: Kettles Yard art gallery: a permanent collection of works by Henri Gaudier-Brzeska and a fine collection of 1920s and 1930s art. Also space for regular showings of modern art or crafts. A domestic and very charming setting. The Folk Museum takes you into bygone days and ways. Scott Polar Research Institute. Museum of Technology: Victorian steam pumping station with other exhibits from the local industrial past.

Theatre: The Arts Theatre: The theatre has been closed for refurbishment but will be open again in 1995. Mumford Theatre: actually on Anglia Polytechnic University's Cambridge campus.

A small theatre, but with the largest stage area in Cambridge: attracts professional as well as amateur productions.

Cinema: The Arts Cinema presents 'art' films - usually around three showings of different films daily. Also 'festivals'. Very high standard. The MGM (central) has two screens. And a multiplex is being built in the Grafton Centre.

Nightlife: Highly college-oriented, and there's a lot of it. The Junction has alternative discos, and attracts big-name and up-and-coming bands. But there is little else in the city. The Corn Exchange has standing capacity for 1,500 and hosts pop concerts, drama and ballet. A reasonably good range of restaurants, a very good showing of teashops and coffee houses and numbers of good pubs, many very pretty, several by the river.

Sport: Lots of boating: rowing, punting, canoeing. Kelsey Kerridge Sports Hall has facilities for five-a-side football, squash, gymnastics, weight-training, badminton, climbing wall. There are a number of public swimming pools and tennis courts and the odd playground with paddling pools. Fenners Lawns for cricket, and Sunday matches on Parker's Piece.

As at Oxford, a bicycle is a tremendous asset here - the whole area is very flat so it's no real effort. Also as at Oxford, bicycle stealing is a well-developed cottage industry.

ESCAPE ROUTES

The area around Cambridge is remarkably flat; a peaty, drained marsh bottom stretching north and east as far as Ely and beyond. Its flatness can be measured by the marvellously named Gog Magog hills which rise a staggering 300 feet and are still noteworthy. The skies are memorable, high, clear, or stacked with clouds. And at night, no city lights obscure the stars.

The fenland to the north is rich farming land, and the towns have grown around markets. Wicken Fen, undrained, gives you some idea of what this land was like when the Danes plundered: ancient land, rich in bird and plantlife.

The Isle of Ely rises above this flat, flat land. Its magnificent cathedral, a lantern, beacon, intricate filigreed structure can be seen for miles and miles and miles.

Wimpole Hall and Maddingley are within easy cycling distance, and across the meadows is Grantchester, where you can see the church clock.

Communications

The **rail links** to and from Cambridge have been restricted for ever by the conviction of the University that railways were a corrupting influence. You can travel directly to London, on fast trains (50 minutes). And directly to Norwich, and generally into East Anglia. Otherwise, you will have to change, probably several times. **Coach** links are better, more general, more direct, and usually faster.

The **M11** links with the **M25**, and otherwise goes into London via Wanstead. The **A640** takes you to the **A1**. Road links are the wheel of a market town in a sparsely populated area. **Stanstead Airport** is nearby, and plans are in hand to make it London's third airport: services.

UNIVERSITY OF LONDON

Imperial College*
King's College*
London School of Economics
Queen Mary and Westfield College*
Royal Holloway College*
University College*

Goldsmiths' College
School of Oriental and African Studies

Single Faculty Colleges

*designated centres for science teaching and research

UNIVERSITY OF LONDON

London University is enormous: over 60,000 full-time students. But the concept of size is largely abstract. In practice you will be conscious of belonging to a college or institution, rather than to the University, although your degree on graduating, whatever college you attended, will be a University of London degree.

Your college is its own world and will be very largely the frame of your student years. The big ones are very like separate universities in size, range of courses, academic, social and Union amenities, and competitive identity.

There are many highly specialised institutions, especially at postgraduate level, and the University spreads its wings as far as Paris (the British Institute) and the Clyde estuary (marine research) - with many other 'outposts'.

THE CHOICE IS YOURS

As a number of the schools, colleges and institutes of the University are small and specialised, for the practical purposes of this guide, we are giving 'full treatment' to the six largest, multi-faculty colleges, plus Goldsmith's College. Less detailed treatment is given to the major medical schools, and smaller academic units.

Which college/institution?

The choice does matter very much, and differences are as significant as those between universities outside the capital. London is quite the reverse of a homogeneous whole. One can cross a street and move from affluence to poverty; some areas are solid urban streets (all traffic, shops and monotonous building); or you can step from a road packed to standstill with traffic, into a quiet of lawns, trees and birdsong, elegantly framed by Regency/Georgian terraces. Student life has spaces between work and lectures when for a short time you can wander and relax - coloured fabric in the memory patchwork of your college years. And London can be magical: what is on your doorstep matters. At Royal Holloway you can lean on the balustrades with the 'chateau'-college behind you and the soft Surrey landscape ahead. From King's you can emerge onto the Embankment to watch the river traffic, or go to Waterloo Bridge to see St Paul's, and Wren's white spires shining in autumn sunlight. Not quite what Wordsworth saw (wrong bridge), but as timeless. University College has Bloomsbury and Russell Square. Imperial College, set in elegant South Kensington, between the Royal Albert Hall and the big museums (Science, Natural History, Victoria and Albert), has Kensington Gardens and Hyde Park on its doorstep; one can hardly imagine a better setting. Or you might prefer the vivid street life of the Mile End Road (QMW College), crossed and contrasted by the walks along the Regent's Canal. Very Bow Bells. Our sections on each college describe its immediate environs.

Central complex

You can't miss Senate House if you are in the vicinity of the British Museum or Russell Square. Its massive bulk towers out of and dominates the green and shady squares and quiet streets of Bloomsbury, one of London's sudden oases between busy thoroughfares. Ten minutes' walk away is Euston Station; another few minutes', St Pancras and King's Cross; 15-20 minutes, the Embankment, in the opposite direction. A central and imposing university complex of eclectic variety covers 35 acres of Bloomsbury. The architecture, dating from this century, is sometimes distinguished and has an air of established confidence and academic solidity. There is University College (one of the original founding colleges of the University); the School of Oriental and African Studies (SOAS); Birkbeck College; the School of Slavonic and East European Studies (SSEES); the School of Advanced Study with its associated institutes of higher research; the Institute of Education; the Careers Service and the Union building. A number of smaller institutions cluster in the grand old houses of the nearby streets and squares, forming an academic heartland. Beyond the other side of Russell Square are the School of Pharmacy, several postgraduate medical institutes and the University's Computer Centre. In addition, the metropolitan presence of academic societies and learned institutions offer unparalleled opportunities to explore broad fields of knowledge.

University services

The library

The University, at Senate House, offers a large library with many specialised collections. There are more than 1,250,000 books and more than 5,000 eminent periodicals. Your college will have its own resources, so the scope is enormous.

The Union

In University Bloomsbury, you will find the University of London Union (ULU), offering a wide range of advice and facilities and political involvement. The Accommodation Service is run in the Union building.

You should certainly investigate the facilities offered by the ULU, housed in a seven-floor building in Malet Street. There are many events and entertainments organised here, and 70 University clubs and societies offer good meeting grounds if your college is small, or if you want a change of scene, or (especially) if you are from overseas and would like to meet a group of compatriots.

The Union building offers a restaurant, winebar and snackbar; a supermarket (a wide range of goods), a travel office, print shop, bank, optician's, concert hall, bars and entertainments complex, heated swimming pool, 'Waves' health centre (sauna, jacuzzi, solarium, gymnasium, fitness centre), launderette, day nursery, badminton and squash courts, music room and meeting rooms. There is also a stage-theatre workshop. ULU publishes the University of London student newspaper, *London Student*.

Sport

Outdoor sports facilities and playing fields: the Motspur Park Athletic Ground (31 acres: 4 soccer, 1 rugby, 2 hockey, 2 lacrosse and 2 cricket pitches, 6 grass tennis courts, a first class running track, grandstand, pavilion); the boathouse on the Thames (University and college boatclubs), with practice tank; the sailing clubhouse on the Welsh Harp reservoir at Brent (space for 70 boats).

In addition to all this, colleges have their own facilities, clubs and sports grounds.

Accommodation

This is the biggest problem. In this guide we tell you in more detail about the position at the major colleges, and more briefly about the rest. In most cases, wherever you go, you will have to find your own roof for part of your course.

Intercollegiate Halls of Residence

In addition to the substantial amount of accommodation owned by the major colleges, the University itself runs seven intercollegiate halls of residence. Two of these halls are for women-only and one is reserved for men-only. All provide breakfast and dinner on weekdays and full meals at weekends. All have quiet study rooms and most have bars, music rooms and libraries. Most have sporting facilities and some offer squash courts. Two halls have photographic darkrooms.

University-managed Flats, Houses and Private Accommodation

The University of London Accommodation Office (at Senate House, Malet Street, London WC1E 7HU; telephone 0171 636 2818) is open from 9.30am to 5.30pm weekdays and 9.30am to 2.00pm on Saturdays (in September only). The Accommodation Office has a register of private-sector and University-owned or managed accommodation - from rooms in private homes to whole blocks of self-catering flats. It also has a list of hostel, inexpensive hotels and accommodation agencies, details of the university centrally-managed properties and other housing information, and a booklet: *Finding Somewhere to Live in London* which is sent to prospective students.

Points to note - housing

1. Check all accommodation before you agree to anything.

2. Check the price per week/month and what exactly is included.

3. Check your liability, and any responsibilities you might have for communal up-keep.

4. Always check your contract with someone from the Accommodation Office or the Students Union.

5. **NEVER view property on your own.** If your friends are not available, ask the Union to arrange for someone to accompany you.

6. Bear in mind the distance and cost of travel from accommodation to campus. You might have to buy a monthly travel card (1995 price, £56.50 per month) - which, although an additional burden in your budget, will give unlimited travel on London Transport (rail or road) within specified zones.

Big advice...
If London is 'unknown' to you, and you cannot afford time and money to spend weeks before the session begins finding a room to suit your needs and your purse; or if you do not have relatives or friends who can accommodate you while you search (or during your course) do not accept a place unless the college can offer you guaranteed accommodation for your first year. (This is the main reason for the percentage of students, far higher here than elsewhere, who remain home-based.)

Out and About

London is a big place. There are whole guidebooks devoted to its treasures, its architecture, its parks, its palaces, its theatres, concert halls, galleries; polemics written in national newspapers on its lifestyle, its people, its events. The population is as large as that of a quite respectable smaller country. So, we are not going to write a gazetteer of information you can easily find anywhere. If you decide to brave this City of Cities, then go to a bookshop and find the guide to suit your needs. That is your first move.

The second is to forget the Underground. You will never get to know this place if you scuttle down escalators with hordes of commuters or people studying stations to find out which is north. To find out where you have been, you should know where you are going, and that you will discover from a bus (particularly the upper deck), or better still, by using your feet. Some hapless travellers cycle. Not a good idea if you value your limbs and lungs.

You should, of course, see the Sights before you leave: the Palace, the Tower, the Houses of Parliament, the Abbey, the Bridges, the Markets...But no lists. A warning. Do not imagine that just because a place is a landmark, listed, historic or beloved, that it is permanent. London's landscape changes perceptibly by the month. It is an evolving city, conscious of the amount of land each building covers. So if you really care about a building which is not occupied by the government or royalty, photograph it.

Fortunately, the city is proud and jealous of its parks. Quite rightly. The inner parks you will explore, no doubt. They are what is left of old hunting grounds, now landscaped, with bandstands and green deckchairs, with lakes and pathways. Regent's Park has an open air theatre which puts on pastoral plays. Further afield is Hampstead Heath, undulating, with marked paths and dozens of dogs; Primrose Hill on the heath's edge is a great place for kite flying. South are Kew Gardens, London's botanical centre. London is full of green spaces: commons, heaths and squares, catching you briefly as you pass: people tend to walk more slowly where there are trees, even if the trees are dusty.

The bridges should each be crossed. In your three years you should endeavour to walk over every bridge and look out over the city in both directions: the views change dramatically even within a few hundred yards. Albert Bridge (Chelsea) is a web of tiny lights which shine from dusk: Tower Bridge might just lift up at any moment: London Bridge...has a long, if unstable, history.

There are river trips from Westminster to Richmond. You should go to Richmond. The Palace is gone, but the Park remains. And to Hampton Court Palace, a placatory gift in return for his head from Wolsey to King Henry VIII. The Palace is haunted and historic; the gardens beautiful and with a maze (perhaps 'the' maze). Neither of these royal thrones of kings is too far from your centre, but will feel another world.

Actually, referring to London as 'the City', is wrong. The City is a quite specific area, and - without going into a long history of the capital - not the whole city at all. It and Westminster are the nuclei: the bodies economic and politic. Otherwise, London is a series of 'villages'. You will pass over boundaries you do not know are there and move from one area to another: and you will feel the difference. So Notting Hill is not Holland Park, or South Kensington: Bloomsbury is not St Pancras, or Holborn. You should discover the full extent of this city, because you will never have the same kind of chance again.

Buy a map. Decide on an area. Sundays are a good time to explore. There is no-one around, and you can look at the buildings without worrying about umbrellas and other feet. Sunday markets (Camden and Petticoat Lane being two) are more relaxed and colourful than those which run day to day. But there is nothing wrong with weekdays. Have lunch in a gallery, or take a picnic to the river, or go to a lunchtime concert. Sit and watch the world go by, because here, there are worlds within worlds, more so than in most cities. You will find idiosyncrasies and layers of humanity wherever you go. And the buildings. Look up at the buildings, because above the shop fronts, some architect bothered to shape them.

Every place has something, if only a capacity to make you want to go somewhere else. Start in the middle and work out. Walking the Regent's Canal is a good way of finding out the northern edges, as long as you take your map and go 'inland' every so often to see where you are.

Imperial College of Science, Technology and Medicine

London
SW7 2AZ
Telephone: 0171 589 5111

University Charter date: 1907

Imperial is a medium-sized college with 5,000 undergraduate students on full-time programmes and 2,500 full-time postgraduates. The College's main campus is in Kensington: other parts - St Mary's Hospital and extensive facilities at Silwood Park near Ascot. Courses - all very prestigious: science, technology and medicine - are divided into value units with some flexibility of choice. There are normally formal end of session examinations: some account is taken of coursework assessment. A Humanities Programme is open to all students, covering a range of human and cultural topics. These courses count as credits in the undergraduate curriculum.

First years are guaranteed a room if offers have been accepted by September 15th in the year of entry.

THE CAMPUS

Not a multi-faculty institution! Hardly surprising since the College was formed in 1907 by merging three institutions (each bringing a 19th century history of distinguished work) which maintain today their separate, though closely linked, identities, dividing the work of the College between them: the Royal College of Science - the sciences; the Royal School of Mines - mining and applied subjects; the City and Guilds College - engineering, computing and management. A fourth School - of Medicine - is being built through major mergers: with St Mary's Hospital Medical School in 1988, with the National Heart and Lung Institute in 1995; in 1997, with the Charing Cross and Westminster Medical School and in 1998 with the Royal Postgraduate Medical School. With the introduction of a new undergraduate Medical course in 1988, Imperial will present a formidable undergraduate and postgraduate Medical School, with a new Medical Sciences building on the main campus. A strong shape of specialisation even within a highly specialised institution.

Imperial's academic prestige is very high. It has close links with government organisations, the Services, professional bodies and industry, with much interchange of advice and knowledge and attracts impressively large sums from independent sources to support research.

The College occupies the kind of London acreage (16) that is worth a fortune, and has even built a residential and social precinct on its site. Most of the buildings are 'new' (1953 and after) and have been designed to harmonise with the gracious South Kensington streets.

This is a very handsome campus, built in light stone (or 'stone'), its well-spaced blocks, balanced in design and height, offset by the tall white tower, green copper domed (the College's landmark), and relieved by lawns and trees. A strong sense of well-being and success pervades.

The College has extensive facilities at Silwood Park, near Ascot. 250 acres of parkland: a lake, marshland, farmland, experimental plots and greenhouses. There are laboratories for atmospheric physics and geophysics and for pure and applied biology. There is also a Centre for Analytical Research in the Environment. Social and residential facilities are here too.

The College also owns a mine, near Truro, in Cornwall, controlled by the Estates Division and used by various academic departments for field studies.

Cars

You are advised not to bring your car. Parking permits are available in exceptional cases (e.g. disability). No parking at residences and local parking charges are very high.

Learning resources

The Central **libraries**, Science Museum Library (a national library) on campus, and the 16 departmental libraries combined have over half a million books and periodicals. The central libraries can seat a total of 500 students and open from 9.30am to 9pm weekdays; 9.30am to 5.30pm Saturdays. The Haldane Library provides for more general reading, supports Humanities interest and has a Music section. The Medical Schools have specialist libraries. A new Biomedical Library will occupy two new floors in the main library building.

The **Centre for Computing Services** provides a campus-wide network, a large number of distributed workstations and local microcomputers for student and staff use. It also provides a help desk and training. Most students have to use computers.

Voluntary classes in **modern languages** are held in the evenings. There is a moderate charge. You can practise your language skills in the two language laboratories, if not already in use, in term time or vacations. Self-teaching materials are available 24 languages.

Academic and technical provision at this College is astounding.

Culture on campus

Drama: There is a strong Drama Society, with good facilities, which runs its own venue at the Edinburgh Fringe Festival each year.

Music: The College orchestra and choir give concerts each term, and the Operatic Society stages several productions each year. There are many smaller music groups: classical, folk, jazz, rock...The Union runs a programme of concerts with up-and-coming bands. Music practice facilities are available in the evenings and at weekends. Lunch time concerts by professional musicians and many more are given at the Royal College of Music next door. There are special music scholarships for talented musicians.

General culture: lunchtime lectures in the Humanities.

Science: any student can take part in research activities in the College to pursue or develop personal interests. A booklet, *Undergraduate Research Opportunities*, is available from the Mechanical Engineering Department.

The Union

In becoming a member of Imperial College Union, you automatically have membership also of your constituent-college Union within Imperial and of London University Union. Each of the four constituent college unions has its own regalia, mascots and social life, including sports, societies and clubs, dinners, parties and formal balls. They are also inter-competitive.

The Union runs over 140 clubs, sports teams and societies. It organises a varied entertainments programme with bands, discos, club nights, cabaret and comedians as well as bar entertainments.

The Union building is situated in a pleasant quad and houses two bars, an entertainments lounge, concert hall, theatre, common rooms, committee rooms and a gymnasium. Films are shown twice a week.

Union shops sell books, stationery and equipment. The Travel Centre provides cheap student fares. Other facilities on campus not run by the Union: refectories, common rooms, a bar and a general shop.

There is a realistic alternative prospectus, giving a helpful breakdown of courses in each department. Also Union produced and run: the IC Rag, *Felix* (the weekly student newspaper), a student TV station and radio and a literary magazine, *Phoenix.*

Sport

The Sports Centre on campus offers a swimming pool, jacuzzi, four squash courts, a gymnasium, weight-training, a full-bore rifle range, climbing wall, exercise studio, club room and a health suite, including steam, sauna and needle massage shower; tennis courts (2) and volleyball (1).

The Sports Centre operates on a membership basis: non-members can use the facilities if they pay a guest fee. Classes in martial arts, yoga and fencing are available.

Nearby are outdoor tennis and netball courts and a free weights room.

The 60 acre Athletic Ground is at Harlington, near Heathrow, about an hour's drive away by special bus on Wednesdays and Saturdays. There are grass pitches for cricket, soccer, rugby and hockey, as well as a full-size floodlit multi-use pitch. There is a bar, numerous changing facilities, and catering is provided on match days.

A second 15 acre sports field at Teddington provides pitches for soccer, rugby and hockey and cricket in the summer.

Putney Boathouse offers rowing and coaching for all levels. Imperial's Boat Club has won all of the top student rowing prizes over the last few years. The College sailing club sails and races its fleet of dinghies on the Welsh Harp Reservoir in north-west London.

St mary's has its own facilities.

The College timetable is free on Wednesday afternoons for sports and other recreational activities. 32 sports clubs.

Student welfare

The Imperial College **Health Centre** is close to the main halls of residence and is staffed by a team of doctors, nurses and administrative staff. Part-time specialist practitioners in psychotherapy, physiotherapy, sports injury and complementary medicine (homeopathy, acupuncture) are also available. Facilities include consulting rooms, a minor injuries room and a sick bay. Full dental surgery facilities are also available. The **student counsellor** is available to discuss your problems. Union advisers extend this support; there is a Nightline service. Two main Christian **chaplaincies** and a Muslim prayer room.

Careers Service

The Careers Service works closely with academic staff: a member of staff in each department acts as a careers advisor and can help with specific queries about careers relating to the department's field. In addition, the Careers Office will help you to appraise your own abilities and skills, to frame CVs and applications, and to cope with interviews. There is a comprehensive programme of careers talks and seminars to help you to decide on a career.

Students with special needs

The College has a Disabilities Officer. Students with disabilities are recommended to get in touch with the College as early as possible and before submitting their application forms. You should write to the Assistant Registrar (Admissions), specifying your disability and indicating any special facilities or arrangements you may require. Some buildings might present problems for the less mobile, although some residential units have been adapted.

Accommodation

Provision here is excellent by London standards. 2,300 live in accommodation either owned or controlled by the College. You are also eligible for a place in London University's Inter-Collegiate halls. Accommodation is guaranteed to incoming first years, provided that they have accepted unconditional offers by September 15th in the year of entry.

Almost 1,000 IC students live in halls of residence on or very near to campus, either purpose-built or in three of the original grand Victorian houses.

There is a further hall in Knightsbridge nearby and another in a late Victorian complex with five sets of student houses in Evelyn Gardens, about a 15 minute walk from College. There are newly built flats and houses on the Clayponds Estate in South Ealing.

The College Accommodation Office keeps lists of rooms available in the private sector and, of course, you can use the UL Accommodation Office. So the prospects for finding rooms in later study years are relatively good.

Halls of residence
All have 24 hour access, and generally study-bedrooms in groups of four to eight, sharing common rooms. There are laundries and small kitchens (you are close enough to use College refectories if you prefer). All halls have a warden presence.

Each hall has its own social life, run by an elected committee: parties, musical evenings, indoor and outdoor games, television, bars and even newspapers. One hall has a dining room.

A number of rooms are shared.

Student houses and flats
Flats are available at Evelyn Gardens, alongside the halls of residence whose facilities can be shared, or in Prince's Gardens, on campus. Newly built flats and houses at Clayponds residential estate in South Ealing (about a 50 minute ride away by tube) accommodates 333 students .

Costs (1995/96)
Rooms on campus cost from £28.28 to £56.49 per week - depending partly on whether you are willing to share and on the standard of accommodation you are looking for. Prices around £50 are common. Costs are for self-catering accommodation: with five evening meals, you should add £14.75 per week.

Private sector
Imperial sends out a comprehensive pack on housing rights: it is well worth sending for; a lot of the information is relevant to all students in all parts of the country, not just in London. Private sector accommodation is expensive in the area immediately around Imperial: you could look at other entries to get some idea of cheaper and still accessible places. Take travel costs into consideration when choosing an area.

Mature students
Minimum age 21. If you lack formally accepted qualifications, you must be able to prove competence as well as commitment.

Nursery
There is a day nursery for 50 children aged between six months and five years. You have to pay the full cost for this service and applications should be made early.

Full-time or sessional care is available for children aged between five and nine years runs in school holidays.

SURROUNDING AREA

You are actually next door to the Natural Science Museum, the Royal Albert Hall, the Science Museum, the Victoria and Albert Museum. The houses, roads, railings and spaces are...gracious. Very solid, very planned. Across from the Albert Hall is the Albert Memorial, with Kensington Gardens and Hyde Park beyond. You are within strolling distance of Buckingham Palace in one direction, and Harrod's in the other.

If, however, you want to shop, a longer walk to Kensington High Street will take you to where it's at, including (if you walk far enough) Olympia.

See also the London Out and About section.

King's College London

Strand
London
WC2R 2LS
Telephone: 0171 872 3434

University Charter date: 1829

King's is a medium-sized college with 7,000 undergraduate students on full-time programmes and 1,600 full-time postgraduates. Courses are modularised within traditional structures, except Law, Pre-Clinical Medicine, Pharmacy and single honours Philosophy and History which remain plain traditional. Assessment is mainly by written examination with the possibility, in some courses, of including a dissertation. The College's main campus is on the Strand; three satellite campuses.

All undergraduates are guaranteed at least one year in a hall of residence.

THE CAMPUS

The Strand campus

Kings' historic main campus occupies space between the Strand and the Embankment, close to Waterloo Bridge, and directly opposite the National Theatre/South Bank arts complex. The lure of this stretch of the river could be a serious threat to dedicated study.

The College was established by George IVth and the Duke of Wellington, given its charter in 1829, and opened in 1831. It was, with University College which very slightly pre-dates it, a foundation stone of London University. The University was set up partly because every capital city should have one, and mostly to break the monopoly held by Oxford and Cambridge. University College aimed to break the social and religious exclusiveness of Oxbridge, and their academic traditionalism. Its independent and liberal stance was in its time shocking enough to provoke the foundation of a second college, backed by the Church and Establishment, in reaction to UC's 'atheism'. Very Gilbert and Sullivan - indeed Gilbert did go to King's.

Both colleges are marked by this early history, and King's today has a lovely Victorian chapel, active in its community life, and an atmosphere of traditional courtesy. The old building shares the stately facade of Somerset House on the riverfront, opening inwards to a courtyard which, together with the dark glass, 'blind' face of the new main building bordering on the Strand, secludes the College from the outside world. The Great Hall is a splendid affair - high spaces and chandeliers - grand enough to be hired out to film-makers.

One of the College's great assets is the Macadam Building which houses the College Union on eight floors, with a high terrace overlooking the river. Facilities are extremely impressive.

Courses on the main campus: all those not listed for the satellite campuses.

A second campus at **Cornwall House,** on the opposite side of the river, relates easily, via Waterloo Bridge, to the main buildings and the Union.

Courses here: Nursing Studies and the School of Education.

The College also has campuses in Kensington and Chelsea; names to be reckoned with and famous throughout the world for elegance and style... and at Denmark Hill.

The Kensington campus

Was Queen Elizabeth College in one of London's most beautiful and gracious areas, amid the tree-lined avenues between Kensington Gardens and Holland Park.

Courses here: Life Sciences

The Chelsea campus

Was Chelsea College, set in the fashionable end of Town, where high style meets quiet squares and the King's Road offsets mansion flats and mews.

Courses here: Pharmacy and Pharmacology (which also operates on other sites)

Denmark Hill

Set in a densely populated multi-ethnic area of south London and offers a rich source of medical and dental working experience for students. The campus adjoins King's College Hospital.

Courses here: Medicine and Dentistry

Cars

None on campus, but some car-parking provision at three of the halls of residence. You are advised not to bring a car; insurance premiums are high.

Learning Resources

The **library** houses 800,000 books, subscribes to over 2,500 periodicals and has space for 500 readers. The library operates on all campuses, with specific provision for campus needs. You also have access to the large Senate House library.

The **computer centre** offers full advice for microcomputer users, as well as providing large computer services to the College. All campuses have departmental terminal rooms, linked to a College network. Computer terminals are also in halls of residence. Introductory courses are run on software and services.

The **Language and Communication Centre** offers courses in a number of languages from beginner to post-A level. There are also specialised courses to back up some subject areas (Science, Technology, Music...). You will have access to a range of computer assisted language learning facilities. Self-study material and advice are usually available for languages not formally taught. Most degree programmes allow you to incorporate a language unit into your course. Alternatively, you can take a certificated course through evening classes. The Centre has a distinguished results record.

The AKC course

The course allows you to study for a respected additional qualification alongside your degree studies. Associateship of the College is gained through an examined course of ethical and philosophical studies. Deeply interesting and well worth the effort.

Culture on campus

Drama: Plays are presented annually by the Classics, German and English departmental societies. There is also a Union Drama Society. The College has a well-equipped, impressive theatre, used for films, lectures and drama.
Film: The Union has weekly showings of recently released films.
Music: There is a college orchestra, departmental choirs and various chamber music ensembles. The BMus in Performance Studies is taught in association with, and principally at, the Royal Academy of Music. Apply through UCAS or direct to the Royal Academy.
Art: The move of the Courtauld Institute into Somerset House gives you next-door-neighbour access to their famous collection of art works.

The Union

The Macadam Building offers exceptionally good facilities: bars open until 11pm and until 1.30am on Fridays and Saturdays; food services (from hot pies to booked tables in a waitress service restaurant, to coffee on the top-floor terrace with river view); pool tables and games machines; shop and a travel shop. Tutu's, the daytime cafe, doubles up as a nightclub. The smart Waterfront bar is open all day. The building also houses student services (accommodation, welfare, information, counselling). There is a host of clubs and societies. The Law Students Society organises debates and moots. The Union provides various publications, including a regular magazine.

Kensington and Chelsea have Union shops and bars which hold regular entertainments.

Denmark Hill's newly refurbished facilities include a large bar, societies room, TV and games rooms and a shop.

Sport

King's has its main sports grounds at New Maldon, and another six acres close to the Denmark Hill campus: the usual range of pitches. There are two gyms at Chelsea, squash courts and a multigym at Kensington. King's Rugby Club was one of the 12 founder members of the Rugby Union; the College's other strengths are its boat/canoe/sailing clubs, and sub-aqua (a top club nationally).

Wednesday afternoons are generally timetable-free to allow time for sports pursuits. Booking fees are low and charges subsidised.

Student welfare

The College has a comprehensive **medical service** staffed by GPs and nurses. A professional staff, including **counsellors**, **psychotherapists** and **psychiatrists**, offers a confidential service. The Students' Union has a welfare unit which hold regular surgeries. Advice and help is available on all campuses. **Religious worship** in the chapel plays an important part in College life at King's. The chaplains of various denominations work as a team; a full programme of activities. Provision is made in catering and there is a prayer room for Muslim students.

Careers Service

The Careers Advisory Service has offices on both the Strand and Kensington campuses. The Service has the added advantage of being part of the University of London Careers Advisory Service which has a comprehensive careers library and runs courses: you can attend lectures and presentations at other London Colleges, as well as those at King's. The range and structure of contact with London's employers and professions is invaluable. There are seminars and consultations on career choice, job application methods and interview skills. Careers counselling is integrated into the curriculum.

Students with special needs

The College has experience of teaching students with sensory disabilities; the College buildings might, however, pose extreme problems for students with mobility difficulties (although this is not true for all schools). You are advised to write to the appropriate school office outlining your special needs, before you apply. Some apartments at Waterloo have been designed for students with special needs.

Accommodation

All undergraduates are guaranteed at least one year in a hall of residence.

If you apply for accommodation before June 30, you will be offered a place in a King's hall of residence or an Intercollegiate hall. In all, there are approximately 2,500 college places, 75% of which are for first years. Another 500 places will be available by September 1997.

The College also manages short life and head-lease schemes, and the Accommodation Office provides lists of vacant properties throughout the year. You should have no problems if costs are within your range.

The halls are a mixture of converted town houses with gardens and modern purpose-built blocks. All halls have recreation rooms, bars, pantries (providing basic cooking facilities) and laundries; most have quiet study rooms, cycle sheds, snooker/pool and games machines; some have music rooms, libraries and tennis, squash and weights facilities.

The College has developed a new student village, housing 550 students, on the former Westfield College site close to Hampstead. 360 rooms are single. All are well served by public transport and journey times (for London) are not excessive.

Costs (1995/96)

Self-catered halls are let for 37 weeks; catered halls for 30 weeks. Costs include heating, lighting, linen and food where provided: Hall fees range from £1,305 for a place in a shared self-catering room in Chelsea, to £3,228 for a single room in the heart of Westminster, including breakfast and evening meal on weekdays.

Average weekly prices for private accommodation range from £50 to £70 per week exclusive for a single room. Weekly rents for head-lease, furnished, £45 - £47 per week excluding bills.

Mature students

All cases considered on merit. There is a possibility of being exempted by the University's Special Entrance Board if you don't have normal qualifications. King's has a nine-month Special Entry Scheme which tackles the groundwork of science subjects. A pass gives you entry to a three-year BSc degree course.

Nursery

Facilities are available at the University of London creche for children over two years old. Places very scarce indeed.

IMMEDIATE SURROUNDINGS

King's is on the river, opposite the South Bank site. New plans are afoot for the South Bank, so that by the time you get to London there might be even more there. To date:

The Royal Festival Hall, with its array of coffee and salad bars, art display areas, free lunchtime concerts, weekend craft fairs; the Queen Elizabeth Hall - smaller than the RFH, but not as intimate as the Purcell Room: these offer concerts of high quality, every night. Next along is the National Film Theatre; you have to be a member to see films, but membership is well worth the cost. The Museum of the Moving Image is great fun. The Hayward Gallery often has two exhibitions running concurrently: the spaces of this gallery are pleasing, the lighting good, the experience - especially in the quiet parts of day. The National Theatre has three auditoria, each running a repertory of productions during a season. Remember that, as a student, you will get standbys and concessionary rates.

The other side of King's opens onto the Strand. If you turn left, you are in the thick of London: Trafalgar Square is five minutes' walk away; Covent Garden with its life, shops, open cafes, markets is again only five minutes off the road. The West End, China Town, Leicester Square's cinemas, the Hippodrome... a list is as pointless as saying 'it's all there': but it is, and it's on your doorstep.

See also the entry for the University of London

London School of Economics & Political Science

Houghton Street
London
WC2A 2AE
Telephone: 0171 405 7686

University Charter date: 1895

LSE is a small, specialised college with 2,700 undergraduate students on full-time programmes and over 2,000 full-time postgraduates. Degree programmes allow study of combined subjects, either as joint honours or as 'major' and 'minor' courses. You may take at least one 'outside' option either from a completely different subject group or from another subject within your chosen area. Almost all degrees have end of year exams; many courses include project reports or dissertations. The School is housed in a small 'campus' between the City of London, Westminster/Whitehall and the law courts.

Students whose home is outside London are guaranteed a place in hall in their first year

---

THE SCHOOL PRECINCT

LSE is compacted into a roughly triangular area just off Kingsway and bordering onto the Aldwych.

The School was founded in 1895 by Beatrice and Sidney Webb, the first Fabians, with the aim of improving society through promoting the study of political and social problems. The School became part of the University of London in 1901, and cornerstone of the new studies of socio/economic/political theory and practice in Britain. Much pioneering work has been done here and, from its beginning, the School has advised government bodies, and generally integrated its work with the needs of those who work in the public service. Its position puts it at a strategically dynamic point between the City, with its powerful banking, financial and legal institutions, Westminster/Whitehall, the centres of government power and the law courts. Interaction is wide, and offers a valuable extended field of awareness to your studies. This is a highly specialised institution, with an impressive list of famous names among its past students and a lasting influence on the shaping of political thought and economic theories.

Worthy of note is LSE's bookshop, which, in its field, has a comprehensive bookstock and some of the best informed and helpful staff we have come across.

LSE is very much in central London, just off the Strand, near the law courts, close to Trafalgar Square: if you want city life, here you will have it.

Cars
There is limited car parking at halls of residence. None at the School. You might have to pay a fee.

Learning Resources

The LSE **library** has a formidable title: the British Library of Political and Economic Science and serves as a national reference library for the social sciences. It contains more than 1,000,000 books, an estimated 3,000,000 'separate items' including collections of government publications from nearly all the countries in the world, including controversial pamphlets and leaflets, and can seat 1,000 readers. The **Computer Service** runs an open-access Advisory Service available to staff and students. There are a number of large open-access microcomputer rooms with 250 IBM PCs and Apple Macintosh workstations. The Service runs Introductory training programmes including computer- and video-based courses. **The Language Studies Centre** runs extra-curricular non-examination classes in French, German, Russian and Spanish from beginner's level upwards.

The Union

The Union, occupying three floors and the basement in East Building, runs a coffee bar, a vegetarian cafe, printing press, two bars and a shop; it organises socials, discos and concerts, as well as a range of student welfare services and funds around 80 societies. In the Union building there are three squash courts and a multigym.

The Union produces its own newspaper and runs a Welfare and Housing Office which gives advice on contracts and housing matters generally. There is an International Resource Centre which gives information on work opportunities and academic exchanges abroad, and acts as a meeting place for multicultural societies.

Sport

On the precinct there are three squash courts, table-tennis, judo etc., and a polygym. You are also, of course, close to the facilities of the University of London Union (ULU). The School has a 25-acre sports ground at New Malden, Surrey (an hour's journey away). Here are pitches for soccer, rugby, hockey, cricket and netball; grass tennis courts and - a rare delight - croquet. You can reach the grounds by train or, on match days, by coach from the School. The School Rowing Club uses the University boathouse at Chiswick, and the Sailing Club goes to Hendon. The Athletics Union funds 27 clubs.

Student welfare

The student **health service** is staffed by GPs and nursing sisters. Psychotherapists provide advice, **counselling** and a **psychotherapy** service. The ecumenical **chaplaincy** team covers the spectrum of churches and religious societies. Two rooms are set aside for Islamic prayer.

Careers service

Seminars and interviews are arranged. Computerised advisory programmes, PROSPECT HE and GRADSCOPE, are available. You have access to the University of London's Careers Service and to talks etc. given at other UL colleges.

Students with special needs

The School is working on improving access to its buildings, and has a Kurzweil Reading Machine and associated equipment. There is a Disabled Students Resource Centre run by the Union, offering advice and help. An advisor helps to ensure that the disabled benefit from IT equipment. Most of the lifts are brailled.

Accommodation

The School has places for around a third of its students in its own halls of residence and flats, plus places allocated to LSE in University halls. First years whose home is outside the London area are guaranteed a place in hall.

Halls of residence

There are four, all within 25 minutes' walk of LSE. All provide breakfast and evening meals, plus weekend lunches: in two halls you can pay-as-you-eat. All also have limited cooking facilities.

Costs (1995/96)

Single: £59.00 to £77.00 per week (30-week session)
Shared: £39.00 to £58.00 per week (30-week session)
(according to amenities and meals taken)

Self-catering

Two accommodation blocks offer flat-facilities shared by two to six students. They are in a complex with one of the halls and share amenities. Fees do not include meals (you buy meal tickets). The third residence, Butler's Wharf, is something special - flats built around courts. Its costs reflect the style of living.

The residences at Silver Walk, Rotherhithe are for 95 students, in 18 shared houses.

Costs (1995/96)

single : £60 to £75 per week (39 weeks)
shared: £45 to £53 per week (39 weeks)

Private accommodation

The School operates a company let scheme, but otherwise you must use the University Accommodation Office. For a reasonably comfortable room you can expect to pay £50 to £80 per week.

Mature students

The School's traditions and the nature of its courses encourage the presence of mature students. Approved Access courses are welcomed as entry qualification.

Nursery

The School provides places for nine babies from the age of six months to two years and 16 places for children aged between two and five years.

IMMEDIATE SURROUNDINGS

LSE is very close to Kings' College, so surroundings are pretty much the same. You will perhaps be more aware of Lincoln's Inn Fields and the Law Courts. You are also closer to Covent Garden with its colour and markets and street performers.

See the entry for the University of London

Queen Mary and Westfield College

Mile End Road
London E1 4NS
Telephone: 0171 975 5555

University Charter date: 1934

QMW is a medium-sized university with c.6,500 undergraduate students on full-time programmes and 1,100 full-time postgraduates. The College has a a single campus near Docklands, on the Mile End Road. Most courses are modularised - and have been for 20 years: there is a long term commitment to learning geared to aptitude and interest. Assessment is a combination of examination and coursework. The College can offer accommodation to all incoming first years, apart from Clearing entrants who will still be considered.

THE CAMPUS

Queen Mary College joined London University in 1915, took its royal charter in 1934 and merged with Westfield College in 1989 to become Queen Mary and Westfield (QMW). The campus, however, remains Queen Mary's, a college which has a history as varied and colourful as the Cockney heritage of its setting. It began as the People's Palace, a philanthropic institution opened in 1888 to bring education and culture to the East Enders of its time. (The fine stone building, in a shallow inset off the busy and noisy Mile End Road, remains the facade behind which the College weaves its world.) The College survived the blitzing of its area slums in World War II; watched the 'replacement' local authority housing which followed, and is now close to the controversial 'yuppie' and office redevelopment of London's Docklands.

In 1995, the College merged with St. Bartholomew's and the Royal London School of Medicine and Dentistry, to create an impressive new School of Medicine and Dentistry which bears the original names.

The College environment is urban in its least attractive mode. The Mile End Road is a noisy thoroughfare, its property run-down, its street markets lively, but inevitably littered. Regent's Canal forms the northern boundary of the campus. Its towpath offers a pleasant walk through to Victoria Park, and also offers a good setting for the new halls of residence.

The campus is well planned, its buildings neatly spaced around its large site: tall new blocks separated by small quads, a few trees, some greenery. A good example of London's capacity to surprise, as you leave the bustle of traffic behind and enter the sudden quiet of an academic precinct. The atmosphere is positive, and collected, and suggests a well-defined sense of purpose. The College is about 20 minutes' ride (by tube) from central London.

Learning Resources

One of the College's main assets is its **library,** which contains 500,000 volumes and subscribes to 2,500 periodicals. It also holds a stock of CD-ROMS and educational videos. The library is recognised as a European Documentation Centre, and receives most of the official publications of the Common Market. The library is open for nearly 66 hours a week during term time. There is seating for over 1,000 students. Libraries also at the Medical sites.

The College gives tuition in **computing** where required for course work: it aims to give all students a working knowledge of IT. The facilities here are excellent and advice is available; some computers laboratories are available on open access, out of hours.

The **Language Laboratories** contain a wide range of self-teaching material, including Computer assisted learning packages, in many languages at all levels of expertise. There are courses in French, German and Spanish, open to all students, which can count towards your degree.

Culture on campus

Drama: Drama here is taught in collaboration with the Central School of Speech and Drama and links are very strong. Student and staff productions are mounted in the Great Hall or in the Department's studio theatre.

More ambitious projects have taken place in professional spaces and small theatres in London and, indeed, have toured abroad. The Department often takes five or six productions to the Edinburgh Fringe.

Music: The Union **Music Society** runs a flourishing choral society, music society and orchestra. A series of lunchtime concerts is open to all.

Film: There is a **film club** in the Union.

The Union

The Union runs and owns its own building, modern and comfortable. Facilities include commonrooms, meeting rooms, TV room, two bars and cafe (prices low) and sauna facilities. Regular discos, bands, cabaret evenings and bar promotion nights. The annual St Valentine's Ball sound spectacular and gaudy. The new nightclub (e1) has a sound system, dance floor, bar and eating area. A Union newspaper, around 30 sports clubs and 40 non-sports clubs and societies. There is a Union shop and travel and insurance offices. A nightline operates from 8pm to 8am every night. A Student Community Action Officer co-ordinates work with the local community or with the nearby Globe Centre.

Sport

The Union building contains a gymnasium, multigym (for which there is a small annual fee), squash courts and weights room, plus facilities for snooker and other indoor games. The College sports grounds are at Theydon Bois, Essex, a tube or coach ride from the College but very close to halls of residence. There are two rugby and three soccer pitches, a cricket square and six tennis courts (three hard and three grass). Hockey is played on astroturf pitches in East London. There are changing rooms and catering facilities at the sports grounds . The Boat Club uses the UL boathouse at Chiswick, and the Sailing Club sails at the Welsh Harp reservoir in Middlesex.

Student welfare

The College **health centre** is staffed by a nursing officer during College hours. A local GP, with whom you may register, visits the College daily in term time. The centre provides a confidential advisory service for all students and staff. There is a College **counselling service** and a team of student advisors. The St Benet's ecumenical **chaplaincy** has a striking meeting room, coffee bar and resources centre. Jewish, Buddhist and Muslim students will find worship centres for their faiths in the local community.

Careers Service
The Service offers individual counselling, computer-based careers guidance and a well-stocked careers library. There are seminars on career choice, job applications and interviews.

Students with special needs
You should write to the Admissions Office before submitting your application and outline your special needs. The library has various equipment for blind or visually impaired students including CCTV. The new buildings on campus have been designed to accommodate students with mobility problems and a number of buildings have lifts.

Accommodation

The College can offer accommodation to all incoming first-years (except Clearing entrants, who will still be considered) in its own accommodation or through London University's Intercollegiate halls, or by providing extensive lists of private accommodation. The College-owned housing stock consists of 700 student places in its catered halls of residence in South Woodford, and 950 places in self-catering residences on or near the Mile End campus.

Halls of residence (catered)
Five halls at South Woodford (seven miles and a 35-minute underground journey from College: a monthly travelcard was £56.50 in 1995). Suburban area: good local shops, pubs and cinemas. Halls are on a 13-acre lawned site, with dining hall, bar and social centre, computer rooms, music and games rooms, and tennis courts. Most study-bedrooms are single, sharing amenity rooms and bathrooms.

Costs (1995/96)
Single: £53.27 per week for 31 weeks
Shared: £43.82 per week for 31 weeks
Costs cover breakfast Monday to Friday and brunch on weekends and a "Pay as you Eat" service during the week.

Students' Hostel at Whitechapel (catered)
Mixed hostel with places for 150 students in single or double rooms. 15 minutes from the QMW main campus. 24 double rooms are available for first years. Breakfast and dinner are provided daily. Utility and ironing rooms on each floor; bed-linen provided.

Costs (1995/96)
Single: £66.36 per week (38 weeks)
Double: £55.51 per week (38 weeks)

Self-catering
There are 950 places in self-catering residences on or near the Mile End Campus. Larger residences, housing between 40 and 125 students, and a number of flats/houses for between 3 and 8 students, all sharing communal facilities. The majority are located on campus or within a 25-minute bus ride; some houses have a very pleasant canal side setting. These rooms are usually given to final year, postgraduate, clinical and overseas students; special pleading may win you one of the few places for First Years.

Costs (1995/96)
Single rooms range between £1,284 and £2,498 for 38 weeks. Costs relate to the quality of facilities and amenities. Includes fuel costs.

Private accommodation
A single room in a shared house costs around £40 to £60 per week. Lodgings can cost £65 to £80 per week.

Mature students

Access courses are run, locally, by Tower Hamlets College, in science, engineering and medicine. Widened access is aimed chiefly at ethnic minorities and women. You are likely to be interviewed.

Nursery
The day nursery has places for the 30 children (from three months to three years) of QMWC staff and students.

IMMEDIATE SURROUNDINGS

The East End and all it conjures; you are, however, only a mile from the City of London and have the advantages of both worlds. The canal walk, turning your feet westward, will take you all the way to Uxbridge, if you really want to go so far. Towards the City, down by the river, the Tower of London is within walking distance. The nearby Docklands development offers leisure and watersport facilities.

See also the entry for University of London.

Royal Holloway, University of London

Egham
Surrey
TW20 0EX
Telephone: 01784 434455

University Charter date: 1898

Royal Holloway is a medium-sized university with 4,500 undergraduate students on full-time programmes and 450 full-time postgraduates. This is the University of London's 'country campus' - a single site in Surrey; the main building is a chateau-style Victorian extravagance set in 120 acres. Courses here are broken into credit units within a coherent, largely traditional structure. Assessment is mainly by examination.

The College can guarantee a place in a hall of residence to all first year undergraduates.

THE CAMPUS

Royal Holloway is one of the six largest colleges of the University. It occupies a 120 acre site, 20 miles from central London, and 32 minutes by train from Waterloo.

The architecture of this College sets it apart: spires, towers, turrets, elegant chimneys - a roofscape to beggar Gormenghast. One simply does not expect to find a 'French chateau' in Surrey, especially not one which houses the student community of part of our metropolitan university. Founder's Building - in chateau style but in an English idiom of particularly warm brick - must be one of the finest examples of extravagant Victorian (W.H. Crossland) architecture. Colonnades, pillars, statuary, a chapel, balustraded terrace walks, and a central green court, sheltered enough for students to be sitting outside - coffee, talk and books - on a sunny November day. There are 500 study-bedrooms in this beautiful abode, if you should be so lucky. The building is used by students and administrators in a comfortable mix, creating a most civilised academic atmosphere. It houses part of the library, a chapel, a dining hall and the famous picture gallery.

New developments are pleasantly set, well planned and, not surprisingly, good quality. They include a library and faculty buildings to contain the College's growing strength in Science. The site is large enough to absorb development, and still retain its lovely woodland walks, green spaces and wide vistas. There is an air of benevolent supervision: a private and privileged world. A number of halls of residence, landscaped into the hillside, provide for a good-sized student community life.

The prospectus describes the College as the 'University of London's country campus': very true, although membership of the University, (as well as the academic and social sharing on offer) gives students here the London Allowance in their grants.

Learning Resources

The **library** has a stock of 500,000 books, takes 1,700 periodicals and seats 630. There are in fact three separate libraries, serving different academic disciplines. The **computer centre** provides an advisory service and gives courses on general and specialist computing, as well as producing user guides and developing special software for research purposes. A card access system permits entry to the Computer Centre at all times. The **Language Centre** has facilities for self-teaching and language practice. There is a language laboratory for computer-assisted learning.

College Certificate Courses are run in Computer Applications, Basic Technology Skills, Creative and Communication Skills and Attainment in a Modern Language. The certificate courses are open to all students. Each Certificate has its own value and carries also a course unit value which will count towards your degree.

Culture on campus

Drama: A well-established drama and theatre studies department here, using its own studio theatre, equipped with flexible seating for 120, lighting and sound systems. A number of plays are presented by the department, as welll as by student societies; the Quadrangles for the outdoor Summer production. There is a separate stage for Japanese Noh drama. Active links with the Music Department (music-drama and dance-drama).

Music: A strong music department ; any student may arrange for tuition in voice or instrument. There are regular lunchtime and evening concerts: the College orchestra and choir, wind band, choral society, chamber orchestra, opera society, 'Big Band', and Savoy Opera group all give performances. The chapel choir broadcasts with the BBC and tours throughout the UK and Europe; its Schola Cantorum specialises in the performance of church music. Music scholarships are available (choral, organ and instrumental).

Art: The picture gallery here houses a collection of Victorian paintings bought by Thomas Holloway - includes Frith, Millais and Landseer. You can also, by arrangement, see, in the centre for the study of Victorian art, stained glass by Burne-Jones and William Morris and a fascinating range of work by eminent Victorians.

The Union

The Union building houses the welfare and information centre, shop, club and society areas (over 100 non-sporting societies are sponsored), and Union offices (there are four sabbatical officers). Staff employed by the Union include a Union manager and trading manager.

The building has a large auditorium, two new bars and a food area. The Union runs two other bars (in halls of residence). One of the main bars is run as a pub, with a real-pub atmosphere. There is a seven-days-a-week entertainments programme, bringing in well-known artists and bands, discos, film showings, cabarets, quizzes, regular formal dinners and a summer ball (with famous entertainers and what a setting!). A late-night minibus will take you home safely (especially women) after the lively social whirlings. Student newspaper: the *Egham Sun*.

Sport

There are grass sports pitches, tennis courts (including four all-weather), squash, a sports hall and a multi-gym. There are more squash and tennis courts at Kingswood. Rowing on the Thames; sailing on Datchet reservoir; automatic membership of local leisure centre.

There are over 40 sports clubs and teams play in the UAU, at regional and local levels. The College has a good performance record in many sports.

Student welfare

Registration with the **health centre** is compulsory for resident students and optional for those off-campus. The health centre has round-the-clock nursing cover and medical officers, as well as a sick bay. Physiotherapy and psychotherapy available. **Counselling** is provided by the student counselling service. There are three Christian **chaplains** (Anglican, Catholic and Free Church); daily worship in the College chapel. The Islamic Society has a room set aside for daily prayers.

Careers Service
The College Careers Service offers seminars to develop personal skills, as well as offering individual guidance and computer-assisted guidance programmes, including PROSPECT (HE). You have access, of course to London University's careers service.

Students with special needs
You should write to the Sub-Dean of Students outlining your special needs. The College will do its best to accommodate you.

Accommodation

The College can guarantee a place in a hall of residence to all first year undergraduates who firmly accept their UCAS offer. Many final year students also live in hall.

Halls of residence
Halls offer mainly single study-bedrooms; only a few larger rooms in Founder's (the 'chateau') and Kingswood halls are shared. Kingswood is the only hall off-campus; it is a whole mile away - above the Thames at Runnymede.

Halls provide kitchens with basic cooking facilities; there is a complicated catering scheme - a blend of 'meals included with fees' and freedom. You can eat in any of the dining rooms. All University rents include the provision of gas and electricity. One hall, Runnymede, is a completely 'no-smoking' hall.

Costs (1995/96)
Costs range from £42.00 to £63.00 per week according to whether you have a single or shared, catered or self-catered room. Tenancies range from termtime only to 50 weeks of the year.

Private sector
The College Lodgings Officer will help you to find accommodation in your second year; not quite so difficult or so expensive here as in central London. The majority of students find accommodation in neighbouring areas. Staines (two miles away) is usually the furthest you might have to travel. Costs: private sector lodgings £45 to £60 per week (no food).

Mature students

Minimum age 21. You must either have normal qualifications or to have followed a relevant course of study recently. A Science Foundation Year operates in conjunction with five local FE colleges.

NEAR-BY

Your nearest centre is Egham, a commuter town which services its community. Near are the M25, M4 and M3.

The College's setting is idyllic: the soft wooded, greenbelt, expensive commuterlands of Surrey, roll in all directions. Virtually on your doorstep is Windsor Great Park, and beautiful stretches of the Thames, weekending territory for Londoners-at-leisure.

University College London

Gower Street
London WC1E 6BT
Telephone: 0171 387 7050

University Charter date: 1826

UCL is a medium-sized university with around 8,500 full-time undergraduates and 2,600 full-time postgraduates. The College has a single campus in the heart of London's academic quarter. Courses are traditionally structured with a range of options. Assessment is through examination with the possibility of including a dissertation or project work.

All first years can be accommodated in College residences

THE CAMPUS

The College stands on Gower Street, in the academic complex of Bloomsbury, with its quiet squares and rapid access to the central resources of the University, the UL Union, and the British Museum. The main entrance is imposing, in neo-classical style with a domed roof, raised by white stone pillars above a flight of stone steps. Period dignity is aided by a semi-circular, lawn-edged forecourt which recesses the College from the traffic of Gower Street. Behind the gracious facade, however, the College's working territory has a make-do, cluttered, utilitarian air, well-used and rather the worse for wear, suggesting a preoccupation with the quality of what is done, rather than how it is seen to be done.

This is the oldest of London's Colleges, set up in 1829, on a wave of liberal principles, designed to bring education to those hitherto debarred by race, religion or class. Its atmosphere retains the dedication and high principle of its origins. There is a sense of a hard-working, absorbed, study-oriented community.

Lectures open to the general public (and to you) are arranged in lunch-hours or early evening in term time; several each week. Distinguished visiting speakers or College academics offer wide horizons of thought and knowledge.

The College incorporates the Slade School of Fine Art, which brings studio and creative art onto campus.

Cars

Car-parking space is very limited.

Learning Resources

The College **library** contains more than 1,300,000 books in the main library plus eight specialist libraries. Added to this are special stocks of books, accessible to students, deposited and housed here by various learned societies: Folklore, Geologists, London Mathematical, Royal Historical and Royal Statistical. The Science library acts as the central Science library for the Bloomsbury institution of the university. There is reciprocal access to their libraries and doorstep access to the University Library in Senate House. The College has a stock of 500,000 periodicals and subscribes annually to almost 8,000. £1 million a year is spent on keeping this impressive book and periodical stock up to date. Open: 9.30am to 9.00pm weekdays; more limited on Saturdays.

The **Computer Centre** gives instruction and advice on how to use the College's full computer services, and has some courses on video. There are terminals in departments and halls of residence ; 200 work-stations in open access.

A new self-access **Language Centre** (open 8am to 10pm) offers cassettes, videos, computers and satellite television. Languages can be included in your pattern of study, or through self-teaching - improving your present languages or learning a new language from scratch.

Culture on campus

Drama: The College has its own purpose-built theatre (The Bloomsbury) used by touring companies. 10 weeks of the year are reserved for student drama. There is also a Theatre Workshop on site.

Music: The Music Society puts on major works in 'prestigious venues' in London, tours abroad and produces an annual opera.

The Union

Premises are very 'cramped but popular', offering seven bars, coffee bars, games rooms, sports and stationery shops, printing facilities, a hairdressers, a welfare advice centre, meeting and music practice rooms, television and minibuses. Bars offer cheap food to supplement the three large refectories in the main building. The Union has a reasonably large permanent staff.

The Union offers a good range of clubs and societies and organises nightly discos, cabaret and College balls. Performances by live bands are rare. Cultural activities include theatre, arts events and films. There is a newspaper and TV station: Bloomsbury TV.

Sport

On campus are squash courts, a multigym, dojo, fencing, gymnasium and snooker room - and of course ULU facilities are practically on your doorstep. The sports grounds at Shenley, reached by hired coaches, are of a high standard, and are used by Arsenal FC as a practice pitch. There are grass tennis courts here.

Student welfare

The College provides a comprehensive health service based on a well-equipped NHS practice. The Health Centre gives advice as well as looking after your physical well-being. The Union Welfare Office gives advice on rate/rent rebates and social security claims. Legal advice is given by the Union's solicitor.

Careers Service

The UCL Careers Service is part of the University of London Careers Advisory Service and has access to its facilities. The team of advisors gives advice and interviews to students. There is a well-stocked, and comprehensive Careers library. UCL has unique Personal Development and Mentoring Programmes which are supported by major companies. These are included in degree programmes.

Students with special needs

You should write to the Secretary to the Committee for People with Disabilities, Registrar Division before submitting your application, outlining your special needs. New buildings have been designed with disability in mind, but older buildings might pose problems. The College will do its best.

Accommodation

The College can offer 3,750 places plus an allocation of places in University Intercollegiate Halls. All pre-results firm acceptance first-years who apply for accommodation by 31 July and who have not spent time in another London University residence can be accommodated, even those whose home address is in London. You even stand a good chance if you are a late arrival.

There are student houses, some in modern, purpose-built flats, some in converted houses close to the College. They offer self-catering (you can eat in College on weekdays - or not) study-bedrooms. Houses have a variety of facilities: bars, libraries, sports facilities, music rooms.

The College has two halls of residence offering (as do the Intercollegiate Halls) mainly single study-bedrooms, common-rooms and dining halls. Breakfast and evening meals are laid on daily at one hall and on weekdays only (the other). Halls also have small kitchens.

Costs (1995/96)
Full board:
Single room in College hall : cheapest £77.00 x 30 weeks
Shared room in College hall: cheapest £56.00 x 30 weeks
Self-catered
Single place in student house: cheapest £37.45 x 38 weeks
Shared place in student house: cheapest £26.95 x 38 weeks

Private accommodation
Many students can spend a second year in College or University accommodation, but if you want to 'go private', suitable accommodation is passed down the years via internal advertising; or the College has 800 places through 'company lets' or 'head-leasing' arrangements. The College also keeps lists of property and lists of approved agencies.

You could expect to pay, on average, £45 to £60 per week for private sector accommodation, but remember you would have to pay for vacation weeks too

Mature students

Minimum age 21. Those who do not meet the 'general entrance requirement' might be allowed exemption if they can prove 'evidence of competence in the relevant field of study'.

Nursery
The day nursery is run by the College and the Union and looks after children of staff and students (24 under 2's and 12 aged 2 to 5): open between 9am and 5.30 pm. Funds are available if you need help.

IMMEDIATE SURROUNDINGS

University College is in the central London University complex, Bloomsbury. The squares around are quiet. The British Museum on your doorstep is an enormous plus. Your nearest green spaces are Russell Square, Gordon Square and Regents Park. Gower Street, onto which the College opens, runs parallel with Tottenham Court Road, which runs down to Charing Cross Road, crossing Oxford Street: in other words, you are very close to the West End - about fifteen minutes' walk away. Just north of the College are three major railway stations - Euston, King's Cross and St Pancras. Quite what will happen to this area when the planned massive redevelopment begins is open to guesswork. The new British Library is still under construction between St Pancras and Euston stations.

See University of London's entry in this Guide.

Goldsmiths College

New Cross
London
SE14 6NW
Telephone: 0171 692 7171

University Charter date: College founded in 1891 and became part of the University of London in 1904

Goldsmiths' is a small if regarded as a university, but a medium-sized college with 3,500 undergraduate students on full-time programmes and 800 full-time postgraduates on a single campus in south-east London. Courses are broken down into Credit units, largely within a traditional degree structure. Assessment is by a combination of examination and coursework. Goldsmiths can accommodate most first years, unless your home is reasonably close to the College or you apply too close to the start of term.

THE CAMPUS

The College was founded in 1891 as a technical and recreative institute and became part of London University in 1904. Its reputation has for many years rested on the strength of its courses in the arts (creative and performing), education and music. It also offers strong courses in the social sciences. Its most unusual characteristic feature is the very large number of part-time students: this is a College bedded into the heavily populated streets of south-east London and thoroughly integrated with its community. Its doors are open to virtually anyone seeking intellectual training.

'Open' is the key word the College would use about itself and certainly the ambience of its main buildings bears this out. The precinct has the size, shape and feel of an old-style comfortable grammar school. The polished corridors lined by classrooms, the traditional stage-equipped hall where the orchestra was busily rehearsing, the attractively designed dining area with the home comforts of carpet and bright colour: all suggest a friendly, easy-going environment where work can be tackled in good spirit.

The area immediately around, from which it draws much of its student life in the evenings and on Saturdays (there are Saturday schools), is not so appealing. Apart from the colour and energy of weekend markets, the surrounding urban sprawl is undistinguished and unprepossessing to a degree; very little to attract you from your own world, unless you aim for Greenwich and the river, Blackheath or central London. This is, however, a cheaper place from which to enjoy the capital.

Cars

There is very little car-parking space and a car would be more a liability than an asset.

Learning Resources

The purpose-built **library** has over 200,000 volumes and takes more than 1,500 current periodicals. Opening hours: 9.15am to 8.45pm weekdays; 9.15am to 11.45pm Saturdays. You also have access to the University of London library.

The **Computing Service** works with departments to provide basic IT skills training when required.

The **Language Resource Centre** offers open access (9am to 9pm Monday to Thursday; 9am to mid-day Friday) to its range of materials and self-learning aids. Tuition and courses are available in a range of languages - sometimes via evening classes.

Culture on campus

Drama: The drama department regularly stages productions and workshops in its studios and in the George Wood Theatre on campus.

Music and dance: The Great Hall offers good space for frequent public concerts, some by the College's own music department and ensembles, and some by external organisations. The Union organises concerts and discos and there is a Sinfonia orchestra and choir.

The University opened a Caribbean Centre in 1992 which holds a regular programme of seminars, lectures and plays.

The Union

The Union runs bars (cheap beer, cheap food) and organises entertainments throughout the week; lively discos and gigs (very well reviewed), jazz, film and LP nights, and over 100 clubs and societies to join. The Union also offers a launderette, coffee bar, shop and a (weekly) branch of ULU Travel. The Union is open to part-time, as well as full-time students. There are five full-time officers on the executive.

Sport

On site at New Cross are two gymnasia, open-air tennis courts, a practice field with cricket nets and a rugby scrummaging machine. The sports facilities are open to the general public; students use them free of charge. The College's sports grounds are at Sidcup in Kent (8 miles away): soccer, rugby and cricket pitches. You can acquire a 'passport' to use local facilities at reduced cost.

Student welfare

The **medical centre** offers a range of services, and is staffed by three medical officers and support team. The College has **counsellors** for any problems and a student welfare officer. **Chaplains** from various denominations are available for counselling.

Careers Service

Goldsmiths Careers Service is part of the University of London Careers Advisory Service. Through the College, the Service offers: individual appointments with advisors; seminars on choosing and planning a career; computer-assisted careers guidance - PROSPECT-HE included; a regular programme of talks and seminars on particular careers, and on application and interview techniques; 'mock' interviews; and a well-stocked careers library.

Students with special needs

The College has scanning equipment for visually impaired students and a loop system. You should contact Kay Francis at the Registry, who will be able to tell you more about what is on offer.

Accommodation

The College can offer around 1,100 place in College halls, flats and conversions, all within a three mile radius. Goldsmiths can accommodate most first years, unless your home is reasonably close to the College or you apply too close to the beginning of term.

There are 314 partial board places available in two halls in mainly single study-bedrooms, plus common rooms and dining halls. Meals are provided on weekdays and it's self-catering at weekends. Some of the self-catering halls are in modern, purpose-built flats, some in converted houses close to the College (you can eat in College on weekdays - or not). Most accommodation is mixed, but there is one all-female residence.

Most rooms are ensuite; some have computer terminal points. A new residence with 400 ensuite rooms will be available for September 1997.

Costs (1995/96)
single catered: £60.00 per week
single self catered: £45.00 to £50.00 per week
You might be asked for a £20 to £30 common room fee for social activities and amenities.

Private accommodation
You should be able to find a room in the range £45 (excluding fuel) to £55 (including fuel) per week. Cheaper rooms are available if you are prepared to suffer. The College accommodation officer keeps a list of local possibilities. Bedsits are in quite good supply; flats are not.

Mature students

There is a wide range of part-time courses on offer here (part of the fabric of Goldsmiths history). At many levels: from Access courses and certificates/diplomas to undergraduate and postgraduate degrees.

Nursery
There is a nursery on campus, taking up to 20 children (of staff and students) aged between three months and five years, between 8.30am and 5.30pm. Fees are subsidised by the Union and by the College and are kept as reasonable as possible. There is a very long waiting list for the few places which become vacant each year.

IMMEDIATE SURROUNDINGS

The immediate area around Goldsmiths is not particularly promising. But you are very close to Blackheath and to Greenwich. Blackheath is one of London's 'villages' with a good range of eating places and the heath. Greenwich is the home of the Cutty Sark, a tea clipper, and the Gypsy Moth, Sir Francis Chichester's boat. Outside the Royal Observatory is the brass strip marking the Greenwich Meridian. You will be here for the Millennium celebrations.

Otherwise, you are on the southern side of the river, which has an atmosphere suitable for student living. There is room to explore, and pubs, clubs and galleries. On the main line train, you are only 20 minutes out of the city centre.

See University of London's entry in this Guide.

School of Oriental and African Studies

Thornhaugh Street
Russell Square
London WC1H 0XG
Telephone: 0171 637 2388

SOAS is a highly specialised college with excellent facilities. Student population: 1,500 full-time undergraduates and 700 full-time postgraduates. Courses are offered either as single or two-subject degrees and are examined in course units. The School is part of the central University of London complex in Bloomsbury.

The School has a hall of residence with 500 rooms.

THE SCHOOL

SOAS has something of a definition problem generated by its title: one expects to find exclusively a range of language and cultural courses relating to Africa and the exotic lands of the East.

But SOAS has far more to offer than this myopic view suggests. Its concentration of staff specialising in African and Asian affairs is the largest of any university's in the world, and in its specialist areas the School is internationally famous.

Courses range over languages, music, anthropology, economics, law, linguistics, politics, management and business studies etc. Language courses are planned on the assumption that you have no previous knowledge of the language, so the door is wide open to a degree which could launch you into the power world of international politics, diplomacy or business: indeed SOAS actually teaches staff from the Foreign Office, other civil service branches and overseas governments, industry and commerce.

The School occupies two very handsome buildings - one 1970s concrete and glass and very imposing; the other, one of the more dignified examples of 1930s architecture. These are part of London University's massive complex in Bloomsbury, and they stand next to the British Museum and British Library, on the edge of Russell Square.

The Brunei Gallery houses both exhibition and teaching accommodation, and was finished in 1995. The School now has its own hall of residence, about a 15 minute walk away, offering 500 single rooms.

Academic services

The library, imaginatively designed, with an atrium and galleried levels for bookstacks and reading rooms, contains 850,000 volumes and has a national lending function. An interesting feature is the ranging of relevant book collections around 12 specialist seminar libraries, in complex with study/reading rooms and the rooms of library staff expert in each particular area. The library takes 5,000 current periodicals. There is a **computer** suite and students have access to the University's mainframe computer as well as to micros and wordprocessors. There are 20 computer workstations.

Life on Campus

You can join in unusual musical activities here or attend the concerts, workshops and instrumental or vocal training offered at the School and elsewhere in London. Occasional whole-day musical events on particular ethnomusicology themes. SOAS administers jointly with the University a remarkable collection (the Percival David Foundation) of Chinese ceramics (1,500 pieces) and a library of Chinese and other books on Chinese **art** and culture.

Student amenities

A refectory serves lunch; two squash courts in the main building; a sports ground at Greenford (shared with Birkbeck College) and close access to the University of London Union. A range of student clubs and activities.

See The University of London for other aspects of university life and University College's entry for the surrounding area.

Single faculty colleges

COURTAULD INSTITUTE

The Institute is a specialist centre for the history of art. It has moved to Somerset House in the Strand, which gives better space to house its fine collections of works of art, books and manuscripts. The Institute's galleries, well worth a visit, are open to the public.

HEYTHROP COLLEGE

Heythrop is a School of Theology, one of the smallest colleges in London University (145 students). It occupies a fine building in Cavendish Square, only a few minutes' walk from the University of London buildings. Despite proximity to noise and hustle, it remains quiet, calm and relaxing.

Although the College is open to students from all denominations, it is expected to make a specifically Roman Catholic contribution to the study of theology within the University.

JEW'S COLLEGE

Jew's College has a small campus in Hendon: it's student body is fewer than 150 students and its courses concentrate, as its name suggests, on Judaism. Entrance is open to all students who have some prior knowledge of Biblical or Rabbinic literature. The College does offer a foundation year in some circumstances.

ROYAL ACADEMY OF MUSIC

The Academy is on Marylebone Road directly opposite Regent's Park and very close to Madame Tussaud's. It is Britain's senior conservatoire and provides training in all aspects of musical performance. All students must be competent pianists, whatever their first instrument. The Bachelor of Music course, run by the University, can be studied in parallel with performance training. Facilities include an electronic studio, a modern opera theatre and a large concert hall.

ROYAL COLLEGE OF MUSIC

The Royal College of Music is sandwiched between the Albert Hall and Imperial College in South Kensington. Also on your doorstep are the Science Museums, the Victoria and Albert and the Brompton Oratory. The College concentrates on performance, and on the teaching of music, although it does stress that classroom technique is not covered. Facilities include a concert hall, opera theatre and electronic studio.

TRINITY COLLEGE OF MUSIC

Trinity College is just off Wigmore Street on the gracious side of the West End. There are two main courses: one three year diploma, and a four year performer course. You can also be admitted to the University Bachelor of Music course. The College has strong performance links with major venues, including Ronnie Scott's Jazz Club.

ROYAL VETERINARY COLLEGE

The Royal Veterinary College is in Camden Town, within walking distance of Hampstead Heath and Regent's Park (including London Zoo). Its other site is a 595 acre campus for clinical studies at Hawkshead in Hertfordshire. This includes an equine unit and a small animal referral hospital. Your first two years are spent in Camden, and the last three in Hawkshead and the College farm.

You should have experience with animals before you apply.

The College has a population of around 400 students.

WYE COLLEGE

Wye College specialises in the study of agriculture, horticulture and the environment. The College is not in London at all, but in Ashford in Kent - rather more than a bus ride out. In fact, it is 57 miles from the capital, situated amid rolling downland. For 'Escape routes' you might do well to scan the Kent section of this guide. The College campus encompasses farmland, orchards, woodland and gardens. A beautiful place.

All first years can be accommodated.

The student population is multinational, and heavily postgraduate.

SCHOOL OF PHARMACY

The School of Pharmacy is a specialist school with a very low 'mature' population. Unusual. This means you will mix with a small population of students, of the same age, studying the same subject at the same pace, although for an actual pharmacy degree there are links with some medical schools. Pharmacy is not the only degree offered, but the School's courses are interrelated and revolve around a science/medical mix.

The School's site is in Brunswick Square, just south of St Pancras and King's Cross stations. The square is on the edge of Bloomsbury, within walking distance of the West End, close to Senate House and the British Museum.

SCHOOL OF SLAVONIC AND EAST EUROPEAN STUDIES

SSEES is concerned with the social/historical/linguistic/ literary aspects of the USSR and Eastern Europe. This School is also integral with the buildings of the University, indeed takes up part of Senate House.

LONDON'S MEDICAL SCHOOLS

The majority of London's Medical Schools, with the exception of St George's in Tooting, have now been merged with each other and with multi-faculty colleges in the University of London. The number of medical students trained within the University will not change, but if you are interested in studying Medicine in London, you should look at the Imperial, King's, Queen Mary and Westfield and University College's entries.

LONDON'S OTHER UNIVERSITIES

Brunel: University of West London
City University
University of East London
University of Greenwich
London Guildhall University
Middlesex University
University of North London
Roehampton Institute
South Bank University
Thames Valley University
University of Westminster

NB: None of the above universities is a member of The University of London. All exist in complete independence.

Uxbridge
Middlesex
UB8 3PH
Telephone: 01895 274000

University Charter date: 1966

Brunel is a small/medium-sized university with around 7,000 full-time undergraduates and over 1,000 postgraduates. The University now has four campuses: the main campus in Uxbridge, Runnymede, Twickenham and Osterley (the latter two were, until recently, the West London Institute). Degrees are modular: module choices are very controlled; courses have strong core studies with some elective options through which students may choose 'outside' subjects - a language, for example. Some courses are interdisciplinary. Assessment: a mix of coursework and examination.

The University houses all main scheme UCAS candidates based at Uxbridge or Runnymede irrespective of their application/confirmation date.

THE CAMPUS

A year or so ago, Brunel began the process of merging with the West London Institute: this merger will be complete in 1997. The Institute was a result of a number of mergers: the London School of Occupational Therapy, the Rambert School of Ballet and Contemporary Dance and the West Middlesex University Hospital School of Physiotherapy; these courses and the Institute's two campuses are now added to Brunel's range and physical presence. The University now has four campuses, distributed along a corridor west of London, between the M40 and the M3.

Uxbridge

Brunel's flagship campus, purpose built in the 1960s to found the University as one of a group of specialist technological universities created at the time from leading Colleges of Advanced Technology. Students from all campuses may use the facilities here and join in the social and sporting life.

The campus is compact and well planned. The plain 'office block' administration building faces a decorative pond with twin fountains. The campus is not very large, and its flat site could produce visual monotony. But a sunken courtyard, with steps and raised flowerbeds, forms a pleasant centrepiece, and the grouping of buildings, though highly functional, uses spaced lawns, trees, walkways and even car-parks, to good effect. The library, Union, refectory, shops and bank are centrally set.

Around the central area, the other academic buildings are geometrically grouped. Their grey brick panels, concrete structural supports and long horizontals of glass give an illusion of balanced space.

A slightly more domestic ambience is created by the warm brick of the halls of residence, screening the rear of the site and softened by the green verges and winding path of the River Pinn (a small stream). Softer too are the clutch of new buildings at the other end of the campus: the low-rise Social Sciences block and the adjacent Mill Hall - the newest hall of residence. Still regularity of line prevails and gives a coherent sense of harmonious design.

This is a pleasant, functional campus which does not try to avoid the sense of institutional living inherent in such a purpose-built complex whose specific aim is to link academic and commercial/industrial life styles: indeed, Brunel makes a virtue out of a paradox.

Courses here: all those not designated elsewhere.

The Runnymede Campus

Eleven miles south of Uxbridge this campus is set in a beautiful estate of 65 acres overlooking the Thames at historic Runnymede (the Magna Carta was signed here in 1215). New building on this site has been designed to be compatible with the stately original hall: a rambling period building with Gothic touches.

The site is wooded and heavily residential, with playing fields, lawns and gardens, near a peaceful stretch of the river. Halls of residence here are also used by students from the Uxbridge campus. There is a regular University free bus service twice a day between the two sites.

Courses here: the Department of Design and some students from the School of Education (the rest of the School being located at the Twickenham campus)

Twickenham and Osterley Campuses

The two campuses are quite close to each other (two miles or so to traverse) and already share facilities and amenities. For the purposes of this Guide, they can be treated as a single complex.

Both campuses have a mix of older and modern buildings; both are set in green space in very pleasant suburbs of London, within 20 minutes of the city centre. Gordon House (Twickenham) fronts onto the Thames; Lancaster House (Osterley) is close to Osterley Park.

Courses here: Twickenham - Faculty of Arts* (including Diploma courses in Music and Dance) plus professional Studies, Education, Health, Social Work and Sports Science; Osterley: the Business School
*Arts Faculty degree courses likely to transfer to Runnymede in due course.

Cars

Student parking space on all campuses is quite generous.

NB: The University is working towards rationalising and combining resources, services and general infrastructure: you can expect changes. The distance between campuses in practical terms (i.e. West London traffic) will, however, mean that much of your student life will remain campus based.

Learning Resources

The University has **libraries** on all campuses. A total of over 500,000 items and subscriptions to around 2,500 periodicals. Uxbridge and Runnymede are open from Monday to Saturday. The Uxbridge campus library is open on Sunday afternoons for study only.

Your course is likely to have a **computing** element and there are regular courses to introduce new users to the University system. Campuses and some halls of residence are linked to the local area network. Brunel's Computer Centre is open to 8am to midnight on weekdays, reduced hours at weekends. Osterley and Twickenham have terminals available centrally or within departments.

You can opt for a language component in many courses. In addition, classes in French and German are available in the **Language Centre**, leading to a Certificate of Proficiency. In your final year you can take Advanced Professional French or German, which includes an appropriate placement. Self instruction is available in most European languages, and some Middle and Far Eastern languages.

Culture on campus

Drama: Uxbridge has a number of student drama groups The University stages annually a major music/drama production; working under a professional director, you could learn all aspects of theatre technique - from lighting to dance. A 420 seat lecture theatre has a full performing licence. Student and staff-directed productions are staged regularly at Osterley and Twickenham.
Music: The University Chamber Orchestra and the Brunel Singers perform regularly. Tuition is available in all orchestral instruments, piano, guitar and voice. Weekly classes are held for early music, brass and wind ensembles; chamber music is encouraged. Music bursaries are awarded annually. Regular professional concerts on campus in the Recital Room or Council Chamber.
Art: The Arts Centre offers many activities. There are weekly classes in photography, ceramics, painting, drawing and etching, given by visiting professional artists, as well as various weekend courses. Here too are studio facilities for print-making, painting and drawing, and etching. Exhibitions of sculpture, fine art and cartography are held regularly in the Brunel Gallery.

The Union

The large Union building at the centre of the Uxbridge campus has an air of lively efficiency and well-kept spaces. Commercial services are run - not necessarily for profit - by a specially formed co-operative-type company: Brunel SU Services Ltd: The Academy (ents venue), a bar club (the main campus social centre), a snackbar and a fast food restaurant. The six bars on the main site are well used; the Academy Bar doubles as the Academy Nightclub five nights a week, offering regular discos, bands and cabaret. The Union supports around 100 societies and the Community Action Group. Concerts, discos and theatre groups are arranged by the Union's full-time Entertainments Officer.

The Union has its own print room; SU managers help students run the presses. The campus newspaper *Le Nurb* comes out every fortnight. Radio B1000 is entirely student-built and run, and broadcasts for 100 hours a week. There is a purpose-built Information and Advice Centre, staffed by trained advisors to deal with a wide range of problems....and a Nightline.

The Runnymede site has a Union shop and a bar where bands perform and other functions happen regularly. Osterley and Twickenham also have their own facilities, clubs and events.

Sport

Uxbridge and Runnymede campuses: The University sports centre has three main playing areas: the main hall (120 x 70 feet) is marked out for a good range of indoor games, and trampolining; the small hall (100 x 40 feet) provides for more individual activities; and seven squash courts.

The centre also has some special features: the basketball facility has electrically operated backboards, scoreboards and foul panels; retractable bleacher seating for 500 spectators in the main hall adds to the excitement of important events; the weight-training area is one of the best-equipped in the country; the climbing wall, 100 x 25 feet, resembles a natural rock face, is partly constructed from a variety of natural rocks, and is constantly being updated in new material. The wall is now rated by the BMC as one of the best in the country.

Outside is a 100 x 60 metre floodlit training area, surfaced with artificial grass. There are two separate playing-field areas close to the campus. The main site adjacent to the Uxbridge campus has four football, three rugby and three hockey pitches, a cricket square, outdoor nets, two netball courts, six hard courts for tennis and a floodlit grass training area. There is also a new pavilion.

The PE staff organise, coach, encourage and generally promote all sporting activities. Over 30 sports clubs in all. Special coaching is provided in about 20 sports, for which the Union pays. Sports bursaries are awarded annually.

Water sports: the University has a boathouse on the Thames near Runnymede for rowing and canoeing. The Queen Mother Reservoir, seven miles from the campus, is used for dinghy sailing and windsurfing.

Osterley and Twickenham: The Department of Sports Science at Osterley ensures high quality resources and a distinguished record in the small Universities Championships. Facilities include a sports centre large enough for indoor hockey, a gymnasium, weight-training rooms and a multigym; playing fields, an all-weather 400m athletics track and tennis courts. Many outdoor facilities are floodlit.

Student welfare

The Uxbridge Campus Medical Centre houses a general NHS medical practice and sickbay; other campuses offer regular surgeries visited by local doctors and run by nursing sisters. All students may use the medical facilities at Uxbridge. Osterley offers a Sports and Dance Injuries Clinic on campus. Qualified counsellors are based at Uxbridge and Twickenham, with a more limited service at the other sites. The multipurpose **chaplaincy centre** has an ecumenical team of chaplains. The Uxbridge campus has a centre for Muslim prayer.

Careers Service

Careers Offices at Uxbridge and Twickenham offer a good range of support services, either by personal appointments or group sessions.

Students with special needs

A part-time Disabled Students' Adviser gives advice prior to your joining the University and during your course.

Accommodation

The University houses all main scheme UCAS candidates based at Uxbridge or Runnymede irrespective of application/confirmation dates. While most students will have a room in an on-campus hall of residence, very late applicants might be allocated off-campus accommodation.

Uxbridge campus

635 single study/bedrooms with en suite facilities and 710 single study/bedrooms in halls of residence; 645 single study bedrooms in five/six person flats. All accommodation is self-catering. Students can buy lunch and evening meals in the refectory at the centre of the Uxbridge site.

Runnymede campus

There are ten halls on the Runnymede campus housing 480 students. Similar conditions prevail as on the Uxbridge campus, but freshers generally share rooms.

Twickenham and Osterley campuses

Most on-site accommodation (340 places) is available to first years. All private accommodation offered here has been inspected.

Costs (1995/96)

Uxbridge and Runnymede: range from £35.00 to £38.65 for a standard room, to £47.00 ensuite (weekly rent)
Osterley and Twickenham: £48.50 (shared) to £54.50 (single) rents include five main meals (Monday to Friday)

Private accommodation

The University headleases a number of properties to be sublet to students. Most students at Uxbridge live in Hayes, three miles away. A room in the Uxbridge or Twickenham/ Osterley area is likely to cost around £50 per week.

Mature students

You should contact the Admissions Tutor about your chosen course before you apply through UCAS. Brunel has initiated Access courses with a number of FE colleges. A successful completion with appropriate grades will guarantee a place at the University. Credit for prior learning (APL or APEL) can be arranged.

Nursery

The Union runs a nursery for children between the ages of one and five years. A Holiday Club for five to twelve year olds also runs.

THE TOWN

The nearest centres for day-to-day shopping and pubs are Hillingdon, a pleasant 'village', typical of the more affluent commuting communities around London, and Uxbridge, which offers a large modern shopping precinct with a good range of chain stores, a cinema and a nightclub. From Uxbridge you can take the Underground (Metropolitan and peak-hour Piccadilly Line trains) into central London.

Osterley and Twickenham have their own pleasant, upmarket, suburban neighbourhoods with parks and shopping facilities.

ESCAPE ROUTES

Brunel is on the very edge of London's urban sprawl; turning west and north you will rapidly find pretty old villages set in the green and pleasant acres of the Chilterns; to the south is Windsor, its Great Park, and the lovelier stretches of the Thames. Although this is now commuterland, many villages are well-preserved, retaining their quiet, rural charm. This is particularly true of the area surrounding Runnymede: 'life' on this campus revolves around the students. Royal Holloway College is near by.

Communications

Regular **British Rail** services from West Drayton into Paddington Station. Underground from Uxbridge to Baker Street takes 40 minutes. The National Bus Service has a London route which goes right past the University, again giving you easy access to most parts of Britain, and abroad. The **M3**, **M4**, **M40** and **M25** are all nearby. **Heathrow Airport** is only three or four miles away from Brunel, although the University is avoided by all its flightpaths.

Twickenham is on the District or Piccadilly lines or British Rail's North London link line. Osterley is on the Piccadilly Line or from British Rail's line from Waterloo (Isleworth station a short walk away). Both are on London's bus routes.

City University

Northampton Square
London
EC1V 0HB
Telephone: 0171 477 8000

University Charter date: 1966

City is a medium-sizes university with around 8,000 students, half of whom are full-time undergraduates; the rest are postgraduates on full and part-time courses. Undergraduate courses are not modularised; some are offered as joint honours programmes. This is a technological university, where even the Music degree is offered as a BSc. Assessment is by a combination of coursework, group-work and examination. The University has a single campus on the edge of the City of London, with an outpost in Whitechapel housing Nursing and Midwifery.

First years are guaranteed a place in a hall of residence provided that you are a 'firm acceptance' by 15 May and you do not normally live within the traditional GLC boundary of London.

THE CAMPUS

City's name marks its close links with the City (London's commercial, financial and business area): the University's Business School puts the 'close links' into practice, and is actually housed within the Barbican Centre complex; support from the City Livery Companies has provided a modern library and sports centre and a number of bursaries and prizes.

City is in one of London's north-residential areas, which for those of you who don't know the capital means its ambience is urban, houses built in terraces mostly at the turn of the century, town-width roads with heavy traffic... It does not have the grace of inner London, but it does have its own atmosphere: that of a neighbourhood, with the low-key charm of preserved Georgian terraces. The area is well-known for its eating places and its range of art facilities - from fringe theatres to craft galleries. The canal towpath is a quiet walking place, and off the main thoroughfares are quiet squares.

City's main building has quite imposing lines and height, and the main entrance is softened by the trees and grass of Northampton Square, a (very small) pretty space, railed and pavilioned. Inside, staff at the vast reception desk are friendly and helpful, but the spaces are a little daunting and impersonal, efficiently signposted and slightly echoing.

The University has a second site, at Whitechapel, housing Nursing and Midwifery. Apart from this, the buildings and residences are within easy walking distance of each other and within easy reach of the City of London.

Cars

You would be better without a car in London. There is very little space for cars at City.

Learning Resources

The University has two libraries: one on the main campus, the other at the Barbican site. The main **library** seats 450 students (to be increased by 865 places in 1997/98), the Frobisher Crescent Library at the Barbican seats a further 80 readers. The University's total stock is 338,000 items. Opening time: 9am to 9pm Mondays to Thursdays; 9am to 8pm Fridays and 10am to 4pm Saturdays.

There is a Programme Advisory Service from which both advice and documentation are given on how to use the **computing** systems, which include a University-wide network. This provides full internet access, with e-mail and World Wide Webb. Workstations: 360 Unix workstations (IBM compatible). All courses include training in transferable skills, including IT

Language courses, at different levels, are offered to all students at City, free of charge. The classes are for two hours a week and you may have your work assessed if you wish. A Language Resource Centre offers self-study facilities. Courses are available in six European languages, Russian and Japanese.

Culture on campus

Music: There are weekly lunchtime concerts: an hour's performance by professionals in music, dance and theatre. The University orchestra and choir perform on and off campus; a number of smaller ensembles - and a jazz orchestra - also give concerts, and there is an annual three day 'Electroacoustic Festival'. Musical activities are often run jointly with the nearby Guildhall School of Music and Drama.

The university has 16 track recording studios. As well as its high-tech facilities, the Music Department has collections of early keyboard instruments, of Baroque and oriental string and wind instruments and gamelan.

The Union

The new, purpose-built Student Union building in Northampton Square houses a cafe/bar, evening venue, traditional pub, general shop, insurance shop, reception and information area and meeting rooms. Open six days a week.

The Union controls the finance of the bars and shop and runs 43 non-sporting societies. Regular events include discos, band concerts, cabarets, films and black-tie balls. Bars and sports facilities are well used by the public, who may become associate members of the Union. This spreads the revenue net.

There is local community voluntary work and a welfare advisory service which gives practical advice on finances etc. The Union publishes a magazine, *Sin City*, approximately eight times a year, covering student issues plus reviews of local restaurants and entertainments.

Sport

The University's sports grounds are in south London and are shared with King's College. There are facilities for most outdoor sports, including cricket and tennis, on an area of 26 acres in total.

The University has a swimming pool, used for canoeing, water polo and sub aqua, as well as swimming.

The Saddlers' Sports Centre has a fitness suite, sauna and a solarium, squash courts and a multi-sport court, facilities for martial arts and fitness, and a climbing wall and provides a comprehensive programme of recreation and sport for all levels of ability.

The rowing club is based in Chiswick, and if you want to sail or sailboard you can use Queen Mary sailing club.

There are 40 sporting clubs in all.

Student welfare

The **Health Service** is run by two doctors, a dentist and a nursing sister. The Health Centre is open from 9am to 5pm on weekdays, and is run on an appointment system. An ophthalmic service is available through the Department of Optometry and Visual Science. Professional counsellors give advice. The University **chaplaincy** has a Quiet Room on campus and there are three Christian chaplains (Anglican, Roman Catholic and Free Church). One of the University buildings houses a mosque and most major religions have a place of worship in the area.

Careers Service

The Careers and Appointments Service offers group talks and discussions on how to make vocational choices, and on application and interview techniques as well as individual counselling. Regular vacancy bulletins and employer visits.

Students with special needs

The University has a policy and a code of practice to promote opportunities for students with disabilities. You should contact the Disability Liaison Officer for information about the University and its facilities.

Accommodation

The University guarantees a place in one of its modern halls of residence provided that you are a 'firm acceptance' by 15 May, and have applied for accommodation by then. If you are a latecomer, the Accommodation Office keeps a register of private-sector accommodation.

Halls of residence

Finsbury and Heyworth Halls (320 places) are very close to campus (five minutes' walk). Single study/bedrooms in groups of 12 sharing common room with elementary equipment. Grouped around a small courtyard at ground level are common rooms, TV rooms and a bar/common room, linking the two hall blocks. These halls are catered, offering light breakfast and dinner on weekdays, brunch and dinner weekends. You will be allocated to a resident tutor, available for advice.

Walter Sickert Hall has 223 single rooms with ensuite facilities. Self-catering and close to campus. Each room has a telephone, tv and computer point.

Peartree Court (142 places) is adjacent to Finsbury/Heyworth Halls and has self-catering cluster flats housing three to six people in single rooms.

Francis Rowley Court offers flats for a total of 296 students and is a few minutes' walk from campus.

Costs (1995/96)

Finsbury and Heyworth: £74.00 per week x 31 weeks
Francis Rowley Court: £67.00 per week x 48 weeks
Walter Sickert Hall: £69.00 per week x 39 weeks
Peartree Court: £67.00 per week x 39 weeks
Costs include heat, light and hot water.

Private sector

Lists of vacancies are available. The University's Accommodation Office is open from 9am to 5pm weekdays throughout the year. Many students have long journeys from 'home' to campus. In this area rents average £57 to £76 per week excluding bills.

Mature students

The University accepts kitemarked Access courses, Open University credits and professional qualifications as entry qualifications. It also considers an applicant's motivation, employment and life experience.

IMMEDIATE SURROUNDINGS

Within walking distance you have the Barbican Arts Centre, which is the London base of the RSC, and the London Symphony Orchestra and whose cinemas show minority films. To the north of City is Islington with antique shops and some good restaurants. The Islington Arts Factory has exhibitions and performances, and runs workshops on the visual arts and music. At weekends, Camden Markets are alive. The area north west - towards Highgate and Hampstead - has wide open spaces.

See the University of London's Out and About section.

University of East London

Longbridge Road
Dagenham
Essex
RM8 2AS
Telephone: 0181 590 7722

University Charter date: 1992

East London is a medium-sized university with 8,000 undergraduate students on full-time programmes, 450 HND students and 460 full-time postgraduates. The University has two campuses at present - one in Stratford, the other in Barking; a third is under construction in Docklands. Most degree programmes are modularised; many courses have a high proportion of continuous assessment, with some written examinations.

Priority for accommodation is given to students from outside the local area.

THE CAMPUSES

The Stratford Campus

The University occupies part of a very handsome complex built in 1898 to house the Municipal Library, College and Museum. The buildings are solid and gracious. But the University in the main has developed on a site behind its frontage. This offers one of the sudden contrasts often found in east London where relatively comfortable style can turn a corner into neglect. The newer University developments centre on a white six-storey concrete and glass tower, rising from a wider base, and surrounded by temporary teaching units.

Other teaching sites in the Stratford area include Maryland House, behind the railway station (Central Line and British Rail), about a five minute walk from the main buildings. This three/four storey building houses the library and the Students' Union.

Three other teaching outposts: Duncan House (Postgraduate Business and Management), Holbrook Centre (Art and Design) and Greengate House (Architecture and Visual Communication) are each a busride from Maryland House.

The immediate vicinity has quite sharp contrasts. The Municipal buildings and some of the wider avenues nearby have a reassuring, civilised air: streets to the rear are, unfortunately, badly neglected. There are several neighbourhood shopping runs and a larger centre at Stratford and Ilford, a short trip away.

Courses here: Design and Built Environment (except for courses listed at Barking), The Faculty of Science and Health and a BSc course in New Technology.

The Barking Campus

The approach to Barking from Stratford takes you into a more affluent area. The site is set back from, and facing, the A124 - dual-carriageway here, lined with modest semis.

The environment is low-key suburban, fairly heavily built-up and undistinguished. A particularly welcome feature of the setting, therefore, is the expanse of Goodmayes Park immediately behind the campus. The area is very flat, and the A124 very busy.

The University's campus is a complex developed behind a large, three-storey, stone-cased brick building in 1930s style. This is both an administrative and teaching centre. The refectory is on the second floor and is connected to the library by a walkway over low level workshops. Other buildings range in style and age: the newest are three halls of residence. All buildings and their grounds are well-maintained. The Students' Union building and most of the University's sports facilities are on this site.

The precinct is a five-minute bus ride from the centre of Barking which has a British Rail mainline station (15 minutes from London), and from where the District Line will take you (slowly) into London.

Courses here: East London Business School, Technology, Social Sciences, and courses in the Faculty of Design and Built Environment Faculty.

Cars

Ample parking on the Barking Campus.

Learning Resources

Each site has a Learning Resources Centre. The libraries have a total of 300,000 books. 1,200 periodicals are taken: seating for 1,300 readers. Opening times: weekdays to 9pm, Saturday to 5pm. Information Services is responsible for your personal **computing** needs as well as for those of the University: open access suites on the two main campuses. The Flexible Learning Unit for Training and Education runs courses covering a wide range of IT skills. The **Languages Unit**, based at Barking, offers German, French, Spanish and Italian at three entry levels - beginners to advanced with something in between. European and Asian languages are available on a self-teaching basis.

Life on campus

Music: The Music Centre (Barking) has music practice rooms, a collection of instruments for loan or hire and runs classes in piano, singing, guitar and chamber music. It organises a programme of lunchtime concerts on both campuses. There is a chamber music group, a wind band and a university choir. The East London Chorus practise at Stratford and students may audition.

Film: Reels, the film society, shows two films a week on the Barking Campus.

The Union

The Union runs shops, bars, coffee bars and a full range of entertainments - fringe bands, alternative comedians, dances, bar quizzes, fashion shows and gigs. Special celebrations at Christmas and Diwali. It also brings out a magazine. In all, the Union runs over 50 non-sporting clubs and societies. The Union has five sabbatical officers and an Executive Committee with a total of 22 members. Decisions are made at General Meetings attended by all interested students.

Sport

The University has a Recreation and Sports Studies Unit which, with the Students' Union, organises a sports and recreation programme. 25 sports clubs in all.

Most sports facilities are on the Barking campus: a self-contained sports centre: swimming pool, two gymnasia, four tennis courts and a squash court. There is a Fitness Centre which offers resistance training systems and loose weight systems, and sunbed and sauna rooms. Also at Barking: playing fields (hockey, football, rugby, tennis and netball).

The University's main playing fields are at Little Heath, three miles from the Barking Campus and have four football pitches and changing facilities.

Stratford uses its main hall, whenever possible, for some indoor sports and has an additional facility for badminton.

There are weekend and vacation courses for sports not catered for by University facilities.

The Sports Council of the Students' Union organises team and club activities, and the University competes in major team events in the British University Sports Association competitions. The University runs an Injuries Clinic with a resident physiotherapist. Fitness screening assessments are undertaken by the Recreation and Sports Studies Unit.

Student welfare

The main campuses have **Health Centres** with an NHS GP service. Each Centre has a full-time nursing sister and a secretary/receptionist. The **University Welfare Service** offers a comprehensive counselling service to all students. The Union also offers advice and support on problems relating to your studies, or housing or finances. The **chaplaincy** offers pastoral, as well as religious care.

Careers Service

There are Careers Development Centres on the Barking and Stratford campuses, with well-stocked careers libraries. You have access to computer-assisted guidance programmes. There is a specialist careers advisor who works with ethnic minorities.

Students with special needs

Advice and assistance is available from Student Services Some accommodation at Barking has been designed to cope with disability. There is a Braille machine and Akenstone readers in libraries.

Accommodation

University residences

The University has 1,275 places. Priority is given to students from outside the local area. All places are self-catering. There are 508 accommodation places on the Barking campus (groups of six students share facilities). All are single rooms with self-catering facilities. The Romford YMCA has 150 rooms which offer breakfast plus one meal a day, also available to Barking students.

At Stratford the University has 540 places in Park Village, two tower blocks and a few houses on the same site which used to belong to the local council. The site is a 30 minute walk (10 minute busride) from campus. Also serving Stratford: Woodlands Hall in West Ham - 225 places in four room flats in four-storey blocks. This is older style accommodation and cheaper. This is also a 30 minute walk from campus.

Costs (1996/97)

£52.50.00 per week (Barking)

£63.71 per week (Romford YMCA)

£36.00 to £51.00 per week (Stratford) according to facilities.

Private accommodation

There are two Accommodation Offices, one on each campus, which offer help and advice. East London is a relatively cheap area in London to find housing. Rents are from £45-£65 per person for self-catering accommodation excluding bills.

Mature students

The University has a high number of mature students and accepts a range of qualifications. Drop-in evening advice sessions are held on the last Tuesday of most months at the Stratford campus.

The University is a member of the North-East London Access Federation and the Essex Access Consortium. Prior experiential learning will be taken into account in some cases as an entry qualification. Contact the Centre for Access Advice and Continuing Education for details.

Nursery

There are playgroups for two-and -a- half to five-year-olds at both the Stratford and Barking campuses, open to children of staff and students. Places for 68 children.

IMMEDIATE SURROUNDINGS

If you do not already know this area, we suggest that you visit the University sites and look around their environments before deciding to apply. The sense of community is very strong here, which can be a plus. You are within 15 to 20 minutes of the centre of London. Stratford's theatre offers a range of new and interesting drama.

See University of London's Out and About section.

University of Greenwich

Woolwich Campus
Wellington Street
Woolwich
London
SE18 6PF
Telephone: 0181 331 8000

University Charter date: 1992

Greenwich is a medium-sized/large university with 9,200 undergraduate students on full-time programmes, 1,133 HND students and 856 full-time postgraduates. The University has a substantial number of students following Further Education courses and around 3,000 part-timers. Degree programmes are very flexible; modules are groups in 'families.

This is a multi-campus, regional university in south east London and north and west Kent with sites along the south side of the Thames.

The University guarantees accommodation to all new students, in University accommodation or in the private sector

---

THE CAMPUSES

Greenwich is a multi-campus regional university in south east London and north and west Kent. The major campuses are Woolwich (45% of all students), Avery Hill, Dartford and Roehampton. Medway Towns Campus in Chatham houses the School of Earth Sciences. Each campus has University and Student Union provision including union shops, catering outlets and bars. The campuses are not easily connected. Courses are strongly site-based: there has been a number of campus switches recently: do check on where a course which interests you is sited.

Woolwich

The University occupies a large complex centred on a handsome example of 1900s municipal architecture. The 'flagship' building is part of a consistently dignified period group which includes the police station, the old town Baths and the Magistrates' Court. The buildings are in stone and terracotta brick and are very reassuring. The University has added modern block extensions to accommodate the mass of its students (nearly half of them are based here). The academic precinct falls into two halves, split by a very convenient shopping street. A few minutes' walk away is the Thomas Spencer hall of residence with a restaurant and snack bars, open to all students, on its ground floor.

Woolwich has quite a good shopping centre and river ferry, but this was a disappointment (we usually like ferries). The old power station has been converted into the Waterfront Leisure Centre, which offers a wide range of activities from water-fun to fitness and dance, at student concession rates. You can reach London in less than half an hour by train.

Courses here: Science, Technology, part of the Business School, and the School of Humanities

Leaving the town towards the south, you are quickly into parks and commonland. Towards Avery Hill, the road passes through affluent residential areas into open countryside.

Avery Hill

This beautiful campus used to be a teacher training college, and now houses the University's Faculty of Education (Primary, Secondary and FE training), the School of Social Sciences and the Law School. The campus is based on both sides of Avery Hill Park. The impressive gateway and the original buildings are very grand; the newer buildings harmonise with the old in quality of fabric and design; the grounds are landscaped - wide lawns and old trees - and beyond playing fields and a golf course stretch broad acres of open country. Immediately next to the campus is a Winter Garden where tropical hothouses grow exotic things. There is an Arts Centre on campus.

A short bus-ride, or longer walk, away is Eltham High Street, where you can shop, or visit restaurants. Sidcup offers alternative facilities; or Greenwich (see the entry for Goldsmith's); or, inevitably, London - trains run from Eltham every 30 minutes and there is a regular bus service.

Dartford

The Schools of Architecture and Landscape, and Land and Construction Management are based here. The campus is rural and is surrounded by heath and woodland. It is centred on an old and beautiful mansion (built 1817). The newer buildings are not in keeping with this period elegance - but no matter. They serve their own purposes and, in any case, there is enough space and greenery here to survive style mixes. The University has negotiated for a regular bus service to run between the town and the campus. London is 45 minutes away by train. You might find yourself needing taxis for late-night returns.

Dartford is an expanding town close to the M25 and on the very edges of London's eastward sprawl. It offers shopping facilities, parks and a theatre, plus easy access to open countryside.

Medway Towns Campus

The Medway Towns Campus at Chatham, in Kent, is the newest University development. The School of Earth Sciences moved here in the Summer of 1994. The campus is based only one mile from the historic cathedral city of Rochester.

The site of the 'new' campus was, until 1984, part of a major Royal Navy dockyard. It was formerly known as HMS Pembroke - a training base for Royal Navy officers and ratings. The grade II listed military buildings have been converted to a high standard. The new laboratories of the large Earth Science department are alongside the internationally renowned Natural Resources Institute. Usual student facilities are available on campus.

Maidstone (Kings Hill)

A campus will be developed here within the Business Park. At present, a range of services for students and businesses is in place.

Roehampton

A range of Business Studies and Accounting courses are taught here. This campus is close to Richmond Park in west London. The area is very pleasant; the 'better' end of south of the river suburbia. There are three sites in all here within easy walking distance of each other. The Manresa site is a medium-sized 'country house', built in the 1760s, standing in 12 acres. The Downshire House site is another restored 18th century residence with two teaching blocks - there is a campus library and computing facilities. The Mount Clare site has 168 study-bedrooms for students.

Cars

Don't bring a car until you have found out where you will be living and whether you will have anywhere to keep it.

Learning Resources

Overall figures are of little value: your own site matters. There are **libraries** on each site. The book stock totals 400,000 volumes and the libraries take 2,000 current periodicals. There is a Guide available which outlines the services of each library.

Woolwich and Dartford campuses have **Computer Centres**; information is also available from advisory services in the Schools, from the libraries and from academic staff. 1,000 workstations across the campuses.

Languages: there is 'open house' at the language laboratories (Woolwich, Avery Hill, Dartford and Roehampton) which can be used by both staff and students to refresh their languages skills. All study 'pathways' allow for a language component.

The Union

The Union has a number of elected sabbatical officers who manage Union affairs. The Union paper perhaps gives the best indication of Union activity at Greenwich: the events section is dominated by Woolwich and Avery Hill which have an extensive entertainments programme; Roehampton and Dartford have weekly parties/discos. The Medway Towns campus is very new and has relatively few students.

The Union funds around 65 clubs and societies. Each site organises its own Rag Week.

The Union at Woolwich occupies the old (converted!) City Baths. The main hall (the Deep End) is the old main pool and provides a good sized function space. There is a snack bar, two bars, function rooms, Union offices and a shop. Avery Hill Union has a bar and limited venue space; Dartford has two bars and also limited venue space. Three of the campuses have Union shops.

Sport

There are recreation classes with professional tuition in basketball, hockey, ski-ing, golf, squash, aerobics, karate and fitness training.

At Woolwich there is a small sports hall, fitness room and two squash courts.

Avery Hill: two gymnasia as well as soccer, rugby and lacrosse pitches. Also, redgra hockey pitch, grass running track, tennis courts and cricket square.

Dartford: an indoor heated swimming pool and the main sports hall, floodlit tennis and netball courts, grass soccer pitches and a cricket square with synthetic practice nets.

Medway: sports hall with five badminton courts, basketball and weights room.

Roehampton: football, netball and tennis and a snooker room.

Student welfare

There are **medical services** at Dartford, Woolwich and Avery Hill. There is a **counselling service** on each site. Occasionally, counsellors run workshops on stress management, exam anxiety, assertiveness skills... The University **chaplaincy** at Woolwich has two chaplains. There is a prayer room on most campuses, used by different religious groups.

Careers service

The service will help you with letters, applications and interview techniques. You will have access to PROSPECT-HE and the opportunity to have individual interviews. The Job Shop provides information on part-time and vacation work for students.

Students with special needs

Greenwich is affiliated to SKILL and is committed to improving facilities for staff and students with disabilities. You should contact the Disability Adviser in Student Services early, to outline your special needs. There is purpose-built accommodation at the Avery Hill site.

Accommodation

The University guarantees University managed housing to all new students, whose parental homes are more than 20 miles from the place of study, and whose application forms have been received before 31 August.

Student village

The new student village at the Avery Hill campus, provides accommodation and facilities for 1,300 students, with approximately 10% of living space being devoted to students with disabilities. Accommodation is in flats for four or five students, or in maisonettes for six with either a shared bathroom or ensuite facilities. You can apply for a room here whatever your site-base. The village has social facilities, shops, a refectory and a launderette.

Halls of residence

Woolwich: a single hall with 255 places in single study bedrooms with weekday breakfast and evening meals provided. The Patio Restaurant is based on its ground floor. The hall is close to campus and has a squash court and weight-training room, TV room, launderette, and snack making facilities.

Dartford: five halls on campus housing 265 students in single study-bedrooms. Breakfast is provided Monday to Friday and there is a cafeteria for evening meals. There is a free minibus service to Dartford railway station.

Medway: two new halls provide 204 ensuite single rooms organised in flats.

Roehampton: 197 single bedrooms arranged in blocks of 12. The site is adjacent to Richmond Park. Small kitchenettes are provided.

A hall is leased from a housing association in Greenwich which provides a further 116 places.

Costs (1995/96)

single room, self catered: £53.50 - £64.00 x 40 weeks
single room, catered: £66.50 x 33 weeks

Private accommodation

The average cost of a single room is £40 - £45 per week, plus bills. The Accommodation Office maintains a list of lodgings, bedsits and shared houses.

Mature students

About 50% of all undergraduates are 'mature'. The University considers applications with a range of post-school qualifications and runs its own Access courses. Alternatively, Study-Link will tailor an educational programme for you to ease you into a University course. The University runs a School of Post Compulsory Education and Training at its Jewry Street Centre.

Nursery

Three nurseries with a total of 79 places available on the Woolwich campus and at Avery Hill, open to any member of the University who needs childcare. There is also a play-scheme for five to eleven year olds at half-term.

THE CITY / ESCAPE ROUTES

Although the University's title suggests a London-based image, most campuses do not have easy swift access to Central London: trains can be slow and irregular; buses likewise. The campuses are set in very varied surroundings: the entry for Goldsmith's College might be relevant for some centres; Roehampton Institute's local area is, of course, relevant to Greenwich's Roehampton site.

London Guildhall University

Admissions
133, Whitechapel High Street
London E1 7QA
Telephone: 0171 320 1000

University Charter date: 1992

Guildhall is a medium-sized university with 6,500 undergraduate students on full-time programmes, 485 HND students and 500 full-time postgraduates. A majority of students come from the London area. The University has several centres distributed through a reasonably compact area of the City of London. Degrees are modular with a variety of possible 'pathways', including single honours. Guildhall was one of the pioneers of modularisation. Assessment is a mix of coursework and examination.

Degrees offered: business, technology, furniture/interiors

The University's three halls of residence are available to first year students

---

THE CAMPUSES

The University's centres are distributed through a reasonably compact area of the City of London, ranging from Moorgate to Whitechapel; the greatest distance between sites is about one and a half miles. The Bank of England, the Lloyd's Building, the Natwest Tower...massively impressive monuments to money: add to these the Tower of London, St Paul's Cathedral, the Barbican, and you have one of the most impressive settings you could wish. As you move eastwards, however, the environment deteriorates sharply; the short spread accommodates a wide range of style and quality.

Moorgate

You will use a very imposing, stone, turn-of-the-century building with enormous glass doors and a dome crowned by a globe supported by stone cherubs. Very grand. The basement has recently been converted into a refectory and cafe area with a myriad arches and alcoves. Around are high-class shops and business premises, and very close, just off Moorgate itself, is Finsbury Circus with its lovely gardens and bowers of trees, complete with bandstand and sundial and encircled by splendid, tall, period buildings.

At Moorgate there is a Students' Union office, snack bar and bookshop.

Courses here are in the Faculty Business.

Tower Hill

Another very imposing building, set directly opposite the Tower of London with a clear, short space between University and the walls of this piece of national history. The University building, lifted on its concrete block pillars, gives clear views of and access to an extraordinarily beautiful curving terrace of Georgian houses.

Tower Hill building itself, four-storey, dark glass and concrete, is a respectable enough presence. It contains a gymnasium on the top floor, basketball, badminton and a bar. A large refectory looks out onto the Tower. The building has a serious air - students around were talking work; the library was quiet and studious.

Courses here: in the Departments of Computing and Information Systems and Civil Aviation Studies.

Jewry Street

Just off busy Aldgate is another building worthy of comment: this used to be the Sir John Cass School of Science and Technology: rather brooding, grimy, three-storey, turn-of-the-century, complete with bell tower. The small-scale entrance hall has a stained glass memorial window, inscribed 'For Empire, King, Good Faith and Liberty'. No facilities here other than vending machines. Courses here are in Business, Social Sciences and Communications.

Central House

The Sir John Cass Faculty of Art, Design and Manufacture occupies five floors above shops in a concrete and glass block along Whitechapel High Street. The surroundings now are veering towards the seedy, but have the advantage of cheaper shopping. Facilities: library and refectory. Courses: Fine Art, Silversmithing and Jewellery.

Commercial Road

Just around the corner is the Sir John Cass Faculty of Art, Design and Manufacture's second site, in Commercial Road, which, although quite close, sits in an efficient-looking building and its own specialised world. Facilities: various workshops, library, refectory and bar. Courses: Music Technology and Furniture and Interiors.

Calcutta House

Close to Central House and the Students' Union sites. This is one of the University's largest buildings and was refurbished in the early 1990s. Facilities: various laboratories, library, the Fawcett Library of Women's Studies, TV studio and the Student Affairs Department.

Other Buildings

The university uses other buildings: the new Admissions Office is in **Whitechapel High Street** which also houses the University's Fitness Centre (aerobics studio and gym) and the Administrative Centre is in **Houndsditch**.

Cars

Not a good idea at all.

Learning Resources

Each site **library** supports the subjects taught. Altogether, they house 200,000 items including videos, books, software and microforms and take 1,200 periodicals. The University holds an important collection of material on women, including the Suffrage movement in the Fawcett Library. The **Computer Service** has units at all main campuses. At Tower Hill there is a support service for all users. The Service is networked and linked to JANET. You can take a **language module** as part of all courses or for a Certificate of Language Proficiency (German, French or Spanish). There are two new open plan language laboratories and computer-assisted language learning facilities.

The Union

The Union has recently moved into new premises, still near Aldgate station: five storeys, offering two bars (one a venue bar) and a diner. The Union also runs offices, shops and bars at teaching sites within the University. A lively programme of entertainment: band night, new dance music, retro disco (the Timewalk) etc. Very popular. Most nights. The Union Welfare Department works closely with the University. There is a night-line. The Union runs around 56 clubs and societies and produces a regular newspaper.

Sport

The University sports grounds are out at Grove Park in Chigwell and offer rugby, football, cricket and hockey pitches and hard and grass tennis courts. Indoor facilities have already been listed in the campus descriptions. Facilities are also hired from local sports centres.

Student welfare

The University has a full-time Occupational Practice nurse and a visiting Occupational Health physician. **Student counsellors** are available to discuss legal, financial and personal problems. The Student Funding Office helps specifically with money problems. The University has an ecumenical **chaplaincy** which operates within a network of college chaplaincies.

Careers Service

The Careers Office is based at Calcutta House and provides aptitude testing sessions, self-marketing workshops, occupational information seminars, an autumn accountancy recruitment programme, individual guidance interviews and computer-guidance programmes (PROSPECT-HE).

Students with special needs

All buildings (except Jewry Street) have lifts and are accessible to students with mobility problems. There is an active policy to improve access.

Accommodation

There are three halls of residence with a total of 461 places available to first year students: John Bell House is managed by the University; Claredale House and Sir John Cass Hall are managed by an independent housing association: Cass and Claredale Halls of Residence Association Limited.

John Bell House (self-catering and housing 92 students in single study-bedrooms) is approximately half a mile from Aldgate East. There is a second self-catering hall, Claredale House, two miles from campus in Bethnall Green. This houses 267 students in flats for between three and five.

Sir John Cass Hall is a catered hall in Hackney, about three miles away from the University, housing 102 students, all in single study-bedrooms.

Costs (1996/97)

John Bell House: £60 per week for a 40 week period. A deposit of two weeks is payable in advance.

Claredale House: £44 per week, including fuel. A deposit of £150 is payable.

Sir John Cass Hall: £65 per week, including heating and meals. A deposit of £200.

Catered hall place includes breakfast and evening meal on weekdays and brunch at weekends.

Private accommodation

The University will advise you about private sector housing; it is quite expensive and not easy to find, so you should allow a lot of time before you come up for the first session. The average cost for a single room is approximately £55 per week excluding bills. This will be out of central London, so budget for travel costs.

Mature students

The University will consider your application if you are over 21 and have good, relevant experience and are likely to benefit from your chosen course of study. The University welcomes students who have studied on Access courses. Degrees are accessible through part-time study. There is a separate Advice Centre for Bengalis and an interpreter is available. You are likely to have an interview and test.

Nursery

Full- and part-time nurseries at two sites available for children between the ages of two and five years (35 places).

IMMEDIATE SURROUNDINGS

As well as the grand, imposing (and dwarfing) mega-presence of the Banking world and its affluent spin-offs in the City end of the University's territory, the area offers Petticoat Lane (with its famous street market), the London Wall Walk, which follows the medieval line of the city wall from the Tower to the Museum of London, various fine churches, one or two designed by Sir Christopher Wren, and the Barbican Arts Centre.

See also the University of London's Out and About section

Middlesex University

MIDDLESEX UNIVERSITY

White Hart Lane
London
N17 8HR
Telephone: 0181 362 5000

University Charter date: 1992

Middlesex is a large university with 13,500 undergraduate students on full-time programmes, 500 HND students and 1,000 full-time postgraduates. The University also has around 4,000 part-time students. This is a multi-campus university with a total of ten sites scattered widely across three north London boroughs. The two largest centres are Bounds Green and Trent Park, one a converted carpet warehouse, the other a manor house set in its own country park - a University of great contrasts. Degree programmes operate within a flexible modular system, offered either in pre-set patterns or as 'design-your-own' degrees. Assessment methods vary. Many modules are assessed on coursework/project only.

Priority for University owned accommodation is given to first year students.

THE CAMPUSES

Middlesex campuses are scattered widely across three north London boroughs: Barnet, Enfield and Haringey. We did not find travelling between the campuses very easy; most roads in this area are very busy. However, we were very impressed by two factors. One is that the campuses we saw - particularly the larger, but to some extent all - did share a common 'Middlesex' style: the environments were bright, comfortable and well-kept; the students confident, friendly and positively engaged in their worlds. The second was the extent to which travel between the campuses was an accepted and easy part of many courses. The University minibuses must work wonders, and, since the campuses have strong and strongly differentiated 'personalities', this kind of flexibility must be a constant stimulus.

There is not really a main campus, but since Bounds Green is centrally set, and houses much of the University's administration, we shall start there.

Bounds Green

This site, close to the North Circular, used to be a carpet warehouse, no less, and although the shell is smartly designed (aluminium-grey, 'blind' tall walls with a gallery of dark glass) one approaches the entrance with some trepidation. But the shock of entry is one of pleasure.

The University has made a virtue from the irregularity of the original purpose-built design. Bold colours, tough surfaces, metal gantries and steps in primary colour paints; the industrial-style roof lights, the exposed pipes - features which could be harsh - all here form a light, bright, exciting atmosphere with a sense of free movement.

The main feature is the central mall, high, wide and dramatic, where sound both echoes and is stilled into the vague background 'busy' hum. Above are carpeted galleries where teaching rooms have been partitioned off, leaving spaces overlooking the mall wide enough to take study spaces (quietly in use on the late afternoon). Vistas off, into workshop regions, are equally impressive.

There is a Health Centre, a small bookshop and a stationery shop, a multigym and fitness area. Courses here: Engineering and Technology

The neighbourhood

This is very much the edge of inner-London suburbia: parades of shops, acres of housing, not a lot to do. Bounds Green underground station gives you frequent Piccadilly Line access to Central London and University minibuses will take you to other campuses.

The Enfield site

The University's complex, large though it is, is almost entirely concealed behind industrial/warehouse units and urban housing terraces. But again, a private academic world is unexpectedly achieved. There is not much to say about the actual site: a large, seven-storey block, a main block with a small tower; single and two-storey extensions, one or two terrapins, a large car-park.

The complex includes a series of lawned or paved courtyards with a few trees. The library is small and specialised - friendly but quiet enough. Subjects here (The Social Sciences) are classroom taught, so the ambience is very much that of a well-run senior school. There is a fitness room and gym, a reasonably kept bar (dense with smoke), a large refectory and a medical centre.

The neighbourhood

Enfield is a suburban town, in the net of London sprawl. There are a few recreation grounds nearby; Jubilee Park and Enfield playing fields are easy walks away, and there are twin reservoirs, with a sailing club, just over a mile away. Slightly further off are the lovely parks of Enfield Chase and Bushey Hill. The tube station is a bus-ride away.

Hendon (Business School)

The site here is part of a complex of handsome civic buildings (jointly known as the Burroughs), set around an inner-crescent court. The setting is semi-urban; green spaces to the rear have been curtailed by a large new housing estate. The complex includes the Town Hall and Library. Turn-of-the-century buildings. Courses here: Business, Economics and Law.

The neighbourhood

Hendon has pleasant enough, affluent town amenities. Not very far from Hampstead, it has its own parks for immediate greenery, and Hendon Central (about 15 minutes' walk from the University) gives you Northern Line access to London.

Ivy House

The University here occupies a small site in a small corner of a small park (Golders Hill) on the very edge of Hampstead Heath (enormous). Pretty chalet style buildings, lots of trees, a refectory and two studio theatres (one, a wooden hut annexe). Scale and ambience are domestic; the environment beautiful and expensive; the access road very busy. Courses here: Drama and Theatre Studies.

Cat Hill

(Between Barnet and Enfield) A small compact site, just off a busy crossroads (the A110 and A111 well north of the North Circular) but well screened by many trees. The buildings to the front are new and stylish with low, tiled roofs and a hint of pagoda. There is a long, concrete-faced, heavy-lined gallery of design studios to the rear. A small pond in front, the trees and Oakhill Park (bowling green, miniature golf course, bandstand) behind create a very pleasant environment. And Trent Country Park, with the University's campus and social life there, is very close. Courses here: Art and Design

Quicksilver Place

Just over a mile along Bounds Green Road from Bounds Green campus, and close to Wood Green underground station and to Wood Green Hall of Residence. Courses here: Art and Design

Health Studies

Nursing, midwifery and Family Health and Transcultural Healthcare are taught in four London hospitals: Chase Farm, the Royal Free, North Middlesex and the Whittington.

Trent Park

(On the A110 between Barnet and Enfield) This is the photo-call, very beautiful treasure of Middlesex's varied sites. Set in the wide acres of the Country Park, with its golf course, woods, streams and ponds, the old Manor House and its complex of buildings - absorbed or purpose-built - has become the University's country home. This is one of London's special deals: a sense of complete rural calm at the end of the Piccadilly Line.

The mansion is stately and large, with Georgian proportions and spacious, elegant interiors. To the rear is a wide, balustraded terrace overlooking lawns, old trees and the designer pond.

There is a small, open-air swimming pool. The mansion itself is in use for teaching groups, and the grounds are your own territory. The library is particularly pleasant, with splendid views.

So, disadvantages? Well - the newer buildings are not really in keeping: there is a large and ugly sports hall (well shielded by woodland and open to the community as well as to students); the Students' Union building (two-storey glass and panels) looks rather shabby in such a setting. But with so much space and so many trees, the landscape wins.

There were intriguing 'performance' hubbubs coming from the Gubbay Hall, and music students on a terrace were making open-air experimental harmonies.

The site has a strongly domestic atmosphere arising from the style of its setting, the nature of its courses and the presence of residential halls.

The walk out to the main gates, and the Piccadilly underground stations (Oakwood and Cockfosters) both take about 20 minutes, and the roads are lovely, tree-lined, and very well-lit. The minibus runs every 15 minutes between gates and mansion-complex until 1.10am (12.20am on Sundays) so you need not worry about late returns from the city.

Courses here: Education Information Technology, Cultural Studies and Performing Arts.

The London College of Dance

The University has recently merged with the London College of Dance: we have not yet visited.

Tottenham

This site was originally occupied by St Katherines College, a strongly Christian foundation: its large chapel remains. The campus has recently been expanded to include a total of around 800 residential places and facilities for 1,800+ students. There are sports facilities which include an indoor swimming pool. The campus will also house a new Graduate Centre and the national Small Press Centre. Buildings are set in well-kept lawns. This campus is intended to link the University to its local community.

Close to the A10, within walking distance of White Hart Lane, and a short bus ride from Wood Green (Piccadilly Line).

Courses offered are a multi-disciplinary mix of English, Humanities, Business Studies and Law

Cars

A car is not necessary. The University's own inter-site transport is good, as is public transport provision.

Learning Resources

Information and Learning Resources Services oversee libraries (with a total of 400,000 books, 2,200 periodical subscriptions annually and 1,300 study places), Computing and the Language Centres.

Microcomputers on each site are networked. Bounds Green has dozens of specialist laboratories and workshops, including the state-of-the-art Microelectronics Centre for advanced teaching and research.

Open access **Language Centres** provide audio and video teaching facilities in around 30 languages.

Culture on campus

Drama: Middlesex students take part in the Edinburgh and Student Drama Festivals. The University has a number of resident performance arts groups made up of staff and students.

Dance: There is a touring dance company which includes staff and students from all courses (probably Performance Arts courses...check if you are a balletic engineer).

Music: It is possible for you to opt for a Music 'set' in the modular programme which caters for students whose musicianship is a little rusty, or who have not learned 'classical' method and who want to do so.

The Union

Middlesex Union is very active and involved with student welfare and well-being. There is a large number of clubs and societies, a busy entertainment programme and a student newspaper *North Circular* and magazine to keep you up to date with what is going on.

Sport

Middlesex's facilities include a sports dome with three tennis courts, three playing field complexes, three gymnasia (with multigym equipment), two sports halls indoor and outdoor swimming pools. A new sports and fitness centre opened at Hendon in 1996. There is a high-level Tennis Centre: you must have reached County Junior standard or equivalent to benefit, and be on a full-time or part-time course. Coaching is free. (There are professional coaches).

The University competes on regional and national levels.

You do have to pay a fee (around £10 for the academic year) to join the Sports and Recreation Club to use equipment, facilities and transport...this does not seem excessive.

Student welfare

There are **health centres** with regular surgeries on all major sites. The health centres are staffed by full-time nurses and visited each week by local GPs.

The University has a **counselling service** and advisors help with any problems, personal or study-related. The Union provides financial and legal advice and helps students from overseas with any difficulties.

The University has an **ecumenical chaplaincy** which serves both students and staff whatever their religion. The Chaplaincy base is in Tottenham, but serve all campuses.

Careers Service

The service operating from Enfield provides help with career planning, including computerised guidance programmes. Technical, personal and intellectual skills are part of the Enterprise programmes which are integral with all courses. Careers libraries are being set up in new 'Single-stop Student Services Centres' at other campuses.

Students with special needs

There is a co-ordinated policy to ensure that, wherever possible, the university will provide for your needs. The Able Centre gives advice on disability benefits and grants and helps students to get special equipment. A member of the Project's staff will discuss your personal disabilities with you. Get in touch.

Accommodation

Priority is given to first year students for University owned accommodation. 2,400 places in all. Most accommodation is in single-study bedrooms. Most hall places are available specifically to their nearby campus. A free, round-trip minibus operates in the mornings between three sites: Trent Park, Cat Hill and Oakwood Gate.

If you are not placed in a hall of residence you will live in private rented accommodation. The Accommodation Services provide information, advice and addresses before you arrive. All new students are sent a booklet 'Finding Somewhere to Live' to help with your search. You should come up early and be methodical. You may stay in University halls of residence while you look.

You will also be eligible to benefit from the services of a Housing Association in Enfield.

Costs (1994/95)

Halls of residence
Self-catering single room: £44 - £49 (en suite) per week

Private sector
Self-catering or lodgings: from £45 per week
(noticeboards suggest that prices might be higher)

Mature students

The modular degree course structure allows full- or part-time study, which is particularly useful to mature students. The University recognises Access courses; some carry guaranteed entry to courses in the University. Accreditation of Prior Experiential Learning (APEL) is working here, and you can switch in and out of part-time study, 'banking' your credits.

Nursery

The University runs four nurseries. Trent Park ,Enfield, Hendon and Tottenham,

THE CITY / ESCAPE ROUTES

See The University of London's entry in this Guide.

University of North London

166-220 Holloway Road
London
N7 8DB
Telephone: 0171 607 2789

University Charter date: 1992

North London is a medium-sized university with 7,000 undergraduate students on full-time programmes, around 1,000 HND students and 250 full-time postgraduates. The University has a number of sites in a fairly compact area. Degrees are mainly modular, with optional subjects offered within approved schemes. Work experience is arranged for all students, although the onus is on each student to find his/her own placement: there is a Placement Officer attached to each Faculty.

The University guarantees accommodation in one of its (around) 900 places in halls of residence to those full-time first years who live more than 25 miles from the University

---

THE CAMPUSES

University buildings are grouped in a fairly compact area.

Holloway Road (main building)

The original building is unassuming, in brick and stone, with a lower link to a concrete and glass 13-storey tower. Windows are either opaque or very narrow, so there is very little sense of 'outside'. Two new major facilities have been developed alongside the main Tower Building: the Learning Centre - an impressive mirrored glass building which houses the majority of the University's learning resources; and the Benwell Road Block which houses the Humanities Faculty.

This 'campus' is on Holloway Road, an urban High Street, with fast-food takeaways, cheap shops and secondhand furniture out on the pavements.

Courses here: Applied Chemistry, Architecture and Interior Design, Humanities, Electronic and Communications Engineering and Applied Physics, Life Sciences, Polymer Technology, Catering and Nutritional Sciences.

Stapleton House

...Across the road. This is a new block in brick and white facing, rising clean and smart above a used-car saleroom. The Business School is housed here, and generates an efficient, though noisy, atmosphere.

Eden Grove

Also opposite the Main building is Eden Grove, another new block, rather quieter since it is just down a side road.

Courses here: Computing and Mathematical Science.

Ladbroke House

Half a mile from the main building, but equally close to Drayton Park is Ladbroke House. Here is the beginning of genteel Highbury/Islington, with its beautiful Georgian and Victorian terraces. The University's building here is a large, functional teaching block, with a coffee bar and refectory, a games room and television room.

Courses here: Geography, Health Studies, Information Studies, Law, Policy Studies, Social Research, Social Work, Environmental Studies, Urban Studies, Communication and Cultural Studies, and Politics.

Learning Resources

The **Learning Resource Centre** on Holloway Road brings together the University's main resources under one roof: the main book and journal collections, open access computing and audiovisual facilities. Similar facilities available at Ladbroke House. **IT centres** throughout the University are networked and allow access to the Internet. The Learning Resources Centre houses the **Language Centre**: its language laboratories are open to all students taking advantage of the Open Language Programme - every student may include a language option.

The Union

A new, self-contained Student Centre in the Tower Building houses the Students' Union offices, bars, shops and welfare facilities. It will also offer a range of social and recreational facilities including the venue for music, clubnights, the Fresher's Ball and other events. The Union runs around 80 clubs and societies, arranges regular dances and concerts and publishes a student newsletter - *FUSE*.

Sport

The University has two gymnasia, a sports hall, a dance studio and fitness room, all sited either in the Tower Building or the Benwell Road Block. These provide the venues for a wide-ranging recreational programme from aerobics to yoga. There are arrangements with local sports centres, squash clubs and other educational establishments to provide facilities for outdoor sports, including canoeing and polo.

Student welfare

The Student Services Centre brings together the University's advisers and counsellors, including the accommodation office, dyslexia support service, disabled students co-ordinator, chaplaincy and childcare co-ordinator. It holds an extensive range of information from journals to CD-ROMs covering careers and other advice and publishes information sheets and a Student Guide covering topics of concern.

Careers Service

The Service offers workshops given by careers staff and employers, as well as presentations, careers fairs and interactive computer guidance.

Students with special needs

Students with physical disabilities should contact Student Services before the beginning of the course. The University has a Kurzweil Reading Edge machine. Study skills are built into the first level of many courses. Writing, communication, Maths and study skills workshops are available.

Accommodation

The University guarantees accommodation in one of its (around) 850 places in halls of residence to those full-time first years who live more than 25 miles from the University and who have accepted a place by mid-August. The majority of students are housed in the private sector. The Accommodation Office publishes daily lists of vacancies and has contacts with landlords.

Halls of residence and University flats

The University has two halls and a block of self-catering flats. Meals: at Tufnell Park Hall a main meal is provided and paid for on a daily basis; at James Leicester Hall the daily main meal is included in your hall fee. Flats are leased for 52 weeks and are fully self-catered - fuel bills are not included in your rent.

University house

Carleton Grange is a converted Victorian house, taking 60 students in single or shared rooms with shared kitchen and bathroom. Leases do not include the summer vacation; bedding is not provided; you must clean your own room.

Costs (1995/96)

Between £46.00 (shared) to £61.00 per week, including heat and light.

Private sector accommodation

You are offered three free nights in a hall of residence to give you time to search for a room. Private accommodation is not inspected so you should be take care and heed the advice given in the introduction to this book. Typically, rents range from £50 to £70 per week for a single room, excluding bills, depending on quality and the degree of self-catering (or not).

Mature students

The University accepts a range of non-standard qualifications for entry. Access courses are recommended for some disciplines; the University runs its own Access courses at local colleges. Drop-in advice sessions are available for prospective students.

Nursery

The University has three nurseries which take a total of 60 children aged between two and five years. There are playgroups for children aged five to eleven during school half-term holidays.

THE CITY/ESCAPE ROUTES

See London University's entry in this Guide.

Roehampton Institute

Senate House
Roehampton Lane
London
SW15 5PU
Telephone: 081 392 3000

Roehampton has around 5,000 undergraduate students on full-time programmes and 500 full-time postgraduates. Degrees are modularised with many Combined honours options. Assessment is a mix of coursework and examination. You would gain a University of Surrey degree. The Institute has a main campus on Roehampton Lane occupied by three of its constituent colleges (by the 1997 intake) and has one 'outposted' college which is a 15 minute walk away.

60% of first years live in College: rooms are allocated on a first come, first served basis.

THE CAMPUS

Roehampton Institute has a well-developed collegiate structure; the Institute is a federation of colleges, each with a long and distinct history; each originally set up as providers of teacher training, following very different philosophies. You apply to a College, rather than just to the Institute, and should spend time in considering which of the four would suit you best. By 1997, three of the colleges will form a single campus on Roehampton Lane; the fourth, Whitelands, is a 15 minute walk away near Putney Heath.

Digby Stuart College
Digby Stuart was founded in 1874 and became a constituent member of Roehampton Institute in 1975. The College is set in its own grounds on Roehampton Lane and backing onto Roehampton golf course. The main College buildings are redbrick, but are more utilitarian than the usual excesses of the late 19th century. They border two sides of a lawned area which runs down to six all-weather tennis courts and a small pond. The main building includes the administrative centre, the staff/student bar and the quiet library. The Union Building is a two storey '60s block and houses a drama studio, common rooms, a refectory and snack bar. Also on site, halls of residence.

Froebel Institute College
The Froebel Institute was founded in 1892 by the followers of the German educationalist Friedrich Froebel. It also became a constituent member of Roehampton Institute in 1975 and is next-door to Digby Stuart. The College's main building is a white Georgian mansion house, gracious and beautiful, set in equally gracious and beautiful grounds. Newer buildings are low-rise and well-spaced, with well-kept connecting paths.

The Gardens are both formal and wild: playing fields and a small lake with noisy geese. On campus are halls of residence, a number of common rooms, a dining hall, snack bar and a Student's Union building.

Southlands College
Southlands College, founded in 1872, will be relocated to Roehampton Lane to a site next door to Digby Stuart. All accommodation will be purpose-built. The artist's impressions are impressive.

Whitelands College
Whitelands College is a 15 minute walk away, near Putney Heath. The College is housed in a listed, purpose-built, neo-Byzantine building designed by Giles Gilbert Scott (a famous Victorian architect), set in twelve acres of grounds. There are windows by Burne Jones and some work by William Morris (two more famous Victorians), taken from the College's original building, Whitelands House in Chelsea. This is a very pleasant working environment: carpeted corridors and views over lawns. As well as teaching rooms, the main building contains residential areas and a refectory and coffee bar. The Union has a separate building nearby.

Planned for Whitelands: an all-weather, multipurpose sports area and a new hall of residence.

Car parking
Students are asked not to bring their cars.

Learning Resources

By 1997, there will be two new Library and Learning Resources Centres, one on Roehampton Lane, the other at Whitelands. These will house the Institute's book collection, will offer increased study space, have computerised access to library facilities and give access to the internet and world wide web.

Culture on campus

Student life is generated through the Colleges. Southlands is, traditionally, the musical College and has both a Steinway grand piano and an Allen computer organ. Student choirs are based here. Froebel Institute has a dance theatre and studio. Digby Stuart has drama facilities, used both by drama students and the Drama Society. All students have access to all amenities.

The Union

Each College has its own Union facilities: Digby Stuart's Union building has administration provision, meeting rooms, a coffee and snack bar and a shop; Froebel Institute' Union building houses a shop, lounge areas and Union offices; Whitelands has a games room, bar, offices and a small club area; no information as yet on the new Southlands facilities. Entertainments are diverse, as are clubs and societies. The Unions hold a number of combined events.

Sport

Sports facilities are housed in the Colleges and their grounds. Digby Stuart has playing fields, a gymnasium and six all-weather tennis courts and Froebel Institute offers playing fields and indoor facilities for basketball, volleyball and badminton. The Colleges have teams who compete locally and in intercollegiate matches. Sports are organised through the Roehampton Recreation Council, which includes the Institute's Recreation Officer. Presently, 22 clubs available.

Student welfare

Medical facilities are available in each College. The Institute has a confidential counselling service. The Careers Service offers information on vacation work, 'Insight Programmes' and work experience schemes. Religion and chaplaincy services vary from College to College. Each College's foundations are in a religious or philosophical movement, and each is very different. All now are ecumenical in approach.

Accommodation

Halls of residence, or other Institute accommodation, are on each College site: at present, the Institute can house 60% of first years in college halls. Most halls are mixed, all are catered. A new 140 place, self-catering complex opened in 1996 at Digby Stuart and more new accommodation will be available by 1997 at Digby Stuart, Southlands and Whitelands. The Institute's Accommodation Office has lists of lodgings and flats.

Costs (1995/96)
Hall of residence
catered: single   £70 per week
self catering: £57 to £60 per week
Private sector:
Self-catered room in a shared house £55 per week plus bills

Mature students

Students should be able to show (in any way) evidence that they could cope with and benefit from a degree programme. Most degree programmes are available on a flexible part-time basis.

Nursery
The Institute's nursery takes a limited number of children between the ages of five months and five years. It is sited both in the Froebel Institute and Queen Mary's University Hospital, and is shared with the Local Authority.

Local area

Roehampton Institute's Colleges lie within a fairly small area around Putney Heath, near to Wimbledon Common, south of the Thames - Hampton Court, Richmond Park, riverside walks...all easily accessible. Putney offers probably the best scope for eating out. Central London and the West End are easily accessible by tube, so look at the entry for the University of London: you have the benefits without the stresses.

South Bank University

Borough Road
London SE1 0AA
Telephone: 0171 928 8989.

University Charter date: 1992

South Bank is a medium-sized/large university with a total of 19,000 students on full and part-time courses. The campus is, effectively, a single site about a mile from the cultural centre of the South Bank complex. Courses here are modular, sometimes assessed wholly by coursework, sometimes by a mix of exams and continuous assessment.

Priority for accommodation is given to applicants who live furthest away from campus.

THE CAMPUS

South Bank University comes quite close to being single campus, since its presence is massively centred on the large complex of buildings in London Road/Borough Road, which is an integral part of that idiosyncratically named area, the Elephant and Castle. The size and quality of the campus and its buildings, so close to (about a mile from) the country's cultural mecca at the South Bank, suggests solid achievement and an ambitious future. The University does have one significant outpost: at Wandsworth Road, about one and a half miles away, where the Faculty of the Built Environment has a smart, purpose-built site. The Wandsworth Road site is big enough to have its own Students' Union offices, sports hall and gymnasium, but all centres are near enough for you to relate to the London/Borough Road campus.

The main campus

Technically, London Road and Borough Road are separate sites, but they achieve such a sense of compact development that intervening 'outsider' buildings can be ignored. Many of the buildings are new or very recent. They balance well the original brick building, dating from the 1890s, with its towering stone pillars and imposing facade. A few other period buildings nearby have been drawn into the academic net, and some of the older campus buildings are dour, in aged concrete and glass blocks. The strongest notes, however, are struck by the new: dark brick trimmed with red or bright green paint, or red-tiled surfaces with dark glass. The Technopark (set up as an independent, small business-promoting enterprise by the University with the Prudential Corporation) is integral with the campus. The new buildings cut smart, distinguished lines into the urban housing blocks and tower flats of the Elephant and Castle.

The Students' Union occupies a splendid building, opened in September 1990, with surfaces designed to withstand student wear and tear. It certainly looks very good at present and generates a friendly community atmosphere. Its bar, the Tavern, is comfortable; the Snug next door is non-smoking.

You are within a two-minute dash (if you can negotiate streets and subways) of the neon joke-pink painted Elephant and Castle shopping precinct: a covered emporium with a range of shops and stalls, and a market atmosphere. The area is heavily urban and drab (apart from the University), with a lot of unattractive post-war development. There is an occasional fine resonance from period terraces of houses, or tops of shops. The area south of the river has streets of good restaurants, and to the west is the up-and-coming yuppidom of Brixton with its winebars. The most important thing about the campus's position is that you are in a cheaper part of London (never been fashionable here), which has a lot to commend it.

You are also within walking distance of the Festival Hall and South Bank centres (three [National] theatres, three concert halls, a major art gallery, the National Film Theatre and the Museum of the Moving Image): coffee bars, free occasional music, book and music shops - there is a regular secondhand book 'market' along the Embankment. A civilised place to meet friends.

Just across the Thames, another ten minutes' walk or so away, are the Houses of Parliament and Westminster Abbey...and about the same energy, across Lambeth instead of Westminster Bridge, will take you to the Tate Gallery, with its national art treasures.

Redwood College...

...has recently been integrated with the University. The College is based in two hospitals in Romford (Essex) and Leytonstone (East London). Courses in health and social care are run here.

Learning Resources

There are two main **libraries** in the University. The Perry Library at the main campus has space for 200,000 volumes and 1,000 study places; Wandsworth Road has 60,000 volumes and 300 study places. There are specialist collections in education, law and computing, bringing the total book stock to 300,000. There are 29,000 volumes of periodicals. You will be encouraged to use the computing network while you are here. The Built Environment Library has the largest single collection in the country in its subject area, and houses an information centre for Construction.

The Learning Resources Centre accommodate 600; you can explore electronically delivered learning materials. All sites are networked.

The **Language Centre** is available to all students for self-study. In addition to formal language degrees modules, language 'pathways' are being offered in an increasing range of courses.

The Union

There are Union offices on Keyworth Street (between Borough Road and London Road) and at Wandsworth Road. The Keyworth Street site is the Union's headquarters and has the main entertainments venues - the Void for discos and parties and the Arc, a large, club-type venue with 1,000 capacity. Here also are three bars, three shops, a recreation room and a student common room The Union funds 22 non-sporting societies. The Welfare Unit gives advice on childcare, housing and many other issues. There is a fortnightly newspaper.

Sport

The University's sports grounds are at Turney Road in Dulwich and cover 21 acres, have a pavilion, a large central hall, changing rooms and a licensed bar. In the winter this area offers five soccer and rugby pitches, and two hockey. In summer, it becomes three active cricket tables, including three artificial wickets.

The main sports hall is on London Road. There is also a gymnasium here with two retractable squash courts and two fitness suites. The Wandsworth Road facilities are shared with the Vauxhall College of Building.

There are around 30 sports clubs. The University competes in UAU national and regional competitions and has a programme of 'internal' events.

Student welfare

The **health unit** has two resident nurses to deal with occasional sickness and a limited back-up service from local doctors. You should register with a doctor near to where you live.

The University has a counselling and advisory service offering advice on finance, grants etc., and help with personal or study-related problems. Two **chaplains,** one Anglican and one Catholic and a prayer-room for Muslim students.

Careers Service

Staff here help with application forms, interview techniques and self-presentation. There is a programme of special events, workshops and presentations.

Students with special needs

The University advises early discussion with the Director of your chosen course who can tell you what learning aids are already available or can be provided. You can also contact Student Services. Six rooms in McLaren hall of residence have been converted for mobility impaired students.

Accommodation

1,100 places in halls of residence; all are self-catering; all are new/recently refurbished and all are managed by 24 hour security staff. Overall not many places in ratio to the number of its students. Priority is given to international students, first years from outside Central London and final year students. The three halls of residence are within ten minutes' walk of the main campus.

The student housing office offers lists of vacancies. You are in an area of London where there are a lot of younger people who are happy to share their living space.

Costs (1995/96)

Halls of residence: £55.00 to £66.00 per week (including heat and light)

Private sector accommodation averages £50 per week.

Mature students

There is a special handbook for mature students available at the beginning of your course. Foundation years offer a bridge into higher education studies. HND courses also provide a pathway to degree status if you do not match pre-entry requirements in terms of qualifications or prior experiential learning. Foundation years presently qualify for a mandatory LEA award (grant).

Nursery

A nursery receives children aged between six months and five years of both staff and students. Fees are means tested.

THE CITY/ESCAPE ROUTES

See the University of London's entry in this Guide.

Thames Valley University

St Mary's Road
Ealing
London W5 5RF
Telephone: 0181 579 5000

University Charter date: 1992

Thames Valley is a medium-sized/large university with 11,500 full-time and 12,500 part-time students following undergraduate, HND, further education and postgraduate courses. The University has two main campuses: one in Ealing and one in Slough. 80% of the student population comes from either one of these two areas. Undergraduate courses are modularised within wide choice bands.

The University does not have its own accommodation.

THE CAMPUS

Ealing College of Higher Education joined with the Thames Valley College (Slough), the London School of Music and Queen Charlotte's College early in 1992, just in time to become a university. Sites have been rationalised, and this is now largely a two-campus University: Ealing and Slough (16 miles apart, along the M4). A free minibus for students and staff shuttles between the two main sites.

Ealing campus

Ealing, in terms of square metres, is not a large campus. The main block, on one of Ealing's main roads, is typical of early 1960s 'technical college' building with wide steps concrete and a ramp leading up to a large, functional reception area from a short drive. Inside, classrooms run off corridors and staircases.

Renovation of the old Student Services building and conversion of lecture halls into bars has created a sizeable Students' Union with its own court area. Student Services (Accommodation, Health Care and Careers) are now housed in semipermanent prefabricated units.

On the other side of the car park, which is small, is the Learning Resource Centre. This new block is very pleasant and includes the library whose atmosphere is one of friendly efficiency. There are polite, but firm, notices about noise control - and they appear to have worked. The interiors are light and comfortable. The Centre also includes learning resources such as computers, audiovisual and electronic information services as well as teaching and group learning facilities.

Grove House, a short walk away, a very smart new building, houses part of the School of European and International Studies. The yellow brick 'tower' occupies a restricted plot on a side street; inside are carpets and smart reception areas, with a businesslike atmosphere.

Vestry Hall houses the University's music studios. The building used to be a primary school: you can still see the old playground, now covered with tarmac.

Ealing itself is a pleasant suburb of London, very leafy and very much its own community. The housing is predominantly late Victorian, with streets of well-kept terraces and semis, and - nearer Ealing Common - larger detached houses set in gardens: London without stress.

Slough campus

A short walk from the station this compact campus consists of predominantly 1960s glass and panel blocks. Surrounding smart modern office blocks accentuate the lack of style of the campus buildings; but, to be fair, there's not much you can do about structures inherited from this decade.

Some of the blocks are several storeys high and overlook the busy roads that bisect the centre of town. Traffic noise is intrusive. The campus has its own library and gymnasium, and a purpose-built Student Union and hall. A new Learning Resources Centre is now open.

The University has links with its local communities, schools and colleges: amenities are open to the public.

Cars

Ealing: very limited parking on campus; Slough: permit parking only, 158 places.

Learning Resources

The Learning Resources Centre at Ealing is open six days a week and contains various multimedia resources. A total of 180,000 volumes, 1,500 periodicals and 650 study places. The new LRC at Slough now houses the campus' book collection (65,000 volumes).

The Ealing campus has a **Computer Centre** whose main computers support 250 interactive terminals. Students are encouraged to take part in computing workshops; practical computing is an essential part of the University's courses.

The prestigious Language Centre is sited at Ealing; this used to be the National Centre for computer Aided Language Learning. There are multimedia self-access **language** laboratories and satellite television viewing laboratories at both campuses.

Culture on campus

The two campuses offer completely different lifestyles. *Music*: Ealing: a number of musical activities on offer - a College Choir and regular evening and lunchtime concerts. The London College of Music gives instrumental and theory classes and holds concerts, open to the public, at the Watermans Art Centre - a community amenity.

The Union

The Union a common room with pool tables and games machines, an entertainments hall, gym facilities, shop, two bars and a cafe. The Union, as well as financing the range of clubs and societies runs regular social events (discos, bands, theatre and cabaret).

The Union at Slough has its own, purpose-built premises which house a snack bar, two licensed bars (one more upmarket than the other) and the student shop. There is a regular entertainments programme. A women's minibus service runs late at night. For large events (usually held at Ealing) the Union provides a bus service for all.

Sport

There are two fitness centres: at Slough a major heavy-duty gym and at Ealing a smaller gym. The University also hires local facilities for the wider range of sports.

Student welfare

There is a **health service** on each main site and the University doctor visits Ealing campus four times a week. You are advised to register with a GP on arrival. The University has a professional **counselling service** which runs classes in stress management, relaxation and exam preparation. The University has three part-time, visiting **chaplains**: Church of England, Roman Catholic and Jewish.

Careers Service
The Service runs ability tests, computerised guidance programmes and occupational interest inventories. The University has its own employment placement service and runs TEMPS, a part-time job agency for students.

Students with special needs
A Guide to Facilities and Sources of Help for Disabled Students at Ealing is available from the Students Administrative Services. The Learning Resources Centres on each campus are equipped for a range students with disabilities.

Accommodation

The University does not have its own accommodation. The Accommodation Office is very helpful and will send lists of private accommodation to you. Both host communities have a good range of flats and bedsits. Prices range between £50 and £59 per week plus bills for a room in a shared house.

Mature students

The University makes no distinction between 'standard' (A-level) and 'non-standard' applicants and decides entry qualifications on 'equivalent' merit, rather than having strict examination entry requirements. All non-standard applicants are interviewed.

Nursery
The Ealing campus runs a creche during school half-terms only, for children between the ages of 4 and 12 years.

LOCAL AREAS

Both Ealing and Slough are quite substantial towns, with a good range of shopping facilities; in the case of Ealing, the ambience is up-market. This was, and to some extent remains, one of London's more gracious areas, far enough out to have its own identity. Tree-lined avenues of Victorian villas, today sometimes run-down and converted to flats/bedsits, trail, nevertheless, the style of another age.

Slough has a less salubrious image, but has quite a good shopping centre. Its surrounding area is covered in the **Reading** section of this Guide.

Both towns relate strongly to London, and you will be able to take advantage of this proximity.

Communications

Both are on/near the M4, and Ealing is also close to the M25, giving access to the country's motorway network. London's airports are close too, and both have access to Intercity rail-links (Slough more easily than Ealing).

University of Westminster

309 Regents Street
London
W1R 8AL
Telephone: 071 911 5000

University Charter date: 1992

Westminster is a medium-sized/large university with 16,000 undergraduates and 3,000 postgraduates, more than half of whom are part-time. The University has a number of campuses, most in central London; one in Harrow. Degrees are modular, offered in single, combined and joint honours programmes. Assessment is a mix of coursework and examination as appropriate.

Priority for accommodation is given to students coming from over 35 miles outside London.

THE CAMPUSES

With the exception of Harrow campus, all the University's sites are in the central London area, within fifteen minutes' walk from the facilities of the Regent Street main building. This is one of London's pivotal central points: main shopping streets, its most famous squares and circuses, the heart of London University, the home-base of the BBC, Hyde Park...the list goes on. A very rich environment for your student years. Because the scatter of buildings is reasonably cohesive, it will be very easy for you to meet a full range of fellow students.

Regent Street
The University's best known original, large, imposing building, opened in 1912, occupies a hub-point in this very hub of London. The spaces of the entrance foyer are dignified, marble pillars and floors and decorated ceilings. The interiors have been undergoing redevelopment: new teaching rooms, the development of the old cinema into a 420 seat auditorium and the refurbishing of the recreational areas was completed in August 1994. Perhaps the most spectacular and eccentric feature is the creation of a cafe in the pool-well of the old basement swimming pool!

Beyond and around the main building in a wide semicircle is a cluster of academic buildings, none more than a few minutes' walk away. The large and modern, block occupied by the Faculty of Engineering and Science is tiered, with narrow balcony spaces. Cantilevered above its sociable foyer, it generates an atmosphere of great energy. The Telecom Tower looms immediately overhead.

The library, in Riding House Street, is a recently built four-floor block - smart and neat; the Faculty of Business, Management and Social Studies is in a five-story office-style block...In fact, the University has kept its expansion well under the wings of Regent Street.

The main Students' Union building, in Bolsover Street, is a six-floor modern block (glass and blue panels): welfare, careers, health, plus a games room and bar.

The Euston Centre
The School of Languages occupies seven floors of a section of this very large new complex - lecture theatre in the basement, pleasant library spaces on the first floor. The atmosphere is calm and competent. Just behind is a small, quiet tree-set court, where you can get very good coffee in the Camden Institute.

Marylebone Campus
This massive complex came as a real surprise, forming, as it does, a mini-campus apart. It sits directly opposite the Baker Street underground station, the Planetarium and a Cannon two-screen cinema. Here are the Faculty of the Environment, the University's London Management Centre and a 21-floor tower block hall of residence. The buildings are solid and imposing, with an inner sculpture court. Regent's Park is a two minute walk away.

Holborn
The library and Information Technology Centre occupies a small stone building very close to the Holborn tube station. A three minute walk away is Red Lion Square, where the Law Faculty occupies floors four to eleven in a plain but impressive block. Very close to you here is Lincoln's Inn Fields (one of London's surprise gifts of green and shady space) and the city's legal acres.

Harrow campus
This site is quite a long and trying drive out. The '60s seven-storey block, in brick, glass and brown panels has been extensively redeveloped. Teaching and research facilities, a new library and information resource centre, computing, a self-access language room, bar, food court, shops and an open air performance space are all now on-site.

A railway line forms one boundary of the site; the grounds of a hospital another. On campus are a sports hall and playing fields. The College Hall seats 480 and is used for drama, music and other activities.

The School of Communication is based here. Courses in Design and Media, Engineering, Computing, Social Sciences and Harrow Business School.

Harrow itself has a large shopping centre, with some high-quality new developments. The town has its own community life but is close enough to London for you to benefit fully from capital-city culture.

Learning Resources

The University has an integrated system of **libraries** serving all faculties. Each of the six site libraries has essential books for the subjects it serves. You can use all libraries. Libraries are open late on weekdays and for shorter periods at the weekend. All major sites are linked into the **computer network** with access to the Internet. There are three Service Centres in all for computing and audio-visual support. 500 terminals over all sites. The University has a Languages for All programme; a foreign language may be an elective module in all courses - 26 languages on offer from beginner to advanced levels. Polymath is also available as an elective module and aims to make mathematics interesting and enjoyable.

The Union

The main Union building is in Bolsover Street; all sites have Union offices. The Bolsover bar offers entertainments six nights and three afternoons a week. Space is hired for larger events. The Union supports a range of activities, including around 25 clubs and societies and runs a shop. The fortnightly magazine, *The Smoke*, is distributed to all students. The Welfare Office is staffed by trained advisors and is supported by the Law Department. Six sabbatical officers in all.

The SU building at the Harrow site has a bar and hall which is used for occasional big events.

Sport

Regent Street has a gymnasium, conditioning room, sauna, solarium, rifle range, billiards room and two other recreational rooms; Marylebone has a small fitness room; and at Harrow, a sports hall, 2 rugby and 2 soccer pitches and a cricket square.

The sports grounds at Chiswick have five hockey, two rugby, one mini-rugby, one dual soccer/rugby and five soccer pitches; four cricket squares, 13 grass tennis courts and 8 all-weather courts (six of which double for netball), an athletics stadium, restaurant, bar, social room and changing facilities. The boathouse with rowing tank is on the banks of the Thames.

The University has a Recreation Unit which provides teachers/coaches qualified at national and international level. 20 sporting societies.

Student welfare

The **Health Service** is based at Marylebone Road. A full-time nurse and a part-time doctor run daily clinics. Services are duplicated at Harrow. The **Counselling Service** provides psychodynamic counselling and courses on Life as a Mature Student, Exam Anxiety, Study Skills and Eating Problems. The **chaplain** arranges discussion groups and services.

Careers Service

The Careers Service offers you individual guidance and group sessions at all sites. Information on vacation work is available.

Students with special needs

The University has a Computer Centre for the Disabled at New Cavendish Street. The Centre is one of the Federation of Access Centres and gives information and advice on grants and other support. Courses are offered for the deaf.

Accommodation

The University's 1,300 residential places are offered on a first come, first served basis with priority given to students coming from over 35 miles out of London. The accommodation service issues housing lists and provides temporary accommodation for you in September and October while you are looking for a place to live.

All hall rooms are self-catering and most are single. One hall is on the Harrow campus, the rest are around London, all, except on, in travel zone one.

Costs (1995/96)
single room self catering (London): £51 to £65 per week
single room self catering (Harrow): £56 per week
private sector (zones two and three): £55 - £60 per week

Mature students

You will be asked for an interview and selection test if you do not fulfil standard entry requirements. The University runs its own Access courses through eight local colleges and recognises courses from other institutions. You might also have the option of a Foundation course, or a conversion one year entry programme to change from Arts to Sciences.

Nursery
The University has a day nursery in Central London for the children of staff and students aged between two and five years. A weekday, term-time nursery also runs at Harrow for two-and-a-half- to five-year olds.

THE CITY / ESCAPE ROUTES

See University of London's Out and About section.

Wales

University of Wales:
University of Wales, Aberystwyth
University of Wales, Bangor
University of Wales, Cardiff
University of Wales, Lampeter
University of Wales, Swansea

University of Wales Institute, Cardiff
University of Wales College, Newport
The North East Wales Institute of Higher Education
Swansea Institute of Higher Education
Trinity College Carmarthen

University of Glamorgan

This country has one old University (with five member colleges), one new University and a number of Colleges of Higher Education, now associate or full colleges of the University of Wales. The original University Colleges now are regarded as universities in their own right - at least nominally - to differentiate them from the ex-CHEs. The Universities making up the University of Wales range in environment from the civic centre splendours of Cardiff to the rural quiet of Lampeter. Bangor is in Snowdonia, looking out over the Menai Straits, with castles all around. Aberystwyth is a seaside town, in one of the most sparsely populated parts of Britain: thickly wooded valleys, waterfalls and rocky rapids inland, and the sea. Swansea borders the Gower Peninsula and the Brecon Beacons, both very beautiful. The University of Glamorgan is only a few miles north of Cardiff, close to the Wye valley, again, very beautiful countryside. Coming to Wales is a special experience. The Colleges of Higher Education in Wales also award University of Wales degrees. Only the University of Glamorgan awards its own degrees.

The University of Wales

There are several misconceptions to be corrected concerning the University of Wales, and quite a lot of information to be sorted out. The structures and practices of the University are idiosyncratic and its constituent universities cannot be measured entirely by the yardsticks used for English universities.

The University is federal in nature, which means that each University (college) is very largely autonomous: you personally will be aware of belonging to the college, rather than to the whole University. Degree examinations and awards are controlled by the University, as are entry requirements (though not course requirements). In other aspects of academic and social life, the colleges have evolved their own style, although it is probably true to say that they are more interested in each other's affairs than are English universities.

The suspicion lurks that the University of Wales is for the Welsh, and expects you to learn Welsh. It is true that there is some special provision, but this is generally low key. Efforts are made to promote the development of the language academically and socially - but you are not expected to participate unless you want to. Bangor offers a number of courses where teaching, studying and examinations are all in Welsh, and actively promotes the language: one of its halls is allocated to Welsh speaking and learning students (181 places), but again English (and other) students are welcome. At Cardiff and Swansea, part of one hall is bilingual, but otherwise the Welsh bias is not pronounced. At Lampeter, about one fifth of the students are Welsh, and half of these are Welsh-speaking. So - it is well worth while for both English and Welsh students to consider Welsh colleges along with English universities, and weigh their special characteristics.

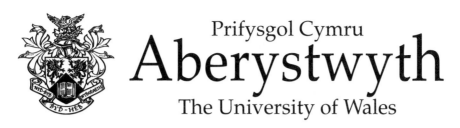

Prifysgol Cymru
Aberystwyth
The University of Wales

Aberystwyth
Dyfed
SY23 2AX
Telephone: 01970 622021

University Charter date: 1872

Aberystwyth is a small university with around 4,500 full-time undergraduates and 1,000 full-time postgraduates. The University has two campuses a mile apart. Degrees are modularised within single, joint or major/minor subject degree structures. A full range of assessment methods: traditional examinations, project work and/or assessed contributions to group and seminar presentations.

All first years are guaranteed a place in University accommodation.

• *New courses*

BSc: Geography (Major)

BA: Economic and Social History (Major), Economic and Social History (Minor), Film and Television Studies, Geography (Major), International Politics and English, International Politics and Welsh, Politics and English, Politics and Welsh.

BScEcon: Information & Library Studies and International Politics, Information & Library Studies and Politics, International Politics (Major), International Politics (Minor), Political Studies (Major), Political Studies (Minor).

• *Areas of Excellence*

To date, as a result of external Assessments of Teaching Quality, the following subject areas in Aberystwyth have been awarded the highest rank of excellence: Celtic Studies, English, Environmental Science, Geography, Geology, Information & Library Studies, International Politics and Welsh.

• *Up to 40 Entrance Scholarships:*

Unconditional Offer and up to £1,800 over three years.

• *50 Merit Awards:*

Unconditional offer plus £100.

Entrance Scholarships and Merit Awards are issued on the strength of applicants' performance in Scholarship examinations which may be held at the applicant's school or college.

THE CAMPUS

In our travels, we have been captivated at some universities by the magnificence of their early buildings, designed with superb Victorian confidence; at others we have been impressed when bold modern architecture has worked well in its environment. Aberystwyth offers splendid examples of both. This is the oldest of the Welsh colleges, founded in 1872, and its Old College, beautifully sited on the seafront, opposite the remains of the castle, was designed by J.P. Seddon, the well-known Victorian architect. It is scheduled as of historic and architectural interest and has turrets, arches, intricate stonework, lofty corridors and winding stairways. The building is still in use, housing some departments and the Registry.

The modern campus is set into the hillside overlooking the town and the sea, only minutes' walk from both, and dominates the view inland from the town. The shapes are mainly blocked, with interesting variations; the light grey and glass units follow level lines along the hillside, blending well into the landscape.

The hill-site is airy - perhaps too airy when the winter blows in across Cardigan Bay - open and exhilarating. The atmosphere is positively friendly and busy, and has the special lift which comes when successful community activity is fully integrated, in right proportion, with student life. The relative inaccessibility of the site becomes a virtue as most students stay on campus throughout the term, interacting with their community to create a special world. Many universities can be quiet at weekends as their students take a break at home or elsewhere: not Aber. The College has a widely based reputation for being a very happy place.

The University is part of an impressive academic composite community: Aberystwyth hosts the National Library of Wales, the Institute of Grassland and Environmental Research, the United Theological College and a College of Further Education.

Llanbadarn Campus

Students taking courses in Information & Library Studies, Information Science and Agriculture are sited here. Llanbadarn is about a mile from the main campus and has its own resources areas, halls of residence, Union facilities, shop and regular bus service.

Cars

No parking problems on the main campus.

Learning Resources

The total **library** stock is around 700,000 volumes and 4,000 periodicals. There is total seating for over 1,200. The Hugh Owen Library on the main campus houses the University's main collections: three specialist libraries - education; physics, maths and computer science; and information and library studies on the Llanbadarn campus. Opening hours: 9am to 10pm: a total of 76 hours per week in term time. You also have free access to the National Library of Wales, just below the main campus, which is one of the country's five copyright libraries.

The **computer unit** runs courses for science students and arts students in aspects of computing relevant to their courses. Open access workstations in halls of residence. The **language laboratory** offers facilities for practice and self-teaching.

Culture on campus

A focal point of the main campus design is the impressive **Arts Centre** complex, housing a concert hall and a theatre, both of which have cinema screens, a gallery, studio, conference facilities, a wholefood cafe, a craft shop and a bookshop.

The Centre is open to the public and is acknowledged by the Arts Council as a Centre of Excellence. The Arts Centre provides an alternative focus and meeting place for students to the Union facilities and offers a programme of courses in art, drama, dance and music.

Drama: The well-equipped theatre hosts productions by professional touring companies, local and college amateur groups, and the College's Drama Department. The Department also presents public performances in its versatile 300 seat studio theatre.

Music: The Music Centre, under the Director of Music, provides practice and teaching facilities. The Centre houses the Joseph Parry Hall where lunchtime recitals are held. There are also regular concerts in the Arts Centre, which has a 1,000 seat concert hall. The Union has its own colourful range of musical activities: Canticum Novum (choral), alternative and rock music, a ceilidh club, Elizabethan madrigals, Gilbert and Sullivan, folk, Morris dancing, Philomusica (serious music in the community) and the Showtime Singers.

The Union

The Union has good accommodation centrally set on the main campus. It represents all the academic institutions in Aberystwyth. The building houses a pizza bar, a catering complex, several shops, insurance and banking services, a games area and a very good travel shop.

The Union's bar and newly revamped hall with c. 700 capacity give space for events. Every Saturday sees the popular 'Up Top Bop' in the Union dance hall. Other entertainments include the annual May and Rag balls; discos put on by various clubs and societies; and there is an assortment of comedy reviews and other acts staged by students and professionals. A range of clubs is financed and run by the Union catering for all tastes. *The Courier*, published two to three times per term, has information on Union activities.

Sport

On the main campus there is a new all-weather playing pitch, and a sports hall, 90 x 60 feet, which has courts and pitches for badminton (three), basketball (one full-size), five-a-side soccer, tennis and volleyball. There are facilities for indoor cricket and athletics, two squash courts, room for weight-training, boxing, dancing, table-tennis, lectures and films. Connected to the hall is a fully equipped heated indoor swimming pool (in use seven days and five evenings a week). A sports 'cage' provides extra courts for badminton (6), basketball (2), tennis (2) and squash (2).

Outdoor facilities are equally impressive. More than 50 acres of playing fields, on two sites on the edge of the town, provide space for numerous College, inter-hostel and interdepartmental teams to play rugby and soccer; there are two well-equipped changing pavilions, 11 tennis courts and a gymnasium used for teaching and coaching.

More than 40 sports clubs and societies are run by the Union's Athletics Board, ranging from athletics to yachting. The Golf Club enjoys special terms at the local golf course.

Student welfare

The College **medical centre** has facilities for clinical examinations and treatment of minor injury. The sick bay accepts students living out of hall. The full-time Welfare Co-ordinator heads a team who help students with financial, family and academic problems. The Union runs a comprehensive **welfare service** maintained by a professional welfare officer. The service includes Nightline. There is a College **chapel** and chaplains are appointed from most denominations.

Careers Service

The Service will help you to define your interests, skills and aspirations and match them with a career. Advisors work closely with academic departments; seminars on the 'Year in Employment Scheme' are timetabled into your course. You can also take confidential psychometric tests which help employers. There are practical and group project learning programmes incorporated into most degree courses to increase your transferable skills. A number of programmes are sponsored by employers and include placements.

Students with special needs

You should consult the Welfare Co-ordinator before you submit your application, outlining your special needs.

Accommodation

The College's halls of residence are either on campus or in a seafront complex. There are 3,248 places: very generous provision. All first years are guaranteed a place.

Halls of residence

For first years, the largest unit is Penbryn, a group of six halls (one for women only), on campus. There is a pay-as-you-eat scheme at the restaurant. Halls have a nice balance between independent character and interconnection (three are physically linked; all are close-knit).

Most study-bedrooms are single, although some first years share. There are several common-rooms, some large enough for meetings, some used as TV or reading rooms. There are recreation rooms, music rooms, library, study, launderette facilities and amenity rooms. Most rooms offer fine views of sea and countryside.

Pantycelyn Hall encourages the use and development of Welsh as the main medium of communication. The hall has facilities similar to those of Penbry, but alternatively a meal is provided six evenings per week. There is a large car-park.

The other main group of 'halls' is actually a string of seafront, early Victorian buildings - very attractive period boarding houses/hotels - converted for hall use. First year students share double rooms: facilities are good (usually a launderette and other amenity rooms) and the prospect of the open sea views across the promenade is a real bonus. A pay-as-you-eat scheme or six evening meals per week.

Students undertaking courses in Agriculture, Information Science and Librarianship are expected to live at the Llanbadarn campus. Here the five halls have amenity rooms, television rooms and libraries. An evening meal is provided. Other meals are on a pay-as-you-eat basis.

Costs (1995/96)

Catered halls: £56.35 per week x 30 weeks
pay-as-you-eat: £48.02 per week x 30 weeks

Self-catering

Cwrt Mawr has ten residential blocks, and houses 545 students. Rooms (mainly single) are grouped for nine or eleven students to share facilities including a kitchen/dining room.

The two new halls on campus, Trefloyne (144 rooms) and Rosser Halls (332 ensuite rooms) are grouped into self-contained flats for 7 and 8 students. There are two small self-catering halls situated at the Seafront hall complex. One of these halls encourages the use of Welsh as the main medium of communication.

Costs (1995/96)

Rosser: £48.51 per week x 30 weeks
Trefloyne: £42.63 per week x 30 weeks
Cwrt Mawr: £32.76 - £38.08 per week x 30 weeks

Pentre Jane Morgan

The University has just completed a student village which accommodates 959 students in individual houses designed to accommodate groups of 5 and 6 students in single study bedrooms sharing kitchen and bathroom facilities. The complex, which has central communal facilities, is accessible from the main campus by means of a footbridge.

Costs (1995/96)

Self-catering, single: £42.21 per week x 30 weeks
Costs include heat and light

Private sector accommodation

A generous list of self-catering or lodging accommodation in the town is kept by the Accommodation Office. Aberystwyth's size (small) and nature (seaside resort) produce pluses and minuses.

Costs (1995/96)

Single study-bedroom in shared house or bedsit: £35 to £45 per week excluding fuel.

Mature students

Enquiries should be made to the Admissions Officer who will give advice and guidance about the necessary preparation for university work, how to apply and how to select university courses. Each student is allocated a personal tutor and there is also a University - appointed mature student counsellor. Study skills courses are available if required.

Nursery

A children's centre provides care for pre-school children from the age of three months to four and a half years. It is run by a committee of parents, volunteers and nursery staff. Coleg Ceredigion Nursery Unit provides facilities for children aged 3 months to four and a half years on the Llanbadarn campus.

THE TOWN (population: 12,000)

Aberystwyth is a seaside resort which manages to combine a lively, busy, friendly atmosphere with a sense of decorum. It has a Euro-blue beach and a promenade lined with tall terraced houses, facing the wide sweep of Cardigan Bay; a small, pretty pier with a pavilion and a headland complete with the longest electric cliff railway in the UK, with the world's largest camera obscura at its top.

The immediate environment includes a number of sites preserved for rare plant and wildlife: you can watch red kites fly over the campus and bottle-nosed dolphins in the bay.

The town is the administrative capital and principal shopping centre of Ceredigion, the most populous town in mid-Wales and the largest resort on the Cambrian coast. Behind the seafront there is a network of intriguing shopping streets with some upmarket boutiques, the usual showing of small-scale chain stores and some really good eating places. The air is sea-bright, the buildings generally well-kept and colourful.

This was once a walled town and its origins are ancient: the Celtic hill fort of Pendinas overlooks the town; Llanbadarn village, close by, marks the religious settlement founded by St Padarn in the sixth century: ancient Celtic inscribed stones are in its church.

College Museum has a rich collection of pottery, glass, china and folk objects. The National Library of Wales, an imposing white building, houses Welsh literary treasures: the Black Book of Carmarthen (late 12th century - one of the earliest books in Welsh), the White Book of Roderick and the Book of Taliesin. The library contains more than two million printed works and three and a half million Welsh historical records.

Opposite the Old College, and now laid out as public gardens, are the ruins of one of the chain of castles built by Edward I after he formally broke the power of the Llewelyns in 1282. These castles were famous throughout Europe for their military architecture. They combined palatial living quarters with complex defensive designs. Today they are strung across Wales, impressive and very beautiful, even when in a ruined state. Some are remarkably well preserved.

The Ceredigion Museum in the town is housed in the Coliseum, a restored music hall, fetchingly ornate, which is itself a listed building. It provides an eccentrically attractive setting for displays showing the history of the district from the Stone Age to the present day.

The Arts Centre on the College campus provides entertainment and culture for the community; there is also a small theatre near the harbour, other gallery areas in the town, and a commercial cinema open all year. The town hosts four professional theatre companies and is visited regularly by some of the best touring companies in the UK. In November there is a Film Festival.

There is an 18 hole golf course, regular agricultural shows, sea angling and pony-trekking. Some activities, it is true, are geared to the tourist season, but most will add to the texture of your own life in Aberystwyth.

ESCAPE ROUTES

The area around Aberystwyth is the most sparsely populated in Britain, apart from the wilder parts of Scotland. The hills inland stretch their vistas wide, and the coastline is one of coves and beaches. It is phenomenally beautiful, still unspoiled in spite of the fact that it is popular with tourists. The river valleys are thickly wooded; waterfalls and rocky rapids cut into the water's steady flow to the sea; rare birds and plantlife survive here. You can walk, sail, fish, ride, explore...

Places to go, other than everywhere, are fairly limited: if you want shops and culture, Aberystwyth is It for miles.

You should go to Strata Florida - an abbey - which was once the Canterbury of Wales and is still beautiful, now in ruins. It is a place of great peace and sanctity.

If you enjoy the Great Outdoors, sea and mountains, then Aberystwyth is one of the luckiest universities in Britain.

Communications

There are rail-links to the Midlands, and from there to the rest of the country. Local roads are not motorways, but neither are they country lanes, and the journey to and from Aber is very beautiful.

University of Wales, Bangor

Gwynedd
LL57 2DG
Telephone: 01248 351151

University Charter date: 1884

Bangor is a small/medium university with a student population of 7,000, 40% of whom are from Wales and 17% of whom are Welsh speaking. Courses here are modularised and assessment is balanced according to the demands of your course (written exams/practicals/ projects/continuous assessment. The University's campus is very much part of the fabric of this small city and has grown from its original 1884 site on the hill to occupy houses and purpose-built faculties and halls of residence.

All pre-Clearing first years are guaranteed a place in hall.

• Excellence in Teaching

Over half of the departments assessed to date in the on-going Teaching Quality Assessments have received the top rating of 'excellent'. These include Chemistry, Music, Ocean Studies, Psychology, Russian, theology and Religious Studies, Welsh.

• Merger

The amalgamation with Coleg Normal Bangor in August 1996 means that BEd Primary Teaching and BA courses in Business and Social Administration, Environmental Planning and Management, and Leisure and Tourism Resource Management will be offered for 1997 entry.

• Accommodation

The final stage of the Ffriddoedd Halls brings the total of single ensuite study bedrooms on this site to 850. The completion of this £12 million building programme also makes Bangor one of the UK's largest providers of ensuite accommodation.

• Sports Facilities

A major development to note is the opening of an £80,000 climbing wall facility at the University's Sports Centre. The wall is part of the continual improvement and expansion of the University sports facilities, and follows closely on the heels of the opening of a new athletics track.

• Special Needs

The opening of two Study Support Centres continues Bangor's commitment to students with special needs. The multimedia resource centres, located in the Arts and Science libraries, include CCTVs, scanners with speech and Braille output, and PCs with software for dyslexic students and students with visual impairments.

• Further information

For more information regarding the University's facilities or courses, please contact Carys Roberts, Schools Liaison Officer, on 01248 383839.

THE CAMPUS

The University began its life as a result of a late 19th-century campaign for better higher education in Wales. Funds were raised by public subscription; particularly generous contributions were made by local quarrymen through voluntary deductions from their wages over a period of years. This sense of dedicated determination and urgency marked also the opening of the University in an old coaching inn in 1884, before a 'proper' building was available.

The present campus area has grown from an original ten acres on a small hill immediately overlooking the city; its main building, an example of the more forbidding style of Victorian institution architecture, was opened in 1911, and today still dominates the site.

The sense of local pride and the community-linked nature of its origins remain characteristics of the University: most of Bangor's cultural life is linked with that of the University, which blends easily into its environment through its occupation of large houses on its site, as well as the newer purpose-built faculty and residential blocks. Academic and domestic buildings pile up the hill, linking one of the city's main roads with an upper area of shops and cafes, forming a small separate community no more than half a mile from the city centre.

The University has a positive policy of encouraging the use of the Welsh language; one of its halls of residence (housing 222 students) is primarily reserved for Welsh speakers and learners, and the University works to develop provision for teaching through the medium of Welsh. The ambience on campus is generally quiet and small-town.

In 1996, Coleg Normal Bangor became an integral part of the University. Its sites relate closely to those of the University and its courses have been absorbed. The join should be seamless.

The University also has three farms, a field station, botanic gardens (where formal garden beds, a rockery, an arboretum, grassland and woodland stretch down to the shores of the Strait), and a research vessel which allows students to gain practical experience and undertake marine research at sea.

Cars

There is a permit system; parking on campus is very limited and permits will be given only to those who can prove special need. A car is, however, a very good idea in this region, and many students do manage to accommodate their vehicles.

Learning Resources

The **library** operates through a number of different sites. Altogether it houses 500,000 items and seats 800 students. Facilities are available for partially sighted students. The science library subscribes to 2,200 current periodicals.

Academic departments organise **computer tuition**, relevant to the demands of your course. A large number of networked terminals are distributed in various buildings. There are also general courses in a range of computer programme skills, plus help in the construction of databases to match your own needs.

Students can teach themselves languages in the three **language laboratories**; the newest laboratory is entirely computer based. The University offers classes to students wishing to learn Welsh.

Culture on campus

Drama: The theatre (seating 343), opened in 1975, was built by the University to serve the community, the region and its own students. It is versatile enough for productions by departments and societies (student or local), and for a varied programme by visiting professional companies (ballet, dance, opera, concerts and drama). The theatre has a small foyer art exhibition area.

Film: A wide variety of films is shown here too; a welcome addition to the single cinema (soon to be five screen) in the city.

Music: There is a good programme of music; the University is proud of its two concert halls and, with the support of the Welsh Arts Council, compensates for its geographical remoteness by offering regular concerts by the resident ensemble and by visiting distinguished artists.

There is also a University orchestra and choir, a contemporary music ensemble, chamber choir, brass ensemble and opera group. The student Music Society puts on its own programme of concerts, often at lunchtimes, by student performers. There is a computer-based electronic music laboratory, of professional standard, which is involved in making records, in doing work for TV and in providing support for some degree courses. The University offers music tuition to all students. The Union organises discos and live music.

The Union

The Union building is conveniently set on the perimeter road where city and College meet; a useful meeting point for students, with close access to the centre of Bangor. The Union works well as the focal point for students; busy at lunchtimes with a happy and welcoming atmosphere.

The Union is active on the entertainment front with different 'events' ranging through karaoke, discos and bands, organised for most nights, with the exception of Sunday. Bangor is on the National Comedy Network.

There are three bars. The main bar has a stage and dance floor. In the basement is a smaller bar.

The Union offers a wide range of clubs and societies. The Athletic Union caters for a variety of sports and there is a flourishing Community Action group. This group does charity work for the benefit of the mentally or physically handicapped, the elderly and children in care, the most successful project being the Bangor Youth Theatre. The Union runs a fleet of minibuses for the use of clubs and societies.

The Union building houses a shop, a bank, a bookshop, a travel bureau, refectory, a fast food restaurant and a printing service. Vegetarian food is available and all food is reasonably priced.

The Union's welfare service is complementary to that provided by the College. There is a full-time Welfare Officer and a Research and Welfare Officer. Counselling, assistance with social security and rent tribunals, information on welfare and tenants' rights and advice on academic matters are all part of the service provided. Various awareness campaigns are run throughout the year. The Union runs a Nightline service which operates for twelve hours most weeknights and seventeen hours at weekends.

There is a regular magazine, *Seren*, containing news, articles and reviews.

Sport

In addition to the University's cachet of Sports Science teaching, Bangor is, of course, an internationally renowned centre for climbing and watersports: few academic institutions can claim to have such spectacular resources fore and aft as the Menai Straits and Snowdonia.

Another advantage is the compactness of this campus: all facilities are on site (it is possible to walk across from one corner of the campus to the other in less than 15 minutes). There are 40 acres of grass pitches, an athletics track, a floodlit 'Dri Pla' pitch, four squash courts, three tennis courts, a gymnastic hall (purpose-built), an indoor climbing wall and the sports centre. Some facilities are close to several of the halls of residence; the main playing field area overlooks the Menai Strait. The sports centre has a main hall (badminton - 6 courts, basketball - 2 courts, tennis and a good range of other indoor activities). There is also a fitness room, well equipped for weight-training and lifting, table-tennis, fencing etc. The Athletics Union organises 40 clubs, many of which take advantage of the College's marvellous setting: rowing, sailing and canoe clubs have a boat house and sailing facilities on the Menai Strait, and the mountaineering club makes full use of the Snowdonia range.

Student welfare

The student **health centre** offers an advisory service - you register with a local GP. A student counsellor and several of the academic staff will help with problems. A student-run Nightline is available most nights. Several local clergymen of various denominations act as **chaplains** to the College. The memorial arch at the entrance to the University is now used as a drop-in centre. The aim is to provide a meeting place, refreshments, a market for world goods and information on varying campaigns for justice and peace.

Careers Service

You will be invited to an exploratory discussion with one of the careers advisors in the Spring term of your second year. The Service offers computer-assisted guidance programmes (Gradscope and Rogetscan) and psychometric testing.

Students with special needs

You should write to the Special Needs Co-ordinator (Academic Office), outlining your special needs. Special learning resources have recently been developed (see the opening panel). A visit is strongly recommended. There is a Dyslexia Unit with a specialist tutor for dyslexic students. The College's Welfare Officer is a member of SKILL and actively campaigns on behalf of disabled students' rights. A book reader for blind students has recently been introduced in the library.

Accommodation

All prospective students who accept a firm or unconditional offer of admission prior to Clearing can be sure of a place in a hall. If you are a later entrant (an 'insurance offer' candidate) you might have to accept temporary accommodation initially. Clearing candidates will be given help in finding private accommodation. You and your parents can stay in hall (bed and breakfast) during the summer to explore.

Halls of residence

The College provides accommodation for over 2,300 of its students in halls of residence (catered and self-catering) or in converted private houses - these are usually allocated to third year and postgraduate students. All halls are warden controlled.

Catered halls

The purpose-built halls are very pleasant buildings and have attractive settings on sites rising above the town, so that many rooms have splendid mountain views. A large majority of the rooms are single study-bedrooms and most halls have common rooms, libraries, games rooms and laundry facilities. One hall (John Morris-Jones) is reserved for Welsh-speaking or learning students. The group of halls forms a close community, just a few minutes' walk away from the academic campus, but relating strongly to the nearby area of shops, pubs and restaurants which provide a lively student-social ambience. The halls provide breakfast and evening meals in the week; breakfast and lunch on Sundays and only breakfast on Saturdays.

Costs (1995/96)

Single room: £56 to £59 (ensuite) per week x 30 weeks

Self-catering halls

Halls have single study-bedrooms. There are kitchen facilities on each floor; a limited number of students from each hall can opt to take meals in one of the catering halls. The new Ffriddoedd site houses 1,500 students: 850 first years are presently housed in ensuite single study bedrooms. Each floor has a shared kitchen with various amenities including a microwave.

Costs (1995/96)

Single room: £34 - £36 per week x 38 weeks
Ensuite single room: £43 per week x 38 weeks

Private accommodation

'Lodgings' usually means here breakfast and a late-night hot drink and biscuits, with domestic care (cleaning and laundry). Flats which have self-contained accommodation are rare; it is more usual to find a single room in houses where you share kitchen and bathroom, or single/double bed-sitters with minimal cooking facilities in the room. If you have problems with landlords or ladies which you cannot negotiate successfully yourself, the Accommodation Office will try to help. You often have to pay a retaining fee over holiday periods.

Costs (1995/96)

Costs vary between £33 and £37 per week for bedsits. If you are interested in private accommodation, consult the Accommodation Office.

Mature students

The minimum age for mature students is 21. Applicants pursuing recognised access courses are welcomed. Mature students study skills groups are organised. A special leaflet for mature students is available.

Nursery

The Union runs a creche for children (aged three months to five years) of students and staff. Fees are subsidised and there is a waiting list, so apply early. The University also runs a day-care nursery with playschemes for after school and the holidays.

THE CITY (population: 17,000)

The city is beautifully contained: caught between the high and wild mountains of Snowdonia and the waters of the Menai Strait, Bangor has been held in natural balance, its shape and size determined by environment. Although a 'city' in status, the community retains the ambience of a small town. In part it huddles round its fishing harbour, in picture-postcard style; in part it offers a pedestrianised small shopping centre where you can find national chain stores, their premises mixing comfortably with those of local business. Facilities are more than adequate for daily needs, though if you enjoy shopping you will have to wait for vacations or plan an expedition. Pubs, particularly near the waterfront, are small and friendly. There is a good indoor swimming pool.

The city centre is dominated from above by the University College Park development, from within by the cathedral, and from beyond by the beautiful Menai Strait usually bright with coloured sails. Across the narrow waters are the gentle wooded island shores of Anglesey, and spanning the Strait are the fine lines of Telford's Menai suspension bridge (a marvel in its time) and Stephenson's Britannia railway bridge, marking the engineering skills of the Industrial Revolution with style.

The city has ancient origins; there is some evidence of a Roman camp and other sites suggest that this was one of the earliest settlements in Wales. The cathedral today, although founded in AD 525, is largely the result of restoration work by Sir Gilbert Scott and his son between 1870 and 1880. It has Victorian stained glass and the 16th century 'Mostyn Christ'; the building itself is small for a cathedral, dark and solid.

The city turns for culture and entertainment to the University.

Theatre: Theatr Gwynedd hosts a variety of performances - professional, students, amateur.

Cinema: Films are shown at Theatr Gwynedd and the Plaza cinema.

Nightlife: The Octagon has live music, bands, discos.

Sport: Bangor is a centre for outdoor pursuits - sailing, board sailing, cruising, angling, sea fishing, bird watching and, of course, climbing. There is a snooker centre with 16 tables.

ESCAPE ROUTES

Bangor is an internationally renowned centre for climbing. Snowdonia rises behind the city offering rock-faces and peaks to be conquered. The views are spectacular. For walkers, the hills are webbed with paths, accessible on foot from the city. Further afield you have museums and railways, castles, mines....

The Menai Strait offers excellent sailing or windsurfing, or any other permutation of watersport. The coast north and east of Bangor is holiday-land: you could escape there in the early season for a whirl. The nearest city of any size is Liverpool, about two hours away.

Communications

There are regular Intercity **trains** to London Euston, Birmingham New Street and Manchester Victoria, from which centres the rest of the country is open. There are direct **coaches** to Bangor from some major centres, and most places can be reached with only one change. The A55 expressway to the M56/M6 gives fast and easy road linking.

University of Wales, Cardiff

PO Box 68
Cardiff
CF1 3XA
Telephone: 01222 874000

University Charter date: 1883
Cardiff is a medium/large university with 13,000 students, 3,000 of whom are postgraduates. The University has an impressive city centre campus. Degrees, apart from Medicine and Dentistry, are modularised. Assessment is by examination and some coursework; a project can replace a module.

Accommodation is guaranteed for all first years.

THE CAMPUS

Cardiff, as it is now, was formed in 1988 by the merger of two long established colleges whose academic history dates back more than a century, and is as large as many of the major universities in Britain. Its main buildings are in Cardiff's central civic park - indeed they are a major part of the civic complex.

One factor which struck us as significant, in our university-hopping tour, was the element of local pride and care invested in these prestige pinnacles of our education system, in terms of land allocation, proximity to and integration with the host town or city, style and quality of buildings, signposting (some are hard to find; some are proudly announced on all major roads) and the profile in the local community (some people don't know they have a university). In Cardiff, the College buildings flank the fine square of Cathays Park, with its lawns, flowers and trees; the square is headed by the splendid city hall, museum and law courts. This civic centre, dating from the first decade of this century, is justly the pride of Cardiff, built in white stone and classical line, with pillared facades, fine domes, a lofty tower and decorative roof-lines. The fair pavilions of Welsh aspiration, providing monuments to its prosperity, the education needed to support that prosperity, and a dream of freedom and brighter horizons for the children of its working community. In our joint (and not always in accord) opinions, this is the finest complex of civic buildings in England and Wales. The interiors of these stately buildings have the rather cold, formal and sombre corridors and spaces of their time: you can't have everything!

The Science and Technology dimension of the University lives in less grandiose surroundings, but is equally central to the city.

'Campus' life is extended in Cardiff by the presence in the city of other academic institutions; the student population reaches a total of around 15,000.

Cars
Although parking facilities are provided at most halls of residence, students are advised not to bring cars because parking in the city is difficult. Local parking vouchers are available.

Learning Resources

The **library service** is split into ten specialist libraries, each close to the department it serves. The service in all has c.1,000,000 books and bound journals, subscribes to almost 9,000 periodicals and can seat 2,000 readers. There are 984,677 monographs/microfile etc. and around 200,000 periodical volumes. Open until 9.30pm Monday to Friday and until 4.30pm on Saturdays and on Sundays during exams.

The **computing service** provides access to computers of all types, from single-user micro computers, through mini and mainframe systems to regional services and national supercomputer systems. Open 8.30am-5pm. Some workstations are available 24 hours a day. There is a range of half day courses on offer and a programming advisory service. Open access computer rooms are open 24 hours daily throughout the year.

Culture on campus

Drama: Cardiff's Sherman Theatre, although now run independently, remains part of the College's main complex of buildings, and offers its range of drama very conveniently. Three Drama Society productions per term.
Music: The music department presents a full programme of musical events: chamber, orchestral and choral concerts, master classes, composers' workshops etc. The Department of Music holds classical music concerts in its own Hall, or the famous St David's Hall in Cardiff, or other venues. Also a series of Tuesday concerts in term time. Concerts by visiting performers, instrumental and voice tuition available, 30 Department practice rooms plus practice rooms in halls of residence (with pianos).

The Union

The Union building is close behind the main College building. The facilities are large and impressive and the atmosphere is positive: one feels at home here, a place where one can meet friends and have fun.

The Union runs over 150 cultural, political, social, sporting and religious clubs and societies (a large number indeed) and organises a Community Action programme.

The Entertainment Programme is impressive. The Union is very active. At regular intervals the Union organises one of its "spectaculars": up to 3000 students attend an array of entertainments which can last most of the night.

'Terminal 396' offers leisure space for meeting and a range of eating places during the day. At night it is transformed into a sophisticated nightclub, with advanced sound and lighting. There is capacity for around 1,400 people. The central feature is the Great Hall, which can seat up to 1,500 and accommodates major rock concerts (open to the public), discos, sports competitions, beer festivals and examinations (an interesting mixture).

There are seven bars in all, including the students' 'local' - the 'Tafarn Bar', furbished with timber beams and stained glass windows. There is something happening every night of term, including jazz and smaller gigs, except on Sundays.

Other facilities are equally impressive: seven different types of restaurant and fast food venues, serving all types; the university bookshop, a travel advice centre and a print shop. There is also a games room, with video arcade and snooker and pool tables.

The Student Advice Centre is situated on the third floor of the building. Confidential guidance is offered by the full time staff on a range of topics. Nightline is available.

The Union produces an excellent weekly newspaper.

Sport

The College Athletic Union runs around 50 clubs, traditional and other indoor facilities at the purpose-built sports complex at Talybont, include tennis and badminton courts, indoor cricket and hockey pitches, a large martial arts dojo and a well equipped weights room. The gymnasium is nearer to the University, has room for badminton and basketball, and has a weights room. A squash and fitness centre is centre campus: eight courts, an activities hall and a Fitness Room.

Outdoor facilities include a floodlit all weather playing surface, six rugby, six football and five hockey pitches, and a small running track.

Snooker, pool, table-tennis, squash and fencing are provided in the Union.

Clubs cover some of the wider outdoor pursuits: hang gliding, caving, mountaineering... The sailing centre is only five miles from campus. Excellent facilities in the city are hired also for club activities.

Student welfare

The College's **Health Centre** offers a range of clinics free of charge, but is intended to supplement the NHS, not to act as a replacement. You should register with a local GP.

The **student counselling service** offers confidential help There is also a money management advisory service. The Dean of Students Office provides advice and help on most problems.

There are **chaplaincies** maintained by the Anglican, Baptist, Methodist, Roman Catholic, Greek Orthodox and Jewish churches. The city is cosmopolitan and will cater for your needs.

Careers Service

The Service offers computer-assisted guidance programmes, a programme of careers talks, presentations and courses, and application and interview workshops. There is a well-stocked careers library. The service works closely with local employers. 'Insight' programmes and application/interview workshops. Individual interviews from first year on. Advice and help is available long after graduation - not always the case in careers centres.

Students with special needs

Some residential accommodation has been adapted for disabled student use. There is a Dyslexia Resource Centre. You should write to the Admissions Office before you submit your application, outlining your special needs.

Accommodation

The College owns accommodation for more than 4,700 of its students and guarantees accommodation for all first years (except Clearing entrants - and you might still be lucky). The mix of buildings and styles is wide: flats, houses, halls traditional, halls self-catering... There are two traditional halls, and ten self catering units (halls, flats or student houses). Over half of the study-bedrooms have ensuite facilities and most are on or close to campus.

Halls of residence

Twelve of the halls are within a mile of campus. Mainly single study-bedrooms, 64% of which are ensuite. Each hall has laundry facilities/common rooms/library. Facilities are not uniform, but include pleasant gardens, indoor games, tennis courts, squash courts, TV rooms, music rooms, bars. Part of Senhennydd Court, on the main campus, is set aside for Welsh speakers and those learning the language. If you want to be sure of specific amenities, apply early.

Costs (1995/96)

single: £1,651 to £1,899 (ensuite) for term time only

Self-catering accommodation

This can be in halls, purpose-built flats, or student houses. The pattern in all is similar: groups of single study-bedrooms (usually 5, but can vary from 4 to 8) share 'flat' facilities. The Cartwright Court complex, half a mile from campus, is close to shops, park, lake and playing fields, and has a clubroom (dining, social space and recreation rooms). A large complex at Talybont, one and a half miles 'out', close to the river Taff and two large parks, has an amenity centre and sports facilities. Student houses are available mainly to returning students and postgraduates: they accommodate four to eleven students. Some accommodation for married students: demand far exceeds supply, so apply early.

Costs (1995/96)

single room: £1,170 - £1,740 (ensuite) term time plus
            Christmas and Easter vacations
single room: £ 1,788 - £2,388 (ensuite) for full year
Married flats: £4,122 (one bedroom) - £5,952 (three
            bedrooms) for full year.

Private accommodation

You are advised to come to the city in good time to conduct your search. Rents on average are around £35 to £40 per week. Married students and those with families are warned that provision is not easily found and are advised to come alone to do the searching. The earlier the better; choice dwindles between June and September.

Mature students

Entry requirements differ between departments, so contact the department which interests you. A foundation or preliminary year is offered in engineering, physical sciences or health and life sciences. The university is a member of the South-East Wales Access Consortium.

Nursery

A day nursery run by the University takes children aged between 10 weeks and 5 years, but provision is limited.

THE CITY (population: c.300,000)

Cardiff - blessed with some very fetching castle ruins of its own - is set in an area thickly studded with castles, ruined, restored or no more than evocative sites; this is an indication of the area's significance until medieval times as an outpost of civilisation. Romans and Normans alike built their fortresses and garrisons in a vain attempt to suppress or contain the colourful Celts. Many were still subject to siege or damage by Cromwell or the Royalists in the Civil War; the history of all is rich and fascinating.

Cardiff fell out of prominence post-Cromwell, and became a remote and quiet market town until the Industrial Revolution swung its sledgehammer of change and catapulted the town into becoming the largest coal-exporting city in the world by the end of the 19th century - with all the concomitant dockland developments and housing and population expansion.

The city was extremely fortunate in having, at this crucial moment in history, leaders who were men of imagination and bold vision. They bought land with astute foresight, preserved the beautiful parkland which still stretches green spaces into the very heart of the city, planned the shape of its growth and left the superb monument to their achievement in the marvellous complex of civic buildings already described.

Cardiff today is a handsome, well laid-out city, full of interesting contrasts; its access areas are grey and urbanised, but its centre is green with parkland and castle-precinct; it has its share of terraced housing acres, balanced by its civic centre, the fine restoration of part of its castle (also central) and its excellent modern shopping arcades and precincts. Cardiff became the capital of Wales in 1955 and has, in suitable measure, the style, elegance and sophistication of a (small) metropolis. There is added interest in the presence of its river and its dockland.

There are four new shopping malls and seven Victorian and Edwardian arcades- providing nice focal points to the range you would expect from a city of this size.

Ambitious plans are under way to develop Cardiff as a major maritime city. The city already scores very highly in independent 'quality of life' surveys.

Theatres: The New Theatre presents a range of dance, musicals and comedy and hosts major touring productions. The Sherman Theatre, in the university area, now independently run, offers drama by professional and amateur groups. The Chapter Arts Centre: a large and enterprising centre for the arts, offers two cinemas, three exhibition spaces, a theatre, a dance studio, and many more amenities.

Music: St David's Hall offers a splendid auditorium for a range classical concerts and recitals. The National Stadium and the International Arena present a range of large-scale concerts, including big-name entertainers. The Welsh National Opera, which is acquiring an international reputation, performs in the New Theatre. Nightly jazz at the Four Bars Inn.

Cinema: Films are shown at the Sherman Theatre and the Chapter Centre, and in three multi-screen cinemas.

Nightlife: On offer is an excellent range of restaurants, and a number of discos and nightclubs. The nightlife you would expect in a major city.

Sport: The city's Empire swimming pool is of international standard; Cardiff Arms Park is one of the most famous international rugby grounds (if you haven't heard of it, you can't know any Welshmen). League soccer at Ninian's Park is also very well known. There is first-class cricket in Sophia Gardens. The Welsh National Institute of Sport, the National Athletics Stadium and the Olympic-standard Empire Pool combine to offer first class facilities. This is one of the few places in Britain where baseball and professional ice-hockey are played, and the icing on the cake comes with the recently opened Wales National Ice Rink. There are eight golf courses in or near Cardiff.

Festivals: The Festival of Twentieth Century Music and the Llandaff Festival are held annually, and in recent years the Sherman Theatre has mounted a New Writing Festival.

ESCAPE ROUTES

Cardiff, at the foot of the Valleys and on a heavily industrialised section of the Severn estuary, does not - on a map - appear to have very much going for it. But, as in so many areas of 19th century British sprawl, the smoke stacks have breathed their last and what was once industry is now industrial archaeology. From your point of view, if not for the local employment figures, this is a Good Thing.

The valleys of the Wye and the Usk are very beautiful. The Usk is nearer, and opens into the Brecon Beacons National Park - all good hiking country. The 'Valleys' as in The Valleys are also worth exploring.

You are close enough to the coastline which runs west to the Mumbles and the Gower (see Swansea), and to the country around Bristol (see Bristol's entry).

Communications

Trains run almost every hour to London (a two hour journey). Regular express **coach services** to London and other main centres.

The **M4** spins a fast route east to Bristol and London, connecting with the **M5** which links the Midlands with the West Country: access to the nation's motorways. **Cardiff Airport** is the local international airport.

University of Wales, Lampeter

Dyfed
SA48 7ED
Telephone: 01570 422351

University Charter date: joined the University of Wales in 1971; founded 1822

Lampeter is a small university with 1,600 students. Courses are modularised with some free modules offered outside the 'parent' department. The University has a single campus on the edge of the tiny market town. 60% of all students are housed in College accommodation

---

THE CAMPUS

Lampeter in unique in the gamut of university institutions: it is the smallest (around 1,600 students); it relates to a tiny market town (3,000 inhabitants); divides its students into only two faculties - arts, the majority, and theology - and is probably the most remote in its setting.

The College buildings are central to the town: most things are! The original building, founded in 1822 and opened in 1827, was designed to prepare youths for the Anglican ministry in Wales. Built around a quadrangle, this is an attractive building, housing today the chapel, library, Students' Union, College offices and residential rooms. Academic units have spread into other buildings, some quite new, functional and purpose-built. The newest buildings are close to the existing hall of residence. The College rests in very lovely countryside, rural, remote, where many inhabitants are bilingual or very fluent in their ancient tongue. The College aims to provide an ambience where Welsh can be learned and spoken.

Learning Resources

The **library** seats 190 students and is open weekdays to 9.45pm, on Saturday morning and Sunday afternoon. The library has a stock of 170,000 books and takes a total of 1,200 periodicals. The Old Library houses 20,000 books and periodicals printed between 1470 and 1850.

The **computing department** runs courses on information systems and word-processing. Open access workstations offer PCs and world wide web access until 10.30pm. The campus is fully networked.

Students can continue with self-teaching in the **language laboratory**, equipped with computer assisted learning.

Culture on campus

Drama: The Arts Hall can seat 400 and is used for drama productions by College societies, by the Welsh National Opera when touring, and by other professional theatre companies and musical groups.

Film: The Union runs a film society. Films are screened twice weekly and there are trips to the UCI in Swansea.

Music: The Lampeter Music Club promotes six professional concerts a year, open to both the College and the town (some famous musicians have played in the College Arts Hall). There is a chamber orchestra (also joint town-and-gown) which meets weekly to rehearse and perform and there is an active choir. Music rooms are available for practice.

The Union

The Union owns its own building and is the social focus of the College. In so small a town, it is important that the College generates its own activity. Discos are held in The Union Hall three times a week; two run until 1am. Most Friday nights of term are dedicated to discos or live bands. Comedy nights are presented three times a term. There are regular cheap beer evenings and quizzes.

The Union has two bars, a games room, a TV room, a print room, shop, insurance and travel agencies and Pooh's Corner, provides good quality food; vegetarian a speciality

The size of the College means that it is very easy to join, organise or set up clubs and activities: the Union runs many clubs and societies with an impressively high club:student ratio, and a Community Action Group.

The Union Welfare service is available 24 hours a day, providing advice and information. The Union's Accommodation Office works closely with the College, giving advice on contracts and how to view properties, in addition to support for students having problems with their landlords. A 'partnering' service is provided for students looking for property on their own.

Counselling is available in all aspects of emotional, financial and legal problems; the Union goes a stage further than most in providing legal representation and safe houses. Altogether, a most comprehensive service.

There is a fortnightly newspaper. The Union also produces an Alternative Prospectus which is well worth looking at. There is a particularly successful Rag here, raising lots of money for charity.

Sport

There is a modern sports hall, rather spartan in appearance, which houses squash courts and facilities for badminton, basketball, volleyball, table-tennis and indoor hockey, cricket and soccer. Pitches for cricket, rugby (women's rugby available since 1995) and soccer are less than five minutes' walk away.

Coaching is available in karate, at black belt level. Students have free use of the town swimming pool and are welcome at the nine-hole golf club, just outside the town. The College sports facilities are open to the public.

Excellent environment for outdoor pursuits!

Student Welfare

The College has a **health service** staffed by two nurses: open daily except Sundays. Minor accidents and ailments can be treated. The town's doctor's surgery is just off campus and students are advised to register there. There is a **mosque** on-campus, as well as, predictably, full provision for **Christian students**. It is important that, being so remote, the College does cater for the dietary requirements of non-Christian students.

Careers service

Careers advice is available at all stages of your course. The College gives you access to PROSPECT HE, the newest of the graduate careers computer programmes. There is a range of seminars and workshops on application procedures and interview techniques.

Students with special needs

Some rooms have been adapted for wheelchairs. The College is committed to providing more ramps for wheelchairs but the location does not lend itself easily to wheelchair access. There may be problems for students with other disabilities.

Accommodation

Around 60% of all students are housed in college accommodation. All new entrants are allocated College rooms: you do not need to ask, unless you are over 21. If for any reason you wish to live out, you should consult the Accommodation Office in good time.

Some of the most popular rooms are in the original building, but there are over 20 small purpose-built halls (mostly taking fewer than 50 residents) and some converted houses close to campus. Some halls are full-board (except for Saturdays); some are pay-as-you-eat. Shared houses have five or six single rooms, kitchen and bathroom. You 'pay-as-you-eat' in the central refectory, the Student Union or the town. There are 350 self catering places of which 132 are ensuite. College accommodation is relatively cheap.

Costs (1994/95)
Halls of residence:
Full board, single: £62.50 x 30 weeks
Pay-as-you-eat, single: £38.00 x 30 weeks
Self-catering, single: £35.40 - £41.75 (ensuite) x 37 weeks

Private accommodation
The College is very supportive if you do decide to 'live out'. Because of the College's location, it is possible you would have to live quite a way from Lampeter. Average costs: around £37.50 per week plus bills.

Mature students

The College runs Access courses and has a range of part-time degrees on offer. Study-skills classes are held weekly. The Centre for Continuing Education mounts a number of pre-university courses and holds open seminars on study techniques. There is a Mature Students' Association and a common room in the Old Building. Mature students over 26 years old can be housed in designated 'quiet' halls.

Nursery
A nursery undergraduates' children (over six months old) is run by the Students' Union and subsidised by the University. Fees are determined on a sliding scale.

THE TOWN (population: 2,000)

Lampeter is a small town, set at the meeting place of little valleys, which creates a very pretty setting. Although small, this is an important market centre, serving the needs of a widely scattered rural and hill community. This means that you should find local shopping adequate to your needs, and market days (once a fortnight) should bring the town to life. You are about 12 miles from the coast and 25 - 30 miles from Aberystwyth and Carmarthen (a larger town).

There are seven pubs in Lampeter, frequented by both students and locals.

Lampeter, however, has a strong sense of remoteness and is very quiet. If you are interested in horses, you will find this a good place to be: the town is known for its breed of Welsh Cob ponies; there is a stallion show in May, and there are lots of riding schools and pony-trekking facilities. Fishing is also a leading activity: the ancient coracle is still in use in the lower reaches of the Teifi - Lampeter's river.

ESCAPE ROUTES

The area around Lampeter is extraordinarily beautiful, with dramatic mountain landscapes, rivers and waterfalls. There are Roman gold mines, a 13th century abbey, the Mynach Falls and many other places of interest: see the Escape section for Aberystwyth, 29 miles away.

Communications

Lampeter does not have a railway station. The nearest is in Carmarthen, or some students use Aberystwyth (both about 25 miles away). There are buses through Lampeter every two hours to and from these centres. At the beginning and end of term, the College provides transport from and to both Carmarthen and Aberystwyth stations. The motorway is 40 minutes away.

University of Wales, Swansea

Singleton Park
Swansea
SA2 8PP
Telephone: 01792 205678

University Charter date: 1920

Swansea is a medium-sized university with a total of 9,600 students. The University has a single campus two miles west of the city. Degrees are modularised and assessed both by coursework and examination.

First years who accept a place by September 1st are guaranteed accommodation

---

THE CAMPUS

The University is set, two miles west of the city, in a large area of landscaped parkland, lifted slightly above the coastal road, with clear views across the wide sweep of Swansea Bay. There is an old original building, Singleton Abbey (a neo-Gothic mansion now housing administration offices), but the campus really consists of a collection of handsome new blocks, often quite dramatic in design. Tones are generally grey, white, soft brick; interiors light and airy (lots of glass) and outlines neatly edged. Grouping is compact and formal, the functional spaces enhanced by wide paved walkways, courts and quadrangles, strategic changes of level and a rectangular pool. The geometric lines are broken and softened by generous screens of trees, by the encircling green spaces of Singleton Park and by the College's own lawns.

With its parkland setting, its wide views, its clean, clear lines and a sense of energy generated by the sea air and by a friendly, busy student community happily housed, Swansea has good cause to count its blessings. The sense of a harmonious balance is probably helped by the fact that a proportion of its residential accommodation (but not too much) is on-campus. Halls add a nice touch of domestic presence without creating the room-based social life of the heavily residential campuses.

Other halls are comfortably close, but you can spread your wings, if you wish, into the self-catering Student Village two miles away at Hendrefoelan. The Department of Education is also at Hendrefoelan, close to the student village.

Cars

You are advised not to bring cars to University: parking is extremely limited. Cycles (hard work or motorised) can be parked. Although Wales inland becomes rather taxing, the coastal area and the Gower offer wonderful cycling terrain. Public transport is reliable, regular and cheap.

Learning Resources

The **library** has over 700,000 books and periodicals. Non-book provision includes audio-visual materials, CD-ROM/network/on-line services. Seating for 880 in the main library, and additional seating for 285 in the four other libraries. Opening hours: 9am to 10pm Monday to Friday; Saturday 9am to 5pm.

The **computer centre** provides advice and terminals in departments and halls of residence. The campus is fully networked with a campus backbone of fibre optic cabling joining all buildings. Open access facilities for use by students are available in locations around campus, between 8am and midnight weekdays and on Saturday mornings. Electronic mail (local and worldwide) and specific courses available in departments. The Multimedia Training Room has a range of learning programmes.

A **language laboratory** is dedicated to self-teaching (open 9am - 5pm). The School of European Languages will advise you on which of the many courses will suit you and your language level. Language teaching is within degree or Access course structures but there is a wealth of material for self-teaching. Introductory materials are available in more than 20 languages.

Culture on campus

The Taliesin Arts Centre, hexagonal, pale-brick, brings interesting lines and a rather stark elegance to the centre of campus. Interior space is stylish and functionally very successful. The Centre, owned and run by the University, also serves the community.

Drama: The theatre seats up to 365 people and presents a mixed programme of professional and amateur drama, dance, opera, film and concerts (classical to jazz and rock). Behind the Centre is the older Arts Hall building, where there is a studio theatre, seating 200, offering flexible space for less formal and experimental music and drama. There is at least one major production each term.

Film: One or two films a week; arts and mainstream. The Union Film Society shows films each week.

Music: Concerts for all tastes are held in both theatre and studio. The Taliesin Centre also has musical instruments (including some early instruments) for student use, and music tuition is on offer. The older Arts Hall building has soundproof practice and tuition rooms and a score and record library.

Art: Tuition is available in painting and ceramics. The University also owns and runs the Wellcome Museum, housing over 2,000 objects, mainly from Egypt.

You may apply for a Cultural scholarship for all arts/cultural pursuits, worth £700 per year.

The Union

The Union building is part of the epicentral blocks which include Fulton House, the main catering building, which has refectory, smaller dining rooms, a bar, snack and coffee bars. Here too: a post office, hairdresser's, shop, travel shop, launderette and medical practitioner's surgery. (The Union runs a second shop at the Student village at Hendrefoelan.) The complex is very busy and lively, and easy to find: just follow the crowds!

The Union has regular discos, quiz nights, bands and party nights. Several concerts, gigs etc. each week. From Indie to jazz, rave to heavy rock. *Bliss*, the Union's own nightclub, takes place fortnightly. The town itself provides many venues for entertainment and some students mix with the students of Swansea Institute. There are over 120 clubs and societies covering the usual political, religious, recreational and cultural spectrum. Community help projects for disadvantaged groups are run by Student Community Action. The Union produces *Waterfront*, a newspaper and a fortnightly broadsheet for Village residents. Also a campus radio station run by students.

The Union Welfare Service offers professional advice and a casework service. The Union also runs a study skills course in conjunction with the Counselling Service. There is Nightline service.

Sport

The University offers a programme of physical activity to suit the casual dabbler or the most dedicated and keen competitive spirit - and everyone else! The sports centre has a multipurpose hall (120 x 94 feet) with a maple strip floor, five squash courts, a weight-training room, a climbing wall and a 100 x 30 feet swimming pool: facilities for a full range of indoor sports are available. A special asset is its lounge area with fine views over playing fields and seascape. The centre is set on the coastal road and separated from the campus by the grounds of the hospital.

Rugby, football and hockey are the pre-eminent team games. There are two sets of playing fields. The 12 acres close to campus include rugby and soccer pitches, a floodlit 'driplay' hockey pitch, a 400-metre cinder athletics track with jumping and throwing areas, six tennis courts and two netball courts. A pavilion houses changing rooms, a refectory and a gymnasium (judo and karate).

The second playing field area is about four miles away. It has its own pavilion (housing a refreshment area and changing rooms), various pitches, a rifle range and a fishing lake. There is sailing at the Mumbles (the promontory shaping Swansea Bay), river rowing and the fine beaches of the Gower for surfing and canoeing.

Courses offered for coaches and referees. If you have outstanding sporting ability, you might be eligible for one of the College's Undergraduate Cultural and Sporting Entrance Scholarships, worth £700 per year each. You should complete the form at the back of the prospectus to receive further details and an application form, or contact the Registry for details.

Some sports facilities are open to the public (fees paid).

Student welfare

You are must register either with a local GP or at the NHS **medical centre** on campus where there is also an emergency service. A number of clinics are available and there is a dental surgery. There is a **Student Counselling Service** which gives professional, personal counselling: counsellors offer either group sessions or one-to-one contact. The Union also provides counselling.

Campus based chaplains cover most Christian sects. There is also a Jewish chaplain. Opportunity for worship for Muslim students is provided.

Careers Service

Students can arrange interviews from their first year, and more organised advice begins in the second year. There is strong practical support, including computerised information, assessment and guidance programmes. Individual advice and group workshops help with interview practice and application techniques. The Careers Service provides information on vacation work and on work and study overseas.

Students with special needs

Most of the newer buildings have wheelchair access and lifts. Neuadd Sibly Hall has a small number of rooms which have been adapted to accommodate students with mobility problems, and some rooms on campus are adapted for students with visual handicaps.

There is a study room for the visually handicapped, a braille embosser, a CCTV reader, a text reader with voice synthesizer, and ten four-track tape recorders. A Recording for the Blind Centre has three broadcast standard studios.

A tutor to disabled students acts as a counsellor to students and adviser to the University. There is a leaflet which outlines all the College's facilities available (also on tape and in braille) from the Admissions Office. You should write to the Registrar outlining your special needs before you apply.

Accommodation

The College accommodates 2,815 students in halls of residence or self-catering units in the Student Village at Hendrefoelan. The University guarantees its own accommodation only to those who have kept it as a 'firm' offer, have met the conditions of their offers and confirm acceptance of their place by 1 September; in the end 95% of initial applicants (firm and insurance offers) are actually allocated Swansea's own accommodation. Post-Clearing entrants should expect to search the private sector. The Accommodation Office will help and try to link you with students who share your interests. Oystermouth, just west of the College, once an old fishing village, now a centre for sailing, water skiing, windsurfing, sea-angling, offers a lively nightlife which has led to a concentration of students living there by choice and forming an independent community of their own.

Halls of residence

Two groups: three off-campus halls accommodate 520 students; three halls on-campus house 600.

Neuadd Beck was converted from a fine terrace of six houses, with new annexes, and is about half a mile east of the campus, close to a good shopping centre. There is a large common room and a library. The two other halls (grouped as the Clyne Halls) are about a mile to the west of campus. They have a parkland setting and the photogenic perk of an 18th century mansion, built in the style of a medieval fortress, as their main building.

Neuadd Gilbertson, with its annexes, balances with its companion, the College's most modern hall, Neuadd Martin, a functional, block design. Of the 490 students living here, 138 occupy shared rooms (by now our gentle readers will know that these, as a rule, go to first years). There is a Gothic common room and a library. Off-campus halls provide breakfast and dinner on weekdays and full board at weekends.

Halls on campus (the three Singleton Halls) are modern ten storey tower blocks housing 200 students in each block. Study-bedrooms are ranged around a central core of services. All are mixed;
one is partly bilingual (Welsh-speakers and learners will have priority). Some rooms are ensuite. There are common rooms. The halls provide breakfast only: other meals are taken in Fulton House, on a cash basis. All halls have laundries for personal use. Rooms are let during vacations, but you might be able to stay in hall (extra fee) over Easter and Christmas if you need to do so.

Costs (1995/96)

catered single off campus: £64.45 x 31 weeks includes all meals except lunch Monday to Friday
bed & breakfast single on campus: £48.95 - £55.95 per week for 31 weeks.

The Student Village at Hendrefoelan

The Student Village houses 1,675 students, mainly undergraduates, in houses which take between four and eleven people . The Village is about two miles north west of the campus and has an amenity centre, run by the Union, where you will find meeting rooms, a bar, fast food, a launderette and a shop. Tennis courts too. There is a regular bus service to and from Singleton Park. Welsh-speaking students and those learning the language can opt to be grouped with other speakers of the language.

The University also manages a number of leased houses shared between four to six students, between one to three miles from campus.

Costs (1995/96)

self-catering single: £33.60 - £35.50 x 40 weeks
All costs include fuel and water charges.

Private accommodation

There are attractive places within reach of College where you can find lodgings or self-catering flats, bedsits or student houses. Bedsits and shared houses cost around £35 per week.

Mature students

You must demonstrate commitment. A range of Access courses are considered for entry.

Nursery

The Union runs a nursery: 20 children aged two to five.

THE CITY (population: 200,000)

Swansea is the second largest city in Wales, after Cardiff. Before the 18th century, the town seemed to have a future as a picturesque watering-place, but its fate was darkened by the intense development of copper and other metals, with the coal and iron mined and worked inland. Swansea became a port-city, with six miles of quays and an industrial centre. Much of the access area around Swansea lies grey and grim: acres of chimneys and cooling towers mar the coastline towards Cardiff, and the northern approaches to the city are not prepossessing.

The bombing devastation in 1941 made necessary the rebuilding which has created modern Swansea - a well provided city with a compact shopping centre housing a full range of good-scale major chain stores, boutiques and other amenities. The personality of the city remains in its many small businesses and its many lively pubs. There is a good market, and some precinct-shopping.

The former dockland area has been transformed into the Maritime Quarter. You can walk or cycle along a seafront track from the Quarter to Mumbles, five miles away.

Theatres: The Grand Theatre has three bars, a restaurant and a bookshop and presents large scale musicals, comedy, drama, dance, Welsh National Opera, TV personalities. The Dylan Thomas Theatre, in the Maritime Quarter, is home of Swansea's leading amateur theatre group, but also presents professional theatre. The Patti Pavilion, in Victoria Park, puts on 'family' shows during the summer months.

Music: The Brangwyn Hall, in Swansea's Guildhall, offers concerts ranging in style from chamber music to 'pop'.

Cinema: Three cinemas and a major cinema complex.

Nightlife: A variety of pubs, bars, dance bars and clubs around the city, and a good range of restaurants.

Sport: The Swansea leisure centre offers a very wide range of activities and facilities. There are sailing and sea-angling schools in the Maritime Quarter, a municipal golf course (and others nearby), rugby, soccer and cricket to watch. A regional Sports Complex just outside the city includes a ski centre and County Cricket, first class rugby and Swansea City Football Club.

Festival: Swansea has a major festival in October.

ESCAPE ROUTES

Inland, and close to the city, rise the Brecon Beacons - not in the Snowdonia league of mountains, but very beautiful.

To the west of Swansea lie the Mumbles and the Gower - a great place for fishing, watersports and walking. You can walk from the Mumbles to Rhossili at the base of the peninsula. The Gower was designated the first area of outstanding natural beauty in Britain. Swansea and the Gower attract around one million tourists every year.

Communications

Trains run almost every hour to and from London: the journey takes less than three hours. There are direct trains to other major centres including Bristol and Birmingham. **Rapide coaches** link most major cities. The **M4** motorway runs within 3 miles of the city centre, giving fast access to Cardiff, Bristol and London. Connects with the M5 at Bristol. **Wales-Cardiff Airport** is a short drive away.

University of Wales Institute, Cardiff

PO Box 377
Llandaff Centre
Western Avenue
Cardiff CF5 2SG
Telephone: 01222 506070

Cardiff Institute has 4,000 full-time undergraduates, 1,200 HND students and 300 full-time postgraduates. Courses here are modular with a 'pick and mix' option (within 'sensible boundaries); modules are more usually within pre-set programmes. Assessment is by coursework/projects/examination. The Institute became a formal member of the University of Wales in 1996.

The Institute has 650 study bedrooms.

THE CAMPUS

The Institute occupies four teaching sites, plus a fifth site devoted to student accommodation, conferences and seminars. The concept of 'campus' should give way to one of student life woven into the fabric of the city - and a very handsome city it is. All sites mark out a rough semicircle around and close to the very centre of Cardiff. Each teaching site has adequate facilities (library, cafeteria, shop), but major student services (welfare, medical care, the Students' Union Office and main bars) are concentrated on Cyncoed, along with sports grounds.

Learning Resources

Each of the four teaching sites has a Learning Resources Centre, with study facilities and materials specific to work located there. The Computer Services Unit provides back-up support, including advice and training.

The Union

The Union Bar is in the Cyncoed Centre. The Union mounts discos and other entertainments - rock bands, comedy nights and video and quiz nights here; major balls at the Cardiff International Arena. There are minibuses to and from other Centres. Clubs and Societies: a range, including the Adventure Club, Christian Union, Remote Control Car Racing Club and the Arts Society. The Union runs two shops selling newspapers, confectionery and stationery, as well as art materials. Welfare advice is available on most issues, from housing to legal.

Sport

Facilities are concentrated at Cyncoed and include outdoor and indoor pitches, indoor tennis courts, a swimming pool, dance studio and floodlit Astroturf. Coaching courses and fitness advisors on hand; free inter-site transport.

Student welfare

The College has a very clear Welfare Pack which is sent to new students. The Medical Centre is at the Cyncoed Centre; nursing staff are also available on each of the Institute's other sites. The Institute has a professional counselling service, as well as a system of personal and course tutors.

The Careers Library at Cyncoed is stocked with various takeaway materials.

Accommodation

The Institute has a present total of 650 study bedrooms: 525 single rooms, some in eight-share flats, some in traditional halls, at Cyncoed; a further 130 rooms at the Fairwater Centre. 275 additional units should be available for October 1997 at Llandaff village.

Costs (1996/97)
Fully catered: £57 - £65 per week
Catered: £41 - £45 (ensuite)

Private sector
The Institute's Accommodation Office has lists of agencies and landlords and will send you a very useful leaflet on finding a flat. Costs: self-catering £35 to £45 per week.

Mature students

If you do not fulfil minimum entry requirements, the Institute will discuss your requirements and abilities, and guide you onto the course best suited to you. You should contact the Access Courses Manager for details of Access courses available through the Institute.

Nursery
The nursery takes children from 18 months to five years.

THE CITY/ESCAPE ROUTES

See University of Wales, Cardiff's entry.

University of Wales College, Newport

Allt-yr-yn Avenue,
Newport
Gwent
NP9 5XA
Telephone: 01633 432432

Gwent has 2,000 full-time undergraduates, 300 HND students and 110 full-time postgraduates. Courses here modularised within linear programmes. Assessment is by coursework and examination. Many of the programmes offered are vocational. The College has two sites - one in Caerleon, the other in Newport.

The College tries to accommodate all first years who request provision: if you apply before September 15th, a place is guaranteed

---

THE CAMPUS

The College has two main sites, one in Newport and one in Caerleon three miles away. A free bus shuttles between the two morning and afternoon.

Caerleon Campus

This campus is housed in a pleasant, imposing building in its own grounds and is the College's Administrative Centre. Also housed here: the Faculty of Education, Humanities and Science. Halls of residence, playing fields, tennis courts and a redgra pitch are all on-campus. The Newport School of Art and Design, a faculty of the College, shares the site in a new, purpose built complex housing studios and workshops.

Allt-yr-yn Campus

This campus is about a ten minute walk from the centre of Newport in a residential area of the town. The buildings are blocks, functional, reflecting the faculties housed here - the Faculty of Technology and the Business School.

Learning Resources

Three **libraries** house a total of 120,000 books and take around 650 periodicals. The Media Resources Unit provides **computing** facilities and video/photographic/audiovisual equipment. There is an open access Language Centre offering independent learning facilities.

The Union

Known as the Guild of Students. Entertainments range from comedy nights to live bands, all organised by the Entertainment Committee. Each campus has a shop, pool tables, televisions and recreational rooms. The Guild arranges free transport between Caerleon and Newport after major social events. 17 non-sporting clubs and societies (including Drama and Music) and 23 sports clubs in all. There is strong co-operation with Student Support Services; Guild officers can help with problems from housing through to financial.

Sport

Most sports facilities - gymnasia, games pitches, floodlit redgra pitch, health and fitness suite and tennis courts - are at the Caerleon campus. Other facilities, including swimming pools, are available locally in Newport. The local landscape and river-ways offer opportunities for most outdoor pursuits: sailing, canoeing, windsurfing, mountain-biking, rock-climbing and hill-walking. College teams are affiliated to national and local organisations (e.g. the Welsh Rugby Union and Welsh Cricket Association) and are involved in competitions both locally and nationally.

Student welfare

The College **Health Service** has bases on both sites. The **Counselling Service** is staffed by professional counsellors; there are also advisers available to help with legal and financial problems.

The **Careers Advisory Service** provides a range of materials and information including computer programmes and video equipment .

Accommodation

The College has a total 700 places, 465 of which are in a new development which has ensuite provision. The halls are on the Caerleon campus and the Accommodation Office try to accommodate all first years who request provision: if you apply before September 15th, a place is guaranteed. All rooms are single and self-catered, in the older halls 15 students share a kitchen, in the newer, five share a kitchen. Licenses run for 37 weeks.

Cost (1995/96)
self-catering: £38.20 pw; £44.50 pw ensuite

Private sector
The Accommodation Office keeps a list of properties near to the campus that are available. Weekly rents average £25-£40 for a room in a shared house.

Mature Students

If you are a mature student, your application will be considered on the basis of relevant experience and evidence of motivation to study. Access courses are also considered for entry: an Access and Foundation Programme runs at Caerleon.

THE CITY (population 128,000)

Newport is on the meeting of two rivers, where the Usk joins the Severn, and has been a settlement since the Bronze Age. Roman legions built the fort at Caerleon, and the Normans a castle around which the 'new town' grew: Newport was granted its charter in 1385 and has been a city ever since. Its architecture reflects this long history, and the explosion of its wealth in the 19th century when South Wales became one of the engines of the Industrial Revolution. The docks still operate today, working bulk cargoes. One of the city's most famous landmarks, along with its castle and medieval cathedral, is the transporter bridge, aerial ferry crossing, currently being renovated.

Shopping is a mix of high street names and specialist shops in covered Victorian arcades and pedestrian precincts. Several markets, including one indoors.

Entertainments: Theatre - The Newport Centre is venue for larger Arts events (rock, pop and classical concerts, opera and big name entertainment); the Dolman Theatre houses amateur dramatics and touring companies, Tredegar House has an open-air theatre and promotes a programme of special events. Cinema - Cannon three screens; Nightlife - a range of clubs and restaurants; Sports - The Newport Centre has a leisure pool with flumes and waves, squash courts and health suite and the city has two other leisure centres and swimming pools.

ESCAPE ROUTES

The Brecon Beacons and Wye Valley are within a twenty minute drive away. The Usk Valley travels into the city centre. This is a marvellous area for all outdoor pursuits and is very beautiful. You are also within easy reach of both Cardiff and Bristol: see their sections in this Guide.

Communications

Rail links with Cardiff, Bristol, Birmingham and London: Newport is on the main Cardiff to London line; trains are fast and regular. Newport is on the M4 with fast links to Cardiff and all points west, Bristol, with links to the M5, and London. Airports: close to Bristol and Cardiff Airports.

The North East Wales Institute of Higher Education

Plas Coch
Mold Road
Wrexham
Clwyd LL11 2AW
Telephone: 01978 290666

> NEWI has 1,250 undergraduate students, 760 HND students and 42 postgraduates on full-time programmes. Courses are modular within a Faculty framework. Assessment is a mix of practicals, assignments, coursework and exams. The Institute has a single campus in Wrexham.

THE CAMPUSES

NEWI is an Associate College of the University of Wales.

The Institute is building a single campus at Plas Coch, near the centre of Wrexham. The Learning Resources Centre and Information Technology Centre are now operating, along with a new base for the Students' Union and the first phase of the Student Village. All courses have moved here, except those in Art and Design which are a short walk away from campus, closer to the town centre.

Learning Resources

The new Learning Resources Centre houses the library, information technology and media services. Open to 9pm, the Centre has open access computers and provides help and advice on the use of facilities. The Centre also has a coffee shop, vending machines and a bookshop.

Culture on campus

The William Aston Hall on campus seat 890 and hosts touring ballet companies, the community Christmas pantomime and children's shows. The hall also hosts concerts by local and national choirs, soloists and the National Orchestra of Wales.

The Union

The Union runs more than 20 clubs and societies and arranges social events - discos, new bands, a Sunday quiz, big parties and the Summer Ball. On campus, the Union runs a shop, print shop, bar and a small recreation room. Welfare, legal and financial advice is available.

Sport

The College relies on local provision. The Union supports a number of sporting societies.

Student welfare

Qualified nurses are on call for emergencies and general health advice. Both the Union and Institute offer counselling and advice on personal and practical problems. There are group sessions on stress-management, exam anxiety, interview technique and relaxation. A full-time Careers Officer keeps information and gives advice.

Accommodation

The first phase of the student village at Plas Coch offers 216 ensuite rooms. The Institute also has halls of residence, all self-catered. Costs (1996/97): £46 pw (new halls); £39 pw (single: old halls); £33 pw (double: old halls).

Student rooms in Wrexham are readily available. Costs: around £33 per week plus bills (self-catering).

Mature students

Experience and commitment are considered alongside formal qualifications and the Institute is developing systems for the Accreditation of Prior Learning (APL).

Nursery
Limited creche facilities are available at Plas Coch.

TOWN (population 123,600)

Wrexham is Wales' fourth largest town, with a number of main shopping areas, indoor markets, high street shops and specialist boutiques. There are clubs, restaurants and pubs. The town's main strength is in sporting activities: the town's provision is remarkable for its size. The river Dee is near by and is one of the best salmon rivers in Wales.

Communications
Wrexham is around three and three quarter hours from London by train, an hour and a half from Manchester and three hours from Holyhead. Chester is less than twenty minutes away. By road: a series of A roads link the town with the national motorway network (M56 and M53)

Swansea Institute of Higher Education

Townhill Road
Swansea
SA2 0UT
Telephone: 01792 203482

Swansea Institute has 1,750 full-time undergraduates, 1,000 HND students and 50 full-time postgraduates. Courses here are modular, usually within named degree patterns. Assessment is a mix of coursework, projects and examination. The Institute has three main sites with two miles of each other in Swansea. The Institute houses 20% of first years.

THE CAMPUS

Swansea Institute is an Associated College of the University of Wales, an Accredited Institution of the University of the West of England and an Approved Centre for BTEC, Higher National and NVQ programmes.

The Institute has three main sites within a two mile of each other.

Townhill: above Swansea has views over Swansea Bay and Mumbles and houses courses in Education, Humanities, Art & Design.

Mount Pleasant and Penybryn Annexe: near the city centre house courses in Applied Design Engineering, Art & Design, Built Environment, Computing, the Business School, Law School, Leisure, Tourism and Transport. The Computer Services Centre is on this site.

Alexandra Road: in the city centre, close to the Glynn Vivian Art Gallery, used to be Swansea College of Art. Courses here: Architectural Stained Glass and the Foundation Year for Art & Design.

Learning Resources

The Institute has three main libraries which cater for the study needs of the Faculties in their immediate areas: total bookstock 130,000 volumes; the Institute subscribes to over 1,000 journals. Groups of computer workstations are located in Faculties across the Institute: about 450 computer are available. Open access on both main campuses: advisory services provided.

The Union

The Islwyn Bar on the Townhill campus is managed jointly by staff and students. Entertainments organised include live bands, barn dances and discos. Big events include the Annual Sports Dinner Dance. The Student Centre at Mount Pleasant offers fast food and a coffee bar. The Welfare Section of the Union includes a Women's Officer, Mature Students' Representative, Overseas Officer and Welsh Officer.

Sport

The Townhill campus has an outdoor tennis court and an indoor gymnasium and fitness centre. Clubs include rugby, football, netball, surfing, cricket, basketball, skiing, women's hockey, men's hockey, gaelic football, Alternative Sports, climbing, caving, canoeing and rambling.

Student welfare

The Student Health Service is run by qualified nursing staff. Daily surgeries are held at Townhill and Mount Pleasant. Counsellors are available for individual consultation. The Institute has several chaplains of various denominations. The careers service provides information and speakers.

Accommodation

The College has 255 places in Halls of Residence which accommodate approximately one in five of first years. Halls are situated on the Townhill campus but students based at any of the campuses may apply for a place. All rooms are single and self-catered. Cooking facilities provided or you may pay as you eat. Costs (1995/96): £35 per week term time only.

Private Sector
Private accommodation is readily available. Costs (1995/96): room in shared house: £35 per week; lodgings (half board): £50 to £55 per week.

Mature students

The Institute will consider applications from candidates over 21 who have no formal qualification. You must demonstrate 'motivation, potential and knowledge to benefit from the course'. Experience and training since school will be assessed.

CITY/ESCAPE ROUTES

See the University College of Swansea's entry.

Trinity College Carmarthen

College Road
Carmarthen
Dyfed SA31 3EP
Telephone: 01267 237971

1 8 4 8

> Trinity College has 1,500 undergraduate students on full-time programmes and 120 full-time postgraduates. The College has a single campus close to Carmarthen centre. Degrees offered: humanities, arts, education, information technology, heritage conservation and the environment.
>
> First years are usually housed on campus.

Trinity College is an Associated College of the University of Wales
Founded in 1848, it retains its historic role as a teacher training institution, but also offers a wide diversity of other courses, including BA and BSc degrees and higher degrees. The BA programme provides for single, joint and combined honours degrees in a range of subjects, including Archaeology, English, History, Religious Studies, Theatre Studies, and Welsh Studies. BSc courses include Health and the Environment, Heritage Conservation and Archaeology, Informational Systems and Technologies, and Studies in the Rural Environment. Trinity degree courses lead to honours degrees of the University of Wales.

Postgraduate study
For graduates, the College offers the Postgraduate Certificate in Education course and a distinctive range of higher degrees, including MA degrees in Bilingual Studies: A European Dimension, Children's Literature, Local History Studies, and Women's Writing and Feminist theory.

The College also offers an MPhil/PhD in Practical Theology and Religious Education.

Internationalism
Students are recruited both from the United States and Europe. The College has links with several universities in Europe.

Accommodation
There are five halls of residence on campus (including two completed recently) and there is also a new library - designed by the Projects Office of the Welsh School of Architecture - with a computerised index linked to an international network. The College has a computer centre, a theatre and concert-hall, laboratories, workshops and studios.

THE CAMPUS

The campus is set in suburban villa outskirts of Carmarthen above the rural roll of an area becoming dramatically remote, with a growing sense of wilderness beyond.

The College was founded in 1848 to train men teachers for Church schools, and its religious bent remains in the focal presence of its original plain, utilitarian chapel and the more beautiful chapel, looking far more 'Victorian' than the real thing, added in the 1930s. Most of the buildings on campus, however, are recently built. Halls of residence, teaching blocks and the new library - all windows, gantries and white spaces - bring sharp clear lines to this compact site. Compact but green and spacious, the lawned campus lies open to hill and sky.

This is a very small college, practically domestic in scale (most large comprehensive schools have more students). Friendly, intersupportive, very rapidly a familiar home from home - these are strong positives of place here.

Trinity is a bilingual college: most courses can be followed in either English or Welsh.

Learning Resources

The College's new library houses 80,000+ volumes. There is a well-equipped computer unit. Most courses have an element of computing; departments are networked.

Culture on campus

There are a number of student productions put on each year, and a programme of visiting professional theatre companies. The Halliwell Theatre is very well-equipped and has the seating capacity and stage area of a small professional theatre. There are also studio facilities here. The College has a choir, orchestra, chamber orchestra and folk groups. The Music Department has music practice rooms and you can ask for private tuition in a range of instruments from beginner to advanced level. Trinity's art collection includes etchings by Rembrandt and Augustus John, and lithographs by Renoir. The Art Department has studios for drawing and painting, textile printing and weaving.

The Union

The Students' Union building is new and is the College's social focal point.

Sport

The College has excellent on-site facilities, including an indoor heated swimming pool, all-weather astro-turf pitches (floodlit) and a weights room. Trinity has a particularly strong rugby tradition. Outdoor pursuits, from windsurfing, canoeing and sailing, to hang-gliding, rock-climbing and hiking, are all on your doorstep.

Student welfare

Trinity College is an intersupportive community. Its Christian foundation is the bedrock of its welfare service. There is a fully staffed sickbay. A local GP holds a surgery here once a week. The Chapel services are open anyone, from all denominations.

The careers library holds literature on postgraduate courses and all major employers, including listings of current teaching vacancies. Individual counselling is given by a careers advisor from the University of Wales who comes to the College. There are regular talks on careers related topics.

Accommodation

The College has five halls of residence on campus offering catered and self-catered rooms. First years are usually housed in halls of residence on campus.

Private sector
Most private accommodation is some distance from college: students may find themselves six or seven miles away.

Mature students

If you do not qualify for standard entry, you should contact the Registrar who will provide details of alternative qualifications and can arrange an advisory interview.

THE TOWN Population c. 15,000

Carmarthen is a small, close community; a market town serving a wide, thinly populated area. Very Welsh, quiet (except for the students) and very traditional. The river Towy is the last place in Wales where you can watch fishing from a coracle (implausible, round, ancient rivercraft). The market is one of the oldest in Wales and operates six days of the week.

There are lots of pubs, two nightspots and a cinema which doubles for live theatre, as and when. For more serious music and drama the town turns to gown: Trinity campus is the hub.

ESCAPE ROUTES

The area around is marvellous for things outdoor - beaches, mountains, rivers, castles: all very beautiful. Pendine Sands, famous for land-speed record attempts, nature reserves and nature trails, ancient sites and buildings, Dylan Thomas' Boat House at Langharne on the beautiful wild estuary flats of the Towy/Taf. Further afield, more spectacular coastalscapes to the west in Pembrokeshire; to the east, Swansea with its city life (see the entry in this Guide) is within range.

University of Glamorgan

Prifysgol
Morgannwg
Pontypridd
Mid Glamorgan CF37 1DL
Telephone: 01443 480480

University Charter date: 1992

Glamorgan is a medium-sized/large university with 10,000 full-time undergraduates and 1,626 full-time postgraduates. 5,000 part-time students also. Courses are modularised: assessment is a mix of continuous assessment, assignments and exams. The University has a single, 70 acre site, just outside Pontypridd.

First years are guaranteed a place in halls if they apply before the closing date.

THE CAMPUS

The University of Glamorgan is about a 15 minute drive from Cardiff in Treforest, just outside the town of Pontypridd, and in many senses is a greenfield campus. Its 70 acre site is tiered into the west side of the valley. There is an exhilarating sense of space even when the student population is moving full-tilt to find lunch.

The campus felt cared for and cared about by its students. Smoking is not allowed in interior public areas: only in commonrooms and staff-rooms.

The atmosphere is very friendly and calmly efficient; the library a good example of balance between the well-ordered and easy informality. New buildings - the Union and Sports Centre - are of extremely high quality, built in a neo-chalet style which fits very well the hillside setting: both were well-used, with active noticeboards. Three halls of residence on campus lend a sense of 'home' to an ambience already domestic. The halls are three storeys high, and cluster on the edge of the site.

Although in many ways the campus feels remote, it has its own station (Treforest) just in the valley, with a regular service to and from Cardiff.

Cars
There is limited car-parking on campus.

Learning Resources

The Learning Resources Centre at Treforest houses the Library, Media Services and bookshop. The **library** has 160,000 books, takes 1,167 current periodicals and seats 740. Open: weekdays to 11.45pm; Saturday to 5pm; Sunday to 6pm. The Centre is also a local information centre with a bulletin board of what is going on in the area. Equipment here for students with special needs.

The library has a **computer room** which - among its resources - has interactive training packages on study skills and is open 24 hours daily. A newly refurbished building at Glyntaff (10 minutes walk from the main campus) provides a similar range of library facilities for Business and Law students based there.

The **Information Technology Centre** offers a range of courses for non-computer-science students - including specific computing skills. A lot of help is available. The campus is networked.

Many courses incorporate a **foreign language**, and the Centre for Language Studies with two audio and audio-visual language laboratories teaches both students and staff. Programmed Language Courses give you language laboratory tuition in Arabic, Dutch, English, French, German, Greek, Hungarian, Italian, Portuguese, Russian, Spanish, Swedish and Welsh. Non-language students have access to facilities in the evenings. Degree course language modules are available in six European languages (including Welsh) and at Beginner or Intermediate level. Evening language courses are open to the public.

Culture on campus

Drama: The School of Humanities and Social Science has a small studio theatre (70 seats), and student drama happens at the Sherman Theatre (Cardiff), The Muni, Pontypridd (700 seats) and the Chapter Arts Centre in Cardiff. You can work with professional standard lighting and sound; all students can participate; there are active links with 'outside' drama groups - and a lot of student productions (four major and 15-20 workshops a year).

Music: There is a University choir and orchestra.

Art: A programme of workshops and lectures by visiting artists, and a connection with the 'Artists Residency Scheme' offers support.

The Union

The Union building has recently been extended. A different social event happens every night of the week: free jazz gigs, discos, film shows, fortnightly quizzes, live bands and Comedy Club night each Sunday. 70 clubs and societies in all. The Union has a pub-type bar, the George Knox, a cafe bar and a nightclub for discos and 'small name' bands. The Municipal Hall in Pontypridd is hired to attract 'big name' bands such as Blur. Also: a fast food cafeteria, a launderette, a travel centre, shop and an insurance bureau.

There is a full-time sabbatical officer responsible for student welfare, who works closely with the service provided by the University. A Nightline service runs every night during term. The Union also runs a Student Employment Service where you can register for full or part-time work.

The Union newspaper, *Leek*, has reviews of local and national events.

Sport

The Recreational Centre, centre campus, is built on three storeys and has a main hall large enough for all indoor sports, a combined sauna/solarium, two large weights rooms, four squash courts (one glass backed), a self-contained climbing wall which includes a totally inverted pitch and is 30 feet high by 60 feet long, a fitness testing area and a small hall for dance and aerobics and six badminton courts.

The University has a 30 acre playing field complex, 3 miles from campus, with a pavilion and floodlit pitches for soccer, rugby and hockey, and a floodlit trim trail. There are additional pitches for cricket, soccer and rugby, practice areas for golf and facilities for boule, croquet and field archery. The floodlit tennis courts on campus double up for five-a-side football, tennis and netball throughout the year.

About 40 sports clubs are sponsored by the Union. Coaching at all levels is available.

You have easy access to the coastline and mountains of Wales, access to two mountain centres and entry permits to local rivers and lakes, as well as to the more usual local amenities. Sailing/water sports: 12 miles away.

Students use the indoor facilities of the local authority for canoeing, subaqua and swimming.

Coaching is available, and there are classes at the Recreational Centre for all levels of sport, from beginner onwards. The University competes at local and national levels, and internationally. Facilities are open to the public, who pay to play.

Student welfare

The **Medical Centre** offers a comprehensive occupational health service. There is a sick bay, but not 24 hour medical coverage. A confidential **counselling service** is available without appointment during the daytime. Self help groups operate. The Ecumenical **chaplaincy** two full-time and one part-time (Jewish) chaplains. The University chapel the centre for many activities and for services. There is an Islamic prayer room.

Careers Service
The Careers Service has a well-stocked careers library and will help you with careers guidance at all stages of your course. The service offered is helpful and practical.

Students with special needs
Facilities provided include a brailling service, full electronic reader equipment, induction loop facilities and a volunteer reader scheme. Some residential accommodation has been adapted.

Accommodation

The University will guarantee a place in halls for first years if they apply before the closing date and accept a firm or insurance offer. The Student Village on campus has 728 ensuite bedrooms, communal dining areas and kitchens. There are three halls of residence on campus which can accommodate 506 students in single study bedrooms. Each hall has a communal lounge and limited snack-making facilities. The majority of these rooms are given to first years. Upper Church Village is a self-catering site less than three miles from campus. This houses 69 students in single study bedrooms with communal lounges, dining rooms and kitchens. All sites are warden controlled.

Costs (1995/96)
fully catered, single: £59.41 x 37 weeks
partially catered single: £49.60 x 37 weeks
self-catered on-campus: £38 - £44 (ensuite) x 37 weeks
self-catered off-campus: £36 x 37 weeks

Private sector accommodation
If you are not given a place in hall, you will be sent a list of private accommodation in the area. Self-catering accommodation costs are around £25 to £40 per week, excluding bills.

Mature students

You should contact the course leader in your chosen subject to discuss course requirements. Access courses and franchised courses in local FE colleges are available.

Nursery
The Play Centre on campus accommodates up to 30 children aged between one and five years (up to seven years during the vacation). During school half-term a Playscheme for children aged between 5 and 13 is run jointly with the Student Union.

THE TOWN (population: 32,000)

Pontypridd, about one mile from the campus, is a small industrial market town built mainly in the 19th century. Markets are held on Wednesdays and Saturdays and there are several pubs and restaurants. The Muni Arts Centre has an art gallery, theatre and cinema.

Treforest, where the campus actually is, can cater for your daily shopping needs.

Cardiff is only 20 minutes away by rail : the University's entry for city amenities and Escape Routes.

Communications

Trains to Cardiff run every half an hour: last train back leaves at 10.10pm. Regular train and coach services from the city. Treforest is 6 miles from Junction 32 on the M4 which spins a fast route east to Bristol and London, connecting with the **M5** and gives access to the nation's motorways. **Cardiff Airport** is international.

Scotland

University of Aberdeen
University of Abertay, Dundee
University of Dundee
The University of Edinburgh
University of Glasgow
Glasgow Caledonian University
Heriot-Watt University
Napier University
University of Paisley
Robert Gordon University
University of St Andrews
University of Stirling
University of Strathclyde

The Scottish universities do not merely add thirteen units to our total: they represent a different educational culture, an independent academic history, a separate definition of what university life is about.

We already knew parts of Scotland well, but were not prepared for the splendour of five of its universities. These fine campuses, distinguished by high architectural style, or by extraordinarily beautiful settings (or both), or by Edinburgh itself (a city to demand and justify hyperbole), are unrivalled by English universities, with the exception of Oxbridge and Durham. Four of them (Aberdeen, Edinburgh, Glasgow and St Andrews) pre-date all England's universities except Oxford and Cambridge. Scotland's educational heritage is long, complex and rich; with law and religion it defines a national culture so differentiated from England's that a trip north of the border is a trip abroad, as is a journey in the opposite direction. The differences should be noted, pondered, and weighed well.

The two systems

Scottish students take the Scottish Certificate of Education, usually in five subjects, at Higher level, after a one year course in the VIth form. The Certificate has more in common, in structure and level, with the International or European Baccalaureates than with the English 'A' level. The difference is significant, not in the definition of calibre of applicants (you will generally perform according to your ability, regardless of the kind of yardstick which measures you), but in the degree to which university study systems are locked into the nature and levels of learning achieved in the schools which feed them.

The Scottish universities accept SCE Highers as entry qualifications so that, although an increasing number of students stay on for an extra year to do the Certificate of VIth Year Studies, or indeed 'A' levels, a substantial number enter university while they are still 17 years old. Scottish first degree courses, therefore, are generally designed to cater for these school leavers and begin at a point which assumes prior knowledge at SCE Higher level.

Some students - those qualified well beyond the standard entry requirement of a particular faculty - might be exempted from all or part of the broad-based first year, and begin the narrowed down course in the second year. This is known as 'accelerated entry'.

Courses at English universities, on the other hand, often assume preliminary learning at 'A' level grade from courses which are longer and more specialised. Candidates normally take three subjects, for two years, and are over 18 years old when they enter university.

Access courses
All the Scottish universities, in collaboration, provide a one year pre-university course leading to the SCE Higher examinations.

Directional considerations

Scottish students entering English universities
The transition to being an undergraduate is a very testing time, even when you are the same age as your fellow students. If you are younger than your intake year, life will be that much more difficult.

Although the SCE Highers are acceptable entry qualifications for English universities, Scottish students might find the first year of traditional courses very demanding, especially in linear learning subjects, and an additional stress factor if they have not taken an 'A' level course. The age difference at 17-18 can also be significant, and might encourage you to think about an additional year in the VIth form.

English students entering Scottish universities
Clearly the converse of many of these points will apply.

In some (not all) Scottish universities, or particular subjects, your fellow students might be markedly younger than you.

Courses geared into SCE Highers might appear slowly paced in the first year. This can encourage a misguided lapse into indolence, which can too easily lead to failure; or you can lose the pace of learning.

In certain subjects, if your own grades are good enough, you might be able to gain exemption from year one. If so, you must be ready to find the second year very hard work, since the mathematics of Life are never straightforward.

Features of the Scottish university system

The Scottish honours degree is generally structured into four years, within which the first two, or even three, years are broadly based. Your decision on the area where you wish to specialise can therefore be delayed until you are entirely sure about your academic orientation. You are not in any way tied to the course you entered on your UCAS form.

This means 'that in the universities which admit by faculty, the same entry requirements are asked of all applicants to the faculty, no matter what UCAS coded specialism they have selected. They will also find that departmental subject requirements are characteristically kept to a minimum' (The Scottish Universities Entrance Guide).

A common pattern is for the first two years to be followed by two years of specialised study (for an Honours degree) or one year (for an Ordinary degree).

Exemption from all or part of the first year curriculum brings the period of study into line with that of English degrees (a factor which will weigh more heavily with the advent of loans), but you will lose out on the virtues of wide-access courses which are an attractive feature of the Scottish system.

A point which might appeal to arts students is that degrees awarded are generally MAs: not easily come by in English universities. This is true even if your performance at the end of your two pre-specialisation years indicates that you should be directed into an Ordinary (one further year) rather than an Honours (two year) course.

University of Aberdeen

Regent Walk
Aberdeen
AB9 1FX
Telephone: 01224 272000

University Charter date: 1494

Aberdeen is a medium-sized university with 9,000 full-time undergraduates and 1,700 full-time postgraduates. Courses here are modularised with the option of building an individual 'portfolio' of modules to create a degree. Assessment is a mix of continuous assessment and examinations. Almost all honours programmes include a dissertation. The University has two campuses, one in Old Aberdeen, the other in Aberdeen centre.

All first years whose families do not live within commuting distance of Aberdeen are guaranteed a place in a hall of residence.

THE CAMPUSES

The University occupies two campuses - certainly not to be described as a split site, since originally both colleges were distinct, rival universities! An interesting history: King's College, in Old Aberdeen, was founded by Bishop, supported by King and confirmed by Pope (in 1494); strengths which enabled its buildings and syllabus to survive the destructive zeal of the Reformation (with a change of staff); although the deflection of this zeal led (in 1593) to the foundation of the rival university (Marischal College) one and a half miles away, dominating the city centre. The two colleges/universities resisted attempts to unite them until 1860, when they were joined to form Aberdeen University.

King's College is set slightly inland, sheltered from the North Sea airs. Some of its medieval buildings are still in regular use. The lines of the lovely crown tower and college chapel are a distinguished centrepiece for the campus. Around it, the University has developed into a nicely planned, compact precinct, many of its new buildings handsome enough to complement the grace of the originals. Surrounded by cobbled streets, Georgian-and-older houses, green spaces and parks, the University has a pervading air of calm. On campus is the historic King's College chapel where staff and students have worshipped and sung together for 500 years - and still do.

Aberdeen, city and University, lies remote, and the solitudes of the sea, and wilderness inland, are in the air. Universities can be places of excessive hubbub, but here the atmosphere is civilised, orderly and friendly.

The present Marischal building, in Aberdeen centre, was rebuilt in the mid 19th century. Its massive splendour is military, castle-like in high granite. Entering the Marischal has the feeling of entering an ancient stronghold. One is daunted by the sheer scale of the architecture. The danger of becoming something of an outpost to King's mainstream is balanced by its city centre locale and by the close presence of the Union building (directly opposite). Marischal also houses the Marischal Museum, the Debater (chamber of the Debating Society - Aberdeen's oldest club) and the Mitchell Hall where evening concerts are held.

The University takes a responsible role in its community, presenting a series of wide-ranging open lectures to broaden the horizons of its students or anyone else in the community beyond.

Aberdeen's Medical School lies equidistant (2 miles) from Marischal and King's. It has the oldest medical chair (dating from 1497) in the English-speaking world.

The advent of the North Sea oil industry, which has changed the face of Aberdeen, has also stimulated change in the University, where a number of specialised courses have developed in tandem with oil technologies.

Cars
Growing problems with bringing a car, but it is useful here to have transport, if you can sort out where to park.

Learning Resources

The **library** contains over 1,050,000 volumes and is one of the largest in Scotland. It is located on six sites, the main one being the Queen Mother Library whose mix of open areas and rooms create an enclosed working environment with 700 study places. Other branches are in King's College, the Medical School, Marischal College, the School of Agriculture and the Taylor Building. Opening hours: to 10pm except Sunday (2pm to 10pm). The libraries take a total of 6,200 periodicals and can seat over 1,400 readers.

The **computing centre** supports the use of computing by all departments of the University. 1,000 workstations are available, some on 'card-carrying' open access. All undergraduate courses include an element of computing and students can gain a qualification in computing.

The facilities of the **language centre** are open to all students for advice. Self-instructional material for beginners is available in over 50 languages, some computer-assisted. Any student in the second year can take a **Television Studies** course which leads to a certificate.

Culture on campus

Drama: Drama flourishes, with different student societies coming to the fore each year. There is also an annual, large-scale, Student Charities Show.

Music: Regular free lunchtime concerts, evening concerts (with student discounts available) and recitals. The University has a chapel choir, symphony orchestra, choral society and various chamber groups. University music is twinned with the Paris Conservatoire and there is an exchange calendar of concerts. In 1995, the Yggdrasil Quartet were appointed to a third year residence to perform and stimulate music-making in the University.

The Union

When you first arrive in Aberdeen you will be met at the station by the SRC's welcoming committee. A tour will help you find your bearings and begin to break social ice.

The Union Building, opposite the Marischal Building in the centre of Aberdeen, has four bars (two serve as club venues at weekends; one serves lunch), a restaurant, two launderettes, a large pool and one of Scotland's largest snooker halls. Showers, autobank, clubrooms, a University travel agency. The shop here is one of three run by the Union, offering very competitive prices.

The Union backs 100-plus non-sporting societies and clubs and produces a weekly newspaper - *Gaudie* . There is a full calendar of events, very well supported.

Sport

The University's Department of Physical Education encourages staff and students to take part in sport, exercise and general physical recreation. In administering services and facilities, the Department works closely with the Student Athletic Association. Sporting club members have the professional support of teaching staff and enjoy quality facilities provided and funded by the University. Fitness classes, instructional classes in a range of sports and an advanced class in swimming are all available.

On campus facilities include the Butchart Recreation Centre, a large sports hall, 4 squash courts, gym and weight-training room. Just across the road the King's Pavilion (containing the swimming pool and 2 more squash courts) is partly surrounded by grass pitches and all-weather tennis courts. The main sports ground at Balgownie, a short bus ride away, provides pitches for rugby, football, hockey and shinty, as well as a bar and catering facilities. There are two ski areas only an hours drive away. Students also have the use of a mountain hut at Lochnagar.

Student welfare

The Student **Health Service** is staffed by four doctors and a dentist, offering treatment under the NHS. The University Counselling Service offers professional, confidential help, whatever your problems, and runs courses in areas of self-support and development. The SRC also employs a Welfare Officer. Full-time Church of Scotland, Anglican and Roman Catholic **chaplains** are always available on campus. Other denominations have part-time provision for the pastoral care of Free Church, Quaker and Muslim students. The Roman Catholic chaplaincy and the University chaplaincy centre are both in Old Aberdeen at the heart of the campus, providing quiet rooms and meeting rooms.

Careers Service

The Careers Service offers various self-assessment aids, including computer-assisted guidance programmes (PROSPECT etc.), and the Service trains you in writing applications and undergoing interviews. The Careers Library is well stocked.

Students with special needs

You should write to the Admissions Office before you submit your application, outlining your special needs: the University will supply you with relevant information on its provision.

Accommodation

All first year students whose family homes are outside Aberdeen are guaranteed a place in one of the University halls of residence if you apply to the Student Accommodation Office by September 9th.

Halls of residence

All halls are within walking distance of the King's site and are in two groups. Crombie-Johnston and Dunbar are close to the main campus and offer single study-bedrooms. Meals are provided in dining halls - breakfast and dinner, Monday-Saturday, brunch on Sunday - but some self-cooking facilities are available, together with laundries, common rooms and shops.

The Hillhead halls complex now accommodates some 2,400 students and is ten minutes' walk away from Kings. It includes three traditional halls very similar to the central halls, two less formal halls containing flats to accommodate six students each and five groups of self-catering flats. The central services block has the dining room, a cafe bar, bar and hall generating some social activity. The regular bus service to town is well used. Additional amenities include a games hall, library, bank and floodlit tennis courts and football pitch.

Costs (1996/97)

Halls of residence: single, catered £63.00 pw

Hillhead flats: self-catering average £44 pw (38 weeks)

Other University Flats

There are several on campus for group applications from two to seven students (£40 to £50 per week 50 weeks).

65 houses at nearby Bridge of Don have been converted into accommodation suitable for older students (£25 to £35 per week)

Private accommodation

For students who opt for lodgings or private flats in Aberdeen lists can be obtained from the Accommodation Office.

Lodgings are all checked, but first year students are advised not to go flat-hunting. Aberdeen is relatively expensive: weekly rents for flats range from £35 to £55 plus bills.

Mature Students

The University is actively committed to admitting mature students (over 21). There is an Access to Degree Studies programme to help mature students prepare for entry in most subjects. Anyone with an interest can, for a small fee, as an associate student, and study individual subjects without undertaking a full degree course, later transferring to a full course if they wish.

Nursery

There is a nursery for 24 children from birth to five years old. Fees are non-profit-making. Some subsidy may be available for students.

THE CITY (population: 204,885)

This is a spectacular city: 'Silver City', 'Granite City' - its sobriquets are inspired by its most notable building material, which does indeed glitter in the northern light. Its major thoroughfare, Union Street, broad and rising to its architectural climax-cluster of civic buildings, is lined by particularly handsome shops and office buildings, nobly proportioned, dressed in this remarkable local stone.

The group of buildings which crowns the city centre - the Marischal itself (one of the world's finest granite buildings), the Town House and St Andrew's Cathedral lift a magical skyline of crenellations and turrets fit for the pages of fairytale or chivalric romance. There is a general air of affluence, in part reflecting the wealth brought to the city by the years of oil trading, but also stemming from the city's solid commercial base in serving the needs of a large area and a widespread (if thinly scattered) population. Taking all this into account, it is not surprising to note that the city offers high-quality shopping. In addition to the established range of good shops, there are three recently developed shopping centres.

A city too of parks and flowers - it has won the Britain in Bloom award year after year. It claims to have a climate milder than its northern latitude would suggest (because the sea warms the coastal area) but when we were there the fine-day air had a sharper edge of frost than in the lowlands where we were based, and generally the North Sea does put a chill on the air, helped by the easterly air flow. But this is not Siberia: we liked it; there is a clarity of line in cold sea air and a brilliance of light.

The city centre is grid-planned and well-ordered, determined in its linear development largely by its two containing rivers. The great Marischal/Town House/ cathedral complex stands virtually at the city's edge: beyond are the docks, heavy now with rather ugly oil tankers and containers, outnumbering fishing vessels, and northward the empty coastal strip of sea-grass, sandy beaches, and the North Sea.

Back in the old part of the city, around King's College, where streets are cobbled and lined with beguiling period houses (one can turn a blind eye to the modern housing estate across the main road into the city) is the 14th century granite St Machar's Cathedral, partly castellated, quaint in design, hardly more than a stone's throw from the campus and some of the halls of residence. It has a 16th century oak ceiling with heraldic motifs, and modern stained glass. The Kirk of St Nicholas, just off Union Street, was first mentioned in 1157 and has a carillon of 48 bells.

Theatres: His Majesty's Theatre has a varied programme with performances by Scottish Ballet, Scottish Opera, drama featuring some famous names and touring repertory companies. The Arts Centre caters for small theatre groups as well as showing work by local artists and craftsmen.

Music: Aberdeen's Music Hall runs a series of concerts by the Scottish Chamber Orchestra. The Scottish National Orchestra and Aberdeen Sinfonietta are featured regularly, as are many other artists of international standing. There is a Choral Society and many choirs. The Capital Theatre presents folk concerts and Country and Western shows.

Cinema: Commercial film screening is at the Odeon (7 screens) and the Cannon (6 screens). World Cinema Club shows minority films; regular video-screenings at the Arts Centre; and the Capitol Theatre shows one film a week.

Nightlife: Aberdeen has a good range of restaurants and pubs, as you would expect from a port city, and many clubs and pubs offering student and promotional nights throughout the week. One very popular place is the Lemon Tree, offering a packed calendar of alternative theatre, comedy, dance and all types of music including bands. Pubs often host smaller names.

Sport: Aberdeen Football Club, rugby, Highland Games for the spectator. Seven public golf courses and facilities for most indoor sports for the more active. The Scottish Premier Division plays at Pitlochrie Stadium.

Festival: the annual International Youth Festival attracts dancers, musicians and performers from many countries world-wide.

ESCAPE ROUTES

Aberdeen lies at the meeting of two rivers on the edge of the North Sea. The Grampian mountains rise inland from the river plains of the Dee and the Don. This is fertile farming land; the rivers teem with fish and the small harbours up and down the coast have been safe haven from the rigours of the sea for centuries.

The land is empty, scattered with small villages and castle ruins. The Grampian foothills are more than 20 miles away, and their heights even further. The Grampian Transport Company offers a day of unlimited travel for £7.50, making some of the places of interest accessible. If you have a car, the Highlands are not too far away - an hour or so's drive; but they are not on your doorstep.

To the north are beaches, some sandy. The bay of Cruden is worth visiting: beaches and a golf course, and Slains Castle (1644). Here too is Bullers of Buchan, a chasm cut from rock, of which Dr Johnson said: 'no man can see [it] with indifference' - English understatement for Scottish magnificence.

Communications

Aberdeen is at the other end of a 125 **Intercity line** to London and from that you can branch out to most of the other destinations in the rail network. The **A94** connects Aberdeen with the south. Northwards A roads radiate into the Highlands. A new **airport** with improved flight schedules brought by the commercial boom. Flights to all UK airports and Norway, Denmark, Holland, France and the Republic of Ireland. P&O **ferries** to Orkney, Shetland and Norway.

University of Abertay

Bell Street
Dundee
DD1 1HG
Telephone: 0382 308080

University Charter date: 1994

Abertay is a small university with around 3,500 undergraduate students on full-time programmes and 200 full-time postgraduates. Courses are modularised and offered in a fairly limited range of subjects (variations on business, engineering, applied science). The University operates from four buildings around Dundee.

Accommodation is guaranteed to first years who apply before September 1st in their year of entry.

THE CAMPUS

Abertay operates from four buildings, all within a quarter of a mile of each other in central Dundee.

The Bell Street Campus is the main teaching campus and houses all three faculties, administrative offices, the library, media and computing centres and the student refectory. **Marketgait** is a five minute walk away and houses teaching accommodation and the Students' Union. **Nicol Street** is five minutes from Bell Street and Marketgait houses teaching and research accommodation. **Dudhope Castle** is a little further away and houses the Dundee Business School (postgraduate management education).

Learning Resources

A new library is planned for 1997. The present **library** (which is also open to the public) holds around 100,000 items, subscribes to 850 periodicals and seats over 440 readers. Opening hours: weekdays to 10pm and on weekend afternoons. The **Computer Centre** is open between 8.45am and 9pm. There are about 800 PCs across the four sites which are networked. The library has a language learning unit.

The Union

The Association elects a sabbatical President annually. The Union building on the Marketgait campus houses the Association offices, a licensed bar and disco, as well as other facilities. There are 50 clubs and societies. A range of entertainment is organised, including a number of special late night events. The Union offers a fitness centre, launderette, video games, meals, snooker, pool table tennis and a shop.

Sport

The Students' Association organises use of Dundee's local sports provision free of charge, both for organised clubs and individual students: three sports centres, the local College of Education's facilities and the city's country parks with fishing and sail-boarding.

Student welfare

A **doctor** visits the university daily and can be seen by appointment: you must register with a local doctor.. Professional **counselling** advice is available. **Chaplains** visit the university on a regular basis.

Careers Service

The Careers Education Programme includes careers seminars, individual interviews and workshops on application and interview techniques. The Careers Information Room has PROSPECT HE, a computerised guidance programme.

Students with special needs

The University has a bank of specialised support equipment, including assistance for students with dyslexia.

Accommodation

The University has 600 places in Halls of Residence or leased accommodation. Accommodation is guaranteed to first years who apply before September 1st. Halls are located: on campus, one and a half miles or three miles from the site. All accommodation is self-catering.

Costs (1995/96)

Range: £33.60 - £43.35 x 38 weeks

Private accommodation

Students are given help in finding accommodation, either with families or in rented flats. £35-£40 per week.

Mature students

The University organises foundation courses aimed at its own degrees and diplomas; there are also a number of Access courses provided by partner institutions.

THE CITY/ESCAPE ROUTES

See the University of Dundee's entry.

University of Dundee

Dundee
DD1 4HN
Telephone: 01382 23181

University Charter date: 1967

Dundee is a medium-sized university with almost 7,000 full-time undergraduates and 800 full-time postgraduates. Courses here are traditionally structured: additional subjects (a language or computing skills) can be taken alongside main subjects. Assessment is usually by end of year formal examinations, although some courses might offer certain exemptions. The University has a single campus, except for its Medical School

The University guarantees a place in hall to all entrant students who live outside Dundee.

THE CAMPUS

The University was founded (as a university college) in 1882, became part of St Andrews University in 1897 and received its independent Charter in 1967.

The outskirts of Dundee offer scope for campus developments in lovely surroundings: indeed the Ninewells Hospital and Medical School occupies such a site: from its hillside setting, two and a half miles from the University precinct, and well clear of the city, it looks over the Firth of Tay to the low hills and green spaces of North Fife. So, in choosing to develop on a small city centre site, straddling the boundary between working and residential areas, Dundee has honoured its origins as a City College and is a university which aims to serve its community.

The campus has a peaceful feel, preserved by its limited-access road system; but its position, a very short walk from the city centre, ensures an easy interflow. Students use the city to balance their campus world, and city folk can share a cultural world with the students in the Rep, a civic theatre built on campus and leased from the University, or in the University-owned Bonar Hall, which offers space for exhibitions (photographs, paintings and crafts) as well as a very fine, if small, auditorium for concerts - classical and jazz - and other dramatic events.

Space is at a premium in this concentrated campus, which has expanded upwards and out to its limits. Trees and green spaces are sufficient to relieve the lines of the functional modern blocks, but they are sparsely present. The site is edged to the north by older, more gracious buildings and some administrative offices are in small terraced houses, but the general impression is of a low-rise, modern campus. The only real example of lavish space is the Student Association building, exceptionally large and well-equipped for a university of this size.

The campus has an atmosphere of low-key camaraderie: its site has its attractions: its buildings command splendid views across the Tay and its famous bridges.

The Tay estuary is one of the least polluted major estuaries in Europe, and the Research Centre there offers ideal conditions for students from many departments to work on aspects of the aquatic environment.

The University maintains strong links with its host community through daytime and evening classes held on campus, in Dundee, or in centres throughout Tayside. Dundees's students attend classes, as well as local people.

The Duncan of Jordanstone College of Art

The College officially merged with the University in 1994 to become a faculty of the University. The faculty has, however, kept its old title and occupies two large post-war, purpose-built buildings on the University's campus.

Cars

Car-parking space is very limited and a permit system is in operation. Enquire before you bring your car.

Learning Resources

The University **library**, holding over 500,000 volumes and taking 3,800 periodicals, is divided between the new main library, the Ninewells medical library, the law library and several departmental libraries. There are reading spaces for about 800 students. Opening times: weekdays to 10pm, Saturday mornings and Sunday afternoons.

In addition to the usual on-campus and inter-University networks run by the Information and Technology Services, the University has a **microcomputer centre** for teaching and research. There are terminals for access to the local area network in most buildings. All students can take certificated courses in aspects of basic computer skills and a more advanced course can lead to a final degree credit.

There are facilities for self-teaching in many modern languages at all levels of ability in the **Language Unit**. Courses in practical French, German and Spanish are available as part of degree courses and there is a series of low cost Open Learning programmes, taught in classes.

Classes, workshops and group work in creative writing are held regularly, tutored by the 'writer in residence'. There are readings by visiting writers through the year.

Culture on campus

Drama: There is a University Dramatic Society and University Revue Group. Touring theatre companies use the Bonar Hall and the city's Rep Theatre.

Film: The student film society offers a programme of over 50 films each year.

Music: Touring musical groups use the Bonar Hall for concerts. There is a weekly programme of lunchtime concerts by visiting, University and local artists. The University has an Operatic and Musical Society, orchestra, chamber choir and jazz group. The Royal Scottish National Orchestra gives monthly concerts at Caird Hall.

The Union

The Student Association building is centrally located on the campus. The building is well-equipped and has a swimming pool, sauna and solarium and two banks. The Association runs two shops, a travel shop, a ('quiet') cafe bar, three other bars, a popular games room (10 pool tables and arcade games) and a pizza place (very limited menu). There is a typing service and you can hire disco equipment.

Events are held nightly, including films and quizzes. The Union is packed at weekends and is by far the biggest venue in Dundee. There are two weekly discos and regular cabaret. There are 60 societies covering most popular pastimes, and meeting rooms are available in the Union. A nightbus is run all week from 11pm at half-hourly intervals, and is free.

Sport

The 33 acre Riverside sports site provides five soccer pitches, three rugby and hockey pitches, a cricket square and floodlit playing area. A mile away is a floodlit non-turf training area.

On campus: a swimming pool, four floodlit all-weather tennis courts and three squash courts. The modern sports centre has courts for volleyball, basketball, netball, badminton and pitches for indoor hockey, soccer and tennis. There is a gymnasium and multigym room with free weights - 15 classes weekly for fitness enthusiasts.

The Water Activities Centre at Newport offers sailing, canoeing and subaqua. The surrounding countryside is good for hill walking, climbing and skiing.

The Sports Union sponsors some 35 clubs, from curling to karate, rucksack to trampoline. Low cost coaching courses are available in a few sports. Intramural sport competitions are held weekly. There is a physiotherapist available through the University's health centre.

The University offers bursaries for golfers worth £1,500 per year, supported by the Royal and Ancient Golf Club in St Andrews.

The P.E.Department serves the local community as well as students and runs a programme of classes.

Student welfare

The University's **health service** is additional to the NHS facilities and responsible for maintaining the health and well-being of students during their academic courses. The Counselling Service provides an advisory service on all facets of student life; as does the Student Advisory Service, which will help prospective as well as in-place students - and their parents. The **chaplaincy centre** has appointed chaplains and offers a chapel, library, common room, coffee bar and quiet room for meditation and prayer. It also hosts many student societies and lunchtime concerts.

Careers Service
Much careers support is offered through the departments and faculties. The Careers Service has two advisors (and four other staff) available for individual interviews. There are careers training courses and a programme of recruitment interviewing, as well as a well-stocked careers library. The service offers computer programmes, GRADSCOPE and Prospect.

Students with special needs
The University is working on making its buildings accessible, and has made 'considerable advances': there are two high-tech study centres for visually impaired and dyslexic students. Computer aided communication systems enable the non-speaking to converse. You should write to the Admissions Office outlining your special needs before you apply and, if possible, visit the campus. The University can normally find accommodation for you and any helper you may need.

Accommodation

The University guarantees a place in hall to all single entrant students in halls of residence (catered or self-catering), or in student houses or flats.

Halls of residence
Three halls provide meals and have common rooms, study areas and launderettes. Most rooms are single. Breakfast and dinner are provided. Each hall has a warden and a residents committee who organise events and represent student needs. All halls are either on or near campus.

Three halls are self-catered. Two are a five minute walk from campus and the third is two kilometres away adjacent to one of the catered halls. Some of the accommodation has ensuite, telephone and computer network facilities. The size of flats varies from four study bedrooms to ten.

Costs (1995/96)
Single room (catered) £53.55 per week x 31 weeks
Single room (self-catered) £31 - £46 per week x 38 weeks

Student houses or flats
Self-catering units to be shared by between four and seven students. Each is self-contained and there is a cleaning and laundry service. The lease may run for the year (50 weeks) or exclude the summer vacation. There are three main sites, all within a 3km radius of campus.

Costs (1995/96)
Self-catering £31.00 per week x 38 weeks.

Private accommodation
The Residences Office can supply you with a list of local private accommodation if you would prefer it: self-catering accommodation costs c.£35 - £40 per week (excluding bills).

Mature students

Sympathetic consideration is given to your career record if you apply as a mature student (over 21) without the usual qualifications. The University looks for evidence of recent study and of your capacity to work to degree level. A 10-week Summer School allows you a fast-track to demonstrate our potential. Access and part-time courses are available in Arts, Social Sciences, Science and Engineering. There is a very active Mature Student Society.

Nursery
Qualified staff supervise the two to five year old children of staff and students in the Association building. The nursery is open daily on weekdays from 8.45am to 5pm.

THE CITY (population: 176,000)

Driving to Dundee from the south west, one is optimistic: the road passes along hillsides, overlooking the broad Tay estuary, with the land rising to the north. The city does have a good setting, dropping to the riverside, framed inland by the gentle green coastal area and low hills.

Crossing to Dundee over the Tay road or rail bridges gives you a better impression. The two bridges stretch across the wide water, and Dundee, ahead, is given shape by its tower blocks and twin hills. The Tay railway bridge is famous: its 'Disaster' (it collapsed shortly after being built, in 1879, killing 75 people) was recorded in well-known verse by William McGonagall - 'The very best of the world's worst poets'.

This is a working city; the waterfront carries the paraphernalia of the docks, serving the oil industry and general cargo trade via a mesh of rails and sidings, and the riverside airport. The old trades of whaling and jute fabric manufacture have gone; the estuary and harbour now receive oil barges and cruise liners. 'Discovery', Captain Scott's ship, built in a Dundee shipyard and launched in 1901, returned in 1986 to rest appropriately here. Dundee's move forward from its history is reflected in the Technology Parks around the city.

Shopping facilities are varied and numerous, catering well for the half million or so people of the Tayside region: there are three shopping precincts in all. As with eating-out places, the shops are adequate and reasonably priced, rather than affluent. The town did not seem to be well endowed with shops that cater for the student market, no sign of the bric-a-brac cum ethnic shop that stocks the unique or slightly eccentric.

Theatre: The Rep is a modern civic professional theatre with a high reputation. The Whitehall Theatre stages local amateur productions, hosts touring companies and is used regularly by the university's Operatic and Musical Society.

Music: The Royal Scottish National Orchestra gives a monthly winter series of concerts and a summer Prom season in the Caird Hall which also hosts concerts by celebrities and bands. Scottish Opera and Scottish Ballet also perform. There is a summer Jazz and Blues Festival.

Cinema: The regional film theatre is the Steps Theatre. The Cannon Centre has 2 screens and the Odeon at the Stacks Leisure Park has 6. The Park is 3 miles from the city centre.

Nightlife: Fat Sam's, the Dundee Dance Factory and De Still's Nightclub are the places for new bands. Many city pubs have live entertainment, especially folk-singing at Broughty Ferry, a bus ride away.

Sport: Dundee has two Premier Division football teams, a rugby team in the top division of the Scottish National Leagues and an American football team. There are 40 golf courses within an hour's drive. The river Tay offers fishing (salmon and sea trout), sailing, canoeing and water-skiing. There are three major sports/leisure centres (one with sauna, health suite and flumes), squash courts and swimming pools. Canoeing, sailing, pony-trekking and (in season) skiing are all within easy range.

ESCAPE ROUTES

Dundee has grown as a port on the Firth of Tay, the land around is rich and fertile. To the north are the Sidlaw Hills, the gentle hills before the rising Grampians. North too are the Angus Glens, climbing country, rocky hills, cascading rivers. The region is wild with historic names (Glamis, Scone, Ossian...), although not always with the castles to go with them. The area is good for outdoor pursuits, and is within easy reach of Edinburgh.

Communications

Dundee is six hours from London by **train**, and has direct lines to Birmingham and the West Country. Fast links to Edinburgh, Glasgow and Aberdeen, all are little more than one hour away. Two **coach companies** run day and night services to London. There are good roads, dual carriageway or motorway, southwards to and beyond Glasgow and Edinburgh. In other directions in Scotland the roads are not so high speed, but are highly scenic.

University of Edinburgh

Old College
South Bridge
Edinburgh
EH8 9YL
Telephone: 0131 650 4360

University Charter date: 1582

Edinburgh is a large university with around 13,000 full-time undergraduates and 2,500 full-time postgraduates. The University's campus is difficult to extract from the city itself, except for the King's Building campus three kilometres out which houses the University's Science courses. Degree structures are flexible and can include trans-faculty study in the first two years. Assessment is usually a combination of assessed coursework and end of year exams.

First years from outside Edinburgh are guaranteed University accommodation.

THE CAMPUS

Although here it us just about impossible to separate the identity and style of the University from that of its host city, there are three major concentrations of university presence: George Square/Old College, the King's Buildings and the Pollock Halls of Residence (a kind of social campus).

George Square
The original square dates from 1776 and elegant houses of the period still stand on its west side; the rest of the buildings are modern. The Square and its close environs accommodate the Faculties of Arts and Social Sciences, some first year and medical-related sciences and the main University Library. The Medical School itself is just to the north. The Square is part of the city's dramatically beautiful central area. Quite a few of the student residences are in the area and the sports centre is nearby.

King's Buildings
The King's Buildings 'campus', three kilometres south, has been developed since 1928. All the University's Sciences are taught here (except first years who are taught in George Square): a third of all students. The buildings are, on the whole, homogeneous, except the Geology Department which would not be amiss in the Old Town. The site has its own academic and student services, including its own Union House (part of EUSA). The surrounding area is partly agricultural land (used by the School of Agriculture) and partly a residential suburb. There is a regular bus service into the Old Town, and the distance is not great.

The Pollock Halls
Half way between the other two sites, the ten-hall complex forms a modern social campus, housing about 1,800 students. Set just south of Holyrood Park and palace - a dream of a city environment.

Identifying these three clusters does not, however, erode the magic of the interweaving of the University's habitation and lifestyle with that of its city. Here, the City section of the Edinburgh text defines the University.

Car parking
Parking is very limited. Permits are available. There is a minibus shuttle from George Square to King's Building: or you could walk or cycle - the best way around this city.

Learning Resources

The main **library** in the Old College occupies what is said to be the largest academic library building in the UK. Its extensive collection is complemented by libraries, in seven faculties, some of which hold considerable stocks. The main library is open 9am to 10pm from Monday to Thursday, until 5pm on Friday and Saturday, and from 2pm to 7pm on Sunday. Hours are shorter at the branch libraries. Library provision is richly extended by major libraries in the city including the National Library of Scotland, which final year students can apply to join.

The **computer centre** offers a full service, access to a large number of networked terminals and general advice. There is access to the local network in some halls of residence.

The **language learning centre** offers a variety of modern languages, mostly through self-teaching programmes. The Institute for Applied Language Studies provides intensive language courses at varying costs. 'Half' courses at intermediate and beginner level in French, Spanish, German and Russian are available as part of all degrees.

Culture on campus

Drama: The Edinburgh University Theatre Company (founded in 1896) has its own 'Bedlam Theatre', one of the very few theatres completely student-run. It offers a wide selection of workshops to help students learn about all aspects of theatre. It produces over 70 shows a year, for both lunchtime and evening performances. The theatre is also used by touring companies. Other drama opportunities are offered by student societies. The University Theatre has a ten day festival of new works: the Febfest. The University also owns the George Square Theatre where University opera productions are staged.

Music: The University offers a wide variety of different types of vocal and instrumental music, from choral and orchestral performances, through more intimate choirs, to chamber music and opera. Lunchtime and evening concerts and recitals in the University's own Reid Music Hall (or in the McEwan Hall) involve both professional and student performers. Close connections are maintained with the Edinburgh Quartet.

Other music societies are less 'highbrow': the Big Band Society gives opportunities for jazz playing; the Great Highland Bagpipe Society caters for both beginners and advanced players; and the Folk Club with its own premises and a thriving membership.

St Cecilia's Hall in Cowgate is Edinburgh's original Georgian concert hall where the Russell Collection of harpsichords and spinets is put to use, and is also the setting for the University's annual summer Bach festival.

Film: The Students' Association has a film club run on membership-only admittance: membership is open to the city too. There are afternoon and evening showings, and some all-night bonanzas of up to ten consecutive films.

The Union

The Union here is the Edinburgh University Student Association (EUSA).

EUSA offers a comprehensive service to students from eight union buildings and provides facilities in six more and is unique in running PAMS house, a Union specifically for postgraduate and mature students. King's Buildings House provides services for students on the Science and Engineering campus. These include catering, games machines, sports facilities and a sauna.

The Student Association runs three Travel Centre branches and a comprehensive print shop service. Each Union has its own shop(s), games and tv rooms and refectories. Teviot Row House has a library, laundry and shower facilities.

Entertainments centre on the Union buildings: Teviot Row House and the Potterrow, and Societies' Centre, all within easy walking distance of each other. There are regular weekly events reflecting a range of interests and styles. All these Unions have bars and discos. Teviot Row House (the oldest purpose-built Student Union in the country) houses the largest nightclub in Edinburgh Societies' Centre has a popular cabaret night.

EUSA funds around 160 societies covering a full range of activities. The Societies Centre has a theatre, meeting rooms, an equipment pool and, of course, a bar.

Student Welfare is staffed by three professional members of staff reinforced by 30 trained volunteers. The Advice Place (Buccleuch Street and King's Buildings House) provides advice and information on a wide range of issues. The Association also organises a Legal Unit, money advice centre and Nightline.

The Association produces a free weekly newspaper, *Midweek* - a review of Association affairs. Also available weekly is *Student* covering both University and general current affairs, and 'what's on' in Edinburgh.

Sport

There are 49 sports clubs in the University and 30 professional coaches will help you raise your standards. There is an extensive intramural competition covering 14 sports and a fitness programme offers assessment, advice and a sports injuries clinic. Each year sports bursaries are awarded for high achievers in a wide range of sports.

The 25 acre Peffermill Sports Ground has grass pitches, a floodlit synthetic pitch, tennis courts, golf teaching and practice facilities and a large clubhouse.

At the Sports Centre (five minute walk from George Square) are sports halls, 10 squash courts, the fitness training centre, a combat salle, and rifle and archery ranges. The centre is open daily throughout the year.

Outdoor pursuits: a well-equipped residential base at Firbush Point Field Centre on Loch Tay. Here you can sail, canoe, ski and hill walk.

Student welfare

The Richard Verney **Health Centre** in the Student Centre provides comprehensive NHS care for students registered as patients. The University **counselling** service is available from 9.30am to 4.30pm every weekday. The University **chaplain** and associate chaplain work from the Chaplaincy Centre. Other religions find a home in student societies or centre in the city.

Careers Service

The University Careers Service has a well-stocked careers library and encourages students to start using the service well before their final year at university. There is a central programme of careers taster courses, plus Insight into Management courses.

Students with special needs

Some halls have adapted rooms. Access is not always easy. Technological support: CCTV, inducter loops; plus a Resource Centre in the Main Library with specialist computer equipment . There is a Dyslexia Adviser and a number of staff contacts who will help and advise. The Disability Officer advises departments and students.

Accommodation

Around 5,800 places available, in a mix of traditional full-board halls, student houses and flats. First year undergraduates from without the city are guaranteed a place in University accommodation provided their application form has reached the Accommodation Services by 1st September, and that UCAS has confirmed their academic place at Edinburgh by that date. However, the University reserves the right to use its discretion in offering students any particular style or type of accommodation.

Halls of residence

One main site: Pollock Halls (1,800 students): about half of all first years are accommodated in Pollock, which is half way between George Square and the King's Building campus. The site is in a beautiful setting, close to Holyrood Park and Arthur's Seat. Almost all rooms are single; 700 have ensuite facilities. There are sports and computing facilities, a library, music library, music practice rooms, a shop and bar. The administration block is a classic Scottish manor house and was once that most famous St Trinians school for girls. Pollock Halls is fully catered.

Student houses

Student houses take an average of 45 students each, a total of some 225 places for first years. They are located throughout the main University areas. Some first years have to share rooms. Self catering facilities are provided in communal kitchens. All houses have a warden

University flats

Over the past few years, the University has invested heavily in a continuing development programme which has resulted in a large amount of new accommodation in flats. Each purpose built or renovated block contains between 80 and 250 students. Around 1,700 places are now available for first years, almost all of them singles, in flats for (mainly) 4 to 6 persons. All are centrally heated and are conveniently located near the main campus areas.

Private accommodation

Accommodation Services keeps a register of approved lodgings and self-catering bedsitters. Most offer single rooms, some are shared. Most are within one and a half miles of the main campus areas. The Service also operates as an agency, putting students in touch with landlords who have vacant accommodation, these are not checked.

Estimated Costs (1996/97)

Halls of residence (full board)
single : £72 pw for 30 weeks
ensuite, single : £82 pw for 30 weeks
Student houses/flats (self-catering) : £46 pw for 37 weeks

All University rents quoted include central heating. Where this is not available (in some student houses) rents are approximately £3 to £4 per week lower. Rents in shared rooms are around 35% lower than those quoted for singles.

In private lodgings, a single room, self-catering, is available for around £46 per week, including bills.

Mature students

The University produces a prospectus for mature students (over 21), explaining the modified entrance requirements. There are special links with Access courses offered at Stevenson and Telford Colleges as well as in the Centre for Continuing Education.

Nursery

The University runs day nursery for the babies and young children (6 weeks - 5 years) of students and staff of the University. Open every weekday, from 8.45am to 5pm, for 48 weeks per year.

THE CITY (population: c. 500,000)

Edinburgh is a city built on seven hills, a city which has grown in two distinct phases, a city with 16,000 listed buildings - more than any other city in Britain outside London. It is the capital of Scotland and hyperbolically beautiful.

The Old Town grew around the castle, and along the high ridge to Holyrood Abbey. The buildings huddled in the shadow of the castle crags were built upwards rather than outwards within the old city walls: the bustle of community did not dare overspill into the hostile world beyond. Lawnmarket's tenements rise ten or fourteen storeys around courtyards. The Old Town is a place of wynds and alleys, small squares, ancient buildings, cobbled streets up steep inclines, brief vistas through archways, glimpses unchanged; and everywhere is the process of Edinburgh's history.

The Royal Mile, the main way from castle to abbey, passes through Castlehill, Lawnmarket, High Street, Grassmarket, Cowgate. Each section has its own history, caught in asides and side alleys. Every place has a story, or several: the surfaces you see now are only one more layer.

Edinburgh's Parliament, cathedrals, law courts all are here, contained in this small area. The City Chambers (built in 1753 as a centre for commercial affairs) was adopted by the town council in 1801 because commercial affairs continued to be centred in Edinburgh's streets and taverns, and such a fine building should never go to waste. It is an architectural curiosity, moulded to Edinburgh's particular geography - three storeys in front, 12 behind. The ridge drops away so steeply that this is not unusual for the great buildings which cling to its side.

Parliament House was home to the Scottish Parliament until the Act of Union in 1707, and is now seat of Scotland's Supreme Law Courts.

Whatever the rights and wrongs of Union, the Act did give Edinburgh city a break. Until then, the citizens remained inside the Flodden Wall - thrown up in 1513 after the disastrous Battle of Flodden. With the main enemy now safely south, Edinburgh could grow. The New Town began to be built in 1767. It was the space, the expansion, the relief of conditions the Old Town needed. And its building coincided with one of the most regal and remarkable architectural phases this island has ever experienced. The result is some of the finest, most elegant, most gracious streets in the world. The grid pattern of streets, with orderly squares and landscaped parks, balances the organic growth of the Old Town.

Three major streets - Queen Street, George Street and Princes Street run parallel, with a square at either end of George Street. Princes Street Gardens occupy what was the Nor' Loch, drained and fertile. Princes Street itself, above the hubbub of its shopfronts, is supremely beautiful - a wide, wide boulevard, expansive, wealthy and recently pedestrainised. Opposite rises the castle ridge, and the castle - night floodlit. Edinburgh is one of Europe's sensations.

We have not touched on the plethora of museums, of churches, gardens, shops and cafes this city offers. Have not even pointed out the obvious tourist attractions of the

Theatres: Edinburgh bursts with theatrical activity during the three weeks of the Edinburgh Festival. During the rest of the year, activity is lower key, but still vibrant. *The Royal Lyceum* is Edinburgh's main theatre, home to the Lyceum Theatre Company. *The French Institute* presents plays and concerts on its first floor. *The King's Theatre* shows ballet, drama and opera, as well as touring productions. *Churchill Theatre* shows for amateur productions. The Festival Theatre is newly opened (1996/97).

Music: The city has a number of concert halls: major concerts, chamber music, recitals are all part of the fabric of city life. Ushers Hall is the principal large scale concert hall which houses weekly concerts by the Scottish National Orchestra. Queen's Hall is a renovated Georgian church and has concerts regularly from the Scottish Chamber Orchestra and Scottish Baroque Ensemble.

The International Jazz Festival held in conjunction with the Edinburgh Festival. Live music happens all over the city every night.

Film: Edinburgh has two art cinemas: the Filmhouse, which gives concessions to students; and the Cameo, now refurbished. Commercial cinemas: the Odeon (five screens); Cannon (three); and Dominion (three).

Nightlife: The Grass Market teems with the city's young at the weekends as they hop from pub to pub; there is a considerable choice! Places of note are the Last Drop, so named as the Grass Market was the site of the gallows, and the White Hart, Edinburgh's oldest pub, which opened in 1740. Almost adjoining is Cowgate, a more enclosed street with good wooden floored, traditional ale houses, and some very popular nightclubs. During the day these areas offer plenty of student specials for food and long happy hours. There is a continental feel on warm nights.

Sport: Edinburgh has excellent sports facilities. The Meadowbank Sports Centre regularly hosts international events in its indoor halls (note the plural) and can cater for 80 sports in all. The Royal Commonwealth Pool in Holyrood Park Road is close to the Pollock Halls. This also has a diving pool, learner pool and sauna facilities. Craiglockhart Sports Centre is noted for its tennis facilities.

You can sail on the Firth of Forth from a number of bases within the city boundaries.

For the spectator, Murrayfield is Scotland's international rugby stadium. Murrayfield Ice Rink is the base of the Murrayfield Racers ice hockey club. Edinburgh has a number of football clubs: Hearts, Hibs and Meadowbank Thistle. Horse racing, steeple and flat, happens at Musselburgh. The motor-racing circuit is at Ingliston.

ESCAPE ROUTES

Should you ever want to go outside Edinburgh, your territory describes a semi-circle south of the Forth, and to the north is the Kingdom of Fife. Fife we leave to St Andrews.

The country around Edinburgh spans the coast out to the North Sea, the band of Forth industry to the west and hill ranges to the south. This is near Border country, the land tussled over by the Scots, French and English for many hundreds of years. Villages of neat houses around well-kept greens sit in the shadow of ruined castles.

Reading the history of the area, one is struck by the frequency of 'gutted', 'destroyed' 'recent restoration' and plain 'knocked down'. Not a stable place. But as well as ruins, Edinburgh's environs have a scattering of stately homes and gardens, gracious and civilised and sensibly built after the brouhaha died down.

South and west of Edinburgh rise the Pentland Hills, and to the east, its sister range, the Moorfoots. This is excellent rambling country, very pretty, not harsh, running down to the Border hills.

Communications

Edinburgh is a capital city. Its **rail-links** are comprehensive. There is an overnight train to London, which is probably the most painless way of doing the journey. Coach links likewise go and arrive from everywhere. Edinburgh is at the northern end of the A1. The M8 gives fast access to Glasgow, the M9 to Stirling and the road bridge to Fife cuts fast routes north to the mountains. Edinburgh International **Airport** is just eight miles from the city centre, with a regular bus-link from Waverley station.

Glasgow University

Glasgow
G12 8QQ
Telephone: 0141 339 8855

University Charter date: 1451

Glasgow is a large university with almost 16,000 full-time undergraduates and 2,000 full-time postgraduates. The University's campus is two miles out of the city centre. Degrees here are traditionally structured and examined.

Priority for accommodation is given to new students, but demand is great. Apply as soon as you can.

THE CAMPUS

The University was founded in 1451 by Papal Bull, and started its distinguished history in the Chapter House of Glasgow Cathedral. A 17th-century move to 'Old College' (a posthumous title) buildings has been lost without trace by the demolition and sprawl of the Industrial Revolution in 1870, when the University was forced to move to its present site by plans to drive a railroad through, close enough to destroy the academic calm.

The result is the finest (post-medieval) campus we have seen, at Gilmore Hill, about two miles west of Glasgow. The main building is zenith-style Sir George Gilbert Scott, a leading Victorian architect. It is a veritable extravaganza of towers, turrets, green quadrangles and amazing cloisters. Some very large buildings are very daunting - and this is very large - but here, as always when the great Victorians took their building zeal to excess, there is a magnetic sense of grandeur and dignity, in scale with the chivalric, monastic and monumental traditions from which the Gothic inspiration was drawn.

The interior offers magnificent halls, and the Hunterian Museum - a surprisingly friendly exhibition space, with Gothic windows; some meeting rooms are adorned by furniture and panelling from major rooms in the Old College. The University retained more of the fabric of its early days by rescuing the Lion and Unicorn staircase, now in Professor's Square beside the beautiful University Chapel (actually built in 1928).

This wonderful building stands on the edge of Kelvingrove Park, with clear views across the park and the banks of the Clyde. Splendid and huge though it is, a giant of a building in its time, today it is a flagship and figurehead to the wide spread of the extended campus, which is graced by many distinguished buildings of more modern design. As well as the purpose-built, impressive blocks - library, reading room, Union building - which extend or face the main building, the University has been fortunate enough to absorb the graciously proportioned period terraces which line the well-planned pattern of streets to the north. This domestic ambience, complete with gardens and trees, offsets admirably the stately quality of the main complex to create a university world which is at once friendly, dignified and dynamic. A number of student houses and flats, and a few restaurants offering good food add to the meld.

It is worthy of note that Glasgow and Strathclyde universities are very much products of their city, far more strongly so than in any other place we have surveyed. Traditions here draw students from home territory; many students live at home, so that family networks have links into university life. (There are parents' Receptions alongside some Open Days.) The universities have grown out of the needs of their city: the move into national (Scottish), UK and international eminence has been a product of time and reputation. Academic doors here are wide open to the community; the range of adult education courses at Glasgow University is quite literally amazing. Dynamic integration on this scale obviously works strongly against town/gown antipathies which shadow life at many universities.

An orientation programme for arts and social sciences students runs for eight days, end of September to early October - talks, bus tours, boat tours, rail trips in and around Glasgow and its environs.

Cars
There is very little car-parking space. You can apply for a permit, but don't be surprised if you're at the end of a long waiting list.

Learning Resources

The University **library**, together with departmental and other specialised libraries, holds over 2,000,000 items, plus a wealth of electronic databases. Those which are most in demand are kept in the undergraduate lending library open to 9.30pm on weekdays and until the early evening at weekends. The Library subscribes to 6,000 periodicals and spends £1.5 million each year on new materials.

The **Computing Service** offers a fast, powerful fibre optic campus network with PC clusters. Responsible use of the Internet is encouraged.

An audiovisual library in the Hetherington **Language Centre** has a collection of tapes which can be borrowed for individual learning by staff, students and the general public. The Centre operates a small TV production studio, a suite of four audiotape laboratories and computer-assisted language learning materials.

Culture on campus

Music: The University's flourishing music department fosters a good deal of musical talent in choirs, bands, orchestras, the Choral Society, chamber music, early music, opera and many other music-making groups. There is a full programme of recitals and concerts by distinguished artists. Composers of international repute visit the campus.

The Union

The Students' Representative Council speaks for the student body on the University committees; gives advice on welfare; produces the student newspaper '*Guardian*' and a termly magazine, *GUM*, and runs a TV service and radio station; funds enough clubs and societies to fill 16 pages in the Student Handbook; and runs shops, a travel bureau, a restaurant, a second-hand bookshop, photocopying and binding services and possible access to financial assistance if you are a worthy cause.

The other two Union buildings began by catering for male and female students separately. Glasgow University Union was a male preserve; Queen Margaret Union, female. Today they remain independent; you may be a member of one or the other and use both, but your gender is not a discriminatory factor. Queen Margaret Union has a casual style and relaxed atmosphere; the University Union is more formal, orderly and well-kept. QMU is the more lively gig venue; the concert hall holds 1,200 and many well-known bands have played there. Other offerings are two bars, catering facilities, discos, quizzes, local bands and - something of a surprise - bingo. UU has four bars, a nightclub (1,000 capacity) a games room with darts and pool facilities and an eight-table billiards hall. There are also concerts, libraries, reading rooms and guest bedrooms.

The Union Debating Chamber is the scene of regular and lively debates in the traditional parliamentary style.

The Union runs a Job Shop (employment bureau) and a night minibus between campus and halls of residence.

Sport

Programmes and classes are organised by the staff of the Sport and Recreation Service; you can also have your fitness assessed and tailor your activities. There are over 50 taught exercise sessions a week and instruction in swimming and various sports. The Stevenson Physical Education building on the main campus has a swimming pool, saunas and two gymnasia (squash, badminton, indoor soccer and pop-mobility). More indoor sports areas are available in the Kelvin Hall sports complex, very close to campus, which has an indoor 200m running track, conditioning room and human performance laboratory.

Playing fields and pavilions at Westerlands and Garscadden; a rifle range, riding school and a boathouse at Glasgow Green.

The Athletic Club offers 45 different sports, including judo, board-sailing, trampolining and mountaineering. Sports bursaries worth £1,000 a year are available.

Student welfare

The University provides a student **health service**, free of charge, to all students, staffed by a medical officer, hospital doctors, GPs, a SRN, a consultant psychiatrist and a clinical psychologist. **Student counsellors** give advice and support on specific problems or general personal difficulties. The **chaplaincy** is in the same building as the counselling service. In addition to the University Chaplain (Church of Scotland) there are Anglican, Catholic, Methodist, Free Church, Jewish, Baptist and Quaker chaplains. Near to the University are a Greek Orthodox church, a mosque and a Hindu temple. The University chapel is very beautiful.

Careers Service

As a supplement to the individual guidance given by your careers advisor, you can use PROSPECT and GRADSCOPE. The Service offers tuition in filling in application forms, presenting CVs and how to be interviewed, in addition to 'Insight into Management' courses, and conducts personal interviews. The Service can keep you informed of vacation work opportunities.

Students with special needs

The University's approach is practical and very positive. A lot of money has been spent on improving access: ramps, purpose-built rooms, additional parking spaces for the disabled. An active support project, VIA (Variety Initiative for disabled Access) is raising money and awareness on campus to improve conditions.

A specially designed library opened in February 1994 with state-of-the-art equipment to help blind and partially-sighted students from all the city's Higher Education establishments. The project was funded jointly by VIA and the RNIB.

You should write to the Registrar before submitting your application, outlining your special needs. Some buildings are still not suitable for students with mobility problems.

Accommodation

The range of accommodation is wide, from traditional halls of residence in Georgian terraces or modern glass and concrete blocks to student houses and flat developments. Murano Street Student Village accommodates over 1,150 students and offers a wide range of facilities and amenities. Priority is given to new students but demand is great. Apply as soon as you can; there are problems in accommodating students who apply after September 1st in their year of entry..

Halls of residence

Accommodation is in single or shared study-bedrooms. Most halls are within walking distance of the campus, although Wolfson Hall is reached by a charter bus service. Maclay Hall is self-catering, the rest provide all meals - except for lunch - Monday to Friday. There are around 1,000 places in halls.

Costs (1996/97)

catered: £1,567.70 - £1,833.69 (varying numbers of meals)
self-catering: single £1,151.29; shared £1,103.80
All leases are for thirty and a half weeks.

Student houses

These house from eight to 28 students, Cairncross House being the exception with 250 places, who cater and clean for themselves.

A new development, Murano Street Village, is slightly more expensive - accommodates 1,000. All are within one and a half miles of the University.

Costs (1996/97)

All houses are on 37.5 week contracts (including short vacations).
single: £1,290.78 - £1,558.59
shared: £1,201.53 - 1,518.24
Murano Street and Cairncross House have the most expensive rooms.

Postgraduate and Family Flats

These are intended for students who sign a 52-week lease for a self-contained flat. It is unlikely that first year students will have this option.

Private accommodation

The Accommodation Office keeps a register of private accommodation and will give general advice on how to find somewhere to live. Costs: self-catering: £160 - £180 per month excluding bills.

Mature students

Various faculties have their own requirements for admission if you are over 21 and without the normal entry qualifications. Experience as well as examination passes will count. The University runs two evening part-time Access courses.

Nursery

There is a nursery which takes up to 58 children between six weeks and five years, on a full- or part-time basis, 8am to 6pm, Monday to Friday throughout the year. Fees are reviewed annually.

THE CITY (population: 750,000)

More than anything else, Glasgow is a city of its people: changing, growing and open. Victorian industrialism, docklands, tenements, parks and pride; the new, the will-be-new, the now of art parading through the city's streets and galleries; beautiful and gracious buildings, a ring of tower blocks and then the hills.

Its streets are a grid pattern, held by dual-carriageways and overspill rebuilding. You should arrive by train into Queen Street Station if this is your first visit to the city, and carry with you the exhilaration of walking down into George Square. This is Glasgow's main square, dominated by the Italianate City Chambers - a celebration of Glasgow's wealth. There are 12 statues in this square, with Sir Walter Scott in prime position.

Glasgow's (now) most famous architect is Charles Rennie Mackintosh, whose School of Art is one of Glasgow's celebrated buildings. The Mackintosh Centre at Queen's Cross (also designed by CRM) celebrates the broader sweep of his work. Mackintosh's own axioms really sum up the style of Glasgow's city centre: 'usefulness, strength and beauty'. Mackintosh was not alone in leaving his mark on this city; Glasgow gave rein to its architects to create a flamboyant, beautiful city.

Heritage trails and walks around Glasgow are chronicled in handbooks which tell you where to look and what you are looking at. Above the shop fronts and down back streets is 'another city'. One route to Glasgow's past is the Firth and Clyde Canal, not a circular ramble, so remember the distance you go in one direction will be there on the way back. Start from Temple Bridge and head east. The canal dates from 1777 and is the branch which links to the Union Canal and Edinburgh.

Your walk will discover the north of the city, beyond the tourniquet of the M8. Glasgow was a city long before the explosion of its population and industry. Its cathedral dates from the 12th century, and is now - near to the Royal Infirmary - rather swamped in the area behind Strathclyde University which has been overtaken by the zealous clearances of post-war re-planning. Here too is the only medieval house left in the city. You will find ancient moments if you look.

This is, unexpectedly for some of you maybe, a green city. Its parks are, for a city of Glasgow's development and history, unparalleled in Europe. Victoria Park has a Fossil Grove of prehistoric tree stumps, Queens Park was the site of Mary Queen of Scots' last great battle (of Langside); Glasgow Green has been common land since the city's beginnings. Glasgow has 70 parks, and - unlike some statistics - it is a number which means something. They are not pocket squares, but areas for the people.

Shopping in Glasgow is contained in the 19th-century grid. Sauchiehall Street is the most famous thoroughfare. As you would expect, shops here offer large city-scale style and quality.

The City will be City of Architecture and Design for 1999.

Theatre: The King's Theatre plays host to touring companies, West End musicals and amateurs, while the Theatre Royal is visited regularly by national companies: the RSC and the National Theatre. There is a resident repertory company which has built up an international reputation, especially for productions of new work, at the Citizen's Theatre.

Traditional music-hall still flourishes at the Pavilion. The newest venue is Tramway, a huge space where many diverse projects in theatre, dance, jazz and the visual arts are planned. There are many small companies, some specialising in new work or alternative theatre. The city's arts festival, Mayfest, has been likened to the Edinburgh Fringe without Edinburgh's gentility - it specialises in provocative social and political comment. There is street theatre (StreetBiz) every August.

Music and dance: The musical life of Glasgow is particularly strong. The Theatre Royal is home to the BBC Scottish Symphony Orchestra, Scottish Opera and Scottish Ballet (all with established, international reputations). The Royal Scottish National Orchestra, with its choir, is also based in Glasgow, and performs in the Glasgow Royal Concert Hall. This wealth of orchestral activity in the city provides a pool of professional musicians for smaller group ensembles: there is a chamber orchestra, string quartets, wind ensembles, specialist groups - the Telemann Ensemble, the Scottish Early Music Consort, and the chamber group Cantilena. An International Jazz Festival is held every summer at the Theatre Royal. Folk and traditional music are also strong. Street entertainment of all kinds abounds.

Cinema: There are commercial cinemas (five in all, with a total of 26 screens) as well as the Glasgow Film Theatre, which shows limited-release films.

Nightlife: Everywhere. Everyway. Many famous acts have originated here and the brewer Tenants sponsors those that are up and coming. Bands for all tastes and venues aplenty. The club scene is equally varied, one very popular place being the Tuxedo Princess, a converted boat on the Clyde. Barrowlands and the Exhibition Centre are the main venues for live acts. Some clubs stay open until 3am...you will not be at a loss for something to do.

Sport: As far as football goes (and this is Scotland, so it goes a long way) you have to support Rangers or Celtic - impartiality is possible by supporting Partick Thistle, the University's nearest team. There are eight public golf-courses as well as private ones, dozens of bowling greens, and fishing in rivers and lochs. Football, rugby, athletics, cricket, wind surfing, horse-riding, mountaineering facilities are available and the city has two dry-ski slopes. The annual half-marathon is a particularly big event. For the less energetic moments, there are river cruises, rowing boats and snooker.

ESCAPE ROUTES

Surrounding Glasgow is some very beautiful country. The Campsie Fells and Kilpatrick Hills to the north are visible from the city centre; Loch Lomond and its bonny banks are only a few miles away; the Clyde winds back to source and to Lanark south east; the Forth and Clyde Canal cruises eastward, joining the Clyde and the Forth (as one might expect); and to the west flows the river, out to its Firth and the Isles of Arran and Kintyre. All around are battlegrounds, historic monuments, routs and routes of marching armies.

Even Glasgow's industrial heartland now has historic interest: the river Clyde, once the wealth bringer, is now being allowed to drop its working harness. Between Lanark and Glasgow, the river is bordered by parks and reserves, with walks and pathways. Beyond Glasgow, the Clyde flows out to sea and the landscape softens.

North of Glasgow Scotland truly begins, with its hills and lochs... We leave the large rest for you to discover: this is one book after all.

Communications

The **mainline stations** have regular services on intercity routes and are only 10 minutes from the University by underground. The scenic West Highland Line, with steamer connections to the islands begins here. **Coach links** are a little more prosaic, but no less accessible. Glasgow is on motorway links to the rest of both countries.

Glasgow Airport is 15 minutes from the city centre by coach link. It receives regular flights from London and other UK cities and there are direct services to the rest of Europe and North America.

Glasgow Caledonian University

City Campus
Cowcaddens Road
Glasgow
G4 0BA
Telephone: 0141 331 3000

University Charter date: 1992

Glasgow Caledonian is a medium-sized university with 8,500 full-time undergraduates and 608 full-time postgraduates. The University has three sites around Glasgow.

Priority for accommodation is given to students who have unconditional offers and live more than an hour from Glasgow.

THE CAMPUS

In September 1992, the Glasgow Polytechnic merged with The Queen's College to become the new Glasgow Caledonian University. The merger gives the new University three teaching sites: the City Campus, Park Campus, and Southbrae Campus.

City Campus
The campus occupies about 30 acres just outside Glasgow city centre next door to the Buchanan bus station. A library block, Students' Union, the Charles Oakley Laboratories, the Hamish Wood Building (Faculties of Business and Social Sciences), the University's administration, Careers, Welfare and Accommodation Offices, and the Science and Built Environment faculties are all based here. Most buildings date from the 1970s. The campus has some green space, but the environment is heavily urban.

Park Campus
A total contrast to the City campus on the edge of Kelvingrove Park (opposite Glasgow University). Trees, grass, quiet roads...only a mile from the City campus, but a different world. Its main building is a fine example of Victorian architecture (seen from the park); less attractive from the rear, where extension building has been haphazard. This was the original College of Technology and retains a collegiate atmosphere, pleasantly domestic. In the basement is a large Student Union room and a main hall, with a stage.

Courses: two departments from the Faculty of Business.

Southbrae campus
Southbrae campus houses the Faculty of Health Studies and is shared with Jordanhill College (see Strathclyde's entry) four miles away. Facilities include a physiotherapy gym and X-ray machines. Social amenities are limited, but you can use those of Jordanhill.

Learning Resources

The **libraries** at City and Park campuses have a total stock of 216,000 volumes, subscribe to 2,200 periodicals and can seat 850. The **Computer Services Unit** acts as support to all computer. Specialist facilities are attached to departments. The campus is networked. **Language learning** is possible only within degree/option structures. Languages available: French, Spanish and German.

The Union

The City Campus Union building has recently been refurbished and has a new diner/restaurant and 450 capacity entertainments venue. There are weekly discos; bands and comedians appear regularly. Park Campus has a bar, common room, multigym and fitness machines. Each site has a small shop. The Welfare Centre has two members of staff and there is a JOB SPOT for undergraduate employment.

Sport

The sports hall on the City campus has facilities for indoor sports (space for six badminton courts) and a recently equipped fitness room. Tuition and guidance are available. Playing fields are two miles away : a hockey pitch and three tennis courts. All sports hall facilities are free to students and open to members of the public. At Park campus has a small gym. The hall is used for aerobics classes. 20 sports clubs in all.

Student welfare

A **GP** visits the University twice a week and there is a full time resident Occupational Health Nurse. The **Welfare and Counselling Service** offer a drop in service. The Educational Development Service offers and study skills workshops. The **Chaplaincy** has one full time Christian chaplain. There is a prayer room for Muslim students.

Careers Service
The Service offers group workshops, computer-assisted guidance programmes (GRADSCOPE, ROGET etc), individual guidance and workshops.

Students with special needs
You should write to the Head of Student Services outlining your particular needs.

Accommodation

Self-catering flats next to City Campus accommodate 320 students in groups of six or eight. The Gibson Hall of Residence offers breakfast and evening meal five days a week and has single and shared rooms for 140 students.

The University leases flats from Glasgow City Council, at Red Road Court (floors 13 to 31): three students per flat; 60 students in all. The flats are well furnished. Next door is the YMCA which houses 120 students. The University also leases accommodation from the NHS.

The Accommodation Service will provide information on local private accommodation (only the lodgings are checked). Priority for University accommodation is given to students who hold unconditional offers and who live more than an hour from the University.

Mature students

The University is keen to encourage mature applicants. You should present evidence that you have the capability to pursue and benefit from your chosen course.

Nursery
There is a nursery on the City campus (22 places), taking babies from six weeks old to school age children.

THE CITY/ESCAPE ROUTES

See Glasgow University's entry.

Heriot-Watt University

Riccarton
Edinburgh
EH14 4AS
Telephone: 0131 449 5111

University Charter date: 1966

Heriot-Watt is a small university with around 4,000 full-time undergraduates and 700 full-time postgraduates. The University has a single campus eight miles from Edinburgh and three Associated Colleges: Edinburgh College of Art, Moray House (Institute of Education, Edinburgh) and the Scottish College of Textiles (Galashiels, about 33 miles south east of Edinburgh). Courses are modularised within coherent, carefully planned programmes.

The University accommodates all eligible first years - those from outside Edinburgh who apply for accommodation by the first Friday in September.

THE CAMPUS

Heriot-Watt had its origins in 1821. It became a chartered university in 1966 and in 1992 completed a phased move from the city centre out to the new, parkland, 380 acre campus at Riccarton, eight miles from the city centre. The site is just off the A71 western access to Edinburgh, set well away from the road, wooded, secluded, quiet. The immediate surroundings are rather featureless.

The campus itself is business-like, geometrically set, with high quality, state of the art (in commercial design) buildings. It has the feel of a large, busy, successful business complex, presenting a sharp image to its market. A generously proportioned site with changing levels and good screening by mature trees, so that the grouping of buildings can be imaginatively planned - and is. The Library now stands on the site of the original manor house; the original garden is still well tended.

The only part of the campus where space is not in generous supply, is the residential section, where the halls of residence are packed in high, neat rows, overlooking the small loch, pretty and tree-lined: indeed you have to cross a rustic wooden bridge to reach them.

A large Research Park is set close to the University. Heriot-Watt has the atmosphere of a practical, efficient place of learning whichhas successfully linked its academic processes to the worlds of technology and business. Links with industry generate millions of pounds worth of research every year.

Cars
There are no restrictions on bringing your car although parking space is limited.

Learning Resources

The Cameron Smail **Library** on the Riccarton campus is open from 9am to 9.45pm from Monday to Friday and from 9am to 5pm at weekends. The Library houses an Internet Resource Centre seating 500.

Computing Services offer advice, instruction, data preparation, programming of language courses and access to JANET. The local area network allows the linking of terminals, departmental computer systems and personal microcomputers throughout the campus, giving access to the Internet and world wide web.

In the **School of Languages**, learning another European language, as part of your degree course, is encouraged within joint degrees, as optional classes within other specialisms, and through private study.

Culture on campus

*Music:*The Music Society is involved mainly in classical music. There is also a choir, and groups catering for rock and folk music, and dancing.

The Union/Association

The Union building is well-equipped and houses a shop and travel agency, food, three bars and a small games room. The main hall holds 500. Entertainments: weekend discos, Wednesday double bill films, quizzes and karaoke.

A second term Freshers Fayre allows first years to launch their own clubs or societies. The Association presently funds around 50 societies, a fortnightly newspaper *Watt's On*, an annual handbook and a teletext-style radio service broadcast campus and Association news.

The Students' Association has offers advice and counselling, in addition to the University's Student Counsellor. An advice centre staffed by trained volunteers is open three afternoons a week.

Sport

The Riccarton campus sports centre and playing fields provide six football pitches, two rugby and a cricket square, a golf practice area, a floodlit training area, three tennis courts and two jogging courses around campus. Tuition is available.

The Tournament Centre for Squash has ten squash courts; also facilities for basketball, badminton, volleyball, indoor football, all-weather tennis, hockey and netball. There is a climbing wall, multigym, weights room and fitness testing room equipped with modern ergometers.

The Sports Union oversees 30 clubs offering coaching, a competitive programme of sports (including a six sport intramural competition), popmobility sessions and social events. Access is also provided to Edinburgh University's outdoor centre at Firbush Point.

Student welfare

Depending on whether your accommodation is on the Riccarton campus or in Edinburgh, you can register with the Heriot-Watt **Medical Centre practice** or with a local GP as convenient. Dental and nursing services are provided at Riccarton.

There is a **professional welfare officer** available to advise on personal and practical problems.

A multi-denominational **chaplaincy** team works from a purpose-built centre with social areas, meditation area and accommodation for any religious group to use. There is a Muslim prayer room.

Careers Service

The Service offers computer-based information, aptitude tests, careers seminars, workshops on job application and interview techniques and a Careers Education Programme, centred on departments.

Students with special needs

The modern buildings of this University should pose few problems for those of you with mobility problems. Some rooms are adapted and there are aid-facilities for sight and hearing.

Accommodation

The University accommodates all eligible first years - those from outside the Edinburgh area who apply for accommodation by the first Friday in September.

The University offers a total of 1,500 places in purpose-built residences on campus. Two main clumps: older residences and the new 'student village'. All the newer rooms (about half the total) have ensuite facilities.

Halls of residence

There are three groups of halls on campus, all are mixed and can accommodate 1,500 students in total in mainly single study-bedrooms. Self-catering accommodation has kitchens and lounges shared by groups of four or five students. Catered accommodation provides breakfast and dinner, and lunch on Sundays, in the central refectory.

The Riccarton flats provide 200 places in 4,5 and 6 person apartments, each containing a bathroom, kitchen and dining area. These are applied for on a group basis by second and subsequent year's students.

Leased flats

The University leases 100 furnished flats on a 'head lease' basis. Places are provided in flats suitable for three, five or six people.

Costs (1995/96)

Halls: catered single: £60 - £65 per week x 32 weeks
self-catering single: £36 - £44 (ensuite) per week x 34 weeks
Flats: £29 (shared) - £32 (single) per week x 38 weeks

Private accommodation

Student Welfare Services can supply a list of private lodgings approved by the University or bedsits. Average costs (self-catering): £40 - £45 per week plus bills.

Mature students

Applicants over 21 may be admitted without the usual formal qualifications but have to give evidence of their ability to undertake the degree course.

Nursery

The nursery on campus takes 12 babies and 28 over two's.

THE CITY/ESCAPE ROUTES

See The University of Edinburgh's entry.

Napier University

219 Colinton Road
Edinburgh
EH14 1DJ
Telephone: 0131 444 2266

University Charter date: 1992
Napier is a medium-sized university with 4,700 full-time undergraduates, 600 HND students and 600 full-time postgraduates. Courses are fully modular: assessment is by coursework and/or examination. The University has seven campuses around Edinburgh. Accommodation is not guaranteed.

THE CAMPUSES

Napier takes its name from John Napier, the inventor of logarithms; the Tower of Merchiston - where John Napier was born in 1550 - is the focal point of the main campus.

The University has seven teaching locations: Merchiston, Craiglockhart, Redwood House, Sighthill, North Merchiston, Marchmont and Craighouse. All are located on the west of the city, in very different areas. There is an inter-site bus service which runs hourly.

Merchiston
The Tower of Merchiston is the ancient centre of a 'wheel' of modern building which is the campus; now renovated, it forms an integral part of the site. Modern tower blocks surround and dwarf their 14th-century hub; for academic purposes, they are the Merchiston site. Before the Tower is a square - a chequerboard of pink, grey and beige concrete paving stones - surrounded by a metal fence .

The Merchiston campus is about three miles from the city centre, in leafy suburbs. The Open Learning Centre, Dunning Library and Faculties of Science and Engineering are mainly housed here. Other courses run include some courses in Applied Arts and one Business School course, Computing and Social Sciences.

Craiglockhart
The Craiglockhart campus is one and a half miles further out into the suburbs, towards the Pentland Hills. The campus is tiered into the hillside, with terraced lawns and views of the Forth Road and Rail Bridges; the central building is a Victorian mansion. This building, and its substantial modern wings, houses the University's administration and departments of Mathematics, Computing, Electrical and Electronic and Communication Engineering.

The site has a large chapel and chaplaincy centre (a relic from its past as a Catholic teacher training college), a hall of residence, a small swimming pool, a putting green, two large refectories and a snack bar. The East Wing of the campus buildings and the residency are both 1950s/60s additions. The main building was used as a convalescent home during the First World War: both Wilfred Owen and Siegfried Sassoon recuperated here.

Redwood House
Situated between Merchiston and Craiglockhart, Redwood House is home to Management Studies. This is set in one of Edinburgh's stately suburbs, and Redwood House does gracious justice to its situation. It is a large Victorian villa with turrets, ivy-clad walls, conservatory and walled garden. Very relaxed.

Sighthill
Off the busy A71, adjacent to an industrial estate and Wester Hailes (one of Edinburgh's larger council estates) stands a six-storey tower block from the 1970s with a small Students' Union building and sports dome.

The main building is well-maintained, clean and light. The library facilities are situated in a more modern extension to the tower block. There is also a very pleasant refectory and a large lecture theatre in the basement.

North Merchiston and Marchmont
Both these sites are former schools: North Merchiston is in rather a run down area; Marchmont in a popular student area of tenement living.

Craighouse Campus
This is the newest of Napier centres and houses 'hospitality' degrees - Hotel and Tourism Management as well as Communication, Journalism, Publishing and Music. The original buildings date from 1894 and are set in extensive grounds. The site is presently undergoing a refurbishment programme to fit it for its new role.

Learning Resources

The **library** contains 210,000 volumes and subscribes to nearly 2,000 periodicals. There are three libraries in all, one on each of the main campuses. All libraries are open until 9pm Monday to Thursday, 5pm on Friday, 10am to 4pm on Saturday and Sunday. The library on the Craiglockhart campus has recently been extended. The **Computer Services Unit** supports users on the three main sites: all open during the week and on Saturday mornings. The network covers the three main sites and Redwood House through terminals and PCs. You can learn a **foreign language** as part of your course; all language courses have an element of class teaching.

Culture on campus

Music: The University has a programme of visiting performers. Music tuition is available, and there are music practice rooms on the Sighthill campus. There is a symphonic wind band, chamber ensemble, big band and there are plans to put together a symphony orchestra. There are lunchtime concerts most Wednesdays, by professional or student musicians.

The Union

The Association funds three sabbatical posts. At present the Association offices are in the Merchiston Union, a converted house close by the site. There are also small Unions at Sighthill and Craiglockhart. In 1993 a new building, the Shack, opened in the heart of Edinburgh's Old Town, and is functioning as the main Union focal point. The building used to be a nightclub and now has two bars.

There are various clubs and societies, and you need a group of only ten students (including yourself) to set up your own. The fortnightly newspaper, *Veritas*, covers University and city news. *Blitzed* is a termly magazine and there are various welfare publications.

Sport

The Physical Education Unit is responsible for the operation and development of sporting facilities (including the sports dome at Sighthill): coaching, expert advice, supervision and support. Facilities include courts for squash, volleyball, badminton, and indoor hockey, a climbing wall, multigym, all-weather tennis courts, judo, fencing and golf tuition. The Unit organises a programme of intramural sport in a wide range of activities.

The Sports Union is a semi-autonomous body and runs the sports clubs: aerobics and aikido through to volleyball - around 25 at present.

Student welfare

The University has an **occupational health service**, staffed by a nurse and a part-time physician. There is a confidential **counselling service**, available daily at Craiglockhart and one day per week at Sighthill. The **Chaplaincy** (one full-time and three part-time chaplains) arranges meetings for worship.

Careers Service
The Service will help you to orient your decisions: there is a careers library and a number of computer programmes on offer. The service works closely with local employers.

Students with special needs
The University's multi-sited composition might make study difficult if you intend to follow a course sited on more than one campus. Students should arrange an appointment with the Special Needs Co-ordinator.

Accommodation

Accommodation is not guaranteed: there are seven times as many applicants as there are places! Priority is given to overseas students and first years who do not live within 25 miles of Edinburgh.

St Andrew's Hall of Residence at Craiglockhart comprises 60 single and 58 twin rooms. The University has 972 beds in student flats around the city in blocks ranging in size from 16 places to 250.

Costs (1995/96)
Halls of residence:

St Andrew Hall: single £42.00; double £32.50 per week
Self-catering flats: single: £48.50 per week

Private accommodation
The Accommodation Office has a register of private accommodation suitable for students. Lists of addresses will be sent to you if you accept an unconditional offer of a place at Napier. Private accommodation is not easy to find in Edinburgh; if you are coming from outside the area, come up early to begin your search. A shared house is likely to cost around £150 to £180 per month plus bills.

Mature students

You should be able to show that you are prepared for your intended course of study and have the potential to complete it successfully. Contact the Admissions Office for help and advice in making an application.

CITY /ESCAPE ROUTES

See The University of Edinburgh's entry.

University of Paisley

High Street
Paisley
Renfrewshire
PA1 2BE
Telephone: 0141 848 3000

University Charter date: 1992
Paisley is a medium-sized university with 5500 full-time undergraduates and 400 full-time postgraduates. Courses here are modularised. The University's main campus is in Paisley with a second campus in Ayr.

Residential accommodation is available to students from more than 25 miles away.

THE CAMPUSES

The University of Paisley has its origins in the Technical College and School of Art founded in 1897. In 1950 the College was designated a Scottish Central Institution and from September 1992 became the new University of Paisley. In 1993 the University merged with Craigie College of Education and has a second campus in Ayr. Students are based at one campus or the other; the distance between Ayr and Paisley makes daily travel impractical. There are special bus services in term time to serve local community-based students.

The Paisley campus

The main campus covers 20 acres in the centre of Paisley, just off the High Street. On three sides the campus is bounded (in part) by 19th century tenements which have been converted into various forms of student accommodation.

Campus building style ranges from the original Gardner Building (the old 1897 College of Technology), through a melee of 1960s and 70s blocks to the new Technology and Business Centre. Some local churches been converted into lecture halls and the town's Museum and Art Gallery is 'on campus'.

The Students' Union is some distance away. A small portakabin bookshop on campus stocks essential texts, and will place orders for you.

Cars

There is car parking at some residences and an NCP car park just off campus on Storie Street.

The Craigie campus, Ayr

This campus was the Craigie Estate - 20 acres of beautiful parkland bordering the river Ayr and close to the centre of the seaside town. The original 18th century mansion still stands in the park and the campus built around it in 1967. Residences and playing fields are located a short walk from the teaching blocks. The Faculty of Education is here.

Learning Resources

Altogether, the libraries at each campus house a total of over 200,000 items and take 1,400 current periodicals. Opening hours: 8.30am to 9pm on weekdays and 9am to 5pm on Saturdays during term time. **Computer Centre** laboratories are available on open access on weekdays until 9.30pm, except when booked for teaching. Students can take a **language module** as part of their degrees.

Culture on campus

Drama: The Craigie campus, Ayr, has a 320 seat theatre which is equipped for both drama and cinema.

The Union

The Union building (known as the Buroo) is a ten to fifteen minute walk from campus close to the town's amenities.

Sunday nights are dedicated to a pool competition and there are occasional theme nights: comedians, films, hypnotists, football or other sporting events. The Association backs around 40 sports clubs and societies; most are sports oriented. The Buroo's TV lounge bar has a small cafeteria, some pool tables and a small annexe for arcade games. The Association runs a small shop on campus. There is a disco hall which also has a large screen. Publications: a weekly newssheet XR, a term-time monthly magazine, and special handbooks for freshers.

The Association employs a Welfare Officer who can offer general advice. Hardship funds are available for rent arrears and single parents.

The Students' Association at the Craigie campus, Ayr organises social activities.

Sport

The sports facilities at Paisley are two miles away from the main campus at Thornly Park. The sports hall facilities include five-a-side football, netball, basketball, volleyball, high jump and table tennis. There is also a multigym. Two Astraturf football pitches have opened. Intramural competitions centre around 5-and-11-a side football.

Student welfare

The **Occupational Health Nurse** for advice and guidance; medication from a local GP, with whom you should register. **Student Advisory Officers** are available to discuss any problems and provide a link to outside organisations. The University **Chaplaincy** providing an inter faith service.

Careers Service

The Service gives guidance on career choices and occupational opportunities, and on self-presentation and communication skills. There are videos on application procedures and interview technique and a well-stocked careers library, plus access to Prospect and Gradscope.

Students with special needs

You are strongly encouraged to contact the University Registrar to discuss your particular needs before you apply. Some accommodation has been adapted for students with mobility problems.

Accommodation

There are five halls of residence and a number of flats in tenement properties around the campus. Priority is given to first years who live more than 25 miles away from campus.

Four halls and the flats are all within easy walking distance of the campus; one hall is two miles away, on a main bus route. All halls are self-catering and have social and recreational amenities.

Craigie campus, Ayr, has 169 places in a hall of residence, 102 catered.

Costs (1995/96)

Range: £25 - £31 per week x 31 weeks

University flats

University flats provide 247 places in single and shared rooms. This type of accommodation is not usually available to first year students.

Costs (1995/96)

£23 £29 per week. Leases run at a month's notice.

Private accommodation

The Residential Accommodation Unit has a register of private accommodation, mainly lodgings and a limited number of flats and bedsits. Self-catering: £35 to £40 per week.

Mature students

Paisley is part of the Scottish Wider Access Programme.

Nursery

The nursery has three places for children under three and 17 places for two and a half to five year olds.

PAISLEY (population: 79,000)

Paisley is seven miles from Glasgow but has its own identity. In the 19th century the town became synonymous with its textile industry, but its roots are more ancient. Part of the Abbey, which stands in the middle of the town, dates back to the 12th century, and is said to be the birthplace of the Stuart dynasty. The Abbey has now been rebuilt and restored. The town, through royal patronage, received its Burgh status in the 14th century.

Paisley Arts Centre has a 165-seat theatre and presents a variety of activities (dance, comedy and music including free jazz each Sunday) throughout the year. The Lagoon Leisure Centre has 'fun' pool complete with wave machines and a 50 metre flume. The Pro-Life fitness centre offers special student rates. The town has several nightclubs.

AYR (population: 50,000)

Ayr is a seaside, fishing and market town situated in the heart of Burns country within easy reach of rolling hills and historical sites (Culzean Castle) and national sporting centres for swimming, skating, golf, rugby, football and cricket. The town has pubs and nightclubs as well as shopping facilities, theatre and concert hall.

ESCAPE ROUTES

Surrounding Glasgow and Paisley is some very beautiful country: the Campsie Fells and Kilpatrick Hills to the north; Loch Lomond and its bonny banks; the Clyde winds back to source and to Lanark south east; and to the west flows the river, out to its Firth and the Isles of Arran and Kintyre. All around are battlegrounds, historic monuments, routs and routes of marching armies.

Even the industrial heartland now has historic interest: the river Clyde, once the wealth bringer, is now being allowed to drop its working harness. Between Lanark and Glasgow, the river is bordered by parks and reserves, with walks and pathways. Beyond Glasgow, the Clyde flows out to sea and the landscape softens.

North of Glasgow Scotland truly begins, with its hills and lochs

Communications

Transport to and from Glasgow is good. There are regular **trains** from Gilmour Street. The **M8** is only two miles away and connects with the national motorway network. **Glasgow Airport** is just a few miles away directly off the M8. You should look at the city section of the Glasgow University entry.

The Robert Gordon University, Aberdeen

Schoolhill
Aberdeen
AB9 1FR
Telephone: 01224 262000

University Charter date: 1992
Robert Gordon is a medium-sized university with 5,300 full-time undergraduates, 500 HND students and 430 full-time postgraduates. Courses here are modularised and the University is part of the SCOTCAT scheme. Assessment varies, but usually includes coursework and examinations. The University has nine sites dispersed around Aberdeen.

A total of 1,500 accommodation places

THE CAMPUS

The University's sites are spread around Aberdeen.

Schoolhill

This is the main University 'campus' - including three sites. Buildings here are part of the fabric of the city centre. University terrain contains the City Art Gallery and Museum and the Robert Gordon's School. Indeed, University and School share the use of the beautiful MacRobert Hall. So...19th century buildings, lawned areas and the dignity of some of the city's fine buildings: this is a handsome context for your studies, even if you do have to share territory with the pupils of the School. The main library is in this complex.

Courses: Applied Sciences; Pharmacy; Mechanical & Offshore Engineering; Electronic & Electrical Engineering; Computer & Mathematical Sciences; plus the Paper Technology Unit.

Woolmanhill

The School of Health Sciences has a base near the Aberdeen Royal Infirmary, close to Schoolhill.

Kepplestone

Occupying the grounds of an old mansion on the inner ring road, a short bus ride, or a longish walk (nearly two miles), from Schoolhill and the city centre.. Buildings here: a five storey 1960's glass-and-panel block, with annexes.

Courses: Offshore Management Centre; Schools of Applied Social Studies; Nursing; Food and Consumer Studies.

Merkland

A small, friendly 'campus'. Two teaching buildings: one used to be a primary school, the other a paupers' hospital (a listed building). The site is a shortish walk from Schoolhill.

Courses: Public Administration and Law. There is an Offshore Survival Centre here and a Survival Tank.

Hilton

Here, the University shares premises with the Northern College of Education, leasing space in their modern buildings. You can use the College's facilities: a Games Hall, four gyms, a Dance Studio, tennis courts, football and hockey pitches and a swimming pool. Two miles or so from the city centre

Courses: Librarianship & Information Services; Public Administration & Law; Business School.

Garthdee

This beautiful riverside site occupies the grounds of a Victorian mansion and its large modern extensions. Together these house the Scott Sutherland School of Architecture. The Gray's School of Art and the School of Surveying are also based here (kilns in the old Gatehouse). The site is 3-4 miles from the city centre. A bus ride.

Courses: Architecture, Art & Design , Surveying.

Foresterhill College of Nursing

Now part of the University's Faculty of Nursing.

Learning Resources

The Central **Library** is on St Andrew's Street (Schoolhill) and caters for all schools on the main site. All other campuses have their own specialist libraries, and the larger ones have CD-ROM facilities. Total bookstock: 180,000; current periodicals 1,600. Opening hours at the main library are Monday to Thursday to 9.45pm, Friday to 5.45pm, Saturday afternoons and to 8.45pm on Sunday. **Computer Services Unit** has an advisory service. Computer laboratories are available on open access, except when in teaching use, until 9.30pm. The University's sites are fully networked. **Languages** can be part of all courses.

Culture on campus

All students can use facilities on all sites. The small hall at Kepplestone houses the occasional drama production.

The Union

The Association building is at Schoolhill and houses a well used refectory, a launderette, shop and small games room. There are two bars. The Association funds around 30 clubs and societies, mainly sports oriented. The Association's 'Review' has articles, sports news and listings. One of the two sabbatical officers takes on Welfare responsibilities. Students here may use the facilities of all higher and further education institutions in the city, including those of the University of Aberdeen. This is a reciprocal arrangement.

Sport

Facilities are on the various sites. Kepplestone has grass pitches for football, hockey and rugby (one of each) and a hall for small court sports and aerobics. St Andrew Street (Schoolhill) has a large hall used for indoor hockey and football. The swimming pool at the Robert Gordon's School is open to students one night a week and good use is made of municipal facilities. There is also a swimming pool on the Hilton site.

Student welfare

Local **GP's** can be seen four afternoons a week at Schoolhill. Health promotion clinics are also arranged. The **counselling service** is based at Schoolhill. The **chaplaincy** is open Wednesdays and Fridays between 12pm and 2pm. The service is ecumenical. The Careers Service offers a weekly CV 'Surgery' helps with application forms.

Students with special needs

A Development Officer and a dedicated Student Counsellor are available. Some accommodation has been adapted for wheelchair users.

Accommodation

The University owns or controls about 1,500 places in all.

Halls of Residence

Two older halls (Queens and Highland, both close to the city centre) offer catered accommodation. Rooms are single or shared (up to four). Each is single sex: one for women, one for men.

Self-catered halls at Woolmanhill, Kepplestone, Garthdee and King Street (close to the harbour area and the city centre) house students in units of six single study bedrooms, with shared kitchen, bathroom, lounge and laundry facilities. Some units at Woolmanhill and Garthdee offer ensuite facilities.

University leased property

A self-catering complex in the Harbour area houses 70 male students.

Costs (1995/96)

Halls: single - £1,938; shared £1,768 - £1,818 per session
Flats: single: £1,445 - £1,972 (ensuite) per session

Private Accommodation

The Student Accommodation Service keeps registers of lodgings (not all checked) and flats/shared rooms. Also look at the recommended solicitors property shops. Costs: self-catering - £40-£50 (exclusive of bills)

Mature students

If you are over 21 and do not have formal qualifications, relevant work experience will be taken into account. Write to the Admissions Office.

Nursery

Treehouse nursery at Kepplestone is non-profit making; places available for students' children.

THE CITY/ESCAPE ROUTES

See Aberdeen University's entry in this Guide.

University of St Andrews

College Gate
St Andrews
KY16 9AJ
Telephone: 01334 463324

University Charter date: 1411

St Andrews is a small/medium-sized university with around 5,000 full-time undergraduates and 500 full-time postgraduates. The University campus is dispersed throughout the small city. Most degrees here are modularised; traditional degree structures in named subjects are also available. Assessment is usually by a combination of examination and continuous assessment.

Many students have three years in residence or self-catering houses provided by the University.

THE CAMPUS

Approaching St Andrews from the Tay Bridge and Dundee (or from the A91 - this is the main access route), one crosses low-lying agricultural land, the sea-line on your left: pleasant enough terrain but unpromising.

Entering the city itself, preferably on foot or cycle, is an experience to remember. A walk (not very long) down ways, following the medieval street plan, lined with old-style shops and ancient buildings, takes you rapidly through and out to the sea shore, to find the twin glories of castle and cathedral ruins standing on the very edge of this rocky coastline.

Inland, the University buildings, even when sought out, come with the shock of beauty found by chance: they blend easily into the old streets of the small city, often half-hidden by high walls. They are built around quadrangles; occupy blocks on street corners; hide behind newer buildings.

The University was founded in 1411, the first in Scotland, and recognised by Papal Bull in 1413. The oldest surviving buildings are St Mary's College and St Salvator's Chapel, both dating from the early 16th century; by this time, the University had (and still has) three colleges.

St Mary's draws its membership from all Divinity students; St Salvator's and St Leonard's have functioned jointly as United College (since 1747) to receive all arts and science undergraduates; and St Leonard's has a dual role in receiving all postgraduates. Staff and students alike are members of these colleges, a feature which determines St Andrews as a collegiate university. Academic life, however, follows the faculty patterns.

There is a modern note struck appropriately by the North Haugh site, housing the Physical, Mathematical and Computer Sciences. This is half a mile out of the city centre - far country in terms of the geography here.

For centuries the University's fortunes were closely bound in with those of the Roman Catholic church: traditionally this was a centre for the cult of St Andrew (there was a legend that the saint's bones were brought here, creating a place of pilgrimage). Consequently, the importance of gown, with 'town', declined sharply after the Reformation and the Union with Protestant England.

Resurgence came in the 19th century and University and city have flourished since then. Many of the buildings date from this time. Naturally enough, tradition carries weight here: you will become involved in the intricacies of wearing the fetching scarlet gowns in the correct way at the correct time; you might join processions along the pier that forms the breakwater for the small harbour; you might join in the Kate Kennedy procession/pageant in April; you might give a bottle of wine to your 'parent' students (and look forward to your own turn) on Raisin Monday, in the first (Martinmas) semester. The second semester, in case you are curious, is Candlemas. The 'parent' tradition is rather a nice one: first year students are assigned to male and female senior students who will introduce you to student life, and a wide circle of acquaintances, and help you find your feet.

But you will soon find your bearings in this tiny city. Mutual city-University dependence is relieved by the complementary summer tourist trade and by the business brought to the city by its internationally famous golf courses. As a student here you will know the nooks and crannies, the main streets and byways, the coastal walks and inland farmland within a matter of weeks.

Many universities create this sense of privileged remove, and here it is intensified by long, historic isolation. The ancient kingdom of Fife was geographically isolated until the Tay was road-bridged in the 1960s. It takes a long time for this sense of isolation to erode, and the separate-world quality lingers for generations.

Cars

Cars in such an environment are obtrusive, and you should weigh this against the fairly remote nature of the University. The newer halls have car-parking space.

Learning Resources

The University **library** has around 780,000 books and seats for 610 readers. Opening times: 8.45am to 10pm Monday to Thursday; 8.45am to 6pm Friday; 9am to noon Saturday; 2pm to 7pm Sunday. The library takes 4,000 periodicals and offers a wide range of computer based information services. There are also specialised branch and departmental libraries.

The **computing laboratory** is open on weekdays throughout the year. Facilities have been recently upgraded; the system is networked with access to the internet and world wide web. Microcomputers available for teaching and self-teaching purposes. Short courses in computing are offered.

All students may use the tape loan service for individual language study. The collection comprises over 3,000 items in around 50 languages. A programme of evening classes is organised by **Language Teaching Services**; classes can lead to qualifications.

Culture on campus

Drama: Four student theatre companies, the most prominent being the Mermaids University Dramatic Association. Activities range from play readings and workshops to full-length productions. The Drama Studio, is also used by visiting professional companies.

Music: The Younger Hall Music Centre contains a concert hall, rehearsal rooms, individual practice rooms with a computerised music workshop. The University Jazz Big Band and University Chamber Orchestra are run by the Centre. Individual tuition is available from qualified teachers in a wide range of instruments. Some choral and instrumental scholarships are available. Special excellence in choral and organ music; preparation for Associated Board Examinations is available in most instruments. The Centre organises lunchtime recitals, evening concerts, masterclasses and study days involving local and visiting musicians. In addition to the student-run University Musical Society, there are many student musical societies, choirs, orchestras, bands and chamber groups, and many concerts plus an annual Gilbert and Sullivan production.

Film: The Film Society is gives popular weekly showings.

The Union

The Union Building is on the city's main street, within easy walking distance of all departments. The Student Association also runs the Old Union next to the main library. The Students Representative Council (SRC) runs from the newer of the two. The Union Building houses a diner, coffee bar, the Salad Bowl and two bars. Here too are a travel service, laundry, reading room, television room, snooker and billiards room, games room and a craft area. The University Bookshop is in the foyer and the Association runs a book exchange and stationery store.

A lively entertainments programme: up-and-coming bands perform on Wednesdays; Thursdays, Fridays and Saturdays see larger bands, bops and events (the main hall has a capacity of 800).

The SRC runs over 100 societies, including folk dancing, fine arts, bridge and mountaineering. There is a vigorous University Charities Campaign and involved Student Volunteer Service. The Debating Society here is the oldest in Scotland and very active.

The Association employs a Welfare Officer who is available between 10.30am and 2.30pm every weekday.

For general information and articles, there is the Association newspaper, *The Chronicle,* and several helpful student handbooks.

Sport

The University Sports Centre, including a sports hall, gymnasium, activities room, weight-training room, squash courts and solarium, is situated on extensive playing fields, where, in addition to the usual sports pitches, there are jogging and trim tracks. The facilities on campus are within convenient reach of academic and residence buildings. Guidance, instruction and coaching are all available.

The town swimming pool offers a concessionary rate to students, and you can play golf (also at concessionary rates) on the five St Andrews courses. St Andrews also has its own extensive beaches and bay for water sports and is within reasonable distance of some of Scotland's mountains, lochs and forests which offer a wide range of outdoor pursuits (climbing, caving and skiing).

Annual or vacation membership of the Sports Centre is open to the public as well as to students and staff.

Student welfare

An NHS practice operates from St Andrews **health centre** and all UK students register there with a local doctor.

Student welfare here is traditional and pervasive and cascades down from professional counselling, through Faculty advisers to the 'academic families' set up in your first year.

The **chaplaincy centre** acts as a meeting place for all denominations. There are regular services, study and discussion groups. The University is sympathetic to the cultural and religious requirements (including dietary) of its students.

Careers Service

The Service runs information sessions and workshops to help you to use the vast array of material available. Individual interviews are arranged from your penultimate year.

Students with special needs

You should write to the Hebdomadar before you submit your application outlining the nature of your special needs. There is some difficulty with access to the University's older buildings, although work has been carried out to facilitate access where possible. A visit is strongly recommended.

Accommodation

There is a strong tradition of community life in the University. Many students have three years in residences or self-catering houses provided by the University. You will normally be guaranteed a place in your first year, in a hall of residence wherever possible and most likely sharing a room. Two thirds of the University's students can be accommodated in University-owned housing.

Halls of residence

An attempt is made to provide a good mix of students from all years and all faculties. Eleven halls in all, with over 2,400 places. Most halls are very near the centre of city; three newer halls of residence (purpose-built) are a little further out of the centre. The newest hall offers 537 ensuite rooms which each have a telephone and satellite television connection. Not surprisingly, this is a hotel out of term time; rents here are higher than other halls. All halls, new and old, are mixed, with mainly single rooms and have space for car-parking. Older halls range from the former Archbishop's House to rather beautiful manor houses. Some rooms (first years of course) are shared.

Each hall is warden controlled, has an elected House Committee and an active social life. Most halls offer full board, apart from evening meals on Saturday and Sunday.

Costs (1995/96)

£2,138.40 to £2,909.28 (ensuite) for 30 weeks

Student houses and flats

If you prefer self-catering there are 86 houses in two complexes on the outskirts of the city. Each house accommodates six students in single study-bedrooms. A set of flats in the city centre is reserved for senior students. Each complex has a launderette and a quiet room for study.

Costs (1995/96)

£1,008.48 to £1,784.64 for 30 weeks

Private accommodation

One third of the student population lives in private accommodation in and around St Andrews, usually in rented rooms. Costs (self-catering) average, £40 per week excluding bills.

Mature students

Mature students (over 21) will be considered on merit and on interview. Standard entrance requirements may be relaxed. The university welcomes applications from students taking approved Access Programme: contact the director of Schools Liaison.

Nursery

The SRC organises an afternoon playgroup for the children of students and staff.

THE CITY (population: 16,000)

This Lilliput city is built on a medieval street plan designed to give processions of pilgrims easy access to the cathedral. Many of its earliest buildings and original 'gates' and walls survive, if only as remnants; the use of stone from cathedral and castle in the 17th century to build houses might have been monumental vandalism, but it created some continuity of materials: much of the expansions came in later centuries, but the effect is totally harmonious.

History is the permeating quality of St Andrews: stones and monuments mark the deaths of martyrs who died here for their beliefs; John Knox was one of the defenders in the castle, captured after the siege of 1546-47, and returned later to St Andrews to preach. His pulpit still stands in St Salvator's Chapel. The story of the siege has a tunnelling episode fit for screen drama.

We can think of no setting in Britain where a university and its host community are so close to a spectacular coastline, where the ruins of a great cathedral and a splendid castle are on the very edge of the sea (the castle walls plunge straight down to rocks and crashing surf). It is no more than a two or three minute walk to break your day's work, or mark the evening, by wandering to the sea's edge, by castle or cathedral, or down to the small coves and sandy shores.

The city is 45 miles north of Edinburgh, 13 miles south of Dundee (with whose University it has historic links) and five miles from the nearest railway station.

Theatre: The Byre Theatre has a programme of productions by touring companies, and there are occasional productions at the Crawford Arts Centre.

Film: Both commercial and 'art' films are shown at the New Picture House (two screens). Late night showings of special films.

Nightlife: Informal music nights in pubs and hotels, plus weekly Scots' nights and folk nights. Big bands and orchestras visit.

Sport: There are no less than six (one 9-, five 18-hole) golf courses in St Andrews (16 within north east Fife) and, apart from the legendary Old Course at the Royal and Ancient Golf Club, there is no requirement that you be a member to play. A paradise for golfers! There is a sports complex offering swimming and other water sports, squash and snooker. It is also possible to go bowling, sand yachting, windsurfing and to play tennis.

Daily life: shops are traditional; there are many restaurants, over 20 pubs and cafes and an all-night bakery.

ESCAPE ROUTES

St Andrews lies on the tip of the peninsula between the Firths of Tay and Forth: the Kingdom of Fife, a kingdom anchored to its mainland north and south by two of the country's longest bridge roads. Fife is easy, rolling country, with a coastal history of fishing and an inland history of farming. It has some of the finest golf courses in the world, is an excellent centre for fishing and is being promoted as a prime tourist area.

Communications

The London-Edinburgh-Dundee-Aberdeen **railway** line serves north east Fife. The nearest station to St Andrews is Leuchars, five miles away: there are two **bus connections** if you are lucky, otherwise taxis. The **A91** and the **M90** lead to Edinburgh and the south and the A91 and A92 and the Tay Bridge to Dundee northwards.

University of Stirling

Stirling
FK9 4LA
Telephone: 01786 473171

University Charter date: 1964

Stirling is a small/medium-sized university with 4,500 full-time undergraduates and 700 full-time postgraduates. Courses here are modularised with a maximum choice of subject combination. Assessment is by periodic testing and examination. The University has a single greenfield campus just outside Stirling.

All first year students who want accommodation will be allocated a room in hall.

THE CAMPUS

In writing this Guide we have tried to avoid the language of hyperbole; but in the case of Stirling, we must yield. Stirling has an exceptionally beautiful campus. Centrepiece - a tranquil, large loch, adding shifting qualities of light, accommodating waterbirds and watersports, dividing the residential blocks from the workplace buildings. Behind the halls of residence, the north frame to this lovely parkland is shaped by the steep, wooded slopes of the hills. Standing guardian to the campus - and the area in general - is the Wallace Monument, a dramatic landmark.

The location of the University, between the town of Stirling and the tiny town of the Bridge of Allan, was agreed in 1963, and in 1967 its first students arrived. This does mean that it is architecturally defined by the style of that period: not one of the best. The buildings are white or grey, flat-roofed, rectangular, generally three or four storeys high; they do not impress the eye with a sense of substance or high quality. But no matter: the long horizontals of glass and concrete sit well on the curves and contours of the site, well screened by the many trees, forming pale regular reflections in the waters of the loch.

The interiors are light, comfortable, with a good sense of space. The site is actually the parkland setting of Airthrey Castle, landscaped by a pupil of Capability Brown (the 18th-century architectural 'gardener' who changed the face of the British countryside by starting the fashion for designing the land-setting of stately homes and palaces as carefully as the buildings themselves). The castle (built in 1791) still stands, used by University departments and offices, adding a nice link with history and a touch of stately solidity with its turrets, towers and bulky dignity. It is set on the edge of the campus development, overlooking the golf course.

The atmosphere of the campus is quiet. Student activity at the busy times of day revolves around the MacRobert Centre and the Union.

Cars

There is ample provision for car parking around the halls of residence; wheels would be an asset at weekends.

Learning Resources

The **library**, which is in the centre of the campus, houses 450,000 volumes, takes 2,500 current journals and seats 1,000 students. Some of the seating is informal, and the windows open onto woodland and loch - working here should be a real pleasure. Open 80 hours per week, including weekends.

A campus-wide **computing network** links hundreds of workstations to central facilities. Should there be any problems, a laboratory staffed by tutors is open 12 hours a day. Open access computer laboratories are available, some 24 hours a day. Information skills training can give you a University certificate. You can buy a computer at special discount from the Micro Shop.

Well-equipped **language laboratories**, sound and TV **studios**, print unit and facilities for **multimedia** presentation are available to support both teaching and private study.

Culture on campus

Drama/music/film: The MacRobert Arts Centre on the campus contains a 500-seat theatre and a small 149-seat studio theatre, both impressively equipped. Professional and amateur productions feature in the programme as well as film, concerts, opera, classical ballet and contemporary dance. The theatre is also open to the town. The University Drama Society produces a play a term.

The Union

The Stirling University Students Association (SUSA) is housed in the Robbins Centre, next to the MacRobert Arts Centre.

SUSA's entertainment programme is most active over the weekend: the Gannochy sports pavilion is transformed into a nightclub and the Robbins opens up its rooms and bars. During the week, events are lower key - quizzes and other bar-based activities. Films are shown twice a week.

SUSA finances over 80 clubs and societies, and runs a shop, four catering outlets, five bars and a disco. There is also a campus radio station - Airthney 963 - and a regular newspaper, *Brig*. Also published is an annual handbook for new students.

The Association's welfare service acts as an intermediary between students and help agencies.

Sport

The generosity of space here, the strong student community centric style of the University and the fact that the University offers a sports studies degree has led to an extraordinary range of facilities on campus.

The sports centre, set in the sweep of the games fields and pitches, houses a 25m swimming pool (Stirling is a National Swim Centre) with sauna and solaria, three squash courts, and a conditioning room (variety of weight-training stations). The sports hall can accommodate eight badminton courts, or be divided to create two full-size tennis or basketball courts. There is a seminar room: the University takes sport seriously, providing instruction for novices and fitness training and assessment.

Outdoor facilities (23 acres of playing fields in all): grass pitches for football, rugby, cricket and American football, a large floodlit all-weather area for hockey and football, an all-weather athletics track and (floodlit) soccer and hockey area.

On the loch (not just an ornament here), you can sail, wind surf, canoe and fish. Beside the loch, beyond the residences, is a nine hole par-three golf course and a putting green.

On and around campus: many paths and tracks for jogging, and a croquet lawn.

For all this you do have to pay a small fee. Facilities are used by staff and their families too: indeed, particular aspect of activity here is the weekly jamboree when over 600 students and staff compete in friendly league and knockout competitions.

The Sports Union sponsors 37 clubs: unusual ones - croquet, curling and wadoryu.

Sports scholarships are well established here. You have to meet normal academic entry standards; a scholarship would allow you to extend your degree programme for a year. Tuition fees, half maintenance costs and specific training and competition fees would be covered.

The Gannochy National Tennis Centre is on campus, with four indoor courts and four outdoor floodlit courts.

Student welfare

You may register with the **Medical Centre** on campus or with other GPs in the area. Student **counsellors** give help on practical and financial problems as well as personal and emotional crises. The Student Information and Support Centre is based in one of the halls of residence.

The **chaplaincy centre** is run on a 'drop in for a chat', informal basis. The ecumenical chaplaincy works to create a pattern of Christian worship and discussion and links into local churches. The Jewish chaplain is based in Glasgow. Muslim students have prayers in the chaplaincy.

Careers Service

The Service offers group sessions on application and interview technique and runs an 'Insight into Management' course each year. You can begin to use the Careers Service even before you come to Stirling: advice is available to you, your teachers and your parents on graduate opportunities related to subject areas. GRADSCOPE and PROSPECT are available.

Students with special needs

University buildings have in general been designed to allow easy access for wheelchairs by means of lifts and ramps, and ground-floor residence can be arranged. The Stirling campus has been progressively adapted for use by students with mobility problems: the University is also well equipped for students who are either blind or partially sighted. You should write to Recruitment and Admissions for advice, outlining your special needs.

Accommodation

2,300 places available in four halls and five blocks of flats and 33 chalets on campus. All first-year students who want University accommodation and apply before September 1st will be allocated rooms, usually in the larger halls (limited catering facilities); rooms are mostly single with kitchen and bathroom shared by groups of students. Segregated accommodation is available if desired. There are no dining rooms in the halls of residence, but there are restaurants on campus. Common rooms, TV lounges, games rooms and a launderette are provided.

Chalets on campus are not normally allocated to first-years. Included in the rent charge are a full warden service, 24 hour portering, regular cleaning, laundering of bedlinen, heating and hot water provision. The University offers 543 places off-campus in new blocks of flats in Stirling . Not normally allocated to first years.

Costs (1995/96)

Halls: single room: £1,150 for 30 weeks
Flats: single room: £1,284 - £1,435 for 37 weeks

Private accommodation

The Accommodation Office inspects private property. There are student houses in the surrounding area, usually occupied by groups of students and taken up very quickly, Bridge of Allan is the nearest area and prices range between £35 - £40 per week excluding bills. Stirling is rather less expensive. If you have a car or do not mind the bus rides, outlying villages have cheaper properties.

Mature students

The University is very active in promoting access to Higher Education both on campus and through a wide range of FE Colleges. Well-developed programmes of study run part-time, or in the concentrated Summer Academic Programme (accredited as an equivalent to a normal 15-week semester course), or in day-time classes where part-time and full-time students work together. Schemes are generous, flexible and imaginative and genuinely offer an open door to the community at large.

Nursery

The playgroup, run by the Students' Association, has places for 42 children (aged three months to five years) of staff and students. There are Easter and summer playschemes for primary school children.

THE CITY (population: 29,000)

Historically and geographically, Stirling is an interesting town. Set in low, flat plains where the Forth once wandered through treacherous marshland to its wide estuary, this was, for centuries, the lowest bridging point on the river. Occupying a kind of crossroads, commanding the narrow space between hills, marshes and rivers, the town grew behind the bulwark of its castle, rising dramatic, impregnable, from the very rock of the sheer 250ft-high crag which still today presents a daunting face to travellers approaching from the south. In its time it must have been impressive indeed. The Stuart monarchs held court here.

Although Stirling has many other attractions, the castle is its crowning glory; there is a visitors' centre on the esplanade (built on a parade ground in 1812) where you can watch and hear an audio-visual programme which tells the dramas of castle and town. There are, needless to say, wonderful views from the castle heights.

The old town, clustered downhill behind the castle, offers many other interesting buildings which mark the trail of history: ruins of an ornate Renaissance palace (Mar's Wark - 16th century); the Church of the Holy Rude (medieval) where James VI was crowned, Mary Queen of Scots worshipped, John Knox very likely preached; the Guildhall (built in 1639 as a hospital, converted in 1852); the Tolbooth (Town House), dating from 1703 and once courthouse, prison and council chamber. Nearby, the Mercat Cross marks the centre of the old town, and was a place of public execution. There are many more old buildings and ways.

But you won't be here as a tourist and much of your interest in Stirling will be less historic. The town has a welcoming ease. Its shops and businesses seem to cater well for their community, without pressure: well stocked, varied in style, with the ambience and quality we associate with county towns. There is a stylish indoor precinct, and the area up towards the castle has older-style craft and antique shops. Even on a busy Saturday afternoon, we felt the pace to be measured, comfortable. The tourist season will bring more people and events, including Beating the Retreat (by pipe bands) on Sunday evenings, or the solo castle piper who plays every day in July and August.

Theatre: The main venue is at the University's MacRobert Arts Centre, but some local amateur drama is presented at the small Cowane Centre and events at the Albert Hall.
Music: Again, mainly on campus, but there is jazz, folk music, etc. in pubs, and pipe bands.

Cinema: There is a cinema with two screens in Stirling.
Nightlife: Discos, folk, country and western, ceilidhs, ballroom dancing. If you have a taste for Scottish flings, this is a place for you. There are two central nightclubs, and popular places in the evening tend to be cafes such as the Bistro which serve continental snacks and drinks.
Sport: The two native obsessions seem to be golf (not a surprise) and bowling (a mild one). There are eight golf courses within easy reach, and the town has at least seven bowling greens, including the oldest in Scotland. There is also a petanque club. The rivers and lochs in the area offer fishing, sailing and rowing, and there are clubs for football, rugby and cricket. The town has a leisure centre with a swimming pool and 200m of water tube slides which have lighting and sound effects, and a multigym. The local football team plays at the Forthbank stadium which also has leisure facilities. Sterling also offers an ice-rink (skating and curling), archery, badminton and tennis.

Bridge of Allan

This town is, in fact, nearer to campus. A regular bus service runs to campus from Stirling and Bridge of Allan. You probably will use Bridge of Allan for your more immediate needs. It is a pretty market town, with a good range of pubs.

ESCAPE ROUTES

Stirling's escape territory is romantic and rugged, a country of lochs, hills and fells, of forests, moorland and rivers, of Rob Roy, Bannockburn and Sir Walter Scott's novels. The hill-ranges around Stirling are not the Highland Grampians, grand and imposing.

To the south west of Stirling is Glasgow, and to the south east, Edinburgh: neither is very far away. Stirling straddles the land between the Firths of Forth and Clyde.

The Trossachs to the west of Stirling are 'the crossing place' or 'the bristly country' depending on your etymological map. It (Trossachs is a collective noun) is a tract of land only five miles wide between three lochs and the lowlands, dominated by the mountainous Ben Venue. Excellent walking country, rambling place, or sit-by-the-loch-and-think. The glens and gulleys of the northern hills are very beautiful, with tumbling streams and woodland leading up to wilderness tops.

Communications

Rail links to Edinburgh and Glasgow, and north, through Perth, to the Highlands. **Coach links** are extensive, although most travel via the major cities. Stirling is on the M9 direct to Edinburgh. The road links to Glasgow are fast, except at rush-hour. The A9 travels north, dividing out to the east and west.

University of Strathclyde

Glasgow
G1 1XQ
Telephone: 0141 552 4400

University Charter date: 1964

Strathclyde is a large university with 10,000 full-time undergraduates and 2,500 full-time postgraduates. The University's main campus is in central Glasgow; Faculty of Education six miles out at Jordanhill. The University accommodates all first years who come from beyond a 25 mile radius of Glasgow.

THE CAMPUS

The University of Strathclyde occupies an area in the centre of Glasgow, just behind George Square, Glasgow's Civic Centre, practically next door to Queen Street station. In 1993, the University took over Jordanhill College of Education and now has a second campus in the west end of the city. The city-centre campus has been named the John Anderson Campus, after the University's founder.

John Anderson Campus

The original Strathclyde building is the Royal College, massive with a reception hall reminiscent of larger municipal art galleries. Behind this edifice the University has grown, taking over the nearby buildings and adding some of its own. The 'precinct' is made up of '60s (and later) blocks in a small area. A touch of historic interest has been added by the acquisition and a restoration of Barony Hall, a Victorian Gothic church modelled on the design of Genoa cathedral. The precinct has, to an extent, a sense of unity, but certainly not of campus 'remove' from its city: Strathclyde is part of Glasgow's inner landscape. The majority of its students are from the city.

A Student Village has taken shape at the east end of the campus. 1,700 students live here, only minutes away from the laboratories, lecture theatres and the city centre.

Jordanhill Campus

Six miles out of the city. The Faculty of Education shares a site with the Health Studies Faculty of Glasgow Caledonian University. Glasgow Caledonian students have access to the facilities at Jordanhill.

The campus occupies a 67-acre parkland site on the west side of the city, with magnificent views to the south over the Clyde estuary and to the Kilpatrick hills in the north-west. The site is dominated by the David Stow Building, pinkish granite with twin green spires. Most teaching takes place in newer buildings on campus.

The campus has two halls of residence, a library, theatre, bank, two shops, refectory, swimming pools, gymnasia and sports grounds all on campus. Students can, of course, also use the facilities on the John Anderson campus.

Learning Resources

The main **library**, the Andersonian, the main campus, the Jordanhill Library and three smaller libraries (Chemistry, Law and Business Information) have a total stock of around 870,000 volumes, subscribe to 5,300 current periodicals and can seat, in all, 2,050.

The **Computer Centre** is in the Curran Building. The campus is networked and equipment is well-distributed: 22 rooms contain a total of 600 microcomputers; 150 high performance graphic workstations are available for project work and there are some AppleMacs at Jordanhill. **Language facilities** are dedicated to EFL teaching.

Culture on campus

Drama: The Strathclyde Theatre Group stages ten to twelve plays a year in the Ramshorn drama centre, which also hosts professional theatre companies. The Group also presents its own festival during Mayfest in Glasgow. There are workshops in all aspects of theatre practice.

Music: Classical and light choral works are performed by the chamber choir and the University chorus. Instrumental music is provided by a brass ensemble, a wind ensemble, a chamber orchestra and a big band group. Regular lunchtime concerts are given by visiting artists.

The Union

Here, as in most Scottish universities, the Union is the Association. There are four sabbatical officers, plus two at Jordanhill. The main Union building has ten floors and is on the western edge of the site. At Jordanhill the Association runs its own calendar of events; facilities include a bar/disco, pool tables and a food outlet.

John Anderson Campus

The Union houses a launderette, travel shop, bank, print shop, insurance broker, and a large games room: nine pool tables, five snooker tables and arcade and fruit machines. Five bars in all. Three ents venues: Level 8 - the main disco and the place for major bands; the Mandela Bar - up-and-coming bands; Level 4 - three discos a week.

The Association runs over 100 societies. There are mature students' and women's group common rooms in the 'Annexe'. The Community Action group, 'Cactus', has 150 members. All bars serve a range of food during the day; Level 5 is specifically vegetarian.

Welfare advice and support is available from a full-time officer, who works with an assistant and volunteers. The student paper, *Telegraph*, covers in-house and other topical affairs and is produced every three weeks.

Sport

The sports centre has a large twin-court games hall accommodating basketball, archery, practice nets and indoor training areas. Two small gymnasia are used for judo and other martial arts, dance and gymnastics. There are six squash courts and a weight-training room. The swimming pool is in the old Royal College building. Jordanhill also has a conditioning/weights room and a squash court.

At Stepps Playing Fields there are seven pitches for soccer and rugby, a new artificial grass floodlit pitch and a pavilion. Future plans include facilities for cricket, golf, tennis and other popular sports. The Jordanhill campus has gymnasia, two swimming pools and outdoor all-weather and grass pitches.

The Athletic Club has over 40 sections catering for most popular sports. The players are drawn from the Jordanhill and John Anderson campuses, a good reason for mixing. Coaching is free of charge.

From Glasgow there is easy access to hill-walking, mountaineering, ski-ing and rowing.

Student welfare

The **Student Health Service** (SHS) deals with physical and emotional disabilities which may interfere with a student's academic performance. Physicians from the Glasgow Royal Infirmary conduct a consultative clinic three times a day and there are close links with the Infirmary's Ophthalmic department and the Dental Hospital. All students must be registered with a local doctor.

The University provides three full-time **Student Advisors**, who are supported by two part-time Welfare Assistants. There is also an 'open door' information service. Full-time and part-time **chaplains** including a Rabbi are available. There is a prayer room for Muslims.

Careers Service

The Service organises a range of group sessions designed to widen your horizons and to develop your job search skills. There are computer-assisted guidance programmes, including PROSPECT-HE. In the Centre for Academic Practice staff are available all year to run seminars, workshops and personal help in a wide and impressive range of tuition in personal and academic skills.

Students with special needs

You should write to the Co-ordinator for Students with Special Needs outlining your problems before you submit your application. Visit the University if at all possible: send for their *'Access Guide to the Campus'*. The whole campus is set into a hill; there might be some difficulty with access to some buildings. The library has a lift and you will have the benefit of access to the extraordinary provision of special equipment at Glasgow University (see their entry).

Accommodation

All University accommodation is mixed and there are three levels of service: fully catered, self-catering with some cleaning, and independent self-catering. Accommodation is limited (around 2,000 at John Anderson and 190 at Jordanhill), but the University accommodates all new, eligible undergraduate and postgraduate students in residence. ('Eligible' means living beyond a 25-mile radius of the University). You should apply as soon as possible, and certainly by September 1st. The Accommodation Services Manager will advise on all aspects of accommodation, including tenants' rights.

Halls of residence

Baird Hall, about a mile from the University, has single and double study-bedrooms and the fees include catering. Murray Hall, on-campus, and Clyde Hall, within walking distance, can accommodate just over 200 students in single or double rooms. These have cleaning services but no catering. At Jordanhill the two halls provide single study bedrooms with weekday catering.

Costs (1996/97)

Catered single:	£60.35 per week
Catered shared:	£55.75 per week
Jordanhill:	£53.85 per week

Self-catering flats

Seven residences in the campus village are divided into shared flats suitable, in most cases, for groups of four to eight students sharing. The provision of cleaning and ensuite facilities varies from residence to residence. Four more sets of flats are a short distance from the campus.

Costs (1996/97)

Self-catering: from £33.50 per week shared to £55.05 per week for a single ensuite.

Leased flats

The University has some leased accommodation, between three and fifteen miles from campus which is suitable for couples and those with families. Normally, demand for these flats exceeds supply. Rents per person are comparable with the University flats.

Private Accommodation

The University's Accommodation Office keeps a list of landlords with accommodation to let. The properties are not inspected. A room in a shared house/flat: £160 - £180 per month plus bills.

Mature students

Mature candidates (over 21) are usually accepted on normal examination performance, or by taking some form of entry test, but special consideration may be given to aptitude and other evidence of academic study. There is a pre-entry course in arts and social science, one evening a week. The Adult Information Service has details.

Nursery

The Students' Association runs a playgroup free of charge for 25 children aged three to five, open from 9am to 4pm.

THE CITY / ESCAPE ROUTES

See Glasgow University's entry in this Guide.

Northern Ireland

Queen's University of Belfast
The University of Ulster

Queen's University of Belfast

The Admissions Office,
Belfast
BT7 1NN
Telephone: 01232 245133

University Charter date: 1845
Queen's is a medium/large university with 9,000 full-time undergraduates and 1,700 full-time postgraduates. The University has a single campus just outside Belfast. Degrees are modularised following fixed pathways within Faculties. Modules are examined at the end of each semester by a combination of examination and coursework.

The University tries to accommodate all first years, but there is no guarantee of accommodation.

THE CAMPUS

Arriving on the road out of the city, you will have a double first impression of the University, which will accurately catch its style. On your left, set back from the busy traffic, beyond calm lawns, trees and shrubs, rise the Gothic towers and solid Victorian splendours of the Lanyon building. On your right, at a balancing remove, are set the large, purpose-built and purposeful rectangular modern blocks of the Students' Union complex.

The Lanyon manages to look more like a domestically scaled mansion than a monumental institution, perhaps because of the proportions of its windows, and the warm russet of its stone-trimmed brick. It does have great dignity and is well anchored into its corridors of time by the wide horizontals of the modern administration block, on the opposite side of the inner quadrangle. And indeed, when the University was opened as Queen's College, Belfast, by Queen Victoria in 1845 its scale was pretty domestic: 20 professors and 90 students.

Perhaps the finest capsule of the University, past and present, is the old library, where you can sit watching light fade from the tall church-like windows with their lovely stained glass, with your back turned to the inner shell which has converted the interior into more practical space. This rare building is linked to a high-rise modern block 'book-stack' where the University library functions quietly and efficiently.

More recent developments have formed an elongated, yet reasonably compact academic precinct in a medley of building styles: beautifully restored Georgian terraces in University Square house the Faculties of Arts and Law; Psychology has spilled into a Victorian mansion; Science, Engineering and Medical courses are suitably housed in modern, functional blocks.

Perhaps the most beautiful feature of the University is the Botanical Gardens, formal, extensive, which frame the main building to the rear. Here, as well as elegant spaces, you will find the spectacular Palm House, with its unbelievable intricacy of curving cast-iron and glass - a masterpiece of mid-Victorian creative design. Here, too, is the Ulster Museum and the Physical Education Centre with its wealth of amenities.

The University has its own Observatory operating from the dark sky precinct of the Malone playing fields.

Cars
There is ample parking in the grounds of the Halls of Residence at Queen's Elms, which is about 7 to 10 minutes walk from the main campus.

Learning Resources

The **Library** at Queen's operates on a number of sites: a Medical Library, a Science Library, an Agriculture and Food Science Library and the Main Library which serves staff and students in the Arts, Law, Education and Social Sciences.

Across the library system there are about 1,000,000 books and pamphlets (and a further 80,000 in departmental libraries). Seats over 1,500 readers. The Main and Science Libraries have computer workstations on which a range of software is available. During term-time the larger libraries are open from 09.00 to 22.00 weekdays and 09.00 to 12.30 on Saturday. Closer to examination time the Main Library is open during extended hours on Saturday and Sunday.

The **Computer Centre** buildings are in the main precinct area. There is an extensive campus network providing fast internal connections and access to external national and international services. Seven open access workstation areas are open for 12 hours a day during semesters.

Taught **language** courses for non-specialists lead to a University certificate and are open to all students. Fourteen languages offered. There are three languages laboratories with TV and audiovisual facilities and a 20 seat listening/viewing room with a tape library.

Culture on campus

Music: The School of Music has a recital room which is the major centre for recital in Northern Ireland. The University has a remarkable collection of percussion and keyboard instruments, plus electronic and computer music facilities. The University Choir and Orchestra give two major concerts a year. The Music Society provides concerts by the Chamber Choir and Orchestra, early music and 20th century ensembles. An Early Music Festival alternates biennially with a 20th Century Music Festival. The University has a Composer in Residence and an Ensemble or Soloist in Residence.

Film: The Queens Film Theatre; a full-time two-screen cinema shows major releases and art house films nightly for ten months of the year (a major attraction). The two auditoria hold audiences of 250 and 160.

Festival: Queen's mounts its own International Arts Festival each November, offering over 200 performances in all fields of the Arts. Visiting orchestras, jazz and folk bands, the Royal Shakespeare Company, the Shanghai Kunju Theatre, Rowan Atkinson, The Gothenburg Ballet...

The Union

The Union building is a mini-world with restaurants, coffee bars, bars and lounges, a launderette, snooker-room (8 full-size), showers, games room, reading room, large shop, travel shop, insurance broker, and a secondhand bookshop.

A regular student paper is produced, with a more frequent news bulletin and an arts and ents supplement. You should be very well informed. The Union runs two bars (food and TV), a snack bar and a disco. The whole area can be opened up to accommodate 2,500. Late night entertainment every night but Sunday. The Union supports 116 non-sporting clubs and societies. There are regular debates, and a lively interaction with local groups, including Community Action Voluntary work.

Three Welfare Officers will help with personal, financial and educational problems. There is a night-line and you can get subsidised driving lessons.

Sport

The Malone playing fields are two miles from the main campus. There are 17 pitches for rugby, soccer, hockey, hurling, Gaelic football and cricket. Four are all-weather pitches including two large artificial grass floodlit pitches. There are also 3 netball and 9 tennis courts, a floodlit training area and an athletics arena. A large pavilion offers 52 changing rooms, as well as social lounges.

The Physical Education Centre has two swimming pools (diving, subaqua, water-polo, canoeing), and an extraordinary range of courts: squash (10), badminton (12), basketball (4), volleyball (3), tennis (2), handball (2), netball (2) and hockey (4). Judo squares, cricket nets, three conditioning rooms, a purpose-built climbing wall, facilities for Olympic gymnastics, athletics, fencing, golf, karate, bowls, yoga, archery and a sauna and solarium...extravagant provision.

Outdoor pursuits include golf at the Malone club, three miles away, sailing, water-skiing, gliding, parachuting, mountaineering, caving and rowing - all at their own centres. 61 sporting clubs in all. The Union provides a free shuttle bus on Wednesday (games) afternoons.

There is a sports injuries clinic, offering physiotherapy and maintenance. Sports bursaries area offered annually. At the end of each academic year, the University Blues Presentation Dinner takes place.

Student welfare

In the **health service** (central complex) there are five doctors, four nurses and a secretariat. One doctor is on 24-hour call. The University runs 'Bodycheck' - a complete physical check available for students and members of the public. It is run in collaboration with the University's Physical Education Centre. The Students' Union runs a **counselling service**, offering confidential advice and support for a wide range of problems. Special financial counselling is available.

Four **chaplaincies** on or close to the campus represent Christian denominations. Support is available for Jewish students. The Belfast Islamic Centre which is close to the University caters for the needs of Muslim students.

Careers Service

The Careers Service stresses the need to start thinking early about your career and will help you in your quest. A well-stocked careers library and advisory service is available.

Students with special needs

You should make clear the nature of your needs on your UCAS form. Provided that your needs are known in advance, the University will do its best to cater for you. Although the University has adapted many of its buildings, there are some which are not accessible. The University is a member of the National Bureau for Handicapped Students. Facilities and provision are continually improving.

Accommodation

The University can accommodate 1,000 students in traditional halls of residence and 1,100 in self-catering halls and houses. About 1,400 places are reserved for first years. The main residential complex of halls, Queen's Elms, is within easy walking distance of the University precinct. The ratio of places to students is relatively low, so you should apply as soon as possible. Private sector accommodation in lodgings and flats is available near by. The University tries to accommodate all first years, and certainly those of you coming from across the water, but there is no actual guarantee of accommodation. Catered halls offer two meals a day.

Costs (1996/97)
Traditional halls: £46 - £54 per week (including heat and light and two meals daily)
Self-catered: £26 - £41 per week (including heat and light)
Some rooms are shared.

Private sector

A list of places is kept by the Accommodation Office. Places are not easy to find close to the campus and you might have to look further out. Prices in the University area are around £100 to £130 per month plus bills.

Mature students

Applications from students over 21 who do not meet the standard requirements are considered individually on merit. Experience and evidence of abilities in other than academic fields may count, but some evidence of recent study is necessary. The University runs a number of Foundation courses and accepts those run by the University of Ulster or which carry the CVCP kite-mark.

Nursery

The Students' Union runs two crèches for around 80 children aged up to four and a half years. They are open from 8.30am to 5.15pm on weekdays. The cost for students is subsidised.

THE CITY (population: 400,000)

This is the only major city (in mainland UK terms) in Northern Ireland. It was - like many of its UK counterparts - a product of the Industrial Revolution, although its early wealth and standing stemmed from the manufacture of linen.

The City Hall, in Italianate palazzo style, is very imposing: completed in 1906, it is built of white Portland stone, has corner pillared domes, a 300ft facade and a central magnificent copper dome rising 173ft above street level. A number of statues, a sculptured 'Titanic sinking' group (the *Titanic* was built here in 1912), and a War Memorial temple are added embellishments.

The City Hall stands in Donegal Square, at the centre of the main shopping thoroughfares which offer city-scale department stores, boutiques, chain stores. There are a number of buildings worthy of note: one of the banks was built in 1769 as a market house and became an assembly place for Irish harpers in 1792. Belfast's cathedral (St Anne's) was built at the turn of the century. The city has a large number of churches (sectarian development and settlement here was far more complex and strongly demarcated than the 'Roman Catholic v Protestant' simplification often accepted in England - the Scots know better). But one of the main distinctive claims of Belfast lies in its pubs and taverns: stained and painted glass, panelled snugs, traditional music sessions: often found down alleyways and entries, they have an atmosphere entirely their own.

Since we last visited Belfast, the city has passed through a major programme of improvements. Buildings have emerged beautiful under the hands of restorers; new shops and precincts add high quality facilities and colour; pedestrianised paved areas slow down the city pace.

The area around the University - your immediate social environment - is only a mile from city-centre life, but offers its own range of varied shopping, good reasonably priced restaurants and lively pubs.

Theatre: As well as the Opera House there are two other professional theatres and one for amateur dramatics.

Music: The major venue for music is the University.

Cinema: There are four cinemas with 10+8+4+4 screens.

Nightlife: The City centre has a good range of restaurants and interesting clubs. The area south of the University has a lot of student-oriented pubs.

Sport: There are 15 leisure centres, all well-equipped.

ESCAPE ROUTES

The Province, Troubles aside, is a very beautiful country. The Antrim coast is warmed by the Gulf Stream. Its roads are hedged with fuchsias and palm trees grow. The coast itself is cliffs and coves, small harbours and villages. Inland are the Glens of Antrim, cut into moorland hills. North and round the coast is the Giant's Causeway, a geological 'roadway' of basalt pillars paved into the sea. There are castles all around the coast, dating back to the first waves of inter-fighting. Most are ruined, standing high above crashing seas. Within short journeys (half to one hour) of Queen's, you can reach marvellous boating waters, the fabled Mourne Mountains, a many-islanded sea inlet and the world's oldest whiskey distillery.

Wherever you go in Northern Ireland, you will find history and literature- the two are often entwined. Northern Ireland is like nowhere else and if you do come here you will find the people, the sea, the hills and the history will be with you always.

Communications

For those of you in Northern Ireland, the **road** system and **rail** network give efficient access to Belfast. For students from the mainland, the best access is either via Larne (**ferry** from Stranraer), or by **air**.

The University of Ulster

Coleraine
County Londonderry
N. Ireland
BT52 1SA
Telephone: 01265 44141

University Charter date: 1984

Ulster is a medium/large (dispersed) university with 11,500 full-time undergraduates, 1,000 HND students and 1,000 full-time postgraduates. Courses here are modularised, usually within Schools; transfaculty structures are possible. A wide range of assessment modes from peer group assessment to formal exams. Usually, course assessment is a mix of methods. Most courses are delivered during the traditional academic year; the University also offers a third 'trimester' over the summer which you can use to add modules to your course or to spread the pressure of study. The University has four campuses, widely dispersed.

Accommodation is reserved for students who live beyond a 25 mile radius of their University campus.

THE CAMPUSES

Three of the four campuses are geographically well distanced from each other: although the Belfast and Jordanstown campuses are only a few miles apart, they are nearly 70 miles from Magee College, in Londonderry, and around 50 miles from Coleraine, just inland from Portrush. The Magee and Coleraine campuses are 30 miles apart, hardly close enough to share facilities. We consider the four campuses separately: their strengths, traditions and identities, and their completely different locales.

There is common ground in that the University's corporate ethic is one of integration with the wider community. This is a wide-access university with doors open to its communities in every possible way.

There are moves towards a measure of integration of university life, in the blocking of some courses to include time on more than one campus and the Union promotes interaction through bookings for concerts and gigs. Minibuses circulate.

Coleraine

This is the headquarters of the University, and was built in 1968 to be the new University of Ulster - Northern Ireland's share of the new universities then set up. It still contrives to look, and feel, very new: a bright, light and colourful set of buildings with an academic but relaxed, friendly atmosphere. One's main reaction is a sense of enormous space. The campus is in open countryside, close to the small market town of Coleraine and not far (about three miles) from the north west coastal resorts of Portstewart and Portrush, where many students choose to live.

Campus buildings have clean lines and well-spaced distribution: the site is planned to give separate identities to its parts, and you can walk a surprisingly long way in your daily routine. Often walkways are sheltered which must be a mercy in the winter. The main complex has a shopping precinct, post office, bank, launderette, travel agency, supermarket, bookshop, refectories, dining rooms and a coffee lounge.

The central Mall is spacious and airy, with high roof lights, lots of natural light, and space to stand or sit and talk. It fulfils well its dual functions of an access spindle and a social meet-your-friends-area. In fact generally, the interiors generate a positive, energetic atmosphere and justify a campus design which does verge on the stark.

Jordanstown

This in terms of student numbers is the University's largest campus and used to be the Ulster Polytechnic. The campus occupies a large 114 acre site in Newtownabbey, a few miles seaward of Belfast. The Antrim hills rise behind, and to the fore the ground slips down quickly to the waters of Belfast Lough.

From the road, the buildings are quite daunting with a repetitive modular system of flat-topped concrete blocks and a series of chimneys. Very factory-style. The impression is off-set by the open spaces of hills and sea-lough, and the scale of the community nearby which is small and easily familiar.

Inside, the buildings continue to be quite daunting: the main feature is a long central Mall, low ceilinged and artificially lit, which gives access to 17 blocks of academic and recreational facilities and accommodation. There is a bank, bookshop, catering, post office, supermarket, the Union and sports centre - all here.

Belfast

Students here can benefit from closeness to Queen's University (a mile away), and Jordanstown, whose facilities they share. The campus is modern block, in a typically city-access environment, but is closely involved in the 'green' development scheme for the area around St Anne's Cathedral. Art exhibitions are held in the foyer.

Courses here: Art and Design

Magee

The College is set on a hillside overlooking the river Foyle, just north of the old walled city of Londonderry and only half a mile from the city centre.

The main College building is neo-Gothic and imposing. Studios, laboratories and workshops accommodate a wide and varied pattern of courses (length and structure) and students (age, social background, experience).

There is a programme of art exhibitions and concerts by folk musicians and other cultural events.

Faculties here: Art and Design, Science and Technology and Informatics.

Learning Resources

The University's joint **library** stock totals around 520,000 books, and 5,000 current periodicals. Books are interchangeable between campuses, but each campus has its special interests. **Computer terminals** and **micro-processing facilities** are in 40 laboratories on the campuses, used by all faculties and providing necessary links to integrate academic work and communication. Use of the Internet is encouraged. Education Services offers a range of courses to improve your skills. Private language study is available in **language laboratories** at all campuses.

Culture on campus

The University has an active Arts policy and a number of very distinguished musicians, writers and a theatre group have joined the University community as Artists in Residence. You can enjoy and learn from talent at first hand.

Theatre: The purpose-built Riverside Theatre at **Coleraine** is used by professional companies, University departments and student groups, and the drama studio base for Theatre Studies. Students make their own scenery, costumes and masks, learn to control the sophisticated lighting rigs and have created their own 'professional style' Green Room. The Theatre proper draws full benefit from its setting: its bar and lounge areas have superb full wall open views over the river to the hills beyond. The programme of events here typically includes professional groups, student productions, film, music, dance, snooker and children's shows - well geared to involving the local community.

Music: **Coleraine's** Diamond Hall - the University's largest - can hold 1,500, has a splendid organ, and is the setting for recitals, choral and orchestral concerts. A smaller hall, the Octagon, offers chamber music and exhibition space for the visual arts.

The Music Department at **Jordanstown** has a separate home in a large 19th-century House. The University's musician in residence and the Brindisi String Quartet are based here. Jordanstown, naturally, is the base for the University's orchestra and choir and has a range of recital rooms and a 1,000 seat Assembly/concert hall.

The Union

The Students' Union represents student views on all four campuses and has seats on the principal decision-making bodies of the University. Facilities at each site vary and are available to all student members of the Union.

There is a thriving network of clubs and societies including amateur radio, caving, Irish music and culture, rock music, transport and youth work... among many others. The Union has good links with the community and does a lot of voluntary work.

Coleraine: a shop, travel shop, coffee bar, two bars and a hair salon. There is a full-time welfare officer. Over 50 clubs and societies. Entertainments events every night in term time; the sports hall is used as a venue.

Jordanstown: the Union promotes big-band events in the University main hall. Facilities include a shop, travel service, insurance bureau, cafeteria, and two bars (one is a venue for bands and discos). There is a Welfare office, nearly 50 clubs and societies and a general recreation area.

Belfast: shop, snack bar, bar, hall for gigs. The bus service to Jordanstown is good.

Magee: shop, banking services, Welfare , two bars (one also a cafeteria, one a function venue) and various clubs and societies.

Sport

Tuition is available in many sports. Watersports clubs have facilities on the Bann, the Lagan and the Foyle rivers. Sports bursaries are available.

Coleraine campus has floodlit hockey and soccer pitches, plus sailing, rowing and subaqua at the Water Sports Centre on the banks of the river Bann; also two sports halls, a fully equipped gymnasium, a dance studio, solarium and steam room, a weight-training room and five squash courts. Playing fields are on the same campus accommodating athletics, Gaelic football, hockey, hurling, rugby and tennis - a floodlit soccer pitch, training area and synthetic pitch. The cross-country course here has hosted the World Student Cross Country Championships.

Jordanstown sports centre has two large sports halls, a fully equipped gymnasium, a dance studio, a weight-training room, five squash courts, a swimming and hydrotherapy pool. Playing fields are on the same campus accommodating athletics, Gaelic football, hockey, hurling, rugby, soccer and tennis. There is a floodlit synthetic pitch. Water-sports are pursued at the local marina and on the river Lagan. Belfast campus students share sporting facilities with Jordanstown.

Magee: a recently constructed complex of sports provision here includes a pavilion, a sand-carpet pitch for soccer and a synthetic training pitch for hockey, five-a-side football and training. Also a multipurpose sports hall, fitness suite and solarium.

Student welfare

Coleraine: The Student Health Service on the Coleraine campus offers a family doctor service and a qualified Nurse. Four chaplains are available, a special suite and a prayer room.

Jordanstown: Medical officers and qualified nurses will treat injuries and minor illnesses and advise you on health matters, in the **Health Centre**. Four **chaplains** serve Jordanstown and Belfast. They also manage a student club in the Student Village.

Belfast: shares with Jordanstown's facilities and has its own part-time nurse.

Magee: A local group **practice** and a part-time nurse on campus. There are four **chaplains** here.

Counselling

Services are well developed and wide-ranging. There are workshops in relaxation and stress control and other personal development areas.

Careers Service

The Careers Advisory Service has information libraries on the Coleraine, Jordanstown and Magee campuses. An advisor visits the Belfast site.

Students with special needs

The different sites have different degrees of suitability: you are advised to contact the Student Services staff. Jordanstown library has a workstation for the visually impaired.

Accommodation

All University accommodation is self-catering. Students living within a 25 mile radius of their University base will not be eligible for University accommodation, although their application will be given sympathetic consideration if they experience daily travelling problems. Approximately five percent of campus places are reserved for students with special needs. For those of you not placed in university accommodation, the Accommodation Office will send you a list of private housing. You will be welcome to stay in university rooms during the first two weeks of September while you look for somewhere permanent to live. The University and student union produce information on the main student residential areas. The Students' Housing Association (SHAC) extends provision.

Coleraine: Residences on-campus for 413 students: mostly with six to nine students sharing communal facilities. A further 700 bedspaces offered in Coleraine, Portrush and Portstewart under a headlease scheme in either houses or purpose built accommodation.

Magee: 276 places in halls on campus or student village closeby. Housing Associations provide a further 100 bedspaces.

Jordanstown: accommodation varies from traditional halls of residence providing 300 places, to self-contained blocks for 30 students and houses for six students sharing. On-site accommodation for over 750 students. First-years take most places. A further 200 bedspaces available near Jordanstown under a headleasing scheme.

Belfast: there is no university accommodation on the Belfast campus but you are eligible for accommodation on the Jordanstown campus, seven miles away. The Student Housing Association provides more accommodation and flats. Furnished houses and lodgings are available nearby or in Belfast.

Costs (1995/96)

Halls of residence:
Coleraine: single: £32.00 - £34.00 per week (31 weeks)
Magee: single: £30.60 - £35.00 per week (31 weeks)
Jordanstown single: £29.80-£35.00 per week (31 weeks)
Jordanstown shared: £23.60 - £29.60 per week (31 weeks)

Private accommodation
Self-catering, single: £25 - £30 per week.

Mature students

Entrance requirements may be modified for mature (over 21) applicants who demonstrate that they have a reasonable chance of completing the course. The Department of Adult and Continuing Education offers foundation courses and support sessions at all campuses.

Nursery

Coleraine has a creche and playgroup for children from one month to five years old; **Jordanstown** - nursery facilities are similar to those at Coleraine. Belfast shares with Jordanstown; **Magee** has a creche/playgroup for children up to five years old.

CITIES and TOWN

Coleraine (population: 16,000)

This is a pretty commodious town which will meet your shopping and social needs comfortably. Most students rapidly begin to focus on the two coastal resorts, Portstewart and Portrush, where a lively student community life has developed.

Magee (Londonderry: population 95,000)

Londonderry is Northern Ireland's second city. The city walls enclose the old settlement and run for a mile in all, punctuated by 17th century cannon. Derry's four main streets radiate out from the centre through the old gates: Bishop's Gate, Butcher's Gate, Shipquay Gate and Ferrygate. These names reflect part of the city's history: as the site of a monastery built here in AD 546, as a place of trade and as a seaport.

Jordanstown and Belfast (population: 400,000)

Jordanstown is actually in Newtownabbey just a few miles out of Belfast. See Queen's University's entry.

ESCAPE ROUTES

The University of Ulster is so scattered that the 'Escape Routes' section would practically cover the whole of Northern Ireland. The Province is very beautiful: the Antrim coast, well within range of campuses, is warmed by the Gulf Stream, its roads are hedged with fuchsias, and palm trees grow. The coast is cliffs and coves, small harbours and villages. Inland are the Glens of Antrim, cut into moorland hills. North and round the coast is the Giant's Causeway, a 'roadway' of basalt pillars paved into the sea. Portrush (Coleraine campus), a popular holiday resort, is the home of the Bushmills Whiskey Distillery, dating from 1608 (officially) and the oldest legitimate still in the world.

Communications

If you are coming from Britain you can either **fly** into Belfast, which is expensive but painless, **drive** and come over by the Larne-Stranraer **ferry**, or travel by **train** - again via Stranraer. Or you could sail to Dublin or Dunlaoghaire from Holyhead and travel up from the Republic. The roads in Northern Ireland are not wide, on the whole: there is only one short stretch of motorway into Belfast from the north.

Appendix I:

The Open University

Walton Hall
Milton Keynes
MK7 6AA
Telephone: 01908 274066

We have not included an entry for the Open University in earlier editions of this Guide because we have always primarily aimed to tell you about place: what it will be like to live away from home; how each university and its area can accommodate your personal needs and style. Clearly, these matters have nothing to do with taking courses with the Open University.

Now, however, the whole academic landscape, including its financial routes and support has changed dramatically. More and more of you will need to consider the cost of a full-time university course spent away from your own base: alternative options become attractive or necessary. You might choose to build a degree through combining full-time residential study in a university for one or two years with a year (or years) of a course completed locally (living at home) by attending a course run by a local college. You can put together blocks of credit units, through part-time or evening study, perhaps over a longish period (which can be sustained by paid employment), and, through the CAT scheme, 'buy' a full-time place at a university for your later or final years. You can, of course, if you wish, complete an entire degree through modular study, adding units at your own pace. (See Introduction sections on Modularisation and CATS).

In this context, Open University degree courses become a very sound option. Distance learning resources (specially-written study texts, tapes, videos, nationally-delivered lectures and seminars on TV and radio) can be of the highest calibre: better than much of the provision in local colleges and night schools which have limited experience of teaching at this level. You can also adjust your times of study by using your own audio/video recorders and the study texts, where journeying to college or night-school at the end of the day can be exhausting.

The problems associated with distance-learning (and this is common to all correspondence courses) are related to isolation: lack of contact with your mentors and the absence of any group activity which gives you support and stimulus. The Open University has overcome this problem by the well-developed system of directed or informal mutual support.

History and objectives

The OU is the largest university in the UK! More than 200,000 people are currently studying its courses; this year's enrolment total: around 30,000. The University began teaching in 1971 and since then 2 million people have studied under its wings. It has opened the doors of Higher Education to those who seek either personal intellectual advancement or the enhancement of their career prospects, but are prevented from following traditional routes by full-time jobs or dependent families or financial constraints.

Structures

The University itself is national, regional, and local in concept and in its structures.

Teaching materials are national: teaching is available to all, in the form of study texts, experiment kits, computer links, TV and radio programmes. The latter are usually on the airwaves either very late at night or very early in the morning. You must either be an insomniac or invest in recording gear if you do not have it already. The quality, naturally, is consistent wherever you are.

Underpinning this national programme is your work with a tutor who is as accessibly close to you as patterns permit. On most courses, s/he will set up a local seminar group; in some cases, self-help groups are set up by the students themselves. There are 293 study centres throughout the country where groups like this operate. Regular day-schools offer additional support and you are free to contact your tutor at any time, within reason, if you have a problem, be it academic or course-related-personal (loss of confidence, depression, despair!).

Between the national and local dimensions, there are 13 Regional Centres which monitor the work of tutors, provide information and advice to applicants and make sure that groups of students can interact either with each other or through a tutor.

Range and structure of courses

All courses are modular and organised into units to allow the widest possible flexibility of study. Since the wider advent of modularisation and the CATS scheme, OU credits have a general national currency and can be 'spent' either within the OU or in other Higher Education institutions.

The range of subjects on offer is equivalent to that of any major university, with the exception of Medicine, Civil Engineering, Veterinary Science and Law. Qualifications other than first degrees can be pursued: these include various diplomas, postgraduate degrees, study-packs for professionals who wish to update their knowledge or skills, courses of personal interest which do not necessarily carry any certification and certain forms of community education.

It is normal for you to take five or six years to complete a degree course. This would mean studying for about 12 to 15 hours a week; a shorter, more intensive three year stint (the equivalent of a normal university degree study period) would require full-time study - which is 24 to 30 hours a week.

In the first year of study, you will follow a widely-based Foundation Course (there is quite a choice), to test your ability to study and allow you time to choose sensibly your final direction. You may be exempted from this course if you already have adequate qualifications...or your existing achievements might be credited against some sections of the course.

You are not obliged to finish your chosen course; you can 'drop out' if you wish; you can stop at a stage short of degree standard, but have earned a creditable Diploma; you could take a year or more off, then continue the course when you feel able, or you could aggregate the credits you have earned and transfer to a course in another university or college. The Open University is, as its title indicates, a truly open route to knowledge.

Entry qualifications

There are none. You must be over 18 years old, and resident in the EC, or other specified countries. Earlier successful study at HE level can be assessed and counted towards your degree; there is nothing to stop you from pursuing other courses at the same time if you wish to do so.

Study methods

Normally you will study at home, receiving packs of learning materials from the OU, which will be fleshed out by TV and radio programmes. Your work will begin in January, or earlier, with the arrival of your first study packs. Teaching begins in February. You will write essays or complete other academic tasks which you will send to your tutor to be marked/assessed. Contact with tutors cannot be clearly described, since it will depend on the establishment, or not, of group sessions, often in the form of evening tutorials or day-schools. Whether you can attend or not will depend on where you live and your personal circumstances. You will certainly have a degree of personal contact. Frequently, relations between tutors and students are very supportive indeed; we hear generally good reports. At an early stage in the course, you will be asked whether or not you wish to continue; if you do, you will pay the balance of fees paid earlier and steam ahead. During your first year you will be expected to attend a one week Summer School, where you will have the experience of studying away from the distractions of ordinary life, spend time with other like-minded and like-oriented students and briefly have fun in regular campus style. The study week is residential and is usually based in an established university in the UK. Some higher-level courses also have residential schools, particularly where laboratory or field-work is involved. Most people enjoy the residential study periods immensely and they are one of the attractions of OU courses.

Social life

You will be able to join in a range of social activities; most study centres in your area will give space to the local branch of the Open University Students' Association (OUSA) and, depending on support, meetings and social events are organised. The Association represents students' interests on OU committees, as Students' Unions do in regular universities; produces its own newspaper to keep staff and students up-to-date and to create a forum for debate and information/opinion sharing. Regular radio and TV magazine programmes have the same function.

How to apply

You can apply for a place at any time, although the closing date for entry in 1997 is September 1996. If there is not room for you in 1997, your application will be carried forward to the following year, unless you opt to withdraw.

Is there help with the cost?

You might be eligible for a training grant if your course is work-related and the OU itself has limited funds to help out in worthy cases: send for the leaflet, Financial Support for Open University Study, available from your region's Open University Enquiry and Admissions office. Another helping hand is offered through the facility to pay your fees by instalments.

Appendix II
Specialist Colleges

Colleges in this section are grouped under their specialisms. It is important to remember that other institutions will offer similar courses within a wider range, and that some specialist colleges which have been adopted by universities appear in other parts of this Guide under the parent university's entry: this is by no means an exclusive listing.

If you are looking at these Colleges, however, it is probable that you have already opted for a particular specialism. That specialism is likely to over-ride your quest for a particular environment: we therefore cover only the bare basics here. You will find fuller entries for these Colleges on the ECCTIS programme.

Agriculture

Askham Bryan College

Askham Bryan
York
YO2 3PR
Telephone: 01904 702121

Askham Bryan is an agricultural college set in the Vale of York, four miles out of the city. The College Farms total 174 hectares and are a mixed arable and livestock system. Redhouse Wood is the College's Forestry Training Centre and the College estate is used by Gamekeeping students. The York Riding School provides equestrian students with experience and it is possible for students to keep their own horses at livery there. The main site houses engineering workshops and applied science laboratories. The library and resource centre, along with the suites of PCs support course learning. Some student residences are on campus and the College's social facilities include a bar, open in the evenings and venue for discos, quizzes and bar games. Sports facilities on site include a four hole pitch and putt, a bowling green, a fitness room and indoor climbing wall. The Union runs a range of clubs and societies - photography, riding, drama, Christian Union and others.

Accommodation: The College has 244 places in Halls of Residence. Halls are situated on the main campus and rooms are single. Catering arrangements are half board seven days a week. There are 22 self-catering places.

City and escape routes: See the University of York entry.

Harper Adams

Newport
Shropshire
TF10 8NB
telephone: 01952 820820

Harper Adams College was founded in 1901, and occupies the farmland of what was the Harper Adams estate, near to the beautiful Ironbridge Gorge. The College is set in the wide countryside of Shropshire, close (but not very) to Newport (Shropshire), Shrewsbury and Telford. This is the largest agricultural college in Britain.

All amenities, accommodation, teaching facilities, farm and woodland are on a single site covering 202 hectares. The campus is well-spaced, with the original buildings (redbrick, solid Victorian, gabled and well-proportioned) balanced by purpose-built teaching facilities and accommodation blocks. All development here is high quality.

The usual range of academic back-up services: library (32,000 books and pamphlets and 700 current periodicals); Languages Resources Centre (optional language modules are available to all students); and computer facilities (CAD facilities, a networked Computer Centre including an open workshop facility).

Teaching facilities also include purpose built science laboratories and glasshouses, and Engineering facilities such as a covered field demonstration area.

The farm and woodland are, in themselves, academic services: the farm is a working unit which will provide you with 'hands on' experience of land management and arable and livestock farming.

The Union runs a range of clubs and societies. There are dances, concerts, discos, barn dances, plays, revues and 'the spectacular end of session ball'. Sports facilities include a sports hall, multigym, heated outdoor swimming pool, billiards, snooker, and squash courts; and outdoors, tennis courts, rugby, hockey, soccer and cricket pitches. Students can also use the National Sports Centre at Lilleshall. The College has a strong reputation for rugby union, with College players achieving national honours.

Accommodation: Harper Adams is a residential college. You will spend your first year on campus in one of the six halls of residence which provide 580 places in all. Most rooms are single, a few are double and 180 are en suite. The College Warden ensures you will have a place to live. Off-campus, in your later College years, you will live in approved accommodation (cottages, houses, flats or digs) locally.

Town and around: The nearest centre is Newport (Shropshire), a small town with pubs and one or two restaurants. You are quite near to Telford, a relatively new conurbation made up of a series of towns. There is a ten screen cinema, and a theatre with a mixed programme, including local groups. Not too far away is Shrewsbury,

Royal Agricultural College

Cirencester
Gloucestershire GL7 6JS
Telephone: 01285 652531

The Royal Agricultural College campus is a mile out of Cirencester in the heart of the Cotswolds, a very beautiful setting. Its elegant Elizabethan buildings, complete with tower and quadrangle, are balanced by purpose built teaching blocks. The College farms 770 hectares, in three separate units eight miles apart which offer contrasting farming conditions. The library houses resources in agriculture, agribusiness and rural land management, and Reading Rooms are open for private study until 11pm daily. Two computer laboratories are available to students. Language tuition in French, German and Spanish is offered to all students in evening classes.

The Union Club manages sports and social activities. There is a common room and bar. The formal Freshers, Christmas, Rag and Burn's Night balls build to the social highlight of the May Ball. The Drama Club puts on an annual play and revue. The College magazine, *Siren*, chronicles College Life; the Journal, published once a year, is the official voice of the Union. Rugby, hockey and cricket are among the most successful of the College's sports. A wide range of other sports on offer, including Beagling and Clay Pigeon Shooting.

The College has a Student Welfare Officer who gives advice and support.

For students without traditional entry qualifications, the College runs a Degree Foundation Programme.

Accommodation: the College has 305 places in fully catered Halls of Residence on campus. Leases cover the three terms. Private sector: within six or seven miles of campus there is a good range of accommodation, (having transport is definitely a bonus here). The Accommodation Officer checks all the properties on the list.

SURROUNDING AREA: The College is in some of the prettiest countryside in England. The M4 and M5 are not far away. Bristol is the nearest large city. Cirencester will suffice for daily needs.

Scottish Agricultural College

581 King Street
Aberdeen AB9 1UD
Telephone
0224 480291

The Scottish Agricultural College is based on three campuses: Aberdeen, Auchincruive (Ayr) and Edinburgh. The College specialises in vocational courses covering Food, Land and Environmental Studies. Some courses are offered in association with the Universities of Aberdeen, Edinburgh, Glasgow or Strathclyde, some are run jointly with Napier and Robert Gordon Universities.

The Aberdeen Campus is located on two sites, one close to the city centre and one five miles away on the Craibstone Estate. As well as libraries and computer laboratories the College has two farms in Aberdeen. Craibstone is a 400 hectare farm with dairy, beef and sheep. The other, students

Tillycorthie, covers 200 hectares and has a range of arable enterprises and a pig unit. Student life on campus revolves around the restaurant, snackbar and bar services. There is a disco. Sports facilities are provided locally.

Accommodation: All first years, who wish to be so, can be housed in the halls of residence at Craibstone. Altogether 88 catered places are provided: breakfast and evening meal are served 7 days per week. A morning and evening minibus service links the two campuses. By September 1995, a further 60 places, in en-suite style, will be provided. Students wishing to find private sector accommodation have full access to the University's accommodation lists. See the entry in this guide.

The main College buildings in **Edinburgh** are on the King's Buildings Campus of the University of Edinburgh, south of the city centre. College farms are seven miles away on the Bush Estate, covering 1,100 hectares and almost all farming activities, including conservation work. Students on the King's Buildings Campus can join the University Union (see the University of Edinburgh's entry). Rural Resources students are able also to join Napier University's Student Association (see Napier University's entry).

Accommodation: All first years can be accommodated in the halls of residence situated north of Edinburgh by the Forth. There is a regular bus service to the College which takes twenty minutes. All rooms are single. Meals are provided five days per week. The private sector housing lists of Edinburgh and Napier universities are available to students of the College.

Auchincruive Campus is three miles inland from the centre of Ayr. The College farmland surrounds the campus; there are further facilities at the Crichton Royal farm at Dumfries and the Kirkton-Auchtertyre farm at Tyndrum. There is a multigym, tennis courts and sports pitches on site. A number of societies are run for and by the students.

Accommodation: Places for 100 students are provided. Rooms in halls of residence are allocated to the youngest and those who are from the greatest distance. Breakfast and dinner are provided during the week. The Accommodation Office keeps lists of private sector housing: lists are sent to all first years who have not been allocated a hall place. Most students live in self-catered or catered lodgings. There are very few houses to rent in Ayr.

CITIES and ESCAPE ROUTES:

For the Aberdeen Campus see the University of Aberdeen; for the Edinburgh Campus see the University of Edinburgh; and for the Auchincruive Campus see the University of Paisley.

Silsoe Campus

Cranfield University
Silsoe
Bedford MK45 4ET
Telephone: 01525 863000

Silsoe is a constituent college of Cranfield University. The College is highly specialised and offers only eight honours degree courses for undergraduates. The bias is vocational and practical, so that a 'sandwich' element is either compulsory or a strong option. The College's specific aim is to apply the principles of science, technology and management to a range of rural activities including agriculture, food marketing and distribution, and environmental planning.

The campus is pleasantly landscaped. Between the two-storey modern blocks of lecture rooms, workshops, labs and student residences are open green spaces. The scale and ambience is friendly - an achievement for '60s buildings.

Almost half the total number of students are on one-year Master's degree courses, so the turnover is quite rapid. This means that the mix of students is not as limited and static as you might expect and as one of the 50 to 70 intake of first-year undergraduates you would be drawn into a community enlivened by students from 50 different countries. The atmosphere is warm and friendly and the drop-out rate is very low.

Shuttleworth College: A large country estate 16km from Silsoe accommodates studies in business management, agriculture and the environment. Administered as part of the Silsoe campus, it offers 3 HND courses and a BSc taught jointly with Silsoe.

Silsoe's **library**'s collection is very closely associated with agriculture, biology, engineering and earth sciences. It includes some 38,000 books, 380 journals, maps and trade catalogues. There are two terminal rooms which give students access to the **computing facilities**. Personal computers are available for general student use and word processing. Computers are linked to Cranfield and to JANET. A European language now forms part of the first year of every course; instruction is given in the **Language Training Centre** where there are facilities for self-study.

Teaching and research are serviced by a 125 hectare **farm** in arable and livestock production. The farm is next to the campus. There are **laboratories** equipped for the study of photography, interpretation, remote sensing, geographic information systems etc.

The Union runs SAFAD (Student Aid For Agricultural Development), a charity supporting Silsoe College students working on agricultural development projects world-wide. This is a unique student activity, operating twice a year (during vacations), using specialist skills to set up small-scale projects in Third World countries.

The Union runs 32 societies including the motor, drama, engineering, ploughing, brewing and international special interest clubs. Dances, discos and a number of formal entertainments are organised by the social committee.

There are soccer, hockey, rugby and cricket pitches, weight training facilities, squash and tennis courts on campus, and an indoor area for badminton, table tennis and snooker.

The **medical centre** holds a daily surgery for treatment and advice. Personal tutors oversee the welfare of each student and a **counselling service** is available. There is a College **chaplain** and a room in College is set aside as a mosque.

Accommodation: First year students are guaranteed accommodation in single rooms in one of the three halls of residence or houses on campus.

Silsoe is very much a country campus. Nearest centres are Milton Keynes or Bedford. A car is really necessary. The M1 and A6 take you to larger centres; the M1 to all points north and south to London.

Writtle College

Writtle
Chelmsford
Essex CM1 3RR
Telephone : 01245 420705

Writtle College specialises in the countryside and amenity industries, and is a Regional College of Anglia Polytechnic University. Its grounds and commercial farms cover 200 hectares of land and are a learning resource. The College is just outside Writtle, a picturesque village in rural Essex. The village is a thriving community with a long history - the settlement long pre-dates the Domesday Book.

The library is a purpose built, modern building; its book collection supports courses taught. There are Flexible Learning Workshops with computers and draughting equipment which are open at all times. Computing and information technology are integrated into all courses: computing equipment, when not in use for teaching, is available on open access. The Design Centre, opened in 1993, has accommodation for drawing office practice and computer-aided design and is also available on open access when not in use for teaching.

Social life on campus is organised by the Union and includes discos, dances, folk nights, jazz, cocktail evenings and quizzes. There is an annual barbecue and beer festival and the Summer Ball. Clubs and societies reflect the interests of students - a four wheel drive club, the 'Green Machine', Writtle Organics Club - and also on offer are the more usual drama, photography and sports clubs. Sport at Writtle is strong. Facilities include two squash courts, a large sports hall, fitness room and multigym; there are extensive playing fields and several tennis courts. Instructional classes in a number of sports are arranged by the recreation manager. Rugby, football, hockey and cricket are the main team games on offer, but are only some of many.

Student Support Services provide counselling and welfare support. College chaplains represent the Free Church, Church of England and the Roman Catholic Church.

Accommodation: the College has 350 places in catered Halls of Residence, all on campus. Rooms are a mixture of single and doubles, with some en-suite. Leases run for 30 weeks. Private Sector: most students can find housing within Writtle village or the Chelmsford area. If you have your own transport then the many farms offering places up to six miles away from College become a viable option too. The Accommodation Office keeps a list of properties available.

SURROUNDING AREA: Writtle is just outside Chelmsford. See the Anglia Polytechnic University's entry.

Art & Design

Cumbria College of Art and Design

Brampton Road
Carlisle
Cumbria
CA3 9AY
Telephone: 01228 25333

Cumbria College of Art and Design in Carlisle offers a balance of BTEC, HND and BA(Hons) courses in the arts. All BA (Hons) courses are validated by the University of Central Lancashire. The College has an 11 acre campus in the centre of Carlisle which includes the Stanwix Arts Theatre - used for touring productions as well as student performances. Fine Art courses are taught in the Caldewgate building on the other Carlisle is a pleasant, small city with fast access to the Lake District and North Pennines (all good hiking country), on the edge of wilderness. Its facilities serve a wide, sparsely populated area and its shopping is above average, as are local pubs, clubs and eating places.

Accommodation: The College has no accommodation stock of its own but the Accommodation Office does keep a list of vacancies, the majority of which are in shared houses.

Falmouth School of Art & Design

Woodlane
Falmouth
Cornwall TR11 4RA
Telephone: 01326 211077

Falmouth School of Art and Design has two campuses, one (the main campus) in Falmouth and one, 12 miles away, in Redruth: both in the wild country which is the western stretch of Cornwall. The Falmouth campus is five minutes from the beach and a short walk from the town centre. Its buildings house studios and workshops, and are mainly purpose-built, many very recently. The Welfare Unit has a register of approved properties. General welfare provision here is good. The Student Union elects one sabbatical officer annually and arranges entertainments throughout the year. Sports and other extra-curricular activities are enhanced by the School's location on the coast and on the edge of some of the country's most beautiful, unspoilt countryside.

Accommodation: the School has a small hall (31 places available) at Lamorva House, adjacent to the Falmouth campus. Priority here goes to overseas students and those with special needs. Private rented accommodation is reasonable and plentiful for both lodgings and shared houses: student living dovetails with the holiday trade.

Kent Institute of Art and Design

Oakwood Park
Maidstone
Kent ME16 8AG
Telephone: 01622 757286

Kent Institute of Art and Design was formed in 1987 by the merger of three long established colleges of art - Canterbury College of Art, Maidstone College of Art and Medway College of Design. Each College retains its identity: although the student body numbers just over 2,000, you should remember that those students are dispersed over three centres. Each of the constituent colleges is housed in purpose-built accommodation. Each college has its own Union and social facilities. Each college also has its own gallery and exhibition area for student work and visiting artists. Canterbury College is a few minutes' walk from the city centre: both the School of Art and the School of Architecture are housed here. Maidstone College is based in Oakwood Park, along with a number of other colleges and schools; Oakwood Park is a residential area about a mile outside Maidstone: this is the Institute's centre for graphic design and communication studies. Medway College is just outside Rochester on a hill overlooking the river Medway. This is the most urban of the campuses. Medway College is the Institute's centre for Three Dimensional Design and Fashion and Clothing studies.

Accommodation: the Institute has a limited amount of its own student accommodation at all three campuses, and also runs a head tenancy scheme incorporating 123 properties. The Accommodation Officers at each campus keep lists of suitable lodgings and shared houses close to their respective campuses.

The London Institute

388-396 Oxford Road
London W1R 1FE
Telephone: 0171 491 8533

The London Institute is a federation of some of the most prestigious and famous art and design colleges in the country: Camberwell College of Arts, Central Saint Martins College of Art and Design, Chelsea College of Art and Design, London College of Fashion and London College of Printing and Distributive Trades. Each College retains its own identity and strengths, while their federation allows interaction and intersupport.

Camberwell College of Arts

The College has grown on the same site, very close to Camberwell Green, in south London since its foundation in 1898. Its courses are divided into two Schools: the School of Applied and Graphic Arts and the School of Art History and Conservation. As well as the usual academic support services of a library, computing centre and media resources, the College has a dedicated drawing facility where students can draw in a calm and relaxed atmosphere. Buses from central London are the most convenient means of city transport; the nearest station is Peckham Rye, about a short 15 minute walk away.

Central Saint Martin's College of Art and Design

Central Saint Martin's College was created by merging the Central School of Art and Design and Saint Martin's College of Art and Design in 1989. The College is on three sites - Southampton Row in Holborn, Charing Cross Road in Soho very close to Trafalgar Square and Long Acre in Covent Garden. No site is far from the others and this really is central London in the West End sense (see the King's College, London and LSE entries in The University of London). Courses are divided into three Schools: the School of Art, the School of Fashion and Textiles and the School of Graphic and Industrial Design. The Photographic Unit's studios and darkrooms are open to all CSM students: first years usually take an Introduction to Photography course. The College also has library facilities, which include a collection of 80,000 art and design books, and 100,000 art and design slides; the library takes 250 periodicals. The Central Computing Unit has been designed as a facility for introducing students to Computer Aided Design methods; courses on computers and Art and Design are available in specialist subjects.

Chelsea College of Art and Design

The Chelsea College has four sites - two in SW6 (near the river), one in SW3 (Chelsea, just off the Kings Road) and one in W12 (Shepherd's Bush). Manresa Road (SW3) is the main site and houses the College offices. The School of Art runs from Manresa Road and Bagley's Lane (SW6). Lime Grove (W12) and Hugon Road (SW6) both house the School of Design. There are three libraries in all, each with specialised collections. Computer-aided art and design is an integral part of all courses: introductory and advanced courses are available. Lime Grove and Hugon Road both have computer suites; Manresa Road houses computer facilities related to film, video and sound production.

London College of Fashion

The London College has five sites in central London: three close to Oxford Street, one close to the Barbican and one near Old Street; this is very much the City of London. Most courses use more than one site. The College has three libraries, foreign languages study areas and six computer rooms, a specialist fashion theatre with permanent catwalk, video suites, radio facilities and a photographic studio, a teaching gymnasium and cosmetics laboratory.

London College of Printing and Distributive Trades

The College is on three sites: Elephant and Castle (School of Printing Technology, School of Graphic Design and School of Business Management), Clerkenwell (School of Media) and Davies Street (School of Retail Studies and School of Professional Studies). All are very close to the centre of London - Elephant and Castle to the south, Clerkenwell to the north and Davies Street in the middle. Each site has a library and computing facilities.

Accommodation

The College has 500 places in Halls of Residence out in Tooting and Battersea. All rooms are single.

Private Sector

The Accommodation Office keeps a list of properties available, both lodgings and shared houses.

CITY/ESCAPE ROUTES

See the London section in the University of London entry.

Norfolk Institute of Art and Design

St George's Street
Norwich NR3 1BB
Telephone: 0603 610561

The Institute, as its title suggests, concentrates on courses in art and design, has two campuses, one in Norwich and one in Great Yarmouth, and is the only centre of art and design honours degree work in the East Anglian region. It regards itself as having a positive regional role and has strong links with the University of East Anglia. Both campuses have buildings of interesting architectural character. The Norwich campus concentrates on Fine Art, Graphic Design, Theoretical Studies and Foundation Studies. Great Yarmouth has workshops for three dimensional crafts and photography. Both campuses have facilities for print-making, ceramics, typography and computer-aided design. The Institute's gallery is on the Norwich campus and promotes local contemporary art, design and crafts. The Students' Union organises parties, pantomimes, reviews and debates. A film programme is shown weekly (Norwich) and the Institute's football team is affiliated to a local league.

Accommodation: The Institute has seven places to offer students, self-catered and single. These are within walking distance of the site.

Surrey Institute of Art & Design

Falkner Road
Farnham
Surrey GU9 7DS
Telephone: 0252 722441

The Surrey Institute is the result of a merger between the West Surrey College of Art and Design and the Epsom School of Art and Design.

The West Surrey campus is close to the centre of Farnham, an historic market town 40 miles from London. The Union has its own bar and organises discos, dances and other events, and runs a number of clubs and societies.

The Epsom campuses are both near the centre of the town (Epsom is 17 miles out of London). The campuses are not far apart. The School has its own bar which is used as a meeting ground.

Accommodation: the College has 300 places in Halls of Residence at Farnham which accommodate approximately 50% of first years, in single, double or treble rooms. There is no College owned accommodation at Epsom. Halls are situated on campus or within two miles of the site. All College accommodation is self-catered. The College has a further 153 places available on the northern edge of campus.

Private Sector: students at Epsom and those without a hall place at Farnham, are sent lists of available lodgings and rooms in shared houses. There is a shortage of rooms close to the Farnham site, but all the accommodation at Epsom is within three miles of the campus. Approximately 75% of students at Epsom live in lodgings.

LOCAL AREA: see The University of Surrey's entry.

Winchester School of Art

Park Avenue
Winchester S023 8DL
Telephone: 01962 842500

Winchester School of Art is an Accredited Institution of the University of Southampton and is an independent specialist art school. All full-time BA courses include the study of a foreign language, and the School has strong European links. There is a specialist collection of learning resources for art and design, including a bookstock of 22,000 volumes and an audio-visual library with 90,000 slides. The Winchester Gallery is on campus and is open to the public; the Gallery offers a programme of contemporary art. The Union organises a range of social events which include discos, video nights, parties and a Summer Ball. There are links with other Students Unions in the region, and with other organisations in the city. The College counsellor can offer confidential advice.

Accommodation: The College has 36 places in Halls of Residence: overseas students are given priority. The halls are five minutes walk from campus and are self-catered. Private Sector: first years are allocated self-catered lodgings. Students of subsequent years find rooms in shared houses. Most live within two and a half miles of campus.

THE CITY/SURROUNDING AREA: See King Alfred's College and the University of Southampton's entry.

Education/ Mainly Education

Bishop Grosseteste College

Lincoln
LN1 3DY
Telephone: 01522 527347

Bishop Grosseteste offers primary teacher training courses in partnership with the University of Hull. The second years of all BEd courses are spent in Hull (see the University of Hull entry). The College was originally an Anglican foundation and still holds to its Christian ethos. The campus is just ten minutes from the castle and cathedral, the historic heart of Lincoln, and twenty minutes from the main shopping centre. College buildings are entirely in keeping with Lincoln's heritage; graceful and tranquil, with newer additions. The Students Union building is on campus, as are playing fields, tennis courts and a small gymnasium. There are purpose built areas, the Primary Bases, which support student learning, as well as the Sibthorp Library and Design Technology Centre.

Accommodation: The College has 230 single rooms in Halls of Residence situated on campus. All places are catered which involves all meals on weekdays and self-catering at weekends.

City (population 75,000): Some cities are more historic than others, and Lincoln is very historic indeed. Its nucleus is the cathedral, one of the very finest in England, and the castle. Around the hill cluster buildings from all ages: medieval, Tudor, Georgian and Victorian. The city even has Roman remains. Brayford Pool, originally a Roman port, is now a marina in the city centre with facilities for rowing, canoeing and river cruises.

Lincoln's present day industry lies below this strata-ed past. The shopping centre is pedestrianised and offers all high street names, and an array of boutiques and specialist shops. **Entertainments:** The Theatre Royal offers a range of theatrical experiences and the city has a range of pubs, clubs, discos and restaurants.

Lincoln is not really on any major road network, and is nearest to the A1. Rail-links with Sheffield and the north and to London are quite regular.

Bretton Hall

West Bretton
Wakefield
WF4 4LG

Telephone: 01924 830261

Bretton Hall College was founded in 1949, concentrates on Arts and Education and is now a College of the University of Leeds.

The College is housed in an 18th century mansion set in 260 acres of sweeping, landscaped grounds. Its more recent additions do not always blend unobtrusively, but the graciousness of the original building prevails.

The Yorkshire Sculpture Park is in the College's grounds; its range of recent exhibitions has been impressive. There is a also gallery - a fixed, airy structure which looks a little like a marquee. You have the benefit of the coffee house, opened to serve the 300,000 visitors annually.

Below the College, in the wide bottom of the gentle valley, are Bretton lakes. The area around the lakes is a nature reserve, jointly run by the Yorkshire Wildlife Trust, which has been designated an site of special scientific interest.

The Union organises most of the entertainments on campus, from balls to folk clubs, cabarets, visits to other venues... The college bar is open at lunchtimes and in the evening. The College has a gymnasium, tennis courts and some playing fields on-site.

The College **library** houses special collections on Teaching Practice, Music and the national curriculum, as well as books, journals and CD-ROM databases to back up the courses taught by the College. The Learning Resources workshop includes facilities for desk-top publishing.

Accommodation: The College has eleven hostels on campus, residential accommodation off campus and a list of private, rented properties. Around 40% of first years can live in College managed accommodation. The Accommodation Office will help you to find a flat or room to rent in the private sector. Hostel common rooms, laundries, study and utility rooms are open to all students.

THE SURROUNDING AREA: Bretton is six miles from Wakefield, its nearest large population centre. Being so near to the M1 (just a mile away) means that Leeds and Sheffield are both easily accessible. The area to the west of the College is hilly and very pretty; 'Last of the Summer Wine' country is about half and hour away in the car. To the east, the countryside is less inspiring, flatter and more urban.

King Alfred's College of Higher Education

Sparkford Road
Winchester
SO22 4NR
Telephone: 01962 841515

The campus site is on the western edge of Winchester, ten minutes' walk from the city centre. The College is set in woodland on a gentle hillside. Its original buildings date back to the 1860s and are of the soft, grey stone typical of this area. Around the original college, new buildings have grown: a purpose built Arts Centre and adjoining theatre, the sports hall, library and resources centre, along with a number of the College's student residences. Other residences are all within a mile of campus.

King Alfred's is part of the Urban Learning Foundation in East London. Teacher education students from the College can have experience of inner city school placements which complement the teaching practice offered by Winchester.

The Martial Rose Library houses 120,000 items, receives 590 journals and seats 375. The Computer Education Centre provides equipment to students for all levels of work and its staff gives help and advice.

The College has a theatre and Arts Centre. The theatre seats 300 and has professional level equipment. The Arts Centre has a large hall with flexible performance area. Both spaces are used by the Drama Department and the Union drama society. There is an annual Open Air Shakespeare put on in the grounds of Wolvesey Castle and the gardens of Mottisfornt Abbey. College productions are also mounted in Winchester Cathedral. The College hosts a programme of professional dance and drama.

A sports hall, a dance studio, a gymnasium, two squash courts, tennis courts and a playing field are on site. In addition, there are 12 acres of playing fields in the city.

Accommodation: A new student village, on-line by 1996, means that the College will be able to house 1,100 students in either self-catered or part-board accommodation.

City & area: Winchester is truly one of the most beautiful cathedral cities in the country. It is still small with a strong sense of history. Its 'life' is in restaurants and pretty pubs. Shopping is generally small shops and boutiques.

Hampshire is a gentle county with a long history of wealth. It contains the New Forest and the beginning of the South Downs. London is an hour away by train.

Liverpool Institute of Higher Education

PO Box 6
Stand Park Road
Liverpool
L16 9JD
Telephone: 0151 737 3000

Liverpool Institute is nominally a dual campus college, a merger of two teacher training colleges which are, in fact, just across the road from each other, with the Art and Design building a short distance away. By most usual criteria it is a single site college, in Childwall - a pleasant suburb around three miles out of Liverpool city centre.

Christ's and Notre Dame is the Catholic half of the Institute. The College was built in the 1960s, glass and brick blocks neatly arranged. Some halls of residence are on campus, as is a gym, tennis courts and all weather pitch.

S. Katharine's College is across the road. Buildings date from its Anglican foundation in the 1930s: warm red brick, two storeys, pitched roofs, large windows and gracious lawns. On campus are playing fields squash courts, student residences and the Students' Union building.

The **library** (sited on both campuses) houses 200,000 books. All registered LIHE students can use the library facilities of the University of Liverpool. Some teaching computer laboratories are available for private use.

Concordia, the Institute's Concert Society, arranges an excellent range of classical music concerts, open to the public. There are regular discos and dramatic productions. The Union funds over 40 clubs and societies, sporting and non-sporting.

Accommodation: The College has over 900 single study-bedrooms in houses which usually accommodate the majority of first years. Houses are either on campus or in Aigburth three miles away. Private sector housing is available within a reasonable distance of campus. The Accommodation Office keeps a list of properties.

THE CITY: see the entry for the University of Liverpool.

Newman College

Bartley Green
Birmingham
B32 3NT
Telephone: 0121 476 1181

Newman College is an accredited college of the University of Birmingham and was founded by the Catholic Education Council in 1968 for teacher training. The College has a pleasant campus on the edge of Birmingham. To the east is the University and City; to the south you can see the Worcestershire hills. The campus is purpose designed and built, with lawns and quadrangles, places to meet between lectures. A large sports hall, gymnasium, squash courts and a health and fitness centre are all on site.

The library houses 75,000 books and subscribes to 250 periodicals relating to the subjects taught at the College. Students also have access to Westhill College's library facilities. Computer facilities are available on open access, including during the evenings and weekends.

Music, although not a subject taught at the College, is very strong. There is a choir, instrumental ensembles, a folk group and pop groups. Informal music evenings happen regularly. Piano lessons are available, and students can study for the College Certificate in Classroom Keyboard Skills.

Union entertainments include band nights, quiz nights, comedy clubs, discos and promotions. A number of balls happen throughout the year, including the formal Christmas Ball.

Accommodation: the College has 280 bedrooms (mainly single) in Halls of Residence which accommodates most first years. Halls are situated on campus and all are catered (full board seven days a week).

CITY: see the University of Birmingham's entry.

Northern College

Aberdeen Campus
Hilton Place
Aberdeen
AB9 1FA
Telephone: 01224 283500

Northern College offers specialised courses in teaching, community education and social work. There are two campuses, one in Aberdeen and one in Dundee.

The campus in Aberdeen is two miles out of the city centre in the quiet area of Hilton. On-site are the library, computer laboratories and a television studio. Culturally, students have access to a theatre and music rooms. Sports facilities on campus are extensive: a games hall, fitness centre, playing fields, tennis courts, gymnasia and a swimming pool. Students' Union amenities are also here. Courses offered: Postgraduate Certificate in Education (Primary and Secondary), BEd (Hons) Primary, BEd (Hons) Music and diplomas in Social Work.

The Dundee campus is north of the river Tay, three miles from the city centre. On-site facilities include: the library, computer laboratories, resource centre, theatre, drama studio, music rooms, dance studio, swimming pool, squash courts, games hall, gymnasia, playing fields and Students' Union. Courses offered: Postgraduate Certificate in Education (Primary), BEd (Hons) Primary, Postgraduate Diploma in Community Education, BA in Community Education and diplomas in Social Work.

Accommodation: The College has 535 places in Halls of Residence of which 256 are at Aberdeen. Dundee: the majority of places are catered, two meals on weekdays and full board at weekends; all halls are approximately one mile from the campus. Aberdeen: 133 catered places offer breakfast and evening meal six times a week, Saturdays breakfast only. Also available are 123 self-catering flats. All halls (Aberdeen) are on campus.

CITIES and ESCAPE ROUTES:
See the University of Aberdeen and the University of Dundee's entries.

College of Ripon and York St John

Lord Mayor's Walk
York
YO3 7EX
Telephone: 01904 656771

Ripon and York St John is a College of the University of Leeds. Degree awards are degrees of the University of Leeds. The College has campuses both in Ripon and York. The two joined forces in 1975.

The main campus in York is a four acre site on Lord Mayor's Walk facing the Minster across the city wall. Its buildings are old and are part of York's historic centre. Gray's Court, a most beautiful historic house nestling in the shadow of the Minster houses the departments of Historical Studies, Language Studies and English Literature. The College's other two York campuses are the Limes and Heworth Croft, both in easy walking distance.

Ripon's campus is close to the Ripon city centre and occupies a 50 acre site. Grounds are landscaped and include gardens, parkland and playing fields. Most amenities are on campus; some cottages and houses nearby are additional residences.

The two cities are 25 miles apart. The College operates a frequent bus service between the two sites on every day during term time.

Each main campus has a Union building with bars and shops. Entertainments happen on each campus five nights of the week. The College has a sports hall, which converts into two gymnasia, a gymnasium equipped for gymnastics and trampolining, a 25 metre swimming pool, squash courts, tennis courts, a dance studio and playing fields (on the York campus); further tennis courts and playing fields are available on the Ripon campus.

There are libraries on both main campuses. The total bookstock exceeds 200,000 volumes and the library subscribes to 1,000 periodicals. There are 500 reading places across all sites. Both campuses have a number of general access computer laboratories and workrooms. All students can take courses in Information Technology. **Accommodation:** the College has 1,089 places in Halls of Residence, 804 are on or within 10 - 15 minutes walk of the York campus. The remaining 285 are located on campus at Ripon. Both sites have an Accommodation Office: lists of available houses and lodgings are provided.

CITIES and SURROUNDING AREA:
For the York Campus see the University of York's entry. This also covers the 'escape routes' for Ripon. The City of Ripon is an ancient cathedral city, significantly smaller than York with a population of 13,000. It is truly charming, with a close community atmosphere. Every night, at nine o'clock the City Hornblower sounds his horn at each corner of the obelisk in the market place.

The city and college join forces for many social events, particularly in music. Ripon is on the edge of the Yorkshire Dales National Park, and is very close to Fountains Abbey: very beautiful country. Excellent terrain for most outdoor pursuits, including caving, pot-holing, climbing and walking. Ripon is on the A1 and is accessible by train.

College of St Mark and St John

Derriford Road
Plymouth
Devon
PL6 8BH
Telephone: 01752 777188

St Mark and St John were, originally, separate colleges, each founded to specialise in teacher training. The two merged in 1923, and the new College of St Mark and St John (Marjon to its friends) moved to Plymouth in 1973.

The new, purpose built campus (53 acres) is around five miles out of Plymouth. The newest buildings are those for primary education and the sports centre. There is both a 'student village' and halls of residence on campus, creating a pleasant, integrated environment for students. The shopping 'mall' on campus includes a launderette, shop and bank. The bookshop is in the main reception area and stocks texts for College courses.

The Union funds and runs over 40 clubs and societies and organises a full social programme, including a May Ball and a fortnight of entertainment when you first arrive. The 'Lion and Lamb', with conservatory extension has a bar and disco area. The College has a theatre with a 'big screen', which doubles as a cinema.

The Centre for Physical Education has recently been extended. Its facilities include: a 25 metre, heated indoor swimming pool, a weight training centre, three squash courts, a gymnasium, three sports halls (each with four badminton courts), a specialist rock-climbing facility, a computer centre, a Fitness and Health Suite with sauna and an outdoor facilities centre. All playing fields are on campus, including an all-weather, floodlit training area and astro-turf soccer/hockey pitch. The College has sailing dinghies on Plymouth quay.

The College is one of the constituent colleges of the Urban Learning Foundation in Tower Hamlets: a base for students on teaching practice

Accommodation: the College has 202 places in the student village and 324 places in halls of residence, all on campus. If you are not housed on campus, the College has a well-developed approved housing scheme. Most students are housed in furnished flats or houses.

CITY and ESCAPE ROUTES:

See The University of Plymouth's entry

Accommodation: a total of 540 accommodation places on, or next to, campus. The College Accommodation Office provides lists of local estate agents and letting agencies for private accommodation. Strawberry Hill's immediate local area's rents are high. You can, however, travel in quite easily from the cheaper areas of south London.

THE TOWN/LONDON: The College is in Twickenham, in the London Borough of Richmond. Central London is only 35 minutes away on the train, and yet you are in an almost country setting. Kew Gardens is a short bus ride away; the Thames flows in its gracious-living mode before it hits the city-proper. You are in the middle of the Royal tract of Surrey, within walking distance of Hampton Court and its famous maze, close to the Royal deerparks of Richmond Park and Bushy Park. Entertainments: Richmond Borough has three theatres: the Richmond Theatre (mainstream touring productions), the Orange Tree Theatre ('alternative') and the Dukes Head Theatre; you can also easily get into the West End. There are also three cinemas in Richmond and one in Kingston. Pubs here are almost 'country' in atmosphere, and civilised. Clubs, the nearest range is probably in Kingston, although, again, London's lights are near enough. Twickenham is, of course, synonymous with Rugby Union. See also the University of London's entry.

St. Mary's College

Strawberry Hill
Waldegrave Road
Twickenham
Middlesex
TW1 4SX
Telephone: 0181 892 0051

St. Mary's was founded in 1850 as a Catholic College for the education of teachers. The College moved to its present site in 1925. The campus is thirty acres of lawns, trees and playing fields, close to the River Thames. Strawberry Hill itself is a 19th century mansion built by Horace Walpole. The house is the main College building; several departments are housed here. It is a wonderful example of Gothic architecture - mini-spires, turrets and crenelations (an ideal college if all you've ever wanted to do is live in a castle). Newer additions are high quality, brick built, and do not pretend to mimic the style of the original building. The College chapel is quite a daunting, squared off block, which inside has height and grace and startling stained glass.

The Drama department has a modern theatre and strong links with professional companies who sometimes perform on campus. The Union organises three discos a week, as well as a range of other social events, including Balls. Sports facilities include a sports hall, gymnasium, dance studio, strength training room and sports injuries clinic, as well as pitches for lacrosse, hockey, rugby, soccer and netball, and tennis courts, all on campus.

The library houses 150,000 books and takes 700 periodicals. There is a model Children's library available to all students and a Primary Materials Room. The Computer Centre provides networked computers as well as booklets explaining how to use the system.

University College, Scarborough

Filey Road
Scarborough
North Yorkshire
YO11 3AZ
Telephone: 01723 362392

The College is a constituent College of the University of Leeds. All degrees are awarded by the University.

The College occupies a single site , one mile south of Scarborough's town centre, on the descending slopes of Oliver's Mount. The main College building is Edwardian and very much a College. The atmosphere is one of a close-knit community: accommodation is totally mixed - residential next to recreational next to teaching rooms. New blocks have been added to the original buildings over the years, and corridors wind from the old to the new. The College bar is on the ground floor and is venue for bands, discos and parties.

The only buildings separate from this burgeoning warren are the new halls of residence, built as a shield from the road in a style sympathetic to the original building (student residences also occupy the attic spaces). A sports hall, tennis courts and playing fields are all on campus.

The College has a theatre studio which provides a year-round programme. Music facilities include practice rooms, a music technology studio and a concert room. The choir, chamber choir, jazz choir, string ensemble, orchestra, recorder ensemble, wind and steel bands are all active. A recital series, featuring student and professional performers, is organised each year.

The main library houses 500,000 volumes and subscribes to 320 periodicals. There are three open access computing rooms, and the College offers introductory I.T. courses.

Accommodation: 290 places in halls of residence, 214 with shower ensuite. Some residential places are in the original building and in annexes across the road; the majority are in the new halls of residence. All halls are catered

THE TOWN (population 65,000): Scarborough is, primarily, a holiday resort, and all the attractions and amenities are there for you in and out of the season; many entertainments are on throughout the year and Scarborough is never a 'ghost town', even in thedepths of winter. The town is built around two bays; Scarborough Castle ruins stand on the headland dividing the two. The coast is cliffs and rocks, with sandy coves and inlets.

Shops are generally the major chain stores. The town has a purpose-built shopping mall. Restaurants are fairly limited - or may-be we haven't yet found the variations... The Stephen Joseph Theatre has recently been rehoused into an impressive conversion of an old cinema: the complex includes an 'arts' cinema and two theatres.

Scarborough is close to the Yorkshire Wolds and the North Yorkshire Moors. The coast to the north is Yorkshire holiday-land: Robin Hood's Bay and Whitby, the Cleveland Way, all very beautiful. Flamborough Head is also nearby with its wealth of birdlife. City life is not too far away, York about half an hour and Leeds 50 minutes by train.

Leeds, Trinity and All Saints College

Brownberrie Lane
Horsforth
Leeds
LS18 5HD
Telephone: 0113 283 7100

Trinity and All Saints is a College of the University of Leeds, but remains independent in many respects. All degrees are given by the University. The College campus is six miles from the centre of Leeds, west of the city towards the Yorkshire Dales. It's setting is pleasant and suburban, with hills in sight. All amenities are on campus - halls of residence, sports fields, learning resources - and the campus style is consistent, mainly flat roofed blocks, well-spaced and purposeful.

There is a wide events programme which includes discos, cabaret, bands, films and plays and a range of extra-curricular courses organised by the Recreational and Cultural Activities Committee. There are extensive sports fields on campus and four squash courts. Netball, basketball, squash, cricket, rugby (men and women's), table tennis, walking and climbing are all popular.

The library houses 100,000 items. The campus is networked and includes electronic mail and bulletin board.

Accommodation: the College has nine Halls of Residence on campus, one with ensuite facilities. Most students can find private accommodation in the area around the College if necessary.

THE CITY: see the University of Leeds' entry.

S Martin's College

Bowerham Road
Lancaster
LA1 3JD
Telephone: 0524 63446

S. Martin's was founded in 1963 by the Church of England. The College is set on a 35 acre site, a mile from Lancaster's centre, overlooking the town and out to Morecombe Bay, with the hills of the Lake District rising in the distance. A beautiful setting. Campus buildings range from the stone Victorian, ivyclad to the very recent, with some 1960s blocks in between. All teaching, recreational and adminstrative resources are on campus, and most of the College's residential units.

The Performing Arts Department has its own studio theatre and invites touring companies. There are three choirs, an orchestra and a jazz group. The Union's main venue has a bar and dance floor and a capacity of 400. Two discos and a quiz night each week.

Grass pitches, two gymnasia, weights room, tennis courts, squash courts and a floodlit all-weather court are all on-campus. Students here also use the facilities of Lancaster University.

The library houses over 100,000 items. An introductory course in computing is available to all first years.

Accommodation: there are 468 catered places on campus and a further 89 self-catered in the town centre. Shared houses are in ample supply in Lancaster's private sector; Morecambe is the best place to find flats and bedsits.

CITY AND SURROUNDING AREA: See University of Lancaster

Westhill College of Higher Education

Wesley Park Road
Selly Oak
Birmingham
B29 6LL
Telephone: 0121 472 7245

Westhill was founded by George Cadbury and George Hamilton Archibald of Quebec in 1907, and remains proud of its Free Church foundation. The campus' green spaces were preserved from the College's inception: Cadbury's environmental philosophy was that no building should take up more than 25% of its plot. Although supplemented now with modern buildings, the original layout and 'human scale' remains. The College's 80 acre campus is landscaped and lawned. Westhill is a fully accredited college of the University of Birmingham.

The Gillett Centre on campus has a heated indoor swimming pool, three squash courts and a small weight training room. The College has seven acres of playing fields and access to ten acres across the road owned by Woodbrooke College.

Accommodation: the College has 300 places in halls of residence which accommodate all first years, mainly in single rooms.

CITY and ESCAPE ROUTES: See the University of Birmingham's entry

Queen Margaret College, Edinburgh

Clerwood Terrace
Edinburgh
EH12 8TS
Telephone: 0131 317 3247

Queen Margaret College occupies a 24 acre site on Corstorphine Hill, about four miles out of the centre of Edinburgh. The campus was purpose-built in the 1970s and houses all teaching, living, learning resource and recreational accommodation. College courses concentrate on Health Care and Arts and Management.

The College library houses 80,000 books and subscribes to 800 periodicals. There is seating for 300 readers. Students have access to eight computer workshops and the College's computer network.

The Students' Association elects three sabbatical officers annually and employs two full-time members of staff. The Association Building houses the Association Offices and College bar. There is a regular entertainment programme throughout the week, its zenith being the 'Wednesday Night'. The Association funds a range of clubs and societies, and provides most equipment.

The College has a heated 25 metre swimming pool, a squash court and outdoor tennis courts. The games hall is equipped for badminton, volleyball and basketball. Transport is provided for access to facilities outside the College. There is a range of sporting societies; the Association has a nominal annual fee for the use of sports facilities.

The College has a counselling service, provided by its professional Student Counsellor. The Careers Service offers help and advice on writing CVs and applications.

Accommodation:
The College has 427 places in three Halls of Residence on the campus. Rooms are mainly single. A third of the places are catered, (half board - 14 meals per week) the rest are self-catered. Leases average 36 weeks.

THE CITY and ESCAPE ROUTES: See the University of Edinburgh entry.

St Andrew's College

Duntocher Road
Bearsden
Glasgow
G61 4QA
Telephone: 0141 943 1424

St. Andrew's College specialises in training teachers to educate Catholic pupils in Scotland. The College has a close association with the University of Glasgow. The 35 acre campus is in the residential suburb of Bearsden, between the city of Glasgow and the Campsie Hills. Buildings are modern, the site open and the views wide. The College is the national Catholic College in Scotland; its book collection and study emphasis reflects this. Computing workshops are available on some applications (word-processing for example).

Students have access to music, drama and art facilities. The Drama Club is open to all; music-making ranges from choral singing to student-organised bands; pottery, photography and print-making equipment are all available.

A licenced bar is venue for parties, discos, live bands and film shows. The Students' Representative Council (SRC) offers help and advice to students and organises social events. The campus has a heated indoor swimming pool, a large gymnasium and facilities for indoor and outdoor games. There is a dry ski-slope close to campus and the outdoor pursuits centre at Garelochhead offers wind-surfing, water-skiing and canoeing, as well as absailing and caving.

The Medical Centre is staffed by a full-time matron, part-time nursing assistant and a doctor visits three times a week. There is a sickbay. Personal counselling is available. The College Chaplain and assistant are resident in the College; Mass is held every day in the Convent Chapel.

Accommodation: The College has 310 places in Halls of Residence which accommodate all first years that want a place. Halls are situated on campus and the catering arrangements are full board, (breakfast and dinner weekdays and brunch and dinner weekends). Most students at the College live at home. Those that need housing tend to find it in Glasgow and commute out.

CITY and ESCAPE ROUTES
See the University of Glasgow's entry.

Westminster College

Oxford OX2 9AT
Telephone: 01865 247644

Westminster College specialises in teacher education and training and the study of academic and applied theology. Its 100 acre campus is set on a hill overlooking Oxford and its undergraduate degrees are validated by the University of Oxford. The College was a Methodist foundation and retains its Christian ethos.

The library houses around 100,000 volumes and subscribes to 450 journals. Students also have access to the Bodeleian Library - a rare privilege. Students have training on and access to Apple Macintosh, Nimbus and BBC microcomputers. Computers are available for student use when not being used for teaching. There is a multi-purpose television studio and an editing suite available to support students' course work.

The Theatre on site houses student productions, musicals and film shows. Art facilities are also good and available to all students. There is a College choir and practice rooms are available. The College has its own Student Union and Westminster's students are eligible to join the Oxford University Union and participate in University activities. Regular entertainments are held at the College - discos, barbecues, live music - and the Union supports a range of clubs and societies.

Sports facilities: six tennis courts, three squash courts, netball courts, cricket, football and hockey pitches, a nine hole golf course and an indoor, heated swimming pool. The two gymnasia have facilities for volleyball, badminton, basketball and dance. Facilities are open to all students, whatever their sporting level.

Medical services are provided by an Oxford Health Centre; surgeries are also held at the College twice a week. A trained counsellor is available two days a week and the Chaplain and Dean of Residence are available at all times. A Careers Officer gives professional advice when needed.

Accommodation: The College has over 500 places in 38 purpose built houses, set in gardens next to the playing fields. At least ten meals are provided each week. Students also have access to microwaves, cookers and fridges. All students who want a hall place will be allocated one.

CITY and ESCAPE ROUTES: See the University of Oxford's entry.

Health

Avon and Gloucestershire College of Health

Glenside
Blackberry Hill
Stapleton
Bristol BS16 1DD
Telephone: 01272 585655

Avon and Gloucestershire College of Health offers courses ranging from degrees and diplomas to short courses and in service training. Specialisms are nursing, physiotherapy, midwifery and radiography. Its main teaching centres are in Gloucestershire Royal Hospital in Gloucester and Glenside, just outside Bristol. Glenside is a solid Victorian building in its own grounds on the banks of the river Frome. Although always an institution, its buildings have been sympathetically converted. The College has a library and computer suite to back up teaching. There are strong links with the University of Bristol and the University of the West of England which give access to a wide range of equipment and resources.

Accommodation: The College has 380 single rooms leased from the local Health Authorities in the Avon area. All places are self-catered. Costs (1993/94): £95 per month

City and Escape routes: see The University of Bristol in this section.

Leeds College of Health

The Leeds College of Health was established in 1992 as a specialist college within the National Health Service and provides training in nursing, diagnostic radiography, therapeutic radiography, ultrasonography and midwifery. The College operates from several sites around Leeds: the General Infirmary, St James' University Hospital and High Royds Hospital being its main locations. Each of the three main sites has a library and information technology centre.

Accommodation: No information available.

City and escape routes: See the University of Leeds' entry.

St Loye's School of Occupational Therapy

Millbrook Lane
Topsham Road
Exeter EX2 6ES
Telephone: 01392 219774

St Loye's is a single subject college (as its name suggests) in Exeter. It enjoys close links with the University of Exeter. The School is housed in a large house just outside the city centre. The library houses 8,500 books (on the School's specific subject!) and subscribes to over 100 journals. Computer terminals are available for student use. The Union organises a range of social events.

Accommodation: the College has 30 places an on campus Hall of Residence. Evening meals are provided. Cost (1993/94): £50 pw for 30 weeks. Private Sector: Occupational Therapists are aided by their good reputations here....many landlords in Exeter will only advertise their properties on the accommodation list of St Loyes. As a result there is a good choice of high quality housing and all students can find places within the city boundary.

CITY and ESCAPE ROUTES: see the University of Exeter's entry.

West Yorkshire College of Health Studies

Lea House
Stanley Royd Hospital
Aberford Road
Wakefield
WF1 4DH
Telephone: 01924 200947

The College is based at Pinderfields Hospital in Wakefield and offers a degree programmes in Health Science. The College is, in effect, a Faculty of Physiotherapy, affiliated to the University of Leeds, and used to be the Pinderfields College of Physiotherapy. The Faculty admits 32 students each year onto courses in physiotherapy, nursing, midwifery and operating department practitioners.

Wakefield is a 'city', but is more of a market town. It is close to the M1 and M62, within 20 minutes of Leeds and has hourly fast (two hours) trains to London.

Accommodation: All first years are found places in shared houses on and around the hospital site. The houses are owned and administered by the Health Authority and rents are subsidised by them.

Performing Arts

Central School of Speech and Drama

Embassy Theatre
Eton Avenue
London NW3 3HY
Telephone: 0171 722 8183/4/5/6

The School was founded in 1906 by Elsie Fogerty and is now housed in a pleasant, residential area of north London. Premises include the Embassy Theatre, a fully equipped 'real' theatre with a seating capacity of 274. The main 'campus' is a small, contained complex of gracious Victorian houses, with purpose built add-ons (and, of course, the theatre).

The campus is in Swiss Cottage, near to Belsize Park and within walking distance of Hampstead and the Heath: one of the best areas of London and one which retains a strong sense of community. There is a good range of cafes, restaurants and pubs; you can have a sophisticated 'village' life while being within twenty minutes of the West End.

The School has a second campus in Camden; very much a student place with its particular range of shops and the weekend markets. There are a number of clubs and lively pubs here.

The library at the Central School is not the normal, quiet study area: here, its mission is to be a communal meeting ground for all departments. The bookstock totals 24,000 volumes and the library subscribes to a number of journals. The media resource unit, as well as training staff and students in the use of video/photography/sound equipment, has a network of Apple Mackintosh word-processors which is on open access to students.

The School puts on a range of public performances in the Embassy Theatre and studios. If you are not involved

Dartington College of Arts

Totnes
Devon TQ9 6EJ
Telephone: 01803 862224

Dartington College of Arts is not so much a place as a way of life. Students are trained to be resourceful, able to work across discipline boundaries and as happy in a team as working alone. The College specialises in the performing arts (music, theatre, visual performance, performance writing) and believes that 'the arts should be practised side-by-side to the highest possible standard'.

The College shares the Dartington Hall Estate in south Devon with the Dartington Centre, the Devon Centre, the Schumacher College and the Dartington Social Research Unit. The setting is beautiful: a medieval manor house and gardens in a wild expanse of phenomenal countryside. Many of the College buildings have been purpose-built for performance arts and include performance spaces, studios, workshops, and sound-proof practice rooms. The medieval Great Hall and the Barn Theatre are also used by the College for particular productions. The Library and

Learning Resources Centre provide course textbooks and backup materials. The Student Centre has a common room, bar, launderette and cafeteria.

Dartington Arts Unit is part of the Dartington complex, although not the College. Its work, however, means that students have access to a year-round arts programmes including concerts, films, theatre, dance, exhibitions, lectures and workshops. The Great Hall is venue for major concerts and the Barn Theatre is a designated Regional Film Theatre.

Accommodation: The College has 155 places in Halls of Residence and guarantees to house all first years who wish to have a place. All but two of the rooms are single and provision for self-catering varies in standard considerably. Private Sector: the rural setting of the College makes accommodation hard to come by and to have a car is a great bonus here. You can expect to have to look as far as eight miles away for a place to live. There are some shared houses but provision is mainly lodgings.

Rose Bruford College of Speech and Drama

Lamorbey Park
Sidcup
Kent DA15 9DF
Telephone: 081 300 3024

Degrees are validated by the University of Kent at Canterbury.

Rose Bruford College is a drama school set on two campuses, one at Lamorbey Park in Sidcup, Kent and one in Greenwich. Lamborey Park's site is a beautiful old house set in parkland. Greenwich buildings offer large rehearsal, performance and teaching spaces. Productions are housed in the College's own Barn Theatre. There is also the Studio Theatre which is used for small scale presentations. The library houses 28,000 volumes, including music scores, and subscribes to over 100 periodicals. The Union offers variety of sporting, social and recreational activities.

Accommodation: the College does not own any accommodation but the Accommodation Officer compiles a list of available properties within a five mile radius of the two sites.

SURROUNDING AREA: Sidcup is a pleasant town which will serve everyday needs. Central London is half an hour away by train, and the Kent countryside is on the doorstep. Greenwich is on the Thames: see the University of Greenwich's entry.

Appendix III
Colleges of Further and higher Education

A large number of Further Education Colleges now offer part or full degree programmes or HNDs which are structured by/franchised from 'parent' universities. Details are in the current UCAS Handbook. If you are interested in studying locally, contact your nearest college and find out what provision is available for Higher Education (degrees and HND) awards.

Appendix IV
Teaching Quality Assessments: Excellent ratings

Anthropology

Brunel University
University of Cambridge
University of Durham
University of Kent at Canterbury
University of London:
    LSE
    SOAS
    University College London
University of Manchester
Oxford Brookes University
University of Oxford
University of Sussex

Applied Social Work

Anglia Polytechnic University
Bradford and Ilkley Community College
University of Bristol
University of Durham
University of East Anglia
University of Huddersfield
University of Hull
Keele University
Lancaster University
University of London:
    LSE

University of Oxford
The Queen's University of Belfast
University of Sheffield
University of Southampton
West London Institute of Higher Education
University of York

Architecture

University of Bath
University of Cambridge
University of East London
University of Greenwich
University College London
University of Newcastle
University of Nottingham
University of Sheffield
University of York

Business and Management Studies

University of Bath
City University
Cranfield University
De Montfort University
Kingston University

Lancaster University
London Business School
University of London:
      Imperial College of Science, Technology and Medicine
      King's College London
      LSE
Loughborough University
University of Manchester
UMIST
University of Northumbria at Newcastle
University of Nottingham
Nottingham Trent University
The Open University
University of Surrey
University of Warwick
University of the West of England, Bristol

Computer Science

University of Cambridge
University of Exeter
University of Kent at Canterbury
Imperial College of Science, Technology and Medicine
University of Manchester
University of Oxford
University of Southampton
University of Teesside
University of Warwick
University of York

Chemistry

University of Bristol
University of Cambridge
University of Durham
University of Hull
University of Leeds
University of Leicester
Imperial College of Science, Technology and Medicine
University of Manchester
University of Nottingham
The Nottingham Trent University
The Open University
University of Oxford
University of Southampton

English

Anglia Polytechnic University
Bath College of Higher Education
University of Birmingham
University of Bristol
University of Cambridge
Chester College of Higher Education
University of Durham

University of East London
Kingston University
Lancaster University
University of Leeds
University of Leicester
University of London:
      Birkbeck College
      Queen Mary and Westfield College
      University College London
University of Newcastle Upon Tyne
University of North London
University of Northumbria at Newcastle
University of Nottingham
University of Oxford
Oxford Brookes University
The Queen's University of belfast
University of Sheffield
Sheffield Hallam University
University of Southampton
University of Sussex
University of Warwick
University of the West of England, Bristol
University of York

Environmental Studies

Bath College of Higher Education
University of East Anglia
University of Greenwich
University of Hertfordshire
Lancaster University
University of Liverpool
Liverpool Institute of Higher Education
University of London
      Queen Mary and Westfield College
University of Plymouth (Environmental Science)
University of Plymouth (Oceanography)
University of Reading
University of Southampton (Oceanography)

Geography

University of Birmingham
University of Bristol
University of Cambridge
Canterbury Christ Church College
Cheltenham and Gloucester College of Higher Education
Coventry University
University of Durham
University of East Anglia
University of Exeter
Lancaster University
University of Leeds
Liverpool Institute of Higher Education
University of London
      King's College London
      Queen Mary and Westfield College
      University College London

346

University of Manchester
University of Nottingham
The Open University
University of Oxford
Oxford Brookes University
University of Plymouth
University of Portsmouth
University of Reading
University of Sheffield
University of Southampton

Geology

University of Birmingham
University of Cambridge
University of Derby
University of Durham
Kingston University
University of Leeds
University of Liverpool
University of London
      Imperial College of Science, Technology and
      Medicine
      Royal Holloway, University of London
      University College London
University of Newcastle upon Tyne
The Open University
University of Oxford
University of Plymouth
The Queen's University of Belfast
University of Reading
University of Southampton

History

University of Birmingham
University of Cambridge
Canterbury Christ Church
University of Durham
University of Hull
University of Lancaster
University of Leicester
University of Liverpool
University of London
      King's College London
      LSE
      Royal Holloway, University of London
      University College London
      Warburg Institute
University of Oxford
The Queen's University of Belfast
University of Sheffield
University of Warwick
University of York

Law

University of Bristol
University of Cambridge
University of Durham
University of East Anglia
University of Essex
University of Leicester
University of Liverpool
University of London
      King's College London
      LSE
      University College London
      SOAS
University of Manchester
University of Northumbria at Newcastle
University of Nottingham
University of Oxford
Oxford Brookes University
The Queen's University of Belfast
University of Sheffield
University of Warwick
University of the West of England, Bristol

Mechanical Engineering

University of Bath
University of Bristol
Coventry University
Cranfield University
University of Manchester
Manchester Metropolitan University
University of Nottingham
University of Reading
University of Sheffield

Music

Anglia Polytechnic University
University of Birmingham
University of Cambridge
University of Central England in Birmingham
City University
University of Huddersfield
Keele University
Lancaster University
University of Leeds
University of London
      Goldsmiths College
      King's College London
      SOAS
University of Manchester
University of Nottingham

The Open University
The Queen's University of Belfast
Royal Academy of Music
Royal College of Music
Royal Northern College of Music
Salford College of Technology
University of Sheffield
University of Southampton
University of Surrey
University of Sussex
Trinity College of Music
University of Ulster
University of York

Social Policy and Administration

University of bath
Brunel University
Edge Hill College of Higher Education
University of Hull
University of Kent at Canterbury
University of London
     LSE
London Guildhall University
University of Manchester
University of Newcastle upon Tyne
The Open University
University of Sheffield
University of Ulster
University of York

INDEX